INTERNATIONAL L
IN A
DIVIDED WORLD

INTERNATIONAL LAW
IN A
DIVIDED WORLD

———

ANTONIO CASSESE

CLARENDON PRESS · OXFORD

Oxford University Press, Walton Street, Oxford OX2 6DP
Oxford New York Toronto
Delhi Bombay Calcutta Madras Karachi
Petaling Jaya Singapore Hong Kong Tokyo
Nairobi Dar es Salaam Cape Town
Melbourne Auckland
and associated companies in
Berlin Ibadan

Oxford is a trade mark of Oxford University Press

Published in the United States
by Oxford University Press, New York

First published 1986
First issued as a paperback 1988

British Library Cataloguing in Publication Data
Cassese, Antonio
International law in a divided world.
1. International law
I. Title
341   JX3091
ISBN 0-19-876194-5
ISBN 0-19-876233-X (pbk.)

Library of Congress Cataloging in Publication Data
Cassese, Antonio.
International law in a divided world.
Bibliography: p.
Includes index.
1. International law.   2. International relations.
I. Title.
JX3091.C34   1986   341   86-16456
ISBN 0-19-876194-5
ISBN 0-19-876233-X (pbk.)

Printed in Great Britain
at the University Printing House, Oxford
by David Stanford
Printer to the University

For Bert Röling,
il miglior fabbro,
in friendship and admiration

Preface

I SHOULD like to thank a few friends and colleagues who have been kind
enough to read individual chapters and offer their criticisms: G. Aldrich,
R. Barsotti, T. van Boven, L. Condorelli, M. Draghi, Sir James Fawcett,
Sir Joseph Gold, B. Graefrath, M. Mendelson, C. Morviducci, F. Rigaux,
B. V. A. Röling, W. Solf, C. Tomuschat, T. Treves, A. Yusuf, D. Zolo.
Without the assistance of so many solicitous gardeners, the plant would no
doubt have been a great deal frailer. However, I alone bear full responsi-
bility for any misapprehensions or mistakes.

I owe a special debt of gratitude to Bert Röling. I read his works many
years ago and was subsequently fortunate enough to meet him and to enjoy
his friendship. I have always been greatly impressed and influenced by his
progressive outlook, coupled with his wisdom and profound insight into
human behaviour. He was so generous as to read a first draft of the whole
book while he was already irremediably ill—a fact of which I was at the
time unaware—and offered very helpful criticism. He died while this book
was going to press.

Finally, I would like to thank Mrs Jennifer Greenleaves Manco for the
skill and forebearance with which she polished up my manuscript. My
English is like a barricade onto which I throw whatever I find close at hand:
old-fashioned cupboards, sophisticated gadgets, brand-new chairs, together
with piles of dusty books. I am grateful to her for helping to tidy up the
first draft. I also wish to thank Mrs A. Knowland for her excellent editing
of the final manuscript, and the staff of the Oxford University Press for
their kind assistance and co-operation.

A.C.

Facoltà di Scienze Politiche
'Cesare Alfieri'
Via Laura 48
50121 Firenze

Contents

SECTION II. CREATION AND EFFECTIVENESS OF
INTERNATIONAL STANDARDS

Principal Abbreviations

AFDI:	Annuaire français de droit international
AJIL:	American Journal of International Law
Anzilotti, *Corso* i:	D. Anzilotti, *Corso di diritto internazionale* (1928), i (4th edn. Milan, 1955)
Anzilotti, *Corso* iii:	D. Anzilotti, *Corso di diritto internazionale*, iii. Part 1 (Rome, 1915)
BYIL:	British Yearbook of International Law
ChYIL:	Selected Articles from Chinese Yearbook of International Law (Peking, 1983)
CYIL:	Canadian Yearbook of International Law
DDR-*Völkerrecht* 1982:	*Völkerrecht, Lehrbuch* (ed. H. Kröger) (2 vols, Berlin, 1982)
GAOR:	General Assembly Official Records
Hague *Recueil*:	Recueil des cours de l'Académie de droit international
ICJ:	International Court of Justice
ICJ *Reports*:	Reports of the International Court of Justice
ILM:	International Legal Materials
ILO:	International Labour Organization
IYIL:	Italian Yearbook of International Law
JYIL:	Japanese Yearbook of International Law
NYIL:	Netherlands Yearbook of International Law
PCIJ:	Permanent Court of International Justice
Schriften:	G. Jellinek, *Schriften und Reden*, ii. (Berlin, 1911)
SCOR:	Security Council Official Records
Tunkin 1974:	G. I. Tunkin, *Theory of International Law*, trans. W. E. Butler (London, 1974)
UNCIO:	United Nations Conference on International Organization
USFR:	United States Foreign Relations
ZaöRuV:	Zeitschrift für ausländisches öffentliches Recht und Völkerrecht

Introduction

Zu fragmentarisch ist Welt und Leben!
Ich will mich zum deutschen Professor begeben
Der weiss das Leben zusammenzusetzen
Und er macht ein verständlich System daraus
Mit seinem Nachtmützen und Schlafrockfetzen
Stopft er die Lücken des Weltenbaus.[1]

Heinrich Heine (*Die Heimkehr*, 1823-4)

THE idea of writing this book first occurred to me in 1980, when a Chinese student from the Florence Postgraduate School of International Affairs, where I then taught, asked me for a book on international law with the advantages of being relatively short and 'not too legal'; in other words, both accessible and appealing to somebody with no legal background yet keen to acquire an understanding of international legal affairs. To my embarrassment, I was unable to suggest a suitable book. A number of excellent manuals which I indicated to my Chinese student disappointed him, for he found them too 'technical'. This set me thinking about the need for a short guide to the intricacies of international law viewed from a historical and political perspective. Much hesitation ensued—after all, I knew all too well that in 1910 the prominent British jurist T. E. Holland, in his valedictory lecture at All Souls College, Oxford, prided himself on not having 'inflicted on the world a new textbook upon International Law'.[2] In the event, I nevertheless decided to try. The reader will decide whether the Peking student should be blamed for involuntarily setting off a process that culminated in the writing of this book.

Perhaps it would be useful briefly to describe the goal I pursued when I embarked upon this undertaking.

First of all, the aim of the book is practical: it chiefly addresses itself to the student of law, history, and social sciences as well as to the layman, and endeavours to provide a guide to the maze of current international realities. It is not intended as a substitute for legal textbooks, rather it seeks to provide a general perspective and some basic points of reference for a better understanding of the role of law in the world community.

---

[1] 'Too fragmentary are world and life!/I shall betake myself to the German Professor./He knows how to recompose life/And makes an intelligible system therefrom;/With his night-cap and dressing-gown's rags/He then plugs the gaps in the world's structure.'

[2] T. E. Holland, *A Valedictory Retrospect (1874-1910)* (Oxford, 1910), p. 17.

Secondly, it adopts a general approach to legal institutions which is different from that prevailing in juridical writings. To explain what I mean by the term 'different' I need to make a short digression. It is almost a truism that positivism, which had its heydey in the second half of the nineteenth century, and the 'normativist' school, which evolved in the early twentieth century in Austria, Germany, and Italy, have two chief merits, especially in the fields of public law and international law. First, they disentangled legal science from other disciplines such as history, philosophy, political science (*lato sensu*), and sociology, with which it was previously associated. Second, they insisted on the need for investigating public law (as well as international law) by a method of enquiry distinct from that which, in the wake of the Roman law tradition, prevailed in the field of private law. However, the first of these undisputed virtues, though it certainly 'purified' legal science, and permitted it to attain very high levels of scholarly elaboration, gradually led to an impoverishment of legal knowledge, despite the fact that the early positivists and such 'normativists' as Kelsen had proclaimed that they did not intend 'to erect a Chinese wall' around the fledgling discipline.[3] As a consequence, legal enquiry was cut off and isolated from other cognate methods of investigation and, in addition, the various branches of legal science were compartmentalized—with the obvious result that today, if one opens a good legal book, one seldom gains any insight into the social, political, and ideological conditions behind the rules, or into the multifarious factors shaping their evolution, or into the impact of legal institutions upon present-day reality. 'Purity' has led to sterility.

In this book an attempt is made to *combine*, rather than merge, the rigorous method of the positivist and 'normativist' schools in their more modern versions, with an enquiry into the historical dimension of international law and the political and ideological motivations behind it. One of the basic, perhaps somewhat naïve, assumptions of the book is that one can draw, with profit, upon various methods of investigation without necessarily betraying the distinct character of each. Let me emphasize that this approach—which one could describe as 'multi-disciplinary'—is intended not simply to render accessible a subject-matter usually considered dry or too technical but principally to examine an area of international relations as part of the complex and multi-faceted reality, with which it is closely connected: to view international legal institutions not as abstract entities 'frozen' in time, but rather as dynamic and continuously changing elements of a whole.

It would, of course, be a mistake to believe that until now no inter-

---

[3] Mention of the 'Chinese wall' was made by V. E. Orlando, 'I criteri tecnici per la ricostruzione giuridica del diritto pubblico' (1889), *Diritto pubblico generale, Scritti varii* (Milan, 1954), p. 19.

national lawyer has drawn upon other disciplines: in some European countries especially, and in the US (where the influence of the two legal schools of thought referred to above has been less marked) many authors have trodden the path before me. In the field of international law a number of seminal works stand out.[4] While deeply appreciating the invaluable contribution offered by them, I feel, however, that there is still a need for an approach which is both radically 'holistic' (to use a fashionable term) and which puts all legal phenomena into historical perspective. I also feel that there is a need for an elementary book to trace the broad outlines and the main issues of international legal relations, viewed from this new angle.

A further general remark seems appropriate. Since the development of the sociology of knowledge, no scholar should claim to be free from 'prejudices' and ideological assumptions: they creep into scientific argumentation often without the writer being aware of them. In a way, scholars are like the character in one of Chekhov's plays,[5] who was meant to lecture on the evils of tobacco but could not help intermingling his cogitations on the drawbacks of smoking with lamentations about his wretched existence and his bullying wife. No student of the social sciences can refrain from interjecting—often unwittingly—his own personal feelings into his work. However, what is universally demanded from any person of learning is that his values should not lead him to manipulate scientific methods to make them suit a particular political philosophy. The reader will no doubt perceive the ideological 'leanings' of this book.[6] They have, of course, conditioned the

---

[4] Suffice it to mention those by the Greek jurist, N. Politis, *Les Nouvelles Tendances du droit international* (Paris, 1927), and the Belgians, M. Bourquin, *L'État souverain et l'organisation internationale* (New York, 1959) and C. de Visscher, *Théories et réalités en droit international public*, 4th edn. (Paris, 1970). Twenty-five years ago B. V. A. Röling, a Dutchman, published his fundamental work which must also be credited with opening the way to a 'progressive' approach to current international law: *International Law in an Expanded World* (Amsterdam, 1960). Other works include those by the French lawyer, M. Virally, *L'ONU d'hier à demain* (Paris, 1961), the Americans, W. Friedmann, *The Changing Structure of International Law* (London, 1964), O. J. Lissitzyn, *International Law Today and Tomorrow* (Dobbs Ferry, 1965), L. Henkin, *How Nations Behave*, 2nd edn. (New York, 1979), as well as (with a different outlook): R. Falk, *The Status of Law in International Society* (Princeton, NJ, 1970), and, most recently, the Frenchman, G. de Lacharrière, *La Politique juridique extérieure* (Paris, 1983), and the Spaniard J. A. Carrillo Salcedo, *El derecho internacional en un mundo en cambio* (Madrid, 1984). I should like to emphasize that the expression 'International law in a divided world' was first used by O. Lissitzyn in the first version of his monograph mentioned above (published in *International Conciliation*, 1963, March issue). It was subsequently taken up by R. Higgins in her book *Conflict of Interests: International Law in a Divided World, A Background Book* (London, 1965).

[5] A. Chekhov, 'Smoking is bad for you', in *Short Plays* (Oxford, 1979), pp. 155–8.

[6] For the 'values' shared in this book, see J. Galtung, 'On the Responsibility of Scientists', *Bulletin of Peace Proposals*, 7 (1976), 186–9, who lists a set of 'positive' values to which the 'negative' values of violence (including war), poverty, and repression can be opposed. See also R. A. Falk, *The Interplay of Westphalia and Charter Conceptions of International Legal Order*, in C. A. Black and R. A. Falk (ed.), *The Future of the International Legal Order*, i (Princeton, NJ, 1969), pp. 33 ff. Falk lists five main 'values': 'the minimization of violence; the promotion

choice of topics, the emphases and omissions, the method of enquiry, the interpretation of legal rules. I have, however, made every effort to avoid disfiguring international reality in a way contrary to scientific rigour.

I have also been induced to neglect certain topics, and to concentrate on others which I felt to be of greater interest within the context of the contemporary development of the international community, both in view of the general approach of this book and the 'values' which lie at its roots. Four general themes underlie the whole. First, the deep crevasses which split the international community along both ideological, political, and economic lines and their prismatic effect on law: in a nutshell, the unhomogeneous character of both the international community and its law today. Second, the coexistence within the community of two distinct patterns of legal order. The former we may call the 'Westphalian model', which grew out of the origins of the international community and lasted until the First, or rather, the Second World War; the latter, which has evolved in our own time, may be called the 'UN Charter model'.[7] Thus international law possesses 'two souls', and the second seems incapable of supplanting the first. Third, the role which international law can play within the international community: what weight legal precepts carry in the decisions of States and to what extent international subjects are guided in their conduct by the rich panoply of present-day legal rules and institutions. Fourth, the diversity and occasional clashes between the old and new 'actors' playing on the international scene: since sovereign States are still the protagonists, how far can we say that individuals, peoples, and non-governmental organizations are allowed to play an active role or that theirs are mere walk-on parts? Is the international community still composed of the 'governors' only or are the 'governed' allowed to have a say?

The choice of these four themes has led me to disregard, as I have already stated, certain classic topics (for example, the relations between domestic

of human rights of individuals and groups, especially autonomy and racial equality; the transfer of wealth and income from rich States to poor States; the equitable participation of diverse cultures, regions, and ideologies in a composite system of global order; the growth of supranational and international institutions'.

[7] For these concepts see R. A. Falk, op. cit. (and, before him, L. Gross, 'The Peace of Westphalia: 1648-1948', *AJIL* 42 (1948), 20 ff.). I should immediately point out that although in the Introduction and in the whole book I have taken up the terminology propounded by R. Falk, I am aware of its flaws. As I shall try to explain in Chapter 3, a main turning-point in the world community occurred in 1917, as a result of the emergence of the USSR and its challenge to traditional international law. (The First World War and the League of Nations were also instrumental in bringing about a gradual change in the international community.) If, by contrast, a main distinction is drawn between two periods (from the Peace of Westphalia to 1945, and from then to the present), those fundamental elements in the history of the world community are passed over in silence; one consequently fails to understand when and how the 'family of nations' split for the first time and profound conflicts (ideological, political, and economic) emerged. Whenever Falk's terminology is used in this book, one should always bear in mind these qualifications.

and international law, the treatment of foreigners, the legal regulation of territory and the high seas, international responsibility, etc.) which, however, I have touched upon tangentially. Should the reader wish for a complete picture of international law, describing each and every aspect of State activity, then he should turn to the textbooks on the subject.

Finally, let me point out, lest the motto quoted on the first page of this introduction be misinterpreted, that of course this book does not intend to ridicule German academics. Far from it, I have relied heavily on their past and present contributions, and hold them in high esteem. In his poem Heine wishes, I believe, to make fun of any man of learning's tendency to manipulate and ossify reality. However critical and vigilant a student of social institutions may be, sooner or later he falls into the trap of believing that his own reconstruction of reality actually reflects it as a coherent and flawless whole and that indeed the object itself is as smooth as the mirror. Reality intrudes continuously, but he glosses over the cracks or simply hides them by theoretical contrivances. The present book is of course not immune from this propensity, nor from other flaws. This I say without any undue trepidation: I remember all too well Hegel's warning[8] that the words of the Apostle Peter to Ananias' wife ('Behold, the feet of them which have buried thy husband are at the door, and shall carry thee out') also apply to all scientific works—which are ineluctably destined to be eroded by subsequent scholarship.

---

[8] G. F. W. Hegel, *Lectures on the History of Philosophy*, trans. E. S. Haldane (London, 1892), i. 17.

Section I

Origin and Foundations of the International Community

Main Legal Features of the International Community

1. We all live within the framework of national legal orders. We therefore tend to assume that each legal system should be modelled on State law, or at least strongly resemble it. Accordingly, and almost unwittingly, we take the view that all legal systems should address themselves to individuals or groups of individuals, and in addition that they should include certain centralized institutions responsible for making law, for settling disputes, and for enforcing legal norms.

However, the picture offered by the international community is completely different. Consequently this enquiry should begin with a note of warning. The features of the world community are quite unique. Failure to grasp this crucial fact would inevitably entail a serious misinterpretation of the impact of law on this community.

The first salient feature of international law is that it aims at regulating the behaviour of States, not that of individuals. States are the principal dramatis personae on the international scene. They are aggregates of individuals dominated by an apparatus which exercises authority over them. Their general goals are quite distinct from the goals of each individual or group. Each State owns and controls a separate territory; and each is held together by political, economic, ethnic, cultural and religious links.

Whereas within States individuals are the principal legal subjects, and legal entities (corporations, associations, etc.) are merely secondary subjects whose possible suppression would not result in the demise of the whole legal system, in the international community the reverse holds true: States are the primary subjects, and individuals play a very limited role (see §§ 43, 57). The latter are as puny young Davids confronted by overpowering Goliaths holding all the instruments of power.

Although the protagonists of international life are corporate structures, of course they cannot but operate through individuals, who do not act on their own account but as State officials, or rather as the tools of the structures to which they belong. Thus, for instance, if a treaty of extradition is concluded by the UK with the USSR, this deal should not blind us to what actually happens, namely that the international instrument is concretely brought into being by individuals and is subsequently implemented by individuals. The agreement is negotiated by diplomats belonging to the two States; their Ministers of Foreign Affairs sign the treaty; the instrument of ratification is formally approved and signed by the Heads of State, if necessary after authorization by parliamentary assemblies. Once the treaty has entered into force, it is implemented by the courts of each country and, if required, also by officials of the respective Ministries of Justice (and, indeed, it is generally for the courts to grant or refuse extradition in each particular case).

Similarly, if a State considers that another country has committed an international transgression, and therefore decides to react by resorting to peaceful reprisals such as the expulsion of all the nationals of the State in question, this response is concretely decided upon and carried out by individuals acting as State agencies: the decision is normally taken, at the suggestion of the Foreign Minister, by the Minister for Home Affairs, after possible deliberation by the Cabinet; the actual expulsion is carried out by police officers or other enforcement agencies.

Indeed, in international law more than in any other field, the phenomenon of 'fictitious person', to which Hobbes drew attention, manifests itself in a conspicuous form: individuals engage in transactions or express their will, not in their personal capacity, that is to protect or further their own interests, but on behalf of groups and collectivities.

It may prove useful to recall Hobbes's penetrating remark on this phenomenon (which of course is also to be found within the domestic setting of States, whenever individuals act as State organs). After pointing out that the Romans applied the term *persona*, or mask, 'like the one tragic and comic actors wore in theatre', to all the individuals speaking on behalf of others, he went on to say, 'Indeed, in the theatre it was understood that it was not the actor who spoke, but somebody else, Agamemnon for example, in that the actor put on the fictitious face of Agamemnon and consequently was Agamemnon throughout the play; this transmutation was later accepted even without the false face (*sine facie ficta*): it was sufficient for the actor to declare which "persona" he would impersonate. Fictions of this kind are no less necessary to the State than in theatre, on account of the negotiations and transactions of the absent (*propter absentium commercia et contractus*). As regards the civil use of the concept of "person", it can be defined as follows: a person is the one to whom either his own words and deeds or those of somebody else are attributed (*persona est, cui verba et actiones hominum attribuuntur vel suae vel alienae*). Consequently, just as one and the same actor can impersonate different "persons" on different occasions, so any man can represent more human beings.'[1]

Why is it that the world community consists of sovereign and independent States, while human beings as such play only a minimal role? We shall

---

[1] T. Hobbes, *Elementorum Philosophiae Sectio Secunda: De Homine* (1658) in T. Hobbes *Opera philosophica quae latine scripsit omnia*, ed. W. Molesworth (London, 1839; repr. London, 1966), ii. 130. The same concept can be found in *Leviathan* (1651), Chap. 16 (see e.g. *Leviathan* ed. by C. B. Macpherson, London 1981, 217–22).

see in Chapters 2 and 3 how the international community evolved and how, after the first modern States (England, France, Spain) came into being between the twelfth and the fourteenth centuries, the various communities in Europe and elsewhere gradually consolidated and 'hardened' into States. It may suffice now to stress that this powerful drive has been a constant and salient feature of the world community since 1300, so much so that all individuals are now monopolized by one State or another: the world population of about five billion human beings is currently divided up amongst nearly a hundred and seventy States. In the Middle Ages it was usual to say that outside the Church no salvation could be found (*extra Ecclesiam nulla salus*)—at least, this was what the Church encouraged people to believe. Today it could be maintained with greater truthfulness that without the protection of a State human beings are likely to endure more suffering and hardship than what is likely to be their lot in the normal course of events—witness the plight of stateless persons, which has only lately been taken up by international institutions.

COLLECTIVE RESPONSIBILITY

2. As in all primitive legal systems where groups play a much greater role than individuals, responsibility for violations of the rules governing the behaviour of States does not fall upon the transgressing official but on the group to which he belongs (the State community). Here again we are confronted with a striking deviation from domestic legal systems.

Within the national legal orders which frame our daily lives, we are accustomed to the notion of individual responsibility: he who commits a tort or any other breach of law shall suffer in consequence; he must either make good the damage or—in case of crime—is liable to a criminal penalty. Such is the rule. There are, however, exceptions, one of which is that of 'vicarious responsibility' which comes into play when the law provides that someone bears responsibility for actions performed by another person, with whom the former has special ties (for example, a parent is legally responsible for damage caused by his or her children); sometimes a whole group is held responsible for the acts performed by one of its representatives on behalf of the group (as in the civil liability of corporations for torts).

In the international legal system the exception becomes the rule. If a State official breaks international law (as when a military commander orders his pilots to intrude upon the airspace of a neighbouring State, or a court disregards an international treaty granting certain rights to foreigners, or a police officer infringes upon diplomatic immunities by arresting a diplomat or maltreating him), the wronged State is allowed to 'take revenge' against the whole community to which that State representative belongs, even though the community has neither carried out nor ordered the infraction. For instance, the State which has become the victim of the international transgression can claim the payment of a sum of money (to be drawn from the State Treasury) or will resort to reprisals damaging individuals other than the actual authors of the offence (for example, the expulsion of foreigners, the suspension of a commercial treaty or of diplomatic immunities, and so on).

Collective responsibility is also borne by subsequent generations. This has been graphically described by Sir John Fischer Williams, who wrote:

> ... The international responsibility of one of those bodies corporate [the State] is carried on from generation to generation of individuals, and the good or bad deeds of previous ages in the international sphere are, without moral justification, credited or imputed to the generation which for the time being supplies the membership of the interested State or body corporate concerned, although no individual now living can be said to have any responsibility for the good or evil deed ... It is even true that in some cases the greater part of a living generation cannot claim that it was their ancestors after the flesh who were the members of the corporate body at the time when the good or evil deed was done.[2]

Hence, collective responsibility means both that the whole State community is liable for any breach of international law committed by any State representative and that the whole State community may suffer from the consequences of the wrongful act.

This form of responsibility is typical of primitive and rudimentary legal systems. H. Kelsen was one of the first authors to draw attention to this phenomenon. Thus he pointed out that:

> ... collective responsibility exists in case of blood revenge which is directed not only against the murderer but also against all the members of his family. Criminal responsibility is established in the Ten Commandments when Yahweh threatens to punish the children and the children's children for the sins of their fathers.[3]

Indeed, the law governing the international community is typical of primitive societies, with the aggravating circumstance—rightly emphasized by S. Hoffmann[4]—that unlike primitive communities (which are, typically, highly integrated, with all the ensuing benefits), the world community is largely based on the non-integration of its subjects, from the viewpoint of their social interrelations (see § 226).

Later on we shall see (§§ 148, 159, 169) that since the end of the last century individual responsibility has gradually evolved in international law as well. It was considered that serious offences committed in exceptional

---

[2] J. Fischer Williams, *Aspects of Modern International Law: An Essay* (London, 1939), p. 23.
[3] H. Kelsen, *Principles of International Law* (New York, 1952), p. 10.
[4] S. Hoffmann, 'International Law and the Control of Force', in *The Relevance of International Law*, ed. K. Deutsch and S. Hoffmann (New York, 1971), p. 36.

circumstances, for example, in time of war, should entail the personal liability of their authors in addition to that of the State to which they belonged. The category of war crimes gradually expanded after the Second World War to include crimes against peace (chiefly aggression) and crimes against humanity (chiefly genocide). However, despite these momentous advances, collective responsibility still remains the rule.

LACK OF ANY CENTRAL AUTHORITY WIELDING EXCLUSIVE POWER: CONSEQUENT DECENTRALIZATION OF THE MAIN LEGAL FUNCTIONS

3. National legal systems are highly developed. In addition to substantive rules, which enjoin citizens to behave in a certain way, sophisticated organizational rules have evolved. A special machinery exists concerned with the 'life' of the legal order. These developments resulted from the emergence within the State community of a group of individuals who succeeded in wielding effective power: they considered it convenient to create a special structure aimed at institutionalizing that power and crystallizing the relationships between the ruling group and their fellow-members. In devising the institutional apparatus, a common pattern evolved in all modern States. First, the use of force by members of the community was forbidden, except for emergency situations such as self-defence (the right to use force to impede unlawful violence which would otherwise be unavoidable). Second, the three main functions typical of any legal system (law-making, law-determination and law-enforcement) were entrusted to central organs acting on behalf of the whole community. Accordingly, the creation and modification of law was vested in an Assembly (generally called Parliament); the ascertainment of breaches of law was entrusted to courts; law-enforcement was granted to special bodies of professionals (police officers; the army).

By contrast, in the international community no State or group of States has managed to hold the lasting power required to impose its will on the whole world community. Power is fragmented and dispersed. Although political and military alliances have occasionally been set up or a strong convergence of interests between two or more members of the community has evolved, this state of affairs has not been consolidated into a permanent power structure. As a consequence, organizational rules—'secondary rules', in H. Hart's terminology[5]—are at a very embryonic stage. They do not set

[5] H. L. A. Hart, *The Concept of Law* (Oxford, 1981), pp. 77 ff. According to Hart 'while primary rules are concerned with the actions that individuals must or must not do, [the] secondary rules are all concerned wtih the primary rules themselves. They specify the ways in which the primary rules may be conclusively ascertained, introduced, eliminated, varied, and the fact of their violation conclusively determined' (p. 92). While I accept this most important

up special machinery for discharging the three functions referred to above, nor do they entrust them to any particular body or member of the international community. All three functions are decentralized—it is for each individual State, acting together with other States if need be, to create and change law, to settle disputes, and to impel compliance with law. Of particular significance is the fact that each State has the 'right' of 'auto-interpretation' of legal rules, a 'right' which necessarily follows from the absence of courts endowed with general and compulsory jurisdiction.

It stands to reason that in *traditional* international law (that is, the law which came into being between the Peace of Westphalia of 1648, and the First World War: §§ 15-17) this state of affairs, coupled with the absence of a ban on the use of force, greatly favoured powerful States. But as we shall see, some minor improvements are to be found in the present international system (§§ 127-8).

THE NEED FOR INTERNATIONAL LAW TO RELY HEAVILY ON DOMESTIC LEGAL SYSTEMS

4. Since international law regulates the conduct, not of individuals but of States, it is not a self-sufficient system. States have no soul, no capacity to form and express an autonomous will; they are 'abstract' structures acting through individuals. Human beings alone can give flesh and blood to State activity. Consequently, if they are to be translated into reality, thus becoming effective standards of behaviour, international rules must be applied by natural persons. Human beings, however, are still subject to national legal systems, which decide of their own accord upon the procedures for choosing or selecting State officials, and establish their field of competence and powers autonomously. International law must bow to municipal authority in this area. Thus, for instance, for an international rule forbidding the use of certain categories of arms (such as chemical or bacteriological weapons) to take effect, the Minister of Defence and the military commanders of a given State must become cognizant of the rule, and take all the necessary measures to implement it. A provision such as Article 29 of the Vienna Convention of 1961 on diplomatic immunities ('The person of a diplomatic agent shall be inviolable. He shall not be liable to any form of arrest or detention. The receiving State shall treat him with due respect and shall take all appropriate steps to prevent any attack on his person, freedom or dignity') obliges the enforcement agencies of a State to refrain from arrest-

distinction, I cannot share Hart's classification of 'secondary rules' (which, for the distinguished jurist, include 'rules of recognition, change and adjudication'). Nor can I share Hart's way of applying these three categories to international law (see ibid., pp. 208-31). For a perceptive criticism of Hart's view of international law see I. Brownlie, 'The Reality and Efficacy of International Law,' in BYIL 52 (1981), 5-8.

ing or detaining foreign diplomats, and to take all necessary measures to prevent undue attacks on them. Similarly, Article 34 of the same Convention ('A diplomatic agent shall be exempt from all dues, taxes, personal or real, national, regional or municipal' except for certain categories of taxes enumerated in the same provision) requires the tax authorities of the receiving State to take the requisite steps to exempt foreign diplomats from all the dues and taxes to which they are not subjected.

It is therefore apparent that international law cannot work without the constant help, co-operation, and support of national legal systems. As the German jurist, H. Triepel,[6] observed in 1923, international law is like a field marshal who can only give orders to generals. It is solely through the generals that his orders can reach the troops. If the generals do not transmit them to the soldiers in the field, he will lose the battle.

5. Since international law cannot stand on its own feet without its 'crutches', that is municipal law, and since national implementation of international rules is of crucial importance, one would expect there to be some form of international regulation of the matter or at least a certain uniformity in the ways in which domestic legal systems implement international law. The reality is quite different, however. International law merely provides that States cannot invoke the legal procedures of their municipal system as a justification for not complying with international rules. There it stops, thus leaving each country complete freedom in the fulfilment of its international duties. A survey of national systems shows a complete lack of uniformity. The reason for this anarchic state of affairs is simple: States consider that the translation of international commands into domestic standards is part and parcel of their sovereignty, and are therefore unwilling to surrender it to international control. National self-interest stands in the way of a sensible regulation of this crucial area. As a consequence, each State decides on its own how to make international law binding on State agencies and individuals and what status and rank in the hierarchy of municipal sources of law to assign to it.

Some national constitutions stipulate that customary international rules become domestically binding *ipso facto*, that is, by the mere fact of their evolving in the international community, and that in addition they override national legislation (see, for example, the constitution of some European countries such as Italy, the FRG, Greece; the same holds true in Japan, as well); others make no such provision. Consequently, should an international custom become applicable in their country, this development could lead to conflict with national legislation, which always prevails eventually. Similarly, some national systems provide that international treaties are to

---

[6] H. Triepel, 'Les Rapports entre le droit interne et le droit international', Hague *Recueil* (1923), 106.

be complied with by domestic authorities upon their publication in the Official Bulletin (see, for example, France and many African countries) or after the enactment of a special legislative measure (see, for example, Italy, the FRG). By contrast, other domestic orders (such as the UK and the USSR) provide that treaties do not bind national authorities unless they are transformed into detailed national legislation. (In the UK, however, this principle does not apply to treaties concerning the conduct of war or to treaties of cession; in addition, as was pointed out by J. Brownlie,[7] 'in recent years the English courts have recognized the relevance of treaty provisions concerning human rights to the construction of statutes'.) The rank and status of treaties varies to a great extent. Thus, in France, Greece, Spain, and a number of French-speaking African countries, such as the Ivory Coast, treaties acquire a status higher than national legislation (and in the Netherlands, one which is even higher than the Constitution, at least in some cases), with the obvious consequence that, in case of conflict, the former prevails; in most countries, however, treaties are equated with laws enacted by parliament; it follows that a later statute can override an earlier treaty. There are, however, many States (such as China and a number of English-speaking African countries such as Ghana, Uganda, Nigeria, Tanzania, etc.) which do not make any provision in their constitutions or national legislation for the implementation of international rules; international law does not enjoy a high standing with them; its application rests on the good will of the domestic authorities, whose fluctuating attitudes and interests may result in the fact that the application of international law remains uncertain and confused.

True, in all cases where national authorities are unable or unwilling to abide by international regulations, the State incurs international responsibility and is duty-bound to make appropriate reparation. However, as we shall see, international techniques for inducing compliance with international law as well as international sanctions are weak and rudimentary. It follows that if the State disregarding international law is powerful or protected by a powerful country, it can be fairly sure of impunity.

However, at least for some Western countries, it may happen that their national system for the implementation of international treaties results in their frequently being the object of international judicial proceedings. Thus, for instance, nearly three out of five cases brought to the European Commission and the European Court on Human Rights (two international bodies set up by the European Convention on Human Rights of 1950), related to the UK. Recently, the President of the European Court, the Dutchman G. J. Wiarda,[8] pointed out that one of the reasons for this state of affairs is 'that while in the constitutional systems of most member countries of the Council of Europe the [European] Convention on Human Rights

---

[7] J. Brownlie, *Principles of Public International Law*, 3rd edn. (Oxford, 1979), p. 51.

[8] G. J. Wiarda, in *Forum* (a Council of Europe quarterly) (1985), 2.

is directly incorporated into the national law, in the UK it is not'. He illustrated further: 'For instance, in my country, the Netherlands, international law always has priority over national law. So when someone in Holland feels his human rights are being violated he can go to a Dutch judge and the judge must apply the law of the Convention. He must apply international law even if it is not in conformity with Dutch law. That is not possible in the UK because the law of the Parliament always has priority over international law. You cannot go to a judge and say that the Government has violated the [European] Convention on Human Rights. The British judge has no competence to apply international law when it is not compatible with national law. So, even though the UK must abide by the Convention and must see to it that its law is compatible with the Convention, a British judge has nothing to do with the Convention. People who think there is a violation of the Convention must go to Strasbourg [that is, to the European Commission on Human Rights].'

6. So much for the *national legal regulation* of the application of inter-national rules. *In actual practice*, States tend to comply with international law out of sheer self-interest; this holds true for bilateral treaties as well as for multilateral treaties or customary rules based on reciprocity (where the undertaking of one party corresponds to and is subject to the fulfilment of a similar undertaking on the part of the counterparty: see § 11). Instead, many States are markedly reluctant to implement (1) multilateral treaties not based on reciprocity, such as those on human rights (see §§ 167-8), and (2) customary rules imposing duties which in actual fact operate 'uni-laterally', or 'asymmetrically', for example, those on the nationalization of foreign property, on non-interference into domestic affairs, and so on, that is duties which in practice are ultimately operative for certain categories of States only. Plainly, obligations deriving from the rules on the treatment of foreign property are incumbent upon those States alone which allow foreign companies to exploit their national resources; consequently, it should not be surprising that these States are markedly recalcitrant to fulfil such obli-gations: clearly, there is no reciprocity here, no *quid pro quo* prompting each partner of a contractual relationship to abide by the agreement for fear the counterparty will disregard it too. The same holds true for the duty on non-interference in domestic affairs: it stands to reason that such duty is unlikely to apply to poorer States *vis-à-vis* Great Powers, for it would be preposterous to think that the former might meddle in the domestic affairs of the latter; by contrast, that duty is highly material to strong States, which tend to encroach upon the freedom of other countries; consequently, it is understandable that Great Powers demur at fully complying with the rule prohibiting such encroachments: after all they are not themselves exposed to a similar disregard by the counterparty.

7. State practice on the matter has not always shown the same features.

Domestic systems have gradually opened the door to international values and States have been increasingly willing to bow to international law. In order to focus on this certain if slow evolution it may be useful to take a cursory glance at the three major theories expounded on the relationship between international and municipal law. Indeed, to a great extent they rationalize and give theoretical justification to the various existing historical and political positions.

The first doctrine in question was propounded in the eighteenth century. It was strongly nationalistic and was put forward by two German scholars, Johann Jacob Moser (1701–85) and Georg Friedrich von Martens (1756–1821), who expounded—albeit somewhat loosely—its fundamental principles. However it was not until the nineteenth century that these concepts were elaborated into a fully-fledged doctrine. Its basis was the strongly authoritarian conception of the modern State advanced by W. Hegel. Hegel's theory was set forth (somewhat confusedly) in his *Encyclopaedia* (1817) and *Philosophy of Right* (1821), and was subsequently expanded on by the German lawyers B. Akzin, A. Zorn, and I. Wenzel. In short, national law subsumed international legal rules, which were 'external State law'. It followed that international law proper did not exist, for it was made up of the 'external law' of the various members of the international community; consequently, each State was free to change the law as soon as this was deemed fit or expedient. International law was not a body of binding standards of behaviour; it was only a set of guidelines whose provisional value disappeared as soon as a 'powerful' State thought that they were contrary to its own interests. Plainly, this doctrine adopted a 'monistic' approach, in that it actually asserted the existence of a single set of legal systems, the domestic legal orders, and denied the existence of international law as a distinct and autonomous body of law. It followed that there was obviously no need for international rules to be incorporated into municipal legislation, international rules being but the emanation of domestic systems. International law did not need to rely on municipal law since it was the outward projection of the various State systems. Clearly, this conception reflected the extreme nationalism and authoritarianism of a few great powers, anxious to protect their respective interests.

At about the same time a less nationalistic view prevailed in such democratic countries as Great Britain and the US—thus proving that theories about the relationship between municipal and international law are strongly influenced by domestic political systems and their reflection in political concepts. English and American courts upheld the principle whereby international customary law was to be regarded as 'the law of the land' and to be applied accordingly. In addition, the principle was authoritatively endorsed in England by such great jurists as Lord Mansfield and W. T. Blackstone. Furthermore, the American Constitution of 1787 laid down in Article

6.2 that the treaties 'which shall be made under the authority of the United States shall be the supreme law of the land; and the judges in every State shall be bound thereby, anything in the Constitution or laws of any State to the contrary notwithstanding'. Although the basic rationale behind this provision was the intent to prevent possible conflicts between federal and state law, the fact remains that, by passing this rule and similar ones State authorities eventually recognized the binding force of international rules (provided they had either been accepted by the great majority of States including, of course, the countries in question or, in the case of treaties, provided the competent constitutional authorities had given them their support). In addition, international law was given domestic guarantees, in that courts and enforcement agencies were called upon to implement it.

This practical approach, too, reflected the interests of Great Powers. However, those interests were safeguarded in a more indirect and sophisticated way than under the 'monistic' conception: that is to say not so much through the explicit admission that each State was free to jettison the law as soon as it no longer served its interests, as by shaping international rules in such a way as to give them a content conforming to all the political, economic, and military demands of the Great Powers.

The latter approach soon appeared to be more consonant with the complexity of international relations and the increasing need for international legal restraints on power politics. In 1899, a prominent German scholar, H. Triepel, developed a new theory based on a 'dualistic' approach ('pluralistic' would, however, be a better term). Among those who adhered to the theory was a distinguished Italian jurist, D. Anzilotti, who contributed greatly to its dissemination in Europe.

As L. Ferrari Bravo has rightly emphasized,[9] the new theory did not come out of the blue: a number of historical developments concurred to, or at least laid the foundations for, its birth. The new constitutions passed in the late nineteenth century in many European countries as a result of liberal trends proclaimed the principle of the rule of law; it therefore became imperative to determine with greater precision, among other things, whether, and on what conditions, international standards of behaviour formed part of municipal law. Furthermore, the number of treaties and conventions entered into by States increased at a staggering pace, thereby raising the problem of the conditions and modalities of their implementation by domestic courts. To these factors one should add that of the growing sophistication of German legal literature, which could not but 'contaminate' fields previously inadequately covered, such as international law.

Dualist doctrines started from the assumption that municipal law and international law constitute two distinct and formally separate categories of

[9] L. Ferrari Bravo, 'International and Municipal Law: The Complementarity of Legal Systems', in *The Structure and Process of International Law*, ed. R. St. McDonald and D. M. Johnston (The Hague, 1983), pp. 728-9.

legal systems. They differ both as to their subjects (individuals and groups of individuals in the case of domestic law; States, in the case of international law) and as regards their sources, that is the means of creating and changing the law, at their disposal (parliamentary statutes being the main source of internal law, while in the international field, treaties and custom are the two principal modes of law-making). Many consequences follow from the fact that these two categories of legal systems are distinct and separate; in particular: (1) the validity of each legal system does not rest on a legal rule belonging to the other category (each system deriving its validity from its own basis), and, consequently, each legal system cannot legally condition the other; (2) within a State system (say, that of the UK) the rules of another legal order, such as international law, cannot be applied as such, but only after being '*transformed*' into legal rules of that system (that is, into English rules). Until this transformation has taken place, international standards merely have the value of 'facts'.

What are the consequences and implications of this view? First, international law is no longer dependent on the will of one single State; it is created by the joint will of members of the international community; each State must abide by it. Secondly, it is for each State to decide whether and in what forms to implement international law within its own domestic system. Implementation is thus made conditional on the will of each State. A State can go so far as to decide not to transform international rules into domestic law, or can even make domestic law override national rules created in consequence of international norms. True, in this case the State would incur international responsibility. The fact remains, however, that on the domestic plane it is free to disregard international rules. Since international law is effective to the extent that it is actually applied within national legal systems, it follows that States may go so far as to thwart the legal import of international prescriptions.

Clearly, the dualist theory was inspired by a moderate nationalism; it endeavoured to face the reality of international society, but at the same time insisted on relying on an 'emergency exit', as it were, in case international law proved to be in harsh conflict with national interests.

The third theory, that of a 'monistic' doctrine giving primacy to international law, was developed in the early twentieth century by the Austrian jurist and philosopher, H. Kelsen. As early as 1899 a German jurist, W. Kaufmann had propounded the basic outlines of such a theory.[10] (At the time his contribution was, for a number of reasons, overshadowed by the

---

[10] W. Kaufmann, *Die Rechtskraft des Internationalen Rechtes und das Verhältnis der Staats-gesetzgebungen und der Staatsorgane zu demselben* (Berlin, 1899). On Kaufmann's view see F. Münch, 'Wilhelm Kaufmann und der ursprüngliche Monismus', *Die Friedenswarte*, 53 (1955-6), 117 ff.

'dualist' approach—the more so because he had not articulated a fully-fledged theory but merely expounded a few general principles.)

As in the case of 'dualism', the best way of accounting for the 'monistic' approach is by drawing attention to the general factors attendant on its elaboration. As Ferrari Bravo[11] has emphasized, a large number of developments after the First World War (such as the punishment of war criminals and the attempt to bring to justice the German Emperor, as well as the establishment of the League of Nations mechanism for the protection of minorities) pointed to the emergence of the role of individuals in the world community; these factors contributed to highlighting the place of individuals in the international community, thus undermining the basic tenet of the 'dualist' doctrine whereby States are solely actors on the world scene and human beings, as such, do not play any role outside their respective domestic setting. Another concomitant factor was the enactment of various constitutions, which solemnly laid down that 'the generally recognised rules of international law' were to be applied by domestic authorities. This proclamation, first made in the Weimar Constitution of 1919 and imitated in subsequent texts, served a political purpose—that of proving to the victors that Germany was willing to live up to the generally accepted standards of the international community, and was, therefore, worthy of entering the League of Nations. The constitutional rules on international law had, however, a side-effect: they showed that the stark separation between the 'law of nations' and municipal systems was an artificial scholarly construction, for in reality there existed national provisions proclaiming the 'superiority' of the former—they made customary international rules immediately binding at the domestic level and in some cases even endowed them with greater legal force than would be the case under ordinary legislation.

Let us now briefly consider the essence of the 'monistic' approach developed by H. Kelsen. His theory postulates firstly, the existence of a unitary legal system, embracing all the various legal orders existing at various levels; secondly, the superiority of international law, which is at the top of the pyramid and validates or invalidates all the legal acts of any other legal system. Consequently, municipal law must always conform to international law; in cases of conflict, the latter declares all domestic rules or acts contrary to it to be illegal. A further corollary is that the 'transformation' of international norms into domestic law 'is not necessary from the point of view of international law'. This is because international and national law are 'parts of one normative system'; consequently, the subjects of international law are not radically different from those of national law and the sources of international law belong to a legal system which is hierarchically superior to municipal systems, not radically different from them. As a result, international rules can be applied *as such* by domestic courts, without any need for transformation. However, allowance is made for certain qualifications. National constitutions (be they written or unwritten) may require domestic

[11] L. Ferrari Bravo, op. cit., 731-3.

courts to apply only statutes enacted by national legislatures; in this case courts will only apply international rules (treaties) after transformation into national statutes. In short: 'the necessity of transformation is a question of national, not of international law'. One of the corollaries of this principle is that, normally, international rules are no longer mere 'facts' to domestic courts; they are binding values emanating from a higher legal system, and should therefore be implemented as such.

Since, according to this conception, the international legal system controls, however imperfectly, all national systems, which are subordinate to it, it follows that international values override national ones and State representatives must always strive to achieve the objectives set by international rules. It is clear that the theory rests on two basic ideological principles: internationalism and pacifism. This was spelled out with great clarity by Kelsen, who concluded, however, that the choice in favour of the primacy of international law cannot be made on the basis of a scientific method but is dictated by ethical or political preferences. This 'non-committal attitude' was largely motivated by Kelsen's adhesion to the philosophy of relativity. There was, however, another reason: Kelsen was aware that the international community is still far from the condition postulated by his theory: it still lacks the machinery for repealing those municipal provisions which are inconsistent with international rules.

Unlike the two preceding theories, the 'monistic' conception of the primacy of international law brought new emphasis to the role of international law as a controlling factor of State conduct. Whatever its logical inconsistencies and practical pitfalls, it has been instrumental in consolidating the notion that State agencies should abide by international legal standards and ought therefore to put international imperatives before national postulates.

THE RANGE OF STATES' FREEDOM OF ACTION

8.   To illustrate yet another typical feature of the international community it is useful to refer once again, by way of comparison, to domestic legal systems.

In most national orders individuals—the basic legal subjects—enjoy great freedom in their private transactions. They can variously enter into agreements with other persons, or refrain from so doing, or they can set up companies, create associations, and foundations, and so on. Their broad contractual freedom is not unfettered, however, in that central authorities usually place legal restraints upon them. Thus, for instance, one cannot make private transactions which are contrary to public order and 'morals' (such as a contract whereby one party undertakes to hand over to another a next of kin, for purposes of prostitution); if it is made, the transaction is null and void. Every domestic system contains a core of values which cannot be disregarded by members of the community, not even when they engage in private transactions *inter se*. In case of trespass, the response of the central authorities is to make the private undertaking devoid of legal effect. *A fortiori* individuals are not allowed to depart from certain basic values which are held in such high esteem as to be embodied in criminal norms. If two or more persons enter into an agreement for the setting up of a criminal association, in addition to their agreement being null and void, they also incur penal responsibility and are punishable accordingly. A third set of restrictions on individual freedom derives from all the norms of public law concerning the functioning of State institutions: thus, for instance, in a State where political elections take place by law once every four years, citizens are not free to vote whenever they would like to do so. Limitations also derive from constitutional rules restraining the exercise of certain rights and liberties (as in the case of freedom of thought or association), as well as from labour laws (which often restrict freedom of contract in labour relations with regard to working time and working conditions, with a view to protecting the weaker party).

Accordingly, in national legal systems two groups of provisions stand out amongst all these rules placing restrictions on individuals' freedom of action: the imperative norms of civil law, usually labelled 'norms of public order' or *jus cogens* (a body of law from which no derogation is permissible, as opposed to *just dispositivum* or 'dispositive' law), and prescriptions of criminal law. It should be noted that *jus cogens* includes norms prohibiting physical persons from disposing of their body or their freedom. Thus, a contract whereby one party undertakes to mutilate his body or to deliver to another party one of his limbs is contrary to 'public order' and consequently null and void. The same consideration applies to a contract whereby one party undertakes to commit suicide or to submit permanently to a position akin to slavery in relation to another party.

By contrast, subjects of the international community enjoy wide-ranging freedom of action. In classical international law their freedom was in fact untrammelled; in modern international law, on the other hand, some legal restrictions have been established.

Under traditional law States enjoyed great latitude as regards their internal set-up. The world community could not 'poke its nose' into how a State organized its political system. All States were free to establish an authoritarian power structure, or to uphold democratic principles; they could create a parliament or do without any representative assembly whatsoever; they could have a monarch or a democratically elected head of State. This was the private business of each country. In addition, international law was not interested in requesting States to give their internal legal order a specific content. With a few exceptions (for instance, international customary rules on the treatment of foreigners), States were completely free to decide upon the tenor and scope of their national legislation. Again, general international law was not involved in the matter.

States also enjoyed complete freedom as regards the conduct of their foreign policy. It was up to them to decide whether or not to enter into international agreements, and they were free to choose their partners and the contents of agreements. They could shape their international relations as they pleased; they could recognize a new State or withhold recognition; they were free to enter into alliance with one or more States or refrain from doing so, and so on. They were even authorized by the legal order to use force as much as they wished and on any grounds they chose. This right was proclaimed in Article 2 of the Hague Convention for the Pacific Settlement of International Disputes (1907),[12] as well as in national documents such as the Spanish Regulations on Land Warfare (1882), Article 836 of which laid down as one of the 'just causes of war', 'the defence of the general interests of the State or of its essential rights'.[13] States could engage in a war or resort to forcible measures short of war (see §§ 121–4) either on the grounds that one of their legal rights had been violated, or because they considered it politically and economically expedient forcibly to attack another State (for example, in order to occupy and annex part, or the whole, of its territory, or to set up a Government subservient to their commands, etc.). Law was so 'generous' as also to allow States to intervene in the domestic and international affairs of other members of the world community, either by political pressure or by threatening the use of force, for the purpose of inducing the 'victim' of the intervention to change its policy (see §§ 121–2). Furthermore, even when they undertook to submit their legal disputes to arbitration, States usually excluded from the obligation to arbitrate all the disputes affecting their 'vital interests', and each of them retained the right to decide whether a specific case fell within that category. J. L. Brierly[14] recalls the remark made by one of the delegates to the Hague Conference of 1907, whereby the effect of those arbitration clauses was that 'though the treaties began with the imperative "thou shalt", they ended with the reassuring words "if thou wilt"'. Freedom in the economic field was even greater. It is worth mentioning the remarks written down by Sir John Fischer William as late as 1939:

---

[12] Article 2 of the Hague Convention on Pacific Settlement of International Disputes of 1907, provides that 'In case of serious disagreement or dispute, before an appeal to arms, the Contracting Powers agree to have recourse, as far as circumstances allow, to the good offices or mediation of one or more friendly Powers.'

[13] See the 'Reglamento de Campaña' of 1882; Article 836 para. 1 provides that 'Entre las causas que ocasionan una guerra, se consideran como justas: La defensa de los intereses generales del estado o de sus derechos esenciales', *Colección legislativa del ejercito*, p. 163.

[14] J. L. Brierly, 'International Law: Its Actual Part in World Affairs', *The Basis of Obligation in International Law* (Oxford, 1958), p. 310.

... It is open to any State without violating a legal rule, except in so far as it may be bound by commercial treaty, to take any measures which it may think fit in the sphere of international commerce. It may stretch out its hand into the economic life of its neighbour by destroying without compensation such part of its neighbour's trade as consisted in export to its own domestic market. The inhabitants of a particular district in one country may have for many years made their living by the supply of some article to another country; that other country may then suddenly and without warning put on a prohibitive duty against the import of the particular article so supplied, and a peaceable group of producers in the first country is ruined without redress, by action over which its own government, in spite of its 'sovereignty', had in fact no sort of control. Such cases have in fact occurred.[15]

Legal freedom went so far as to allow States to agree with other subjects that one of them must extinguish itself: they could conclude an agreement whereby one of them was incorporated into the other; or they could merge; or else, one of them could agree to cede a portion of its territory to another State. No imperative rule prohibited self-mutilation or self-destruction.

I have, of course, been speaking of *legal* freedom. Power politics, the constant need for a balance of power, economic and social considerations, the geographical situation of States, prestige and traditions as well as other factors—all these conspired to reduce that freedom. Nevertheless, the legal order adopted a *laissez-faire* attitude, thereby leaving an enormous field of action to States.

It is not difficult to understand why international law took this turn: as no State or group of States proved capable of wielding permanent control over the world community so as to impose a set of basic standards of behaviour calculated to govern the action of members, it was necessary to fall back on a negative regulation, leaving all members free to act as they liked, provided they did not grossly and consistently trespass on the freedom of other members. Clearly, this approach could not but favour the Great Powers. In actual fact, international law was modelled in such a way as to 'codify', legitimize and protect their interests.

9. The unrestricted freedom of States has been encountering increasing qualification since the First World War. Three factors account for new developments in this area. First of all, there is the ever expanding scope of the network of international treaties. So many States are now party to so large a number of treaties impinging upon their domestic legal systems that, at present, most members of the world community are bound to obey a number of duties which greatly restrict their latitude, both as regards their own internal systems and concerning their freedom in the international sphere. Many of them have assumed obligations in the field of commercial, political and judicial co-operation, in the realm of human rights, etc. Similarly, as far as international action is concerned, many of them are

[15] J. Fischer Williams, *Aspects of Modern International Law*, pp. 108-9.

parties to international organizations, to treaties of alliance, etc. True, all these undertakings derive from treaties; in theory, States can therefore get rid of them if they wish to do so. However, in practice, it is difficult for them to release themselves from all their various commitments—political, economic, diplomatic, military, and psychological factors stand in the way.

A second important reason is the increasing number of legal restrictions on the right to use force. Considerable restraints on the power to wage war were placed on a number of States by the Covenant of the League of Nations in 1919; they were reinforced and extended to a larger (and, in some respects, different) group of States in 1928 by the Paris Pact, promoted by the US and France; they became radical and sweeping in 1945, when the UN Charter required members to refrain from using or threatening the use of any sort of military force, with or without the label of 'war'. The ban on the use of force has now turned into a principle encompassing the whole international community but unfortunately, the resulting limitation on State freedom is beset with loopholes which chiefly affect the enforcement mechanisms—of which some members of the world community take full advantage (see §§ 135, 145).

A third development has proved instrumental in limiting the freedom previously enjoyed by States. In the 1960s a customary rule evolved in the international community to the effect that certain general principles have greater legal force than other rules, in that States cannot derogate from them through international agreements. This set of peremptory norms was called *jus cogens*. It follows that States are now duty-bound to refrain from entering into agreements providing for one of the activities prohibited by peremptory norms; if they still do so, their agreements are null and void. We shall see, however, that this all-important advance has only manifested itself in the normative field; no specific international machinery has been set up to impose the observance of *jus cogens*, and—as stated above—the present mechanisms for law-enforcement are still very deficient (see § 145). We can therefore, conclude that at least in some respects, the condition of the present international community is not far from that of classical international law.

THE OVERRIDING ROLE OF EFFECTIVENESS

10. International law is a realistic legal system. It takes account of existing power relationships and endeavours to translate them into legal rules. It is largely based on the principle of effectiveness, that is to say, it provides that only those claims and situations which are effective can produce legal effects. A situation is effective if it is solidly implanted in real life. Thus, for instance, if a new State emerges from a secession, it will be able to claim international status only after it is apparent that it undisputedly controls a specific territory and the human community occupying it. Control over the State community must be real and durable. The same consideration holds true for insurgents. If civil strife breaks out within a State, the rebellious group cannot lay claim to international rights and duties so long as it does not exercise effective authority over a part of the territory concerned. Similarly, in case of military occupation of a foreign territory, the occupant cannot claim all the rights and privileges deriving from the international law of warfare, until the territory is actually placed under its authority and until he is in a position to assert himself. As pointed out in the US Department of the Army Field Manual (The Law of Land Warfare, 1956): 'occupation ... is invasion plus taking firm possession of enemy territory for the purpose of holding it'.[16]

The principle of effectiveness permeates the whole body of rules making up international law. One of its corollaries is the fact that legal fictions have no place on the international scene (this holds true for the 'old' law; for examples of legal fictions typical of the 'new' law, see *infra*, § 133). New situations are not recognized as legally valid unless they can be seen to rest on a firm and durable display of authority. Rebellions, the splitting up of existing States, the emergence of new entities, and so forth: none of these new situations can claim international legitimacy so long as the 'new men' fail to demonstrate that they have firmly supplanted the former authority. Force is the principal source of legitimation in the international community. The formal 'endorsement' of power tends to legalize and crystallize it.

One may well wonder why force plays such an overriding role in the world community, giving the international legal system a 'conservative' slant. The answer probably lies in the fact that power is diffused and a superior authority capable of legitimizing new situations does not exist, nor have States evolved a core of principles serving this purpose (they are too divided to be able to do so); as a consequence, legal rules must of necessity rely upon force as the sole standard by which new facts and events are to be legally appraised.

It should, however, be added that these observations apply primarily to the traditional setting of international society. Since the First World War (the main impetus having been given by the 'Stimson doctrine' of 1932: see § 133), an attempt has been made by a number of States to make 'legality' prevail over sheer force or authority, by withholding legitimation from certain situations which, although effective, offend certain values which are increasingly regarded as fundamental. This doctrine was defined by the British jurists L. Oppenheim and H. Lauterpacht in the following terms:

A State confronted either with an attempt by another State to bring about a new title, treaty or situation by means of an illegal act or with an actually consummated

[16] US Department of the Army, *The Law of Land Warfare* (Washington, DC, 1956), p. 138 (para. 352).

act of that nature, may expressly declare that it will not in the future validate by an act of recognition the fruits of the illegal conduct.[17]

We shall see to what extent 'legality' can displace 'effectiveness' (§§ 45, 133).

INDIVIDUALISTIC TRENDS

11. The political structure of the international community and the lack of strong political, ideological, and economic links between its members (the Christian principles prevailing in the 'old' community were not allowed to override national interests), have resulted in the tendency for every State to be self-seeking. Self-interest holds sway.

This phenomenon is also apparent in the way substantive rules govern the behaviour of States. Most customary and treaty rules confer rights or impose duties on pairs of States only. As a result, each State has a right or a duty in relation to one other State only. Such rules can also be termed 'synallagmatic' in that they impose reciprocal obligations. This feature, self-evident in the case of a bilateral treaty, holds true for other rules as well. Take, for example, the provisions of multilateral treaties on diplomatic immunities; although they are general in character and address themselves to all the contracting parties, in actual fact they split into a number of binary rules, each regulating a pair of contracting States. Thus, for instance Article 31.1 of the 1961 Vienna Convention on Diplomatic Relations ('A diplomatic agent shall enjoy immunity from the criminal jurisdiction of the receiving State') entails that in the relations between, say, the UK and Indonesia, either State has the right to claim from the other that its diplomatic agents be immune from the criminal jurisdiction of the other State; the same applies to all other pairs of States making up the totality of the contracting parties. In practice, this multilateral treaty can be broken down into a set of substantially similar bilateral treaties, each regulating the relationships between a particular pair of States. It is as if each contracting party were bound by as many bilateral treaties as there are other contracting parties.

There are, however, general rules which confer on each member of the international community *rights erga omnes*, that is, towards all the other States. Conspicuous instances are the rule on sovereignty (each State has the right to claim from all other States full respect for its territorial integrity and political independence) and that on the free use of the high seas (each State has the right to enjoy freedom of navigation, fishing, overflight, as well as freedom to lay submarine cables and pipelines in all parts of the sea which are not under the jurisdiction of a coastal State). It should, however,

---

[17] L. Oppenheim and H. Lauterpacht, *International Law*, i, 8th edn. (London, 1958), pp. 142-3.

be noted that as soon as one of these norms is violated, the ensuing legal relationship links only the aggrieved State and the offending party. In other words, the character *erga omnes* of the substantive rights is not accompanied by a procedural right of enforcement belonging to all the members of the international community. Once a State has infringed upon the sovereignty of another State, it is for the victim to claim reparation; no other State can intervene on his behalf or on behalf of the whole international community to claim cessation or reparation of the wrong. Plainly, we are far from the system obtaining in all national legal systems, where, in case of serious breaches (for example criminal offences), a representative of the entire community (the Public Prosecutor or a similar institution) can initiate legal proceedings irrespective of the attitude or the action of the injured party. The system prevailing in international law has a number of serious drawbacks, among them the fact that the reaction to a wrong ultimately depends on whether the victim is stronger than or at least as strong as the culpable State. In the final analysis, respect for law is made dependent on power.

12. However, these observations should be qualified, for in the *present* international community States have agreed upon new rules with a different content and import. A number of treaties, many of which came into being after the First World War, and more particularly in the aftermath of the Second World War, provide for special international duties. They are, firstly, *duties erga omnes*, that is towards all the other contracting States, and, in addition, they are attended by a correlative right belonging to every other contracting State. Consequently, if a State disregards one of the rules, its failure to fulfil its duty towards all other parties gives each of them a right to insist on its fulfilment, or in any case to demand that the offence must not be repeated. A right exists quite independently of any damage which may be inflicted on a party. In other words, a contracting State can require respect for the treaty by the delinquent State regardless of whether or not the former has suffered any prejudice from the infraction.

Some treaties confine themselves to proclaiming a particular right, without specifying by which means it can be exercised. It follows that in case of infraction the traditional means of redress (diplomatic steps, diplomatic pressure, peaceful reprisals) must be resorted to. By contrast, a number of other treaties set up special procedures or a special machinery for facilitating the task of the claimant State. We shall return to this point later on (see §§ 115–16, 178, 182). But it seems appropriate at this juncture to comment on the content of this category of treaty. It evolved from the emergence of new values which have come to be regarded by the international community as worthy of special protection. Thus, after the First World War, as a result of the ideological and political pressure of socialist doctrines, and also because, following the catastrophe of war, it came to be believed that the condition of workers was growing worse, the lot of workers deserved greater international concern (see, however, § 168). Similarly, after the Second World War, as a reaction to the mass murder of ethnic and religious groups by the Nazis (chiefly Jews and Gypsies) and the total disregard for the basic human rights of thousands of individuals both in Germany and elsewhere, the Allies decided to create better safeguards against genocide and other egregious violations of human rights. By the same token, the Nazi aggression against a number of European States and the attack of Japan on the US prompted the UN to enact a sweeping ban on all forms of aggression. All these new values resulted in a number of international treaties (§ 169).

Nevertheless, the value of the recent emergence of 'community duties', though important, should not be over-emphasized. For one thing, the treaties or customary rules laying down these duties are still relatively rare. For another, even those rules are seldom put into effect. A typical feature of the international community, namely the huge gap between the normative level and that of implementation, is more conspicuous in this area than anywhere else. Although States are offered the opportunity of acting in the interest of the whole international community, they usually prefer to avoid meddling in other States' internal affairs. They end up by exercising their 'community rights' only when their own economic, military, or political interests are at stake. In the final analysis, most procedures based on State-to-State complaints have ended in failure, or, at least, have not been exploited fully (see §§ 115-16, 178). However, this pessimistic assessment is somewhat attenuated by the fact that there are international procedures which can be set in motion either at the request of the aggrieved individuals or *ex officio*, that is by the international body responsible for supervising compliance with the treaty concerned (see §§ 115, 116). In these cases fulfilment of the duty *erga omnes* is sought by entities other than the various contracting States. Their action eventually compensates for the lack of consideration shown to ideals of a common good.

COEXISTENCE OF OLD AND NEW PATTERNS

13. Every legal system undergoes constant change, for law must steadily adjust itself to new realities. This sometimes results in old and new institutions living together: even in the case of revolutions, it is difficult to get rid of all the existing legal structures overnight. However, the rule is that outmoded pieces of the legal fabric are supplanted by fresh ones so as to eliminate the most glaring inconsistencies.

In the international community two different patterns in law, one traditional, the other modern, live side by side. The new legal institutions, which

have developed within the setting of the international society approximately since the first World War (and with greater intensity since 1945), have
not uprooted or supplanted the old framework; rather, they appear to have
been superimposed on it (even though their main purpose is to attenuate
the most conspicuous deficiencies of the old one). This in a way reminds us
of what happens in the modern mind, where highly sophisticated intellectual
capabilities coexist with archaic modes of feeling: as Jung once remarked,
a 'modern European' can feel and behave like 'the child of a troglodyte'.[18]

What are the main features of the traditional system? For our present
purpose, and subject to the qualifications to be made in the following
chapters, they can be summarized as follows: force as the primary source
of legitimation; the extreme decentralization of the legal functions; unfettered freedom of States; the unrestricted right to resort to armed violence,
either to enforce rights or to protect interests. The resulting picture is that
of a community where law does not place any major restraint on power; on
the contrary, it gives its official blessing to power. Economic, social, and
military inequalities fail to be taken into account. Formally, all States are
equal in that they can all claim respect for their sovereignty. In practice, if
a powerful State tramples upon the rights of a weak State, the latter will
derive very little benefit from law. If the offending State refuses to settle a
dispute by peaceful means (for example, by entrusting an independent body
with the task of determining if, and to what extent, the law has been
broken) no sanction can be taken against it, lest the stronger State should
decide to go to war.

If we were to take up the distinction drawn by H. Bull[19] between what
he considers the three competing traditions of thought put forward throughout the history of modern States (namely the *Hobbesian*, or realist tradition,
'which views international politics as a state of war', the *Grotian*, or internationalist conception, which emphasizes the element of co-operation and
regulated intercourse among sovereign States, and the *Kantian*, or universalist outlook, 'which sees at work in international politics a potential community of mankind' and lays stress on the element of 'transnational solidarity'), it is difficult to avoid the conclusion that in its first stage of
development the international community was shaped on the pattern of the
Hobbesian and Grotian traditions.

On the other hand, the 'new' international legal institutions which appear
to be largely patterned on the 'Kantian' model of thought, try to mitigate
the most striking defects of the old system, by introducing certain improve-

---

[18] C. G. Jung, *Die Beziehungen zwischen dem Ich und dem Unbewussten* (Zurich, 1928); trans. R. F. C. Hull in Jung, *Two Essays on Analytical Psychology* 2nd edn. (Princeton, 1972), p. 201.
[19] H. Bull, *The Anarchical Society: A Study of Order in World Politics* (New York, 1977), pp. 24–7.

ments such as the creation of international organizations, the placing of sweeping restraints on the use of force and so on. In particular, the new 'setting' has endeavoured to attenuate (see §§ 107, 114-18, 128-134) the shortcomings of the decentralization of the three legal functions referred to above (§ 3).

The extent to which these imaginative devices have proved effective will be examined further on. For the time being it is sufficient to repeat that the new pattern has not replaced the old one. The latter is deeply rooted in international society and reflects its basic tendencies. Very often, particularly in periods of crisis, the old structure rises to the surface and instantly obliterates all the mechanisms set up with painstaking care. It is like a human skeleton that can only be seen on an X-ray being covered by flesh and skin and clothes. Though momentarily concealed, it is still very much there, constituting the framework on which all the rest is based.

THE INTERNATIONAL COMMUNITY: A DIVIDED WORLD

14. Many of the features on which I have dwelt are characteristic of the old international community, even though they have been somewhat alienated since the First World War. I shall now turn to one distinguishing trait which has arisen in the latest stage in the development of the world community. For a long time the 'family of nations' was relatively homogeneous (at least between the Peace of Westphalia (1648) and the end of the nineteenth century): all its dominant members had a common ideological and religious background and, what is even more important, they shared a common socio-economic outlook: they were all geared to a market economy and free competition.

Since 1917, the world community has, in many respects, lost its homogeneity. The emergence in the 1960s of numerous developing countries delivered the fatal blow to its former cultural and ideological unity. At present, the community is split into three main segments, each with a distinct socio-economic philosophy, a fairly fully developed ideology, and diverse political motivations—and even within each of these groups there are many divisions and differences. What is particularly relevant to the present enquiry is that the profound rifts existing in the international arena have also had a profound effect in the realm of law. In the following chapters we shall see that the three existing groupings of States are in full agreement on only a very small number of crucial issues of international law.

This disturbing situation raises the question of whether there are certain principles capable of holding the various States together, whether there is such a thing as a cement which prevents the world community from falling into utter chaos. We shall see that a core of very general legal standards acceptable to all States does indeed exist: it has evolved in recent years, and all States, irrespective of their ideological, economic, or political orientation, tend to rely on them (see Chapter 6).

The existence of broad areas of dissent or only partial agreement on the one side, and the emergence of certain fundamental standards of behaviour acceptable to all States on the other, makes it useful to draw a distinction between three categories of international norms: *universal* (principles applicable to all States belonging to the three main groupings referred to above), *general* (customary rules or norms of multilateral treaties accepted by only two groups of States), and *particular* (bilateral treaties, as well as multilateral treaties, adhered to by one segment only of the international community).

2

Historical Evolution of the International Community: The Former Setting (1648–1918)

15. WE should now ask ourselves how it came about that the international community acquired the unique features it currently shows: as a result of what historical events and what forces did it evolve in such a way as to appear so markedly different from all domestic legal systems?

In tracing the historical evolution of the world community, it is useful to divide it into various *stages*. Periodization is, of course, always arbitrary; nevertheless, it may prove helpful for a better understanding of some major turning points.

BIRTH OF THE PRESENT INTERNATIONAL COMMUNITY AFTER THE PEACE OF WESTPHALIA (1648)

16. The origin of the international community in its present structure and configuration is usually traced back to the Peace of Westphalia (1648), which concluded the ferocious and sanguinary Thirty Years War. However, it was not then that international intercourse between groups and nations started. From time immemorial there had been consular and diplomatic relations between different communities, as well as treaties of war and peace and treaties of alliance; reprisals had been regulated for many years and during the Middle Ages a body of law on the conduct of belligerent hostilities had gradually evolved. A peace treaty going back to approximately 3100 BC has come to light—concluded in the Sumerian language between Eannatum, the victorious ruler of the Mesopotamian city State of Lagash, and the representatives of Umma, another Mesopotamian city State, which had been defeated.[1] And yet all these relations were radically different from current international dealings, for the body politic itself was different. Even in the late Middle Ages, when international relations of a kind resulted from the splitting of communities into various groups headed by feudal lords, the fabric of international society differed from the present one, and this for two reasons. First, fully-fledged States—in the modern sense—did not yet exist (centralized structures, which had gradually come into being

[1] See A. Nussbaum, *A Concise History of the Law of Nations* (New York, 1962), p. 1.

in Europe between 1100 and 1300, did not assume the typical features of a modern State until after 1450).

Of the various historical enquiries into the origin of the modern State, it may suffice to quote here those of J. R. Strayer.[2] In his view, what characterizes the modern State and differentiates it both from 'the great, imperfectly integrated empires' of the past and 'the small, but highly cohesive units, such as the Greek city State', are the following characteristics: 'the appearance of political units persisting in time and fixed in space, the development of permanent, impersonal institutions, agreement on the need for an authority which can give final judgments, and acceptance of the idea that this authority should receive the basic loyalty of its subjects'. Underlying them are 'a shift in loyalty from family, local community, or religious organization to the State, and the acquisition by the State of a moral authority to back up its institutional structure and its theoretical legal supremacy'. In addition to these features, the modern State shows a very important distinguishing trait: the emergence of centralized bureaucracies, which gradually turn into ministerial departments. It is no doubt a slow evolution; nevertheless, in the seventeenth century, 'the permanent core of the State was by now the bureaucracy' (Finer)[3] although, as has been pointed out by Jellinek,[4] one must wait until the adoption on 25 May 1791 of the French 'décret' establishing the various ministries for the 'principle of division of labour to be completely carried through in public administration, and for ministers in the sense of administrative law to side by the monarch'.

The period following the Peace of Westphalia inaugurated a new era in a second respect; previously there had been the overpowering presence of two poles of authority: the Pope at the head of the Catholic Church, and the Emperor at the head of the Holy Roman Empire (which had been set up as early as AD 800 by Charlemagne and had encompassed most of Europe to dwindle in the seventeenth century to the German territory in central Europe). Two sorts of law (ecclesiastical and imperial) corresponded to the two power structures. They left little room for a legal system akin to the present body of international law.

True, after the fourteenth century the Pope gradually lost power and his own authority, like that of the Emperor was eroded little by little, so much so that in the sixteenth century it was more formal than real. However, the fact remains that, as Jellinek[5] rightly pointed out, in order to emerge, the modern State had to fight against three powers, namely 'the Church, the Emperor, and the authority of trade-guilds' (*ständische Macht*). The birth of the modern State cannot be dissociated from the struggle against those three 'powers', for 'the modern State is a unitarily closed-up entity, in which all the authority that individuals or guilds may possess can only be granted by the State itself'.

[2] J. R. Strayer, *On the Medieval Origins of the Modern State* (Princeton, NJ, 1970), pp. 10, 9.
[3] S. Finer, 'Civil Servants and Bureaucrats' in *Faces of Europe* (London, 1981), Chap. 25.
[4] G. Jellinek, 'Die Entwicklung des Ministeriums in der Konstitutionellen Monarchie' (1833), *Schriften*, p. 98.
[5] G. Jellinek, 'Die Entstehung der modernen Staatsidee' (1894), *Schriften*, p. 46.

Thus the necessary premise for the development of the present international community is the rise of modern national States between the fifteenth and the seventeenth centuries. This momentous phenomenon, indisputably favoured by the discovery of America (1492) and the dissemination of Protestantism after the Reformation, led to the formation of a number of strong States, all of which sought to be independent from any superior authority. Western countries such as England, Spain, and France, followed by the Netherlands and Sweden, as well as the Ottoman Empire, China, and Japan in the East, increasingly regarded each other as separate and autonomous entities, and each struggled to overpower the other. New standards of behaviour became necessary. Consequently, either the old rules were given a new shape or, alternatively, new norms were developed. In this respect an important contribution was made by a number of imaginative and forward-looking jurists, such as the Spaniards Francisco Vitoria (1480-1546) and Francisco Suarez (1548-1617), the Italian Alberico Gentili (1552-1608), a Protestant who fled to England, where he taught at Oxford, and above all the Dutchman Hugo Grotius (1583-1645). They set out to lend a lucid legal justification to the interests of the emerging States in general, and of their own country in particular.

The new situation crystallized in 1648, when the Peace of Westphalia concluded a most appalling war, which had caused 'great effusion of Christian blood and the desolation of several provinces' (preamble to the Treaty of Münster). The major countries of Europe had been involved in it; the conflict had started in 1618 for religious reasons, namely the struggle between Catholic and Protestant countries, but it soon turned into an all out struggle for military and political hegemony in Europe. The treaties of peace were signed in the Westphalian towns of Münster and Osnabrück (questions of prestige accounted for the choice of two places for negotiating peace: France and Sweden, the former Catholic, the latter Protestant, quarrelled over the question of precedence; consequently France was given priority in Catholic Münster and Sweden in Protestant Osnabrück. However, from the legal point of view, the two treaties were considered as one single instrument). They constitute a watershed in the evolution of the modern international community. First, they recognized Protestantism at an international level and consequently legitimized the existence of States based on Calvinist or Lutheran faith. Henceforth, even from the point of view of religion, it was recognized that the State was independent of the Church. Second, the treaties granted members of the Holy Roman Empire (three hundred odd small States) the *jus foederationis*, that is the right to enter into alliances with foreign powers and to wage war, provided that those alliances or wars were neither against the Empire 'nor against the public peace' and the 'treaty' (Article 65 of the treaty of Münster). Thus, a number of small countries were upgraded to the status of members of the international community with almost sovereign rights. Third, the treaties crystallized a political distribution of power in Europe which lasted for almost a century. France, Sweden, and the Netherlands were recognized as the new emerging big powers, Switzerland (and the Netherlands) were given the status of neutral countries; Germany was split up into a number of relatively small States. In short, the Peace of Westphalia testified to the rapid decline of the Church (an institution which had already suffered many blows) and to the *de facto* disintegration of the Empire; by the same token it recorded the birth of an international system based on a plurality of independent States, recognizing no superior authority over them.

17. The view whereby international law goes back to the period after the Peace of Westphalia is the most widespread in Western legal literature, and has recently been taken up by a Chinese jurist, Chen Tiquang. But a different view was put forward by three Western international lawyers, the German M. Zimmermann,[6] the Austrian A. Verdross,[7] and the Italian G. Balladore Pallieri.[8] In their opinion international law as we know it today was born in the eleventh century, when a community of Christian States evolved. A different view has been taken by R. Ago,[9] who holds that international law evolved even earlier, namely in the ninth century, when three 'different worlds' began to coexist and to have international relations: the French-Lombard empire of Charlemagne, the Byzantine, and the Islamic empire: hence, for Ago, the origin of the international community has not been exclusively Christian, but pluralist and multicultural; indeed, as early as the ninth century, it encompassed three different civilizations.

A different approach is taken by most of the jurists from Eastern Europe. For example, the Soviet E. Korowin[10] and the *Manual* of the GDR[11] (the latter being more articulate and detailed) start from the assumption that there have been as many historical stages as there have been 'class societies' and corresponding 'types of States': consequently they divide the historical evolution of international law into the phases of the 'slave States' (the ancient world), that of 'feudal States', that of 'capitalist States' (starting, according to Korowin, in 1789), that of 'socialist States' (starting in 1917), and finally the stage of the 'passage from capitalism to socialism'. This

---

[6] M. Zimmermann, 'La Crise de l'organisation internationale à la fin du moyen-âge', Hague *Recueil* 44 (1933-II), 352 ff.

[7] A. Verdross, *Völkerrecht* (Berlin, 1937), pp. 5 ff; 5th edn., ed. S. Verosta and K. Żemanek (Wien, 1964), pp. 51 ff.

[8] G. Balladore Pallieri, *Diritto internazionale pubblico* (Milan, 1937), pp. 4 ff. (8th edn., Milan 1962, pp. 4–7).

[9] R. Ago, 'Pluralism and the Origins of the International Community, *IYIL* 3 (1978), 3 ff.; id., 'The First International Communities in the Mediterranean World', *BYIL* 53 (1982), 213 ff.

[10] E. Korowin (ed.), *International Law* (Moscow, 1962), pp. 27 ff.

[11] DDR-*Völkerrecht* 1982, i. 69 ff.

view, largely based on ideological premises, is shared by the Chinese international lawyer Zhou Gensheng.[12]

It is worth pointing out that, logically speaking, none of the aforementioned views is wrong. Each puts a premium on different turning-points or historical phenomena and is consequently valid in the light of its basic assumptions. Nevertheless, to my mind the traditional view, which regards the period around the Peace of Westphalia as the main divide separating the traditional setting from modern international law, is the view which takes the best account of the fundamental circumstance that the body of law under discussion governs 'sovereign and independent States', namely sovereign entities possessed of the centralized structures typical of the modern State.

STAGE I: FROM THE PEACE OF WESTPHALIA TO THE FIRST WORLD WAR (1648–1918)

Composition of the International Community

18.   Since its inception, the world community has, needless to say, encompassed States belonging to different geographic, cultural, and religious areas. While the most intense intercourse took place between European States, treaties were also concluded with non-European States with which Europe had come into contact, chiefly the Mogul Empire in India, the Ottoman Empire, Persia, China, Japan (since 1854), Burma, and Siam (which acceded to independence in 1880 and has been called Thailand since 1939), as well as with the States of Ethiopia and Liberia (the latter being independent since 1847), and Haiti (independent since 1804). Suffice it to mention that only one year after the Peace of Westphalia, namely on 1 July 1649, the Holy Roman Empire concluded a treaty with Turkey for the continuation of the peace which had been agreed in 1642.

Nevertheless, for many centuries the most active and prominent members of the international community were the European States, joined by the United States of America in 1783 and by the Latin-American countries between 1811 and 1821. Paraphrasing Hegel's description of the role of Greece and Italy in the past, one might say that in this period Europe was the 'theatre of World History' and that there the 'World Spirit' (*Weltgeist*) found its home.[13] All the States above-mentioned had a common religious matrix: they were Christian. This common ideological background made for a better understanding. Despite political, economic, and military conflicts, culture and religion acted as a cement uniting all of them. Another strong unifying factor was the pattern of internal economic and political development. All Western States were the outgrowth of capitalism and its

---

[12] Zhou Gensheng, as quoted by Chen Tiqiang, *Ch YIL*, 247.
[13] G. F. W. Hegel, *The Philosophy of History*, trans. J. Sibree (New York, 1956), p. 102.

matching phenomenon in the political field: absolutism (followed in sub-sequent years by parliamentary democracy).

19. In a number of respects non-Christian States lived for many years on the margin of the international community, in the sense that they did not take a very active part, nor did they play any major role, in it. According to the Dutch historian J. C. van Leur[14] and the Polish-born British inter-national lawyer C. H. Alexandrowicz[15] followed by the Israeli jurist M. Mushkat,[16] for roughly three hundred years (from the sixteenth to the eighteenth centuries) a few Asian powers (namely all State entities in the East Indies, as well as Persia, Burma, and Siam) had social intercourse with European countries on a footing of complete equality. However—so the argument goes—the industrial revolution which took place in Europe in the late eighteenth century created a gap between Europe and non-European States; in the nineteenth century the latter were left far behind and were gradually conquered by the former or at any event fell under their domi-nation. Thus, in the nineteenth century, a previously universal international community narrowed to a European one (to become again universal as a result of the decolonization process in the 1960s). The aforementioned authors consequently insist that newly independent States should not be termed 'new', for many of them were 'original' members of the international community; furthermore, their belonging to such a community from the outset is a further reason why they should enjoy full equality in their current participation in the world community. This view has also been taken up by some States. Thus, for example, in 1968, when the issue of the succession of States in respect of treaties was discussed at the UN, the representative of Ceylon (as it was then called) questioned the use of terms such as 'new State' and 'old' or 'predecessor' State. He made the following observations:

The term 'new' could not properly be applied in the case of an ancient State which was subjugated and exploited for three or four centuries and then gained political independence in the twentieth century. In his delegation's view, the so-called 'new' State should rather be termed the 'original' State. His delegation was concerned that the principles finally stated should have a sound historical and economic basis. Not only the pre-independence phase of a country's past but also the period of independence prior to colonial rule might perhaps be relevant in determining the principles applicable in respect of State succession.[17]

---

[14] J. C. van Leur, *Indonesian Trade and Society* (London, 1955), as quoted in C. H. Alex-androwicz, 'The Afro-Asian World and the Law of Nations (Historical Aspects)', Hague *Recueil* 123 (1968-I), p. 125.

[15] C. H. Alexandrowicz, 'The Afro–Asian World and the Law of Nations', cit., 123 ff.

[16] M. Mushkat, 'L'Afrique et les problèmes du droit des gens', *Verfassung und Recht in Uebersee* 7 (1974) i. 3 ff.

[17] See UN document A/C.6/SR.1036.

The historical reconstruction propounded by the three scholars referred to above has been challenged by other authors, for instance by the German W. G. Grewe.[18] Be that as it may, three points are difficult to question: (1) since its inception the world community has not consisted only of European States, but has embraced other countries and nations as well, and there was some degree of intercourse between all sections of the community, although, of course, many factors including geographical distance and the slowness of communication and transport rendered transactions between European and other countries particularly difficult; (2) for various reasons, the European Powers set the tone from the outset and played a dominant role throughout; (3) Western jurists have consistently theorized and buttressed the idea of 'European' superiority.

The relations between European States and the 'outside world' have been aptly characterized by H. Bull[19] on the basis of his distinction between 'systems of States' (which are formed 'when two or more States have sufficient contact between them, and have sufficient impact on one another's decision, to cause them to behave—at least in some measure—as parts of a whole'), and a 'society of States' (which comes into being 'when a group of States, conscious of certain common interests and values, forms a society in the sense that they conceive themselves to be bound by a common set of rules in their relations with one another, and share in the working of common institutions'). At least until the late nineteenth century, when they were gradually assimilated to the international community, Turkey, Japan, China, Siam, etc. were part of a 'system of States' in their relations with Europe and the US: they were in contact with the latter without, however, conceiving themselves as part of a common world sharing the same values or setting up stable bonds of co-operation, let alone common institutions.

20.   As pointed out above, non-European States bowed to Western 'superiority' and eventually submitted to the rules elaborated by European countries and the US. Western States tended to develop two distinct classes of relations with the 'outside' world, depending on whether this 'world' consisted of States proper (the Ottoman Empire, China, Japan, etc,) or was instead made up of communities lacking any organized central authority (tribal communities or communities dominated by local rulers, in Africa and Asia). With the former, Europe and the US to a large extent based their relations on the 'capitulation' system; they considered the latter mere objects of conquest and appropriation, and consequently turned them into colonial territories.

[18] W. G. Grewe, 'Vom europäischen zum universellen Völkerrecht', *ZaöRuV* 42 (1982), 450 ff.
[19] H. Bull, *The Anarchical Society*, pp. 8–20.

Let us first consider the capitulation system. Capitulations were agreements (so called probably because they were divided into numbered *capitula* or brief chapters) concluded by Western States with Moslem rulers (later on with the Ottoman Empire), with some Arab countries (Egypt, Iraq, Syria, Morocco, Palestine), with Persia, Thailand, China, and Japan ever since the sixteenth century. The capitulary regime was consolidated in the seventeenth to eighteenth centuries: the treaty of 1740 between France and the Ottoman Empire is usually mentioned as being of great significance for the delineation of the main traits of this regime. Capitulations served to regulate the conditions of Europeans (*lato sensu*, that is including the US) on the territory of non-European countries. They tended to include the following basic provisions: (1) Europeans having the nationality of the party to the agreement could not be expelled from the country without the consent of their consul; (2) they had the right to practise public worship of their Christian faith; to this end they could erect churches and have their own graveyards; (3) they enjoyed freedom of trade and commerce and were exempted from certain import and export duties; (4) reprisals against them were prohibited, especially in case of insolvency; (5) jurisdiction over disputes between Europeans belonged to the consul of the defendant or, in criminal cases, of the victim (hence not to the territorial court), while in case of disputes between a European and a national of the territorial State it devolved upon the judges of the latter State.

Three features of this legal regime are striking. First, Europeans came to make up a legal community completely separate from the local one and actually subject to their own national authorities (which thereby extended their control beyond their own territorial range, and to a foreign country). Second, this regime was not based on reciprocity: it consisted of a number of privileges granted to Europeans on non-European territory, without there being any counterpart in favour of non-European nationals (the few instances adduced by Alexandrowicz of privileges granted in Europe to non-European partners are exceptional and of scant relevance). The crying inequality on which capitulations rested was clearly indicative of the kind of relationship existing between European States and the outside world. Third, at least in the eighteenth and early nineteenth centuries certain non-Western States did not see capitulations as detrimental to their sovereignty. Thus, for instance, it was stated by a Japanese author[20] that 'The Japanese authorities in those days, which had little knowledge of the concept of extraterritoriality, regarded national laws of Japan as something sacred, for the benefit of which foreigners were not worthy of enjoyment.' And Alexandrowicz has pointed out that capitulations rested on an ancient

---

[20] H. Otsuka, 'Japan's Early Encounter with the Concept of the Law of Nations', *JYIL* 13 (1969), 56.

Asian tradition ('ancient custom in Asia allowed foreign merchants to govern themselves by their own personal law instead of submitting to the jurisdiction and the law of the host country and possibly to a different way of life.)[21] None the less, the fact remains that Western rights of 'extraterritoriality' constituted in reality serious restraints on the sovereignty of the 'territorial' State and later on, towards the end of the nineteenth century, they were deeply felt as an undue encroachment even by the Japanese authorities.

21. Let us now turn to the relations of European States with another class of 'other' countries, namely those lacking any state-like structure, or governed by a great number of local authorities normally feuding with one another. These countries fell victims to Western Powers and were gradually subjected to their colonial domination.

It is well known that Europeans first colonized the Americas in the fifteenth century. As soon as the first signs of rebellion were apparent in America, Asia became a desirable area. In the eighteenth century first France and then the UK appropriated large portions of India, until in 1773 most of India actually became a British colony. In the early nineteenth century, when the successful revolt of the US was followed by the independence of South America, Europeans turned to Africa, while at the same time intensifying their interest in Asia. Africa was split up among the UK, France, Portugal, Belgium, Germany, and Italy; Asia was appropriated by the UK, France, the Netherlands, and even by a State formerly under colonial domination, namely the US (which seized power over the Philippines in 1898 as a result of the war with Spain, which was concluded by the Peace Treaty of Paris in 1898).

While it is also true that in a few areas and under certain conditions colonial domination proved fairly beneficial (for instance, occasionally it was economically advantageous to at least a section of the colonial population: see § 204), the question which should be raised here as particularly germane to the present enquiry is that of the role of international law in the process of colonial conquest. In short, it can be argued that this body of law greatly facilitated the task of European powers, offering them, as it did, a large number of legal instruments designed to render conquest smooth and easy. First of all, international law authorized States to acquire sovereignty over those territories, both by downgrading the latter to *terrae nullius*, namely, territories belonging to no one, and by depriving the local communities or rulers of any international standing; effective occupation and *de facto* control over the territory (coupled with the intent of appropriation) were sufficient for the acquisition of sovereign rights. Second, if

[21] C. H. Alexandrowicz, 'The Afro–Asian World', 150 ff.

local rulers opposed the colonial conquest, international law offered two instruments: either war (without all the legal restraints applicable to wars between 'civilized' States), or the conclusion of treaties (indeed a great number of agreements with 'local rulers' or chieftains were entered into by European States, and they, of course, lacked any reciprocity: see, for example, the treaty drawn up in 1841 between the UK and the Ruler of Cartabar; that in 1847 between the UK and the Ruler of Rowallah; and the treaty of 1884 between France and the Sultan of Tajuran).

The same legal instruments were available in case of conflict with other Western countries wishing to appropriate the same territories: either the waging of a war or the conclusion of an agreement settled the matter.

Allocation of Power

22. Throughout the whole period under consideration power was spread out: no single State became so strong as to subject all the other countries to its will. Legally, all members of the international community were on an equal footing. In actual practice, a group of great powers (France, the UK, Spain, Portugal, the US, Russia, Austria, Prussia, the Netherlands) dominated the international scene. However, this group never unified into a closely knit front because of constant rivalries. A balance of power proved necessary, and was in fact established.

It is against this general background that two experiments in collective systems for restraining power and enforcing the law should be considered. The first was made as early as 1648, in the Treaties of Westphalia which provided that peace should be enforced—after a threat to peace or any serious violation the victim was not to resort to war but should 'exhort the offender not to come to any hostility, submitting the cause to a friendly composition or to the ordinary proceedings of justice' (Article 123 of the Treaty of Münster). A cooling-off period, lasting as long as three years, was envisaged and if at its expiry no settlement had been reached, the injured State was entitled to wage war, and all the other contracting States were to assist it by the use of force (Article 124). In addition, States were duty-bound to refrain from giving military assistance to the offender, nor could they allow its troops to pass through or stay in their territories (Article 3). In other words, the collective security system envisaged in 1648 hinged on the following notions: (1) a sweeping ban on the use of force; (2) a prohibition on individual self-defence, except after the expiry of a long period; (3) the duty of all States other than the victim of a wrong to act in collective self-defence. This normative scheme, which strongly resembles the one set up in 1919 (see § 32), was never put into effect. Though weak and rudimentary by modern standards, it was too far ahead of its time and in harsh conflict with the interests and predispositions of most States. The latter eventually followed a different pattern of behaviour based on the untrammelled right of the individual State to resort to war whenever appropriate and on the lack of any duty to give military aid to the victims of attacks by third States.

A less unsatisfactory experiment was made in 1815 after the defeat of Napoleon. The French revolution and the genius of Napoleon had shattered deep-rooted principles and upset the existing order. The victors felt they had to protect the interests of European monarchies against the seeds of revolution. To this end they met to devise a system capable of putting a strait-jacket on these new forces, which were urging the abolition of inequitable practice and the dismantling of aristocratic privileges. The new system was set up in a series of treaties worked out in 1815 and supplemented by subsequent agreements. It rested on three principal elements:[22]

(1) *A declaration of principles.* It was embodied in the Treaty of Paris of 26 September 1815, instituting the Holy Alliance between Austria, Russia, and Prussia. The Treaty, to which all States adhered except for England, the Papal States, and the Ottoman Empire, proclaimed that the contracting parties would adopt as standards of behaviour, both in their internal orders and in international relations, the precepts of Christian religion (Preamble to the Treaty); accordingly, the contracting States undertook to help each other with a view to preserving religion, peace and justice, and to behave towards their own citizens and armies as 'fathers of a family' (*pères de famille*: Article 1); in addition, the three Governments pledged to consider themselves as members of the same 'Christian family', which they undertook to govern in their capacity as 'delegates of Providence' (*délégués par la Providence*: Article 2).

(2) *A military alliance.* This was instituted by the Treaty of Paris of 20 November 1815, concluded by Austria, Prussia, Russia, and England, to which France acceded in 1818.

A unique feature was the fact that it envisaged a system for collective security based on the agreement of the big powers which was designed to forestall or stifle any recurrence of Bonapartism, either in France or elsewhere. Under Articles 2 to 4 of the Treaty, the contracting States undertook to agree upon the measures to be taken against those infringing upon the 'tranquillity' and the 'established order' in Europe; they also pledged themselves to agree upon the number of troops which each of them was bound to provide 'for the pursuit of the common cause'. While at the outset the main object was that of averting any threat to the stability of post-Napo-

---

[22] For the discussion on the system established in 1815 I have drawn upon an excellent essay by M. Bourquin, 'La Sainte-Alliance: un essai d'organisation européenne', Hague *Recueil* 83 (1953-II), 381 ff.

leonic France, the system was subsequently extended so as to function against any revolutionary movement likely to overthrow European monarchies (see the treaty of 1818 and the protocol of 1820). The latter, ratified by Austria, Russia, and Prussia, provided for three measures in case of revolutions: first the State where a revolution broke out would cease to be a member of the Concert of Europe; second, the new government resulting from a revolution would not be recognized; and third, the States directly concerned, or otherwise the Holy Alliance, would intervene to put an end to the revolution.

This system proved quite effective in practice. It was actually resorted to on two occasions: in 1821, when Austrian troops were sent to Naples and Turin to suppress liberal insurgents on behalf of the Holy Alliance; and in 1823, when French troops were dispatched to Spain, again to thwart a liberal attempt at independence. On both occasions one State only—the one directly concerned—made a military intervention. But the right to take action was considered as delegated by all the partners of the Holy Alliance, and was actually authorized by a general meeting (the Conference of Troppau and Laybach in the former case, the Conference of Verona in the latter).

(3) *A new procedure for the settlement of political questions.* This was envisaged in Article 6 of the Treaty of Paris of 20 November 1815, which provided for meetings of all the Sovereigns concerned where they might discuss 'great interests in common', consider measures conducive to the 'tranquillity and prosperity of peoples' and attempt the maintenance of peace in Europe. In short, a new diplomatic method was propounded: multilateral diplomacy, based on periodical summit meetings. It proved most useful and was indeed resorted to on a number of occasions in later years.

23. As soon as European monarchies came under strong attack from nationalist movements and were gradually overthrown or forced to turn into parliamentary democracies, the system set up in 1815 was replaced by the traditional policy of *balance of power*: only the diplomatic method of summit meetings survived. Protected—at least in some respects—by this policy, great powers revived their tendency to exercise hegemony, endeavouring not to trespass upon the respective spheres of influence in order to avoid friction and conflict.

Within this general framework, the emergence of the US set a limit to European influence and power in the Americas. The new trend was formally proclaimed by the American President Monroe in the doctrine propounded in the famous message to Congress of 2 December 1823.[23] This Message stated, first, that 'the American continents ... are henceforth not to be considered as subjects for future colonization by any European power'; second, that while the US would not intervene in European matters, by the same token it could not allow European powers to intervene in America. Thus a check was placed on European expansionism and at the same time the basic principle was enunciated that the American continent was under the control of the most powerful State of the area.

Legal Output

24. The majority of present principles and rules of the international community go back to the period under consideration. The legal backbone of the community was created in the seventeenth and eighteenth centuries; in the nineteenth century other basic rules were added, such as those on warfare.

The very expression 'international law' dates back to this period. It is well known that it was first used in 1780 by J. Bentham in his *Introduction to the Principles of Morals and Legislation*. Since then it has increasingly replaced the previous terms 'law of nations' and 'droit des gens'. As has been shown by the Italian philologist E. Peruzzi,[24] other factors besides the strictly linguistic motivated this change or were instrumental in making it widespread—the emotional appeal and the growing importance of the concept of 'nation', the spread of 'international industrial exhibitions', and the setting up in 1864, in London, of the 'International Working Men's Association', commonly known as the 'First International', or simply, 'The International'.

The principal standards regulating the delimitation of power among the various members of the international community evolved very soon: the rules on territorial sovereignty (whereby each State has a right of exclusive control over the territory, the airspace and the territorial sea over which it actually wields authority), on the acquisition of sovereignty over territories belonging to no one (the intention of appropriating the territory, as well as the actual display of exclusive control over it, were necessary elements for the acquisition of a legal title), and on the free use of the high seas. Further norms were created to ensure mutual respect for the political structure of each State; in particular, two rules set up a formidable shield for the protection of sovereignty: those on State representatives' immunity (a State

---

[23] The text of the Monroe declaration, as well as many other related documents, can be found in the appendix to H. Kraus, *Die Monroedoktrin in ihrer Beziehungen zur amerikanischen Diplomatie und zum Völkerrecht* (Berlin, 1913), pp. 403 ff.

[24] E. Peruzzi, 'A European Word-Formation Pattern', *Archivio glottografico italiano* 41 (1976), 76–85.

cannot punish individuals for acts they have performed in their capacity as representatives of another State), and on immunity from the jurisdiction of foreign courts for acts or transactions performed by States. Other rules served the purpose of facilitating international intercourse, in particular those on diplomatic and consular immunities and privileges, on diplomatic protection of foreigners and on the conclusion and the binding force of treaties. Even friction and conflict were regulated: important standards were developed on how a State could react to what it considered a wrong perpetrated by another State. Norms on reprisals (acts constituting a reaction to wrongful behaviour) and on war evolved; in particular, standards for the purpose of placing restraints on the most inhuman aspects of conduct in warfare were elaborated.

Main Features of the Law

25. The legal regulation created in this period possesses two salient features:

(1) International rules and principles were the product of Western civilization and bore the imprint of Christian ideology and of a 'free-market' outlook (they rested on a *laissez-faire philosophy*, that is on the idea that all States should be legally equal and free to pursue their own interests, irrespective of any economic or social imbalance).

(2) international norms and principles were mainly framed by great powers or middle-sized States, particularly by those States which built up extensive colonial empires by dint of conquest and expansion. They elaborated the rules to serve their own interests. Among the norms of this category, particular emphasis should be laid on those concerning force: they placed no restraint on the threat or use of force.

Two qualifications should be made however. First, in some cases big powers were impelled to make concessions to smaller States. A few illustrations may prove useful. For example, the rule on the freedom of the high seas whereby any State is at liberty to navigate and fish everywhere beyond that portion of the sea which is under the jurisdiction of the coastal State, was strongly advocated by great naval powers (the UK, Portugal, Spain, the Netherlands, and France) after it had become apparent that none of them could appropriate large portions of the high seas. Although it was in the economic and military interests of such great powers to restrict as much as possible and even to suppress any authority of the coastal States over a portion of the seas off their coast, these attempts were thwarted by smaller countries, eager to submit a belt off their coast to their jurisdiction, both for security purposes, and also to ensure their exclusive exploitation of fishing resources in those areas. In consequence, the rule on territorial sea evolved whereby States could exercise jurisdiction over a narrow portion of sea off their coast, that is, within the range of cannons, or three miles (as C. Bynkershoek put it in 1702, 'Terrae potestas finitur ubi finitur armorum vis', territorial sovereignty extends as far as the power of arms carries). This, however, was not the end of the story, for bigger countries succeeded in ensuring the right of 'innocent passage' in the territorial sea, that is to say the right to send both their merchant ships and their men-of-war through that area, for navigational purposes. Thus, in the end their concessions to lesser countries did not turn out to be too detrimental to their own interests.

Similarly, with regard to war, it was in the interest of big powers to exclude from the category of lawful combatants any other than members of the regular army (as powerful States usually rely on standing armies of professionals and are likely to invade the territory of the adversary, they do not wish members of the enemy civilian population to be upgraded to the status of lawful combatants); in addition, in the case of military occupation, since great powers normally find themselves in the position of the occupying power, it is to their advantage to place as many restrictions as possible on the rights of the population of the occupied territory. However, the opposition of a number of small and middle-sized States succeeded in the nineteenth century in extracting concessions for militias and volunteer corps as well as for the whole civilian population (on certain conditions: see § 148), all of whom were upgraded to lawful combatants, and in excluding the possibility that the occupying power should acquire *ipso facto* sovereign rights over the territory it invaded.

The influence which minor States could exert, albeit to a limited extent, on the formation of international rules can be explained by the need of powerful States to take into consideration demands and aspirations of smaller States with which they had alliances or privileged relations. That influence can also be traced back to the practice of convening international diplomatic conferences for the adoption of multilateral treaties. (The first important conference was held in Brussels in 1874 but did not result in any treaty; it was followed by those convened at The Hague in 1899 and 1907.) These gatherings were open to smaller States as well (participation in the Brussels conference was extended to Belgium, Denmark, Greece, the Netherlands—whose importance had been dwindling since the eighteenth century—Sweden, Norway, and Switzerland; the Hague conferences were attended by a number of Latin-American, and some Asian States). As the rules of procedure required that the treaties being drafted be adopted unanimously (subject, however, to the dissenting States' right to append reservations upon signature of the treaty), lesser States were in a position to participate in the negotiating process and press forward their views. If their demands were not dealt with satisfactorily they could enter reservations

which the other States had to accept if they desired the treaty to be unanimously ratified. In this way, the views of smaller States, if rejected at the
law-making stage, could still be accommodated at the stage of signature or
ratification. However, precisely this rule of unanimity could play into the
hands of great powers, since it was sufficient for one of them to object to
the reservation entered by a small country for this country to be excluded
from the treaty. Nevertheless international diplomatic conferences were certainly to some extent instrumental in gradually democratizing the legal
framework of the world community. Although they were of course dominated by the great powers, the lesser States were given the means and
opportunity to voice their concern, and their demands could no longer be
passed over in silence.

The second qualification is that while a number of treaties were dictated
by humanitarian demands, others met the exigencies of all members of the
international community, whether powerful or weak. The former include
not only treaties on the slave trade (see § 27), but also some international
agreements placing restraints on the use of weapons causing inhuman suffering (see §§ 145, 155).

At least one of the treaties banning weapons should be mentioned at this juncture,
namely the Declaration prohibiting the use of expanding bullets, adopted by the
Hague Conference in 1899. Soft-nosed bullets which expanded on contact, thus
causing gaping wounds and appalling suffering, had been developed by the British
at the Dum-Dum arsenal in Calcutta in the nineteenth century. As E. M. Spiers
recalled,[25] the British authorities justified their production by saying that 'the demands of small colonial warfare warranted this deviation from the standards of
European armaments. The enemies whom Britain encountered were not armies from
the European countries who had signed the St Petersburg Declaration [of 1868,
prohibiting the use in time of war of explosive projectiles under 400 grammes
weight], but "fanatical natives", "savages", and "barbarians". The difference was
deemed substantial: "civilised man is much more susceptible to injury than savages
... the savage, like the tiger, is not so impressionable, and will go on fighting even
when desperately wounded"'. Although the UK assured other Western powers that
it would not use those bullets in European wars, they managed to have the Hague
Peace Conference pass the Declaration referred to above. The UK grudgingly adhered to it in 1907, and the prohibition gradually expanded so as to cover any
international armed conflict.

The other category of rules intended to meet the demands of all States
irrespective of their strength included treaties such as those on diplomatic
and consular immunities, as well as the norms, both general and conventional, on neutrality and the neutralization of States. Although some of
these norms were also motivated by particular interests or were designed to

[25] E. M. Spiers, 'The Use of Dum Dum Bullets in Colonial Warfare', *The Journal of
Imperial and Commonwealth History* (1975), 6–7.

meet the demands of specific States, their intrinsic significance for the whole international community transformed them into lasting principles which continue to display their effects today.

Efforts to Restrain Great Powers' Dominance

26.   One should not pass over in silence the first timid attempts at restraining the domination of great powers by international or national legislation. The first and probably the most important one was the clause which many Latin-American States began to insert into concession contracts with foreigners from the middle of the nineteenth century, at the instigation of the Argentine jurist C. Calvo. It stipulated that in case of disputes arising out of the contract, foreigners relinquished the right to request the diplomatic and judicial protection of their national State and agreed to have the dispute settled by local tribunals. Plainly, the Calvo clause sought to limit the legal and political interventions of western capital exporting countries, which often constituted the pretext or the occasion for armed expeditions, strong political pressure, or other forms of interference. The attempt was ill-fated: numerous international courts and claims commissions ruled that the clause was legally ineffective, in that it could not deprive States of their rights of protection, since the latter derive from international law only. Consequently, the clause was either set aside or downgraded to a (superfluous) proviso requiring the exhaustion of local remedies before international diplomatic or judicial action could be initiated. No doubt the refusal to apply the clause was legally correct in the light of the international rules applicable at the time. The failure of the Calvo stipulation only proved that it was vain to seek to undermine existing conditions by means which fell short of a radical change in the legal regulation of the treatment of nationals abroad.

Another important attempt to place restraints on great powers' hegemony was made by the Foreign Minister of Argentina, Luis Drago, in the early twentieth century. The unfettered right of States to resort to force entailed their right forcibly to recover payments due by foreign States to the nationals of the former. Three European countries, the UK, Germany, and Italy made use of this right against Venezuela in 1902. They had requested Venezuela to pay both compensation for damage caused to their nationals during the civil strife which raged between 1898 and 1900, and for the seizure of fishing boats and other commercial ships by the Venezuelan authorities, and to repay loans made to Venezuela for the building of its railway. Venezuela demanded that the European claims be settled by a Venezuelan commission. This commission, however, partly rejected and partly reduced the European demands. The European Powers found the settlement unacceptable and, after imparting an ultimatum, sank three Venezuelan ships, bombarded the locality of Puerto Cabello and, on 20 December 1902 instituted a naval blockade off the coasts of the Latin-American country. Venezuela then gave in. A few days later, on 29 December, Drago sent a diplomatic note to the US State Department, in which he claimed first that the European armed intervention was contrary to the Monroe doctrine (which he declared to be willing to uphold), and, second, that financial troubles and the consequent need to postpone payment of debts, was no justification for foreign military intervention, since 'the collection of loans by military means requires territorial occupation to make them effective, and territorial occupation signifies the suppression or subordination of the governments of the countries on which it is imposed'.[26]

This note, which enunciated what was subsequently termed the 'Drago Doctrine', elicited a lukewarm response from the US. In his note of 17 February 1903, the US Secretary of State P. Hay substantially dismissed Drago's claims and pointed out that so long as Latin-American countries fulfilled their international duties towards foreign States, they need not fear any foreign intervention; Hay quoted a message sent to Congress by President Theodore Roosevelt on 2 December 1902, which stated:

it behooves each one to maintain order within its own borders and to discharge its just obligations to foreigners. When this is done, they [the independent nations of America] can rest assured that, strong or weak, they have nothing to dread from outside interference.[27]

In sum, the US considered protection of foreign property to override the need to keep Europeans from intervening militarily on the American continent. It is hardly surprising that the so-called Drago doctrine was assailed by leading European jurists such as the Englishman J. Westlake[28] and the German C. L. von Bar[29] as being at variance with international law—a proposition which was indeed correct, in the light of the rules obtaining at the time.

No substantial headway was made in 1907, when Latin-American countries endeavoured to pass at the second Hague Peace Conference, a convention forbidding the use of force for the recovery of contract debts. The ideas put forward by Drago in 1902 were taken up, but also watered down, by the US delegate, General H. Porter. He proposed to make resort to force conditional on the non-acceptance by the debtor State of international arbitration or its failure to carry out an arbitral award. The proposals of General Porter were largely accepted by the Conference, which went on to set up a Convention on the matter. Significantly, it was not ratified by any European country, thus showing again that even in an emasculated form,

[26] *See AJIL*, Supplement 1 (1907), 1–6.
[27] For the note by Hay, see USFR (1903), 5.
[28] J. Westlake, in *Revue de droit international et de législation comparée*, 35 (1903), 608.
[29] C. L. von Bar, in C. Schücking, *Das Werk vom Haag*, 2nd ser., i (1912), 281.

the efforts of Latin-American countries to restrain international legitimation of force were to no avail.

Rise and Fall of Slavery

27. Against this general background, one particular historical phenomenon, with noteworthy legal implications, should be emphasized: the emergence and the later gradual waning of *slavery*. The attitude adopted by the
international community towards slavery is conspicuously indicative of the
trends of this first stage of historical evolution.

Unlike the slavery practised in antiquity in Greece and Rome, which—
ironical as it may seem—was based on principles of equality of a kind (all
the enemies conquered following a war were enslaved, irrespective of their
colour, sex, social origin, or religion), the slave-trade which started immediately before the discovery of America, in the early 1440s, and developed
fully after 1492, was essentially based on a racist attitude: only (African)
blacks were enslaved. They were raided by Europeans, by Arabs, and even
by African chieftains and transported to Brazil, the West Indies and the
French and English colonies in North America. The main reason behind
this infamous practice was economic: colonial powers needed a cheap labour force to exploit the wealth of the Americas and to produce cotton,
tobacco, sugar, minerals, to be imported into Europe. The native Americans, used from the outset as a tool for exploiting the rich natural resources
of the Americas, had been decimated by over-exploitation and by the ex-
hausting labour in the gold and silver mines. Consequently, Spanish and
Portuguese rulers gradually turned to the practice of importing blacks from
Africa.

No international rule prohibited the slave-trade, much less slavery: the
laissez-faire attitude of international law left great latitude to States. In
particular, the rule on the freedom of the high seas proved an excellent
instrument for facilitating and legitimizing the slave-trade, and after two
centuries of slavery, States determined also that the agreement (*asiento*) by
which they gave licence to individuals or private companies to import black
slaves from Africa into the Americas could also be concluded between
themselves.

In the late eighteenth century a movement against slavery gathered momentum in various States, chiefly the UK, France, and Denmark, and laws
banning the slave-trade were passed. The UK soon took the lead in the
abolitionist movement and promoted the conclusion of international treaties against the trade. What were the causes of this unexpected change of
attitude? The role of Christian doctrine has often been emphasized in this
respect, but Christian principles had not impeded this inhuman practice for
three centuries. The increasing importance in the eighteenth century of the

Quakers (founded by George Fox in 1671) was no doubt instrumental in spreading awareness of the heinous nature of slavery. But the following factors are no less important: (1) the successful rebellion of the American colonies against English rule and the consequent interest of the English in stopping the flow of slaves towards French, Spanish, and Portuguese colonies in the Americas, which made those colonies increasingly rich, much to the detriment of the British interests; (2) the British conquest, during the years 1750 to 1784, of India, and the consequent opportunity for the UK to get hold of cheap manpower without resorting to slavery; (3) the Legislative Union with Ireland (1800) which, by according a hundred seats in the House of Commons and thirty-two in the House of Lords to Protestant Irishmen, allowed representatives of Irish voters (none of whom had commercial interests in the slave-trade) to plead in the British Parliament for equality and justice.

The French Revolution (1789), and the principles proclaimed in the Declaration of the Rights of Man also played a role; yet, when it turned out that those principles clashed with the interests of French planters in the French colony of San Domingo, the Paris Assembly passed in March 1790 a resolution stating that the constitution framed for France was not intended to embrace the internal government of French colonies. And a liberal decree passed on 15 May 1791, was repealed on 24 September when the French Assembly feared it would lose the colony.

The reaction to the slave trade was aptly summed up by a great French jurist, G. Scelle—the author of a searching analysis of that odious phenomenon—as follows:

The evolution of international law is very instructive on this point. The struggle against slavery, the protection of the bodily freedom of individuals only begin in international law when it is clearly demonstrated that slave labour has *economic* drawbacks and that the progress of modern technology allows it to be *replaced*. Whenever human manpower has not been replaced, slave labour and forced labour still exist, despite all efforts made to proscribe it. This proves that a *moral conviction*, even if of a general character, does not override the necessities of economic life in the formation of legal rules.[30]

It should be added that in antiquity as well, slavery did not disappear for moral or religious reasons, but—as was proved by the French historian H. Bloch[31] in a masterly essay (substantially borne out, albeit on the basis of

---

[30] G. Scelle, *Précis de droit des gens* (Paris, 1934), ii. 55. The monograph by G. Scelle on slavery is: *La traite négrière aux Indes de Castille: Contrats et traités d'asiento—Etude de droit public et d'histoire diplomatique puisée aux sources originales et accompagnée de plusieurs documents inédits*, 2 vols. (Paris 1906).

[31] M. Bloch, 'Comment et pourquoi termine l'ancien esclavage', *Annales et études de sciences sociales* (1947), 30-44, 161-70. English trans. in M. Finley (ed.), *Slavery in Classical Antiquity* (Cambridge, 1968), pp. 204-28.

different arguments, by an authority such as M. Finley[32])—only when changed economic relations rendered slave labour increasingly unnecessary.

Besides passing domestic legislation banning the slave-trade, a few European States started entering into international agreements to the effect that in some areas of the high seas ships suspected of indulging in that trade could be visited and searched. However, throughout this period, that is to say until the First World War, no international treaty was concluded for the prohibition of slavery as such. International agreements confined themselves to proscribing, within certain limitations, the slave-trade solely.

All in all, it can be argued that international law, after being greatly instrumental in facilitating slavery, to some extent contributed to its prohibition.

[32] M. Finley, *Economy and Society in Ancient Greece* (Harmondsworth, 1981), pp. 97 ff,; *Ancient Slavery and Modern Ideology* (Harmondsworth, 1983), pp. 123 ff.

3

Historical Evolution of the International Community: The New Setting (from 1918 to the Present)

28. IN the previous chapter an attempt was made to set out the main features of the world community in its first stage of development. If one sought to isolate its most idiosyncratic trait, emphasis should first of all be laid on the existence of deep factual inequalities and widespread relations of domination, both among the various members of the world community and in the community itself. This state of affairs was not felt to be intolerable, but rather to be part and parcel of the human condition. The concept of inequality was pithily, succinctly, and painfully expounded in 1773 by Dr Johnson:

... Mankind are happier in a state of inequality and subordination. Were they to be in this pretty state of equality they would soon degenerate into brutes; they would become Monboddo's nation; their tails would grow ... All would be losers were all to work for all: they would have no intellectual improvement. All intellectual improvement arises from leisure; all leisure arises from one working for another.[1]

This condition was not only accepted and taken for granted; it was legitimized by legal standards of conduct. This legitimation is the second remarkable characteristic of the epoch. Law endorsed and consecrated force, inequality, and hegemony. The role occasionally played by smaller States in the elaboration of a number of international rules, the attempt by some leading Latin-American politicians and diplomats to push through the demands of less powerful countries, the plea for social justice made in a number of States by certain segments of public opinion—all these were peripheral phenomena incapable of impairing the substance of international relations.

After the First World War a host of events (see § 30) set in motion a

---

[1] J. Boswell, *The Life of Johnson*, ed. C. Hibbert (London, 1980), p. 164. James Burnett, Lord Monboddo (1714-99), Scottish judge and anthropologist, put forward the idea that men could be descended from monkeys.

lengthy process which was to effect a radical transformation of the world community as well as of the domestic setting of a handful of States. It was a process towards equality. Not that international relations changed rapidly; on the contrary, the change was very slow and, in fact, did not become obvious until the 1950s. What is striking about the new period following the first world conflagration is that disparity and domination were no longer taken for granted. The view that these should be suppressed or gradually tempered became strong. Needless to say, unequal relations continued to exist; in some instances they became even more deeply entrenched. However, this state of affairs was no longer accompanied by acquiescence; growing demands for change arose in a number of fields, including that of legal institutions. The new tendency was best expressed by Nehru, who said in 1956: '... The spirit of the present age is opposed to any kind of domination of one over the other, whether it is national domination, economic, class or racial. There is a strong urge to resist this kind of domination.'[2]

29.   A second major feature of the period following the First World War is the gradual imposition of restraints on the use of force by States.

After that dramatic turning-point the conviction emerged that the best means of forestalling new horrors and devastations was to place restrictions on the right of States to engage in military hostilities. At first the trend was shared by most countries, both powerful and weak. However, in time, the failure of international mechanisms designed to enforce prohibitions and restrictions, coupled with the return to traditional power politics, eroded the legal restraints to the point at which a Second World War proved unavoidable. At its conclusion both great and lesser States once again came to feel that no member of the world community should be allowed to use force any longer. Again legal restraints were established and again the failure of enforcement techniques revitalized traditional tendencies of individual States to settle political and legal disputes by military coercion. But despite many set-backs and loopholes, the new international regulation proved so well attuned to a widely shared conviction that it gradually turned into customary international law. As a result, traditional rules authorizing force were cancelled and it is extremely unlikely that they will ever be revived. Admittedly, the defective system established in the event by the UN led Great Powers to exercise a wide measure of discretion and dominance in international relations. The fact remains, however, that if they adopt forcible measures contrary to existing rules their conduct can be assessed in the light of those rules and condemned by public opinion and by such international gatherings as the UN General Assembly.

[2]   T. Mende, *Conversations with Mr Nehru* (London, 1956), p. 44.

STAGE 2: FROM THE FIRST TO THE SECOND WORLD WAR

The Turning-point: The First World War and its Consequences

30. Two major events mark the beginning of a new era: the First World War which, although fought in Europe solely, involved the greater part of the international community and caused its members to strive to rebuild it on better foundations; the Soviet revolution and the consequent rise of a 'new State'—the first State openly to oppose the economic and ideological roots of other States and of international relations.

The War had many important repercussions. It marked what was termed 'the passing of the European Age'.[3] When the War was over it became apparent that Europe no longer played a crucial part in the world community: the gradual erosion of its importance, initiated long before as a result of the growing importance of the US, culminated in Europe's demotion to the rank of merely *one* of the areas of power. Among the chief factors affecting its position were not only the rise of the US but also the emergence of the Soviet Union and the end of colonial expansion—a striking phenomenon which marked the beginning of that long process of erosion of the European Powers' colonial empires, and culminated in their collapse in the 1960s. The decline of Europe made itself felt in the field of economic, military, and political power, but also in that of culture and ideology. Europe's pivotal role in the previous centuries as the world's store-room of values, institutions, political concepts, standards of behaviour, came to an end.

The War united the whole world—albeit in a forced and somewhat sinister way. For the first time a conflict assumed such magnitude as to involve all major members of the international community. As a consequence, the international community no longer consisted of groups of States often ignoring one another. The war proved that some major events were crucial to the world community at large; consequently it became difficult for States to remain 'neutral' or keep aloof from what was happening in other areas of the world.

But even more crucial to the life of the world community was the rise in 1917 of the Union of Soviet Socialist Republics (as it was called after 1923). The substantial ideological and political unity of the 'old' community fell to pieces. As a leading Soviet jurist, E. Korowin stated in 1928, 'the tower of Babel of world-wide unity is left in ruins'.[4] This is an issue deserving our attention.

---

[3] See R. Albrech-Carrié, *The Meaning of the First World War* (Englewood Cliffs, 1965), p. vi.

[4] E. Korowin, 'Soviet Treaties and International Law' *AJIL* 22 (1928), 753.

The Soviet Union's Presence Splits the International Community

31. It has already been pointed out that although some members of the international community (Turkey, China, Japan, Persia, Siam) had a different economic and ideological outlook to that of European States, they had actually yielded to the Christian majority geared to market economy, which indeed set the tone throughout the development of the international community. After 1917 a State existed with an ideology and a political philosophy radically at odds with those upheld by all other States. In the international field, the USSR advocated the following principles:

(a) *The self-determination* of peoples, to be applied both to national groups in Europe (for example, the nationalities in Austria–Hungary) and to peoples under colonial domination (see §§ 80, 81).

(b) *The substantive equality* of States (in contradistinction to their legal equality). Point 6 of the proposals forming the basis for negotiations submitted by Adolf Joffe, the head of the Russian delegation to the Brest-Litovsk peace Conference (which opened on 22 December 1917), proposed that

... the contracting parties should condemn the attempt of strong nations to restrict the freedom of the weaker nations by such indirect methods as economic boycotts, economic subjection of one country to another by means of compulsory commercial agreements, separate customs agreements, restricting the freedom of trade with third countries, naval blockade without direct military purpose, etc.[5]

Thus, for the first time, economic coercion as a means of subduing weaker States, and unequal treaties were outspokenly condemned.

(c) *Socialist internationalism*, whereby the USSR pledged itself to help and assist the working class and the political parties struggling for socialism in any State. Thus, again for the first time, a member State of the international community proclaimed a policy aimed at disrupting the fabric of other States and their colonial possessions (and such a policy was officially pursued until at least 1927). This new state of affairs was soon fully appreciated by the American Secretary of State Lansing, who pointed out that the Soviet regime was 'productive of disorder and anarchy', and that Lenin's programme threatened not only 'the existing social order in all countries' but also the 'stability of the future world order by applying the self-determination principle to the colonial world'.[6]

(d) *The partial rejection of international law*. The USSR proclaimed that since all the existing legal norms and institutions of the international com-

---

[5] A. Joffe, in *Soviet Documents on Foreign Policy*, ed. J. Degras, i (1917–24) (London, 1951), pp. 21–2.
[6] R. Lansing, *Papers Relating to the Foreign Relations of the US 1917–19* (Washington, 1932) ii. 253, 247–8.

munity were the upshot of 'bourgeois' and 'capitalist' tendencies, they were by definition contrary to socialist interests, and would be endorsed by the new regime only to the extent that they proved useful to it. Consequently, many existing treaties were denounced. In his 'Fourth Letter from Afar' (25 March 1917) Lenin set forth a programme of action including the following tenets:

1. [The Petrograd Soviet] would immediately declare that it was not bound by any treaties concluded by either the tsarist monarchy or by the bourgeois governments; 2. It would forthwith publish all these treaties in order to expose to public obloquy the predatory aims of the tsarist monarchy and of all the bourgeois governments, without exception.[7]

And the famous Decree on Peace (8 November 1917) stated that the Soviet Government:

... declares rescinded, immediately and unconditionally, the entire substance of these secret treaties [ratified or concluded from February to 25 October 1917, by the Government of the landlords and the capitalists], directed as they were for the most part to the advantage and privilege of the Russian landlords and capitalists and to the maintenance or the increase of the annexations of the Great Russians.[8]

In fact, the Soviet Government did not reject international law wholesale — indeed, it could not have done so without becoming an outcast in the world community: one cannot be a member of a social group and at the same time dismiss all its rules; at least some of them must be complied with since otherwise international relations become impossible with the group as a whole ostracizing the recalcitrant member by condemning it to complete isolation. The USSR rejected a number of bilateral and even multilateral treaties, but it tacitly or expressly bowed to a great many international standards. Thus, for example, it invoked a general norm (the rule *rebus sic stantibus*; see §§ 101, 104, 105) to justify its repudiation of unacceptable treaties. The Soviet argument was put forward by Korowin in the following terms:

Every international agreement is the expression of an established social order, with a certain balance of collective interests. So long as this social order endures, such treaties as remain in force, following the principle *pacta sunt servanda*, must be scrupulously observed. But if in the storm of a social cataclysm one class replaces the other at the helm of the State, for the purpose of reorganizing not only economic ties but the governing principles of internal and external politics, the old agreements, in so far as they reflect the pre-existing order of things, destroyed by the revolution, become null and void ... Thus in this sense the Soviet doctrine appears to be an

---

[7] Lenin, *Collected Works*, xviii (New York, 1929), pp. 54-5; xx (New York, 1930), pp. 60-1.
[8] For the Soviet decree on peace see, for instance, G. F. Kennan, *Soviet Foreign Policy, 1917-41* (Princeton, NJ, 1960), pp. 116-19.

extension of the principle *rebus sic stantibus*, while at the same time limiting its field of application by a single circumstance—the social revolution.[9]

Similarly, the USSR upheld many customary rules on treaty making (witness its entering into a great number of bilateral and multilateral treaties), on respect for State sovereignty, on diplomatic and consular immunities and privileges. In addition, it tacitly accepted at least the bulk of customary rules on the treatment of foreigners, as is proved by Articles 8 and 9 of the Soviet-German Treaty of 6 May 1921, which stated that Germany guaranteed Soviet citizens 'the prescriptions of international law and of the German common law'.

Nevertheless, the basic Soviet attitude towards the legal instruments of the international community inevitably undermined some of the community's basic doctrines. The USSR eroded—to a greater or lesser extent—many sacred principles (such as 'sanctity of treaties', the protection of investments abroad, etc.) while it resolutely opposed others, such as the rights of colonial powers. Although in the end the Soviet Union gradually came to adhere to a number of traditional rules, in 1917 it set in motion a far-reaching process for the revision of numerous legal standards considered contrary to its own interests or to what it regarded as the exigencies of the international community as a whole.

Another Experiment in Collective Co-ordination of Force: The League of Nations

32.   Following the First World War the victors decided to set up an international institution designed to prevent the recurrence of world-wide armed conflicts. The League of Nations was created, with a relatively small membership (42 States including five British Dominions: India, New Zealand, Canada, Australia, and South Africa). For domestic reasons the US held aloof. Its absence undisputedly weakened the institution from the outset.

The system set up in 1919 greatly resembles that devised in 1648 in the form of the Settlement of Westphalia. Recourse to force was prohibited, except for a limited number of cases. Articles 12, 13, and 15 of the Covenant subjected resort to war to a cooling-off period of three months. If a dispute was submitted to the League Council or to the PCIJ or an arbitral tribunal, war could only be resorted to three months after the arbitral or judicial decision or the Council report. Consequently, there was a general prohibition on wars initiated before that delay or waged against a State which was complying with an arbitral award or a judgment of the PCIJ, or with a report adopted unanimously by the League Council.

Major flaws in the League system were that, first, no ban was put on

[9] Korowin, art. cit., 763.

resort to force short of war. This qualification manifestly induced States to engage in war operations while claiming that they were merely using coercion short of war and were therefore not breaking any Covenant provision. An instance of this practice is the case of Manchuria, when Japan attacked China (1932). Second, war was not banned altogether, but only subjected to a cooling-off period, in the naïve hope that States would calm down and get less excited after a certain delay, and that the procedures for the settlement of disputes provided for in the Covenant would meanwhile induce them to refrain from using force. This proved illusory, as is shown by the case of the Italian aggression against Abyssinia, 1935–36. Third, no collective system was set up for enforcing law against a State breaking the procedural prohibitions of the Covenant. If a member State made war contravening the Covenant's stipulations, all the other member States were duty-bound to assist the victim against the aggressor—on condition, however, that they considered the use of force in the case at issue to be a breach of the Covenant. The League of Nations Assembly or Council had no power to send in troops against the aggressors; they could only recommend the use of force to member States. In short, the Covenant merely envisaged joint voluntary action on the part of States. No institutionalized enforcement procedure was provided for, no monopoly of force was granted to the League organs, much less was an international army for the maintenance of peace and order set up. Plainly, the League system was a far cry from the enforcement machinery existing within each State system. Indeed, in the only case where sanctions were resorted to (namely against Italy, 1935–6) they proved a failure, for political reasons. Fourth, the Covenant's prescriptions remained treaty law; consequently they did not bind States extraneous to the League (the US, as well as a number of European and Asian countries at a certain stage, including Germany, the USSR, and Japan). As a result, the customary international rules authorizing war remained unaffected as far as third States were concerned.

Differences between member States, the lack of co-operation, the fact that the League gradually became a political instrument of the UK and France only, along with its inherent institutional deficiencies—all these account for its failure. A number of States resorted to force without being the subject of military sanctions or at any rate without the League bringing about a satisfactory settlement.

The US and France endeavoured to obviate the most conspicuous deficiencies of the League by promoting the Paris Pact of 27 August 1928 on the Banning of War. The Pact, however, did not make much headway, for once again only *war* was prohibited (although the ban was now more sweeping), and in addition an enforcement mechanism failed to be provided. Furthermore, the correspondence exchanged before signing the Pact made it clear that the right of self-defence was unaffected, and that a very liberal construction was placed on that right. Thus, the UK stated that it included its right to defend 'certain regions of the world, the welfare and integrity of which constitute a special and vital interest for our peace and security'. And the US contended that self-defence embraced any action decided on by the US Government to prevent an infringement of the Monroe doctrine. The conspicuous merits of the Pact were that it laid down a more general prohibition of war, and that it was binding on States which were not parties to the Covenant such as the US. However, the Pact itself was unable to supplant the customary rule authorizing war, in that it did not turn into a customary rule abrogating the previous one.

The failure of both the League system and the Pact of Paris proved that in the international community it is not sufficient to impose a prohibition on the use of force on the one hand, and rely on the voluntary co-operation of States, should the ban be disregarded, on the other hand. States are still substantially motivated by self-interest. Consequently, they are ready to co-operate in the enforcement of sweeping prohibitions on the use of force, to the extent that this co-operation furthers their own interests. In order to place effective restraints on such a fundamental and basic right, States or international institutions ought to set up an international machinery which is independent of the will or co-operation of member States. Such an arrangement, however, presupposes a radical change in the political structure of the world community.

In short, even in the period between the two World Wars, States gradually endeavoured to retrieve their traditionally unfettered right to use military force in international relations. The League served to slow down the process and reduce the instances of recourse to force. It was, however, unable to introduce a radical change in one particular structural element of the old international community.

Legal Output

33.   During this period no conspicuous result was achieved in the elaboration of new rules. In its isolation the Soviet Union remained to a great extent on the defensive; on a number of occasions it attacked the existing international institutions, but was unable to leave an imprint on new rules. The only area where marked progress was made was that of the arbitral and judicial setttlement of disputes. In the inter-war period international arbitration was in full bloom. The PCIJ, set up in 1921, delivered 32 judgments, and 27 advisory opinions. The parties to the contentious proceedings were mostly European. Similarly, the members of the Court were mostly from European countries or from the US (from 1922 to 1930, four out of 16 judges were non-Western, while from 1931 to 1942 the proportion changed to 7 out of 21). Several *ad hoc* arbitral tribunals were also set up.

This was because most European States strongly believed that arbitration was the best means of settling disputes and preventing the outbreak of wars. However, it was an illusory view, both because on a number of occasions arbitral awards were not heeded, and because arbitration was, of course, unable to forestall the plunging of mankind into a second and even more devastating world-wide conflict.

However, frequent recourse to arbitration made it possible for international courts, particularly the PCIJ, to pronounce on many international issues and the case-law which evolved was instrumental in filling many gaps in international legislation. Principles and rules were specified, elaborated, and clarified. This, by itself, was a remarkable contribution to the improvement of the technicalities of international rules.

Even though the overall picture is gloomy, we should not jump to the conclusion that no progress whatsoever was discernible during the second stage. In actual fact, after the First World War, a new wind began to blow through the international community, bringing with it a drive towards limiting inequalities between States (see above, §28) and towards a greater concern for the demands of individuals.

The tendency to do away with the most glaring forms of inequality can be seen in the gradual abolition of capitulations. The only country where this regime had already been dismantled before the Great War was Japan (in 1899). Capitulations with other countries were gradually abrogated: with Turkey in 1923 (in 1914 Turkey had already unilaterally announced their abolition), with Siam in 1927, with Persia in 1928. In the case of China the Soviet Union renounced in 1925 its so-called extraterritorial rights and privileges, thereby lending impetus to the repeal of treaties by other countries as well. This movement continued until 1943 when the UK and the US relinquished their rights in that country. As for Egypt, after a transitory period when mixed courts were instituted, capitulations were definitively abolished by the Montreux Convention of 8 May 1927.

The emergence of a fresh concern with the exigencies of individuals manifested itself in two forms. First, in addition to prohibiting the slave trade, States began to ban the *institution* of slavery as such. Second, groups of individuals were granted the right to lodge complaints with international bodies: religious, ethnic, and linguistic minorities protected by post-war treaties were authorized to submit to the Council of the League of Nations 'petitions' designed to inform it of alleged violations of minority rights, and under Article 24 of the ILO Constitution trade union associations were entitled to lodge complaints with the ILO Governing Body. As we shall see (§57), at least in the short run, these normative innovations turned out not to be very significant. Nevertheless, they were indicative of the new tendency to pay greater attention to the interests of human beings, who until then had had no say whatsoever in the international community. As was stated in 1927 by the leading international lawyer, N. Politis:

beforehand, the sovereign State was for its subjects an iron cage whence they could communicate legally with the outside world only through narrow bars. Under the pressure of the necessities of life, those bars have progressively loosened. The cage is starting to wobble. It will eventually fall to bits. Men will then be able to communicate beyond the frontiers of their respective countries freely and without any hindrance.[10]

STAGE 3: FROM THE UN CHARTER TO THE ACCESSION OF MOST FORMERLY DEPENDENT COUNTRIES TO POLITICAL INDEPENDENCE (1945–60)

The Consequences of the Second World War

34. In 1945, within a few months or even days of one another, three momentous events occurred: on 26 June the Charter of the United Nations was signed in San Francisco (it came into force on 24 October 1945); on 6 August the atomic bomb was dropped on Hiroshima (on 9 August a second bomb was dropped on Nagasaki); on 8 August the Agreement on the International Military Tribunal (IMT) for the Punishment of War Criminals was signed in London (the first session of the Tribunal was held in Berlin on 18 October). Although these three events were not formally linked to one another, and did not result from a unitary design, all of them were destined to have a radical effect on the future of the international community.

The dropping of the atomic bomb began a new era: the use of atomic and nuclear energy for warlike purposes meant that States were now capable of annihilating the entire planet or huge portions of it. The question of how to place restraints on the use of means of destruction, which had exercised the international community since at least the middle of the nineteenth century, now became the central issue.

The setting up of the United Nations was the first radical attempt at creating an international institution designed to introduce law and order into the international community. Although, as we shall see (§§ 128–30), the UN has failed in its main purpose of maintaining peace, it has, nevertheless, greatly influenced international relations, chiefly by encouraging and speeding up the emergence of new States, so much so that as a consequence of its action the make-up of the international community has changed profoundly in the last thirty years.

The creation of the IMT and the subsequent trial at Nuremberg of the great German criminals (followed in 1946 by the Tokyo Trial), may appear to be a less conspicuous event, or, at any rate, something which has left a

[10] N. Politis, *Les Nouvelles Tendances du droit international* (Paris, 1927), pp. 91–2.

lesser imprint on the international community. Admittedly, what appeared to be a radical turning-point at the time, later failed to display its full potential. Nonetheless, the importance of the trial should not be under-estimated. Until 1945 (with the exception of the provisions of the 1919 Treaty of Versailles relating to the German Emperor), State officials had never been held personally responsible for any wrongdoing they might have per-petrated. Until that time States alone could be called to account by other States. The only exclusions were military people (in actual practice, low-ranking servicemen) accused of misconduct during international wars. This deviation was warranted by the exceptional character of war (in a way a pathological occurrence in international dealings, leading through abnormal degeneration into utterly inhuman behaviour). In 1945, for the first time in history, the principle was laid down—and carried through, unlike what had happened in 1919, when the provisions of the treaty of Versailles on the punishment of the German Emperor has remained a dead letter—that other State representatives (high-ranking officers, politicians, prominent admin-istrators or financiers, as well as men in charge of official State propaganda) could also be made answerable in international gatherings for gross mis-conduct. Those men were no longer protected by State sovereignty (see §24); they could be brought to trial before organs representative of the international community and punished by States. For the first time the basic principle was proclaimed that, faced with the alternative of complying with national legal commands or international standards, State officials and individuals should opt for the latter. As the IMT forcefully stated, 'the very essence of the Charter [instituting the IMT] is that individuals have international duties which transcend the national obligations of obedience imposed by the individual State'.[11]

What was the general effect of these seemingly disparate events? In a way, they increased the already existing tension between the opposite poles of law and force. This tension was now dramatically enhanced: on the one hand, States came to possess potentially unrestricted physical power; on the other hand, new rules and principles were proclaimed and acted upon with a view to placing an ever increasing number of legal restraints on State sovereignty. The dramatic clash between law and force was destined to cast its long shadow over the international community in the years ahead.

35. At this point it seems useful to dwell upon a theme mentioned briefly above. During the Second World War, and in its aftermath, peace became the principal goal of the international community at large. The reasons behind this major development can easily be grasped if one remembers that in the past, wars had never been of world-wide magnitude, and that, in

---

[11] The text of the judgment delivered by the International Military Tribunal at Nuremberg is in *AJIL* 41 (1947), 127 ff. The passage quoted here is on p. 221.

addition, States had never possessed the means of destruction capable of destroying mankind. The new appalling advances in man's ability to wreak havoc made it necessary to regard peace as the fundamental purpose of all States, a purpose to which all others—including the goals of respect for international law and promotion of justice—ought to be subordinated. However, when the framers of the UN Charter upgraded peace to such high rank, they did not naively pursue the goal of permanent and universal peace, for they were aware that international friction and interstate armed conflict would not disappear by legislative fiat. They more realistically set about to build up a system designed to keep armed clashes within the bounds of exceptional events, to be controlled and put an end to by means of international institutionalized co-operation. In short, States aimed at achieving a condition where the absence of war was to be the norm—although they knew that this would be a relative state of affairs.

One means of pursuing this new purpose was to render the unleashing of wars more onerous than before. Waging war in breach of international law (that is a war of aggression), was made an 'international crime' entailing the personal responsibility of its authors (in addition, of course, to that of the State for which they acted).

36. The Second World War had yet another remarkable consequence: it precipitated the downfall of colonial empires. In the opinion of the Swedish economist G. Myrdal this was indeed the most conspicuous upshot of the War. As he wrote in 1963:

Indeed, the collapse of that [colonial] political power system will one day be seen as by far the most important result of the Second World War. The reverberations of it will change conditions for life and work in every corner of the world and will in a decisive way determine world development till the end of this century and even beyond. Its importance cannot be overestimated. We have as yet only seen the beginning of its world-shaking effects; and ... we have by means of biased scientific approaches protected our minds from grasping the seriousness of what has happened and what will happen.[12]

In the view of this great scholar, the freeing of colonial peoples from metropolitan rule, which started with a snowballing effect after 1945, showed striking similarities with the emancipation of slaves which had taken place in the second half of the nineteenth century in the US. In both cases the people gaining emancipation were black: and in both instances freedom came as a result of a big and devastating war which had not been waged for the specific purpose of liberating slaves or colonial peoples respectively, and in which the black or colonial peoples themselves did not

---

[12] G. Myrdal, 'The Worldwide Emancipation of Underdeveloped Nations', in *Assuring Freedom to the Free*, ed. A. M. Rose (Detroit, 1964), p. 99.

have the opportunity to participate actively. Be that as it may, it is un-
questionable that the Second World War accelerated a process which had
started earlier, and whose principal components were the gradual economic
and political decline of European Powers (§ 30), the disrupting presence of
the Soviet Union on the world scene (§ 3), and the growing political and
economic power of the US which, despite its colonial domination of the
Philippines (§ 21), and the *de facto* direct or indirect exploitation of some
Latin-American countries, propounded an anticolonialist ideology. These
were the international factors which contributed to the demise of colonialism. There were, however, also domestic reasons, and they have rightly
been stressed by various authors. After the First World War, at least some
Western-European countries had witnessed both a gradual opening to
democracy (which through universal suffrage led to greater participation of
the whole population in the decision-making process) and also a drive
towards the 'Welfare State', largely motivated by greater sensitivity to and
concern for the underprivileged. Thus, when the cost of maintaining colonial rule over distant territories increased (among other things because of
rising unrest there), the metropolitan masses were able to transmit a clear
message to their rulers: since the principal profits from colonial exploitation
went to limited groups of people, whereas—in Myrdal's words—'the general
costs—military costs and also some welfare costs—were rising rapidly and
more and more becoming costs on the budget of the metropolitan country',
it was no longer in the interest of the population to hold on to colonial
domination, the more so because it now appeared to be at variance with
the welfare ideology at home.

Composition of the International Community

37. Following the Second World War, the make-up of the world community changed radically. First, a handful of Eastern European countries
became socialist 'democracies' (the German Democratic Republic, Poland,
Bulgaria, Hungary, Romania, Czechoslovakia, to which Yugoslavia should
be added); as a consequence, the Soviet Union no longer felt isolated in its
ideological and political fight against capitalist States. Second, a number of
countries subjected to colonial domination gained political independence as
a result of the erosion of the colonial empires of France, the UK, Belgium,
the Netherlands, Portugal, and Italy.

Syria and Lebanon were granted independence in 1945 and 1946 respectively;
India and Pakistan became formally independent in 1947; in 1948 the state of Israel
was founded, and Burma became independent; an independent status was granted
to Libya in 1951, to Tunisia, Morocco, Sudan and Ghana in 1956, to the Federation
of Malaya in 1957, and to Guinea in 1958.

These events had a strong impact on the political life of the international community. Western countries no longer dominated. While in many respects they continued to exercise a strong influence on the shaping of international and domestic policies, they were now compelled to come to terms with two groups which were characterized by strong ideological motivation. Eastern European States were guided by most of the principles referred to above (§ 31). Although they differed widely as to their economic, political, and cultural backgrounds, developing countries found a unifying factor in their desire to get rid of their colonial past and the attendant Western outlook. While they were at the outset tributaries to the industrialized countries on a great many scores, they gradually learned to propound new ideas and concepts, more often than not at odds with Western political philosophy.

Along with newly independent States, a new category of international subjects became active in the international arena: intergovernmental organizations. They mushroomed in a short period of time, covering several fields (political, economic, social, technical, etc.) with a broad variety of activities which had considerable impact on international affairs. Their existence had many consequences. It may suffice to emphasize one which relates to the political field. Previously, some States, particularly middle-sized and small powers, were to some extent able to refrain from getting involved in international affairs which were not directly relevant to them. Once they started participating in the activity of international organizations where all major world events were discussed, often to form the subject of resolutions or some sort of joint action, it became almost impossible for them to hold aloof. They were constrained to express their views on the matter, to take sides, to join in praising, condemning or exhorting. In short, the creation of a wide network of intergovernmental organizations aroused or strengthened, if not a sense of solidarity, at least the sense of belonging to the same community and therefore of being concerned by any crucial event occurring in it. If the First World War made each State feel that it could no longer live in relative isolation, the emergence of organizations buttressed this trend and definitively established the notion that certain occurrences (an act of aggression in one area of the world, a policy of destabilization of other States pursued by one particular country, widespread injustice in economic relations between two or more groups of States, etc.) are of concern to the whole international community.

The Attempt at Institutionalizing the Pre-eminence of Great Powers

38. As a reaction to the devastations of the Second World War and the unfettered recourse to violence marking those dark years, the Allies decided to set up an international organization capable of placing far-reaching restraints on the use of force. The political premise to this major turning point was the *rapprochement* between two former political opponents, the US and USSR, which had gradually come about during the war and had led to some form of political co-operation.

The system for collective security created in 1944–5 bears a strong resemblance to the Concert of Europe of 1815 (see § 22). As in the post-Napoleonic era, in 1945 the big powers considered it necessary to assume control of international affairs and to decide themselves on joint action to be taken in case of serious threats or breaches of peace. They therefore set up a 'directorate', consisting of the two Superpowers (US and USSR) plus a few other States which, although already on the wane, could still be regarded as indispensable to any effective direction of international affairs (the UK, France, and China, the latter being at that time formally represented by the 'nationalist' Government of Chang-Hai-chek). The superiority of a few powerful countries was formally acknowledged in law: Article 27.3 of the UN Charter lays down that no deliberation on matters of substance can be adopted by the Security Council unless all five permanent members agree (either by voting in favour or by abstaining, according to the practice evolved later). This is the so-called veto by any of the Big Five. By the same token, the Charter envisaged a system of collective security: if the Security Council, with the concurring vote of the Big Five, agreed that there was a threat to peace, a breach of the peace or an act of aggression, it could dispatch UN armed forces against the offending State.

As we shall see below (§ 128), the disagreement between Western Powers and the Soviet Union, which immediately surfaced in 1946, with the Cold War spreading everywhere, prevented the collective security system from working. As a consequence, the international community had to fall back on the traditional devices for preventing war or enforcing international law. Once again, an attempt at centralizing the use of force ended in failure, and the old institution of self-help acquired new importance, albeit with a number of qualifications.

The International Legal System in Transition

39. One of the salient features of this phase is the massive participation of newly independent countries in the world community. One may wonder what stand these new countries took in relation to international law. In fact their behaviour was not unlike that of the USSR in 1917. While they rejected some general rules (such as those on the protection of foreign property) and a multitude of treaties made by colonial powers on their behalf, the bulk of international law they did accept, either tacitly or expressly. Yet, they soon became aware that many international rules did not fully respond to their needs (for example the principle of freedom of the sea, under which Great Powers were free to exploit the natural resources off the coasts of developing countries, while the latter were unable to do so for want of the requisite technology). By the same token, they realized that the whole body of international rules rested on the sacred tenets of freedom and formal equality of States, and that there was no 'community duty' which stipulated that disadvantaged States should be assisted by industrialized countries. Here again was a huge area where legal change was needed.

It will therefore not come as a surprise that developing countries, backed up by socialist States, prompted a revision of the principal rules of international law. The UN General Assembly, where Western or pro-Western States were gradually losing control, was the ideal forum for ventilating new ideas and denouncing the injustice behind many traditional norms.

One of the consequences of the influence of the two groups of States was that the need for progressive development (and codification) of international law gained momentum. The adjustment of the old rules of international law to new political realities made it imperative to recast those rules in multilateral treaties. The process of reformulation allowed the needs of the newly independent countries which had not participated in the previous law-making process to be taken into account. At the same time, codification of international law ensured greater certainty and stability, for in many instances customary rules were put into writing and were consequently given greater precision and made more specific.

The codification process started in 1958 with the four Conventions on the Law of the Sea, where the whole of this intricate matter was clarified and partially revised, except for the issue of the width of territorial sea, over which no agreement was reached. The four Conventions of 1958 are, indeed, indicative of this stage of development of the international community. Although in a number of respects new demands were taken into account (codification of the legal regime of the continental shelf, introduction of the idea of protection of natural resources at sea, etc.) no radical change was made in the existing law. Developing States were still too weak to be able to press the points they were to make in the early 1970s.

STAGE 4: FROM THE EXPANSION OF THE THIRD WORLD (1960) TO THE PRESENT DAY

Composition of the International Community

40. After 1960 the bulk of the international community consisted of Third World countries. Together with socialist States they could easily muster a two-thirds majority in any international gathering.

The new make-up of the world community differs radically from that represented in its first phase (see Chapter 2). While between the seventeenth and the eighteenth centuries a number of European countries dominated the world scene, and non-Western States were far less numerous and of marginal importance, now non-Western States constitute the overwhelming majority. However, one should refrain from jumping to the conclusion that the present position is the exact reverse of the former. In actual fact the current Western minority still wields enormous economic and military power, while the majority is chiefly endowed with political and rhetorical authority. Hence, the situation is now rather more complex and fragmentary than in the past.

41. It should be added that during this time the People's Republic of China (henceforth: China) opened up to the international community. It increasingly took part in international gatherings and expounded its views on a number of subjects.

At first China had confined itself to denouncing unilaterally all the treaties concluded by the previous regime which it regarded as 'unequal' and 'at variance with international justice' (this position was among other things laid down in the 'Common Programme' adopted in 1949 as an interim constitution at the first session of the Chinese People's Political Consultative Conference). Subsequently, in 1954, China launched, together with India and Burma, the famous five Principles for the regulation of international relations[13] ('mutual respect for each other's territorial integrity and sovereignty', 'non aggression', 'non-interference in each other's internal affairs', 'equality and mutual benefit', 'peaceful coexistence'). Plainly, they only constituted political guidelines for international action and, in addition, were geared to coexistence rather than to co-operation. In later years China's policy appeared to be increasingly marred by the use of catchwords, which often proved to be nothing more than formulas. No thought-out contribution was made to the reshaping of international institutions. China appeared to be content with hurling accusations instead of contributing constructively to the rebuilding of the international legal order on more democratic foundations. This is the period subsequently dubbed by Chinese leaders as dominated by the 'ultra-Left ideological trends of Lin Piao and the Gang of Four', which led, among other things, to the predominance of the 'nihilist and liquidationist points of view regarding the study of international law'.[14] This attitude gradually changed and at present China is greatly instrumental in shaping Third World strategies. There is now a greater opening towards the international community and its legal instruments (as is shown, *inter alia*, by the fact that China has recently sought a

[13] The text of the 'Five Principles' is in *Documents on International Affairs 1954* (London, 1957), pp. 312 ff.
[14] For the phrase 'nihilist and liquidationist conceptions', see *Ch YIL*, pp. 256, 260.

post in some legal bodies of the UN, such as the ILC and the ICJ, as well as by the setting up in 1980 of a Chinese Society of International Law).

Some Chinese jurists have pinpointed the main reasons for the opening up of China to international law. Thus Huan Xiang, Vice-President of the Chinese Academy of Social Sciences, stressed in 1980 that China felt the need to study in depth various aspects of international law in order to cope with the intensifying diplomatic activity and the increasing international contacts. He pointed out that 'China's economic and cultural exchanges with foreign countries involved increasingly complicated legal relations, as could be seen in the assimilation of foreign investment, the importation of advanced technology, the joint development of resources with foreign countries, the establishment of joint ventures and other forms of economic co-operation, the contracting of loans, foreign trade, maritime affairs, insurance and tourism, all of which had to be governed and regulated through various forms of law. It was [therefore] necessary to step up the study of these questions and relevant international conventions, regulations and customs'. Another Chinese scholar, Chen Tiquiang, Professor of international law at Peking University, has pointed to the political, ideological, and diplomatic reasons why, in his view, international law should be studied and drawn on by China:

... The struggle around international law was closely related to international political struggles; in particular, many of the struggles at the UN, which are political struggles in essence, often took the form of judicial struggles. Though struggles in international law could not replace political, military or economic struggle ... [the struggle around international law] was important as a struggle by means of argument and reasoning. The correct use of international law, a criterion acceptable to a third party in distinguishing between right and wrong, would help a country win international sympathy and would contribute to the defence of world peace and the struggle against hegemonism. It was one-sided to dismiss international law as something unimportant because it had failed to stop the Soviet invasion of Afghanistan and to compel Iran to release hostages.[15]

Legal Change

42. Once developing countries had, with the active support of socialist States, firmly established their command over the assemblies of most international organizations, they started devising and propounding a complex strategy. First, UN potentialities were enhanced, except for the area of collective security. Second, developing and socialist States kept insisting on self-determination and racial equality, and demanded that they be turned into legal principles. These were achieved, in 1965, when the UN Conven-

[15] For the remarks of Huan Xiang, see *Ch YIL*, pp. 255-6; for those by Chen Tiquiang, p. 258.

tion on Racial Discrimination was adopted, and again in 1966, when the two 1966 UN Covenants on Human Rights included Article 1 which laid down the principle of self-determination. These instruments were followed and amplified by a number of resolutions and other treaties laying down ancillary rules. Third, the two groups of States proposed that all the basic principles governing international relations should be recast in such a way as to take account of their views. This was achieved in 1970, after many years of labour, when the General Assembly adopted the Declaration on Friendly Relations (see § 177). Fourth, codification was expanded to cover a wide range of subjects (see § 106). Finally, developing countries began to realize the importance of effecting radical changes in the economic set up of the international community. As soon as political independence was attained, they became aware that they also had to press for a change in international economic relations so as to achieve socio-economic and political progress. After long and untiring efforts the so-called 'Group of 77' (in 1964, when they first united their efforts on an institutional basis, African, Asian and Latin-American States numbered 77) succeeded in having the General Assembly adopt a declaration and a plan of action on the New International Economic Order (NIEO). The developing States opted for a resolution, for it would have been both unrealistic and premature to impose new economic principles with legally binding force on industrialized countries. The adoption of resolutions was seen as the stage preceding the gradual transformation of political guidelines into international legal rules (§ 213).

4

International Legal Subjects

43. WHILE national systems encompass many legal subjects (all the citizens, plus the corporate bodies set up by them, the State institutions, as well as foreigners), only a limited number of legal persons make up the international community. The fundamental or primary subjects are *States*. They possess paramountcy because they are the only international entities controlling *territory* in a stable and permanent way. All other subjects either exercise effective authority over territory for a limited period of time only, or they have no territorial basis whatsoever. States, therefore, are the backbone of the community. Should they disappear, present international society would either fall apart or change radically. For historical reasons, no more than some one hundred and seventy States have come into being—including a few mini-States which, in recent years, have become independent as a result of the gradual disappearance of colonialism. One particular class of such subjects—a handful of States with strong economic and military systems—are the real holders of authority in the international community. Beside States proper there is another category of international subjects, namely insurgents, who come into being through their struggle against the State to which they formerly belonged. They are born from a wound in the body of a particular State, and are therefore not easily accepted by the international community unless they can prove that they exercise some of the sovereign rights typical of States. They assert themselves by force, and acquire international status proportionate to their power and authority. However, their existence is by definition provisional: they either turn into fully-fledged States or they are defeated and disappear.

States and insurgents are 'traditional' subjects of the international community, in the sense that they have been the dramatis personae on the international scene since its inception. Since the Second World War, other poles of interest and activity have gained international status. They are: *international organizations*; *peoples* finding themselves in certain conditions (§§ 51, 52) and endowed with a representative structure; and *individuals*. The emergence of these 'new' subjects is a distinct feature of modern international law and requires a few words of comment.

The reasons behind the international recognition of intergovernmental organizations are different from those motivating the granting of international standing to peoples and individuals. As far as the former category is concerned, States have been motivated by reasons of expediency and practicality. Instead of looking after certain areas of mutual interest individually, they have preferred to set up joint bodies charged with the carrying out of international action on behalf of all the participating States. This phenomenon had already occurred in the first half of the twentieth century. What is remarkable is that after the Second World War a step further was taken and intergovernmental agencies were endowed with autonomous powers, with rights and duties distinct from those belonging to each member State. In addition to these reasons, an ideological factor contributed to strengthening the role of intergovernmental organizations and to allotting international standing to them. This factor centred on the idea that to ward off the scourge of a third world war, a strong network of international instrumentalities should be created so as to impose heavier and more far-reaching restraints on States. However illusory and naive this 'internationalist' outlook may have been, there is no denying that it led to the proliferation of organizations and contributed to their increasing importance.

In the case of individuals and (organized) categories of peoples, the ideological factor was decisive. A different ideology accounts for the emergence of each of the two classes. A Western, liberal–democratic theory lay at the root of the appearance of individuals on the international scene: the human rights doctrine, championed by western countries such as the US and a few Latin-American countries as early as 1945 and subsequently taken up by a number of other Western or Western-oriented States. This doctrine did not only result in the drafting of a number of international treaties protecting human rights; its logical corollary was that individuals were granted the opportunity to call States to account before international bodies whenever they felt that their rights had been disregarded. As we shall see, although States belonging to the two other groups (socialist and Third World) were gradually (albeit grudgingly) won over to the Western human rights doctrine, most of them did not go so far as to accept its corollary: to them State sovereignty should predominate; according to this view, individuals can only play a role within each municipal legal system. As a consequence, the breaking of the traditional ruler–ruled relationship and the (occasional and limited) placing of the ruled on an equal footing with the rulers in the international arena has only materialized with respect to the Western component of the international community, together with those developing countries willing to accept the Western outlook. Socialist States do not merely deny individuals recognition as subjects of international law; they also *oppose* their international subjectivity. A typical reflection of this stand is the view set forth in the GDR Manual of International Law of 1982, which states that doctrines on the international status of physical persons 'are extraordinarily dangerous, for they provide support and apparent justification to attempts or practices of some imperialist States, calculated to encroach upon the domestic affairs of other States, in blatant violation of the international prohibition on intervention'.[1]

The doctrine of the self-determination of peoples—a 'formula of collective freedom and human progress', as Scelle[2] termed it—resulted in the emergence of peoples on the international scene. However, what gave impulse to the appearance of this category of subjects was the anticolonialist version propounded by Lenin as early as 1917, not the more moderate one put forward by the American President Woodrow Wilson (§ 80). After the Second World War and the acquisition of independence by many developing countries the doctrine came to command wide support despite the opposition of some Western countries, and gradually gave rise to a legal principle. It is on the strength of this principle that some categories of peoples—if possessed of a representative organization—have been able to acquire international status (although, as we shall see, their international status tends to be admitted by socialist and developing countries, while Western States are reluctant to do so).

Thus one of the basic principles of the traditional international community has been undermined, stating that only sovereign (or quasi-sovereign) States are international subjects and that the populations over which they wield power do not have any say in the world scene. At present the international community is no longer an exclusive club for rulers; it also allows some categories of the ruled to participate in international action with a distinct and autonomous legal status. In the case of 'organized' peoples and individuals, the 'umbilical cord' connecting those under the authority of a sovereign power to the State apparatus has been partially severed, and the former are allowed to put forward their own claims and demands without having to go through any State agency.

In the next few paragraphs we shall see how sovereign States have placed restrictions upon the international status of these new classes of international subjects.

CATEGORIES OF INTERNATIONAL SUBJECTS

44. One specific feature common to international organizations and individuals must be borne in mind.

Unlike other subjects, they only exist as international legal entities if groups of States decide to grant them legal rights; in addition, these rights remain dependent on the will of those who granted them. These two categories perform activities delegated to them by States, which consider it convenient or appropriate to institute distinct centres of action for the

---

[1] DDR-*Völkerrecht*, i (1982), 22 (see also p. 157).
[2] G. Scelle, *Précis de droit des gens*, ii (Paris, 1934), p. 257.

furtherance of goals agreed upon by them. On this score organizations and individuals can be styled 'ancillary' subjects of international law. This, however, also means that they are but instruments in the hands of States. They cease to exist internationally the very day the groups of States which begot them decide to get rid of them.

It follows from these observations that international organizations and individuals are 'derivative' subjects, in that they draw their existence from the formal decisions (normally a treaty) of other subjects. States, together with insurgents and peoples endowed with a representative organization, make up the category of 'original' subjects (whose existence follows primarily from a *de facto* process, independent of any formal decision of existing subjects). It is possible to draw a further distinction based on the relative importance of the subjects and the degree of their indispensability to the present structure of the international community. Consequently one can distinguish between 'primary' and 'secondary' subjects (the former embracing States, the latter encompassing all other international subjects).

TRADITIONAL SUBJECTS

States

45. Generally municipal law lays down rules establishing when an individual or a body acquires legal status—that is when they become holders of rights and duties. To this effect, most States provide that individuals become legal subjects at birth, although they can only exercise their rights and obligations when they come of age. As for entities (corporations, foundations, public agencies, etc.) domestic law usually specifies the requirements they must meet in order to be granted rights and duties. In short, municipal law normally includes special provisions on the 'birth' of juridical subjects. In a way, the application of such rules constitutes a kind of precondition to the operation of all other substantive and procedural norms.

By contrast, there is no international legislation laying down detailed rules concerning the creation or identification of original subjects, namely States, insurgents and organized peoples (it stands to reason that the position of derivative subjects is somewhat different: as they are instituted by treaty or international resolutions, they derive their origin from specific provisions which may set forth the characteristics they are expected to display in order to possess rights and duties in relation to the instituting States). Yet, on careful analysis, it is possible to infer from the body of customary international rules granting basic rights and duties to States that these rules presuppose certain general characteristics in the entities to which they address themselves.

They usually require the following elements: first, a central structure capable of exercising effective control over a given territory; the bodies endowed with supreme authority must in principle be quite distinct from, and independent of, any other State, although some forms of international interference by other subjects have in the past been considered compatible with statehood (for instance, protectorates, where the protecting State—say France in relation to Morocco and Tunisia—was authorized to control the defence and foreign policy of the protected State); second, a territory which does not belong, or no longer belongs to any other sovereign State, with a community whose members do not owe allegiance to other outside authorities. Let it be said with emphasis that territory is an essential element to this class of subjects. Territory may be large or small, but it is indispensable if an organized structure is to qualify as a State and an international subject. International law always exacts possession of, and control over, a territory. Only in exceptional circumstances does it allow corporate entities which have lost effective control over territory to survive as international entities for some time (this was the case of the so-called 'Governments-in-exile' created during the Second World War: they were hosted in Great Britain and represented countries occupied by Germany, that is Poland, Norway, the Netherlands, Belgium, Luxemburg, Yugoslavia, Greece). Even in those cases the 'survival' of the international subjects rests on a legal fiction— politically motivated—and is warranted by the hope of recovering control over a particular territory. Once this prospect vanishes, the legal fiction is discarded by the other States.

If these requirements are met, then all the rules governing international dealings become applicable.

Plainly, the norms referred to above do not provide very specific criteria. They merely provide a general yardstick. It is, therefore, difficult to ascertain in practice whether a State fulfils all the requisite conditions. Two factors prove of great help here: the principle of effectiveness, and the attitude of existing States, as reflected in their recognition, or non-recognition, of the new entity.

It follows from the principle of effectiveness (§ 10) that every member of the international community, in assessing the new situation, should ascertain whether the apparatus exercising authority in a given territory over a given population does effectively constitute a separate and distinct entity from other States and in addition holds *de facto* control within the limits of its jurisdiction. The principle of effectiveness thus affords broad guidelines to existing States. Often, however, it is not sufficient. The attitude of States towards the new entity should then be taken into account.

This attitude is generally manifested in the granting or withholding of recognition.

The act of recognition has no legal effect; it does not confer rights, nor does it impose obligations on the new entity. The view that recognition entails 'constitutive' effects, that is that it creates the legal personality of

States, has been advocated by many jurists, chiefly in the past. It is, however, fallacious because it is in strident contradiction with the principle of effectiveness whereby 'effective' situations are fully legitimized by international law (according to the theory of constitutive recognition a State would not possess legal personality if not recognized even when possessing effectiveness); furthermore it is inconsistent with the principle of sovereign equality of States, for existing States would be authorized to decide when a new entity can be admitted to membership of the world community. The theory is also logically unsound, for it implies that a certain entity is an international subject in relation to those States which have recognized it, while it lacks legal personality as far as other States are concerned; thus international subjectivity would be split quite artificially, in defiance of reality. The theory under consideration is an outmoded survival from the nineteenth century, when, as I pointed out above (§ 19), European States claimed the right to admit or exclude other States to the 'family of nations'. I have already emphasized that even at that time such a right was questionable and that the policy was devoid of formal legitimation.

At present, the recognition of States has a twofold significance: first, it is politically important in that it testifies to the will of the recognizing State to initiate international interaction with the new State and second, it is legally relevant for it proves that the recognizing State considers that in its view the new entity fulfils all the required conditions for becoming an international subject. Of course this assessment is not at all binding on other States. It is, however, indicative of the attitude of States and can therefore prove useful in deciding whether the new entity may be regarded as an international legal subject. In a community lacking any central authority responsible for formally passing judgment on legally relevant situations, the attitude of single States acquires considerable weight as evidence for or against the existence of new legal subjects.

In actual practice new States hardly ever succeed in being recognized by all members of the international community in a short period of time (unless they are States which were granted independence by peaceful means). Usually, only a few States grant recognition and accordingly initiate dealings with the new entity, exchanging diplomatic envoys, entering into agreements, and so on. A segment of the international community may decide to hold aloof for some time—this attitude is usually motivated by political considerations (a lack of ideological or political affinity, or even open opposition, or else strong economic or geographic obstacles to the subsistence of the new entity). If this is the case, the new State will not be able to enter into active relations with those States: no treaties are concluded, there is no exchange of diplomats, the nationals of the new State are not allowed to enter other countries and vice versa. This does not, however, necessarily mean that the new entity is devoid of legal identity in relation to the non-recognizing nations. General international rules on the co-ordination of States (as opposed to those on co-operation), such as the norm on the high seas, or respect for territorial and political sovereignty, etc. do apply to the relationships between the new State and all other members of the community. It follows that non-recognizing States are duty-bound to refrain from invading or occupying the new State or from jeopardizing its political independence; they must refrain from subverting its domestic political system; they must also respect the right of the new State to sail the high seas (in particular, no interference in the navigation of its warships is allowed).

It should be added that extreme situations may exist whereby a State, although it exhibits all the necessary requirements, is still not recognized by the overwhelming majority of the members of the world community. This actually happened in the case of Southern Rhodesia, from the moment of its Unilateral Declaration of Independence (UDI, 1965) to the moment when its internal political system accepted majority rule (1980). During these years all States (except for South Africa) withheld recognition on account of Southern Rhodesia's racist policy. This attitude was dictated by the aforementioned principle to the effect that new situations contrary to basic principles of the international community should not be legitimized, even though they may prove to be effective (see § 10). This general stand did not imply that Southern Rhodesia was devoid of legal personality in relation to other international subjects. It only meant that no other State (except South Africa) was ready to enter into relations with it so long as it did not change its domestic policies. Southern Rhodesia was regarded as a social outcast, a pariah State. It did, nonetheless, possess rights and duties, although it was unable to make use of most of them. This anomalous condition resulted from the clash of two conflicting principles: the old principle of effectiveness and the new principle of withholding legitimacy to facts and situations inconsistent with the general values of the present world community. The coexistence of these two principles, that is, the fact that the latter has not been capable of displacing the former, brought about this disconcerting situation.

There have also been cases in which it was doubtful that a new State had actually been created, and indeed the international community withheld recognition. This, for instance, occurred in the case of the 'Turkish Republic of Northern Cyprus', proclaimed on 15 November 1983 and recognized by Turkey only. The UN Security Council, the Commonwealth heads of government and the Committee of Ministers of the Council of Europe declared the proclamation of independence illegal and called for its withdrawal.

Insurgents

46. Often political and military dissidence within a sovereign State results in large-scale armed conflict, with rebels succeeding in controlling a modicum of territory and setting up an operational structure capable of effectively wielding authority over the individuals living there. When this happens the insurrectional party normally claims some measure of international subjectivity.

Insurgency has been a frequent occurrence since the inception of the international community. Civil strife raged in North America between 1774 and 1783: the fight between American settlers and the British colonial power (today it would be styled a 'war of national liberation') lasted a long time and wrought havoc; it ended with the victory of the rebels. Between 1810 and 1824 other rebellions broke out on the same continent: in this case against Spanish and Portuguese rule in Latin America. Once again, the insurgents got the upper hand. It was as a result of insurrection that the Greeks freed themselves from Turkish domination after fighting from 1821 to 1829. In the nineteenth century a number of civil wars also erupted in Europe, chiefly in Poland, Hungary, and Italy; most of them led sooner or later to the formation of national States. Yet the most important civil war of all took place in the US between 1861 and 1865, and was attended by such appalling devastation and cruelty that the contestants felt it did not differ from a war proper, and consequently applied to it the bulk of the rules governing armed conflict between States. On the American continent other civil wars broke out: in Cuba, on two occasions (1868-78 and 1895-8), in Chile, in 1891, and Brazil, in 1894. In the same period Europe was also the theatre of uprisings: France in 1871 (but the Commune of Paris was short-lived) and Spain, between 1873 and 1875.

In the present century there have, perhaps, been fewer internal conflicts but they have been particularly serious, protracted, and destructive. The Russian civil war (which started in 1917 and did not end until 1920)—the anti-Soviet forces being supported by the British, French, Japanese and, for some time, by the US Governments—and the Spanish Civil War 1936-9—in which Italian and German forces played a conspicuous role—stand out for their magnitude and far-reaching repercussions. After the Second World War, apart from internal conflict in Greece (1946-9), in Northern Ireland, in Hungary (1956), and in Czechoslovakia (1968), all major insurrections have broken out in Third World countries—the Congo (1960-1), Yemen (1962-9), Nigeria (1967-70), Nicaragua (1978-9), and El Salvador (1979-83).

What is the reaction of international law to civil strife? Later on (§ 163-5), I shall show how international rules govern the conduct of hostilities. Here it is my purpose to enquire into the extent to which rebels acquire some standing in the world community.

States have traditionally been hostile to insurgents in their territory, on the obvious grounds that they do not like the status quo to be disrupted by people who seek to topple the 'lawful government' and possibly to change the whole fabric of the State. Consequently they prefer to treat insurgency as a domestic occurrence and the rebels as common criminals; in their eyes, any 'interference' from the international community is bound to bolster insurgents and make them even more dangerous. Traditional reluctance to grant civil upheaval the status of international armed conflict has become even more marked in recent times, for two reasons: first, the existence of tribal feuds or other forms of conflict in many Third World States, particularly in Africa, where the arbitrary borders decided upon by the colonial powers are likely to lead to secession, and second, the growing tendency of Great Powers to replace direct confrontation with war by proxy, through support for 'loyal' or 'friendly' political and military groups in small or middle-sized countries. Consequently, feeling more and more insecure, the overwhelming majority of States, and, above all, developing countries, show a growing tendency to withhold the granting of international legal standing to rebels and to treat them under the criminal laws of each country concerned.

The inimical attitude of States towards insurgents has manifested itself in three principal forms. First of all, the current regulation of insurgency is rather confused and rudimentary. International law does not specify when a group of rebels starts to possess international rights and duties. It only establishes certain loose minimum requirements (those indicated in the definition above) for being eligible to international subjectivity. It is for States (both the State against which civil strife breaks out and other parties) to decide—by granting or withholding recognition of insurgency or belligerency—whether these requirements have been fulfilled. In actual practice, the very existence of rebels as international legal persons largely depends on the attitude of other subjects. Theoretically, if all members of the international community were to decide that a certain insurrectional party is devoid of the requisite conditions, that party would not acquire any international status, however strong, effective, and protracted its authority over a portion of the territory belonging to a sovereign State. In practice, things are different, for two main reasons. First, in the international community there are several political and ideological alignments; any insurrectional party is likely to enlist the support of one or more States on account of political, religious, or ideological affinities, or because of military or strategic considerations. Consequently there will always be one or more States inclined to recognize certain rebels. Second, even other States may at a certain point find it useful to concede that a group of insurgents has become a legally independent subject: this may occur when the rebellious party exercises effective authority over a territory where foreigners live. Since it would be unrealistic for third States to claim respect for their nationals from the incumbent Government, they are forced to address their claim for protection of their citizens and their property to the rebels. They thus implicitly admit that rebels have a duty under international law to protect the lives and assets of foreigners.

Be that as it may, there is no gainsaying that in the case of rebels, recognition by existing States plays a more significant role than in the 'birth' and legal personality of new States. The conspicuous reluctance of States to admit rebels to the 'charmed circle' of the family of nations, the inherently provisional character of insurgency, the embryonic nature of most international rules concerning civil strife, are all factors determining the practical and legal importance of recognition.

There is a second way in which hostility to rebels comes to the fore. While third States are authorized to provide assistance of any kind, including the dispatch of armed forces, to the 'lawful' government, they are duty-bound to refrain from supplying assistance (other than humanitarian) to rebels. Plainly, the current international regulation looks on insurgents with disfavour while granting the incumbent Government the right to enlist foreign help for wiping out rebels.

A third consequence of this hostility is the paucity of international rules applicable to the rebellious party. All in all, it can be argued that only very few general rules address themselves equally to rebels and to States (provided of course that the former prove they have control over the territory, and civil commotion reaches a certain degree of intensity and duration and that, in addition, at least a few States grant them recognition).

For example, the norms on treaty making: rebels are empowered to enter into agreements with those States which are willing to establish rapport with them. Similarly, the rules on the treatment of foreigners: rebels are to grant foreigners the treatment provided for under international law. In his Report on the Draft Convention on State Responsibility, R. Ago[3] drew attention to three 'examples' of State practice where third States requested insurgents to make compensation for damage caused by the insurrectional authorities to the nationals of the States concerned. These cases relate to the American civil war (1861), to an insurrection which broke out in Mexico in 1914, and to the Spanish Civil War (on three occasions in 1937 the British Government addressed a formal request for reparation to the Nationalist authorities, as a consequence of the destruction of a British destroyer, a merchant vessel, and two seaplanes at the hand of the insurgents). At the same time, rebels do not have a full correlative right to claim respect for their lives and property from all third States where their 'nationals' (that is, people owing them allegiance) may find themselves. Such respect can be exacted only by way of reciprocity. If a 'national' from an insurgent territory lives in a State unwilling to recognize rebels, that State's duty to protect that 'national' only exists in relation to the 'lawful' Government, of which the individual has citizenship. With regard to the rules on the immunity of foreign representatives: insurgents must treat as State organs all officials of third States in the territory under their control (they owe a special duty of protection, and must grant them immunity from jurisdiction for official acts, etc.). As to the persons acting for the rebellious party, they can claim international protection only in relation to those States which have granted them recognition.

[3] See *Yearbook of the International Law Commission*, 2 (1972), 139.

Other States are entitled to regard them simply as nationals of the country where civil strife is in progress.

A few rules on the enforcement of international law (unarmed reprisals and other peaceful sanctions) can also be applied. Insurgents can resort to all lawful sanctions both to enforce international agreements entered into with third States or the general international rules on foreigners and respect for officials, when applicable. Finally, there are rules concerning the conduct of hostilities with the 'lawful' Government (§§ 164-5).

As I pointed out above, the insurrectional party is provisional in character (insurgents are either quelled by the Government, and disappear; or they seize power, and install themselves in the place of the Government; or they secede and join another State, or become a new international subject). It follows that they cannot claim rights contingent upon the permanent character of international subjects. Thus, *inter alia*, insurgents do not possess any right of sovereignty proper over the territory they control (they cannot lawfully cede the territory or part of it to another international subject). They merely exercise *de facto* authority.

To conclude, insurgents are State-like subjects, for they exhibit all the major features of States. However, they are transient and, in addition, they have a limited international capacity in two respects: first, they have only a few international rights and duties; second, they are only 'associated' to a limited number of existing States (those which by granting them recognition adopt the view that they fulfil all the conditions for international personality, and consequently engage in dealings with them).

47. At this point a few words should be added on the current condition of civil war in world affairs. At present we are confronted with an odd situation. On the one hand, for the reasons hinted at above, insurrections break out with greater and greater frequency, and big powers or even middle-sized States increasingly meddle by providing assistance to one side or the other. On the other hand, whereas political reality would make it imperative to enact international legislation on the matter, international law-makers hesitate before passing rules designed to control insurgency legally. As a result, the present international situation is less and less favourable to insurgents—witness the stand of 'lawful' governments in recent civil wars (for instance, in Nigeria and Ecuador) and the attitude taken by States at the Geneva Diplomatic Conference of 1974-7 (see § 151): after developing and socialist States succeeded in upgrading wars of national liberation to the category of international armed conflict (see § 161), the former countries closed the gates, as it were, in the face of insurgents not falling within the class of liberation movements (as far as insurgents were concerned, most Western and socialist States followed suit). In sum, whereas uprisings and domestic disorders are becoming a much more common occurrence, rebels are less and less likely to enjoy international standing and benefit from international regulation. Plainly, States prefer to deal with insurgency outside the realm of law, in the hope that the lack of legal trammels will allow them to dispose of the phenomenon more quickly.

NEW SUBJECTS

International Organizations

48. States increasingly find it convenient to establish international machinery for the purpose of carrying out tasks of mutual interest.

International organizations were first created in the late nineteenth and the early twentieth centuries; they were, however, very rudimentary, and primarily concerned with technical matters—for example, the Universal Postal Union, set up in 1875; the Union for the Protection of Industrial Property, established in 1883; the International Institute for Agriculture, created in 1905; and the various 'River Commissions', for the Rhine, the Danube, etc. They were merely collective instrumentalities for the joint performance of actions which each member State would otherwise have had to undertake by itself.

The League of Nations and the I L O—political institutions established after the First World War—were of greater importance. Yet they, too, were conceived by member States as 'collective organs', that is as structures possessing hardly any independent role or existence of their own in relation to their members. It is, indeed, no coincidence that the question of their possessing international legal personality either did not crop up, or, when raised by certain jurists, was usually turned down. The problem of the proper role and weight of intergovernmental organizations in international affairs only arose after the Second World War, when many organizations were created and were endowed with sweeping powers. International institutions were set up in various fields, including: political relations—for example, the United Nations, which has universal scope; the Organization of American States, the Council of Europe, the Organization of African Unity, and the League of Arab States, all of which are regional in character; military relations—for example, NATO and the Warsaw Pact Organization; economic co-operation—for example, the IMF and the World Bank (on the universal level), and the EEC or COMECON (on the regional level); cultural relations—for example, UNESCO; social co-operation—for example, I L O, F A O.

At present there are 378 intergovernmental organizations (30 of which have a world-wide scope, 51 intercontinental, 296 regional and 1 a 'federation of organizations').[4]

Usually, these organizations consist of a permanent secretariat, an assembly in which all member States take part when it meets periodically, and a governing body which is made up of a limited number of member States, and is entrusted with managerial tasks.

---

[4] The figures relating to international organizations cover the year 1984 and are taken from *Yearbook of International Organizations 1985-6*, ii, pp. 1478-9.

What are the international rights and duties of such organizations? Needless to say, it is impossible to give a definite answer, for it is left to the instituting States to decide in each case what powers and obligations to grant to the specific institution they set up. Bearing this caveat in mind, some general remarks can be made.

First of all, a distinction should be drawn between the rights conferred and the duties springing directly from the instituting *treaty*, and those deriving from general international law. The former are normally provided for in the 'constitution' of the Organization. Of course, they give the institution a status in relation to member States only: it stands to reason that since such rights and duties issue from the instituting treaty, they only produce effects with regard to the contracting parties (on account of the principle that *pacta tertiis nec nocent nec prosunt*, that is, international treaties are only binding on the States which are parties to them).

Often, the treaties in question grant the Organization the right to make treaties and to send or receive diplomatic missions to and from States.

As to *general* rules, the international practice which evolved after the Second World War shows that at least a handful of international rules do confer rights on Organizations in relation to non-member States on condition that the former are sufficiently autonomous from the latter and have a structure enabling them to act in the international field. Among the rights which can safely be regarded as belonging to international bodies, the following should be mentioned:

(1) *The right to enter into international agreements with non-member States.* Treaties concluded by the Organization with third States have all the legally binding effects of international treaties proper—provided, of course, that this was the intention of the parties to the agreement. In actual fact, Organizations have concluded numerous treaties covering a host of matters: headquarters agreements, conventions on privileges and immunities of international civil servants and members of international organs, treaties relating to activities performed by the organization concerned (for instance, those on technical assistance entered into by the UN), agreements with other organizations for the co-ordination of their fields of action, etc.

(2) *The right to claim immunity from jurisdiction of State courts for acts and activities performed by the Organization.* Domestic courts of many States have held that disputes relating to employment with international organizations cannot be submitted to States' jurisdiction, for they concern activities falling within the purview of the Organization concerned.

(3) *The right to protection for all the Organization's agents acting in the territory of a third State in their official capacity as international civil ser-*

vants. This right was authoritatively upheld by the ICJ in its Advisory Opinion on *Reparation for Injuries* (1949).[5]

On 17 September 1948, the UN Mediator, a Swede, Count Folke Bernadotte, and the UN Observer, a Frenchman, Colonel André Sérot were assassinated by a Jewish terrorist organization while on an official mission for the UN. The murder took place in the Eastern part of Jerusalem (then under Israeli control) after Israel had proclaimed its independence, and before it was admitted to UN membership. The Israeli authorities tried to discover and bring to justice the perpetrators and instigators of the crime but, as was stated by the Israeli representative to the UN General Assembly on 5 May 1948, 'the results of the investigations had been disappointingly negative'. The Government of Israel admitted that 'failure had been reported in the functioning of its security system in the past' but 'could not admit that any conclusions could be drawn from that event with respect to its present capacity to fulfil its international obligations'. Whatever the reasons behind its stance (it has been contended that it made a point of honouring its international obligations because it was keen to enter the UN), the fact remains that Israel declared itself to be ready to make reparation for its failure to protect the two UN agents and to punish their killers. However, because the victims had been acting not in their private capacities but as UN agents, the question arose whether the right to claim reparation belonged to the national State of the victims under the relevant rules of customary international law (see §24), or rather to the UN. The question was brought to the Sixth Committee of the UN General Assembly, where a lively, albeit fruitless, debate took place, after which the Assembly decided to ask the ICJ for an Advisory Opinion. The Court held that the UN had the capacity to bring an international claim against a State (be it a UN member or a third State). However, it correctly implied that this right was procedural in character and presupposed the violation of a substantive right of the Organization, that is the right to claim respect for and protection of its agents by any State in whose territory they performed their official functions. The Court stated as follows:

As this question [concerning the capacity of the UN to bring an international claim] assumes an injury suffered in such circumstances as to involve a State's responsibility, it must be supposed, for the purpose of the [Advisory] Opinion, that the damage results from a failure by the State to perform obligations of which the purpose is to protect the agents of the Organization in the performance of their duties.

(4) *The right to bring an international claim* with a view to obtaining reparation for any damage caused by member States or by third States to the assets of the Organization or to its officials. This right too was upheld by the ICJ in the same case. The Court held unanimously that the Organization could bring an international claim for damage caused to its assets, and held by a large majority (eleven to four), that the Organization could also bring a claim for reparation due in respect of the damage caused to an agent of the Organization or to persons entitled through him. It should be stressed

[5] On the Bernadotte case see *Yearbook of the United Nations 1948*, p. 400. The Court's judgment is in *ICJ Reports 1949*, pp. 177, 186.

that the Court's majority adopted a very progressive stand on this last issue. Instead of endorsing the traditional view whereby States alone can put forward claims on behalf of their nationals, the Court held that when an individual acts on behalf of an Organization, the 'functional' link between himself and the Organization takes precedence over the national link with his State. Accordingly, it was up to the Organization to bring claims on behalf of its agents, even in the case of the offending State being the national State of the victim. This view, needless to say, greatly privileged the functional bond as opposed to national allegiance. It was felt by some that this view actually undermined the authority of States over their citizens and constituted a dangerous precedent. The socialist countries, in particular, strongly resented and criticized the Court.

These various rights are not, however, attended by the capacity of Organizations to enforce them in case of breaches by member or non-member States. Although, as has been pointed out, they have substantive rights, as well as the right to seek remedies before international bodies (provided of course that the defendant State has accepted the competence of such organs), international organizations are impotent in case of non-compliance by States either with their own obligations or with international decisions ascertaining their wrongful acts. In these extreme situations international institutions can only rely on their moral and political authority, or on the pressure which powerful member States can bring to bear on the lawbreakers.

49. It should be added that the attitude of member States towards the international status of Organizations varies to a great extent. Great Powers as well as a few middle-sized States *tend* to take an unfavourable view of the allotting of extensive powers to international Organizations. Indeed, in their eyes this practice is likely to render Organizations increasingly independent. Plainly, the more limited the powers and functions of Organizations, the greater the control of powerful member States over them. This is best illustrated by the attitude adopted by certain countries on the occasion of the Bernadotte incident.

Before the ICJ was requested to deliver its Advisory Opinion, a few States (Brazil, Venezuela, the Netherlands) declared in the GA that in their view the responsibility of a State towards the UN for the death or injuries of a UN official could be admitted and that consequently the Organization could claim reparation.[6] States such as the US and the USSR thought otherwise. The former pointed out that only the national State of an individual was qualified to present a claim in his name for any physical injury inflicted on him. If the national State consented to present the claim, it could do so in conjunction with the claim for damages presented by

---

[6] See *Yearbook of the United Nations 1948*, quoted in n. 5.

the UN on its own behalf. But if the State concerned refused to take action on behalf of one of its nationals, the UN could not assume that right. The USSR took an even more 'conservative' stand. It affirmed that the UN Secretary-General should make claims on behalf of the UN in the national courts of the offending State. To avoid making concurrent claims, the Secretary-General should first reach an agreement with the State of which the victim was a national.

Both the Soviet and the US judges subsequently dissented from the Advisory Opinion and emphasized in their Separate Opinions that the UN was not authorized to bring an international claim against a State on behalf of an individual. When the matter was again considered in the General Assembly, in September 1949, the USSR, supported by Poland and Czechoslovakia, reaffirmed its thesis and added that the Court's view would impair the sovereignty of States. They argued that the capacity to claim damages for losses suffered by persons was the exclusive right of a State and could not be transferred to any other body. In their view the Court, by stating that the UN possessed such a capacity, had intervened illegally and without valid reasons in the domestic affairs of States; they stressed that it was necessary to guard against interpreting reparation as a punitive measure and against interfering in the jurisdiction of sovereign States. The US, on the other hand, ultimately bowed to the Court's opinion. Its representative stated that the Opinion was an authoritative expression of international law on the question with which the Court had dealt.

Although in 1949 socialist countries adopted a negative attitude on this issue, more recently jurists from the socialist area—whose views tend to agree with the official stand of their Governments—have argued in favour of the international legal status of intergovernmental organizations. Thus, for instance, the majority of Soviet writers agree that universal organizations possessing certain objective characteristics do have a limited international subjectivity; but they insist that these organizations are 'secondary' and 'derivative' entities, subject to the will of member States.

50. Finally, an interesting sociological phenomenon deserves our attention. International organizations, like other political and bureaucratic institutions at every level, tend to consolidate their authority once they come into operation. They tend to turn gradually into autonomous centres of power, one contributing factor being that they rest on the consent of a number of States which are politically neither homogeneous nor united. Thanks to divisions and conflicts among member States, international organizations end up by gaining a strength and effectiveness which would otherwise be beyond their grasp. It follows that even powerful members are unable to influence Organizations decisively or to make them take a path different from that agreed upon by the majority of members. They are faced with institutions which, although formally dependent on States, eventually wield authority over individual members. To condition the life of an Organization radically, all the major members would have to unite and take joint action within the institutional structure. Whenever it proves impossible to harmonize their political stand, single members must resort to devious procedures or devices. This is best illustrated by the attitude of the US towards ILO.

In November 1977 the US withdrew from this Organization. Among the reasons for this step President Carter mentioned the erosion of the tripartite principle (the alleged diminution of independence of employer and worker delegates attending ILO Conferences), the ILO's selective concern for human rights (the relative immunity of socialist countries from criticism for violating workers' rights), and the increasing politicization of the Organization (the introduction into ILO debates of extraneous political issues, such as those relating to the Middle East question). It is significant that a great power such as the US felt unable to make the ILO change its policies while still a member of the Organization and felt that the only way out was withdrawal from ILO. As a result the US ceased to pay its financial contributions and since they represented about one-quarter of the whole Organization's budget, the US withdrawal made many States ponder its demands anew. In February 1980 the US, considering that a majority of ILO members had 'successfully joined together to return the ILO to its original purposes', decided to re-enter the Organization.

Simply by standing aloof from the Organization and withholding its financial contributions the US had used its influence to prompt the ILO to change its politics. (As is well known, a similar stand was taken by the US and the UK with regard to UNESCO.)

Peoples under Colonial, Alien, or Racist Domination, Endowed with a Representative Organization (National Liberation Movements)

51. The emergence of organized groups fighting on behalf of a whole 'people' against colonial powers is a characteristic feature of the aftermath of the Second World War. The geo-political areas where liberation movements arose were first Africa, then Asia; they are now in the process of mushrooming in Latin America and—to a lesser extent—in Europe as well. Africa, however, still remains the principal home of this striking phenomenon. Along with the gradual expansion from Africa to other continents, liberation movements also broadened their objectives: in addition to colonialism, new goals were invoked by liberation movements, namely the struggle against racist regimes and alien domination.

Algeria was the first country to witness the emergence of a liberation movement (the FLN, in 1954). Other African movements were: PAIGC (African Party for the Independence of Guinea and Cape Verde), FRELIMO (Liberation Front of Mozambique), the three movements in Angola (MPLA, UNITA and FLNA), the two movements which fought in Zimbabwe (ZAPU and ZANU); those fighting against South Africa (ANC: African National Congress and PAC: Pan African Congress); SWAPO (South West Africa People's Organization), which is struggling for the liberation of Namibia; MOLINACO and SPUP, which advocated the liberation of Comores and the Seychelles respectively; the FLCS (Front for the Liberation of the Somali Coast); the two fronts fighting in Eritrea against Ethiopian domination (FLE and FNLE); POLISARIO struggling against Morocco in Western Sahara, and others.

In the Middle East the PLO was founded in 1969 and is still active. In Asia the FNLV actively participated in the struggle against South Vietnam from 1960 to 1974; the FRETILIN sprang up in Timor in 1975 to fight against Indonesian rule. In Latin America similar movements are in the process of emerging, starting from El Salvador (where the FLMN operates). In Europe, along with the IRA in Great Britain, self-styled liberation movements are emerging in France (Corsica) and Spain (Basque movements).

It is well known that many of these movements eventually acquired statehood (for instance, in Algeria, Zimbabwe, Comores, Seychelles, Angola, Mozambique, Vietnam) but also legal and political legitimation has been granted to some of the movements mentioned above by socialist and a number of developing countries. The fundamental principle on which legitimation rested was the right of peoples to self-determination (§ 80).

Control over some part of the territory in which they were fighting characterized a few of these movements (for example, the FLN in Algeria, the two movements in Zimbabwe, the two liberation movements in Eritrea, POLISARIO in Western Sahara); however, most of them are, or were, hosted in a friendly country, from where they conduct, or conducted, military operations against their adversaries (for example, the PLO, SWAPO, ANC). *Control of territory*, therefore, is not their distinguishing trait. Their chief characteristic is their *international legitimation based on the principle of self-determination*. They are given international status on account of their political goals: their struggle to free themselves from colonial domination, a racist regime or alien occupation. However, this does not mean that the territorial factor is ruled out altogether: it is present, albeit in a very singular way. Liberation movements are elevated to the rank of international subjects because they tend (or at least strive) to acquire control over territory. In this context territory amounts to a 'prospective' factor. Liberation movements could not be recognized as members of the world community if they did not aspire to possess (once their struggle is over) the basic feature proper to primary subjects of the community, that is, effective control over a population living in a given territory.

However, one should not jump to the conclusion that there is full agreement in the world community on the need for liberation movements to control some territory. On the contrary, this is one of the numerous issues on which the 'family of nations' is split. This rift came to the fore in the Geneva Diplomatic Conference on the Humanitarian Law of Armed Conflict (1974-7). The majority (socialist and Third World States) passed a provision stating that armed struggles conducted by liberation movements against colonial States, racist regimes, or alien powers were to be considered international armed conflicts (Article 1.4 of the 1977 Protocol I: § 161). In other words the majority did not see control of territory by liberation groups as a prerequisite to the status of being party to an international conflict. By contrast, the same majority, with the support of a number of Western countries, adopted a norm (Article 1.1 of the 1977 Protocol II) on internal armed conflict providing that the conflicts covered by Protocol II were solely those involving insurgents which 'exercise such control over a part of its territory [i.e. of a contracting party] as to enable them to carry out sustained and concerted military operations and to implement this Protocol'. In other words, authority over territory was required for insurgents but not for liberation movements. As stated above, this distinction reflected the views of the vast majority of members of the world community. However, when Article 1 of Protocol I was adopted, the UK delegation entered a 'reservation' to the effect that, in their opinion, to qualify for the status of belligerent party a liberation movement should meet at least the same requirements as insurgents, that is to say the conflict should have the same, or greater, intensity as the operations to which Protocol II would apply. It follows that, in the opinion of the UK (an opinion most probably shared by other Western countries), control of territory was one necessary condition for a liberation movement to be eligible for international status as a lawful belligerent.

52. Since the legitimation of national liberation movements derives from the principle of self-determination, and since at present the latter only covers the three categories of peoples referred to above, liberation movements fighting for peoples other than those three classes are not entitled to international status. As a consequence, representative organizations of a people living in a sovereign State and oppressed by an authoritarian government fall outside the category of international subjects under discussion; the same holds true for the population of a sovereign State dominated by a despotic élite controlling the country with the economic and military support of a foreign Power (a frequent occurrence, for example, in Latin America). This may no doubt appear to be a serious deficiency in the current international regulation. However, as a dispassionate examination of reality should not be confused with political or ideological aspirations, one ought to take account of the present limitations of the international legal system. The truth of the matter is that most members of the world community are reluctant to accept a form of international legislation which might eventually undermine their own power structure. The same preoccupations which militate against granting international status to insurgents also apply to a possible expansion of the role of peoples and their representative organizations in the international community.

None the less, a gradual evolution and indeed expansion of the principle of self-determination should not be discarded out of hand: new classes of peoples may become entitled to international status in the not too distant future. One likely development is perhaps a liberal interpretation of the words 'colonial' and 'alien domination' enshrined in the current regulation. It is possible that 'colonial' be so construed in international practice as to encompass, under certain conditions, neo-colonial forms of domination as well (otherwise the almost complete demise of traditional colonialism would eventually render this particular international norm pointless; on neo-colonialism see § 213). Furthermore, 'alien domination' could gradually be given a broad interpretation so as not to be limited to foreign military occupation only but to extend to some particularly conspicuous forms of hegemony of one country over another (such as the foreign military and economic conditioning of an undemocratic government, where the foreign country ultimately props up and buttresses an authoritarian government which is contrary to the interests of the population).

53. Although the principle of self-determination grants a right to *peoples*, one should co-ordinate that principle with all the other rules of international law, in order to grasp the scope of peoples' international personality. International rules cannot have as their addressees loose aggregates of individuals. Since in this context the term 'a people' refers to a group of human beings united by ethnic, religious, cultural and historic ties, one may legitimately ask oneself which members of such a group can act upon international rules, put forward international claims, and so on. Some sort of organization or structure is necessary for the activation and implementation of international norms. Indeed, all the other international subjects (except of course for individuals), present a structure or apparatus capable of putting into effect international rights and duties. The same consideration applies to peoples. In order to be owners of rights and subjects of obligations, it is necessary for them to have an apparatus, a representative organization which can come into contact, as it were, with other international legal persons. Once a people falls into one of these three categories and is endowed with a representative organization or apparatus, it can claim to possess international status. This was clearly spelled out in Article 96.3 of the First Geneva Protocol of 1977, mentioned above. In indicating the categories of peoples entitled to make a declaration for the purpose of being bound by the Protocol, it was specified that such a declaration could be made by '*the authority representing a people* engaged against a High Contracting Party in an armed conflict of the type referred to in Article 1.4', that is, a conflict against a colonial, racist or alien Power.

54. Who decides whether a certain organization is representative of a people and consequently falls within the category of subjects under discussion? It should be noted that this assessment is particularly complex and tricky, for international rules concerning liberation movements do not clearly specify the various requirements. The problem is exacerbated by the fact that the requirements themselves are rather evanescent; thus, for instance, while a condition such as effective control of territory (required for insurgents) is relatively objective and verifiable, a requirement such as 'representativeness of a people' is difficult to appraise. As a consequence, so long as international rules (or rather the majority of States behind them) do not specify and elaborate upon the various requisite conditions for liberation movements, concrete evaluation of whether or not they have been met in a specific instance must of necessity fall upon the existing members of the world community, namely States and intergovernmental organizations. Hence, the recognition granted by such subjects acquires enormous importance, almost as great as that which according to a few jurists, accrued to the recognition of States by existing Powers in the nineteenth century, when the international community was actually monopolized by a small group of countries wary of 'admitting' new subjects into the 'family of nations'. The U N through the General Assembly has delegated to regional organizations the task of recognizing national liberation movements: through resolution 2918 (XXVII), of 1972, followed by other resolutions adopted the subsequent year, the G A requested the O A U to pass judgment on the existence of the requisite conditions for liberation movements; by resolution 3102 (XXVIII), of 1973, the same task was entrusted to the Arab League. Of course, the G A has itself the power of pronouncing upon the 'representativity' of a given liberation movement existing in an area not covered by the two regional Organizations just mentioned.

The U N and the other two Organizations have so far recognized a number of African movements and the PLO. SWAPO and the PLO have even been granted observer status within the U N, a number of specialized agencies, and at a handful of diplomatic conferences. In 1981 the European Parliament (an organ of the European Community) declared that the liberation movements fighting in Afghanistan against Soviet occupation were the legitimate representatives of the Afghan people.

Some authors (e.g. Lazarus,[7] and Freudenschuss[8]) have concluded that the recognition accorded by intergovernmental organizations has 'constitutive' value—it creates the international legal personality of liberation movements. However, this view is not entirely acceptable. There are a number of liberation movements which for political reasons have not been (and will never be) granted recognition by the regional organization con

---

[7] C. Lazarus, 'Le Statut des mouvements de libération nationale à l'Organisation des Nations Unies', *A F D I* 20 (1974), 173 ff.

[8] H. Freudenschuss, 'Legal and Political Aspects of the Recognition of National Liberation Movements', *Millenium: Journal of International Studies*, 11 (1982), 115 ff.

cerned; nevertheless, they have been recognized by a few States and show the basic requirements for being treated as international subjects. Take, for example, the two Eritrean liberation fronts, which have not been recognized by the OAU on account of Ethiopia's strong opposition (as was rightly pointed out by Abi-Saab[9] 'the regional organizations, for obvious reasons, only recognize liberation movements whose adversary lies outside the membership of the organization'). Furthermore at the Geneva Diplomatic Conference of 1974-7 on Humanitarian Law of Armed Conflict, a Turkish proposal which was calculated to entrust to regional intergovernmental organizations the task of selecting the liberation movements entitled to invoke Protocol I, was never followed through. Had the proposal been championed and eventually accepted, it might have been inferred that the world community considered the 'screening' by intergovernmental organizations as a prerequisite for the admission of liberation movements to this community. The lack of any such 'screening' in the Geneva Protocol proves that, however important it may be, it is not the *only* way of legitimizing liberation movements. The view seems therefore warranted that although recognition by international organizations is of great importance, it is by no means a *sine qua non*; recognition by States too is important for assessing whether a liberation movement qualifies for international subjectivity.

Clearly recognition—be it granted by regional organizations, the UN or by single States—is not 'constitutive' of the international legal personality of liberation movements; the latter, like all other international subjects, can claim international status as soon as all the requisite conditions are satisfied. Nevertheless—as I have already pointed out—in the case of liberation movements the views and attitudes of States and organizations play an even more crucial role in appraising whether those requirements are met than in that of other international subjects. In actual practice, a liberation movement not recognized by any State, or recognized by only a very limited number of States, could hardly be considered eligible for membership in the world community at large.

55. What are the rights and duties of the peoples referred to above? To get a fair idea of what they are, it is appropriate to list the most important rules addressing themselves to such peoples:

(1) The principle of self-determination. Since it is general in character and consequently affects all member States of the international community, the right to self-determination devolving to a people is a right *erga omnes*. (On the principle that even States which do not recognize a particular movement are affected by certain general rules concerning liberation movements, see

[9] G. Abi-Saab, 'Wars of National Liberation in the Geneva Conventions and Protocols', Hague *Recueil* 165 (1979-IV), 408.

below.) Consequently all States are duty-bound to respect this right; in particular, the occupying or colonial State or the State with a racist regime has an obligation to discontinue its unlawful denial of self-determination and to grant this right. Third States must refrain from assisting the offending State. They must not give it any assistance likely to prop up or consolidate its oppressive domination. In particular they must refrain from providing any military aid to the Government in question. Furthermore, according to a number of States, national liberation movements representative of one of the three classes of peoples referred to above have the right to use force against the oppressing Power.

It should be emphasized that this right has never been accepted by Western countries. For many years in the UN, socialist and developing countries insisted that liberation movements had a right to use force but the staunch opposition of the West resulted only in the adoption of rather loose formulas such as: 'the right [of those movements] to resist forcible denial of self-determination by all means in conformity with the UN Charter'. These were interpreted by those favourable to liberation movements as making legitimate the use of armed force; Western countries read them as permitting 'peaceful means' only. The tug of war between the West and the other two groups has been interpreted as having gradually led to the acceptance of the majority view, although—so the argument goes—this occurred in a roundabout way and through the adoption of general formulas. Neither the 1970 Declaration on Friendly Relations nor the Definition of Aggression issued by the GA in 1974, explicitly lay down the right in question, nor do they use phrases pointing in that direction. Article 7 of the Definition of Aggression, for example, provides that nothing in the Definition prejudices the 'right' of peoples fighting for self-determination 'to struggle to that end and to seek and receive support, in accordance with the principles of the Charter and in conformity with the above-mentioned Declaration [on Friendly Relations]'. This provision was interpreted by States such as Algeria, China, Egypt, Ghana, Kenya, Senegal, the USSR, and Yugoslavia, as recognition of the legal use of force.[10]

It should be stressed that while both the Declaration of 1970 and the Definition of 1974 prohibit the use of force to deny the self-determination of peoples they fall short of adding in specific terms that peoples have the right to oppose such a forcible denial. It could be argued, however, that this right logically follows from the fact that States are forbidden to use force against liberation movements (since force is prohibited by Article 2.4 of the Charter 'in international relations' solely, and Western countries claim that this means 'interstate relations', colonial, racist or foreign powers would otherwise be allowed to use military force for the purpose of crushing

---

[10] See *Yearbook of the United Nations 1974*, pp., 845-6.

liberation movements); however, no parallel prohibition is laid down for liberation movements, which in addition are 'entitled to seek and receive support' from third States in their 'action against and resistance to' the forcible denial of their right of self-determination.

The fact of having an international *right* to use force would imply that engaging in armed violence against the dominating Power must not be regarded by third States, or by the international community as a whole, as a breach of the prohibition on using force (§83), or as a justification for third Powers for resorting to coercive measures to help wipe out the liberation movement in question.

However, it should be added that the interpretation given above has been challenged by a number of Western States: Canada, Belgium, the UK, the US, Italy, the Netherlands, the FRG, Portugal and Israel objected to Article 7 of the Definition of Aggression of 1974, maintaining that such a provision can only be interpreted as permitting the struggle for independence by liberation movements 'by peaceful means', not through armed violence.[11] Their view about the inadmissibility of national liberation movements resorting to armed violence has been increasingly shared by Latin-American countries.[12]

However, confusion about the standing of liberation movements does not have any major *practical* consequences. While socialist and many developing countries take the view that liberation movements have a right proper, Western and many Latin-American countries actually downgrade those movements to insurgents and implicitly argue that their use of force does not constitute the exercise of a right but a mere fact which—as is also the case with insurgents—is neither inherently lawful nor unlawful under international law.

(2) General principles on the conduct of hostilities (*jus in bello*) (see § 162).

(3) Rules on treaty-making. Organized peoples have the power to enter into agreements with States and international organizations. Such agreements are regulated by the international law governing treaties proper.

The Argentinian jurist J. A. Barberis[13] has recently drawn attention to numerous

[11] See GAOR, XXIXth Session, VIth Committee, 1473rd Mtg., para. 15 (Canada); 1476th Mtg., para. 11 (Belgium); 1477th Mtg., para. 24 (the UK); 1480th Mtg., para. 73 (US). See also 1472nd Mtg., para. 27 (Italy); 1473rd Mtg., para. 5 (The Netherlands); 1478th Mtg., para. 19 (FRG); ibid. para. 22 (Portugal); 1480th Mtg., para. 60 (Israel).

[12] See for instance the views put forward in 1978 by such countries as Argentina, Bolivia, Brazil, Chile, Colombia, Costa Rica,. Peru, Trinidad and Tobago, Venezuela, Uruguay (*Yearbook of the United Nations 1978*, p. 695). Similar views were expressed also by Singapore in 1978 and Papua New Guinea in 1979 (ibid., 1979, p. 835). See also the statements made in 1980, in the plenary meetings of the General Assembly, by Argentina (GAOR, XXXVth Session, 98th Mtg, para 67), Chile (para 197) and Uruguay (para 198), as well as the views expressed in 1984, in the IIIrd Committee of the General Assembly, by Uruguay (A/C.3/39/SR. 35, para 32), Peru (para 36), Chile (para 43) and Honduras (para 63).

[13] J. A. Barberis, 'Nouvelles questions concernant la personnalité juridique internationale', Hague *Recueil* 179 (1983-I), 259 ff.

treaties and agreements concluded by liberation movements with States in one or other of the following areas: conditions for the cessation of hostilities and the granting of independence (for instance, the Evian agreements of 1962 between the Algerian FLN and France; those of 1974 between Portugal and PAIGC, and Portugal and FRELIMO, as well as the agreements of 1975 between Portugal and the three Angolan movements FLNA, MPLA, and UNITA); border questions (for instance, the agreements between the Provisional Algerian Government and Morocco in 1961, and that in 1979 between POLISARIO and Mauritania); the stationing of armed forces belonging to liberation movements on the territory of States (for instance, the agreements of 1969 and 1970 between the PLO, Lebanon, and Jordan).

(4) Rules on the protection of official representatives. Organized peoples have the right to claim respect for and protection of the persons acting in their official capacity as organs of the people's representative structure.

Finally, it may be interesting to ask ourselves how all the rules listed above operate in actual practice. To put it differently, to what extent do organized peoples take advantage of the pertinent rules and, by the same token, to what extent do States comply with the rules in relation to organized peoples? It is not easy to answer these questions satisfactorily, for international practice is of necessity fragmentary, given the plurality of liberation movements claiming international standing on the one side, and the multiplicity of groups of States having, or not having, relations with them, on the other. On balance, it may be said with some approximation that very few organized peoples have been able to benefit from the rules mentioned above—the PLO and SWAPO being exceptions. For one reason or another, all other movements have aroused a certain hostility or at least a reluctance to accept them into the various alignments and groupings, particularly among Western States. Thus they have failed to enlist support from the world community at large. They are recognized and actively assisted by only a very small number of States, totally ignored by most other States, and in some instances even heatedly opposed. It follows that, subject to one or two exceptions, organized peoples occupy a very precarious position in the world community.

56. By way of conclusion, it may prove useful to point briefly to the main differences between insurgents and liberation movements. First, the former derive their international legitimation from control of territory, whereas the latter primarily benefit from ideological legitimation (the principle of self-determination of peoples). Second, while the former have no international right to use *force*, the latter possess such a right—at least according to a large segment of the world community. This differentiation is accounted for by the considerable hostility of the overwhelming majority of States to rebels, while socialist and the bulk of Third World countries at least tend to accept the aspirations of liberation movements.

However, in practice, this distinction is difficult to operate, the more so because there are borderline cases which are hard to classify which may gradually shift from one category to the other. For example, the Angolan group known as UNITA had been regarded as a liberation movement until 1975, when Angola gained independence; after that date it 'turned' (under the proposed classification) into an insurrection group. As is apparent from this illustration, what really matter are the goals pursued by the fighters and the principal features of the adversary: in the case of UNITA, until 1975 the adversary was a colonial Power and the purpose of the struggle was to obtain independence; since 1975, the adversary has been the Government of a sovereign State and the goal has become its overthrow (or, in the words of UNITA itself, the liberation of Angola from foreign—i.e. Cuban—troops).

Individuals

57. Over a long period of time—in fact during the whole of the first stage of development of the international community (1648-1918)—human beings were under the exclusive control of States, each State exercising total control over its own citizens. If, in time, individuals acquired some degree of relevance in international affairs, it was as mere 'objects' or, at best, as 'beneficiaries' of treaties (treaties of commerce and navigation, or conventions on the treatment to be accorded to foreigners); or else, they constituted the 'reference point' of States' powers (think, for example of the customary rule granting States the right to exercise diplomatic and, if legally possible, judicial protection of their nationals wronged by a foreign country).

Recently States have started to allow individuals under their jurisdiction the possibility of playing a small part in the world community. This trend began after the First World War, when the framers of ILO decided to confer on industrial associations of workers and employers the right to demand compliance with ILO Conventions by member States. At the time this was a great improvement indeed. It went hand in hand with another similar development in the field of the international protection of (racial, religious or linguistic) minorities: representatives of such minorities gained the right to lodge 'petitions' with the League of Nations, if in their view the States concerned failed to honour their international undertakings. In both cases the rationale behind this significant change can easily be accounted for—as ILO Conventions and international treaties on minorities were calculated to protect workers (or employers) and minorities respectively, it was quite logical to grant their beneficiaries the right to protest in case of alleged violations. This appeared all the more sensible since the treaties in question did not lay down any synallagmatic rules (§11), but merely imposed obligations *erga omnes* (*contractantes*) relating to acts to be performed by each contracting State within its own municipal order, regardless of any direct interest or benefit accruing to other contracting States. Consequently, had the groups of individuals directly concerned not been authorized to denounce possible violations, no State would have been likely to protest and the treaties would have remained a dead letter.

However, the practical benefits of this important new right failed to fulfil its potential. Associations of workers and employers lodged very few complaints with the ILO, while minorities made scant use of their right of petition. Historical conditions were manifestly not yet propitious to a legal development that was in many respects far in advance of its time.

After the Second World War the ILO principles were solemnly reaffirmed and the implementation machinery was gradually given greater strength and influence. Treaties on minorities, which had collapsed long before the outbreak of the war, were replaced by a number of conventions on human rights, which no longer protected groups of individuals as such, but rather single human beings. Some of them granted their beneficiaries the right to make States accountable for possible misbehaviour. Individuals consequently came to possess a certain measure of international status.

On close scrutiny, it appears that this status is characterized by the following major limitations:

(1) Individuals are given only *procedural* rights: the right to initiate international proceedings before an international body, for the purpose of ascertaining whether the State complained of has violated the treaty providing for substantive rights benefiting individuals. In addition, this right is usually limited to forwarding a complaint: the complainant is not allowed to participate in international proceedings (a notable exception is the European Convention on Human Rights of 1950). Much less has the individual a right to enforce or to promote the enforcement of any international decision favourable to him (again, a limited deviation from this rule can be found in the practice relating to the European Convention). Once the international body has pronounced upon the alleged violation, the applicant is left in the hands of the accused State: cessation of, or reparation for, the wrongful act will substantially depend on its good will.

(2) The procedural right in question is only granted by treaties (or, in a few instances, by international resolutions). Consequently, it exists only with respect to certain well-defined matters (labour relations, human rights).

As to ILO, Article 24 of its Constitution grants associations of workers or employers the right to submit complaints with respect to any ILO Convention ratified by the State complained of; in addition, a few resolutions adopted in 1950 provide for the right of associations of workers to petition an ILO body (the Committee on Trade Union Freedom of Association) for alleged violations of the

ILO Conventions on the matter, regardless of whether the accused State has ratified them.

In the field of human rights, mention should be made of the Optional Protocol to the UN Covenant on Civil and Political Rights of 1966, the Convention on the Elimination of Racial Discrimination of 1965 (Article 14), as well as of two procedures set up by ECOSOC in 1967 and 1970 respectively, whereby individuals or groups of individuals can submit 'communications' to certain human rights bodies (§ 178). On the regional level, the most noteworthy treaty is the European Convention on Human Rights, referred to above. An Inter-American Convention on Human Rights was adopted in 1969, one of its provisions (Article 44) granting 'any person or group of persons or any non-governmental entity legally recognized in one or more member States' of the OAS the right to lodge with the Inter-American Commission on Human Rights petitions containing denunciations or complaints of violation of the Convention by a State party to it.

(3) Another limitation on the right at issue lies in the fact that not all States that are parties to the above treaties have accepted being made accountable to individuals.

To enable States notoriously opposed to the presence of individuals in the international community to ratify the treaties concerned without submitting to supervisory procedures set in motion by individuals, a special device has been resorted to: the authority of international bodies to consider individuals' petitions has been laid down in particular clauses of the treaties. Consequently, only those contracting States which *also* explicitly accept the clauses submit to the control mechanisms. In practice, so far no socialist State has subscribed to that competence, being generally opposed to allowing individuals the possibility of calling the State to account before international forums. The States declaring themselves competent to hear individuals' petitions are mostly Western plus a few Latin-American, African, and Asian countries.

(4) A further weakness in the international status of individuals is that the procedures they are authorized to set in motion are quite different from those existing in domestic law.

Three things in particular should be stressed. First, international bodies responsible for considering petitions are generally not judicial in character, although they often behave in conformity with judicial rules. True, most of them consist of independent experts acting in their individual capacity; nevertheless, diplomats in office as well as other national civil servants can be elected to those bodies, and one may wonder whether all of them remain immune from the pressure of their own Governments. Second, international proceedings are themselves often quite rudimentary; in particular, there are notable limitations concerning the taking of evidence. Third, and even more important, the outcome of the procedure is not a judgment proper, but a fairly mild act, such as a report setting out the views of the international body; a recommendation, and the like: no legally binding decision is envisaged (again, the European Convention is an exception).

It is apparent from the points made above that the role of individuals is very limited on many scores. In addition, it is precarious, for it rests on the will of States. As soon as they decide to repeal the treaty or the international resolution granting procedural rights to individuals, the latter cease to have any existence of their own in the international arena. Similarly, as soon as a State which has ratified one of the treaties in question withdraws its acceptance of the international bodies' authority to deal with complaints of individuals, the latter can no longer attack that State on the international plane.

Despite these deficiencies, one should not underestimate the importance of the actions of individuals on the international scene. First, they are granted the right to petition international organs irrespective of their nationality, whether they be citizens of the State complained of, or nationals of other States (be they parties to the treaty or not), or even stateless persons. The right of petition is therefore granted to physical persons *qua* human beings. No bond of nationality nor any other form of allegiance is taken into account. This in itself represents a momentous advance in the world community.

Second, one should bear in mind that it is not easy for States to deprive themselves of some of their sovereign prerogatives, such as their traditional right to exercise full control over individuals subject to their jurisdiction. Given the present structure of the world community and the fact that States are still the overlords, the limited status of individuals can be regarded as a remarkable progress. True, they only play a small role in the theatre of international relations; they only play a walk-on part which lasts so long as States do not decide to regain their freedom of action. However, at present the world community is not prepared to grant the individual greater freedom.

Third, in a great many cases where States have accepted the authority of international bodies to consider the complaints of individuals, they have eventually come to respect the decisions by which those bodies have determined violations. In other words, international techniques of supervision set in motion by physical persons or non-governmental groups have indeed proved effective. This is hardly surprising. Once a State has taken the serious and momentous step of accepting the jurisdiction of international bodies acting at the request of individuals, it does not find it too difficult to attend to the decisions of those bodies and, if found guilty of violations, to take all the necessary measures for terminating a breach, or paying compensation to the victims.

All things considered, the existing international systems for protecting human rights which depend on the initiative of the very beneficiaries of the rights in question are no less effective than other international devices for ensuring compliance with international law. One should therefore not be discouraged by the paucity of international mechanisms based on individuals' petitions. Like all international instruments denoting a bold advance, treaties granting procedural rights to human beings are destined to be fruitful in the long run.

MULTINATIONAL CORPORATIONS: ARE THEY INTERNATIONAL SUBJECTS?

58. It is well known that amongst the entities participating in the daily life of the world community a few big multinational corporations (Unilever, Texaco, IBM, ITT, etc.) stand out. Three of their principal features are relevant to us, namely the fact that they are very powerful economically and politically (they are more powerful than many member States of the UN); their activity is not confined to one single State, but extends over a great number of countries, in almost all areas of the world; they make transactions not only with private companies but also with States and international organizations, and their disputes with States are often submitted to international arbitration. In spite of these characteristics, States have not upgraded these entities to international subjects proper. Socialist countries are politically opposed to them and the majority of developing States are suspicious of their power; both groups would never allow them to play an autonomous role in international affairs. Even Western countries are reluctant to grant them international standing; they prefer to keep them under their control—of course, to the extent that this is possible. It follows that multinational corporations possess no international rights and duties: they are only subjects of municipal and 'transnational' law.

CONCLUDING OBSERVATIONS

59. It is apparent from the foregoing discussion that the position of subjects of the world community has greatly changed in time. During the first phase of the community sovereign States were in practice the only 'actors'. Membership was largely homogeneous. The dominant figures were European countries and the US. Other States, if they were admitted at all into the 'family of nations', had no option but to bow to European values. Insurgents were occasionally given access to the 'charmed circle', but then only as 'half-brothers'. Generally speaking they were treated as dangerous subversives to be got rid of as soon as possible.

Since the watershed of the First World War, membership in the international community has gradually changed in three respects. First, although States remained the primary subjects, they no longer made up a homogeneous group. New values and ideologies were embraced by old subjects (the USSR, rising from the ashes of Russia) or by newcomers (the Afro-Asian countries, increasingly emerging after the Second World War). Second, new entities were given the status and rank of international legal subjects: inter-governmental organizations, individuals, organized peoples (liberation movements). No doubt these three classes were not put on a par with States, but rather confined to the rank of secondary subjects; two of them (organizations and individuals) were endowed with ancillary or subsidiary roles only, and individuals have so limited a standing that they can be regarded as the 'poor relations' on the world scene. However, expediency in the latter case and ideological principles in the case of peoples led States to accept association with all three categories of subjects. Third, like insur-gents, the new categories of subjects did not become equal partners in the eyes of all States (they are not universal subjects). Although theoretically there is general agreement concerning the legal personality of international organizations, most of them have been associated to some States only. More striking is the case of individuals and peoples. The former are rec-ognized as international subjects by some Western and developing countries only; the latter are regarded as international subjects by socialist and most developing countries only. I have tried to show that under certain strict conditions, these categories of entities might be regarded as possessing rights and duties in relation to *all* members of the international community. None the less, the fact remains that in actual practice physical persons are associated with one segment of the world community while organized peoples are associated with others.

5

Attitudes of States Towards International Law

60. ACCORDING to Jean-Paul Sartre[1] man is 'une liberté en situation' (freedom in a given situation), that is, man is free to choose his own destiny, but within a social, economic, and political context which imposes a set of restraints and pressures on him, limiting his freedom as much as his 'human condition', which consists in the need to earn a living, to inhabit a world shared by others, and to face the ineluctability of death. In a way, States are not unlike men. They too are free to choose their own destiny; their freedom, however, is not boundless. In fact it is greatly restricted by many considerations like geographical location, economic conditions, and historical traditions. States are free, but only within a network of limitations which greatly reduce their field of action. They tend to seek alliances on the strength of economic and geographical affinities, as well as of ideological or political leanings. Thus, groups and alignments take shape within which each member feels much stronger and better protected. Yet, while enhancing the role of each and cementing the relations among all members, the groups are placing an array of constraints on the members which act as further limitations on their individual freedoms.

To gain insight into how States behave in the international arena it is therefore necessary to look upon them not as isolated monads existing in a meta-historical world but against the background of their real condition and within the context of the groups to which they *de facto* belong.

Of course I cannot delve here into the historical, geographic, and economic situation either of individual States or of the major alignments in the world community; I shall merely point to the political objectives and legal strategy of the principal groupings, namely their attitude towards that body of legal standards which we concisely refer to as 'international law'.

Let it be said right away that there are three main groups in the world community: Western countries, socialist States and developing or Third World nations. These groups, however (particularly the first and the third), are rather disparate for they consist of States whose historical and political conditions are often widely divergent. Nevertheless, there are some unifying factors which warrant the usual classification under the three headings just

[1] J. P. Sartre, *Réflexions sur la question juive* (1954; repr. Paris, 1982), p. 109 and *passim*.

mentioned. What is no less important, the States themselves use these labels and identify with one or other of the alignments. The undeniable differences within each grouping should, however, induce us to use great caution. The generalizations made in the following paragraphs must therefore be read with these qualifications in mind.

WESTERN COUNTRIES

61. Particular caution is needed when speaking of this class of States. It encompasses countries with widely different attitudes towards the international legal institutions: countries ranging from those content with the status quo or 'law and order' such as the US, the FRG and the UK, to Scandinavian States, which tend to be quite responsive to Third World demands and which support the need for sweeping social and legal change. In spite of these differences, some general trends can be discussed. Considering that for two and a half centuries the principal international lawmakers were the European States—and those States moulded in the European tradition—it comes as no surprise that today most of them are interested in maintaining the traditional legal framework as intact as possible. Their primary concern is for stability. However, as the modern international set-up and the new realities call for profound alterations in that framework, they are disposed to accept legal change, provided it does not take the form of a radical break, but is gradual, and so long as it is effected with their active participation and co-operation.

Western countries are not simply motivated by their own interests. Their action is also strongly influenced by their concept of law. This is a unique feature, and it is therefore worth dwelling on it at some length.

There are several reasons why in the West law is regarded as a highly esteemed value to be cherished and respected *per se*. Law was among the driving forces behind the moulding of modern States in Europe in the fourteenth and fifteenth centuries. Roman law and ecclesiastical law were important parts of the University curriculum in the Middle Ages, influencing all those who had a hand in building up the State structures.

Furthermore, the two primary unifying factors leading to the creation of the State in England and France between the late 1200s and the fourteenth century, were the administration of justice by central courts and the levying of taxes by national authorities. In the words of a prominent American historian, J. R. Strayer,[2]

the fact that there was such a strong emphasis on law at the very beginning of Western European States was to have a profound influence on their future development. The State was based on law and existed to enforce the law. The ruler was bound morally (and often politically) by the law ... In no other political system was

[2] J. R. Strayer, *On the Medieval Origin of the Modern State* (Princeton, 1970), pp. 23-4.

law so important; in no other society were lawyers to play such an important role. European States did not always attain their ideal of being primarily law-States, but that this was their ideal was an important factor in gaining the loyalty and support of their subjects.

Another significant consideration is that law played an important role in the birth of capitalism (which in turn was decisive for the formation of strongly centralized national States). The economic system evolving in the fourteenth and fifteenth centuries was based on free enterprise and free competition. One of the social mechanisms necessary for the new system was a body of predictable and ascertainable standards of behaviour allowing each economic factor to maintain a set of relatively safe expectations as to the conduct of other social actors (including the State authorities, in cases of transgression). Thus law became one of the devices permitting economic activities and consolidating and protecting the fruits of such action. It soon appeared to be one of the major agencies of social relations, and no one raised the question as to whether it was necessary or not.

A further consideration is that a large section of law in Western States was the fruit of political struggles between contending groups. The first 'bills of rights' resulted from wranglings between a King and his barons, who protested against what they regarded as the King's arbitrary behaviour. Constitutions, first 'conceded' by the King, then wrenched from him by the middle classes, represented a way of placing restraints on the power of the aristocracy and its feudal privileges. By the same token, modern labour law is to a great extent the result of hard-fought battles by the workers against the propertied classes. In short, law is often the consecration and formal evidence that political strife has been waged and has ended in some form of compromise between two embattled social groups. It therefore becomes the *symbol* of social progress and equilibrium.

The importance of legal rules in the economic and political process favoured the emergence of a social group of legal experts, who practised law in the courts either as judges or as advocates. This new group, which, of course, needed the support of law teachers and law schools, gradually led to the formation of a social category strongly interested in law *per se*.

Yet another element is more general in character and less palpable, but by no means less significant. The birth of modern European States goes hand in hand with the secularization of religion, chiefly Christianity in its Catholic and Protestant versions. This process entailed the gradual erosion of the metaphysical component of religious tenets and their absorption into daily life as general moral precepts. Resting on religious or ethical principles, legal rules acquired an *extra-legal dimension* which strongly enhanced their value and which made it imperative for members of a State community to be law-abiding. O. J. Lissitzyn[3] points out that, in the West, self-interest

[3] O. J. Lissitzyn, *International Law Today and Tomorrow* (Dobbs Ferry, 1965), p. 64.

as the main motive for compliance with law 'is sometimes reinforced by a sense of moral obligation. Observance of the law is a symbol of rectitude'.

This concept of law could not but influence the attitude of Western States towards international law and impel them to take it relatively seriously. One should not, however, overemphasize the role of the Western legal stance. At least three qualifications are called for. First, as was shown above (§§ 18-19), at least in the first stages of development of the world community, law was moulded by Western countries in such a way as to suit their interests; it was therefore only natural for them to preach law-abidance and to attempt to live up to legal imperatives which had been forged precisely to reflect and protect their interests. Second, in many countries jurists, politicians, and diplomats tended to draw a distinction between municipal law—regarded as a distinct social value *per se*—and interstate law—which was to be complied with so long as it did not turn out to be in conflict with national political goals. In other words, especially in the eighteenth and nineteenth centuries, a deep-rooted sense of national sovereignty prevented many States from consistently widening the attachment to law advocated and practised at the domestic level to include international rules as well. It is indeed no coincidence that it was Western countries which invented the practice whereby international arbitration did not extend to those disputes which affected the 'independence', the 'honour' or the 'vital interests' of States (§ 112). Differences touching upon fundamental interests were settled not by virtue of law but by resorting to economic, political, or military force. Third, one should not forget that the three most abominable violations of international morality and legal principles perpetrated in the present era—Nazi genocide during the Second World War, the dropping of the atomic bombs on Hiroshima and Nagasaki, and the heinous system of apartheid in South Africa—have all been or are being perpetrated by Western Powers. Fortunately, however, examples such as these of gross misconduct or even of lesser transgressions, are the exception.

62. This description of the Occidental outlook allows us better to understand the legal strategy adopted by Western States in the international community. They are prepared to accede to the request for legal change put forward by other groups, on condition that this change be effected within the sphere of diplomatic conferences and by the adoption of international treaties (written instruments are perceived as providing better guarantees than international custom because by definition they cannot impel States to accept something contrary to their own interests). In addition, they favour the procedure of consensus (§ 108) as a technique of negotiation and decision-making in international bodies and diplomatic conferences, for it ensures that they will not be left out of the negotiating process. Finally, when it comes to drafting international legislation, they insist on two major points, which in their view are crucial to the acceptance of new legal rules: first, legal provisions ought to be clear and precise if they are to serve as reliable standards of behaviour; in other words, the margin of discretion which legal prescriptions leave their addressees should be as narrow as possible, so as to ward off the danger of easy evasion; second, substantive rules should always be attended by norms providing for mechanisms or techniques of implementation, that is devices calculated to spot possible instances of disregard, and to impel transgressing States to abide by law. To Western States any form of international legislation lacking both, or even one, of these elements is of scant value and should be discouraged as much as possible.

SOCIALIST STATES

63. The attitude adopted by the socialist Eastern European countries towards international law is profoundly different from that of Western nations. (I am referring to the socialist countries of the European area only; other States such as Cuba, Nicaragua, Angola, Mozambique, Ethiopia, etc., with strong pro-Soviet leanings, together with China, I do not class under this heading. For present purposes these must be categorized as 'developing nations'.) Unlike the West, Eastern European countries are relatively homogeneous and closely-knit, both for ideological reasons and because of the political authority wielded by the USSR (even though, as is well known, States such as Romania and Hungary tend to adopt an autonomous stand in many respects.)

64. The concept of law shared by socialist countries is to a great extent governed by Marxist ideology and by the role of law in their domestic systems. For Soviet authors, law serves to consolidate the socialist social order and helps society advance towards communism. According to P.S. Romashkin, Soviet law is 'one of the important forms through which the policy of the communist party and the Soviet State is carried out'.[4] In short, law is a means of ensuring peaceful social intercourse and direct control by the State authorities, which are bound by legal rules to the extent that this does not run counter to supreme State interests. Law must, therefore, give way to the demands of the State as formulated and interpreted by the leading force of the society, namely, the communist party. The role of law as subordinate to the party is reinforced by the fact that the State actually monopolizes all economic activity: the lack of competing economic classes or groups eliminates the need for autonomous categories of lawyers capable of defending the interests and concerns of those classes or groups.

[4] P.S. Romashkin is quoted by I. Lapenna, *State and Law: Soviet and Yugoslav Theory* (New Haven, 1964), p. 115.

Thus, law does not become a tool in the hands of conflicting social strata but merely one of the means of exercising control available to the dominant social structure.

For the purpose of understanding the socialist attitude towards the body of international rules, this general philosophy of law is to my mind more important than the socialist nations' specific concept of international law. For the latter has been less fully worked out and its elaboration is mainly due to the need to explain how it is that whilst in Marxist doctrine law is but the reflection of the economic structure, one single body of law can embrace and govern both 'capitalist' and socialist countries. According to the leading Soviet jurist G. Tunkin,[5] general international law is made possible by the peaceful coexistence of the two systems: it results from the 'concordance of wills' of both 'capitalist' and socialist States, with the difference that in the former case the international will of the State is in fact the reflection of the economic and political demands of the ruling class in that State, whereas in the case of socialist countries their foreign policy reflects 'the will of the entire people led by the working class'. Thus, according to this view, international law is merely a contractual relationship between two different worlds which have to come to terms with each other for the purpose of living in peace and engaging in mutually beneficial dealings.

65. Socialist States are also motivated in international relations by their political interests, which largely amount to the following aims: strengthening the 'socialist camp'; averting any intrusion of Western States into their own domestic affairs; maintaining relatively good relations with the West so as to ensure a satisfactory economic and commercial interchange and keep open a channel of communication on matters of security and disarmament; attempting to convert developing countries as much as possible to socialist ideals. These political objectives lead Eastern European countries to insist on three main tenets in the field of international legal relations: sovereignty; peaceful coexistence with other groups of States; and new principles allowing a reshuffle of the international community along lines more acceptable to socialist political philosophy. Let us consider these three points separately.

One of the primary concerns of socialist States is to forestall any possible interference of other States in their own territorial integrity and political independence. They therefore consistently refer to sovereignty as the key concept in international relations and the principal legal means of shielding their freedom of action from external interference. Tenacious clinging to sovereignty has led socialist scholars to adopt a doctrine which was highly popular in Europe (chiefly in Germany and Italy) between the end of the

[5] G. Tunkin, *Theory of International Law* (London, 1974), pp. 3 ff.

nineteenth and the beginning of the twentieth centuries, namely, legal positivism. Its principal postulate is that international law is exclusively created by the will of States; anything which does not stem from the State cannot be binding law. At its inception this doctrine was clearly the ideological reflection of the interests of the great powers in Europe and the US. At a time when a number of strong States had emerged, none of which was capable of overpowering the others, it proved necessary to rule out the possibility for any one of them to be bound by standards of behaviour it had not previously accepted. State sovereignty was the linchpin of the whole body of international rules and one of the basic postulates of legal literature.

It is not accidental that these theories—long since replaced in Western countries by more flexible views which tend to attenuate the role of the will of States and to give pride of place to the binding force of the international community as such—have been adopted and elaborated upon by socialist lawyers. Today the latter find themselves in a position closely resembling that of Western jurists about a century ago. Consequently, they consider it appropriate and profitable to use positivist concepts, albeit with some necessary updating. They have espoused positivist views in the following three fields: First, international subjects. In the view of socialist diplomats and jurists, beside sovereign States, only international organizations—that is entities created by States—possess international legal personality, which is, however, limited in that it markedly depends on the will of the constituent States and consequently comes to an end as soon as the latter so decide; by contrast, individuals and private organizations cannot be regarded as international subjects, for they remain under the control of States. Second, sources of law. According to socialist authors all international law has an exclusively consensual basis; therefore to them custom is but tacit agreement, and general legal principles can be considered as binding only to the extent that they are the product either of treaty or of custom. One explanation of this legal doctrine is that Eastern European countries still constitute a minority in the world community, and do not want to be bound by majority 'decisions'. Third, the relationship between international and municipal law. Socialist States adopt a strict 'dualist' approach (see §7), with the consequence that international rules apply in their domestic legal orders only to the extent that this is allowed by municipal law; in addition, in case of conflict international rules yield to domestic law (subject to a few exceptions, for example in the USSR).

As well as emphasizing sovereignty, Eastern European nations uphold the need for peaceful coexistence with other States and in particular with Western countries. A natural consequence of this doctrine is their insistence on the principles prohibiting the use or threat of force and intervention in domestic affairs, as well as the doctrine of equality of States and of peaceful settlement of disputes. (The recent resort to the so-called Brezhnev doctrine (see below, §145), has entailed a serious deviation from some of these postulates.) This is crucial to socialist countries in that it allows them to engage in international affairs without the fear of being hampered by the 'aggressive' drive of other States. The importance of these and similar principles for Eastern European States was tellingly spelled out in 1961 by the representative of Czechoslovakia to the UN General Assembly. He pointed out:

> The international pluralism deriving from the present structure of the world community not only did not preclude the possibility of regulating international relations by general international law but, on the contrary, emphasized the need for such a course. Thus, the principles of peaceful coexistence between States with different social and economic systems had become the cornerstone of present-day international law ... The inevitability of the recognition of the legal principles of peaceful coexistence was determined by two factors: first, the threat of devastating nuclear war and, secondly, the development of the productive forces of society which compelled all countries to maintain economic and cultural ties with one another.[6]

However, adherence to the doctrine of peaceful coexistence does not prevent socialist countries from vigorously propounding a few general principles which ultimately run counter to the interests of at least certain Western countries: racial equality (with the corollaries of prohibition of racial discrimination and apartheid), self-determination of peoples, and all other anti-colonialist postulates.

66. It may be useful here to describe briefly the strategy followed by socialist States for the development of international law, or rather their methods and means in the realm of law for attaining their political objectives.

Like Western States, and for the same reasons, they tend to favour the elaboration of new legal standards by means of treaties. However, unlike Western countries, they are keen to develop general principles as well. In the previous paragraph I mentioned the crucial importance of these principles to Eastern European nations. Their basic significance was forcefully expressed by one of the leading jurists of the area, the German B. Graefrath. After pointing out that the existence of general principles constitutes a characteristic feature of contemporary international law, for they are designed to allow the peaceful coexistence of differing socio-political systems, he argued that, generally speaking, principles are such (and consequently differ from mere rules) because they correspond to 'historical laws'; in the case of current international principles, they correspond to 'the historical laws of transition from capitalism to socialism': they both reflect this tran-

---

[6] See GAOR, XVIth Session, VIth Committee, 723rd Mtg., pp. 170-1.

sition and allow it to flow unimpeded.[7] According to Graefrath, international principles, unlike norms, have a 'guiding character'; they impinge upon and 'determine the structure' of the international society. They possess a threefold significance: they are themselves standards of behaviour; they constitute criteria for assessing the lawfulness of other rules (since they override all other norms, which are null and void in case of conflict); they embody 'instructions and guidelines' to the international subjects for the creation and development of other rules.

It is interesting to note that in order to work out general principles, socialist countries prefer a combination of the traditional custom-creating process with resort to negotiation in international forums, where they can press their points and agree upon new developments. This tendency was reflected in the elaboration by the U N General Assembly of the Declaration on Friendly Relations of 1970 (see § 77). Over a number of years socialist States, with the support and the decisive contribution of the Third World, have succeeded in restating, developing and elaborating a set of principles on a universal level, which for the most part had already been embodied in the U N Charter. The Declaration did not create new law, for to Eastern European States, as to the West, it seems unacceptable to endow the G A with law-making powers (see §§ 95, 107). However, in the view of the socialist group, it enshrined a sort of authentic interpretation of the U N Charter and in addition, it laid down a set of new guidelines which had the support of the whole international community by dint of common consent. Socialist scholars do not ask themselves if such consent took the form of custom or agreement, for in their view the two processes amount to the same thing, namely the manifestation of State will.

Here we touch upon a characteristic feature of socialist legal philosophy. Generally speaking there appears to be strong disinclination in the advocates of extreme positivism to concede that there is a place for general principles in international law. Indeed, in domestic systems legal principles proper (as distinct from 'principles' which can be inferred by the jurist from legal norms and have therefore a merely scholarly value; see § 76) are normally laid down in norms having general character and enjoying a higher status than ordinary legal rules. By contrast, according to traditional positivists, international law consists of the sum of particular norms, that is, treaties or tacit agreements, binding only on those subjects which consent to them; as a consequence, universal rules proper can exist only in the exceptional case of having been adopted by *all* community members. Furthermore, in their view international law does not rank certain rules

---

[7] B. Graefrath, *Zur Stellung der Prinzipien im gegenwärtigen Völkerrecht* (Berlin, 1968), pp. 3–8, 12–15. I have used the expression 'historical laws' to translate Graefrath's expression '*historische Gesetzmässigkeiten*'. In fact, the German word '*Gesetzmässigkeiten*' means 'law-governed regularities', with law here in the sense of the Marxist laws of history.

higher than others. This being so, for traditional positivists it did not make much sense to speak of international legal principles, for first, they were hardly binding on all members of the world community and, second, they could be easily derogated from by express or tacit agreement. By contrast, socialist States have come to reconcile positivism and general principles. This has been facilitated by the emergence of the class of peremptory norms or *jus cogens*, that is, the body of precepts overriding all other norms of international law (§ 96), at whose birth socialist countries have acted as the principal midwives. Socialist jurists maintain that principles can be said to exist to the extent that they are begotten by treaties or custom. Thus, for instance, at the Vienna Diplomatic Conference on the Law of Treaties the Hungarian representative insisted that principles of *jus cogens*, on which a heated discussion was taking place, no doubt did exist, but that they undisputedly rested on the 'will of States'.[8]

67. Another feature of the socialist States' strategy is that they insist on the development of the normative aspect of law, and are less interested in improving techniques of scrutiny. On the whole, they prefer to leave the task of implementing international rules to each of the States concerned, with the consequence that if after the elaboration of new norms a certain State is no longer willing to respect them, no specific or *ad hoc* mechanism exists for prompting compliance with the law. Their marked reluctance to support the creation of international supervisory machinery stems to a great extent from their fear that international bodies or mechanisms might unduly encroach upon their own sovereignty. This lack of confidence—quite unwarranted, as we shall see later (§ 115)—highlights one of the distinguishing features of present international legislation: the swelling of the normative network without any corresponding development in supervision. Their consistent distrust of international monitoring also derives from their general concept of the aims of international law. To socialist countries this body of rules may serve three different purposes. First, in the forms of bilateral treaties, of multilateral treaties covering reciprocal interests (treaties on consular and diplomatic immunities, on trade and commerce, on the law of treaties, on the law of the sea, etc.), and of general principles for peaceful coexistence, law serves to consecrate and formalize their interest in unimpeded intercourse with Western and other States. Second, in the form of general principles impinging upon the interests of the West (self-determination, racial equality, sovereignty over national resources, etc.), law serves as an instrument in the Third World political struggle against the West. Third, in the form of multilateral treaties on 'non-reciprocal' matters (such as human rights) international legal rules may prove useful in that, in some instances, they can be used in the ideological struggle against the West; on

[8] For the Hungarian statement, see Vienna Conference on the Law of Treaties, *Official Records*, First Session, 54th Mtg. of the Committee of the Whole, para. 46.

the whole, however, these rules do not possess an absolute value for socialist countries, for, in case of conflict, they ought to yield to State interest.

Let us now apply these three categories to the practice of supervision. Plainly, in the case of the first set of rules and principles, law is based on reciprocity. Consequently, States do not need any special devices for ensuring compliance: the threat of disregarding an international standard in the event of another State's failing to abide by the same standard may suffice. The second class embraces rules which are primarily political in scope and are used as 'instruments of attack'. In this area any mechanism for legal supervision would be superfluous. This leaves us with the third set of rules, where techniques of investigation and scrutiny could prove particularly helpful; here, socialist States prefer to shun international monitoring not only out of fear of a possible bias against their conduct of domestic affairs, but also because they ultimately regard those rules as loose standards possessed of no greater value than their own corresponding constitutional provisions—as stated before, they are rules which are expected to give way to the superior interests of the State whenever this proves necessary.

It should, however be stressed that recently the Soviet Union has proved more amenable to international scrutiny, at least in some areas; for instance, in development, production, and stockpiling of chemical weapons (as demonstrated, among other things, by the Soviet draft treaty submitted to the Geneva Conference on Disarmament in 1982[9]), as well as in the nuclear field (this is proved for example by the Agreement entered into in 1985 by the USSR with the International Atomic Energy Agency for the application of IAEA safeguards in the Soviet Union[9a] and by the recent Soviet decision to allow, on certain conditions, foreign inspectors at its nuclear test sites[9b]).

DEVELOPING COUNTRIES

68. It is well known that these countries, which make up the so-called Third World and constitute the overwhelming majority of the international community (about 130 out of 170 States), exhibit a great diversity.

The expression 'Third World' usually covers African, Asian and Latin American nations, in contradistinction to the First World (Western States) and the Second World (Eastern European countries). It was coined by the French political scientist A. Sauvy[10] in 1952. It has been recently attacked by the British sociologist P. Worsley[11] for its being based on the confused use of a twofold criterion (economic

[9] The Soviet draft treaty on chemical weapons of 29 July 1982 is in UN document CD/ 539, 28 August 1984, Annex III.

[9a] See text of the Agreement in 24 ILM (1985), pp. 1411 ff.

[9b] See *International Herald Tribune*, 20 December 1985, pp. 1 and 7, and *Le Monde*, 20 December 1985, p. 3.

[10] A. Sauvy, as quoted by S. Angelopoulos, *The Third World and the Rich Countries* (New York, 1972), p. 9.

[11] P. Worsley, 'How Many Worlds?', *Third World Quarterly*, 1 (1979), 100–1.

and political): the First and Second Worlds are differentiated by a historical and political criterion, whereas the Third World is distinguished from the other two by virtue of an essentially economic criterion. It is worth noting that a different interpretation of the phrase under consideration was propounded in the 1970s by Mao Tse-tung:[12] in his view 'the US and the Soviet Union constitute the First World; Japan, Europe, and Canada—the middle section—are the Second World; and we [namely, Asia except for Japan, Africa and Latin America] are the Third World'. This definition was taken up in the statutes of the Chinese Communist Party of 28 August 1973.

A different expression was launched in 1957-58 by the OECD: that of 'developing countries'. It is now the one which the countries concerned like best. Nevertheless, even this expression has been criticized, for example by T. Mende,[13] who holds that it is based on a 'polite fiction', namely the notion that those countries are in a process of development and are filling the gap with industrialized nations. The same strictures have been set forth by E. Jouve.[14]

In this book both expressions will be used interchangeably: although aware of their limitations, I believe that terminology is ultimately a matter of convention; the main thing is for agreement to be reached on issues of substance.

Developing countries are in many respects very diverse: they differ in their cultural and ideological backgrounds, in their degree of economic or social development, in political alignment, in their respective systems of public order, and so on. In spite of these huge differences, they do possess certain common traits, namely: first, before reaching independence they were all subjected to some sort of Western domination, either direct or indirect; second, they all suffer from economic underdevelopment (none of them has an advanced industrial economy comparable to that of the major Western powers, Japan, the USSR or the GDR); third, they owe their independence not only to an armed or political struggle against domination but also to a whole arsenal of ideas borrowed from or moulded on Western or socialist philosophy, such as the concepts of nation-State (developed by Bodin), of sovereignty (elaborated by Bodin and Locke), of equality (propounded by Rousseau and the French revolutionaries), of self-determination of peoples (advocated by Western political leaders such as Woodrow Wilson and by Lenin). Furthermore, as emphasized by the British historian Fieldhouse,[15] 'the concept of a permanent unitary State with fixed frontiers was largely a European importation into other parts of the world and "nations" based on such concepts and demarcations are the product of colonialism'.

---

[12] Mao Tse-tung, as quoted by Wang Tieya, 'The Third World and International Law', *Ch YIL*, 8.

[13] T. Mende, *De l'aide à la recolonisation. Les leçons d'un échec* (Paris, 1972), p. 8.

[14] E. Jouve, *Relations internationales du tiers monde*, 2nd edn. (Paris, 1979), p. 15.

[15] D. K. Fieldhouse, *Colonialism 1870-1945* (London, 1981), p. 15.

As was to be expected developing countries share no common cultural traditions or uniform political systems. Thus, Latin-American countries had their original culture almost completely wiped out by the Spanish and Portuguese invaders in the late fifteenth and in the sixteenth centuries (Hegel wrote in 1837, without the least shade of irony, that the pre-Columbian civilizations, particularly in Mexico and Peru, were 'totally natural' and they were therefore to disappear 'as soon as the Spirit (*der Geist* [to wit, the European war machine]) approached them': 'the indigenous populations gradually faded away at the breath of European activity').[16] In consequence, they are strongly geared to European traditions and tend to uphold the Western legal philosophy, except, of course, for countries such as Cuba and Nicaragua, which have recently turned to socialism.

By contrast, most African countries have a rich cultural tradition. Their social structure (based essentially on family, lineage and tribe), as well as their autochthonous culture, were not completely obliterated by colonial powers.

As for Asian countries, they too are very diverse, ranging from States with socialist leanings such as the People's Republic of China to countries relatively close to Western democracy, such as India and the Philippines.

69. Third World countries have two other features in common: a concept of law which, while differing from one culture to the other, is always profoundly distinct from that predominating in the West, and a tendency towards authoritarian structures in their respective domestic legal systems. Let us consider them in turn.

I have already suggested that in the West law was primarily an outgrowth of capitalism and the ensuing social and political struggles; furthermore, the tradition of Roman law coupled with the philosophical trends of the eighteenth century engendered a view of law as a systematic, logical, and rigorous set of clear and distinct social rules, structured on the pattern of a hierarchical society. By contrast, in all Western cultures law failed to acquire an equally great significance and status. Thus, it was suggested by A. Bozeman[17] that in the Islamic Middle East, law evolved 'neither under the impetus of practical needs, nor under that of juridicial technique, but under that of religious and ethical ideas.' As for Africa, '... everywhere [law] is the product of non-literate ways of thinking, emanating not from abstract juristic or philosophical cerebrations but from social practice, and nowhere can it be separated from the kinship system and belief in supernatural agencies.'

---

[16] G. W. F. Hegel, *The Philosophy of History*, trans. J. Sibree (New York, 1956), p. 81.
[17] A. Bozeman, *The Future of Law in a Multicultural World* (Princeton, NJ, 1971), pp. 62, 105-6, 123-4.

Again, according to Bozeman, yet another concept of law can be found in India and in 'Indianized' Asia:

Hindu law (not unlike Muslim law in this regard) originates in myth and religion, not in human intelligence. Neither secular jurisprudence nor legislative enactments responsive to changing human needs are thus fathomable here. Furthermore, and for the same built-in reasons, Hindu law does not know the idea of the person either as a citizen possessing civil liberties and responsibilities, or as the bearer of what we call human rights. Since it exists primarily as an emanation and protection of the caste system, this law makes different provisions for life in different castes, stressing in each case the duty of conforming with one's appointed *dharma* [the duty of following the laws of one's birth] and thus making inequality a fundamental legal axiom.

The other characteristic shared by all developing countries is, for a number of historical, economic, and political reasons (as investigated in particular by Fieldhouse),[18] that they have 'inherited' from the colonial Powers 'highly centralized and basically autocratic' systems of government which tend to rely on power structures where law is easily disregarded whenever it suits the ruling group. This is often in consonance with their original culture. Thus, for instance, most of them are community-oriented countries, where the leader is not viewed as a sort of possible oppressor, and his being in a way *legibus solutus* (or unbound by law) is not regarded, as it would be in the West, as an outrageous deviation from the sacred postulate of 'rule of law' (see also § 180). Furthermore, the State—which in the West is almost the incarnation of law—is often felt to be an extraneous entity. To quote a Nigerian publicist, B. O. Nwabueze[19] 'The State itself is an alien, if also a beneficial creation; its existence is characterized by a certain artificiality in the eyes of the people and it is remote from their lives and thought.'

The attitude of citizens towards State representatives in some black African countries has been described by the Senegalese jurist K. M'Baye[20] in terms applicable to other African countries as well:

Whilst in Western countries the citizens' vigilance, their gusto for putting forth claims and their attachment to legal litigation often prevent abuses against public freedoms, in the countries of black Africa passivity is instead the rule. The majority of the population lives under constant fear of the State and indeed outside the State. The African peasant takes pride in saying: 'I have never set foot in a court of law or in a police station'. The lack of education accounts for this attutide. Africans are not conversant with the mysteries of justice; frequently, they do not grasp either the meaning or the scope of legal rules.

---

[18] D. K. Fieldhouse, op. cit., 41. See also § 180, 204–5.
[19] B. O. Nwabueze, *Constitutionalism in the Emergent States* (Rutherford, 1973), p. 24.
[20] K. M'Baye, 'Les Réalités du monde noir et les droits de l'homme, *Revue des droits de l'homme* 2 (1969), 391.

The adoption of authoritarian structures in their domestic political systems (either in the form of military regimes or in that of one-party systems), leads developing countries to look upon law in a manner different from that current in the West. To most of them law does not represent the embodiment of a set of basic values acquired by one social group in its struggle against another group, or a covenant agreed upon by various social classes or political parties for the purpose of laying down the fundamental guarantees for each individual and for the whole community. In short, law is not primarily a contractual undertaking endowed with binding force; it is a means of exercising social control which must give way to power whenever superior State interests make it imperative to disregard legal obligations. Law is one of the instruments for exercising authority.

These differences in legal philosophy and domestic power structures are important, for developing countries, almost unwittingly, tend to extend their concept of law to their conduct in the world community.

70. What unites their conduct is the basic strategy adopted by developing countries. To them international law is relevant to the extent that it protects them from undue interference by powerful States (see §85) and is instrumental in bringing about social change, with more equitable conditions stimulating economic development. Their legal strategy in international relations consequently hinges on two important principles: State sovereignty and radical legal change. Since the first part of this two-pronged doctrine is self-explanatory (see, however, §§218 and 226), I shall dwell mainly on certain aspects of the second one. (For the contents of Third World legal strategy, see above, §§40–3.)

A major feature of developing countries' strategy is their insistence on the need to elaborate general principles as opposed to detailed and precise legal rules. At this point it seems apposite to quote the words of a leading Egyptian international lawyer, G. Abi-Saab[21] who, in commenting on the attitude of Third World countries to the development of international humanitarian law, made a few general remarks which are also applicable to the position assumed by those States towards the whole of international law:

... in dealing especially with the Western countries, anything which could be formulated in the very precise terms of an operational rule was considered nonsense [by developing countries], while Third World representatives in general attached great weight to general principles which sometimes could not be refined into operational rules. If we look at the same thing from a different point of view, I would say that in most cases the attitude of the Third World was defined by the total effect of a proposed solution. This is a really special legal outlook: what is law? Is law a

[21] For the remarks by G. Abi-Saab, see *The New Humanitarian Law of Armed Conflict*, ed. A. Cassese (Naples, 1980) ii. 249–50.

principle or value directive of behaviour, or is it a mere mechanism? ... I think that the Western powers put too much emphasis on the mechanistic elements while for Third World countries if by going through all the motions and respecting all the procedural rules you end up with an unjust solution, this would be bad law. And if you have a general directive, even if you cannot reduce it to very precise procedural rules, it still is good law, though it may be imperfect in terms of application.

What accounts for this marked preference for general principles? One possible reason is the 'dislike of legal technicalities',[22] expressed chiefly by Asian countries. This dislike is partly due to cultural tradition. To some extent, perhaps, it is also motivated (or was motivated until recently) by the relative lack of skilled lawyers capable of wrangling with the sophisticated experts from industrialized countries. For fear of being outwitted by those experts, developing countries often tend to play down legal sophistication. Apart from the fact that at present these countries can count on the services of a few outstanding lawyers, in no way inferior to those belonging to other areas, one can discern some more specific reasons behind their attitude. First, there is the fact that principles, being general and sweeping in character, are more acceptable to Western countries than detailed rules in areas where they oppose new developments demanded by the Third World. Often the West accepts a principle but enters the explicit or tacit reservation that in any case it is no more than a political guideline or that it is too woolly to possess definite legal content. (This, for instance, happened in the case of self-determination of peoples, adhered to by Western countries on the assumption that it did not impose legal obligations but only expressed a policy line and set a standard of achievement.) Yet, their misgivings and reservations notwithstanding Western countries do not ultimately oppose the reaffirmation of principles in official documents. Developing countries count this as a considerable success, for it makes room for the gradual transformation of general tenets into definite standards of behaviour to be used in appraising the conduct of States and exposing it to public condemnation in case of violation. As far as developing countries are concerned, the adoption of a principle in an official document is not the end of the story. Quite the contrary, it is the starting-point of a long process in the course of which the principle is restated, specified, elaborated, expanded, updated, in short gradually made workable and operational as an international parameter.

Another advantage of general principles is that, being loose and flexible, they are more likely to be interpreted and applied in such a way as to allow for future developments and demands. By contrast, detailed rules may crystallize and even ossify the circumstances for which they were enacted. In consequence they are often not capable of being adjusted to fresh situations.

[22] J. Syatauw, *Some Newly Established States and the Development of International Law* (Leiden, 1960), p. 23.

A third merit is that, even to developing countries, principles leave greater latitude than hard and fast rules. Consequently, the Third World feels that by upholding them it commits itself in a way permitting greater leeway should unforeseen circumstances arise.

71. Another distinguishing feature of Third World strategy is the fact that these countries show a definite preference for normative developments in substantive rules whereas they are less inclined to accept international procedures of supervision or compulsory modes of settlement of disputes. This came out clearly in 1966, when the U N General Assembly adopted the two Covenants on Human Rights (§ 177). Along with socialist States, a number of developing countries opposed the creation of international machinery for scrutinizing the observance of the Covenants; in the face of strong Western insistence, they eventually succeeded in watering down the Western proposals to a considerable extent, rendering the most incisive procedures of implementation optional. A similar attitude was adopted by a number of developing countries in Vienna in 1969, when the Convention on the Law of Treaties was adopted (§§ 103, 105). The reasons behind this attitude are to a great extent akin to those motivating the stand adopted by socialist countries (§ 67). As in the case of socialist countries, this particular attitude of the Third World deserves criticism, for in the long run it proves to be short-sighted. Here again it is appropriate to quote a few remarks made by Abi-Saab on the Vienna Convention of 1969, which can, however, be considered of general value: in distrusting the procedural guarantees for the observance of the new law on treaties, advocated by Western States,

... the Third World gave primacy to transient considerations over fundamental long-term interests. For as long as Third World States participate effectively in the choice or election of arbitrators and judges, and as long as the rules to be applied are substantively in conformity with their interests, the procedural guarantee can only be an added protection for these interests. The progressive rules which are the result of hard-won battles risk being ignored in bilateral relations, unless there is a compulsory procedure ensuring their application, and which can be put into motion by the weaker party, a role in which Third World States are more often than not likely to find themselves.[23]

It should however be noted that recently developing countries have shown a tendency to submit legal disputes to the International Court of Justice—a happy development that one hopes will gain increasing momentum.

72. As stated above, a further characteristic of Third World strategy is its tendency to expand national jurisdiction. This tendency has been apparent

[23] G. Abi-Saab, 'The Third World and the Future of the International Legal Order', *Revue égyptienne de droit international* 29 (1973), 55.

in claims over the high seas, which exhibit a marked insistence on the institution of the patrimonial sea or exclusive economic zone (§ 218) under national jurisdiction. One of two possible objectives appears to stand behind the claims in question: either that of appropriating areas belonging to nobody, or, alternatively, to have them declared, 'the common heritage of mankind' (see Chapter 14). The latter applies chiefly to areas where the countries in question would be unable to exploit for want of technology (this consideration also applies to outer space and celestial bodies). Both objectives have been reinforced by the need for these countries to develop their economies and by their hope to reap the benefits from new areas of the sea; the second objective is also motivated by the wish to prevent developed countries from increasing their economic advantage to the detriment of less developed nations.

Closely linked to the objectives just described are the Third World's attempts to restructure international economic relations with a view to acquiring a greater share of wealth. Developing countries have pursued this goal by advocating new international standards on economic relations (§ 213), international institutions more sensitive to development than the traditional economic and financial organizations (§§ 207–8), and the exploitation of important assets such as the ocean bed and its subsoil and outer space, in the interest of, and on behalf of, the whole of mankind.

73. It will not come as a surprise that the Third World is the segment of the world community which presses most assertively and consistently for legal change. More clearly than others, developing countries have chosen between the two goals (respect for international law; upholding of justice) set by the UN Charter for the achievement of better international conditions. They have bluntly opted for justice and are endeavouring to bend all other goals to the realization of this purpose. It therefore comes as no surprise that they consistently seek to change international law by making it less unjust. They have already achieved much; they have brought about fairly satisfactory changes in the rules governing such important areas as treaty-making, the law of the sea, the humanitarian law governing armed conflict, the law of State succession—often with the decisive support of socialist countries. Nevertheless, they still have a long way to go as regards the introduction of more equitable conditions in international economic relations and the acquisition of greater political power. For instance, they are not satisfied with the fact that China is the only developing country endowed with veto power within the Security Council; in their opinion this power should be extended to other countries of the group. To strike a balance with Western States, three of them, in their view, should be vested with the right to cast a veto. Their attempts at changing the provisions on the veto power have, however, met with very strong resistance on the part of the two super-powers. In particular, the Soviet Union has made it clear that efforts at revising Article 27 of the Charter stand no chance, the more so because, in its view, the present system already protects developing countries. As it was put by the Soviet delegate in the General Assembly in 1980:

Any attempt to amend the rule of unanimity [of the permanent members of the Security Council] could undermine the very foundations of the United Nations. The principle did not represent a privilege but a historical necessity, and it reflected the need for consensus in the Council's decision-making on matters relating to the maintenance of peace and security. The unanimity rule had been and continued to be a reliable mechanism for preventing particular groups of States from using the Security Council and the Organization as a whole for purposes which contravened the Charter. Experience had shown that the rule was of particular importance for new developing countries, for small States.[24]

74. It should be added that, although Third World countries tend to adopt a legal strategy which is in many respects similar to that pursued by socialist States, there are nevertheless a number of notable differences. While at present Eastern European countries prefer to proceed gingerly, believing as they do that legal change should be brought about gradually, and as much as possible through mutual agreement, developing countries press instead for quick, far-reaching and radical modifications. What is even more important, they ardently demand a basic restructuring of the world community, in particular a shake-up of its economic foundations. If we take up the distinction between the Hobbesian, the Grotian, and the Kantian 'traditions' referred to above (§ 13), we might say that socialist countries tend to stick to the Grotian vision of an international community consisting of sovereign States inspired in their dealings by the demands of both co-existence and co-operation; by contrast, developing countries show a tendency to give pride of place to the Kantian conception of a universal community where co-operation and moral imperatives of solidarity should play an overriding role and peoples should matter at least as much as sovereign States.

CONCLUDING REMARKS

75. It would, of course, be quite wrong to conclude that the differences in attitude towards international law between the three groups of States prevent them from engaging in peaceful relations, or stand in the way of smooth and unimpeded transactions. As a matter of fact, despite divergences in outlook, ideology, and political or legal philosophy, States get

[24] UN document A/C.6/35/SR.68, at 10 (para. 37)

together in international forums, no matter what group they belong to, and agree upon a modicum of 'rules of the game'. A striking feature of the current international community is that along with groups of States whose conceptions and ideologies are wide apart, there are important international forums (chiefly the U N and all the specialized agencies) where those States can iron out divergences and gradually reach agreement on at least a number of basic principles or rules. It is likely that international organizations will continue to serve the inestimable purpose of gradually smoothing out the discrepancies between rival groups of States. Hitherto they have already enabled States to come closer together in a number of fields. Apart from international law-making (where the drafting of the Vienna Convention on the Law of Treaties of 1969 stands out as a remarkable achievement), this 'rapprochement' has occurred in many areas, including that of human rights, and the humanitarian law of armed conflict. As for the former, suffice it to stress that the doctrine of human rights, primarily propounded by the U S in 1945, with the strong support of a few Latin-American countries, was soon accepted by other States, thereby becoming one of the pillars of the U N. It was subsequently gradually transformed into a broader doctrine, upheld by all international subjects. Admittedly, each of the three main segments of the world community tends to place greater emphasis on some classes of human rights than on others (such as civil or political rights rather than economic, social or cultural rights, or vice versa). Yet there is now broad agreement on at least the bulk of principles laid down in the more important international instruments (see §§ 78 and 92). The same holds true for the humanitarian law of armed conflict. Thus, for example, as the American anthropologist R. Benedict[25] pointed out in 1946, during the Second World War the Japanese attitude towards such things as treatment of prisoners of war, treatment of the wounded, and the rescuing of the shipwrecked or servicemen in distress differed radically from that of the Americans. The Americans were at a loss to understand Japanese behaviour, and tended to jump to the conclusion that Japan simply disregarded international standards on P O Ws, medical care of the wounded, and so on. In fact, as Benedict has demonstrated, the Japanese attitude stemmed from their patterns of culture, which led them to consider surrender to the enemy as a disgrace. Consequently Japanese servicemen preferred to kill themselves rather than be captured, and tended to grant American P O Ws a treatment which the U S regarded as below international standards. Similarly, 'Japanese scorn of materialism' contributed to their downplaying medical care and the rescue of servicemen in distress: Japanese soldiers 'were taught that death itself was a victory of the spirit and [that] our [American] kind of care of the sick was an interference with heroism—

[25] R. Benedict, *The Chrysanthemum and the Sword* (1946; repr. New York, 1974), pp. 20–42.

like safety devices in bombing planes'. Yet all these culturally motivated differences did not prevent both Japan and the West from accepting the Geneva Conventions on War Victims of 1949, or from contributing to the Geneva Conference on the Reaffirmation of the Humanitarian Law of Armed Conflict (1974-7) and subscribing to the international instruments hammered out by the Conference (see §§ 150-1). This, therefore, is a significant illustration of how culturally and ideologically different States can come to accept the same international standards—thanks to the efforts of international organizations and the existence of multilateral forums where they are able to get together and reach agreement.

Even at the risk of seeming too sanguine, I conclude that the present cultural, ideological, and philosophical differences do not prevent States from agreeing upon a common body of international standards by which to be guided in their transactions; it seems probable that these differences will even gradually narrow down, provided no major disruption of the world community is caused by the present political and military conflicts.

6

The Fundamental Principles Governing International Relations

INTRODUCTION

76. MOST States have written constitutions which lay down the fundamental principles regulating social intercourse. Principles are the pinnacle of the legal system and are intended to serve as basic guidelines for the life of the whole community; besides imposing general duties and obligations, they also set the policy lines and the basic goals of State agencies. Furthermore, they can be drawn upon for the construction of norms, in case the rules on interpretation prove insufficient.

The position is different in the world community. When it came into existence, no State or other authority set forth any fundamental principles for regulating international dealings, for the simple reason that no member State had enough power to impose standards of behaviour on all other members. A body of law gradually evolved under the impulse of interests and exigencies of single States, but no general principle was agreed upon. However, the increase in the corpus of rules by the gradual accretion of new norms made it clear that States spontaneously and almost unwittingly based their lawmaking on a few fundamental postulates from which they drew inspiration. Close scrutiny of the legal standards emerging in the first stages of development of the international community shows that States were substantially guided by at least three principles: freedom, equality, and effectiveness. As was rightly pointed out in 1943 by Ago—the first writer to shed light on the matter—these standards differ from the general principles of national legal systems, which are legally binding and are usually laid down in constitutions. They merely express 'a sort of guiding line that manifests itself in the legal content of the various norms of the international legal order; they represent principles which inspire the rules and co-ordinate them around a certain goal, but which do not themselves constitute binding norms'.[1] Plainly, they are merely theoretical constructions, reached through an inductive process based on the examination of international rules and the generalization of some of their distinguishing traits. Through such a theoretical process, the conclusion can be reached that most international norms grant a wide sphere of action to States (§§ 8–9); proclaim, or start

[1] R. Ago, *Lezioni di diritto internazionale* (Milan, 1943), p. 65.

from the assumption of, the legal equality of all States (§ 3); and tend to legitimize situations which have acquired *de facto* force (§ 10).

The three principles just mentioned are clearly the synthesis of what could be concisely defined as the 'laissez-faire approach' of classical international law. According to this approach, all States are equally free to do what they like irrespective of their real conditions, provided they abide by certain 'rules of the game'. Moreover, if in the exercise of this almost unfettered freedom, they bring about new situations by force, the law is ready to give these situations its blessing.

77. The adoption of the UN Charter in 1945 heralded a very significant change, for the draftsmen laid down in Articles 1 and 2 a set of fundamental principles by which all the members of the Organization were to abide. Thus, for the first time, an international treaty set forth the fundamental standards governing States' action and establishing the main goals of international institutions. This new state of affairs was the direct consequence of the reshuffle in the world community brought about by the Second World War, in particular of the keen desire of all States to lay the foundations of an international system more conducive to peace and justice. Major contributing factors were the political convergence of the US and the Soviet Union and the awareness of the great Powers of the importance of enacting new standards of behaviour calculated to avert plunging the world into a cataclysmic war.

In spite of the tremendous impact of the Charter principles on the evolution of the international community, it gradually emerged that they suffered from two shortcomings. First, they were not applicable to States outside the UN, for which they were merely a *res inter alios acta* (a thing made between others). Second, the radical and far-reaching revolution which took place in the international community in the aftermath of the Second World War, and especially the assimilation to the community of numerous new members whose political outlook differed substantially from that of older States, led the former to question the majority of international rules.

Socialist and developing countries initiated a process of revision which involved the expansion and updating of the Charter principles, with a view to turning them into new general standards of universal value. Both groups of countries were motivated by two basic factors. On the one hand they were keen to inject their own basic demands into international law so as to make it more consonant with current international realities. On the other hand, they felt that, in order to satisfy the need for predictability and security underlying social relations, they had to discuss, negotiate, and agree upon the basic standards of behaviour with the traditional members of the world community. The marked preference of socialist and developing countries for general principles rather than detailed rules emphasized in the previous chapter, accounts for the opting for principles in this case as well.

The process of formulation of universal principles was initiated in the UN in the late 1950s and reached its climax in 1962, when a Special Committee was set up. Its work lasted several years, and in 1970 a Declaration on Friendly Relations was adopted by consensus (Resolution 2625-XXV). It should not be thought, however, that only those principles laid down in the Declaration make up the body of fundamental principles of international law. Similarly, it should not be held that the mere fact of belonging to the list included in the Declaration upgrades a standard of behaviour to the rank and status of a universal and fundamental principle. In actual fact, a wide range of factors (treaties; General Assembly resolutions; declarations of States; statements by Government representatives in the UN; diplomatic practice, if any) should be taken into account when trying to determine whether certain international pronouncements have engendered a principle of universal scope and legally binding force.

78.   Before considering each principle in some detail, it seems useful to assess their basic significance in the current international setting. (For the sake of clarity, the general features they possess in common will be delineated later on: see §90.)

In the present world community, where States are divided economically, politically, and ideologically to such an extent that their relations are daily beset with friction and tensions, the principles at issue possess tremendous importance, for they represent the only set of standards on which States are not fundamentally divided. They constitute the core of the 'rules of the game' on which all States basically agree and which allow a modicum of relatively smooth international relations. The three major segments of the world community are aware of the existence of differences and of conflicting views on numerous international issues. These disagreements make the principles all the more indispensable, for without them the world community would resemble a tower of Babel where, in addition to confusion and difficulties in communication, there would be a lot of dissent and contention. The principles make up the apex of the whole body of international legislation. They are fundamental, or 'structural' standards (in de Visscher's terminology)[2] in that they reflect the 'political structure of the relations among States' and are 'inherent in their coexistence' as sovereign entities. The erosion or disruption of one or more of them would have very perilous consequences indeed (see, however, §91).

---

[2] Charles de Visscher, *Théories et réalités en droit international public*, 4th edn. (Paris, 1970), p. 412.

SOVEREIGN EQUALITY OF STATES

79. Traditional international law was of course based on a set of rules protecting the sovereignty of States and establishing their formal equality in law. In 1945, while drafting the UN Charter, the 'founding fathers' decided to proclaim 'sovereign equality of all its members' (Article 2.1) as one of the Organization's principles. It is apparent from the preparatory work that this new terminology was agreed upon 'on the assumption and the understanding' that it covered four 'elements', namely, to quote the words of the Syrian *rapporteur* of Committee I/1,

... first, States are juridically equal; second, ... each State enjoys the right inherent in full sovereignty; and third, ... the personality of the State is respected as well as its territorial integrity and political independence.... And the fourth element [is] that the States should, under international order, comply faithfully with their international duties and obligations.[3]

These four elements were considered by the draftsmen 'as a basis for international relations between member States and between the Organization and these States'. This formula was not adopted without opposition. The Belgian delegate in Committee I/1 pointed out:

... the smaller States would regard it as somewhat ironical, in view of the striking inequalities evident in the Organization, to find at the head of the statement of principles a bold reference to the 'sovereign equality' of all members.[4]

He therefore proposed to delete the word 'sovereign'. His motion was rejected, as was the proposal by Uruguay to replace 'sovereign' by 'juridical'.

However, the Belgian delegate was right: the UN is not based on the full equality of all its members, for Article 27.3 grants the so-called right of veto to the permanent members of the Security Council only. Consequently, the principle of equality laid down in Article 2.1 is to be interpreted merely as a general guideline which is weakened by the exceptions specifically laid down in law.

Neither the labours of the Special Committee on Friendly Relations (1962-70) nor the debates in the General Assembly reveal any radical differences on this principle, so much so that it was reaffirmed in the Declaration along the lines of Article 2.1 of the Charter. However, in the Declaration, it was extended to *all* States, irrespective of their membership in the UN.

Of the various fundamental principles regulating international relations, this is unquestionably the only one on which there is unqualified agreement and the support of all groups of States, irrespective of ideologies, political leanings, and circumstances. All States agree upon both the crucial impor-

[3] See UNCIO, VI, 69 (see also ibid., 70, 457, 717-18).
[4] Ibid., 332.

tance of the principle and its basic contents. The conclusion is therefore warranted that sovereign equality constitutes the linchpin of the whole body of international legal standards, the fundamental premise on which all international relations rest.

This being so, what is its present purport? On close consideration, it turns out to be, first of all, a principle typical of the Westphalian model, that is of the old pattern of international legal order; indeed, it legally sanctions the existing power relationships in the world community and formally acknowledges and endorses the claim that all States, regardless of their actual 'stature', ought to be treated as equal. Secondly, it is an umbrella concept, covering various general rules, of which it provides a synthesis and restatement. Consequently, it can only be fully appreciated if these general rules are spelled out. As the principle embraces two logically distinct notions (sovereignty and legal equality), it makes sense to consider them separately.

Sovereignty, in addition to granting each State a set of powers relating to the territory under its jurisdiction, includes the following sweeping rights: first, that of claiming respect for the State's territorial integrity and political independence by other States; second, that of claiming sovereign immunity for State representatives acting in their official capacity—acts performed by State officials must be imputed not to the individuals acting on behalf of the State, but to the State itself; consequently individuals cannot be brought to trial and punished by foreign States for any such official act if the latter proves contrary to international law (the exceptions being international crimes: see §§ 1, 148, 159, 169); third, that of claiming immunity from the jurisdiction of foreign courts for acts or actions performed by States in their sovereign capacity (the question, however, of the *extent* to which the immunity must be granted is at present controversial).

Legal equality implies that no member of the international community can be placed at a disadvantage: all must be treated on the same footing. As de Vattel stated as early as 1758, 'a dwarf is as much a man as a giant; a small republic is no less a sovereign State than the most powerful kingdom'.[5] Consequently, possible legal hindrances or disabilities may only be the result of factual circumstances (e.g. land-locked States; States without any natural and mineral resources, and therefore heavily dependent on foreign aid) or, alternatively, the legal constraints in question must be accepted, in full freedom, by the State concerned (e.g. the status of a neutralized State, which entails a series of limitations on freedom of action in international relations; the legal condition of member States of the UN other than the permanent members of the Security Council; mention can also be made of the Treaty on Non-Proliferation of Nuclear Weapons, of 1968. As was rightly pointed out by B. V. A. Röling, 'The Non-Proliferation

[5] E. de Vattel, *Le Droit des gens, ou principes de la loi naturelle*, i (Paris, 1830), p. 47. ('Préliminaires', para. 18.)

Treaty, by which the non-nuclear-weapon States, party to the Treaty, relinquished their sovereign right "to go nuclear", was concluded ... [for the maintenance of peace]. The Treaty made the nuclear "have-nots" into nuclear "have-nevers". It was resented because of that negative discrimination, but adopted in the interest of peace. A world with many nuclear-weapon-States was considered too dangerous for mankind.'[6]).

It follows that the principle of sovereign equality does not produce all the effects of peremptory principles, or *jus cogens* (see thereon §96). For instance, it can be derogated from by treaty, and this is demonstrated by the numerous conventions providing for restrictions on State sovereignty, or on States' equality. Derogations are, however, permissible to the extent that they are freely accepted by the State on which the limitations are placed. By contrast, two or more States are not allowed to enter into an agreement providing for impairment or restriction of the territorial integrity or political independence or legal equality of a third State. Such an agreement, even before it is implemented, is null and void.

SELF-DETERMINATION OF PEOPLES

80. Like the principle of sovereign equality, the principle of self-determination relates to international subjects. In particular, it touches upon both the inner structure and legal legitimation of subjects on the international plane. However, unlike sovereign equality the principle of self-determination strikingly reflects the new trends emerging in the world community (in other words, it expresses the 'Charter model') and, in addition, it has a markedly ideological matrix (this is why its transformation into a legal standard of behaviour has been a gradual process and has elicited strong opposition from Western countries).

It was first proclaimed at an international level by the USSR in 1917. It was intended to apply both to nationalities in Europe (chiefly those under the Austro–Hungarian monarchy) and to colonial peoples. Its first forceful enunciation dates back to Lenin's *Theses on the Socialist Revolution and the Right of Nations to Self-Determination* (January–February 1916) which advocated self-determination not only for 'Austria, the Balkans, and particularly Russia', but also for colonial peoples ('Socialists must ... demand the unconditional and immediate liberation of the colonies without compensation'). This proclamation was reiterated in a number of documents, among which was Lenin's *Fourth Letter from Afar* (25 March 1917), which listed 'the liberation of all colonies; the liberation of all dependent, oppressed, and non-sovereign peoples' among the conditions for peace.[7]

[6] B. V. A. Röling, 'The History and the Sociological Approach of the NIEO and the Third World', *Thesaurus Acroasium*, 12 (1982), 192.

[7] Lenin's essays are in *Collected Works*, xix (1916–17; repr., New York, 1930), 192.

About the same time, self-determination was also proclaimed as a valid principle by the American President Woodrow Wilson. However, the significant differences between the views of the two statesmen should not be underestimated. Although they both meant to apply self-determination to Europe and to colonies, the American conception of how it should be extended to colonial countries was greatly qualified by the need to take account of the interests of colonial powers: the fifth of the famous fourteen points proclaimed by Wilson in his address delivered before a Joint Session of Congress, on 8 January 1918, requested:

A free, open-minded, and absolutely impartial adjustment of all colonial claims, based upon a strict observance of the principle that in determining all such questions of sovereignty the interests of the populations concerned must have equal weight with the equitable claims of the government whose title is to be determined.[8]

The wide gap between the two conceptions was also apparent in the criticisms of the Soviet views voiced by the American Secretary of State R. Lansing. He wrote that Lenin's programme menaced 'the stability of the future world by applying the self-determination principle to the colonial world', and went on to note that:

... however justified may be the principle of local self-government, the necessities of preserving an orderly world require that there should be a national authority with sovereign rights to defend and control the communities within the national boundaries.[9]

In the period between the two World Wars the principle was to a large extent implemented in Europe, whereas the staunch opposition of colonial powers prevented its application to colonies (the Mandate system established by the Covenant of the League of Nations was an able attempt to keep control of the three categories of dependent peoples provided for in Article 22 of the Covenant, while accepting the idea of the 'sacred trust of civilisation'). When the Second World War was drawing to a close and the problem of reshaping international relations cropped up, the US and the UK agreed upon the Atlantic Charter (1941), where the principle was upheld in a mild form (Articles II and III). Churchill, however, hastened to state in the House of Commons that the notion of self-determination proclaimed in the Charter did not apply to colonies but only aimed at restoring sovereignty and self-government to the European States and nations which had been under the Nazi yoke.[10]

[8] W. Wilson, *Public Papers: Wars and Peace*, i (Washington, DC, 1927), pp. 155–62.
[9] R. Lansing, *Papers Relating to the Foreign Relations of the US*, ii (Washington, DC, 1939–40), pp. 247–8.
[10] The text of Churchill's declaration to the House of Commons is reported by E. R. Stettinius, Jr, *Roosevelt and the Russians: The Yalta Conference* (New York, 1949), pp. 244–5.

. Thus, when the UN Charter was drafted, the USSR had to take account of Western opposition. It proposed a draft to the US, UK, and China—three States with which it was discussing the proposals to be submitted to the San Francisco Conference.[11] Later on the Belgian delegate tried to have the norm deleted, but strong opposition from States such as Egypt, the Ukraine, Iran, Syria, and Colombia thwarted the move.[12] The result of the discussion was the acceptance of the principle in Article 1.2, providing that one of the purposes of the Organization was 'to develop friendly relations among nations based on respect for the principle of equal rights and self-determination of peoples'. Through this provision the principle had made great strides, for it was now embodied in an internationally binding treaty. However, it had a number of weaknesses: (1) it did not lay down a legally binding obligation to be fulfilled immediately but merely set forth a goal for the Organization and propounded a policy that member States pledged to pursue by taking joint and separate action in co-operation with the UN (Article 56); (2) generally, self-determination was taken to mean 'self-government' only,[13] and not independence; independence was set as one of the possible goals for trust territories solely (Article 76b), while mere self-government was envisaged for non-self-governing territories (Article 73b); (3) in actual practice, colonial empires were allowed to survive, albeit in the guise of the trusteeship system, or subject to the general commitments set out in Article 73; (4) self-determination was conceived of as a means for ensuring peace and friendly relations—it was not considered an independent value—with the obvious consequence that it was to be set aside whenever its fulfilment gave rise to tension and conflict between States; (5) the principle was upheld only in so far as it did not bring about or authorize secession:[14] as early as 1945 the territorial integrity of States was held to be paramount, a fact which confirms that—in actual fact—self-government only was envisaged, not independence.

In subsequent years, especially after the late 1950s, the action of socialist States, vigorously supported by an increasing number of Third World countries, succeeded in gradually transforming the woolly and moderate provisions of the UN Charter into a universal principle having a direct impact on international reality. While colonial empires were gradually being dismantled, the principle was given a normative value which upgraded it to the highest standards of the international community. It was first sanctioned in a stream of General Assembly resolutions, notably that on colonial

[11] The Soviet draft is in UNCIO, iii. 622.

[12] The criticisms to the Belgian proposal voiced by the various delegates are quoted in A. Cassese, 'Political Self-Determination: Old Concepts and New Developments', in A. Cassese (ed.), *UN Law: Fundamental Rights* (Alphen aan den Rijn, 1979), pp. 161–2 (where I quote the unpublished microfilms of the debates).

[13] See UNCIO, vi. 296.

[14] Ibid., 296.

peoples (1514-XV) of 14 December 1960 and that on permanent sovereignty over natural resources (1803-XVII) of 14 December 1962. Then, in 1966, it was upheld in Article 1 of the UN Covenants on Human Rights, in 1970 in the Declaration on Friendly Relations, and in the First Protocol Additional to the four 1949 Geneva Conventions on War Victims, in 1977 (Article 1.4). These resolutions and treaties, together with the statements made by Government representatives on the occasion of their adoption, testify to the crystallization of a general principle endowed with binding force.

Socialist and Third World countries managed not only to bring about this remarkable achievement in spite of the opposition of Western countries, but also to determine the general terms propounded by the principles. Self-determination became applicable to three categories of people only: those under colonial, alien, or racist domination. By contrast, it was ruled that the principle could not apply to the population of a sovereign State with a Government which, however oppressive and authoritarian, did not practise systematic racial or religious discrimination. This exclusion, proposed by socialist countries and accepted by all other groups of States in the course of the discussion on the Declaration on Friendly Relations of 1970, greatly limited the scope of the principle, and confined its application to three types of situations stated—all of which are becoming rarer and rarer. This restriction was plainly due to the fear of States that by authorizing an unqualified right of self-determination they might allow secession and dismemberment in sovereign States.

As a result, the principle had only a limited pertinence to 'internal' self-determination (that is, the right of a people in a sovereign country to elect and keep the government of its choice). With regard to the population of sovereign States, self-determination was restricted to peoples of sovereign States under a racist regime (for example, South Africa). Consequently, 'internal' self-determination amounts to the right of an ethnic, racial or religious segment of the population in a sovereign country not to be oppressed by a discriminatory government. By the same token 'external' self-determination (that is, the right of a people or a group to choose freely in the field of international relations) was granted to colonial peoples and peoples under foreign domination only. They were offered the following choice: 'the establishment of a sovereign and independent State, the free association or integration with an independent State or the emergence into any other political status freely determined' by the people (1970 Declaration, Principle V, para 6).

81. At this point it may be useful to contrast the various political concepts of self-determination propounded after 1917 with those eventually upheld on the legal plane.

Briefly, self-determination, in the guise of a political postulate and *idée force*, has been advanced in three different 'versions'. In an essentially anti-colonialist form it was propounded above all by Lenin. His obvious aim was to disrupt colonial empires and redistribute power in the international community on the basis of the idea of equality among nations, thereby assisting in the emergence of new international subjects consisting of those very peoples which had previously borne the colonialist yoke. In a more moderate version the principle was put forward as a criterion for 'reshaping' existing States, with due emphasis on national and ethnic groups, by proposing such instruments as plebiscites and referendums. Seen from this point of view the principle carried a less destructive charge with regard to the international community. It essentially addressed itself to sovereign States, and invited them to rearrange their territorial order so as to make allowance for the aspirations of various groups and communities. Lastly, especially in recent years, the principle has been interpreted—largely in the West—as impinging upon the internal self-determination of peoples belonging to sovereign States. In other words, as a criterion for the democratic legitimation of the governments of sovereign States.

The only thing linking these three different versions is that all three 'intrude' upon the domestic affairs of sovereign States and concern themselves, more or less intrusively, with communities which are subject to those States.

In the previous paragraph I showed how, faced with these various politico-ideological formulations, present-day international law has sanctioned self-determination as: (1) an anti-colonial postulate; (2) a criterion for condemning those forms of oppression of a people involving the 'occupation' of territory; (3) an anti-racist postulate. The principle has therefore promoted the emergence of new international subjects, thereby radically modifying the social foundations of the world community. Self-determination, however, has not been accepted as a principle protecting national or ethnic groups or as a postulate for defying autocratic regimes: State sovereignty, infringed in the case of colonialist and similar regimes, has shielded States from the demands of ethnic minorities and the demand for democratic legitimation which could have had a radically unsettling effect on a significant number of States in all three of the present groupings (though mainly on the Soviet bloc and on the Third World).

I should add that this principle, despite the limits I have just outlined, should not be accused (as R.-J. Dupuy has done[15]) of being predominantly anti-colonial and anti-racist. If this were so, self-determination would inevitably lose its force (since colonial regimes have slowly disappeared and racist ones are, one hopes, dying out). In fact, as I attempted to pinpoint

[15] R.-J. Dupuy, in *AFDI* 28 (1982), 337 ff. Cf. also M. Virally, in 183 Hague *Recueil* (1983-V), 68.

above, this principle possesses at least one other virtue endowing it with a value and a potential which have nothing to do with historical colonialism (and its racist derivations): the condemnation of that form of oppression of another people involving occupation of its territory. This 'dimension' of the principle is destined to have effect even after the numerous contemporary historical situations have vanished. It will continue to lend a 'liberating' (or, if one prefers, 'libertarian') charge to the idea of self-determination.[15a]

82. What are the rights and duties deriving from the principle? In a nutshell, it can be said that first, States which oppress peoples falling within one of the three categories are duty-bound to allow the free exercise of self-determination; in particular they are enjoined not to deny them this right forcibly; second, the peoples entitled to self-determination have a legal right in relation to the oppressor-State, as well as a host of rights and claims in regard of other States (§ 55); lastly, third States are duty-bound to support peoples entitled to self-determination, by granting them any assistance short of dispatching armed troops; conversely, they must refrain from aiding and abetting oppressor States; and furthermore, they are entitled to claim respect for the principle from the States denying self-determination. If self-determination is forcibly denied they can bring the question before the competent UN bodies and can even resort to peaceful sanctions, provided there has been a previous finding by the Organization to the effect that the right at issue is illegally infringed. Plainly, in this case, the universal principle is closely bound up with the 'enforcement' system of the UN, which serves the important purpose of guaranteeing the implementation of the principle and preventing any abuse or 'perversion' by individual States.

To conclude, it should be recalled that States have clearly expressed the view that the principle is part and parcel of *jus cogens* (see § 96). Consequently, any treaty calculated to place restrictions on its exercise or to deny

---

[15a] It should be added that various Western countries have insisted time and again that the principle under consideration applies to *all* peoples. Suffice it to mention the declaration made in 1983 by the FRG on the occasion of the ratification of the UN Convention on the Elimination of All Forms of Discrimination Against Women, of 18 December 1979. The German Government declared that in its view the principle of self-determination *does not apply only to peoples under alien or colonial domination or under foreign occupation*: any different interpretation was unacceptable to the FRG (see text of the declaration in 45 *ZaöRuV* (1985), p. 743). In view of the importance of this declaration, it is worth quoting the relevant passage: 'Das Recht der Völker auf Selbstbestimmung, wie es in der Satzung der Vereinten Nationen und in den Internationalen Pakten vom 19. Dezember 1966 niedergelegt ist, gilt für alle Völker und nicht nur für diejenigen, die "unter Fremd- und Kolonialherrschaft sowie ausländischer Besetzung" leben. Deshalb haben alle Völker das unveräusserliche Recht, frei über ihren politischen Status zu entscheiden und frei ihre wirtschaftliche, soziale und kulturelle Entwicklung zu gestalten. Die Bundesrepublik Deutschland könnte eine Interpretation des Selbstbestimmungsrechts, die dem eindeutigen Wortlaut der Satzung der Vereinten Nationen und der beiden internationalen Menschenrechtspakte [...] widerspricht, nicht als rechtsgültig anerkennen'.

it should be deemed null and void. Thus, it has recently been claimed by two French jurists (Chemillier-Gendreau and Colin)[16] that the Camp David Agreements of 17 September 1978 are null and void inasmuch as they adopt a restrictive and inaccurate conception of the right to self-determination of the Palestinian people.

PROHIBITION OF THE THREAT OR USE OF FORCE

83. The prohibition of the threat or use of force was first laid down in the UN Charter (Article 2.4). That this principle was proclaimed and strongly emphasized in 1945 is hardly surprising. As I pointed out above (§ 35), after 1945 peace became the supreme goal of the world community and States decided to agree upon serious and sweeping self-limitations of their sovereign prerogatives in the form of the mutual obligation to refrain from using or threatening force. The need to avert armed conflict likely to endanger the very survival of mankind prompted the international community to take a step which would have been unthinkable a few years before.

Let us briefly consider Article 2.4. Both the textual and logical interpretation of this article and its drafting history make the following provisions clear beyond any doubt. First, the ban on force is an 'absolute all-inclusive prohibition', as was stated by the US delegate at San Francisco.[17] Force was banned in all circumstances except for those provided for in: Chapter VII (collective enforcement measures); in Article 51 (self-defence); in Article 53 (enforcement action by regional agencies); and in other provisions in Articles 106 and 107 which have by now become obsolete. Second, only military force was proscribed; a Brazilian amendment calculated to prohibit also 'the threat or use of economic measures in any manner inconsistent with the purposes of the UN' was rejected, for reasons which unfortunately were not reported.[18] Third, only the use or threat of force in interstate relations was banned; consequently, member States were by implication allowed to resort to forcible measures to suppress insurgents on their own territory, or to fight against liberation movements struggling for independence in territories subject to colonial domination—territories considered by colonial powers as an integral part of their own territory inasmuch as they were under their exclusive authority.

After 1945 the ban in Article 2.4 was gradually transformed into a general rule of international law, binding on non-member States as well. Among

---

[16] M. Chemillier-Gendreau et J.-P. Colin, *Les Accords-cadre 'pour la paix au Moyen-Orient' conclus à Camp David le 17 septembre au regard du droit international*, paper submitted to the 'Association internationale des juristes démocrates' (Brussels, n.d.), pp. 9-10.

[17] See UNCIO, vi. 355.

[18] The Brazilian amendment is ibid., 559 (see also pp. 334 and 720-1).

other things, the statements made by the FRG[19] in April 1968—when it had not yet gained UN membership—and also those by the US in a memorandum on the war in Vietnam on 4 March 1966,[20] are indicative of this transformation which was finally confirmed by the Declaration on Friendly Relations. A number of developments subsequently attracted the attention of socialist and Afro-Asian countries. First, the spread of wars of national liberation in colonial territories as well as in territories under foreign occupation (for instance, the Arab territories occupied by Israel following the war of 1967), or under racist regimes (for example, in Namibia and South Africa as well as in Rhodesia during the period 1965-80). Under existing law the Powers against which liberation wars were being waged were authorized to use force to quell liberation movements, and this seemed to socialist and developing countries a negative feature of the Charter. Second, economic coercion was increasingly used by powerful States to subjugate developing countries which easily fell prey to economic pressure; the lack of any rule prohibiting such behaviour was profoundly resented by the Third World, which managed to command the support of socialist States for the purpose of changing the existing legal regulation. Third, in some instances strong States resorted to war and managed to conquer foreign territory without there being any effective sanction on the part of the international community capable of bringing about the evacuation of the occupied territory (for example, the Arab territories occupied by Israel in 1967 and later on in 1973). Thus, the need arose at least to specify that conquest could not legalize the annexation of territory.

Western countries strongly opposed the views propounded in the UN by socialist and by most developing countries since the early 1960s. The whole Western strategy hinged on two points:

(1) They rejected those views, by clinging to the Charter which banned military force in relations between States only, thereby objectively favouring the interests of bigger Powers. The West opposed any changes to the Charter lest the whole system it had set up and the careful balance it had introduced should collapse. Western countries also emphasized that the concept of 'economic force' was too loose and general and that its acceptance in international law might therefore result in dangerous consequences. In addition, they expressed the fear that the prohibition of the use of economic force might authorize States which had fallen victim to such force to resort to self-defence, thereby bringing about a dangerous broadening of the concept of self-defence. Western States also took exception to the granting of the right to use force to liberation movements. In particular, they contended that (i) the Charter did not deal with relations between States

---

[19] See *Europa-Archiv* 23 (1968), D-375.
[20] See M. Whitemann, *Digest of US Practice*, 12 (Washington, DC, 1968), p. 122.

and non-State entities; (ii) it was extremely difficult to define the objective criteria for determining when a political group claiming to be a liberation movement was actually eligible for such status; (iii) as wars of national liberation were but internal armed conflicts—conflicts taking place within the territory of a sovereign State—to claim that unlike other civil wars, rebels were in such cases entitled to *jus ad bellum* that is, the right to wage war, would introduce the concept of *bellum justum*, or just war, into international relations, a concept rightly abandoned since the end of the Middle Ages; (iv) one of the legal consequences of socialist and Third-World doctrines was the fact that liberation movements would enjoy the right of self-defence against the 'dominant' Power, with the corollary that any State would be empowered to invoke the right of collective self-defence to come to their help, thereby seriously jeopardizing international peace.

(2) On the other hand, Western countries realized that their interests would best be served by a broadening of the clauses authorizing the use of force by individual States: in actual fact, they were increasingly confronted with situations where armed force offered the best protection to their interests. Consequently, they endeavoured to expand the scope and purport of those Charter clauses. This they did in two ways. First, they interpreted Article 2.4 to the effect that it authorized resort to force whenever the latter was not directed against the territorial integrity or the political independence of another State and was in conformity with one of the purposes of the Charter. On this score a few Western countries, or at least some distinguished jurists of the Western area, argued in favour of using force to vindicate international legal rights, to protect nationals abroad, to enforce judgments of the International Court of Justice, or even to carry out armed reprisals against wrongdoings of other States. Second, many Western States tried to broaden the scope of Article 51, by contending that self-defence also embraces any pre-emptive strike against an imminent armed attack, and military reaction against indirect armed aggression—aggression effected through various forms of assistance (for example, concession of military bases, military help such as the provision of arms and ammunitions, dispatching of so-called 'volunteers' etc., to groups of individuals fighting against the State which has fallen victim to the aggression).

The clash between the demands of the West, sometimes backed up by a few of the Latin-American States, and those of socialist and developing countries, resulted in lengthy and tiresome discussions within the UN. The ensuing compromise was set forth in the Declaration on Friendly Relations of 1970 and in the Declaration on the Definition of Aggression of 1974. None of the competing groups gained the upper hand. Rather, an agreement was reached which, to some extent, reconciled the opposing interests or gave pride of place to the demands of one or more groups of States in a specific area while giving priority to the exigencies of the other group or groups in another area. The resulting situation can be summed up as follows:

(a) the threat or use of armed force must not be resorted to against (i) *States* or (ii) *peoples* having a representative organization (that is, a national liberation movement) and falling within one of the categories entitled to self-determination (colonial peoples, peoples under foreign occupation or under racist regimes);

(b) *economic force* is also proscribed, but it does not follow that in case of resort to economic coercion the aggrieved State is authorized to make use of military force in self-defence, or to react by way of countermeasures consisting of economic coercion. In other words, a violation of the ban only legitimizes resort to peaceful sanctions (§ 143).

How to define 'economic force'? Arguably, what is prohibited is resort to economic coercion as a means of compelling a State to adopt a course of action contrary to its will and advantageous to the coercive State. Not every form of economic pressure, be it direct or effected through international economic institutions, can be regarded as forbidden. Thus, for instance, the decision simply to withhold economic assistance to developing countries or the financing of international institutions promoting development, does not amount to an infringement of the principle, if it is warranted by serious difficulties on the part of the granting State or by a change in its policy exclusively motivated by domestic considerations. Only those economic measures designed 'to coerce another State in order to obtain from it the subordination of the exercise of its sovereign rights and to secure from it advantages of any kind' (para. 2 of principle III of the U N Declaration of 1970) run counter to the principle.

It is not easy to ascertain whether the conditions outlined above are fulfilled in specific cases: often the nexus between economic measures and the intended subjugation of the will of another State is impalpable. Frequently States are not explicit about making economic action conditional on the behaviour of the recipient. The conditioning is not stated in so many words, but can only be inferred from a host of clues. In these instances it is indeed arduous to demonstrate that undue economic coercion has been effected. However, the difficulty of verifying compliance with the principle does not detract from its importance.

(c) territory belonging to a particular State cannot be 'the object of *acquisition* by another State resulting from the threat or the use of force' (1970 Declaration, principle I, para. 10). This means that conquest does not transfer a legal title of sovereignty, even if it is followed by *de facto* occupation and authority over the territory. Furthermore, all other States are enjoined to withhold recognition of the territorial expansion resulting from the threat or use of force;

(d) subject to some exceptional circumstances force must not be used for the purpose of forestalling an imminent attack by another State (that is, an attack which is presumed to be imminent). This is the concept of *anticipatory self-defence* (see § 137).

(e) force must not be used to repel an indirect armed aggression (see however § 138).

The principle in question should, of course, be considered in the light of the general rules which *exceptionally* allow the use of force. As this subject will be dealt with at length in Chapter 9, it may be sufficient to mention now that force can be lawfully resorted to by individual States in self-defence (§ 136), and also that liberation movements may use it under certain strict conditions (see § 55). It should be emphasized that it is precisely the need for the general principle prohibiting force to be supplemented by these exceptional rules which constitutes its 'Achilles heel'. Indeed, it is by dint of a broad interpretation or even by bypassing those rules that various States—particularly the Great Powers or the countries certain of their support—have endeavoured to dodge the principle, thereby also abusing the 'exceptions' laid down in the rules (see Chapter 9).

Finally, it should be stressed that the ban on the use of force has become part of international peremptory law or *jus cogens* (§ 96), as was affirmed by various States at the Vienna Conference on the Law of Treaties and has been repeatedly asserted in subsequent years in the UN. (Furthermore, in a memorandum of 29 December 1979 to Acting Secretary of State W. Christopher, the Legal Adviser of the US Department of State, pointed out that 'while agreement on precisely what are the peremptory norms of international law is not broad, there is universal agreement that the exemplary illustration of a peremptory norm is Article 2.4'.[21]) It follows that any treaty providing for the use of force contrary to the principle is null and void.

It may be interesting to recall that a number of authors have held that the Zurich Agreement on Cyprus, of 16 August 1960, is contrary to the principle, in that Article 4.2 stipulates that in the event of a breach of the provisions of the Treaty, 'in so far a common or concerted action may not prove possible, each of the three guaranteeing Powers [that is, Greece, Turkey, and the UK] reserves the right to take action with the sole aim of reestablishing the state of affairs created by the present Treaty'. Interestingly, in February 1964, when Turkey invoked this provision, threatening to intervene militarily on Cyprus in the conflict between the Turkish-Cypriot and the Greek-Cypriot communities, the Cypriot government claimed in the Security Council that Article 4.2, if construed in the sense advocated by Turkey, could not but be contrary to *jus cogens*.[22] However, on 20 July and 14 August 1974, Turkey drew on the treaty under consideration in the Security Council to justify its invasion of some areas in Cyprus.

[21] See *AJIL* 74 (1980), 418–20, 419.
[22] Security Council, 19th Year, *Official Records*, Supplement for January–March 1964.

It should be added that the memorandum of 1979 of the Legal Adviser of the US Department of State, referred to above, stressed that if the Treaty of Friendship, Good neighbourliness and Co-operation between the USSR and Afghanistan, of 1978, lent itself 'to support of [sic] Soviet intervention of the type in question in Afghanistan, it would be void under contemporary principles of international law, since it would conflict with what the Vienna Convention on the Law of Treaties describes as a "peremptory norm of general international law" (Article 53), namely, that contained in Article 2.4 of the Charter'.[23]

PEACEFUL SETTLEMENT OF DISPUTES

84.   The principle of peaceful settlement of disputes, too, emerged in the international community after the Second World War. It is based on the same political and historical motivations as those standing behind the ban on force, that is, the need to forestall threats or breaches of the peace as much as possible.

The UN Charter imposed on member States the duty to settle their disputes, both political and legal, by peaceful means, and also stipulated that the settlement should be effected 'in such a manner that international peace and security, and justice, are not endangered' (Article 2.3). The machinery of the Organization was made available for any dispute teetering on the edge of disaster, that is a dispute or situation 'the continuance of which is likely to endanger the maintenance of international peace and security' (Article 33.1). However, since the Security Council was empowered by Article 34 to investigate any dispute or situation in order to determine whether it fell within the category in question, in practice the Organization was entrusted with the task of stepping in whenever a dispute might lead to serious friction. Consequently, this duty is assisted by and made enforceable through the collective system set up in 1945 with respect to practically any serious international dispute.

It is apparent that while the principle imposes on States a host of sweeping duties, it stops short of enjoining them to select *one specific* mode of settlement and to settle the dispute peacefully *in any event*. States retain their freedom in these two all-important areas: if a State is unwilling to accept one specific mode of settlement proposed by the other litigant, or else if, after having agreed on a certain form of settlement, one party believes that the terms suggested are unacceptable, it cannot be obliged to reach agreement. Nor can a party be considered in breach of the principle, if it has acted in good faith, thereby fulfilling the various duties following from the principle, to the best of its ability.

Plainly, this is one of the main pitfalls of the principle. These restrictions may appear very striking indeed to any lawyer not accustomed to inter-

[23] *AJIL*, 74 (1980), 419.

national realities. If, however, one does not lose sight of the ideological and political conflicts currently besetting the world community, the disquieting features of the principle under consideration can be easily accounted for.

Whenever the principle does not suffice to ensure a satisfactory outcome, it is for the UN to play a significant role in the interest of the whole of the international community, including the few non-member States. Specifically, it is up to the relevant UN organs (the Security Council and the General Assembly) to step in and act as collective organs for putting pressure on the parties to bring about a peaceful settlement. Indeed, a third State is unlikely to enmesh itself in a specific dispute between two international subjects unless there are special political, ideological and other links between the three of them. This situation can be compensated for by the UN, as the World Organisation is in a position to bring to the fore and give voice to the interest of the whole international community in the peaceful solution of international conflicts.

So far no official pronouncement has been made on whether the principle in hand has the character of *jus cogens* (§ 96). However, it would seem that its main traits, its contents and implications, leave room for considering null and void any treaty authorizing the contracting parties to resort to coercive means of settlement of disputes before trying out the peaceful ones.

NON-INTERVENTION IN THE INTERNAL OR EXTERNAL AFFAIRS OF OTHER STATES

85.   The principle of non-intervention in the internal or external affairs of other States brings us back to the old pattern of the world community. Indeed, it constitutes one of the most significant tenets of the 'Westphalian model'. Together with the principle of sovereign equality (§ 79) it is designed to ensure that each State respects the sovereignty of the other members of the community.

The principle exhibits two main features. First, in the period of 'classical' international law, it primarily took the form of a general tendency of the international community, and was concretely sanctioned in three specific customary rules. Second, in the 'post-Westphalian' period, that is the period after the First World War, particularly the years following the Second World War, instead of losing its significance and impact, it has continued to 'work through', as it were, the three customary rules and has even acquired new vigour—mainly at the request of developing and socialist countries. Indeed, it has assumed such importance that it has gradually turned into one of the fundamental standards of behaviour of international subjects.

The principal reason behind this development is easily explained: in 'classical' international law non-intervention merely reflected the structure of the world community, based on the postulate of the formal equality of States and the *laissez-faire* doctrine. In that period, the principle of non-intervention was the outgrowth and logical consequence of State sovereignty and State equality; however it also suffered from all those shortcomings resulting from the fact that restraints on State action, as laid down in international law, were precarious. They could be legally set aside whenever paramount interests of a political, economic or military nature materialized. In the 'new' international community two major developments have brought new life and authority to the principle: first, the introduction of far-reaching legal restraints on the use or threat of force (conferring on the principle of non-intervention a less precarious existence); second, the drive towards international co-operation, entailing increasing opportunities for States for meddling with the interests of other States. The principle of non-intervention has thus acquired the fundamental value of a solid and indispensable 'bridge' between the traditional, sovereignty-orientated structure of the international community and the 'new' attitude of States based on coexistence geared to more intense social intercourse, and closer co-operation. The principle currently plays the role of a necessary shield behind which States can shelter in the knowledge that their more intense international relations will not affect their most vital and delicate domestic interests.

Let us now briefly consider the three customary rules referred to above. The first one is the rule prohibiting States from encroaching upon the internal affairs of other States. Thus, for instance, a State is not allowed to bring pressure to bear on the national bodies of other countries (the legislature, enforcement agencies, or the judiciary), nor can it interfere in the relations between foreign government authorities and their own nationals.

Another rule designed to safeguard domestic affairs from foreign intrusion is that enjoining States to refrain from instigating, organizing or officially supporting the organization on their territory of activities prejudicial to foreign countries.

In the diplomatic field, the following measures to enforce compliance with this duty can be mentioned: the expulsion of foreigners who take advantage of the asylum granted to them to conspire against foreign countries; the inposition of restrictions on the traffic of arms and ammunitions; the prohibition against the creation of armed bands and the supply of the means of disturbing the domestic order of foreign countries. It should, however, be pointed out that this rule is not as sweeping as it may appear. For instance, it does not go so far as to prohibit any kind of subversive activity; in particular, it does not prohibit subversive activity against foreign States carried out by private persons without State involvement.

The third customary rule has a more specific purport, in that it only deals with the case of civil strife: it stipulates that whenever a civil war breaks out in a foreign country, States are duty-bound to refrain from assisting the insurgents (§ 46).

These rules are still in force. What is characteristic of the period before 1945 is that they were only to be complied with so long as a State did not consider that its interests overrode them. As soon as the interests of the State were affected, the State was legally authorized to disregard the rules in question and intervene by force, or by the threat of force, in the domestic or external affairs of another State, and impose a certain course of action. As Anzilotti stated authoritatively in 1912:

... if States, in order to satisfy non-legal interests, can resort to war, i.e., attack the integrity and the very existence of international subjects, it is easily understandable that they are also allowed to impel—not by war but by the threat to wage a war—another State to adopt a certain behaviour either within the ambit of its own authority or in its relations with other States. This is what is called intervention.[24]

Consequently, as I pointed out above, the protection afforded by the three rules was utterly precarious.

Things changed considerably as soon as States began to hammer out international treaties designed to ban resort to war. The Covenant of the League of Nations of 1919 and the Treaty of Paris of 1928, prohibited war, subject to certain limitations (§ 32). This prohibition also implied that States were no longer authorized to use force to impose their will on other States, although they were still allowed to *threaten* the use of force as well as to resort to all forcible measures short of war. A radical turning-point was the adoption of the UN Charter, which in Article 2.4 proscribes any threat or use of force, thus creating *inter alia* a right of all member States (subsequently of all States: § 83) to non-intervention in their internal or external relations by the threat or use of force.

While Western States were satisfied with this international regulation, Latin-American States and socialist countries, soon joined by an increasing number of African and Asian nations, since the 1950s have made more and more frequent demands for the prohibition of other forms of intervention as well. In their view illegal interference by powerful States in the freedom of other countries does not only take the form of sending, or threatening to send, military aircraft and warships; these States can and do also impose their will on weak or ideologically incompatible nations through economic pressure or even economic coercion; through political destabilization; by instigating, fomenting, and financing domestic unrest. In addition, powerful States resort to more subtle forms of undue interference, such as radio propaganda, economic boycott, withholding economic assistance, or influencing of international monetary and financial institutions with a view to stifling weak States economically. Furthermore, according to socialist and

---

[24] D. Anzilotti, *Corso di diritto internazionale*, i (Rome, 1912–14), p. 315.

certain developing States, Western countries increasingly interfere in their domestic affairs under the guise of concern for human rights: they disturb the national set-ups of the former regimes applying pressure in various ways on State authorities under the pretext that they are disregarding human rights. (For example, in 1977 the Argentinian foreign minister stated that the decision of the US to reduce military aid as a sanction against alleged human rights violations, implied 'an intrusion into the internal affairs' of Argentina. Uruguay reacted in the same way, stating that the American decision constituted 'an intolerable meddling in [its] domestic affairs'. The Soviet Union's reaction was similar, also in 1977, when the US delegation to the Commission on Human Rights of the UN proposed to send a telegram to the Soviet authorities expressing concern about the reported arrest and detention in the USSR of persons who had been active in the cause of human rights.)[25] Yet another form of illegal intervention is, in the view of this vast group of States, forcible interference in the life of colonial peoples or peoples subject to alien domination or racist regimes, with a view to denying them their cultural identity and their right to self-determination.

One point should be stressed: traditional international law did not afford any protection against these new forms of intervention. As I have already pointed out, one of the three aforementioned customary rules simply banned interference in the domestic affairs of States; international practice was very confused, if only because until the gradual emergence of prohibitions on the use or threat of force, States were at liberty to disregard the duty of non-intervention. In addition, the classes of encroachment on the freedom of States and peoples arousing the strong opposition of developing and socialist countries were in many respects *new* ones. Consequently, even assuming that the customary rule just referred to could be extended so as to cover such new manifestations, the extension by no means went without controversy. Indeed, quite the contrary, the West strongly held that traditional law did not formulate any restriction along the lines demanded by the other two groupings. In fact Western countries flatly rebuffed all the claims put forward by the other States. They repeatedly asserted that present international law only prohibits intervention by force or by the threat of force ('dictatorial intervention'). They also maintained that States are and should continue to be free to influence the policies and actions of other countries. Furthermore, they rejected the idea of extending any ban on intervention so as to benefit peoples. On top of this, the West took exception to the criticism by which socialist countries alleged Western interference in their domestic affairs, by retorting that the Soviet Union itself

---

[25] The statements of the Argentinian and Uruguayan Foreign Ministers are reported in the *International Herald Tribune*, 2 March 1977, p. 2. The Soviet statement is in UN document E/CN.4/SR.1416, paras 65–74.

was not immune from attack for its consistent policy of intrusion into the internal sphere both of other socialist countries and of States belonging to other groupings.

However, there were at least two points on which the West was in agreement with the other States: first, the need to extend the traditional prohibition of 'indirect armed aggression', to cover any 'toleration' by States of subversive activities against other States organized in the territories of the former; second, the necessity to proscribe the 'exportation' of revolutions and counter-revolutions, by proclaiming respect for the right of any people freely to choose its political, economic, social, and cultural system.

The clash between these opposing views manifested itself in the 1960s in the debates of the General Assembly, and in the Special Committee on Friendly Relations. The upshot of the lengthy discussions and negotiations was the adoption on 20 December 1965 of Resolution 2131 (XX), containing the 'Declaration on the inadmissibility of intervention in the domestic affairs of States and the protection of their independence and sovereignty', passed by the General Assembly by a very large majority (109 to 0, with 1 abstention: the UK), and the inclusion in the Declaration on Friendly Relations of 1970 of a principle on this matter. Subsequently, on 9 December 1981 the General Assembly adopted (by 120 votes against 22—Western countries—with six abstentions) Resolution 36/103, containing a general Declaration on this matter, thereby arousing strong opposition in the West, mainly for the restrictions on the promotion of respect for human rights, derived from the principle of non-intervention in domestic affairs.

The text of the two resolutions on which general consensus was reached shows that, all in all, it was the Third World and the Eastern European countries which prevailed in the end: both embody the prohibition of 'indirect' (that is, coercive, non-armed) intervention—as well as the concept that peoples too enjoy the right to be free from any form of forcible intervention. To a certain extent, however, this was a Pyrrhic victory, for the price paid by the two dominant groups of States was the extreme looseness of the wording. The provisions proscribing non-armed intervention are so woolly that it proves difficult to establish what categories of interference are actually prohibited.

The importance of this principle for States leads one to believe that it has by now become part and parcel of *jus cogens* (§ 96). This view is borne out by a pronouncement of the General Assembly. Operative paragraph II *h* of Resolution 36/103, quoted above, provides that one of the consequences of the principle is the duty of States 'to refrain from entering into agreements with other States with a view to intervening or interfering in internal or external affairs of other States'. Arguably, this provision, by declaring those agreements to be contrary to non-interference, aims at rendering them null and void; it therefore implies that the principle belongs to *jus cogens* (no objections or misgivings were voiced when the resolution was passed, nor was its purport challenged—not even by the Western States which voted against it or abstained).

RESPECT FOR HUMAN RIGHTS

86.   Unlike the principle we have just discussed—a typical expression of the Westphalian order, to which the politico-ideological divisions and dissensions in the world today have given a new lease of life—the principle of respect for human rights is typical of a new stage of development in the international community which can largely be traced back to the Second World War. This principle is one of the most significant aspects of the post-war phase: in a sense it is, in fact, competing—if not at loggerheads—with the traditional principles of respect for the sovereign equality of States and of non-interference in the domestic affairs of other States. As we shall see (§91), it is for this very reason that the principle of respect for human rights is so difficult to co-ordinate with the other two.

The adoption of the UN Charter and the subsequent enactment of such fundamental international instruments as the Universal Declaration of 1948 and the two Covenants on Human Rights of 1966 had such an impact on the international community that no State currently challenges the concept that human rights must be cherished and respected everywhere in the world. As a result of, on the one hand, those general texts and a host of specific conventions and international resolutions, and, on the other hand, the consistent practice of international bodies—especially the multifarious activities carried out by various UN organs—a general principle has gradually emerged prohibiting gross and large-scale violation of basic human rights and fundamental freedoms. It was primarily the West which provided the impetus to its establishment and sustained support for international action in the field of human rights. As we shall see in Chapter 11, the gist of the 'philosophy' of human rights emanates chiefly from Western countries and represents their major ideological contribution to the shaping of modern international law. Socialist States and most developing countries—which have traditionally shown less enthusiasm than the West for upholding human rights (although see §§170 and 180), and were probably instrumental in excluding human rights from the 'Principles on Friendly Relations' in 1962—have gradually come to accept the idea that massive infringements of basic human rights are reprehensible and make the delinquent State accountable to the whole international community. Single instances of violations, on the other hand, are not necessarily of international concern. At the outset, that is to say in the early 1960s, Eastern European and Afro-Asian countries emphasized that massive violations chiefly took the form of apartheid, colonialism, racial discrimination, genocide, and similar acts.

However, they gradually agreed to expand the category of violations to include large-scale disregard of any class of human rights, including civil and political freedoms or trade union rights.

The principle at issue does not impose on States the duty to abide by specific regulations on human rights or to respect individual instances of human rights. Rather it requires States to refrain from gross violations: they must abstain from seriously and repeatedly infringing on a basic right (for example, the right not to be subjected to torture; or the right to a fair trial; or freedom from arbitrary arrest), and from trampling upon a whole series of rights (for instance, the fundamental civil and political rights, or social, economic and cultural rights). In other words, the misbehaviour proscribed by the principle does not consist of an isolated or sporadic occurrence, but must take the form of repeated and systematic transgressions.

Two points should be stressed. First, as in the case of other general principles, respect for human rights derives its most solid guarantee from the UN system. Legally, any State whatsoever is entitled to insist that the offending party discontinue its violations (and make reparations, as the case may require). For a number of historical, political, and diplomatic reasons, however, States eschew bilateral action and prefer to bring the issue of gross disregard for human rights before international organizations, chiefly the UN. This practice is, to some extent, a healthy phenomenon, for in the UN a more dispassionate, or less partial, examination of allegations can be made, and 'collective sanctions' (§§ 131-4) may be resorted to, which tend to be more effective than individual (peaceful) sanctions.

Second, this principle too belongs to the category of *jus cogens* (§ 96). For one thing, this character derives logically from the fact that certain general rules protecting specific human rights (those on racial discrimination, apartheid, slavery, genocide, self determination of peoples) have had the nature of peremptory norms ascribed to them in official statements by Government representatives (§ 184). Logically, if a treaty providing for genocide, slavery, racial discrimination, etc. is null and void on account of its inconsistency with *jus cogens*, there is no reason for denying the same character to a treaty providing for large-scale infringements of similar gravity of human rights (for instance, massive denial of civil and political freedoms, of trade union rights, of basic economic, social, and cultural rights). Such a treaty too should be branded as 'illegal', on account of its incompatibility with the basic values of the international community. Even more important, however, than the logical argument just set out, is the fact that there is ample evidence in pronouncements by various States that the principle at hand is regarded as having a peremptory character. A number of statements to this effect were made by countries belonging to various groups at the Diplomatic Conference on the Law of Treaties in Vienna (§ 103). In addition, one should mention the authoritative dissenting opinion of the Japanese Judge Tanaka in the South West Africa case (1966), where he expressed a view all the more interesting for having been pronounced by an Asian jurist (although of course the view of a judge is no full substitute for the opinions of a group of States, it may nevertheless be regarded as indicative of the 'feelings' and tendencies of that group). Judge Tanaka stated: 'surely the law concerning the protection of human rights may be considered to belong to the *jus cogens*'.[26]

INTERNATIONAL CO-OPERATION

87. Until 1945 there was no general duty of co-operation in the international community. Indeed, such a duty would have been at odds with the whole structure and basic configuration of the community. The individualistic trends permeating the community (§§ 11 and 12), the fact that international rules were exclusively designed to delimit the allocation of power and permit coexistence, the lack of a central authority pursuing general aims on behalf of the whole community—all these explain the absence of the duty of co-operation. The appearance of the League of Nations did not change much, although of course member States were prompted to intensify relations and assist one another. Yet, co-operation still rested on the will of States and was contingent on their inclination, or interest, in making arrangements of mutual benefit.

A notable turning-point was the UN Charter, which in Article 56 explicitly obliged member States to take 'joint and separate action in co-operation with the Organization' to achieve the purposes set forth in Article 55 (including economic and social co-operation). Admittedly, the obligation deriving from Article 56 was not stringent and precise. It stipulated that member States must do their utmost, either by themselves or with other States, to co-operate with the UN in solving international and domestic problems in the social and economic fields as well as in the area of human rights. Nevertheless, the whole apparatus of the Organization and the powers allotted to its agencies have gradually rendered the general pledge of Article 56 operative. States cannot refuse to co-operate; if they fail to do so, they must explain and justify their behaviour to the relevant UN body. Moreover, UN organs are authorized to call upon member States to intensify their co-operation by indicating the policy to be followed, by suggesting guidelines and goals, and by propounding possible methods for attaining the purposes set out in Article 55.

After the accession of many African and Asian nations to independence, their growing demands for economic and other assistance rendered the question of international co-operation increasingly urgent. In the discus-

[26] ICJ *Reports* (1966), p. 298.

sions for the elaboration of the Declaration on Friendly Relations 1962–70, Third World as well as socialist States proposed that a duty to provide aid and assistance to developing countries be proclaimed. The strong opposition of Western States prevented it from being upheld. The ensuing formulation of the principle of co-operation, which has by now become widely accepted by States, merely extended the principle proclaimed by the Charter in 1945 to the whole international community.

As a consequence, any State is duty-bound to co-operate with other States and with the UN and its various agencies specializing in the economic and social field. The principle of course does not indicate how a State should co-operate and by what means it should lend its support to international efforts to solve the major economic, social, and military problems of the international community. At the present stage of development of the world community, to go beyond a generic duty would have meant infringing upon the sovereignty of States. Yet, the duty is of notable significance, at least from a negative viewpoint, in that a State's refusal to co-operate, which is not accompanied by a satisfactory explanation to the relevant UN organ or agency, can be held as a breach of the duty. Against such a State only 'collective sanctions' are available and permissible ('sanctions' open to the UN and consisting of exposure to public opinion, condemnation by stern resolutions, pressure on the State by reiterated appeals).

It seems clear that the principle at issue constitutes the fragile thread of the whole normative texture of international principles. While a fair amount of respect for the other principles is a *sine qua non* for (relatively) orderly international affairs, co-operation is not strictly needed for the survival of international relations. Or, to put it in more accurate terms, principles regulating 'co-existence' must be observed by any State, including mutually hostile countries, lest the international community be paralysed by dangerous rifts and eventually plunge into utter chaos. By contrast, co-operation can remain at a minimum level, or may be absent, between (ideologically or politically) hostile States without the world community as such suffering any major disadvantage. There is, however, another and perhaps even more important reason underlying the tenuity of the principle. Given the present social and economic conditions of the world community, it is in the interest of States to have a modicum of contact with other international subjects. Economic and other forms of co-operation serve the interest of all contracting parties. However, the kind of co-operation urged by some developing countries—one-way assistance and economic aid, not necessarily serving the interests of the donor or grantor State—is something different. It is precisely this kind of co-operation which developed countries (Western or socialist) are reluctant to engage in for chiefly economic reasons. The substantial reserve of Western and socialist countries is responsible for the striking weakness of the principle. The coalition of ideologically disparate industrialized nations has succeeded in watering down the principle or, to put it more precisely, in preventing it from acquiring vigour and incisiveness. It is no coincidence that while the other principles have substantially emanated from ideological and political groups (or, as in the case of the principle on sovereign equality, have from the outset mustered the support of all such groups), the principle on co-operation bears the imprint of an extra-ideological alignment, based on economic policy lines.

It goes without saying that, being still in a rudimentary form, the principle cannot rank among the peremptory norms of international law (§ 96). Consequently, a treaty by which two or more States undertake to refuse to co-operate with a certain group of States should not be considered as null and void, although of course it might arouse the concern of the UN and prompt it to call the States in question to account.

GOOD FAITH

88. In any political system there will be a good many legal rules which leave some discretion in their application. Although the rules specify the content and modalities of the behaviour authorized or enjoined, the addressees enjoy some leeway in the exercise of their rights or the fulfilment of their duties. Consequently, a legal subject can choose not only whether or not to execute the rule, but also between different ways of implementing it. He can choose either an application strictly in keeping with the prevailing standards of the social community or an application which, although not contrary to the rule, is more beneficial to himself.

The existence of a certain 'margin of appreciation' left to legal subjects acquires conspicuous importance in the international community, for two principal reasons. First, the addressees of most international norms are sovereign States, entities which by definition tend to stake out a claim to freedom of action and which will, consequently, endeavour as much as possible to take advantage of the relative discretion granted to them, even in applying international rules. Second, the international community lacks judicial bodies endowed with compulsory jurisdiction; if a State allegedly abuses its rights, there is often no judicial remedy available.

The principle of good faith is intended to 'invade' the penumbra of discretion left by international rules and guide the conduct of States (and other international subjects) in applying norms. While States are enjoined by the general norms, known as *consuetudo est servanda* (customary rules must be observed) and *pacta sunt servanda* (treaties must be complied with), to fulfil their duties, the principle in hand prescribes how to carry out the performance of such duties. The principle does not specify how States must behave but merely conveys the idea that international subjects must not take advantage of their rights (or discharge their obligations) in such a way as to thwart the purpose and object of legal rules. States must not betray the expectation created in other States by those rules, nor must they stultify by their behaviour the confidence which the relevant norms have given to their fellow-States. As the International Court of Justice pointed out in the *Nuclear Tests* case in 1974,

... one of the basic principles governing the creation and performance of legal obligations, whatever their source, is the principle of good faith. Trust and confidence are inherent in international co-operation, in particular in an age when this co-operation in many fields is becoming increasingly essential.[27]

It is thus apparent that the principle of good faith aims at buttressing the binding force of international rules. To be more precise, it is designed to broaden the reach of legal norms by restricting the freedom of international subjects.

How can one deduce that good faith has acquired the features of a general principle governing international relations? The answer is that a number of important treaties and resolutions of international Organizations enshrine the principle in question.

Suffice it to mention Article 2.2 of the UN Charter; Article 5 litt. *c* of the Charter of the Organization of American States of 1948; Article 26 of the Vienna Convention on the Law of Treaties of 1969; the Declaration on Friendly Relations of 1970; and Article 300 of the Convention on the Law of the Sea of 1982. In addition, the principle has been invoked in many judicial decisions.

We should now ask ourselves why it is that the international community—which appears to reflect the Hobbesian pattern on the 'state of nature' (*homo homini lupus*) in the extreme, and which at any rate is made up of States steadfastly clinging to the Machiavellian view of the relationships between morality and politics (with law as its appendix)—upholds and legally sanctions an essentially ethical postulate such as 'good faith'. To try to answer this question we must establish what international political forces were behind the proclamation of the principle. The best way of doing this is to pinpoint the attitude of the various groups of States by examining the debates surrounding the adoption of the UN Charter and the Declaration on Friendly Relations.

In 1945, in San Francisco, the provision on good faith was strongly advocated by the representative of Colombia, who succeeded in having his proposal adopted unanimously. The Colombian move, made in Commission I, was essentially based on three arguments. First, before and during the Second World War bad faith had been the basis of the conduct adopted by States, especially by Germany, and had plunged the world into chaos:

... the United Nations must react against such inadmissible concepts and must

[27] ICJ *Reports* (1974), p. 268.

proclaim that international life requires a minimum of morality as a normative principle of conduct for peoples. This minimum cannot be anything else than full good faith and respect for the pledged word . . .

Second, the legal tradition of the international community tended towards the acceptance of the principle. Third, the legal tradition of municipal law of most States was also favourable to the principle. Other delegates, particularly from the US and the UK, stated that the principle seemed superfluous to them, as it was implicit in other norms of the Charter. Nevertheless, they agreed not to oppose it. The Belgian president of the Commission rebutted that the principle was far from superfluous, because it proved useful for interpreting legal obligations ('If two interpretations are possible but one allows a literal carrying out of the obligation which is not consistent with "good faith", it must be rejected'). Interestingly, the representative of the Ukraine remarked that at first his delegation too had considered the principle unnecessary but added that lately there had been signs of attempts at violating the Yalta agreements and that this should be prevented. For that reason he was in favour of upholding the principle of 'good faith'. The discussion was wound up by the Australian delegate who stressed that the principle seemed superfluous to the States of Anglo-Saxon tradition, but since it was advocated by Latin-American countries as well as by States of civil law tradition, Australia too would support it.[28]

Clearly, all States concerned eventually agreed on the acceptance of the principle, though the motivations differed widely. If in the course of the debate misgivings were voiced, this was not on account of any opposition to the principle, but only because, in the view of some delegations it was implicit in a number of provisions, and there was therefore no need to spell it out in a specific norm.

No less instructive was the debate surrounding the adoption of the UN Declaration of 1970. The proposal to include 'good faith' among the fundamental principles to be elaborated was made in the General Assembly by developing and socialist countries in 1962, in a Czechoslovak draft, in a draft submitted by nine African countries plus Canada and Denmark, and in a draft put forward by fourteen non-aligned countries (African and Asian countries together with Yugoslavia). All mentioned 'good faith'.[29] The conspicuous difference between them was that the one tabled by Czechoslovakia qualified 'good faith' by stating that only obligations assumed 'freely and on equal footing' were to be fulfilled in good faith. Interestingly, before the discussion on principles governing friendly relations was resumed in the

---

[28] The statements of Colombia are in UNCIO, vi. 72–3; of Belgium, ibid., 74; of Ukraine, ibid., 75; of Australia, ibid., 76–7.
[29] The draft put forward by Czechoslovakia is in UN document A/C.6/L.505. The draft of the nine African countries is in A/C.6.507 and add. 1. The Afro-Asian draft is in A/C.6/509 and add. 1 and 2.

UN, the Second Conference of Non-Aligned Countries, held in Cairo in 1964, proclaimed nine fundamental principles of peaceful coexistence, the ninth of which related to 'good faith' ('necessity of States to meet their international obligations in good faith in conformity with the principles and purposes of the [UN] Charter') without making any qualification. The 'socialist' proviso was later taken up in a proposal made in 1966 by nine non-aligned countries in the UN Special Committee,[30] and became the dominant theme of the statements of socialist as well as Third World delegates. They all argued that the principle could not be invoked with regard to treaties not concluded freely on a basis of equality, that is treaties resulting from aggression, colonial domination, 'inequality among States', the threat or use of military force, and economic coercion. This view was strongly opposed by Western countries, and the outcome was the adoption of a compromise formula which, to a great extent, did not uphold the socialist and Third World countries' views ('Every State has the duty to fulfil in good faith its obligations under international agreements valid under the generally recognized principles and rules of international law.') Indeed, its clear implication was that only with respect to *valid* treaties can good faith be invoked. Consequently, the principle does not cover treaties rendered void or voidable through having been concluded under military coercion (threat or use of force) of the State or the relevant organ (Articles 51 and 52 of the Vienna Convention of the Law of Treaties), or because they are contrary to a rule of *jus cogens*. Plainly, by implicitly referring to the general rules on treaties laid down in the Vienna Convention, the Declaration eventually excluded from the ambit of its applicability those treaties challenged by socialist and developing countries which, however, were not impugnable under existing law (treaties 'resulting from colonial domination', or imposed by economic coercion). In short, the Declaration stated the obvious, for it would not make sense to uphold good faith with regard to treaties to which no obligation is attached, for the simple reason that they are not valid or binding.

In sum, from the outset all States, regardless of their political or ideological alignments, were agreed on the importance of the principle; on the initiative and at the behest of socialist countries (which as early as the 1950s had elaborated a whole doctrine on the matter in their scholarly literature), developing countries soon used the whole debate on the principle as a roundabout means of wrenching from Western States the cancellation of certain categories of so-called unequal treaties, which in their view, were flawed by injustice. This struggle ended however, in failure, for the provisions which were eventually adopted did not affect the treaties in question. Thus, the principle was neither undermined nor jeopardized by political or ideological clash, but came to be clearly restated and specified.

[30] The proposal of the nine non-aligned countries is in A/AC.125/L.35.

It is interesting that the legal writers of East European countries continue to 'interpret' this principle as if it included the political requests advanced by them during the diplomatic negotiations preceding the drawing up of the Declaration on Friendly Relations. Thus, for example, the GDR's *Manual* (1982)[31] announces that, by virtue of this principle, '... the Declaration ties the obligation to perform international duties to the assumption that these duties are in line with the principles laid down in the UN Charter and other principles and rules generally accepted by international law [for example, the principle of the freedom of the high seas]. Consequently, the Declaration does not admit as legally binding those international agreements that conflict with generally recognized international principles, and underlines once again the practical significance of the system of the fundamental principles of international law in force as a yardstick by which to measure the validity of international agreements.... Thus, for example, "unequal" treaties, or treaties obtained by force such as colonial or neo-colonial ones, and agreements in which intervention is foreseen, or those drawn up under threat or violent pressure of any kind, cannot be the basis for international obligations.' The *Manual* goes on to note that socialist countries withdrew their proposals for including some reference to 'unequal' treaties in the principle of 'good faith' because, in the meantime, the Vienna Convention had already accepted the principle that treaties contrary to *jus cogens* (see §96) are null and void. In my opinion, by referring to *jus cogens* at this point, the *Manual* is widening the scope of the principles of self-determination of peoples and of the prohibition on the use of economic force. In reality these principles, even though they constitute peremptory norms, do not go so far as to invalidate either 'colonialist' or 'neo-colonialist' treaties or treaties drawn up under economic pressure. This is because the Vienna Convention merely provides for the nullity of treaties 'wrested' by the use or threat of *military* force and does not mention the so-called unequal treaties. The views set forth in the *Manual* amount to an interesting attempt to widen the scope of international rules no longer through the concept of good faith, but with the help of *jus cogens*. It is not unlikely that other States will gradually come to accept these views.

89. This principle raises the question of what cases 'good faith' can be applied in and whether it can, in practice, play a useful role. The answer can be inferred from international case-law, which shows that it was, in the main, introduced in international courts in the period between the two World Wars, but that in subsequent years it has been somewhat silently passed over. It has mainly been used as a limitation on the discretionary power of States, but has only in actual fact played a peripheral role. It has not served as a *basis* for the decision of the case at issue or *ratio decidendi*, but as an argument *ad abundantiam* or as an *obiter dictum*—that is, as a proposition of no direct relevance to the decision. More often than not the principle has only been invoked to note that it was not applicable in the case.

Although so far the practical results in the judicial application of the

[31] DDR-*Völkerrecht* 1982, i. 127–9 (the quoted passages are from p. 128).

principle are not of great consequence, one should not underestimate its possible role and impact. In a community where legislation is expanding and States are ever more frequently vested with rights and powers, while at the same time judicial bodies continue to lack compulsory jurisdiction, good faith may increasingly serve as a useful means of placing restraints on States' discretion, so as to ensure that international legislation is not frustrated by devious means.

I have already said (§ 88) that by virtue of this principle no rule can be applied in a way designed to frustrate its intended purpose. I should add that, as Virally has pointed out,[32] in ascertaining whether in a specific case 'good faith' has been flaunted, it is sometimes possible to apply the rules on interpretation laid down in the Vienna Convention on the law of treaties; in fact, the principle merely indicates the *general aims* that the parties should pursue in applying legal rules.

A recent illustration of a breach of the principle of good faith, that is of the abuse of rights, can be seen in the declaration made on 6 April 1984 by the US to the effect that its acceptance of the International Court of Justice's compulsory jurisdiction (of 26 June 1946) 'shall not apply to disputes with any Central American State or arising out of or related to events in Central America'. This declaration was made three days before Nicaragua instituted proceedings against the US regarding its responsibility for military and paramilitary activity in and against Nicaragua. Regardless of any other grounds for invalidity, it seems to me that the US declaration, intended to deprive the Court of its jurisdiction over a dispute that it knew would presently be submitted to it, amounts to an abuse of its right to terminate or revise the 1946 declaration (albeit with six months' notice). To my mind the US declaration being contrary to the principle of good faith must be regarded as inapplicable to the dispute submitted to the Court by Nicaragua.

It is common knowledge that in its judgment of 26 November 1984,[33] the International Court of Justice disregarded the US declaration for reasons other than the doctrine of abuse of rights. However, it mentioned good faith in passing, stating that 'the principle of good faith plays an important role' for unilateral acts as well. It is interesting to note that in its statement of 18 January 1985 on US withdrawal from the proceedings initiated by Nicaragua, the American Department of State in turn accused Nicaragua of having abused its rights: 'Nicaragua's suit against the US is a blatant misuse of the Court for political and propaganda purposes'.[34]

DISTINGUISHING TRAITS OF THE PRINCIPLES

90. Now that the various principles have been discussed separately we should examine their common features.

First, these principles, except for that on sovereign equality of States, do

---

[32] M. Virally, 'Good Faith in Public International Law', *AJIL* 77 (1983), 133.

[33] ICJ *Reports* (1984), pp. 418–20 (paras 60 and 63).

[34] See ILM 24 (1985), p. 247.

not address themselves to States solely, but are binding on other international legal subjects as well—insurgents, and peoples represented by liberation movements, and international organizations. As they constitute basic standards of behaviour in the world community, all the legal entities operating in that community must abide by them. For instance, insurgents, liberation movements, and international organizations must comply with the principle of good faith to the same degree as do States. If they want to benefit from the advantages and privileges of international legal affairs they must also bow to the general standards designed to restrain the freedom of international subjects. The same holds true for the principle of non-intervention in the internal affairs of States, which must be respected not only by States but also by insurgents and liberation movements (needless to say, in relation to States other than the one against which they struggle), as well as by international organizations (their 'constitutional texts' include a rule forbidding undue trespass on the domestic jurisdiction of member States; but international organizations must also refrain from unlawfully interfering in the internal affairs of third States).

Second, except for the principles on sovereign equality, on non intervention and on good faith, the rights and claims deriving from the principles accrue to all members of the international community, all of which are entitled to exact their observance by other international subjects. In other words, while *all* principles impose obligations *erga omnes*, *most* of them also grant *rights erga omnes*.

Thus, for instance, any State can claim respect for the principle on the use of force by any other State and in case of violation, it is entitled to insist on its cessation or, if need be, reparation of the international offence. Similarly, the principle on respect for human rights grants to all members of the community the right to demand full compliance and, in case of gross and large-scale infringements, to request their cessation (and the punishment of the responsible authorities if allowed by the circumstances).

In other words, observance of most principles is a matter of concern for *all* international subjects: these are entitled to step in whenever principles are violated (although of course they may deem it politically expedient to remain aloof). To put it differently: the principles are of *universal applicability* not only in the sense that they are binding on all States and on other members of the world community, but also in the sense that they concern and involve each and all of them, and give rise to a deep sense of solidarity and of joint interest among international subjects.

Third, practically all the principles save for that on co-operation and the principle of good faith belong to the category of peremptory rules or *jus cogens*, that is to say, to those principles and rules accepted and recognized by the international community as a whole as standards from which no derogation is permitted and which can only be modified by subsequent norms or principles of general international law having the same character (compare Article 53 of the Vienna Convention on the Law of Treaties). As will be specified later on (§ 96), the special force of such peremptory principles lies in rendering null and void any international treaty contrary to them.

Fourth, certain of the principles reflect the 'classical' pattern of the world community, that is the traditional structure based on equality of States and marked by strong individualism; others are the product of the new trends which emerged after the First and particularly after the Second World Wars, and denote the innovations introduced in the world community by various States, primarily by the socialist and developing countries. The principles strongly embedded in the 'old pattern' are those of sovereign equality, of non-intervention (at least in its role as a precept designed to protect States from interferences of the traditional type in their domestic affairs); and the principle on good faith (which has, however, been 'revitalized' in recent debates and now enjoys wide support among developing countries). The principles which are indicative of the 'post-Westphalian-model', that is of the changes brought about in the international community by the new values which have emerged in recent times, are those on self-determination of peoples, on the ban on force, on the peaceful settlement of disputes, on respect for human rights, and on co-operation among States. We shall shortly see that the 'coexistence' of principles of such diverse origin and motivation raises many problems and tends to affect the operative force of the 'new' principles.

Finally, a common feature of the principles is that, although valid for and applicable to every State, they rely heavily for their implementation and enforcement on the UN organization whose membership does not as yet include the whole world community. Plainly, the momentous advance represented by the emergence of a network of normative standards has not gone hand in hand with a commensurate progress in the international instruments of law enforcement. In other words, no *specific* machinery has as yet been set up in the international community to give strength to the basic prescriptions destined to act as the backbone of the community. In this vacuum, the UN has been called upon to play the role of implementation mechanism. As we saw while considering each specific principle in turn, the UN has been entrusted by the world community with the task of scrutinizing and enforcing the observance of the principles. In doing so, the UN ultimately acts in the interest and on behalf of the whole world community, of which it is the legitimate representative. This is hardly surprising. For one thing, the UN is gradually becoming a World Organization in the full sense of the word, embracing all the members of the international community. Moreover, even before it coincides completely with the international community, the Organization already acts on behalf of all international subjects.

THE CLOSE LINK BETWEEN THE PRINCIPLES AND THE NEED FOR THEIR CO-ORDINATION

91. The eight principles discussed above are closely intertwined, not only in the sense that international subjects must comply with all of them, but also in the sense that in the application of any one of them, all the others must simultaneously be borne in mind. They supplement and support one another and also condition each other's application. By way of illustration one may mention that the ban on force, the principle on the peaceful settlement of disputes, and that on good faith are closely bound up with one another. For in case of dispute States must refrain from using force and must also endeavour to settle their disagreement peacefully; by the same token, in seeking a peaceful solution, they must act in good faith. Similarly, the principles on human dignity, on non-intervention in the internal affairs of States and on co-operation, are tightly connected. For example, the question as to whether States can intervene to prompt a third State to discontinue alleged violations of human rights can only be settled in the light of and on the combined strength of, the three principles, which—taken together—can provide a correct solution to the question in specific cases. By and large, a useful criterion can be found in the distinction drawn by Hoffmann, according to whom

We must make a distinction between what one can normally call interference or meddling, which is practiced by every sovereign State, and which essentially consists of trying to change a sovereign regime so as to make it more favourable to one's own political or economic interests, and the kinds of measures I am advocating here [that is, peaceful steps to be taken on the bilateral and multilateral level, and within international organizations] and which are essentially aimed at getting governments to observe rules of behaviour to which they have committed themselves.[35]

It follows that any peaceful initiative aimed at requiring a State to discontinue large-scale and gross violations of human rights does agree with the principle on intervention. Such initiative can also take the form of a proposal, within an international organization, that non-coercive sanctions should be taken against a State systematically engaging in violations of basic human rights. The situation is different in the case of sporadic infringements, or single occurrences of serious disregard for human rights. In this case a balance between the two principles may consist in allowing foreign countries to take steps solely via diplomatic channels; consequently, the State where the alleged violations have occurred must not regard as an unfriendly act the *démarche* by another State aimed at expressing concern and calling upon the former State to do its utmost to end the violations. By contrast the State where the violations have occurred can reject as undue

[35] S. Hoffmann, *Duties Beyond Borders* (Syracuse, 1981), p. 124.

interference any attempt by other States to exercise direct pressure on its State representatives or on individuals or groups and associations acting on its territory.

As an illustration, mention can be made of the letter sent on 5 February 1977 by President Carter of the US to the Soviet citizen Andrei Sacharov on the occasion of alleged violations of human rights in the USSR.[36] The letter was considered by the Soviet authorities as an unlawful interference in their internal affairs. On the same occasion the French foreign minister stated that in his view diplomatic steps through official channels in regard of the Soviet authorities were lawful.[37]

Similarly, in 1977, the Soviet delegate to the UN Commission on Human Rights expressed strong criticism of the American proposal that the Commission send a telegram to the USSR expressing its concern about the detention of some Soviet human rights activists. He then pointed out that 'if the US was concerned about the human rights situation in the Soviet Union, it could act through its embassy in Moscow, but not in [sic] an international body'.[38]

It should be stressed that in this area the views of the various groupings are far from consistent. By and large, Eastern European countries cling to the doctrine expounded in San Francisco in 1945, by the framers of the UN Charter, to the effect that 'if rights and freedoms were grievously outraged so as to create conditions which threaten peace or to obstruct the application of the provisions of the Charter, then they cease to be the sole concern of each State'.[39] This doctrine, according to socialist States, applies both to the action of the UN and to interstate relations. They feel that instances where alleged violations of human rights do not threaten peace, States can only use diplomatic channels. As Hannikainen, a Finnish jurist very close to the Soviet views, has written,

the expression of an opinion by a State and its requests to another State should not be considered to constitute intervention but to be part of the normal communication between States. It should be clear that such communication should not include demands, pressure or campaigns. A State has a wider power of expressing opinions about the human rights policy of another State only if some treaty specifically so decrees. More general statements about the inadequacies of a specific socio-political system do not constitute intervention as far as they are not directed in an accusing form against some specific State.[40]

---

[36] The letter of President Carter is in *Le Monde*, 19 February 1977, p. 2. See also *Keesings Contemporary Archives*, 1977, 28255.

[37] The declaration of the French Minister is in *Le Monde*, 2 March 1977.

[38] UN document E/CN.4/SR.1417, para. 40.

[39] The passage quoted in the text is taken from the report submitted on 1 June 1945 by Subcommittee I/1/A to Committee I/1, at the San Francisco Conference, in UNCIO, 6, p. 705.

[40] L. Hannikainen, 'Human Rights and Non-Intervention in the Final Act of the CSCE', *Acta Scandinavica Juris Gentium* 48 (1979), 34. (Reference is made here to various writings by socialist jurists.)

African, Asian, and Latin-American countries tend to share the views of Eastern European countries, although they try to take a less rigid stand. (This emerged in 1977 in the discussions in the UN's Human Rights Commission on the aforementioned American proposal to send a telegram to the Soviet Union.)[41]

There are significant differences in the views of Western countries too. At one extreme is the position adopted by President Carter, to which I referred above; at the other end of the spectrum is the statement made in 1977 by the Federal Republic of Germany:

The ban on intervention is valid in international law today as much as it was before, and this in principle also in the field of human rights. On the other hand, the increasing importance of human rights in international law has led to the result that in this field the threshold of prohibition of intervention has been lowered. However, in international law human rights have not achieved a rank superior to that of the prohibition of intervention.[42]

More recently (on 20 March 1985), the twenty-one Western members of the Council of Europe adopted at Vienna a Declaration on 'Human Rights in the World at Large', in which they reaffirmed *inter alia*, 'the conviction that the protection of human rights and fundamental freedoms is a legitimate and urgent concern of the international community and its members and that expressions of concern that such rights and freedoms are not observed in a certain State cannot be considered an interference in the domestic affairs of that State'. On close scrutiny, this statement appears to be rather vague; it does not make clear first what 'level of violation' of human rights in another country legitimates the expression of concern, and second, how concern can be specifically expressed. In particular, the Declaration does not mention the possible legitimate reaction to 'a systematic pattern of gross violations'.[43]

---

[41] For the various statements by representatives of Third World countries in the UN Commission on Human Rights, see E/CN.4/SR.1416, para 92 and SR.1417, paras 1-29.

[42] The passage from the statement of the FRG is in *ZaöRuV*, 39 (1979), 576.

[43] See text of the Declaration in: Council of Europe, European Ministerial Conference on Human Rights (19-20 March 1985), *Texts Adopted*, doc. H(85)7, pp. 9-11.

It should be noted that a previous draft stated that 'the principle of non-interference in the domestic affairs of States does not apply when such rights and freedoms are seriously threatened' (Council of Europe doc. MDH-HF(85) 2, p. 22). This wording seems more sweeping than the one eventually adopted. A stand substantially along the same lines as the draft just mentioned was taken in Vienna by Denmark and Norway. The Danish Minister of Justice stated among other things that 'The principle of non interference "in matters which are essentially within the domestic jurisdiction of any State"—to quote the UN Charter—does not apply when human rights are seriously violated' (unpublished text of statement, p. 2). The Norwegian Secretary of State for Foreign Affairs stated *inter alia*: 'As a result of the increasing international obligations in this field, respect for human rights is no longer a domestic concern only, which could be considered free from interference from the outside world. We should, therefore, bring up, in multilateral fora as well as in bilateral relations, our human rights concern' (unpublished text of statement, p. 2).

The various principles must also be combined with regard to categories of international subjects other than States. Thus, for example, although liberation movements (§ 51-5) are entitled to—or, according to another school of thought, may *de facto*—use force in order to oppose the forcible denial of their right to self-determination, they must refrain from resorting to force for the settlement of disputes, if any, with other members of the international community, and seek a peaceful settlement instead.

CONCLUDING REMARKS

92. As the discussion above should have made clear, most principles are ideologically motivated, but the motivations can differ substantially. Thus, the right of peoples to self-determination owes its origin and its present impact on the world community to socialist and Third World demands, whereas, at the other end of the spectrum, one can find that the principle of respect for human rights derives essentially from Western political philosophy. Similarly, the principle on co-operation is primarily advocated by developing countries and it is founded on political and economic, rather than on ideological motives.

It may prove useful at this juncture to take up a theme which has already been touched upon a few times in this Chapter, namely the notion that certain of the fundamental principles reflect the 'Westphalian model' whereas others are indicative of the new trends which emerged in the world community after the decline of that 'model'. It is no coincidence that, on carefully appraising the various principles, it should become apparent that the less controversial principles (which are predictably the ones most strongly supported by State practice), are those firmly rooted in the 'Westphalian model'. Plainly, being the expression of the most elementary demands of States' coexistence, they tend to command greater respect among sovereign subjects. By contrast, those principles which reflect the 'Charter model' are relatively weaker, either because certain segments of the international community are, for political, ideological, or even military reasons, reluctant to adopt them, or else because, owing to the conflicts and divergences underlying their formulation, they are loosely worded and can hardly operate as legal precepts. (This holds true, also, for the principles on co-operation and on peaceful settlement of disputes.)

A second difference between the two categories of principles—which is but a corollary of the first one—is that in case of conflict the principles belonging to the old model tend to override the 'new' ones.

We have also seen that since they were first formulated, many principles have received the support of all the main groupings. However, not all of them have commanded unqualified support; what is even more important, not all of them have been consistently interpreted in the same way. Actually, as I pointed out above (§ 79), the concept of sovereign equality is the only one which has always been construed by all States along the same lines and which has never given rise to any major differences in its interpretation. By contrast, in the elaboration of the other principles, conflicting views have come to light and opposing demands have been put forward by rival groups. In certain cases, such as that of non-intervention, the eventual formulation had to accommodate sharply conflicting claims; as a consequence many problems were left unsolved.

This being so, one may wonder whether the ideological and political dissensions, which the principles were designed to lay to rest, did not surface once more at the moment of implementation and interpretation. If this was the case, the principles would clearly have lost some of their weight, for their importance as a basic nucleus of consensus in the world community would have lessened.

On close scrutiny, international practice shows that differences did indeed emerge, not so much, however, with respect to the interpretation of the principles, but rather with regard to their co-ordination. I showed above (§ 91) that the principles ought logically to be co-ordinated along certain sensible and rational lines allowing for their coherent and harmonious joint operation. Those observations are, however, somewhat at odds with what occurs in practice. Thus, for instance, socialist States tend to overemphasize non-intervention, while at the same time playing down the importance of respect for human rights. In their view, when it comes to the co-ordination of the principles, the former must of necessity take pride of place. Similarly, on many occasions States belonging to different groups have argued about how to co-ordinate the right of peoples to self-determination with that of sovereign equality of States (inasmuch as the latter safeguards the territorial integrity of States).

A recent case in point is the conflict over the Falkland Islands (Malvinas). In the General Assembly, Western countries, spearheaded by the U K, con- sistently argued that the crucial issue was whether or not the inhabitants of the Islands ought to exercise their right to self-determination. In contrast, Third World and socialist countries, following in the wake of Argentina, contended that the right to self-determination was not applicable owing to the historical circumstances of the occupation of the Islands by the U K, and that, therefore, the principle of territorial integrity should be overriding. This was to the advantage of Argentina, which maintained that the Islands should be legally subject to its territorial jurisdiction because the Argentines had been unlawfully evicted by the British in 1831.

This instance, and numerous others, proved that the struggle between competing groups has shifted from the formulation of the principles to their practical co-ordination. It stands to reason that the jurist can only suggest the solutions he considers most sensible and in keeping with the principles themselves. Of course, he cannot substitute for the will of States, which he must take into account. The present international conditions indicate that no grouping has succeeded in imposing its own 'interpretation' on the others. Thus the tug of war will go on, albeit on a different plane than before, until a new equilibrium, if any, is reached.

Section II

Creation and Effectiveness of International Standards

7

International Law-making

The Traditional Law-making Processes: Custom and Treaties

93. E VER since the beginning of the international community States have spontaneously evolved two methods for creating legally binding rules: treaties and custom. Both were admirably suited to the exigencies of their creators. Both responded to the basic need of not imposing duties on such States as did not wish to be bound by them. No outside 'legislator' was tolerated: law was brought into being by the very States which were to be bound by it. Consequently there was complete coincidence of law-makers and law-addressees. Treaties in particular, being applicable to the contracting parties only, perfectly reflected the substantial individualism of the international community. As to custom, it did admittedly give rise to norms binding on all members of the community, but any member could object to the applicability of a customary rule at the moment of its formation, thereby avoiding being restrained by any rule which was not to its liking. Custom too, ultimately rested on a consensual basis.

The unbridled freedom of States was reflected in another feature of international law-making; namely the absence of a hierarchy between custom and treaties as sources of law. In other words, rules created by means of bilateral or multilateral treaties were not stronger or superior to customary or 'general rules', and vice versa. Both systems possessed equal rank and status. Thus two or more States could elect to derogate *inter se* from customary international law; by the same token, a new customary rule could supplant a treaty concluded by two or more States.[1] The complete interchangeability of the two sources plainly sanctioned the wish of sovereign States to regulate international relations as they thought best, without any obligation being imposed from outside. States did not tie their hands for good; they were able to get rid of them by mutual agreement as soon as their undertaking proved contrary to their interests.

The resulting picture justified the principle propounded since the late 1890s by the positivist school whereby in the international community 'all that was not prohibited was by this mere fact permitted'. This is merely

---

[1] See for instance D. Anzilotti, *Corso di diritto internazionale*, i, 4th edn. (Milan, 1955), p. 94.

another way of saying that freedom of States (or sovereignty) was the fundamental feature of the international community.

As I shall show (§ 97), this legal regime is still largely valid today.

The Attempt at Expanding the Traditional Law-making Processes in 1921
The General Principles of Law Recognized by Civilized Countries

94. After the First World War the strong feeling that something should be done to avert another similar cataclysm led statesmen and diplomats to contrive devices likely to channel conflicts and differences along less dangerous paths. One of them was the Permanent Court of International Justice (see § 33), which was intended by its creators or inspirers (among whom was American President Woodrow Wilson) to exert a powerful influence as an agency for resolving conflict. When the statute of the Court was being drafted by an 'Advisory Committee of Jurists' appointed by the Council of the League of Nations and made up of ten members (eight from the West, a Brazilian, and a Japanese), one of the issues that cropped up was that of the law to be applied by the Court. A proposal was put forward by the Committee Chairman, the Belgian E.E.F. Descamps, to the effect that, in addition to treaties and custom, the Court should also apply 'the rules of international law as recognized by the legal conscience of civilized nations'. In commenting upon and reacting to the proposal, the Committee split into two groups:[1a] The majority favoured it, but three members—the American Root, the Englishman Lord Phillimore, and the Italian Ricci-Busatti— strongly opposed it. The majority had two aims in mind. First they wished to expand the sources of international law, by making applicable 'the fundamental law of justice and injustice, deeply engraved on the heart of every human being and which is given its highest and most authoritative expression in the legal conscience of civilized nations' (Descamps). Plainly, the advocates of this doctrine endeavoured to introduce natural law principles in international relations. Second, in case a dispute was not governed either by a treaty or by custom, they wished to avoid the possibility of the Court declaring itself incompetent through lack of applicable rules. They claimed that by rendering applicable 'principles of objective justice' in addition to treaties and custom, actions at law would not be dismissed and international justice would be properly administered.

It is apparent that the supporters of the new source were politically motivated. They intended to go beyond the traditional limitations of the international legal system by broadening the existing legal network through the addition of principles reflecting Western legal philosophy. It was, of course, impossible to impose new rules on States. The purpose of the Com-

---

[1a] For the various statements in the Consultative Committee of Jurists referred to in the text, see League of Nations, Permanent Court of International Justice, *Advisory Committee of Jurists*, 1922, pp. 287 ff., 306 ff.

mittee's majority was subtle: to wedge between the crevices of existing law principles derived from Western civilization. However modest the scope of the principles, the attempt was revolutionary, because for the first time an international heteronomous law (that is, rules imposed from outside and not resting on the free will of States) was to be created (it stands to reason that the 'natural law' upon which jurists relied in the seventeenth and eighteenth centuries, although universal and heteronomous, was not a binding body of law in the modern sense). The role of the new law was self-evident: it was meant to restrict State sovereignty as much as possible whenever the absence of treaties or custom left States free to behave as they liked.

The proposals made by the Committee majority did not go unchallenged, however. The minority of three adopted a markedly positivist approach: in a previous meeting its leader, the American Root, had emphatically stated that 'Nations will submit to positive law, but will not submit to principles as have not been developed into positive rules supported by an accord between all States.' They claimed that the proposal exceeded the bounds of existing legal precepts. As Root asked, 'Was it possible to compel nations to submit their disputes to a Court which would administer not merely law, but also what it deems to be the conscience of civilised peoples?' And Lord Phillimore suggested that 'disputes which could not be settled by the application of rules of law should be taken before the Council of the League of Nations' (that is, a political body). The Italian member Ricci-Busatti put forward a powerful argument based on a consistently positivist approach. He noted that the fear of a *non liquet* (that is, a declaration to the effect that the Court could not pass judgment upon a dispute for want of legal rules relevant to the matter) was imaginary; he argued that since 'that which is not forbidden is allowed', the lack of a positive rule allegedly prohibiting a certain State from behaving in a given manner simply meant that that form of behaviour was permissible. It could therefore be said that in a way, the law regulated the matter, for it implicitly authorized a form of conduct which one of the disputants wrongly deemed unlawful.

In short, the minority clung to the traditional concept that the Court should solely apply rules and principles derived from the will of States and embodied in treaties or custom. Given this radical difference of views, Root and Lord Phillimore decided to try to retreat from what appeared to be a blind alley by proposing a compromise formula: they suggested that the Court should be empowered to apply 'the general principles of law recognised by civilised nations'. The proposal was accepted both by the Committee's majority and later on by the League Council, and eventually became Article 38.3 of the Court's Statute.

According to Lord Phillimore the general principles referred to were those 'which were accepted by all nations *in foro domestico*, such as certain principles of procedure, the principle of good faith, and the principle of *res judicata,* etc'. In other words, the rule covered principles which were first, general in character and second, upheld in the domestic legal systems of all 'civilised nations'. Clearly, the formula agreed upon followed a middle course between the two opposing views. The Court was empowered to apply something more than treaties and custom, and was thus able to go beyond the law resting on the will of States. However, it could not apply general and vague 'principles of objective justice' (in which case it would ultimately have been endowed with the power to create law), but only those principles which were clearly laid down in the municipal law systems of dominant States.

The looseness of the formula adopted in 1920 and the fact that international courts previously had not consistently and deliberately drawn upon general principles of law proclaimed in national legal systems, warrant the view that Article 38.3 did not codify an unwritten rule on general principles. Rather, an attempt was made to create a new, albeit secondary, source of international law. As the rule adopted by the League of Nations' Council was not challenged by States, being either explicitly or implicitly accepted by them, there gradually evolved a 'general' rule establishing this secondary source of law.

It should again be emphasized that, unlike treaties and custom, this new source did not produce rules based on the will of States. Principles were actually to be formulated by the Court by a process of induction along the lines indicated by Article 38. It may be interesting to recall the remarks made in 1928 by Anzilotti:

Inasmuch as [Article 38] makes reference to general principles that belong to municipal law alone, one is bound to admit that the [international] judge is referred by the international legal order to a different source, to a material source; this source can only provide the elements necessary for the formulation of the rule that he will apply to a specific case as a rule of international law; thus the judge will create the law for a special case and for that only ... by following certain criteria and in particular the general character of the concepts which he may draw upon. Thus conceived, the function granted to the Court by Article 38 para. 3 is not different—except for the greater limitations it encounters—from the function that some recent codes vest in the judge, when they stipulate that when other sources are lacking, the judge shall apply the rule that he would apply if he himself were the law-maker ... One could say that to the very new *jus gentium* there corresponds an even *newer praetor,* who has, however, powers much more limited than those belonging to the Roman praetor.[2]

What use was made of the new source of law by the Permanent Court of International Justice? Even a cursory glance at the Court's case-law makes it clear that first, the Court very seldom resorted to the principles and, what

[2] D. Anzilotti, *Corso di diritto internazionale,* i, cit., p. 107.

is more important, that it actually relied on principles of legal logic or general jurisprudence, such as the duty of reparation for international wrongs ('it is a principle of international law, and even a general conception of law, that any breach of an engagement involves an obligation to make reparation' (PCIJ *Chorzow Factory* case (Merits), 1928), and the principle *nemo judex in re sua* ('The well-known rule that no one can be judge in his own suit holds good', *Mosul* case, 1925). Second, the principles themselves were not identified through a detailed investigation of the legal systems of the various members of the international community. This, in itself, corroborates the view that they were actually not applied *qua* general principles obtaining *in foro domestico*, but as general tenets capable of being induced from the rules of international law or deduced from legal logic. Third, the principles resorted to were not indispensable for the final decision in the case. They were only mentioned *ad adjuvandum*, that is to bolster a proposition that could already be formulated on the basis of other rules or principles.

When the Permanent Court of International Justice was replaced by the International Court of Justice the principles were even less frequently resorted to. In addition, their formulation, especially the outmoded and discriminatory reference to 'civilised nations', was harshly, and rightly, criticized by the Lebanese Judge Ammoun.[3] Furthermore, socialist legal literature attacked them on the substantial grounds of their failure to reflect the will of States. (See, for example, the group of Soviet jurists led by Tunkin[4] as well as the authors of the 1982 GDR Manual.)[5]

The socialist jurists claimed that the principles as conceived by the prevailing legal doctrine could not constitute a separate source of law first, because 'there cannot exist normative legal principles which would be common to socialist and bourgeois law', and second, because only treaties and custom, being based on the will of States, produce binding norms. Consequently, socialist jurists have concluded that the 'principles' referred to in Article 38 may either consist of general principles of international law deriving from treaties and custom, and elevated to the rank of fundamental doctrines of the world community (see §§ 77–8), or else they refer to non-normative standards, that is, 'general legal concepts, logical rules, modes of legal techniques, which are used in interpreting and apply ing law in general', such as the maxim *'lex specialis derogat generali'* (a special rule prevails over a general one), *'nemo plus juris transferre potest quam ipse habet'* (no one can transfer a right that he does not possess), and so on.

All these factors warrant the view that after establishing a third source in the 1920s, the general rule gradually withered away to such an extent that it has now fallen into disuse. (It should be noted that even Verdross—

---

[3] ICJ *Reports* (1969), pp. 133–4.
[4] G. Tunkin, *Theory of International Law* (London, 1974), pp. 195 ff.
[5] DDR-*Völkerrecht* 1982, i. 208–10.

one of the most authoritative and staunch advocates of the importance of Article 38, conceded in 1968 that the role of the 'principles' had greatly dwindled as a result of their gradual absorption into treaty and customary law.)[6] At present, in addition to the two traditional sources, it is possible to have recourse to those general principles which can be inferred by way of induction and generalization from conventional and customary rules of international law (see § 76) or which have been laid down by States for the purpose of setting out the fundamental standards of behaviour of the international community (see §§ 77 ff). The reference to the 'principles' laid down in Article 38 of the ICJ Statute should be interpreted to the effect that it adverts to the two categories just mentioned: if this were not the case Article 38 would turn out to be meaningless, and, as such contrary to the principle on interpretation whereby in case of doubt a rule should be so construed as to be given a legal meaning and purport (this is the so-called principle of effectiveness: see § 105).

Finally, I would like to draw attention to the fact that recently a Chinese jurist, Li Haopei, after forcefully criticizing the positivist approach to international law which, in his view, overemphasizes the role of the will of States, has contended that the 'principles' mentioned in Article 38 constitute a third source of international law: according to him they 'represent the common legal conviction and experience of all mankind' and are 'universal' 'for the very reason that [they] are universally recognized by all civilized nations'.[7]

The Attempt at Granting Legislative Powers to the UN General Assembly in the late 1950s

95. A second attempt at instituting a new source of law or at least greatly expanding the existing law-making process was made by a number of developing States in the early 1960s. It was not systematic or well organized, nor did it assume the form of definite and articulate proposals. Rather, it consisted of suggestions and views propounded on a number of occasions but without a general design within the UN.

The aim was to upgrade resolutions adopted by the UN General Assembly to the rank of law-creating instruments. By so doing developing countries hoped that their command of a strong majority in the General Assembly would enable them to pass new international legislation and do away with what they considered the most blatant injustices or inadequacies of traditional international rules. However, as the UN Charter clearly embodies the concept that recommendations by the General Assembly do not possess any binding force (Article 10-14), the consent of all States was

---

[6] A. Verdross, 'Les principes généraux du droit dans le système des sources du droit international public', in *Hommage Guggenheim* (Geneva, 1968), p. 530.

[7] Li Haopei, 'Jus Cogens and International Law', *Ch YIL*, pp. 61–3.

required for those recommendations to be turned into legally binding acts. The strong opposition of the West and the substantial, albeit cautiously expressed, resistance of socialist countries precluded the emergence of such a consent. As a consequence, a general rule bestowing the requested legal force upon General Assembly resolutions never saw the light. (On the legal value of G A resolutions, see § 107.)

The Upgrading of Certain Fundamental Rules Produced by Traditional Sources of Law: The Introduction of Jus Cogens in the 1960s

96. More successful was a further attempt made in the late 1960s by the socialist countries—with the strong support of a number of Third World States—in a different area of international legislation. The socialist countries and their allies claimed that certain principles governing States' relations should be given a higher status and rank than ordinary rules deriving from treaties and custom. Consequently, it was held that treaties must not deviate from those supreme principles and, if they did, were to be regarded as null and void. In the view of the proponents of this view, the principles in question covered self-determination of peoples, the prohibition of aggression, genocide, slavery, racial discrimination, and, in particular, racial segregation or apartheid.

Plainly, unlike the previous two attempts—that regarding 'general principles recognized by civilised nations' and the one concerning resolutions of international organisations—this endeavour sought not to create a new source of law, but rather to upgrade certain of the norms produced by the traditional sources. The different aim helps to explain why on this occasion the initiative was successful.

It should be noted that the proposal advanced in the 1960s was not new. It had previously been suggested by a number of jurists that international treaties must not derogate from certain international standards. Some of them were, to some extent, motivated by the underlying desire to challenge the validity of the Versailles Treaty, felt by Germany to be an iniquitous imposition on the part of the victors. A case in point is that of the German judge Schücking, as can be seen from his views on the PCIJ *Wimbledon* and *Oscar Chinn* cases of 1923[8] and 1934,[9] respectively. Others, such as Verdross,[10] were primarily impelled by their bias in favour of natural law, which prompted them to assign a high rank to rules upholding moral tenets. Finally, a number of scholars with a strong positivist outlook were probably influenced by the distinction usualy upheld in most domestic legal systems between *jus cogens* (rules or principles of public policy which cannot be derogated from by legal subjects) and *jus dispositivum* (norms which can be replaced by subjects in their private dealings). For example, in 1912, Anzilotti contended:

[8] *PCIJ*, Series A/1, 47. [9] *PCIJ*, Series A/B, 63 at pp. 149–50.
[10] A. Verdross, 'Forbidden Treaties in International Law', *AJIL* 31 (1937), 571–7.

... the will of States must not be aimed at something forbidden by international law. Thus, for instance, a treaty under which two States were to undertake to share control over a part of the high seas, or under which a State were to dispose in favour of another of the territory belonging to a third State, would be null and void.[11]

In 1914 the same author pointed out that two States were legally barred from undertaking by treaty to kill prisoners of war. In 1905 Oppenheim wrote:

... if, for instance, a State entered into a convention with another State not to interfere in case the latter should command its vessels to commit piratical acts on the open sea, such a treaty would be null and void, because it is a principle of International Law that it is the duty of every State to forbid its vessels to commit piracy on the high seas.[12]

During 1968 and 1969 socialist and Third World States succeeded in having an important provision of the Convention on the Law of Treaties adopted by the Diplomatic Conference of Vienna. It was Article 53, which defines *jus cogens* and provides that treaties contrary to peremptory rules of general international law are null and void (see also Articles 64 and 66).

What were the political and ideological motivations behind this move? It seems that the Third World and socialist countries were impelled by slightly different, though somewhat overlapping, motivations. To developing countries, the proclamation of *jus cogens* represented a further means of fighting against colonial (or former colonial) countries—as was made clear in 1968 at the Vienna Conference by the representative of Sierra Leone, who pointed out that the upholding of *jus cogens* '... provided a golden opportunity to condemn imperialism, slavery, forced labour, and all practices that violated the principle of the equality of all human beings and of the sovereign equality of States ...'[13] To the socialist countries, on the other hand, the peremptory rules represented the hard core of those international principles which, by proclaiming the peaceful coexistence of States, permitted and safeguarded smooth relations between States having different economic and social structures. The upgrading of such principles to *jus cogens* further reinforced them, as it offered them protection against the risk of being nullified by any future treaty. In short, to socialist States, *jus cogens* was a political means of crystallizing once and for all the 'rules of the game' concerning peaceful coexistence between East and West. This concept stood out most clearly in the statements made at Vienna by Romania and Ukraine (which, curiously, were echoed by Mali).

[11] Anzilotti, op. cit., 202–3; and *Rivista di diritto internazionale* (1914), pp. 78–9. (See also Anzilotti's opinion in *Austro-German Customs* case, *PCIJ*, Series A/B 41, p. 64).

[12] L. Oppenheim, *International Law: A Treatise*, i (London, 1905), p. 528.

[13] See Vienna Conference on the Law of Treaties, *Official Records*, Ist Session, 53rd Mtg. of the Committee of the Whole, para. 9.

From the outset Western countries were on the defensive: some of them (for instance, France and Switzerland) immediately expressed strong doubts, while others—such as the Scandinavian countries and a number of others, including Italy, Greece, Spain, and Canada[14]—became aware of the need to bow to the will of the majority, either because of their strong humanitarian or legal tradition, or under the influence of national jurists who had supported the concept of *jus cogens*. In the event, Western countries, with the support of some Latin-American and Afro-Asian States, accepted the socialist and Third World initiative on condition that some mechanism for the determination of peremptory norms be set up. This mechanism was embedded in the ICJ. Article 66(a) provided for resort to the Court in the event of disputes on the actual content of *jus cogens* in specific instances. Thus, in late 1969 a very broad measure of consent was achieved on *jus cogens* (only France voted against the rule, but it appears that it subsequently came to accept the concept of peremptory norms as well).[14a] The agreement resulted not only from the adoption of Articles 53, 64 and 66, but also from the statements made in the Conference, and was borne out in later years by the declarations concerning specific peremptory norms made by a number of States in the UN. The view is therefore warranted that in that short space of time a *customary* norm evolved to the effect that certain rules of international law (created either by multilateral treaties or by custom) possess special legal force, that is the capacity to prohibit any contrary norms and to quash those made in spite of this prohibition.

Can we hold that the general rule on *jus cogens* embodies the reference to the ICJ's compulsory jurisdiction laid down in the Vienna Convention? Arguably, a negative answer must be given, because all Eastern-European countries, though often relying on the Vienna Convention (see § 103), have failed to ratify it, primarily on account of the clause on the Court's compulsory jurisdiction. In addition, at least one State, namely Tunisia, entered a reservation to Article 66(a) to the effect that the consent of all the parties concerned is necessary before a dispute on *jus cogens* can be submitted to the Court (however, the US, the UK, New Zealand, and Sweden objected to this reservation).

The *general* rule on *jus cogens* differs in another respect from that laid down in the Vienna Convention, for whereas the Convention confines itself to providing that peremptory norms render contrary treaties null and void,

[14] For all these declarations see ibid., 54th Mtg., paras 55–6; 56th Mtg., para. 70; 56th Mtg., para. 35; 54th Mtg., para. 41; IInd Session, 20th Plenary Mtg., paras 37–8.

[14a] This proposition should, however, be qualified. On 20 March 1986, at the end of the UN Conference on the Law of Treaties between States and International Organizations, France voted against the draft convention on the same subject and put on record that its negative vote was, among other things, motivated by its opposition to the two provisions (Articles 53 and 64) on *jus cogens*.

the general rule on the matter relates also to *customary* rules conflicting with peremptory norms (although of course it would be difficult for such customary rules to evolve).

By contrast, a fundamental element common to both rules is the fact that a peremptory norm can only take shape if the three main groupings of States consent to it. (It is in this sense that Ago authoritatively interpreted the formula of Article 53 of the Vienna Convention.)[15] This means that for a peremptory norm to be undisputably regarded as existent, at the very least the most important and representative States of the Western, socialist, and Third World areas must be in full agreement with each other.

It should be underscored that at the time of their proclamation, the provisions of the Vienna Convention on *jus cogens* aroused greater hopes, in some, and fiercer opposition and fear, in others, than was warranted by a realistic prospect of their application. This was rightly observed by an outstanding jurist, E. Jimenez de Arechaga, who, speaking as the representative of Uruguay at the Vienna Diplomatic Conference, said:

In supporting the principle [of *jus cogens*], care must be taken not to exaggerate its scope, either in a positive direction, by making of it a mystique that would breathe fresh life into international life, or in a negative direction, by seeing in it an element of the destruction of treaties and of anarchy ... It was in the nature of things that, in practice, that type of treaties [sc. contrary to *jus cogens*], a flagrant challenge to the international conscience, would be infrequent and that instances of treaties that would be null and void as the result of the application of that rule [on *jus cogens*] would be rare.[16]

The caution of the Uruguayan jurist is warranted, all the more so because peremptory norms suffer from the limitations inherent in the sources to which they owe their existence, namely custom and treaties. Like the rules generated by these two sources, peremptory norms bind States to the extent only that the latter have not staunchly and explicitly opposed them at the moment of their emergence (see §97). It follows that a State which has clearly and consistently expressed its dissent at the stage when a peremptory norm was taking shape, and has not changed its attitude subsequently, is not bound by the norm even if it comes to possess the overriding role proper to *jus cogens*. Such a State can make an agreement contrary to the peremptory norm with another State which also consistently objected to the norm, without the agreement becoming void. The ultimately *consensual* foundation of *jus cogens* clearly indicates the limitations of this class of norms (as well as of all international law-making). No doubt much headway has been made, in that a body of supreme or 'constitutional' principles has been created; however, they are not necessarily endowed with universal

---

[15] R. Ago, 'Droit des traités à la lumière de la Convention de Vienne', Hague *Recueil* 134 (1971-III), 297.
[16] Vienna Conference, *Official Records*, loc. cit., para. 48.

force, nor are they 'heteronomous' for, as stated before, they ultimately rest on the will of the members of the world community. However, two qualifications should be made. First, for a State other than a Great Power it is, in point of fact, difficult to oppose the formation of a peremptory norm: too many political, diplomatic, or psychological factors dissuade States from assuming a hostile attitude towards emerging principles which most other States consider to be fundamental. Second, it is a fact that the various peremptory norms that have evolved so far and on whose content and purport there is general agreement, have a universal scope, for no State objected to them at the moment of their formation. (It follows that, for example, South Africa is bound by the norm prohibiting racial discrimination, and Israel is similarly bound by the principle of self-determination of peoples.)

Interestingly, a Chinese international lawyer, Li Haopei, has recently argued in favour of a 'universalist' approach to *jus cogens*.[17] In his opinion this class of norms is provided for by a 'general principle of law recognized by civilised nations'; Article 53 of the Vienna Convention 'does nothing more than formally proclaim a general principle of law which has in fact existed for a long time'. Since for Li Haopei a 'general principle of law' is 'necessarily universal', it follows that peremptory norms are always universal. As he puts it, 'no States, including those not parties to the Convention, may reject [the] binding force [of a peremptory norm] on them by any statement or objection'.

Finally, it should be noted that considerable agreement has evolved among States to the effect that certain rules belong to *jus cogens*: the prohibitions of the use or threat of force (see §83), of genocide, slavery, of gross violations of the right of peoples to self-determination (§82), of racial discrimination.

PRESENT SOURCES OF INTERNATIONAL LAW
General

97. As I have already stated, treaties and custom are the two sources of international law. What I pointed out above (§93) when describing the main features of 'traditional' international law holds true also for the present stage of the world community—subject, however, to the qualifications relating to certain new trends that have come to light in recent years, and to which attention will be drawn in the next paragraphs.

It should be noted, first of all, that, characteristically, international rules do not define in detail the processes by which treaty and customary rules come into being. (As we all know, in the domestic legal order the position is quite different: there, constitutional and similar legal precepts normally regulate the complex procedures for legislating—they define the subjects and bodies called upon to make law, the various stages of the law-making

---

[17] Li Haopei, op. cit., 62–4.

process, and so on.) This is not accidental. States wished to be as free as possible in their dealings. Only recently, as a result of the need to codify, reshape, and develop traditional rules, did States agree to devote a whole treaty to the 'birth', 'life', and 'death' of international agreements. This was the 1969 Vienna Convention, referred to above.

Second, custom has substantially maintained its largely 'consensual' features. As the ICJ pointed out in the *Fisheries* case,[18] any State which consistently and explicitly opposes a customary rule *in statu nascendi* (at the moment of its formation), and subsequently does not discontinue its opposition, is not bound by the rule. As the world community still lacks a superior authority, no law-making body capable of enacting 'heteronomous' legal precepts exists.

Third, since treaties and custom are on the same footing, it follows that the relations between rules generated by the two sources are governed by those general principles which in all legal orders govern the relations between norms deriving from the *same* source: *lex posterior derogat priori* (a later law repeals an earlier law), *lex posterior generalis non derogat priori speciali* (a later law, general in character, does not derogate from an earlier law which is special in character), and *lex specialis derogat generali* (a special law prevails over a general law). Furthermore, both categories of norms can regulate any subject matter and in any manner be decided upon by the parties concerned: the only limitation derives from peremptory rules or *jus cogens*; they place a clear restraint on the otherwise unbridled freedom of States.

Custom

General

98. Article 38.1(b) of the Statute of the ICJ lists among the sources of law upon which the Court can draw 'international custom, as evidence of a general practice accepted as law'. This is the most authoritative definition, although it has been questioned by a number of scholars. It also reflects the widely held view that custom is made up of two elements: general practice, or *usus*, and the conviction that such practice reflects (or is imposed by, or amounts to) law. Of course, the two elements need not be present from the outset. Usually, a practice evolves among certain States under the impulse of economic, political, or military demands. If it does not encounter the strong and consistent opposition of other States but is

[18] ICJ *Reports* (1951), p. 131. See also the separate opinion of Judge Gros on the *Nuclear Tests* case, ICJ *Reports* (1974), pp. 286-9. On the role of the 'persistent' and 'subsequent' 'objector', see the authoritative view of I. Brownlie, *Principles of Public International Law*, 3rd edn. (Oxford, 1979), 10-11 (who places a different interpretation on the famous *dictum* in the *Fisheries* case from the one upheld here).

increasingly accepted, or acquiesced in, it is gradually attended by the view that it is dictated by international law—in other words, States begin to believe that they must conform to the practice not so much or not only out of economic, political, or military considerations, but because they are enjoined to do so by an international rule. At that moment—difficult to pinpoint exactly, since it is the result of a continuous process—a customary rule may be said to have evolved.

Present Crisis of Custom

99. Since the Second World War custom has increasingly lost ground in two respects: existing customary rules have been eroded more and more by fresh practices, and resort to custom to regulate new matters has been relatively rare. These developments are largely due to the growing asser- tiveness of socialist countries and the massive presence of Third World States on the international arena. Both groups have insisted on the need radically to revise old customary rules, which appeared to them to be the distillation of traditional Western values; indeed, custom has come to repre- sent the quintessence of the outlook they oppose. Legal change has been demanded. Custom is not the most suitable instrument for achieving legal change. The insecurity inherent in its unwritten character and its protracted process of development rendered it disadvantageous to the Third World. As we shall see (§ 106), treaty-making, by contrast, exhibited a number of merits. The majority of States accordingly turned to codification and pro- gressive development of international law through treaties.

A second general reason why custom has been demoted is that the world community's membership is far larger than in the heyday of international customary law (in the space of one hundred years it has risen from 40 to 170) and, even more important, it is deeply divided economically, politi- cally, and ideologically. It has, therefore, become extremely difficult for general rules to receive the support of the bulk of such a large number of very diverse States. By the same token, it nowadays proves exceedingly difficult to ascertain whether a new rule has emerged, for it is not always possible to get hold of the huge body of evidence required.

Current Role of Custom

100. Custom, however, is far from being on the wane everywhere. There are at least three areas where it plays a significant role, and is indeed acquiring growing importance. First, in emerging economic interests such as, for example, the law of the sea. There, the rapid growth of new economic demands often cannot be as rapidly co-ordinated and regulated by treaties on account of numerous conflicts between groups of States and the com- plexity of all the closely interrelated matters to be taken into account. By contrast, solutions of specific issues propounded by one or more States happen eventually to meet the interests and needs of others and thus bring about the gradual appearance of customary rules. Typical illustrations of such newly emerged norms are those on the continental shelf, whereby each coastal State has exclusive jurisdiction over the natural resources of the subsoil and the sea-bed of the continental shelf beneath the high seas but contiguous to its coast, and the very recent one on the exclusive economic zone, whereby States have the exclusive power to exploit fishing and natural resources in a zone reaching out as far as 200 miles from their coasts.

Second, there is the area of fundamentals, where newly emerged needs in the international community give rise to conflicts between groups of States, and it therefore proves extremely difficult to achieve regulation via treaty rules. The only option open to States is, therefore, to engage in a complex negotiating process for the purpose not of bringing about legally binding rules but rather of delimiting areas of broad consent. In this field a major contribution is offered by the UN, where States are able to exchange and, where possible, wed their views to arrive at some form of compromise with other groups. Within UN representative bodies, chiefly the General Assembly, as well as in other international forums, general consent on the least common denominator is often evolved: the majority of States eventually succeed in overcoming opposition of individual States, and in achieving general standards of behaviour. The latter come to constitute the normative nucleus forming the basis for subsequent practice as well as the drafting of treaties. In other words, those general standards of behaviour represent a sort of bridge between the previous normative vacuum and the future detailed regulation afforded by treaty-making. They provide basic guidelines; the treaty provisions which usually follow in time provide the nuts and bolts, as it were—the technicalities calculated to bind international standards together and make them more detailed—besides setting up the necessary techniques of supervision.

Examples of customary rules evolved in this area in the last two decades are: the fundamental principles governing international relations (see §§ 77–90) and the norms prohibiting racial discrimination (§ 183) and torture (§ 184).

A third area where custom is relatively thriving is the updating and elaboration of those parts of the body of customary law which have been considered more or less acceptable by newly independent States, although in need of some revision and clarification. Illustrations of this broad area are several rules on warfare and on the law of treaties. Here, the updating has been carried out by means of codification and 'progressive development'. However, the codificatory treaties have often embodied provisions possessing a legal value going beyond that of conventional undertakings; in other words, by a process that I shall presently focus upon, certain parts of traditional law have been supplemented and elaborated upon by conventional rules carrying the imprint of general rules in spite of their being consecrated in treaties.

101. An interesting feature of the present stage of development of the world community is the fact that customary international law develops on the margin, as it were, of diplomatic conferences set up to codify and progressively develop international law. This is a striking instance of how general law is formed and is therefore worth emphasizing.

As will be pointed out below (§ 106), there is an increasing tendency today for States to enter into multilateral treaties for the purpose of restating, clarifying, and progressively developing rules of customary law. The making of such treaties provides States with an opportunity for crystallizing emergent rules of customary law, or for agreeing upon how to develop, supplement, and improve existing law; and international diplomatic conferences serve as catalysts for the formation of new custom. As a consequence, a number of the provisions of the treaties hammered out at the conferences acquire a twofold legal status: they lay down both conventional undertakings and also general commitments which are binding upon all States (except of course for those which do not participate in the law-making process or express drastic dissent).

There are four basic processes through which general law comes into being on the occasion of, or as a result of, international conferences. (1) States agree to develop and supplement existing customary rules, and in so doing they lay down rules eventually affecting the whole corpus of general law. Examples can be taken from the various rules that emerged in the 1974-7 Geneva Diplomatic Conference on the updating of the laws of warfare and include: the provision defining 'military' and 'civilian' objectives (§ 156); the rules of Article 59 on 'non-defended localities' (§§ 148 and 156). Another significant instance is Article 62 of the Vienna Convention on the Law of Treaties (concerning the 'fundamental change of circumstances') (§ 105). In the process of rediscussion and remodelling of traditional law, States need both to reaffirm old rules which prove to be vital and acceptable to all groups, and at the same time to update, develop, and elaborate upon old rules in such a way as to render them equally binding on all States. It would be incongruous if only the old rules were to possess binding effect on the whole world community, while their updating in international gatherings were to take effect for ratifying States alone. In fact, very often the reaffirmation of the old law goes hand in hand with its development; it is therefore only logical for States to take the view that they are equally bound by the whole corpus of rules. (2) In international diplomatic conferences States crystallize incipient rules of customary law, thereby lending such rules the concreteness and incisiveness they previously lacked. Before the diplomatic conference, international practice was not consistent, the views of States differed, and doubts on the purport of the nascent rules existed. Once the diplomatic conference agrees upon the exact content of the relevant prescriptions, the rule 'solidifies' and at the same time acquires a general value transcending the contractual bonds laid down in the treaty elaborated by the conference. Examples can be drawn from the 1974-7 Geneva Diplomatic Conference referred to above: Article 1.4 of Protocol I, equating wars of national liberation with 'international armed conflicts' (see §161) and Art. 44.3 of the same Protocol laying down the requirements guerilla fighters need to meet to be considered lawful belligerents (see §153). Mention can also be made of the rules on the continental shelf adopted at the 1958 Conference on the Law of the Sea (see §218). The Conference crystallized an incipient rule which upheld and defined the criterion of exploitability for the measurement of the seaward extension of the shelf and so served to consolidate an emergent rule whilst at the same time acting as a catalyst for the creation of an important element pertaining to the definition of the shelf. (3) States agree upon new rules in areas where international practice does not exist or is fragmentary and contradictory. In the course of negotiations there evolves, both among the negotiating States and in the world community at large, the legal conviction that the rules thus elaborated are binding upon any State, irrespective of the ratification of the treaty; as an illustration we can take the rule whereby the territorial sea of States has a maximum breadth of 12 miles, laid down in Article 3 of the 1982 Convention on the law of the sea (cf. §25), as well as the rule on the width of the exclusive economic zone, laid down in Article 57 of the same Convention (see §218). (4) States work out treaty rules which before or after the treaty comes into force, gradually generate corresponding rules of customary law which are binding upon all member States of the international community. Important illustrations of this process are Article 3 common to the four 1949 Conventions on war victims (see §164) as well as the rules on *jus cogens* of the Vienna Convention on the Law of Treaties (see §96).

The main factor currently underlying this norm-creating process is that at present the three principal segments of the world community have to get together and agree upon standards of behaviour acceptable to all. Diplomatic conferences open to all States have therefore become a necessity. Within them States endeavour to elaborate or reshape rules governing international relations in such a way as to accommodate the basic demands of all the major alignments. The necessity to renegotiate the fundamentals of various issues (the law of treaties, the law of the sea, the law of warfare, and so forth) prompts States to achieve agreement on major areas in a complex process of bargaining and bartering. Very often the major points where an equilibrium between conflicting demands is established are so important that they form the subject of general consent. States cannot afford to leave major points of agreement in the form of treaty regulations with the consequence that any State would be free to evade the treaty regulation merely by withholding ratification. This would entail a lack of general standards in crucial areas of international relations. There are, therefore, compelling reasons for States to bestow the imprint of *general* rules upon those standards of behaviour.

In sum, agreement upon general norms by dint of multilateral negotiation in international forums is a fundamental necessity for the world community. Its very division into different and often conflicting groups of States renders it necessary for them to make an effort to co-operate and contrive generally acceptable rules of conduct within gatherings where all the geo-political areas are represented. The norm-creating effect of nineteenth-century treaties was based on unequal relationships between hegemonic and minor States; the custom-creating process of the present century bears a potentially democratic hallmark, in that it involves practically all States.

Treaties

General

102. The most frequent means of creating international rules is the conclusion of agreements. They are also called treaties, conventions, protocols, covenants, 'acts', and so on. The terminology varies but the substance is the same: they all denote a merger of the wills of two or more international subjects for the purpose of regulating their interests by international rules.

States and other international entities enjoy full freedom as regards the modalities and form of agreement, for there are no rules *prescribing* any definite procedure or formality. However, over the years two main classes of treaty—bilateral and multilateral—have evolved in State practice.

First, treaties concluded in 'a solemn form'. They are negotiated by plenipotentiaries (that is, diplomats endowed with 'full powers' to engage in negotiations) of the contracting States. Once a written text is agreed upon, it is signed (or initialled and subsequently signed) by the diplomats and then submitted to the respective national authorities for ratification. Usually modern constitutions require the intervention of the legislature before the head of State—or some other prominent State agency—signs the instrument of ratification. ('Ratification' does not mean endorsement or confirmation of the State's will to be bound by the treaty. Until the instrument of ratification is drawn up, signed and exchanged with the other parties, or deposited with one of them, or with an international organization, the State is not formally bound by the treaty, although it must refrain from acting in such a way as to stultify the object and purpose of the treaty.)

Second, treaties concluded 'in simplified form' (also called 'executive agreements'). They are normally negotiated by diplomats, but become legally binding as soon as they have been signed either by the negotiators themselves or by the Foreign Ministers of the contracting parties. Sometimes they take the form of an exchange of notes between the Foreign Minister of a given State and the ambassador of another State accredited to the former. This class of agreement does not call for ratification by the Head of State, and consequently does not involve parliaments in their elaboration. The reasons behind their appearance are self-evident: they are the need to regulate urgent matters by procedures which have the merit of being expeditious, and the advantage of bypassing national legislatures in areas where the Executive prefers to preserve a certain flexibility and latitude of power.

The 'Old' and the 'New' Law

103. As mentioned above, the formation, the 'life' and the 'death' of treaties is currently regulated by an all-important agreement, the 1969 Vienna Convention on the Law of Treaties, which greatly modifies existing law. To show how international law has evolved, and under the impulse of what demands, a short account of the international law of treaties of the classical period (1674-1918) will be given below (§ 104), contrasted with a brief summary of the present law in force (§ 105).

Emphasis should, however, be laid on the fact that the 'old' law has not been completely superseded by the 'new'. First of all, the Convention itself, in Article 4, lays down that 'it applies only to treaties which are concluded by States after the entry into force of the present Convention with regard to such States'. It follows that treaties made before that date are still governed by the 'old' law. Second, not all members of the world community have become parties to the Convention: thus, as pointed out above (§ 96), so far no Eastern European country has ratified it,[18a] although they frequently invoke certain of its provisions as reflecting customary law (see, for instance, the Soviet memorandum of 31 March 1983 on chemical weapons);[19] it follows that treaties made by Eastern European countries are governed by the Convention to the extent only that it is declaratory of customary law.

The exposition below is therefore of both historical and legal relevance.

[18a] However, reliable sources report that in mid-1986 the Soviet Union ratified the convention, but appended a reservation concerning Art. 66(a) on the competence of the ICJ to pass upon matters relating to *jus cogens*.

[19] UN document A/38/131, 31 March 1983. In this document the Soviet Union objected to General Assembly resolution 37/98D, which among other things provided 'for the establishment of procedures for verifying observance' of the 1925 Geneva Protocol on chemical weapons. In the view of the USSR, this provision entailed 'an increase in the scope of obligations assumed by States parties to the Protocol' by a process (the adoption of a resolution without the support of all the parties to the Geneva Protocol) not allowed by international law; as the Soviet document put it: 'such a practice of amending agreements is in blatant contradiction to the 1969 Vienna Convention on the Law of Treaties, particularly its Article 39, which permits the amendment of treaties only by agreement between the parties' (doc. cit., p. 3).

The 'Old' Law

104. The 'old' law upheld the principle of States' freedom in the field of treaty-making. This sort of regulation ultimately played into the hands of stronger States, as is apparent from a survey of a few of the major features of the body of rules governing the matter:

(1) *Conclusion of treaties.* Legally all States were put on an equal footing, despite obvious inequalities. The law also turned a blind eye to possible coercion of stronger States over weaker ones. Thus duress—economic, political, or military coercion exerted by one State over another to compel it to enter into a given agreement—was not considered to invalidate a treaty. Similarly, corruption of the State officials negotiating or, more generally, concluding a treaty did not render it null and void. The only grounds of invalidity were minor ones: using force or intimidation against the State representative making the treaty; inducing the other party through misrepresentation to enter into an agreement (for example, the conclusion of a boundary treaty based on a map fraudulently manipulated by one of the parties); the slipping in of errors as to facts (for example, an incorrect map, in the case of a boundary treaty). The fact that there are few examples is ample proof of the relative irrelevance of these grounds of invalidity.

(2) *Participation in treaties.* Traditionally, when a State participating in the negotiations for a multilateral treaty found that some of its clauses were too onerous but none the less wished to enter into the treaty, it made 'reservations' to it for the purpose either of excluding the application of one or more provisions, or of placing a certain interpretation on them. Reservations, however, had to be accepted by *all* other contracting parties for the reserving State to become bound by the treaty. The principle of unanimity favoured the 'integrity' of treaties, but in practice it gave a sort of right of veto to all other contracting States. Consequently broad participation in multilateral treaties was *de facto* discouraged. This proved totally inadequate when membership in the international community increased and the newcomers belonged to political, economic, and cultural areas different from those of Western Christian countries.

(3) *Contents of treaties.* No rules placed restrictions on the freedom of States as to the object of treaties. States were therefore allowed to regulate their own interests as they thought best, and even to agree upon offences or attacks upon other States or on the partition of their territory. A few jurists took the view that treaties at variance with certain basic general rules were invalid (see § 96) but these and other similar views, however, were not supported by State practice. No case was ever brought where a State challenged the validity of a treaty for the alleged inconsistency of its contents with international principles.

(4)   *Interpretation.* As was rightly pointed out by Anzilotti as early as 1912,[20] there were no binding rules on the matter. The criteria for construing treaty law were merely 'rules of logic', borrowed from national law or developed by arbitral courts, or 'those very general criteria which could be inferred from the nature and character of the [international] legal order'. The adverse consequences of the lack of legally binding rules in such a delicate area are self-evident; furthermore, it proved ultimately to be to the advantage of bigger States. It is hardly surprising that one of the few maxims on interpretation which evolved in this period stemmed directly from the structure of the world community and the overriding principle of States' freedom: the criterion whereby international obligations should be so construed as to place fewer curtailments on States (*in dubio mitius*: if in doubt, the least unfavourable interpretation to the subject of an obligation must be chosen, or, in other words, limitations of sovereignty were to be strictly construed).

(5)   *Termination of treaties.* To an even greater extent than the 'birth' and life of treaties, their 'death' was regulated by a handful of rules containing numerous loopholes. This explains the scepticism expressed as early as the eighteenth century by Frederick the Second of Prussia on the weight of treaties in relation to State interests (which in his view must always prevail in the final analysis),[21] as well as the following comments made by Bismarck, in 1879:

Observance of treaties between Big States is relative indeed, as soon as it is put to the test 'in the struggle for existence'. No big nation will be prompted to sacrifice its existence on the altar of fidelity to a treaty, if obliged to choose between the two. The [maxim] *ultra posse nemo obligatur* [no one is bound beyond what he can do] cannot be invalidated by any treaty clause. Similarly one cannot ensure by treaty the measure of earnestness and employment of force necessary for treaty compliance, as soon as the interests of the party which is to fulfil the treaty no longer support the undersigned text and its previous interpretation.[22]

More specifically, it was not clear under what circumstances the material breach of treaty provisions authorized the other contracting party to consider itself released from the treaty obligations. Similarly, it was unclear whether the outbreak of war between two contracting States terminated all treaties between them or whether it left some of them unaffected. The import of the clause *rebus sic stantibus* (whereby a change in the basic conditions underlying the making of a treaty could terminate it) was also

---

[20]   Anzilotti, op. cit., 103, 104.

[21]   Frédéric II, 'Histoire de mon temps. Avant-propos', in *Oeuvres posthumes de Frédéric II, roi de Prusse*, i (Berlin, 1788), pp. 11, 14.

[22]   Otto Fürst von Bismarck-Schönhauser, *Gedanken und Erinnerungen*, ii (Stuttgart and Berlin, 1924), p. 287.

confused, for international practice on the matter was not conclusive. The most widely accepted mode of terminating treaties consisted of the denunciation by one of the contracting parties. However, even in this field it was questionable if and under what circumstances a State could denounce a treaty when the right of denunciation was not provided for in the treaty itself.

The 'New' Law

105. Under strong pressure from socialist and Third World countries momentous changes were introduced, and to a large extent 'codified', in the 1969 Vienna Convention.

Two observations are apposite here, one concerning the formal aspects of the law enacted through the Convention, the other regarding the political and ideological concepts underlying it.

As for the status of the Convention, it was pointed out in § 103 (see also § 101), that only some of its provisions attest to existing customary law, or have given rise to rules belonging to the corpus of general law; consequently, those which do not will retain their status of treaty stipulations as long as they do not pass into the body of customary rules. It follows that, for the time being, the Convention as a whole does not yet constitute general international law. Nevertheless, it seems most likely that, as the 'old' law withers away, the 'new' one, destined gradually to replace it, will evolve along the lines set forth in the Convention. To put it differently, it is extremely improbable that future customary rules will be markedly different from the provisions of the Convention. The latter is therefore endowed with great significance, even in those areas where it only appears to be potential customary law.

Let us now ask ourselves about the 'political' or ideological philosophy underlying the main innovations of the Convention.

Three principles inspire the bulk of the text. First, it introduces restriction of the previously unfettered freedom of States. States are no longer free to do whatever they wish but must respect a central core of international values from which no country, however great its economic and military strength, may deviate. Second, there is a democratization of international legal relations. While the previous oligarchical structure allowed Great Powers formally to impose treaties upon lesser States, this is no longer permitted. Moreover all States can now participate in treaties without being hampered by the fact that a few contracting parties can exercise a right of veto. Third, the Convention enhances international values as opposed to national claims. Thus the interpretation of treaties must now emphasize their potential rather than give pride of place to States' sovereignty.

We may now turn to certain novelties introduced by the Vienna Convention which deserve special attention:

(1) *Conclusion of treaties.* A major cause of injustice in the making of treaties—coercion exercised by a powerful State—was regarded as making the treaty null and void. Thus Article 52 of the Convention covers coercion by the threat or use of military force, while a Declaration adopted by the Vienna Diplomatic Conference calls upon States to refrain from economic and political coercion as well—so laying the foundations for the gradual emergence of a customary rule on the matter. In addition, Article 50 stipulated that corruption of a State representative of one of the negotiating parties was a cause of invalidity. Furthermore, significant clarification was provided as regards error (Article 48), fraud (Article 49) and use of coercion against the State representatives negotiating the treaty (Article 51).

What is very significant and marks a momentous advance in the field of the law of treaties, is the distinction drawn in the Convention between 'absolute' and 'relative' grounds of invalidity. The former (coercion against a State representative, coercion against the State as a whole, incompatibility with *jus cogens*) imply: that any State party to the treaty (that is, not merely the State which has suffered from possible coercion or which might be prejudiced by actions contrary to a peremptory rule) can invoke the invalidity of the treaty; that a treaty cannot be divided into valid and invalid clauses, but stands or falls as a whole (Article 44.5); and that possible acquiescence does not render the treaty valid (Article 45). The distinction between the two classes of grounds of invalidity is of great importance, for it points to an area of values which the international community has upgraded by establishing specific regulation: the use of force as well as any behaviour inconsistent with a peremptory rule have been condemned in such a way as to render treaties concluded by resorting to either of them particularly vulnerable.

(2) *Participation in treaties.* The very liberal doctrine of 'universality of treaties' was upheld in the field of reservations. Thus, a regime was envisaged whereby States can formulate reservations, unless they are expressly prohibited by the treaty or prove incompatible with its object and purpose; the treaty comes into force between the reserving State and the other parties, unless the latter have objected to the reservation, in which case the entry into force of the treaty may be precluded as between the objecting and the reserving State (Articles 19–23). This legal regime which can, no doubt, impair the integrity of multilateral treaties (they end up being split into a series of bilateral agreements) has, however, the great merit of allowing as many States as possible to take part in treaties which include provisions unacceptable to some of them.

(3) *Contents of treaties.* The fundamental upholding of *jus cogens* (§ 96) in Articles 53, 64, and 71 for the first time introduced major restraints on

States' freedom for the sake of safeguarding certain basic values which have now become paramount in the international community.

(4) *Interpretation*. This tricky area received a balanced and satisfactory regulation in Articles 31-3. Although some important questions, such as intertemporal interpretation, were left out, the rules on construction upheld the most advanced views. Basically the Convention gave pride of place to literal, systematic, and teleological interpretation. Thus, great weight was attributed to the purpose pursued by contracting parties and, by implication, to the principle of 'effectiveness' (*ut res magis valeat quam pereat*), whereby a treaty must be given an interpretation which enables its provisions to be 'effective and useful', that is to have the appropriate effect. This principle is plainly intended to expand the normative scope of treaties, to the detriment of the old principle whereby in case of doubt limitations of sovereignty were to be strictly interpreted.

(5) *Termination*. One of the major advances in this area was the clarification of the concept of 'material breach' justifying the termination of a treaty. Thus, under Article 60.3 such a breach consists in '(*a*) a repudiation of the treaty not sanctioned by the present Convention; or (*b*) the violation of a provision essential to the accomplishment of the object or purpose of the treaty'. Furthermore, the clause *rebus sic stantibus* was restated, clarified, and elaborated upon. In particular two exceptions to its operation were enunciated (under Article 62.2 the clause cannot be invoked '(a) if the treaty establishes a boundary; (b) if the fundamental change is the result of a breach, by the party invoking it, either of an obligation under the treaty or of any other international obligation owed to any other party to the treaty'). *Jus cogens* was called into play for the termination of treaties as well. Under Article 64 'if a new peremptory norm of general international law emerges, any existing treaty which is in conflict with that norm becomes void and terminates'. Besides, the Convention spelled out a cardinal principle, namely that, except for what is stipulated by Article 64, the various causes of termination do not make treaties come to an end automatically but can only be invoked by one of the parties as a ground for discontinuing the treaty. It was also provided that, in addition to authorizing a party to claim that a treaty should cease, the above clauses could have a more limited effect too; that is to say they could authorize a party to claim the mere suspension of the treaty.

Codification

106. As pointed out above (§§ 66, 72-3), the vast majority of the international community, especially socialist and developing countries, infinitely prefers treaties to custom. Western States too, though previously very attached to custom, currently show a tendency to opt for treaty-making

(§62). This can be easily understood if one bears in mind that they now form a minority in the international community and are therefore interested in negotiating with the majority any revision or updating of the old law, or any regulation governing new situations.

This general convergence of interest accounts for the expanding role of codification and progressive development of law through international agreements and conventions.

So far, two major channels have been used to this end. In the more traditional and classical areas of codification (law of the sea; diplomatic and consular immunities; law of treaties; State succession; State responsibility) draft treaties have been elaborated by the International Law Commission (made up of forty-two experts with great diplomatic experience, and, therefore, particularly sensitive to States' demands) and subsequently discussed by the Sixth Committee of the General Assembly; they were subsequently the subject of negotiation in diplomatic conferences. In other, or even in the same, areas when existing law was more in need of radical change, or major differences persisted, the technical co-operation of the ILC was shunned: States preferred to keep the discussion and negotiation under their direct control; accordingly, a Special Committee consisting of their representatives was set up to report to the General Assembly. In some instances where the matter was too controversial for a detailed agreement to be reached, the upshot was the adoption of a Declaration (such as the 1970 Declaration on Friendly Relations). In other cases the General Assembly, after taking account of the discussions in the Special Committee, referred the matter to a diplomatic Conference. An important illustration of this process is the laborious work carried out from 1973 to 1982 on the new law of the sea. In 1958, when four Conventions on the matter were adopted, the main purpose was to restate, codify, and update existing law, and consequently the co-operation of the ILC proved indispensable. By contrast, in the 1970s the main object was to change the law radically; to this end direct negotiation among States was regarded as a more suitable method.

The Role of General Assembly Resolutions in Law-making

107. I stressed above (§95) that owing to the opposition of Western and socialist States, the tentative endeavour made in the 1960s by developing countries to turn General Assembly resolutions into legally binding acts ended in failure. Resolutions are therefore still governed by the UN Charter provisions, which grant the Assembly and other bodies (except, of course, for the Security Council) hortatory powers only. And, indeed, most General Assembly resolutions produce very limited effects because, in addition to the intrinsic limitations deriving from the Charter, their very contents and the sort of majority behind them frequently result in their carrying little weight. As was said in 1983 by a prominent representative of Jordan, 'UN resolutions are unfortunately seldom landmarks in history; they are more often mere "footprints in the sands of time" '.[23] Nevertheless, some resolutions can be fitted into either of the traditional law-making processes: treaty-making or custom.

I have already given a few illustrations of UN resolutions which accelerated or at least testify to the formation of customary international law (see § 77 on the UN Declaration on Friendly Relations of 1970). Other illustrations include: the turning of wars of national liberation into a special category of international armed conflicts, as distinct from civil wars (§ 161); the gradual transformation of mercenaries into war criminals, in derogation from the traditional standards of international law (the long process of General Assembly resolutions on this subject was compounded by the adoption of a provision on the matter in 1977, in the Geneva Diplomatic Conference on Humanitarian Law: Article 47 of Protocol I (§ 154)). It stands to reason that the unique opportunity afforded by the UN for practically all members of the world community to get together and exchange their views cannot fail to have had a strong impact on the emergence or reshaping of customary rules. In addition, the UN encourages States to develop their views on matters on which they are often called upon to comment. This again ensures that a host of pronouncements are collected which would otherwise only be obtainable with difficulty.

In some instances General Assembly resolutions can also be tantamount to interstate agreements, more specifically to agreements concluded 'in simplified form' (§ 102). This, of course, depends on the intention of the States supporting the resolutions, and can emerge from their declarations as well as from the tenor of the text adopted. It stands to reason that the 'resolution-agreement' only binds those States which voted for it, or at any rate did not voice their opposition explicitly.

The view that, except for a few well-defined cases, resolutions do not possess a legally binding value *per se* is by far the most widespread in the Western legal literature. The same view is also upheld, to a very large extent, by the jurists of Eastern European countries,[24] and is also reflected in the official attitude of those countries (see, for instance, the Soviet Memorandum to the ICJ for the *UN Expenses* case).[25] Some international lawyers from the Third World also tend to regard UN resolutions as devoid *per se* of binding force, although they strongly emphasize the importance that resolutions can acquire in many respects with regard to the customary

---

[23] See, the Declaration of the Prince of Jordan, Hassan Bin Tallal, to the 'Independent Commission on International Humanitarian Issues' (Geneva), p. 3.

[24] The view of socialist jurists on the legal value of recommendations is set out in Tunkin, 162–76. See also DDR-*Völkerrecht* 1982, i. 206–8.

[25] The Soviet memorandum is in ICJ *Reports* (1962), pp. 270–4 (see also pp. 397–412).

process, or even from the viewpoint of treaty-making. For instance, this stand has been taken, with variations, by the Mexican Castañeda,[26] the Egyptian Abi-Saab[27] and the Chinese Wang Tieya.[28] Wang Tieya recently observed:

In some instance, General Assembly resolutions—particularly the declaratory documents therein—may specify and systematize rules of customary law and they may reflect or even reaffirm and develop existing principles and rules of international law. If such declaratory documents creatively clarify new principles and rules of international law, no one would be able to deny their law-making effect just because they are, strictly speaking, not legally binding. At least they have been approved by the majority of countries and represent their legal consciousness, thus clearly pointing to the direction in which international law is developing.

Some of the Third World jurists go so far as to contend that the 'cumulative effect' of resolutions may prove sufficient for the creation of new law. A contrary view has recently been propounded by the distinguished Argentinian jurist Barberis,[29] in whose opinion for a rule of customary law to come about or for it to undergo a legal change it is always necessary that the passing of resolutions be attended by the *actual practice* of States.

Interestingly, many a developing State steadfastly argues in the UN that General Assembly resolutions are binding *per se*. Suffice it to quote the statement made in 1982 by the delegate of Zaire in the Security Council, in the course of the debate on the South African raid in Lesotho:

There is not the shadow of a doubt that all decisions of the UN, through the GA, the SC and all the other bodies which in one way or another deal with the situation in South Africa, in particular, and in southern Africa, in general, are binding on all Member States of the UN. Under other circumstances I have had the opportunity of recalling that UN decisions and resolutions which are in keeping with the principles and purposes of the UN are binding on all Members of the UN whatever position they may have taken on a particular resolution. If that were not recognized, then it would mean that any Member could disown the mission, the goals and the objectives of this universal Organization.

As for the way of assessing the possible impact of resolutions on customary or treaty law, the most appropriate and sensible criteria have been suggested by Abi-Saab:

Three indices can help us gauge the real value or weight of the contents of a resolution beyond its formal status as a recommendation and chart its progress

[26] J. Castañeda, 'La valeur juridique des résolutions des Nations Unies', Hague *Recueil* 129 (1970-I), 211 ff.
[27] G. Abi-Saab, 'The Newly Independent States and the Rules of International Law: An Outline', *Howard Law Journal* 8 (1962), 109-10.
[28] Wang Tieya, 'The Third World and International Law', *ChYIL*, pp. 23-4.
[29] A. Barberis, 'Nouvelles questions concernant la personnalité juridique internationale', Hague *Recueil* 179 (1983-I), 252-3.

towards becoming part of the *corpus juris* of international law. The first refers to the circumstances surrounding the adoption of the resolution, and in particular the degree of consensus obtaining over its contents. The second is the degree of concreteness of these contents, and whether they are specific enough (by themselves or in addition to those of prior related resolutions) to become operational as law, i.e. identifiable prescribed behaviour. The third is the existence (and effectiveness) of follow-up mechanisms generating a continuous pressure for compliance.[30]

Consensus as a Means of Facilitating Agreement within International Organizations and Diplomatic Conferences in an Age of Deep Divisions

108. In the early 1960s, it became apparent that developing States mustered a broad majority within the UN and that, by siding with socialist countries, they could easily command a two-thirds majority. Consequently, they were in a position to pass resolutions to their liking, overcoming any possible opposition from the West. However, the Third World soon became aware that scoring such easy victories would be self-defeating. It was evident that in consistently losing the support of a powerful segment of the international community they would alienate it for good and doom any international action to failure. Socialist countries too were reluctant to be impelled to make a show of strength with Western States, lest the latter should impair the process of *détente* initiated in the early 1960s—a process the former intended to pursue and even step up. Western countries, on their part, were eager to co-operate for fear of remaining isolated. Thus, a new device gradually evolved in the UN for narrowing down differences and reaching solutions acceptable to everybody—that of the consensus procedure.

After being frequently resorted to both in the UN and in other organizations, as well as in diplomatic conferences, consensus was defined in one of the rules of procedure adopted in 1973 by the European Conference on Security and Co-operation. Rule 69 stipulated that 'Consensus shall be understood to mean the absence of any objection expressed by a Representative and submitted by him as constituting an obstacle to the taking of the decision in question'. A similar definition was included in the Rules of the 1974 World Population Conference, whereby consensus was 'understood to mean, according to UN practice, general agreement without vote, but not necessarily unanimity'. Reference to consensus was also made in subsequent instruments, among which was a famous 'gentleman's agreement' adopted by the Third UN Conference on the Law of the Sea, in 1974.

Consensus therefore denotes a negotiating and decision-making tech-

---

[30] G. Abi-Saab, *Analytical Study on Progressive Development of the Principles and Norms of International Law Relating to the New International Economic Order*, A/39/504/Add.1, 1984, 36-7.

nique, consisting of a collective effort to agree upon a text by reconciling different views and smoothing out difficulties. This process culminates in the adoption without vote of a text basically acceptable to everybody. Consensus is different from *unanimity*, for in the latter case there exists full agreement on a given text and in addition the general consent is underscored by a vote. Consensus is also different from *acclamation*, for although normally texts approved by acclamation are not voted on (as in the case of consensus), they are, however, the subject of unqualified agreement. Often 'reservations' and objections are expressed either before or after it is declared that a consensus decision has been taken. What distinguishes consensus from the usual adoption of decisions by a *majority vote* is that, in the case of consensus, possible 'reservations' do not affect major points of the decision (whereas when there is a split between States favourable, those opposing, and those abstaining, the States casting a negative vote or abstaining usually entertain and express basic differences with the States supporting the text). Moreover, as a consequence of the lack of fundamental divergencies, and with a view to emphasizing the existence of a substantial convergence of views, no vote is taken.

The political and ideological premises on which the consensus procedure rests are clear: first, the fact that at present the world community is deeply divided in many respects; and second, the desire of the various groups of States to refrain from widening the gaps by resorting to traditional methods which under the present circumstances would produce ineffective international 'legislation', valid only for the majority of weak States. Consensus is therefore a decision-making process characteristic of the present stage of development in the world community.

The advantages of the new technique are self-evident: it implies that the prospective minority becomes involved in the process and can therefore see to it that its interests and concerns are safeguarded; it fosters negotiation and compromise; and it means that neither the overpowering (but only rhetorical) force of the many, nor the veto of the few powerful States, are made use of. This in turn increases the chance of resolutions being implemented and of conventions being ratified and observed by a large number of States. The drawbacks of consensus are no less evident, however: divergent views are often ironed out only on paper, by dint of vague compromise formulas which each of the draftsmen subsequently interprets in his own way; international instruments become tainted with ambiguity; and negotiations tend to get bogged down in interminable discussions and trade-offs, because each State or group feels that the more it holds out, the more likely is its counterpart to abandon its initial bargaining position and make substantial concessions. In addition, no benefit derives to the interpreter from preparatory work, for consensus is usually reached through informal consultations, of which no record is taken.

Generally speaking, it can be said that consensus proves beneficial provided the decision reached is not couched in such equivocal terms that it
represents only a means of papering over real differences. Whenever such
a stage is reached, the States concerned would do better to choose the more
clear-cut and straightforward position of calling for a vote, and thus determine exactly where the majority and the minority stand. It should be noted
that no formal difficulty stands in the way of such an option. Under the
rules of procedure of most international bodies or conferences, whenever a
State wishes a vote to be taken, it has a right to ask for it. In some instances
the passage from the consensus procedure to the traditional techniques of
decision-making has been formalized. Thus, for example, the 'Gentleman's
Agreement' of the Third Conference on the Law of the Sea, quoted above,
admitted that when the attempt at reaching a consensus decision failed, a
vote could be taken on a certain matter (the Agreement, however, stipulated
that States 'should make every effort to reach agreement' and that 'there
should be no voting ... until all efforts at consensus have been exhausted';
Rule 37 of the Rules of the Procedure of the Conference set out a large
number of devices to defer a vote should consensus fail, and to put pressure
on States to come to an agreement without voting).

Unfortunately, on more than one occasion States have chosen the
short-sighted approach of attaining consensus in spite of unbridgeable divergencies. This pays dividends in the short run only, for it creates confusion,
in addition to revealing to any impartial observer a substantial lack of
agreement. Furthermore, it merely postpones until after the adoption of the
consensus text the settlement of all the problems the text was intended to
overcome. As soon as the question of implementing international decisions
comes up, differences arise again, with all the attendant political problems.
A telling illustration of the snares set by consensus can be seen in the
circumstances surrounding the adoption in 1974 by the U N General Assembly of two resolutions on the New International Economic Order.[31]

Emphasis must, however, be laid on certain imaginative techniques evolved within the Third Conference on the Law of the Sea for facilitating
and accelerating consensus—techniques which have been termed 'active
consensus procedure' (Buzan),[32] and are primarily designed 'to extend the
process of consensus formation'. It is not improbable that they will be
adopted by other diplomatic conferences, thus proving instrumental in promoting international co-operation.

Finally, let me add that consensus, being only a modality of the negotiating and decision-making process, has no bearing whatsoever on the legal

---

[31] See A. Cassese, 'Consensus and Some of its Pitfalls', 58 *Rivista di diritto internazionale*,
1975, 756-61.
[32] B. Buzan, *AJIL* 75 (1981), 324 ff.

force of the decision reached. The legal standing of the final text is quite independent of the manner in which the decision is achieved; rather, it depends on the general provisions governing the value of resolutions and other acts of international organizations or diplomatic conferences—provisions to be found in the charter of the organizations or in the terms of reference of conferences respectively, as well as in rules of customary international law. Thus, for instance, a decision taken by the Security Council under Article 25 of the UN Charter is legally binding irrespective of the modalities of its passing. By the same token, a General Assembly resolution concerning matters other than the internal functioning of, or membership in, the UN has only hortatory value, whether or not it has been adopted by consensus. If it fulfils the requisite conditions for being regarded as an agreement entered into by all the States participating in the consensus, this special status would only follow from the general rules concerning treaty-making. The same holds true for resolutions susceptible to being considered as evidence of a customary process of international law.

International Law-making in a Divided World

109. It is apparent that at present all States agree on a basic nucleus of conceptions as to how law is made in international relations. There is full agreement on treaty-making and on the importance of this source of law.

By contrast, States are divided on the way international *custom* becomes binding (§ 65), on the significance and purport of the 'general principles of law recognized by civilised nations' (§ 94), and also, albeit to a limited extent, on the legal relevance of resolutions adopted by international organizations. Whereas most developing States tend to attribute quasi-legislative force to resolutions, claiming that their 'cumulative effect' can give rise to binding rules, by contrast, Western and socialist States cling to the traditional view that, subject to certain well-defined exceptions, resolutions have a hortatory value only.

As has been rightly stressed by Condorelli,[33] these differences have often led States eventually to agree upon solutions on a *regional* level, where there is frequently greater homogeneity, and where it is therefore easier to reach agreement. At a universal level the difficulty of attaining substantial arrangements and consequently of passing legally binding rules has often brought about the weakening of the legal force of precepts resulting in the creation of so-called '*soft law*', that is to say, general declarations, resolutions, acts, agreements, and rules so loose in content as to prove virtually ineffective.

---

[33] L. Condorelli, *Droit international public* (Geneva, 1984–5), p. 26.

However, the present rifts and conflicts, both ideological and political, and the differences on the law-making processes, as well as the two trends just stressed do not prevent States from engaging in peaceful relations and should therefore not be overestimated. In actual practice States tend to play down their disagreements over sources of law to such an extent that only in extreme cases do they surface. In addition, divergences are to some extent narrowing down. It is therefore possible to cherish the hope that in the not-too-distant-future the three main segments of the world community will reach greater agreement on how the principal sources of international law operate.

8

Settlement of Disputes

INTRODUCTION

110. IN every national legal system there are various rules establishing the authority of courts of law to adjudicate disputes arising between members of the community. By virtue of these rules a person can be brought to trial even if he is unwilling to submit to court. Indeed it is the case that for the institution of proceedings a suit by another subject is sufficient. In addition, the system for determining whether in specific instances substantive rules are violated is so elaborate and complex that a basic dichotomy exists between civil and criminal proceedings. In the latter, most offences can be submitted to court by any individual who happens to be cognizant of the offence, or by central authorities, or on the initiative of enforcement officers. While this is the rule, there is also the exceptional procedure of arbitration whereby disputes can be settled by a third party chosen by the litigants. The main feature of arbitration is that it rests on the agreement of the contending parties: the arbitrator cannot pronounce on the dispute if he has not been granted the power to do so by both sides.

By comparison, the position of the international community appears utterly rudimentary. A general duty to settle legal or political disputes peacefully has emerged since the Second World War, as we saw in § 84. (Until then, the lack of any such duty meant that States were authorized to resort to force to impose the terms of settlement, unless they had entered into treaties requiring self-restraint on the matter.) This duty is a major breakthrough in another respect as well. Before it evolved, States were authorized to make use of force without previously endeavouring to seek a peaceful solution of their differences. Thus, while in municipal systems third-party ascertainment of whether the law has been broken as a rule precedes resort to enforcement measures, in international law this intermediate stage was not necessary, and in fact was often skipped. By contrast, since the general duty referred to above took shape in the world community, States have been enjoined to try to resolve their disputes peacefully, before taking any enforcement action (see § 84). The need to go through this intermediate stage means *inter alia* that States may find it advisable to have the dispute settled by an arbitral court empowered to determine whether the law has been breached and, if it has, to determine what remedial action can lawfully be taken.

In spite of its momentous importance, this general duty is marred by the absence of any provision establishing by what modalities conflict and disagreement should be solved. No general rules have evolved to the effect that States must submit to the authority of bodies empowered to dictate the terms of settlement; in particular no adjudicating organ endowed with general and compulsory jurisdiction has ever been created. Hence, States are at liberty to choose any means of peaceful settlement they prefer. Thus, whereas States are duty-bound to settle their differences by means other than force, on the other hand, such stringent obligation is accompanied by complete freedom as to the choice of the means of settlement.

It is not difficult to grasp the reasons for this utterly unsatisfactory state of affairs. All members of the world community have come to realize that it is too dangerous to allow disagreements to be resolved by force; the threat or use of force between two States can easily involve other countries as well, since international subjects are interconnected by a variety of links. Hence, the establishment of the general duty referred to above. However, if one then turns to the prescription of definite modalities for settlement, one stumbles on a profound chasm between States. On the one hand, many Western countries claim that conciliation and judicial review are the best means of settlement and that they should therefore be rendered compulsory for all States. By contrast, many socialist and Third World nations contend that negotiation is more appropriate; more generally, they argue that States should be left free to choose the best means in each specific case.

One of the consequences is that the only international entities created for the purpose of settling disputes by judicial methods are arbitral courts or tribunals such as the International Court of Justice. As we shall see, they vary in effectiveness and technical sophistication and, in addition, possess a jurisdiction limited to a relatively small number of States. They all share, however, the characteristic of resting on the *consent* of States: they are set up by means of treaties and their jurisdiction is accepted by means of unilateral or contractual obligations. In short, the system representing the exception in domestic legal systems, that is arbitration, is the rule in the international community.

TRADITIONAL MEANS OF SETTLEMENT

111. The most elementary means of settling international disputes is resort to negotiation between the contending parties. Characteristic of this method is the total absence of a third party, be it another State or an international institution. The advantage of this practice is that the solution is left entirely to the parties concerned, without any undue pressure from outside. Furthermore, as the goal of the negotiation is to achieve an amicable understanding by reaching a compromise over the conflicting claims, a further and more important merit is that there will be no loser and no winner, for both parties should derive some benefit from the diplomatic exchange. It seems that it is precisely because of these features that negotiation is the method preferred by socialist and some Third World countries. However, one should not underrate its two major shortcomings: first, negotiation seldom leads to an in-depth determination of the facts or, when legal disputes are at issue, to the identification of the rules applicable in the specific case— negotiation being a question of give-and-take, a compromise is reached to patch up the differences between the parties; second, the stronger party is more likely to apply pressure to its counterpart than the other way about— more important still, the stronger State may easily subdue the other litigant by resorting to a host of means available to it on account of its *de facto* superiority. This, of course, implies that negotiation may reveal itself to be a way by which powerful States bend the will of lesser States and ultimately settle the issue to their own advantage.

Whenever the parties decide to depart from direct diplomatic exchanges and to involve a third entity in the dispute, they have various methods at their disposal: enquiry, good offices, mediation, conciliation, or arbitration.

112. In many respects, arbitration involves a qualitative leap. First of all, the dispute is no longer settled only for the purpose of safeguarding peaceful relations and accommodating the interests of the conflicting parties in a mutually acceptable manner. An additional goal is pursued—that of settling a dispute on the basis of international legal standards previously accepted by States. In short, arbitration aims at maintaining peaceful relations among States by applying existing standards of conduct endowed with legal force. A second salient trait is that a thorough examination of both the facts at issue and of the law governing them is made by the court. A third significant feature is that the court's findings both concerning the facts and the law are legally binding on the contending parties. It is, therefore, hardly surprising that the heyday of arbitration was the period between the two World Wars, when Western States still made up a relatively homogeneous group and were still paramount in the world community. Tradition, domestic legal philosophy and attachment to the principle of the rule of law, all prompted Western States to submit to adjudication. Even more important, during that period States were under the influence of the Wilsonian concept of 'open diplomacy', according to which the 'reign of law', and voluntary submission to impartial judgment would save the world community from another conflagration by relaxing dangerous tensions.

The substantially favourable attitude of Western nations should not, however, lead us to believe that the West has always and whole-heartedly upheld international arbitration. Indeed, European States have often voiced misgivings about accepting the jurisdiction of international courts.

Suffice it to mention here the objections expressed in 1899 by the German Foreign Minister, Bernhard von Bülow, which are particularly interesting in that they rely to a great extent on concepts taken up fifty years later by socialist and newly independent countries. When the negotiators at the 1899 Hague Peace conference put forward the idea of establishing a Permanent Court of Arbitration, the German Foreign Minister instructed his delegate to refrain from participating in the undertaking, for the following reasons. As he put it:

As far as this question is concerned, we find ourselves confronted with an equation with two unknown quantities. One unknown quantity is the objectivity of the judge, the other is the uncertainty of the legal rule which would constitute the legal basis of the judgment. It is an open and doubtful question to what extent a judge, faced with a question involving his country, will maintain his full personal independence and hold aloof from patriotic instincts. Even judges who belong to third, neutral States will be unwittingly influenced by consideration of the possible consequences of the judgment for their own country. In addition, in each individual dispute the parties concerned are uncertain as to which legal conception will prevail in the formulation of the judgment. One must take into account the possibility that, in the case of a court consisting of three judges, each will base his views on different norms. In consequence, so long as there does not exist a unitary, codified international law, States will find themselves worse off than any individual—in case of dispute, the latter can make sure, either by himself or with the help of legal counsel, what position the laws of his country adopt concerning the question at issue.[1]

The German delegate to the Hague Conference, the international lawyer Zorn, had previously shared von Bülow's ideas, which were common among statesmen and diplomats of the Great Powers.[2] Zorn himself recalled a few years later:

I was under the influence of the concept then prevailing in Germany, that a strong State in no way needed the strengthening of international arbitration. In case of an international dispute, if it regarded resort to an arbitral tribunal as useful, the road to it was always open. For a State rightly aware of itself, however, what really mattered was its diplomatic skill and, indeed, primarily its military strength.[3]

Yet various factors, including the strong diplomatic and psychological pressure of other States, led Zorn to change his mind, and he became so firmly convinced of the advisability of favouring the setting up of the Court that he became instrumental in attenuating the German Government's intran-

---

[1] The passage from the instructions issued by von Bülow is in E. Fürst (ed.), *Die grosse Politik der europäischen Kabinette 1871-1914*, xv: *Rings-um die erste Haager Friedenskonferenz* (Berlin, 1924), no. 4308.
[2] On Zorn's attitude, see his book: *Deutschland und die beiden Haager Friedenskonferenzen* (Berlin, 1920), pp. 23 ff.
[3] P. Zorn, 'Zur neuesten Entwicklung des Völkerrechts', in *Festgabe für K. Güterbock* (Berlin, 1910), p. 213.

sigence (see § 228). The establishment of the Permanent Court of Arbitration was in the event accepted by Germany on condition that, among other things, its jurisdiction be not compulsory and that it consist only of a panel of judges (see § 113).

In order not to lose sight of the limited extent to which Western countries traditionally accepted arbitration, it is useful to recall that in the period of 'classical' international law, arbitration treaties normally included a clause whereby the arbitral tribunal was not authorized to pass judgment upon disputes affecting the 'independence', the 'honour', or the 'vital interests' of States. As the decision whether a certain dispute fell within the purview of the clause often belonged to each disputant State, the contending parties were left free to prevent the court from pronouncing upon issues which in their view touched upon their essential interests.

To fully grasp the significance of the aforementioned clause, mention can be made of what Zorn (whose role in the development of arbitration has been mentioned) stated in 1910:

I hold impossible and contrary to the very foundations of current international law a treaty on compulsory arbitration which fails to include the so-called clause on the honour of States. Indeed, whenever such a clause is not explicitly laid down, under modern international law it must nevertheless be deemed to constitute an essential element of any treaty on compulsory arbitration.[4]

Before him, in 1906, a prominent Italian international lawyer, Fusinato, who had contributed much to the working out of numerous arbitration treaties between Italy and other States, had gone to the length of observing that the international conventions which included the clause

... have naturally only a moral value, in that they constitute the manifestation of a lofty trend. Since they practically leave to each contracting State the power to avoid the arbitral pronouncement, they do not lend to arbitration any greater guarantee than those following from the general trends of Governments and public opinion, which regard arbitration as the most civilised means of settling disputes.[5]

I would like to add that, although those clauses are no longer embodied in arbitration treaties (they were all the rage mainly between 1880 and 1920), a few remnants can still be found in a handful of treaties. Arguably, a partial adumbration of the traditional clause can be seen in the declaration made in 1946 by the US under Article 36 of the Court's Statute for the acceptance of the compulsory jurisdiction of the International Court of Justice. Under that declaration the US excluded the Court's jurisdiction 'with regard to matters which are essentially within the domestic jurisdiction of the US as determined by the US'. (A similar proviso can be found in

---

[4] Ibid., 228.

[5] C. Fusinato, 'Ultimi progressi dell'arbitrato internazionale', *Rivista di diritto internazionale*, 1 (1906), 16.

the declaration made under Article 36 by a few other States, which in fact imitated the US declaration.)

In sum, one should not overrate Western adherence to international arbitration for even today many Western countries hold rather lukewarm views on the matter.

113. The attitude of socialist and developing countries has long been very close to that adopted in 1899 by the then German Foreign Minister (see § 112). For a number of years the main reasons behind their marked reluctance to accept adjudication have been the following: first, international courts of arbitration apply a law still strongly influenced by its sires, the Western capitalist States, and consequently unacceptable to socialist and newly independent countries; second, members of international courts are required to be unbiased and independent, which is, in the view of these States, a condition all but impossible to achieve.

In this respect one should mention a famous statement made in 1922 by the high-ranking Soviet diplomat Litvinov (who subsequently became Foreign Minister) on the occasion of international negotiations at The Hague concerning recognition by the USSR of its foreign debt. When the British delegate to the 1922 Hague Conference suggested that an impartial authority should be appointed to arbitrate in the event of differences between the Soviet Government and foreign bondholders, Mr Litvinov observed:

It was necessary to face the fact that there was not one world but two, a Soviet world and a non-Soviet world ... Because there was no third world to arbitrate, he anticipated difficulties ... The division he had mentioned existed, and with it existed a bias and a hatred, for which the Russian Government must decline the responsibility ... Only an angel could be unbiased in judging Russian affairs.[6]

Third, the idea that socialist and developing States are underrepresented on international courts, and that therefore Western judges can easily outvote or (owing to the stronger legal tradition in the West) outwit them. Finally, the fear that losing a case might have adverse consequences on public opinion or, at any rate, tarnish the State's good image in foreign affairs (clearly, the domestic legal philosophy of States where the principle of the 'rule of law' is not very strong greatly influences State behaviour in the international arena).

Most of these conditions have changed today. A large segment of international law has been revised in such a way as to uphold the claims of socialist and developing countries (although admittedly the new law is often ambiguous); very often international judges have proved to be genuinely independent and even-handed; socialist and Third World countries are no

[6] See Conference at The Hague: I. Non-Russian Commission; II. Russian Commission, June 15-July 20 1922, *Minutes and Documents* (Department of Foreign Affairs, The Hague, 1922), p. 302.

longer underrepresented on international courts. However, despite all these changes, international arbitration is still far from enjoying wide support. It will probably take some time for States to depart from old habits and views and to come to accept a method that is unquestionably commendable in many respects. What is, however, surprising is that Western countries—whose general legal philosophy should predispose them to submit to adjudication—are very often no less reluctant than other States to resort to this mode of peaceful settlement.[7] Equally striking is the fact that, in recent years, developing countries have with increasing frequency submitted their disputes to the ICJ (while socialist countries persevere in their reserved attitude).

The (initial) opposition of socialist and Third World States and the disinclination of some Western countries to institute proceedings before international courts have not prevented arbitration from undergoing a notable process of improvement and sophistication. Treaty rules providing for resort to arbitral courts have become more numerous; they envisage better means of bringing suits to international courts; and, what is more important still, courts have become institutionalized—that is to say, permanent bodies have been set up and a whole corpus of rules of procedure has been developed. This process began in 1899, when the First Hague Convention for the Peaceful Settlement of International Disputes set up the Permanent Court of Arbitration (still existent), which consisted of a standing panel of arbitrators from which conflicting States could pick up the names of the persons to be selected for each specific dispute, plus an administrative infrastructure (the Permanent Administrative Council and the International Bureau) created to act as a secretariat in the event of the Court being called into being. The features of the Court were described in 1907 by the Russian jurist and diplomat Fëdor Fëdorovich de Martens who had played a central role in setting it up in 1899. He said that 'The Court of 1899 is only a shadow which, from time to time, materialises, only to fade away once again'.[8] Actually, since 1900 the PCA has only heard 23 cases, 20 of which were dealt with between 1900 and 1932.

Less imperfect was the Permanent Court of International Justice created in 1921 and replaced in 1946 by the International Court of Justice. The Court is really a permanent body, has a fixed set of rules of procedure, and has developed an important case-law over the years. In addition, means for facilitating a wider acceptance of the Court's jurisdiction were devised, the most significant being the so-called 'optional clause', by virtue of which

[7] See, for example, the *Statement of the US Withdrawal from the Proceedings Initiated by Nicaragua in the ICJ*, in ILM 24 (1985), p. 247. See also the *Observations on the ICJ's 26 November 1984 Judgment on Jurisdiction and Admissibility in the Case of* Nicaragua v. US, ibid., 249 ff.

[8] The statement by F. F. de Martens is quoted in League of Nations, Permanent Court of International Justice, *Advisory Committee of Jurists* (1922), p. 22.

every State can declare that it accepts *ipso facto* and without special agreement the compulsory jurisdiction of the Court in relation to any other State accepting the same obligation (Article 36.2 of the Court's Statute).

Notwithstanding all these improvements, the ICJ is still a court of arbitration, and there still exists a remarkable unwillingness among States to submit legal disputes to it. Out of about 170 States only 47 (17 Western and 30 Third World) have declared that they accept its compulsory jurisdiction. (For the data relating to the PCIJ, see § 33.)

NEW DEVICES FOR PROMOTING COMPLIANCE WITH INTERNATIONAL LAW

Handling of Disputes by UN Organs

114. One major feature of the present world community is the intervention of UN organs—chiefly the Security Council and the General Assembly—in interstate controversies for the purpose of promoting a peaceful settlement. The machinery provided for in the UN Charter refers both to legal and to political disagreement, although, as we shall see, in the case of legal disputes a specific mode of settlement is suggested. The lack of distinction between the two classes of disputes is a sound development, for all too often clashes between legal claims are politically motivated, or they have strong political implications, whereas political feuds frequently present legal overtones, or else one of the parties or even both of them employ legal arguments to buttress their political demands. If one of the major purposes of the world community is reconciliation of disputants so as to prevent them from crossing swords, the better course of action is that followed in 1945 of not making the selection of a certain mode of settlement conditional on the intrinsic character of a dispute.

The basic philosophy underlying the Charter is that every effort should be made to maintain peace and security. An obvious corollary is that whenever disagreements between States threaten to become explosive, and to endanger peace, the UN must step in and endeavour to defuse the situation. This, of course, implies that the Organization must always watch out for possible cracks in the fragile edifice of peace. Put in another way, the UN must concern itself with any dispute which, although not posing an immediate threat to peace, might develop into a clash such as could jeopardize peaceful relations in the future. The field of action of the Organization thus becomes very broad, for any disagreement evidently may escalate into a major conflict, except for the very minor and peripheral ones. The great novelty of the Charter system was aptly stressed by Ross in the following terms:

The essence of the Charter, the point where it definitely breaks with the rules of traditional international law, is that it establishes the principle that *every dispute* (the continuance of which is likely to endanger the maintenance of international peace and security) *is a public matter*, so that whether the parties wish it or not, they must accept the fact that the dispute may be debated in the SC ([or] the GA), if that organ considers such debate to be in the interests of peace. The parties are not obliged to seek the assistance of the Organisation, but they are obliged to put up with its intervention.[9]

International Supervision

115. To obviate all the deficiencies of the international order in the resolution of conflict, since the First World War a new system—which I shall succinctly term 'international supervision'—has gradually been introduced for the purpose of scrutinizing the behaviour of States which are parties to specific treaties. It differs from international adjudication in many respects. First, the *composition* of the organ responsible for monitoring the implementation of international rules is normally different from that of judicial bodies, for the supervisory body may also be made up of representatives of States instead of individuals acting in their personal capacity. Second, control functions are frequently entrusted to *more than one body*, and in this case the various organs often differ as to their composition, for one or more are composed of independent individuals, whereas others consist of State officials. Third, the *initiative* of the supervisory procedure is not normally left to the aggrieved State, but can be taken either by the beneficiaries of the international rules (for instance, individuals or groups of individuals), or even by the supervisory organ itself acting *motu proprio*. Sometimes there is no need for anybody to initiate the proceedings, for the simple reason that the procedure is automatic, consisting in a periodic scrutiny of the behaviour of the States concerned. The obvious consequence is that while in the case of adjudication the existence of a dispute (that is, a clash of opposing views and demands as to the facts and their legal appraisal) is necessary for the proceedings to be initiated, in the case of supervision the existence of a dispute is almost never a necessary prerequisite of the international action. Fourth, while the hearings of judicial bodies are public, normally the debates between the contending parties before a control body (or, when the procedure is not contentious in character, the investigatory activities of the body) are carried out *in camera*, so as to avoid attracting publicity to possible violations committed by the State under scrutiny while the investigation is under way. Fifth, the outcome of the procedure *does not consist in a binding decision* but takes various forms (report, recommendations, etc.), which, whatever their official label, have only moral and hortatory force.

Why did States resort to this ingenious system for inducing compliance

[9] A. Ross, *The United Nations: Peace and Progress* (New York, 1966), p. 190.

with international law? There are two closely interrelated reasons. First, in the aftermath of the First World War, States started to resort to international treaties to regulate matters which until then had remained within their domestic jurisdiction. These included issues such as the protection of minorities, the regulation of labour conditions and the rights of workers; the establishment of international mandates over territories which up to that time had been under the exclusive control of sovereign Powers; the regulation of narcotic drugs; and unique matters such as the relations between the Free City of Danzig (now Gdańsk) and Poland and more generally the protection of the rights of the City laid down in the Treaty of Versailles. The new international legislation presented one remarkable feature: it did not impose reciprocal obligations—that is to say obligations entailing each contracting party to be interested in complying with the rule for fear the other contracting State might feel free to disregard it. Rather, the new rules belonged to that unique class of norms which protect the interests of entities other than the subjects assuming the rights and obligations in question— such as individuals, groups, populations subject to the mandate system, associations of workers and employers, and so on.

The second reason is that in these new areas it was difficult to establish mechanisms for ensuring that the new international rules were faithfully observed. Resort to adjudication was not feasible on a number of grounds, including the fact that, whenever States had accepted such new and bold obligations, they became reluctant to submit matters to judicial bodies. Furthermore, the unique features of the subject-matter rendered adjudication scarcely appropriate. Indeed, the non-reciprocal character of the obligations laid down in those rules meant that infringement upon one of them might be passed over in silence, if only the other contracting States were granted the right to demand conpliance with them. It was, therefore, only logical to bestow the right to exact respect for the rules upon the very entities for whose benefit they had been agreed upon. However, it would have been impossible for States to accept the granting to individuals of *locus standi* before international courts. A compromise was reached. It consisted in allowing individuals to petition international bodies devoid of any judicial function and powers.

To satisfy all the requirements mentioned above, imaginative monitoring systems were contrived. However, to make them acceptable to States, it was deemed necessary to water down their possible impact on State sovereignty. To this effect, no binding force was attached to the final assessment of supervisory bodies. In addition, side by side with organs consisting of impartial individuals, bodies composed of State representatives were set up (plainly, they are more sensitive to States' exigencies and, therefore, more inclined to attenuate possibly harsh evaluations by other supervisory bodies). In addition, as was pointed out above, it was decided that the meetings or sessions of the monitoring bodies should normally be held in camera, for the manifest purpose of shielding States from public exposure.

Supervisory systems proved a balanced and relatively effective means of impelling States to live up to their international undertakings. It is, therefore, not surprising that certain of them survived the Second World War. (For example, the International Labour Organization mechanisms for supervising the application of international labour conventions, and the systems for scrutinizing conventions on narcotic drugs.) In other areas new control machinery was instituted. The fields in which supervision is at present most widespread are those concerning international labour conventions; treaties and other international standards on human rights; trusteeship agreements; the peaceful use of atomic energy; the Antarctic and outer space. Monitoring mechanisms exist in the field of international and internal armed conflict as well. Plainly, the expansion of supervision to so many important areas testifies to its responsiveness to States' needs. In addition, it also proves that all groups of States are ready to submit to supervision, for even those countries which are more recalcitrant in respect of other international means of investigation, do not oppose international control. This, of course, is mainly due to its flexibility and to the fact that supervisory bodies do not put States in the dock, but tend to persuade them by dint of cautious diplomatic and moral pressure to abide by those rules which they may be inclined to disregard.

116. To give a fairly clear picture of supervision, it seems useful to indicate briefly the four principal modalities through which this process is effected:

(1) The examination of periodic reports submitted at predetermined intervals by the States concerned. For example, reports by the member States of the ILO concerning the application of international labour conventions under Article 22; the reports provided for in various human rights conventions, such as the 1965 Convention on Racial Discrimination (Article 9); the 1966 Covenants on Human Rights (Articles 16 and 40 respectively); the 1956 Slavery Convention (Article 8).

(2) Inspection—provided for in, for example, the treaty on the International Agency For Atomic Energy (Article 12.6), the Antarctic Treaty (Article 7), and the 1967 Treaty on the peaceful use of outer space (Article 12). Of course, this form of supervision is more effective and penetrating by far than the examination of States' reports where the inquiring body must confine itself to the data provided by the State concerned. In the case of inspection, on the other hand, on the spot investigations allow international organs (or, as in the case of the treaties on Antarctica and on outer space, the other States which are parties to the treaty) to satisfy themselves whether a State respects or disregards the treaty.

(3) Supervision carried out through a contentious procedure where the parties to the dispute, or the State under control and the supervisory body, engage in a contentious examination of the case. See, for example, the procedures provided for in Articles 22-3, 24-5, and 26-9 of the ILO Constitution; in Article 41 of the Covenant on Civil and Political Rights; and in the Optional Protocol to the Covenant (the Human Rights Committee is entrusted with looking into alleged violations of the Covenant, either at the request of a contracting State or of individuals subject to the jurisdiction of a party to the Protocol).

(4) Adoption of measures designed to forestall the possible commission of international delinquency by a State. So far this unique form of 'preventive' supervision has been established only in the area of the peaceful use of atomic energy. The special nature of the subject-matter accounts for the exceptional characteristics of this class of international scrutiny. Take, for example, certain bilateral agreements such as those between Canada and the FRG of 11 December 1957; between Canada and Australia of 4 August 1959; between the UK and Italy of 28 December 1957, or the treaty instituting EURATOM (Article 103). All of them make the delivery of nuclear material conditional on a preventive control of the facilities of the recipient party by the granting State. Only if those facilities are considered consistent with the general standards set in the agreements can the material be delivered. In this case, the extreme importance of the matter, that is, the danger that nuclear material might be used for military purposes, warrants the resort to a very advanced type of supervision which States would otherwise find unacceptable.

Compulsory Conciliation or Adjudication

117. Another important way of providing for the settlement of international disputes is—by means of a multilateral treaty—to impose the duty to submit disputes to conciliation or adjudication. From a strictly formal viewpoint, the laying down of this duty is no different from the traditional system of providing for the compulsory jurisdiction of conciliation bodies or arbitral tribunals. What markedly differentiates, however, the procedures I am about to illustrate from the traditional ones (and this from a *substantial* viewpoint) is the twofold circumstance that they are laid down in multilateral treaties of great importance and, above all, that they rest on the basic consent of the three major groupings of States.

In the case of conciliation, the conclusions and proposals of the conciliatory organ are not binding on the parties. In spite of this major shortcoming, the mere facts of providing for a right to initiate, or the duty submit to, conciliation; establishing a procedure to be followed in the conciliation stage; and setting up a body responsible for seeking to induce the contending parties to reach an amicable settlement, represent a major step forward, given the present state of the world community. The establishment of compulsory conciliation is the upshot of two conflicting views: on the one hand, those of the Western countries, which argue that the drafting of new international substantive rules can only make sense if some compulsory means of settling disputes is established, and, on the other hand, the views of socialist and of most developing countries which, while conceding the paramountcy of the general principle on peaceful settlement of disputes, do not wish to tie their hands by accepting a priori the obligation to have recourse to one or another of the specific methods of settlement and, in particular, strongly oppose any settlement procedure leading to a 'win or lose' conclusion. Faced with this profound rift, States have eventually struck a balance by rendering resort to conciliation compulsory.

It should be noted that even this modest advance is not general, but has been achieved in certain very definite areas only, namely where new international legislation has been agreed upon by all the three major groups of States.

Indicative of this trend is the conciliation system devised by the Vienna Convention on the Law of Treaties in 1969. (The substantive rules of the Convention partly codify traditional law and partly innovate it by giving serious consideration to the demands of socialist and Third World countries (see § 105).) Under the Convention, disputes concerning any provision other than those on *jus cogens* can be submitted to conciliation within twelve months of their beginning (Article 66(b)). Any party to the dispute can set in motion the conciliation procedure by submitting a request to this effect to the U N Secretary-General. The Conciliation Commission, appointed from a list drawn up by the Secretary-General, 'shall hear the parties, examine the claims and objections, and make proposals to the parties with a view to reaching an amicable settlement of the dispute' (Article 5 of the Annex to the Convention). Clearly, the Commission has quasi-judicial powers, for it can look into both the facts and the law. However, its findings and proposals are not binding, for the report of the Commission 'shall have no other character than that of recommendations submitted for the consideration of the parties in order to facilitate an amicable settlement of the dispute' (Article 6 of the Annex). Nevertheless, the authority of the Commission's conclusions and recommendations cannot fail to have a great impact on the parties. It is likely, therefore, that in actual fact the weight of the Commission's report will be no less than that of a legally binding judgment.

118.   In some exceptional cases States have decided to make adjudication compulsory. A number of devices have, however, been introduced to render the system more acceptable to those States which oppose judicial review. Furthermore, the very unique character of the substantive law to which the system for compulsory adjudication relates, accounts for the exceptional acceptance, in principle, by all groups of States, of a method of settlement still looked upon with suspicion by so many States. The system is provided for in two important treaties, the 1969 Vienna Convention on the Law of Treaties and the 1982 Convention on the Law of the Sea, which updates, codifies, and, in many areas, radically revises the law of the sea. The complexity and intricacy of the subject-matter as well as the need of developing countries to take account of the views of industrialized (notably Western) States in shaping a new law, explain why socialist and newly independent countries had to barter advanced modes of settlement of disputes with developed countries for the acceptance by those countries of many of the Third World's demands.

A quick look at how compulsory adjudication works with regard to the two Conventions should be sufficient at this point.

Under the Vienna Convention disputes relating to *jus cogens* can be submitted to the ICJ at the request of one party only, after 12 months have elapsed since the start of the dispute without any settlement being reached (Article 66 a). In keeping with Article 33 of the UN Charter, Article 279 of the Convention on the Law of the Sea of 1982 reiterates the duty of States to settle their differences peacefully. It then imposes on them the duty to 'exchange their views' as to the mode of settlement to be adopted (Article 283). If no other method is agreed upon, each contending party has the right to propose resort to conciliation. If the offer is not accepted or the parties do not succeed in agreeing upon the conciliation procedure (that is, under Article 284), any party to the dispute is entitled (under Article 287) to initiate judicial proceedings before one of four courts, namely, the International Tribunal on the Law of the Sea (established under Annex VI to the Convention); the ICJ; an arbitral court set up under Annex VII to the Convention; or a special arbitral tribunal created under Annex VIII. These provisions are, however, subject to the limitations provided for in Articles 297-9.

It should be apparent from this short survey that the system under consideration is much stronger than the one laid down in the 1969 Vienna Convention. Whilst conciliation is not compulsory, adjudication becomes obligatory if the parties fail to agree upon another method of settlement. In view of the present political leaning of the various groups of States, one may safely assume that many States will do their utmost to avoid the makeshift solution of judicial redress, and will, therefore, try to insist on conciliation. This, together with the fact that resort to conciliation is a necessary step before moving on to adjudication, tends *de facto* to strengthen the position of conciliation.

CONCLUSIONS

119. To recapitulate, in the international community we are confronted with a striking contradiction: on the one hand we are faced with a general obligation to settle political and legal disputes peacefully; on the other hand, States enjoy complete freedom to choose the appropriate means of settling disputes. Specific modes of settlement, if any, are provided for in treaties only: no *general rule* on the matter has emerged. As I have already pointed out (§ 110), States are too divided politically and ideologically to

reach agreement on the creation of universally acceptable devices. They
have, however, a general scheme of settlement at their disposal, namely,
that provided for in the UN Charter. Although the Charter does not impose
any specific mode of reaching a solution, it does require States to endeavour
to attain agreement. In addition, it stipulates that, in the case of 'dangerous'
disputes (those which might jeopardize peace), contesting parties must submit to UN machinery (or, at any rate, must not oppose an 'intervention'
by the Organization). Thus, a multilateral diplomatic forum is made available to the contending parties (and even to third States) which, in many
instances, proves more suitable than direct negotiations, or third-party settlement. Its strength lies in the interplay of States of different origin, with
varying degrees of ideological or political involvement, which come into
play and put pressure on the litigants. In many instances the UN scheme
has turned out to be vital, and it has also served as a model for other
multilateral conflict resolution techniques developed by a number of specialized agencies (for instance, FAO, ICAO, UNESCO).

Furthermore, States have set up a host of techniques applicable to individual treaties which have proved very useful. Among the traditional modes
of settlement, arbitral or so-called judicial courts stand out, many of which,
including the ICJ, have proved indispensable. Modern devices are represented by international supervision, as well as rules on compulsory conciliation or adjudication. Although here one is again faced with merely conventional bonds, they work in a fairly satisfactory manner.

Even though this is an area where international law is particularly deficient, the picture resulting from this survey is not, all things considered,
too dispiriting. First, there is general consent that efforts must always be
made to solve differences without resorting to force. Second, the UN plays
a vital role in promoting agreement between contending parties and has
been successful in a great many instances (except, of course, those where
political, military, or other rifts were unbridgeable, or where one of the
contending parties was determined to use force). UN machinery has proved
particularly useful to weak States, for whom appeal to the World Organization is often the only means of preventing conflicts from degenerating into
armed clashes. Third, many Third World States are increasingly departing
from their previous opposition to international adjudication, and seem more
and more amenable to this important method of third-party settlement.
Fourth, a number of ingenious systems and techniques of solution (chiefly
methods of supervision) have been contrived by States, and they have
yielded considerable results (although usually only for contracting parties).

In short, although serious disagreement persists concerning the creation
of specific techniques with general applicability, advances have been made
in a number of areas, and this might gradually bring about the eventual
institution of a stable system endowed with general validity.

9

Enforcement

INTRODUCTION

120. BEFORE starting the enquiry, a note of caution should be sounded. In this as in other areas, one cannot transpose concepts elaborated within domestic systems onto international realities. In municipal legal orders enforcement strictly denotes all those measures and procedures, mostly taken by public authorities, calculated to impel compliance with the law; consequently there exists a clear-cut distinction between those coercive measures and procedures (that is, sanctions) on the one hand, and, on the other hand, forcible acts which, since they do not amount to an authorized reaction to a wrong, are unlawful. By contrast, as we shall soon see, for reasons which I have already tried to set forth (§ 8) the world community has, for a long time, not made this distinction. It follows that the word 'enforcement' used in this chapter is taken in a broad sense, as covering both action designed to ensure compliance with law and instances of resort to force which are not prohibited even though they do not seek to impose the observance of law.

TRADITIONAL LAW

121. As I have just pointed out, since the law applicable before the First World War did not place any sweeping restraints on the use of force, there was no substantial difference between sanctions and resort to force for the protection of one's own political or economic interests. States were only to respect certain modalities: if they decided to engage in war, they were to express their *animus belligerandi* (that is the intent to wage war) in some way, with the consequence that all the rules on war and neutrality became applicable. If, instead, they preferred to resort to coercion short of war, they were to make it clear that they did not mean to render the laws on war and neutrality applicable, but to remain within the province of the laws of peace. Other modalities concerned the proper use of force: in case of war, various rules on warfare placed restraints on the conduct of hostilities; in case of forcible measures short of war, a few general principles gradually evolved (see § 125).

Such were the main trends of State practice. Some international lawyers, probably motivated by ethical considerations or inspired by natural law principles, denied that States could use force for the mere protection of their own interests. Similarly, some powerful States, especially when they interfered in the affairs of middle-sized or weak countries, endeavoured to show that their action was warranted by unique circumstances; they affirmed that but for these circumstances they would have respected the sovereignty of the State attacked or otherwise interfered with. However, one should not be misled by such statements, for they were primarily dictated by political, diplomatic, or even psychological reasons.

A distinguished jurist, the Italian Anzilotti, voiced a realistic line of thought. In 1915 he rejected the views of those who upheld sweeping curtailments of the right to use force, and wrote:

International practice includes a number of cases, especially concerning relations between strong and weak States, where violence short of war has been resorted to, not for the purpose of reacting to the violation of a legal right of the State using force, but for the purpose of safeguarding its interests which were not protected by law ... Even the most cursory examination is sufficient to show that States consider themselves perfectly free to act in this way, that is to say that there does not exist a rule imposing on States the duty not to use physical coercion instead of war proper. And ... it would indeed be peculiar that such a rule existed. Since States are at liberty to resort to war for any purpose, one is at a loss to see why they should not use, for any purpose, acts of coercion constituting a *minus* with respect to war. It is sheer absurdity to think that a powerful State is free to declare war against a weak State in order to impose a new agreement for the regulation of certain interests, while it would be legally barred from merely blockading its ports, occupying its provinces, seizing its ships, refusing the implementation of certain treaties, and so on.[1]

These and similar scholarly propositions by prominent German jurists such as Jellinek,[2] and British jurists such as Phillimore,[3] Hall,[4] and Oppenheim,[5] reflected the actual conduct of States—which was also spelled out in unambiguous pronouncements by statesmen such as Lord Castlereagh[6] in 1821, and by the American President Theodore Roosevelt,[7] in 1904.

[1] D. Anzilotti, *Corso di diritto internazionale*, iii. 155–6.
[2] G. Jellinek, 'China und das Völkerrecht' (1900), *Schriften*, 490.
[3] R. W. Phillimore, *Commentaries upon International Law* iii.i (London, 1879–89), p. 559.
[4] V. E. Hall, *A Treatise on International Law*, vi (Oxford, 1909), p. 279.
[5] L. Oppenheim, *International Law*, i (London, 1905), p. 185.
[6] Lord Castlereagh, *British and Foreign State Papers 1820–1921* (London, 1830), p. 1162. In a circular letter of 19 January 1821, Lord Castlereagh wrote: 'It should be clearly understood that no Government can be more prepared than the British Government is, to uphold the right of any State or States to interfere, where their own immediate security, or essential interests, are seriously endangered by the internal transactions of another State'. He continued with a number of qualifications.
[7] T. Roosevelt, in *US Congress: A Compilation of the Messages and Papers of the Presidents*, xiv (New York, 1905), pp. 6923 f.
In his message to the US Congress of 6 December 1904, Roosevelt stated: 'Chronic wrongdoing, or an impotence which results in a general loosening of the ties of civilized society, may

A further distinguishing trait of traditional law was that even when a State resorted to force in order to react to a wrongful behaviour of another State, no prior exhaustion of peaceful remedies was requested; much less was the State to wait for a third party to pronounce on the fact that international law had actually been broken. Thus, while in domestic legal systems enforcement is normally carried out *after* judicial ascertainment that a breach of law has indeed occurred, in traditional international law, by contrast, States were authorized to judge by themselves, that is to base their possible resort to force on their own unilateral assessment of wrong-doings by other countries.

Both before and after the First World War State practice and legal literature tried to identify the various forms which the use of force could take. The classification which I shall set forth below is primarily intended to serve practical purposes and to unravel the maze of States' conduct. Except for the differentiation between the use of force short of war and war proper, which is based on legal differences between the two categories and is therefore of scientific value, all the other distinctions serve a classificatory purpose only. In particular, the distinction between intervention (whereby States act to protect their own interests) and reprisals (reactions against wrongful acts of another State), which States often relied on, was rather blurred in actual practice, for two reasons: first, because States were, in any case, authorized to use force to pursue their interests, and so it did not make much difference whether they engaged in military action to react to an instance of unlawful conduct on the part of another State, or to safe-guard their own interests; second, all too frequently States invoked legal considerations as a cloak to cover their action in cases where they acted out of mere political interest; conversely, in some instances, when they were the victims of breaches by other States, their reaction was not explicitly based on legal arguments.

Intervention

122. By forcible interference in the internal or external affairs of another State, is meant compelling this State, by the threat or use of force, either to do something (for example, to change its government, to enter into a treaty with a third State, to cede territory, etc.) or to carry out actions in its territory in the interest of the intervening State.

Usually intervention taking the form of a mere threat to use force was

in America, as elsewhere, ultimately require intervention by some civilized nation, and in the Western hemisphere the adherence of the US to the Monroe Doctrine may force the US, however reluctantly, in flagrant cases of such wrongdoing or impotence, to the exercise of international police power'.

exercised through diplomatic channels. Forcible intervention took the form of military occupation of the territory of another State, naval demonstrations, naval blockade (that is to say the blocking by men-of-war of a portion of the coast of another State), seizure of assets belonging to the other State or its nationals, embargo (in the old sense, that is—the seizure of ships belonging to the other State or its nationals), arrest and detention of foreigners, expulsion of foreign diplomats, etc. International practice is replete with cases of armed intervention. As was aptly emphasized by the German jurist Staudacher in 1909,[8] this practice gained momentum after 1820 as a result of two things. On the one hand, there was a growing tendency among major European countries to get together and police international relations by sending troops to trouble spots; this tendency, evolved during the Napoleonic wars and dictated by the need of other European Powers to counteract Napoleon's hegemony, was consolidated after his downfall in the form of a strong feeling of solidarity linking reactionary monarchies, and led to the formation of the Holy Alliance (§ 22). On the other hand, the gruesome devastation entailed by the Napoleonic wars impelled States to shun getting involved in wars proper. The combination of the two trends led European States to intervene on a number of occasions both in Europe and elsewhere, without, however, engaging in fully-fledged wars. So, for instance, after the downfall of Napoleon, the Holy Alliance provided for military intervention in European countries menaced by revolutions—Austria sent troops to Italy; France to both Italy and Spain (§ 22). Later on interventions were carried out by Great European powers against Turkey and Egypt and in the colonial territories of other States, and by the US in Latin-American countries.

123.   It should be noted that in some instances intervention in the territory of other States was officially justified by the intervening State on the grounds of 'self-defence and self-preservation'.

As early as 1817 the US occupied the island of Amelia, then under Spanish sovereignty, on the grounds that it had become a centre of illicit trafficking which was damaging to the US and that the Spanish authorities were unable to wield control. In 1818 the American troops invaded Western Florida which was also still under Spanish sovereignty, to repel the Seminole Indians living in Florida.

Mention should also be made of the famous incident of the *Caroline*.[9] On the occasion of the Canadian rebellion of 1837 against the British authorities (Canada being at the time under British sovereignty), rebels were assisted by American citizens who several times crossed the Niagara (the border between Canada and the US) on the *Caroline* to provide the insurgents with men and ammunitions. A party

[8] H. Staudacher, *Die Friedensblockade* (Leipzig, 1909), pp. 29-31.
[9] See R. Jennings in *AJIL* 32 (1938), 82 ff.

of British troops headed by Captain McLeod was then sent to attack the ship. They boarded it in the US port of Fort Schlosser, killed a number of men, set the ship on fire, and set it adrift towards the Niagara Falls. The US Government protested against this violation of its territorial sovereignty. A characteristic feature of the *Caroline* incident is that England saw no need to justify its behaviour by invoking a breach of international law by the US. Rather, it claimed that its violation of US sovereignty had been rendered necessary by the fundamental right of 'self-defence and self-preservation'. However, the ensuing diplomatic correspondence enabled the two States to agree upon a delimitation of the instances in which armed attack on the territory of another State was allowed. According to the definition by US Secretary of State Webster, the attacking State must show a 'necessity of self-defence, instant, overwhelming, leaving no choice of means and no moment for deliberation'. This formula, which became famous and was taken up in subsequent years, initiated an international practice which gradually led to placing some restrictions on the unfettered freedom of States to use force for the protection of their interests.

124. A typical example of resort to force against alleged violations of international law by another State, is the decision on the part of a State to send armed troops abroad for the purpose of protecting its nationals. In such a case the justification normally invoked by the invading State was that the territorial State had failed to take all the precautionary and other measures necessary for safeguarding the life and property of foreigners, and it, therefore, proved imperative to substitute for this omission, and exercise the requisite measure of control. Plainly, this sort of justification lends itself to many abuses.

According to the American writer Offutt,[10] between 1813 and 1928 US troops were sent abroad at least seventy times in order to protect US nationals or 'US interests'. Not unexpectedly, most military expeditions were effected by the US in Latin-American countries, but US troops also landed in other countries, such as Japan (1853, 1854, 1863, 1864, 1868); China (1854, 1856, 1859, 1900); Egypt (1858 and 1882); in Kisembo (on the west coast of Africa) in 1860; Formosa (1867); and Korea (1871, 1888, 1894). During the same period British forces landed in the Honduras in 1873 and in Nicaragua in 1895 and 1910, and German forces in Samoa in 1899.

Reprisals

125. Reprisals are acts or actions in response to an unlawful act by another State. They seek either to impel the delinquent State to discontinue the wrongdoing, or to punish it, or both.

[10] A. Offutt, *The Protection of Citizens Abroad by the Armed Forces of the US* (Washington, 1928), pp. 12 ff. See also the US document *Right to Protect Citizens in Foreign Countries by Landing Forces*, Memorandum of the Solicitor for the Department of State, 5 October 1912, 2nd edn. (Washington, 1929).

They are usually divided into peaceful reprisals and military reprisals. The former term implies the avoidance of the use or threat of force; thus, it can consist in the failure to apply a treaty or a customary rule (for instance, on the treatment of foreigners), in the mass expulsion of foreigners, and so on. The latter category includes any act implying coercion, or the threat or use of force against the State responsible for a wrongful act. This category, therefore, covers all the actions indicated above under the heading of intervention (blockade, embargo, and so on).

International law does not impose the choice of one form of reprisal rather than another. It only sets forth a few general criteria States must respect when carrying out a reprisal. Until the First World War international law did not exercise any restraints. However, according to Anzilotte,[11] reprisals implying the use of force were subject to the very restrictions which apply to similar acts when performed in time of war. Thus, bombardment of undefended localities, wanton destruction of places of art, religion or science, pillage, etc. were not allowed by international law. The reason was that this class of action is a *minus* with regard to war; hence, the will of States to rule out their admissibility in time of war for humanitarian considerations should *a fortiori* apply to the use of force short of war.

After the First World War the restrictions on war laid down in the Covenant of the League of Nations and the concomitant limitations on intervention led States to reduce the instances of resort to armed reprisals as well.

The famous *Naulilaa* case ought to be mentioned.[12] In 1914, while Portugal was still neutral, German forces from German South-West Africa crossed the border with Angola, then under Portuguese domination, in order to meet Portuguese authorities and initiate negotiations concerning the importation of food and the setting up of postal relations with Germany through Angola. At the Portuguese post of Naulilaa, on the southern border of Angola, two German officers and the interpreter were killed following a misunderstanding caused primarily by the German interpreter. By way of reprisal German troops were sent to destroy Portuguese posts and kill Portuguese soldiers. The Special Arbitral Tribunal instituted by Germany and Portugal determined in 1928 the following concerning reprisals: first, they comprise acts which would normally be illegal but are rendered lawful by the fact that they constitute a reaction to an act of international delinquency; second, they must be 'limited by considerations of humanity and the rules of good faith applicable in the relations between States'; third, they must not be excessive, although they need not be proportionate to the offence; fourth, they must be preceded by a request for peaceful settlement (they must 'have remained unredressed after a demand for amends'); fifth, they must 'seek to impose on the offending State reparation for the

[11] Anzilotti, op. cit., 166–8.
[12] The judgment on the *Naulilaa* case is in *UN Reports of International Arbitral Awards*, ii. 103 ff.

offence, the return to legality and the avoidance of new offences'. It is interesting to note that in this case, the Tribunal held that Germany had violated international law because: (1) the Portuguese had not acted contrary to international law, since the killing of the three Germans was not a wilful but a fortuitous, if deplorable, incident; (2) the Germans had not made a request for peaceful settlement before resorting to force; (3) the force used by Germany was 'excessive' and 'out of any proportion' to the conduct of Portuguese authorities.

Clearly, the requirement whereby reprisals are lawful only to the extent that they constitute a reaction to a wrong committed by another State, presupposes the emergence of a rule prohibiting *coercive* intervention, that is to say, any interference in another State by the threat or use of force (see § 127). So long as such intervention was admitted, reprisals—in actual fact—hardly made up a separate category, for it did not matter very much whether forcible measures short of war were to be labelled 'intervention' or 'reprisals'.

War

126. As stated above, until 1919 States were free to resort to war whenever they considered it fitting. In 1899 a Convention adopted by the Hague Peace Conference prescribed a declaration of war or an ultimatum (namely a declaration making the beginning of hostilities contingent on the non-observance by the other party of the conditions set forth therein). The 1899 Convention, which was restated in 1907 and soon turned into customary international law, can, however, be violated without this breach implying that war, in the full sense of the word, has started: if a State initiates war-like action against another State without complying with the Convention, it only makes itself answerable for a breach of international law; nevertheless the so-called 'state of war' (namely the entering into operation of the laws of war and neutrality) comes into force.

NEW TRENDS FOLLOWING THE FIRST WORLD WAR

127. After the First World War, for the historical and political reasons set out above (§ 29), sweeping restrictions on resort to *war proper* were laid down in the Covenant of the League of Nations and later on in the Kellogg-Briand Pact of 1928 (§ 32). In addition, it was felt that force should not be used to settle international political or legal disputes. This view resulted in three major developments between 1918 and 1938: (1) a customary prohibition of war as a means of protecting one's own interests slowly evolved; (2) a gradual process circumscribing the grounds for coercive intervention in the territory of another State, led to the formation of a rule prohibiting 'dictatorial intervention', that is, the threat or use of force for the purpose of imposing on the will of another State; (3) a set of rules evolved permitting force under exceptional circumstances (reprisals; self-defence; protection of nationals abroad whose life and assets are in peril because the territorial State is unable or unwilling to protect them).

THE NEW LAW

An Overview

128. The *rapprochement* effected during the Second World War between the Western Great Powers and the USSR led to an agreement between these countries on a new scheme for the maintenance of international security. At Dumbarton Oaks, in 1944, the Four Powers (US, UK, China, and the USSR) hammered out a collective security system based essentially on the concept that from then onwards no State must use force or threaten the use of force; and that they would take care to safeguard international peace and intervene on behalf of the world community in any dangerous crisis. In San Francisco in 1945 other countries accepted the scheme, both because it was in the interest of mankind and on account of the fact that it stemmed from the States wielding real power in international relations. However, they pressed the Big Four to lay down explicitly an important exception, namely the right of (weaker) States to defend themselves in case of armed attack, pending intervention by the UN.

The system inaugurated in 1945 was revolutionary indeed. It postulated that in future States ought to settle their disputes peacefully and never use force, subject to the exception of self-defence; and that an international authority, the UN, would act as a world police and enforcement agency. Thus, self-help, traditionally a characteristic feature of the international community, was done away with (except for self-defence), and a centralized body was vested with broad powers of forcible intervention. There were two momentous consequences: first, whereas before the distinction between lawful and unlawful use of force either could not be made or was blurred, it had now become possible to say—at least in theory—whether a specific instance of use of force was lawful; second, whereas before force could be used without any previous *ascertainment of the illegality of another State's behaviour*, now enforcement must come after an assessment by a third party (see § 110), except in the case of self-defence (§ 136).

That the system has not proved effective is well known. What are the causes for this failure? And what substitutes have been contrived by the majority of States? Before going into the details of the present regulations for the use of force, it may be useful to point out the major flaws of the system and how it has evolved in recent years.

The basic deficiencies of the UN Charter system were fourfold. First, the idea of a collective monopoly of force by the five permanent members of the Security Council was, of course, based on their continuing agreement; in case of dissent the so-called veto power (strongly advocated by the US and endorsed by the USSR at Dumbarton Oaks) gave any of the Five the right to cripple the collective security system. Second, the 'army' which should have been put at the disposal of the UN was not envisaged as an international army proper, exclusively dependent on the Security Council: it was to be composed of contingents placed at the disposal of the Security Council by the various member States and destined to remain under their control (although at the same time the Security Council would exercise its authority over national contingents); the 'dual allegiance' could not but result in a dangerous likelihood of the 'army' being paralysed by national States. Third, force was only banned in 'international relations' (Article 2.4); it was consequently allowed in 'internal' relations (for example, against rebels in case of civil strife), and in the relations between colonial powers and dependent territories; as tensions within the various colonial empires had already become apparent and were to increase, the Charter left a huge host of potentially dangerous strains to be dealt with at the discretion of individual States, should political dissension and demands for change intensify to the point of armed conflict. Fourth, to a large extent the UN Charter upheld a concept of 'negative peace', or absence of war, rather than 'positive' peace, or the introduction of justice for the purpose of preventing as far as possible political tensions from degenerating into armed conflicts. This is not to say that the UN closed its eyes to political reality and refrained from suggesting political solutions calculated to prevent armed conflicts. Indeed, co-operation in the economic, social, and political fields was promoted, obligations were imposed on colonial powers and it was also envisaged to further co-operation as regards disarmament. However, this part of the UN Charter proved rudimentary and weak. Particularly unsatisfactory were the provisions concerning colonies and economic relations.

The basic disagreement between the Western Powers and the USSR, which emerged a few months after the signing of the Charter and soon spread, resulted in the substantial failure of the collective security system. The UN 'army' was never set up: the two Superpowers crossed swords in the special body charged with elaborating the criteria for the institution of the 'army' and never reached an agreement. It soon became apparent that the great hopes entertained in 1944–5 would never become a reality. The two contending blocs set up separate organizations for 'collective self-defence' (NATO in 1949 and the Warsaw Pact in 1955). The world community returned to the old system of opposing political and military alliances which only a few years previously had helped to avoid total disintegration. In addition, a trend emerged which was to become one of the distinguishing features of the present international community, namely, the tendency of States to make increasing use of the right of individual self-defence, to such an extent that they now feel relatively confident to engage in war under the cloak of 'self-defence', without having to fear any decisive hindrance from the UN. At the same time States have endeavoured to broaden the concept of self-defence so as to include major forms of use of force short of war not covered by Article 51 of the Charter (see, for instance, § 140).

The UN has not, however, been cast aside altogether. Its presence could still serve a useful purpose although under unique circumstances in which a few groups of States might consider it politically expedient to make use of the UN machinery. In the face of Soviet opposition, the majority, dominated by the US, first contrived to enhance the role of the General Assembly by the famous resolution 'Uniting for Peace' (377-V, adopted on 3 November 1950). The General Assembly was empowered to recommend member States to adopt coercive measures against another State held responsible by the Organization of a breach of the ban on use of force. The new system was put into force during the Korean War, 1950-1. Subsequently, the temporary convergence between the two Superpowers led to the elaboration of a new and imaginative scheme: the creation of a 'peace-keeping' force (see § 130).

Collective Enforcement

Coercive Measures

(i) The UN Charter System

129. As stated above, the Charter hinges on the notion of collective security, that is, the monopoly of force by the Organization which should render superfluous military alliances created to protect weak States from possible attacks.

In addition to prohibiting force in Article 2.4 (§ 83), in Chapter VII the Charter set up a system calculated to enforce the law, that is to force States violating Article 2.4 to discontinue the breach (and make reparation, if necessary) as well as to police international relations. (As was cogently demonstrated by Kelsen[13] and Verdross,[14] under Article 39, the Security Council has the power to declare that a breach of the peace, a threat to the peace, or an act of aggression has occurred, even in instances where Article 2.4 is not violated, as in cases of civil wars menacing peace or of acute tensions between two States jeopardizing peace without either State having threatened or actually used force.)

[13] H. Kelsen, *The Law of the United Nations* (New York, 1950), pp. 727 ff., and *Principles of International Law* (New York, 1952), pp. 54-8.

[14] A. Verdross, 'Idées directrices de l'Organisation des Nations Unies', Hague *Recueil* 83 (1953-II), 52 ff.

The Security Council can decide upon provisional measures (Article 40), or measures not involving the use of armed force (such as complete or partial interruption of economic relations and of rail, air, postal, telegraphic, radio, and other means of communication, and the severance of diplomatic relations, under Article 41), or military sanctions, under Article 42. Besides, it had been the intention of the draftsmen for the armed forces on which the Security Council was to draw to be made available to it by member States by virtue of agreements to be concluded under Article 43. But for the political reasons mentioned above, these agreements were never entered into. However, we have seen that, even if they had been concluded, the UN 'army' would have been very weak indeed.

In order fully to expose the flaws of the Charter system, let us recall a metaphor used in 1950 by Ross to characterize that system.[15] He referred to the case of a densely wooded district whose inhabitants wish to co-operate for the purpose of combating the risk of forest fires. They will have to choose between three different ways of coping with the problem, each denoting a certain degree of social integration. They could institute automatic co-operation (each of them merely undertakes to put out the fire, by using his own fire-extinguishing appliances; if a fire council is established, its only function will be to make suggestions on how that duty should be performed). Alternatively, they could set up an organized form of co-operation (the fire council is authorized to decide if a fire has broken out and what must be done to put it out; the means for extinguishing it are not, however, owned by the council nor used by a special body of persons under its authority, but by the various inhabitants of the area, each of whom will use his own fire-extinguishing appliances). Finally, they could resort to institutionalized joint action (the fire council creates a regular fire brigade endowed with its own appliances and under the exclusive authority of the council). Now, while the first stage is reminiscent of the League of Nations, the second calls to the mind the UN. The third stage has not yet been reached by the world community; indeed, it is not even in the offing.

(ii) *UN Peace-keeping*

130. In 1956, on the occasion of the Anglo-French and Israeli armed attack on Egypt following President Nasser's nationalization of the Suez Canal Company, the changing relations between the two Superpowers and their convergence of interests begot a new form of UN intervention in case of serious crisis. As the UK and France had vetoed a Security Council resolution, the General Assembly was convened on the strength of the procedural provisions of the 'Uniting for Peace' Resolution and a group of States led by Canada suggested a new formula, that of 'peace-keeping operations', destined to be used on subsequent occasions.

[15] A. Ross, *Constitution of the United Nations* (New York, 1950), pp. 137 ff.

So far, UN peace-keeping operations have been carried out in the following cases: in the Middle East (1956-67); the Congo (1960-1); Cyprus (1964 onwards); the Middle East (1973 onwards).

These operations show the following distinguishing traits: (1) UN forces, that is armed forces put at the disposal of the UN by member States, are sent to a troubled area with the consent of the territorial State. (2) They are not composed of contingents provided by any of the Five Permanent members of the Security Council so as to avoid the involvement of any of them (an exception was the case of Cyprus, in which UK troops contributed to the UN forces, on the unique ground that they were already stationed in Cyprus under bilateral agreements). (3) They are not under the exclusive authority of the Security Council—they can be under the authority of the General Assembly whenever the former is paralysed by a veto. In addition, their direction is normally entrusted to the UN Secretary-General, who is given extensive powers of control, although he always acts under the supervision of the Security Council or the General Assembly. (4) The forces have no power of military coercion, but can use force in self-defence. (A notable exception took place during the conflict in the Congo, as can be seen in Resolution S/4741 A, adopted by the Security Council on 21 February 1961: the use of force beyond self-defence was authorized 'if necessary, in the last resort' to prevent 'the occurrence of civil war in the Congo'.) Essentially, the function of the UN forces consists in separating the contending parties, forestalling armed hostilities between them, and maintaining order in the area. (5) Except in the case of Suez, financial support for the Forces is provided by voluntary contributions of member States. (In the case of Suez the expenditures of UNEF were allotted to the regular UN budget although the socialist countries and France protested, claiming that this was contrary to the Charter. In 1962, the ICJ in its advisory opinion on *Certain Expenses of the UN* supported the Western view. There has been no recurrence of the line of action resorted to in 1956.)

Clearly, the 'peace-keeping' system is at odds with that envisaged in the Charter, which hinges on the Security Council only. The Council has authority over the armed forces of the Five Powers, which can enter the territory of member States without their consent and use force to repel the aggressor, or put an end to a breach of the peace or a threat to the peace. Finally, under the Charter system, the relevant expenditures are assigned to the ordinary budget of the Organization.

On balance, peace-keeping operations have proved useful for the purpose of making the contending parties stop fighting thereby avoiding more bloodshed. They are not designed to compel the parties to accept a solution imposed by the UN, but serve to help putting into practice, on the spot, the solution agreed upon by the contending States. However, in the long run, peace-keeping operations may turn out to be counter-productive, for they freeze the situation without providing a real solution to the basic problems lying at the root of the conflict (as in the case of Cyprus). This drawback can perhaps explain why U N peace-keeping is currently on the wane.

Non-coercive Measures

131. The almost complete failure of the U N collective system, and even of the imaginative substitutes subsequently set up, has, of necessity, led to magnifying the role and importance of 'sanctions' not involving the use of force. We shall presently take a quick look at these so-called 'sanctions'. At this juncture, it may be useful to point out that resort to them is inversely proportionate to their coerciveness; in other words, the less coercive they are, the more frequently and effectively they are used. The reason is simple: States and international institutions cannot do without 'sanctions'; in the face of growing dissent between groups of States and the consequent paralysis of collective enforcement machinery, the solution lies in mild forms of pressure or exposure, which serve to express collective condemnation of States' misbehaviour.

132. In a few cases the Security Council has decided that member States could take certain measures not involving the use of armed force. Cases in point are Rhodesia (1966-77) and South Africa (1977), when the Security Council explicitly acted under Article 41 of the Charter. In other instances either the Security Council or the General Assembly have recommended the adoption of measures such as the breaking off of diplomatic or economic relations: for example, against South Africa (since 1962 on account of apartheid and later on also because of its illegal occupation of Namibia) and Portugal (between 1963 and 1975 because of its colonial policy).

Unfortunately, most of these decisions or recommendations have gone unheeded, owing to the lack of unanimous and substantial support by the whole international community (often the target State was aided by one or more major Powers, which inevitably undermined U N condemnations).

133. On several occasions, faced with unlawful behaviour of States it was not in a position to terminate, or against which it proved unable to recommend or enjoin effective sanctions, the U N has fallen back on non-recognition of the illegal situation.

This doctrine was first enunciated in early 1932. After the Japanese invasion of the Chinese province of Manchuria, H. L. Stimson, the U S Secretary of State, declared that his Government

... cannot admit the legality of any situation *de facto* nor does it intend to recognize any treaty or agreement entered into between these Governments or agents thereof which may impair the treaty rights of the United States ... and ... it does not intend to recognize any situation, treaty or agreement which may be brought about by means contrary to the covenants and obligations of the Treaty of Paris of August 27, 1928.[16]

A resolution along the same lines was adopted by the Special Assembly of the League of Nations on 11 March 1932. In 1938 the Conference of American States adopted at Lima a Resolution on the non-recognition of acquisition of territory by force.

So far the Security Council and the General Assembly have resorted to the sanction at issue with respect to three States: Israel, South Africa, and Rhodesia.

What is the import of UN pronouncements on non-recognition? Politically they rest on the idea that all actions contrary to certain basic values commonly accepted by the world community amount to deviations which should not be legitimized. Their aim is to isolate the delinquent State and compel it to change the situation which has been condemned. They constitute a last-resort measure in those cases where the UN proves unable to bring about a return to legality by resorting to the sanctions provided for in the Charter: since the international organized community cannot nullify power, it must confine itself to emphatically withholding its endorsement.

Legally speaking the UN pronouncements mentioned before entail a mutual undertaking on the part of the supporting States. States pledge themselves to avoid any international or internal act capable of turning the *de facto* situation into an internationally legal one. It follows that domestic courts of all those States must treat acts and transactions with the unlawful authority as null and void; on an international level, no act should be performed that might result in legalizing the situation in any way. The ensuing state of affairs is likely to be very complex: although many customary rules of international law have in fact been modified to such an extent as to take account of the universal principles which have recently emerged (§§ 77–89), those States which do not vote in favour of the UN resolutions cannot be forced to take the view that the effective situation is contrary to international law; in fact, invoking the principle of effectiveness (§ 10) they can claim that they are entitled to consider that situation lawful and act accordingly. By contrast, the States who support the UN resolutions are authorized to regard the effective situation as unlawful, and to behave accordingly. Here, as in many other instances, one is confronted with a split in the attitude of the world community. Current international law makes allowance for this rift: although it does not render both tendencies legally warranted, it affords no means of making the majority view prevail.

[16] *AJIL* 26 (1932), 342.

134. The failure of the UN to come to grips with the tremendous problems posed by forcible implementation of international law has impelled it to fall back on yet another 'sanction': public exposure of gross violations. This sanction normally consists in the adoption by the General Assembly of resolutions condemning the unlawful conduct of States and in calls for the discontinuation of the deviant behaviour. So far resolutions of this class have been passed by the General Assembly on several occasions, chiefly when member States have violated human rights (see §§ 178, 182) or when they have disregarded basic principles of the Organization (as in the case of South Africa and Israel).

The fact that mere resort to exposure is seen as a sanction need not surprise us. Time and again States themselves have admitted the importance that public exposure can have as a means of exercising leverage on States. Thus, for instance, in 1975 the Greek representative said in the General Assembly:

Only intervention by various international and national organizations or protests of foreign Governments which truly respected the principles of freedom and democracy could exert an influence on dictators and guarantee some protection to political prisoners under totalitarian regimes.[17]

In the same vein, the UK delegate pointed out

If it was accepted that exposure was the most potent weapon available for combating torture, then the responsibility of the UN was very great indeed and there was cause to be grateful for the response to the GA's resolution [on torture, passed in 1975].[18]

Of course, one should not expect too much from this category of 'sanction', for more often than not the State concerned turns a deaf ear to international organizations. However, the beneficial effects of public condemnation can be appraised in the long term. It appears that States increasingly endeavour to avoid public strictures and, in particular, try to avoid being the target of repeated moral chastisements (see also § 145).

ENFORCEMENT BY INDIVIDUAL STATES

135. Another logical consequence of the malfunctioning of collective 'sanctions' has been the gradual 're-appropriation' by individual States of their right to react to wrongful acts by taking coercive or other measures designed to impel the delinquent party to discontinue its misbehaviour or to make reparation, as the case may be. Thus, individual States' 'sanctions', provided for by the Charter in absolutely exceptional circumstances only,

---

[17] See GAOR, XXXth Session, IIIrd Committee, 2160th Mtg., para. 14.
[18] Ibid., 2167th Mtg., para. 1.

have become more and more frequent, and currently constitute the rule. It stands to reason that this development has, in the event, damaged lesser States, which obviously cannot retaliate against violations by Great Powers. The latter, in turn, have tried to make use of force without grossly infringing upon the relevant provisions of the UN Charter. In actual fact, they have tried to circumvent the Charter prohibitions by skilfully stretching their interpretation in such a manner as to enjoy greater latitude in their right to react to the (real or alleged) misconduct of other States. As we shall see, lesser States have *normally* preferred to resort to peaceful 'sanctions', also to avoid conflicts escalating into open war.

Coercive Enforcement

Individual Self-Defence

136. Article 51 of the UN Charter, now general international law, only allows the use of force in order to repel an 'armed attack', and subject to the procedural requirements to the effect that the Security Council must be immediately informed of the armed action in self-defence. The text and drafting history of Article 51 make it abundantly clear that the provision did not intend to leave the pre-existing right of anticipatory self-defence, if any, unaffected. Under a strict interpretation of the Charter, self-defence can, therefore, be resorted to only *after* an armed attack by another State has actually been initiated.

Since aggression by another State constitutes a violation of the sovereign rights of the victim, in resorting to self-defence the latter engages in *legal enforcement*. This implies that self-defence must limit itself to rejecting the armed attack; it must not go beyond this purpose. Consequently, the victim of aggression must not occupy the aggressor State's territory, unless this is strictly required by the need to hold the aggressor in check and prevent him from continuing the aggression by other means. Furthermore, self-defence must come to an end as soon as the Security Council steps in and takes over the task of putting an end to the aggression. If the Security Council fails to take action, self-defence must cease as soon as its purpose, that is, to repel the armed attack, has been achieved. In other words, Article 51 and the corresponding norm of general international law do not authorize or condone any military action overstepping mere rejection of aggression. In particular, they prohibit prolonged military occupation and annexation of territory belonging to the aggressor.

137. A problem which has cropped up on several occasions and which has aroused great interest in the legal literature is whether Article 51 allows *anticipatory self-defence*, that is a pre-emptive strike, once a State is certain that another State is about to attack it militarily.

A favourable view has been maintained by Israel, which has actually resorted to anticipatory self-defence on various occasions: for example, in 1967 against Egypt, in 1975 against Palestinian camps in Lebanon, and in 1981, against Iraq (Israeli aircraft bombed the Iraqi nuclear reactor near Baghdad). Similarly, in 1980, in the UN Security Council, Iraq justified its armed attack on Iran by relying upon the pre-emptive right to strike at other countries preparing for War.[19] The admissibility of this class of self-defence has also been advocated by States such as Japan (1968 and 1975),[20] the US (1981),[21] and Canada (1981).[22]

The rationale behind the doctrine of 'anticipatory' self-defence, stressed by all those who advocate it, amounts to arguing that in an era of missiles and nuclear weapons and of highly sophisticated methods of reconnaissance and intelligence, it would be naive and self-defeating to contend that a State should await the attack by another country, in the full knowledge that it is certain to take place and likely to involve the use of very destructive weapons. As McDougall, one of the leading proponents of this view, has stated, to impose on States the attitude of 'sitting ducks' when confronted with an impending military attack 'could only make a mockery, both in its acceptability to States and in its potential application, of the Charter's main purpose of minimizing unauthorized coercion and violence across State lines'.[23] In 1981 the Israeli delegate echoed this doctrine in the Security Council when he declared that the scope of the concept of self-defence had:

... broadened with the advance of man's ability to wreak havoc on his enemies. Consequently the concept took on new and far wider application with the advent of the nuclear era. Anyone who thinks otherwise has simply not faced up to the horrific realities of the world we live in today, and that is particularly true for small States whose vulnerability is vast and whose capacity to survive a nuclear strike is very limited.[24]

This meta-legal rationale has been given a legal foundation by claiming that Article 51 did not suppress the pre-existing international rule on anticipatory self-defence, which was, therefore, left unaffected by the Charter. The argument, developed by some eminent jurists (Waldock, Stone, Bowett,

---

[19] The Iraqi thesis on anticipatory self-defence is in UN document S/PV.2250, 23-5.

[20] See *The Practice of Japan in International Law 1961–1970*, eds. S. Oda and H. Owada (Tokyo, 1982), 383-4; *JYIL* (1984), 109 and 111.

[21] The US view was put forward in the Security Council, on the occasion of the debate on the Israeli attack on the Iraqi nuclear reactor (see UN document S/PV.2288, 12 and 58).

[22] The Canadian view is in *CYIL* 20 (1982), 303-4.

[23] M. McDougall, 'The Soviet-Cuban Quarantine and Self-Defense', *AJIL* 57 (1963), 597, 601.

[24] The Israeli statement is in UN document S/PV.2288, 40.

Schwebel, McDougall, Kaplan, Katzenbach),[25] was cogently refuted by Brownlie, Lamberti Zanardi and Röling'[26] who rightly emphasized that first, the alleged customary rule did not envisage a right of anticipatory self-defence proper, but a right of self-defence and self-preservation; and second, Article 51 wiped out all pre-existing law, and did not leave any room for self-defence except in the form it explicitly authorized. Be that as it may, what matters more than scholarly views is the attitude of States. It is striking that when in 1981 the Israeli attack on the Iraqi nuclear reactor was discussed in the Security Council, the only State which (implicitly) indicated that it shared the Israeli concept of self-defence was the US. Although it voted for the Security Council resolution condemning Israel (Resolution 487—1981), it pointed out after the vote that its attitude was only motivated by other considerations: 'Our judgment that Israeli actions violated the UN Charter is based solely on the conviction that Israel failed to exhaust peaceful means for the resolution of this dispute.' All other members of the Security Council expressed their disagreement with the Israeli view, by unreservedly voting in favour of operative para. 1 of the resolution, whereby '[the Security Council] strongly condemns the military attack by Israel in clear violation of the Charter of the UN and the norms of international conduct'. In addition, Egypt and Mexico expressly refuted the doctrine of anticipatory self-defence. In particular, Mexico said:

... It is inadmissible to invoke the right to self-defence when no armed attack has taken place. The concept of preventive war, which for many years served as justification for the abuses of powerful States, since it left it to their discretion to define what constituted a threat to them, was definitively abolished by the Charter of the UN.[27]

The Mexican statement neatly brings out the main reason why many States interpret Article 51 as not authorizing pre-emptive strikes, and are not disposed to accept a new norm authorizing that sort of strike. However unrealistic and ineffective Article 51 may be, those States are deeply concerned that the interpretation they oppose might lead to abuse.

Arguably, recent State practice shows that a trend is emerging towards recognition, under certain strict conditions, of the right to resort to antici-

---

[25] H. Waldock, 'The Regulation of the Use of Force by Individual States in International Law', Hague *Recueil* 81 (1952-II), 495 ff.; J. Stone, *Aggression and World Order* (London, 1958), pp. 43-4; D. Bowett, *Self-Defence in International Law* (Manchester, 1958), pp. 187 ff.; S. Schwebel, 'Aggression, Intervention, and Self-Defence in Modern International Law', Hague *Recueil* 136 (1972-II), 479 ff.; M. A. Kaplan and N. Katzenbach, *The Political Foundations of International Law* (New York, 1961), pp. 210 ff.

[26] I. Brownlie, *International Law and the Use of Force by States* (Oxford, 1963), pp. 264 ff.; P. L. Lamberti Zanardi, *La legittima difesa nel diritto internazionale* (Milan, 1972), pp. 191 ff.; B. V. A. Röling, 'On the Prohibition of the Use of Force', *Legal Change: Essays in Honour of J. Stone* (New York, 1983), pp. 276 ff.

[27] The statements by the US, Egypt, and Mexico on the Israeli attack on the Iraqi nuclear reactor are in ILM (1981), 985, 980, and 991-2, respectively.

patory self-defence. In this connection, special emphasis must be placed on three cases: the pre-emptive strike of Israel against Egypt in 1967, the Iraqi attack on Iran in 1980, and the Israeli bombing of the Iraqi nuclear reactor in 1981. In the first two neither Israel nor Iraq was condemned by the world community, while in the third case all members of the Security Council, including the US (for the reasons indicated above), considered the Israeli attack contrary to the Charter. Arguably, the attitudes taken by the bulk of the world community in these instances are not as inconsistent as they might appear at first sight. Indeed, in 1967 Israel carried out its pre-emptive strike in the face of an imminent armed attack by Egypt; all indications supported the imminence of this attack. Israel had no other means to fall back on, in particular peaceful means of settling disputes, and an urgent meeting of the Security Council seemed of little value. The same might hold true for the Iraqi attack on Iran, at least in some respects. Indeed, no condemnation of Iraq was issued by the Security Council in 1980 for its armed attack. By contrast, in 1981 the Iraqi–Israeli situation was totally different: Israel had no certain evidence that the Iraqi nuclear reactor would be used in future for warlike purposes, and in addition the IAAE had been keeping the reactor under close scrutiny. Instead of turning to the Security Council or to other international bodies, Israel launched an armed attack. In this case the almost universal condemnation seems to indicate that the factual circumstances did not justify the Israeli attack. One might perhaps draw the conclusion that a concensus is now growing to the effect that under Article 51 anticipatory self-defence is allowed, but on the strict conditions that: (1) solid and consistent evidence exists that another country is about to engage on a large-scale armed attack jeopardizing the very life of the target State, and (2) no peaceful means of preventing such attack are available either because they would certainly prove useless owing to the specific circumstances, or for lack of time to resort to them, or because they have been exhausted. However, the risks of abuse make it imperative to take this construction of Article 51 very strictly and consider it as giving only very exceptional licence. On balance, the conclusion of the Polish judge Lachs seems warranted. As he said in 1980: 'I accept the view that one has to be very careful in regard to anticipatory action and in principle exclude it in view of the risks involved.'[28]

138. While Article 51 clearly refers to an actual use of force taking place at a definite time (the crossing of frontiers by military troops, the bombing of territory by foreign aircraft, large-scale attack on foreign ships on the high seas, etc.) international practice shows that military aggression increasingly takes the form of gradual infiltration of armed forces and groups of

[28] M. Lachs, 'The Development of General Trends of International Law in Our Time', Hague *Recueil* 169 (1980-IV), 163.

'voluntaries' supported by a foreign Government into the territory of another State (the 'invasion' of the territory of a State does not take place all of a sudden and on a large scale, but over a long period and piecemeal). It can also consist in organizing, assisting, fomenting, financing, inciting or tolerating subversive or terrorist activities carried out against another State, either to overthrow its Government or to interfere in civil strife (so-called indirect armed aggression). The problem arises whether international law extends self-defence to include reaction to invasion through infiltration of troops and to indirect armed aggression.

It should be recalled that the former category of aggression was invoked by the US in the case of Vietnam: the American Government consistently held that individual self-defence by South Vietnam and collective self-defence by the US were legitimized by the gradual infiltration of North Vietnamese troops and Vietcong into South Vietnam. However, the attitude of other States towards this view does not show that a customary rule has come into being which justifies self-defence in the event of armed infiltration.

As for indirect armed aggression, various States (chiefly the US, Israel and South Africa) have claimed that it warrants self-defence. In particular, Israel, on the occasion of its attacks against Palestinian camps in Lebanon (in 1970–83) and in Tunisia (in 1985), Rhodesia (when it attacked Zambia in 1978–9), and South Africa, on the occasion of its attacks on Swapo camps and troops in Angola and its raids into Lesotho, Zambia and Swaziland (between 1976 and 1985) have claimed that the violation of sovereign rights of the attacked State was justified by the fact that the latter tolerated or actively supported terrorist activities of guerrilla groups against the territory and assets of the attacking States.

However, the reaction of the international community has never been one of full and convinced acceptance of the legal justifications propounded by Israel, Rhodesia and South Africa. In addition, the discussions on the principle of non-intervention which took place in the UN Special Committee on Friendly Relations in 1966–70 were revealing.

In 1964 the UK proposed to proclaim the right of any country to seek military assistance from third States, should it become the victim of unlawful intervention in the form of 'subversive activities leading to civil strife in which the dissident elements are receiving external support and encouragement'. In 1966 a group of Western countries (Australia, France, Canada, Italy, the UK, and the US) took up and broadened that proposal, suggesting that the

... right of States in accordance with international law to take appropriate measures to defend themselves individually or collectively against intervention is a fundamental element of the inherent right of self-defence.

However, this proposal was strongly attacked in the Special Committee by a number of socialist and Third World countries, including Czechoslovakia, the United Arab

Republic, Ghana, India, Lebanon, Algeria and Mexico. They argued that the proposal was 'a dangerous departure from the UN Charter and from international law as generally accepted'; in particular, it ignored Article 51 and led to

... a dangerous broadening of the range of eventualities in which [self-defence] could be exercised under that provision of the Charter.

As a result of that criticism, the proposal was withdrawn by its sponsors and the final text of the Declaration on Friendly Relations simply refers to the 'relevant provisions of the Charter'.[29] It should also be noted that the UN Special Committee for the Definition of Aggression eventually took the same stand, as is apparent, in particular, from the debates which took place within the Committee and to which L. Lamberti Zanardi has drawn attention.[30]

It thus seems difficult to contend that a general rule has evolved authorizing States to invoke self-defence to repel indirect armed aggression, or else that self-defence against this type of aggression is authorized by Article 51.

Attention should, however, be drawn to a recent and very significant trend in State practice. The Soviet Union has intervened militarily in two instances (Czechoslovakia in 1968, and Afghanistan in 1979) claiming that it was acting both at the request of the State concerned, and on the strength of Article 51, that is, in 'collective' self-defence (see § 139), to repel an aggression against the State to whose territory it sent its troops. Now, it is apparent from reliable circumstantial evidence that in fact no armed attack proper by a third State had been committed—one could at most speak (in the case of Afghanistan) of military aid of some sort by third countries to rebels. It is, indeed, no coincidence that in the UN the USSR never made it clear by which specific State the alleged aggression had been carried out, but simply spoke of 'external interference in Czechoslovakia's internal affairs' and of 'subversive actions by external forces' in Afghanistan. It can therefore be said that in fact the Soviet Union has gradually been getting closer and closer to an interpretation of Article 51 not very different from that advocated by Israel, South Africa, the US (as well as the UK and other Western countries), that is to say, that Article 51 also authorizes collective self-defence in case of 'indirect armed aggression' (and, indeed, it is significant that recently an Hungarian international lawyer, Bokor-Szego, has propounded precisely this view in a scholarly publication).[31]

---

[29] The British proposal is in UN document A/AC.119/L.8, 8; the proposal put forward by various Western countries is in A/AC.125/L.113 subpara. 2D. As for the various statements against the Western proposal, see A/AC.125/SR.14, at 10 (Czechoslovakia); ibid., 12 (UAR); SR/15, 5 (Ghana); ibid., 8 (India); ibid., 10 (Lebanon); SR/16, 7 (Algeria); ibid., 16 (Mexico).

[30] Lamberti Zanardi, op. cit., 250-5.

[31] H. Bokor-Szego, 'The Attitude of Socialist States Towards the International Regulation of the Use of Force', in *Legal Restraints on the Use of Force Forty Years After the Charter*, ed. A. Cassese (Doordrecht, 1986), pp. 466 ff.

'Collective' Self-defence

139. Article 51 grants any member State of the UN the right to use force in support of another State which has suffered an armed attack. This right, now incorporated in a general rule, has been interpreted to the effect that the intervening State must not be itself a victim of the armed attack by the aggressor (in which case it would act by way of 'individual' self-defence). Both the NATO treaty and the Treaty on the Warsaw Pact point in this direction. However, what is required is a prior bond (for example, a treaty) between the two States acting in self-defence or, if such a bond is lacking, an express request by the victim of the attack. In other words, a State cannot use force against a country which has attacked another State, without the request or the previous consent of the latter.

So far 'collective' self-defence (that is intervention by one or more States in favour of the victim) has been invoked by the US in the case of Vietnam (in various official pronouncements, in particular the State Department Memorandum of 4 March 1966, the US relied upon Article 51 for their military action in support of South Vietnam),[32] and by the Soviet Union in the case of Czechoslovakia (1968) and Afghanistan (1979).

The relative paucity of instances of 'collective' self-defence—in itself no doubt a felicitous feature of the present world community—is due to the tendency of States to hold aloof as much as possible from international armed conflicts or to side with one of the contending parties merely by sending arms and military equipment.

Protection of Citizens Abroad

140. In various instances States have used force for the purpose of protecting their nationals whose lives were in danger in foreign territory.

In certain cases force has been used without the consent of the territorial State: Belgium intervened in the Congo in 1960; the US in the Dominican Republic in 1965; Israel in Uganda in 1976; the US in Iran in 1980, and in Grenada in 1983. In the first two cases the territorial State was not responsible for the threat to the life of foreign nationals, for such threat resulted from the collapse of the public order system; by contrast, in the third and fourth cases the local Government was answerable, for it did not protect the lives of foreigners, but tolerated or even aided and abetted the activity of private individuals endangering foreign nationals; in the fifth case (that of Grenada) independent reports disclosed that there was actually no imminent threat or danger to the lives of American citizens, and the fact that US troops were stationed in the island after evacuating the American na-

---

[32] The US memorandum of 4 March 1966 is in *The Vietnam War and International Law*, ed. R. A. Falk (Princeton, NJ, 1968), pp. 583 ff., 584-6.

tionals confirmed that the ground for landing troops adduced by US authorities was indeed a mere pretext for unlawful forcible intervention.

In four other cases military intervention was effected with the consent of the territorial State: the US sent their troops to Lebanon in 1958;[32a] Belgium did the same, with help from the US in the Congo in 1964; the Federal Republic of Germany sent a commando to Mogadishu with the consent of Somalia in 1977, and, in 1978, French and Belgian troops intervened in the Shaba area at the request of Zaire.

In addition, there is the case of the Larnaca incident of 1978. It is, however, quite unique and anomalous and can therefore not be put into the same category as the others just mentioned. In February 1978 two terrorists killed the Egyptian Secretary-General of the Afro-Asian Peoples Solidarity Organization during a meeting of the Organization in Nicosia. After seizing hostages, among which there were a few Egyptian nationals, the terrorists left Cyprus by aeroplane but, being refused access by various countries, were obliged to return to Larnaca airport. While negotiations were under way between the Cypriot authorities and the terrorists, an Egyptian aircraft was allowed to land at Larnaca. When the Cypriot authorities realized that it carried a commando, they refused to authorize it to intervene. The Egyptians nevertheless opened fire against the terrorists, whereupon the Cyprus national guard in its turn fired against the Egyptians. As a result of the shoot-out several Egyptians and Cypriots were killed or wounded and the Cypriot authorities arrested the terrorists. A dispute between Egypt and Cyprus ensued. The former, while conceding that Cyprus had not authorized the use of force, claimed that it had not violated Cypriot sovereignty and had acted upon the principle of fighting terrorism. Cyprus, however, rejected Egyptian claims and firmly asserted that its sovereignty had been violated. The case clearly does not fit into the class of incidents where States use force to protect their own nationals, first, because Egypt claimed its sole aim was to combat terrorists, and, second, because it contended that it had used force after being authorized by Cyprus to send a military aircraft to Larnaca.

One thing is striking: in cases of use of force to protect nationals, the intervening State is invariably a Western Power, and the State on whose territory the military action is carried out is a Third World country. This situation is indicative of the present constellation of power in the world community and of the relations between the West and developing countries. Of course, there is no denying that in nearly all the cases at issue there was either a real breakdown in the territorial system of public order, or an inability on the part of the local Government to prevent the perpetration

---

[32a] Although the principal grounds for American intervention adduced both by the US and Lebanon were the request of the Lebanese Government as well as the applicability of Article 51 of the UN Charter (see the statement made in the Security Council by Lebanon on 15 July 1958, in SCOR, 827th Mtg., para 84, as well as the US statement: ibid., paras 34 and 35), the US delegate to the Security Council also emphasized that US troops had been sent to Lebanon in order to protect American lives (he pointed out that US forces 'will afford security to the several thousand Americans who reside in that country': ibid., para 35).

of unlawful acts against foreigners. Admittedly, this inability testifies to the relative backwardness of some developing countries. It is nevertheless striking that developed States only intervene when their own nationals are imperilled. As long as the lives of local people alone are at stake, the world community, and developed countries in particular, tend to turn a blind eye; it does not occur to them that the best way of forestalling regrettable attacks against nationals of developed States is to help 'backward' countries improve their domestic system of law and order—which, of course, presupposes, and goes hand in hand with, the improvement of social and economic conditions.

The second remarkable thing is that only Western States have expressed the view that armed intervention for the protection of nationals is internationally lawful, being authorized either by Article 51 of the UN Charter or by a customary rule unaffected by the Charter. (The US went so far as to adopt in 1948 national legislation laying down the right of the US to use force abroad to protect 'the lives and property' of American citizens 'against arbitrary violence': Article 0614, US Navy Regulations.) By contrast, developing and socialist countries have consistently opposed the legality of this class of resort to force. Except for the German intervention in Somalia (where the territorial State gave its consent), foreign intervention has consistently been attacked by Eastern European and Third World countries as contrary to international law. Thus, for instance, on the occasion of the armed action by the US in Lebanon in 1958, Ethiopia stated in the General Assembly:

Ethiopia strongly opposes any introduction or maintenance of troops by one country within the territory of another country under the pretext of protection of national interest, protection of lives of citizens or any other excuse. This is a recognized means of exerting pressure by stronger Powers against smaller ones for extorting advantages. Therefore, it must never be permitted.[33]

On the same occasion Poland argued that the protection of nationals abroad constituted an 'old pretext'.[34] And in 1978, on the occasion of the French and Belgian military operation in Zaire, the Soviet official news agency Tass stated that 'humanitarian intervention' was merely 'a fig leaf to cover up an undisguised interference in the internal affairs of Zaire'.[35]

The reasons for the strong opposition of these two large groups of States are obvious: States fear that the protection of nationals may serve as a means of using leverage on developing countries; in other words, as a form of neo-colonialism. Be that as it may, it seems certain that the tenacious

[33] See GAOR, IIIrd Emergency Special Session, 742nd Pl. Mtg., 20 August 1958, para. 75.
[34] Ibid., 740th Pl. Mtg., 19 August 1958, para. 84.
[35] The dispatch of Tass is in *Keesing's Contemporary Archives* (1978), 29128.

resistance of so many States has prevented the general rule on the matter, evolved after the First World War (see §127), and later obliterated as a result of the impact of the UN Charter on customary law, from being revived in the world community. However, when the territorial State genuinely and spontaneously grants its consent and both the situation obtaining in its territory and the attitude of the intervening State are such as to rule out the possibility of a neo-colonialist intervention in disguise, the use of armed force can be considered lawful.

Armed Intervention With the Consent of the Territorial State

141. Let us deal at greater length with a topic until now only touched upon—that of whether the principle *volenti non fit injuria* (an illegal act is no longer such if the party whose rights have been infringed previously consented thereto), which is universally enshrined by State law, is also acknowledged as valid by the international community.

In traditional international law this principle was obviously in full force— each member being on a par with the others, there were no limits to the freedom of States and all rules could be derogated from. Thus each State was free to allow another to use force in any form on its own territory. Just as a State was able officially to sanction its own mutilation, dismemberment, or even its total extinction, so it could agree to allow another international subject to use force on its own territory.

Did the situation change once the use of force had been explicitly forbidden in the UN Charter and this ban had been enshrined as one of the pivots of the international community, with only a few very circumscribed exceptions? Since these exceptions did not include consent, can consent become an implicit exception? A close scrutiny of the Charter allows for only one conclusion: by explicit consent a State may authorize the use of force on its territory whenever, as the object of an 'armed attack', it resorts to individual self-defence (by giving its consent the State authorizes a form of collective self-defence). What if the consenting State is not in fact the object of an 'armed attack'? For example, what if there has been an insurrection within its territory, or if it is faced with serious disorders, and would like to appeal for help to another member of the international community?

Not a few States tend to consider *traditional* law still fully valid and consequently hold that consent legitimizes the use of force because it precludes the violation of Article 2.4 of the Charter. In 1958, for instance, the British Foreign Secretary asserted:

The structure of the Charter preserves the customary law by which aid may be given to a nation of the kind which I have described [in the face of civil strife fomented from abroad] ... I do not believe that either the spirit or the letter of the Charter takes away the customary, traditional right....

However, in 1963 Brownlie,[36] the distinguished English jurist, stated that one should tread very warily, especially in the case of civil war, and never lose sight of certain general principles which were emerging at that time within the international community, and which were tending to restrict the freedom of States.

Brownlie felt that, as a rule, it was necessary to ascertain that consent had not been vitiated by illegal pressure and to establish that it had been issued by the legitimate authorities. Once these preliminary enquiries were completed, with specific reference to intervention in civil war or internal disorders, one ought to distinguish between three main hypotheses. First, that in which consent to the use of force was given by a State on whose territory an organized movement was *not* fighting the government 'with a general political object of replacing it; in this case the use of force was acceptable'. Second, that in which a substantial body of the population supported the insurrection 'and there is no question of foreign aid, moral or material, to the insurgents'; in such a case the use of force by a third State in support of the Government *can provoke objections* 'on considerations of principle' because it could conflict with the principles of self-determination and non-interference, or for reasons of policy (the danger that these internal disturbances could escalate into an international conflict). Third, that in which the rebels receive military aid from third States. According to Brownlie, under these circumstances, the use of force at the behest of the Government is legitimate.

Certain States all too readily claim their own military interventions to be lawful. Remember, for example, the Soviet intervention in Hungary (when the USSR did not invoke Article 51), that of the US in Lebanon, and of the UK in Jordan, both in 1958 (when both States invoked Article 51, as well as receiving consent), that of the US in the Dominican Republic in 1965 (when the Americans also invoked the Charter of the OAS), in Grenada in 1983 (when the US also referred to a regional treaty and to the 'right to protect nationals abroad'), not to mention Soviet intervention in Czechoslovakia in 1968 and in Afghanistan in 1979 (when the USSR both invoked Article 51 and allegedly received the consent of the territorial State in question). Thus, on more than one occasion, in cases of subversion in the territory of one State, other States have considered it quite legitimate to intervene, after a request to do so, either because the rebels were said to receive aid from third States, or because the consenting State was said to be the object of an 'armed attack', as laid down in Article 51. In fact it would appear that many of these cases of so-called armed intervention were unlawful, either because they were based on a misinterpretation of the relevant rules, or because the concrete situation adduced to justify intervention differed in reality from the one depicted by the intervening State. Often the rebels were not in fact receiving any 'external' aid, and certainly not in

[36] I. Brownlie, op. cit., 317–27. Ibid., 326 for the quotation of the British statement.

the form of massive 'military assistance'; or else, the individuals requesting or authorizing foreign intervention could not be regarded as the lawful authority of the 'inviting' State. Furthermore, whenever the intervening State (not to mention the 'consenting' State) justified the use of force by the need to repulse, in conformity with Article 51, an 'indirect armed aggression', the justification was based on a questionable interpretation of Article 51 because, as we have already seen (§ 138), it should not allow the use of force against that particular form of 'aggression'.

Clearly State practice makes extensive use of the consent exception, even though this practice hardly conforms with present-day international law. Let us not forget that the latter has evolved as a consequence of the affirmation of *jus cogens*, a development to which the momentous Article 29 of the Ago Draft Convention on State responsibility (approved by the UN International Law Commission) bears witness.

The present legal system may be summarized as follows: First, consent must be *freely given* (that is, it cannot be wrested by any form of force whatsoever); it must be *real* as opposed to merely 'apparent', and it must have been given by the lawful Government, that is, by the authority empowered thereto by the constitution. Second, consent cannot validly legitimize the use of force when it is contrary to principles of *jus cogens*, for example if its use tends to deny or to limit the right of peoples to self-determination, or if it turns out to be a case of interference in the domestic affairs of the State on whose territory force has been used (on the legal basis of the link between consent and *jus cogens* see the comment of the ILC on Article 29, mentioned above).

Non-coercive Enforcement

142. It will come as no surprise that this category of measures is mostly resorted to by lesser States (because of the obvious lack of military power) or by middle-sized or Great Powers in respect of other powerful States (with the aim of avoiding dangerous clashes which might easily degenerate into armed conflicts).

Characteristically, most of these 'sanctions' are taken by States in conjunction with other States, often with the endorsement of international institutions. Indeed, the weight of these measures is so small that they can become effective only if resorted to by more than one State and with the support of an international organization, which enhances the 'symbolic' value of the 'sanction'.

Peaceful Reprisals

143. In the event of a breach of international law, the injured State can disregard any international obligation to the delinquent State (for instances of this kind of reprisal, see above § 125).

Peaceful reprisals are subject, however, to three basic limitations:

(1) States are not allowed to resort to them as soon as the wrong occurs; the injured State must first exhaust all possible means of peaceful settlement of disputes (provided for in Article 33 of the Charter). This requirement follows from the general principle, already referred to (§ 84), whereby States are duty-bound to settle their disputes peacefully. When can a State consider that it has complied with this duty and feel justified in resorting to reprisals? If, prior to the dispute, both parties had not accepted as compulsory a specific mode of settlement, the aggrieved party must propose negotiations, or may bring the dispute before the relevant UN bodies. Only when the author of the wrongdoing *refuses* to engage in negotiations or *wilfully hampers* the working of other means of adjustment available, can the injured State consider in good faith that no other choice is available, and resort to peaceful reprisals.

(2) Reprisals cannot disregard international rules for the protection of human rights or, more generally, the dignity and welfare of human beings.

This serious limitation follows from the general principle on human rights discussed above (§ 86). Respect for human dignity has acquired such importance in the world community that it is no longer possible to sacrifice the interests and exigencies of human beings for the sake of responding to wrongs caused by States. Consequently, if a State breaks an international rule, the aggrieved party is not authorized to violate international rules protecting the rights or interests of nationals of the delinquent State. Human beings are no longer objects of State action; States cannot dispose of individuals at their discretion any longer; they cannot make the consequences of international misbehaviour fall upon innocent people.

The principle was partially codified in the 1969 Vienna Convention on the Law of Treaties. Article 60.5 lays down that material breach of a bilateral or multilateral treaty cannot be invoked by a party as a ground for terminating the treaty or suspending its operation, *in toto* or in part, in case of '... provisions relating to the protection of the human person contained in treaties of a humanitarian character, in particular to provisions prohibiting any form of reprisals against persons protected by such treaties'. Interestingly, the provision was proposed by Switzerland, whose primary purpose was to safeguard the observance of humanitarian conventions on war victims (§§ 149 and 157), and was strongly supported by other Western countries, as well as by a few Latin-American States plus India. Tanzania, on the other hand, expressed serious misgivings. In the event the rule was adopted by a large majority (eighty-seven to none, with nine abstentions).[37]

The provision codifies only in part the general limitation upon reprisals, for it rules out disregard of a treaty whenever the treaty itself is broken by another party. By contrast, the general limitation set forth above is intended to protect human beings even in case the breach relates to a rule other than that which might be violated by way of reprisal. International rules designed to protect human beings must be observed under any circumstance, whether or not they themselves are the subject of a breach.

It should be added that the general qualification under discussion does not apply solely to treaties or general rules on human rights or to the humanitarian law of armed conflicts. It also extends its reach to rules protecting the interests or needs of human beings. Thus, for instance, if a State acts contrary to international law (for example, by mistreating foreign diplomats, or unlawfully hampering the innocent passage through its territorial sea), the injured State cannot reciprocate by terminating (or suspending the application of) a treaty which provides for economic aid to the defaulting State for the purpose of alleviating the plight of a segment of its population, as this kind of reprisal would ultimately damage the needs and interests of human beings. Similarly, if a State unlawfully expropriates the assets of foreigners, the national State of the expropriated companies cannot react either by expelling all the citizens of the expropriating State or by terminating a commercial treaty intended to benefit poor segments of the population of that State (in this instance, we are also dealing with the breach of an international rule protecting interests and rights—those relating to property—which are considered by the two 1966 UN Covenants as not worthy of the same international protection as other interests and needs of the human person. Consequently, we are faced with two conflicting interests, one of which outweighs the other in international consideration. This situation reinforces the obligation not to disregard the rule protecting human interests by way of reprisal). In a nutshell, the reciprocity principle does not apply when interests and exigencies of human beings are at stake.

(3) A third limitation upon reprisals is that they must not be out of proportion to the breach by the delinquent State.

As the arbitral tribunal in the *Naulilaa* case stated, no strict proportionality was required at the time in case of coercive reprisals. The same consideration holds true for peaceful reprisals, if only because it is always difficult to ascertain whether reprisals are strictly commensurate with the wrongdoing. What is exacted by international law is that reprisals be not

[37] For the views put forward by States on Article 60.5 of the Vienna Convention on the Law of Treaties, see *Conference Records, First Session*, 61st Mtg. of the Committee of the Whole, para. 12; *Second Session*, 21st Plenary Mtg., paras 21 and 26–47. The views of Tanzania are at para. 53.

grossly disproportionate in gravity and magnitude: the importance of the rule disregarded as well as the duration and global effects of its non-application should roughly correspond to those of the unlawful act to which one retaliates.

Joint Economic Sanctions

144. The current international practice of States includes cases where countries, individually or jointly, have decided to react against gross violations of basic international norms by other States by initiating economic sanctions against the delinquent State. Thus, for example, the US put into effect economic sanctions (suspension of deliveries of corn, withholding of industrial goods, etc.) against the USSR as a consequence of the Soviet 'invasion' of Afghanistan in 1979. Also, the US decided to call the USSR to account for the Soviet attitude towards Poland in 1981. In 1982 the ten EEC countries decided upon economic sanctions against Argentina for her invasion of the Falklands/Malvinas.

Such economic measures are to be regarded as *reprisals proper* to the extent that first, they are taken in consequence of a breach of international rules imposing duties *erga omnes*, hence conferring on *any* State a right to claim respect for the rules; and second, the economic measures run contrary to previous legal commitments of the sanctioning States. It may, however, prove useful to discuss them jointly, both because they are often lumped together with other forms of reaction to international wrongs (for example, they are frequently not contrary to binding obligations previously undertaken by the sanctioning State), and also because they constitute a notable and distinctive trend in the present international practice.

Legally speaking, the basic assumption on which such measures must rest for them to be considered legitimate, is that an international representative body must have pronounced authoritatively on the illegal acts which originally provoked them.

In the case of the Falklands/Malvinas the resolution adopted on 3 April 1983, by the UN Security Council, to the effect that Argentina had committed a 'breach of the peace' (Resolution 502), can be considered sufficient international authority for imposing economic sanctions on Argentina. Of course, the decision of the EEC Council of Ministers gave added weight to the Security Council pronouncement. In the case of Afghanistan, the resolution adopted by a very large majority on 14 January 1980 by the UN General Assembly (Resolution ES-6/2), 'deploring' the 'armed intervention' in Afghanistan as being contrary to the fundamental principle of respect for sovereignty, territorial integrity and political independence of States (the USSR, however, was not named), can be regarded as warranting the economic sanctions taken by individual States or a group of States.

It seems that a second basic requirement should be met by economic 'sanctions': they must aim at inducing the delinquent State to discontinue its misbehaviour; they ought not to be used as an instrument in bloc politics or as a new weapon for gaining political or diplomatic advantages. In short, they should not be abused.

The difficulty of making an impartial and balanced assessment of the economic sanctions taken so far by States outside any prior *specific* authorization of a representative international body helps to explain why sanctions produce such widely varying reactions in the world community. Thus, for example, the USSR has consistently rejected as unlawful the sanctions applied by the US in response to the Soviet 'invasion' of Afghanistan.[38] As for Argentina, a few socialist countries (GDR, Bulgaria, Albania, Belorussia, Czechoslovakia) plus Laos, argued in November 1982 in the General Assembly that the 'collective sanctions' imposed by some European countries were unlawful (however, they did not specify to which international norms they ran counter). Poland, the Soviet Union and Panama had contended in May 1982, in the Security Council, that the sanctions violated the UN Charter.[39]

Let us now look at the current international practice from another viewpoint and ask ourselves what motivated economic sanctions, and whether these sanctions have proved effective. It seems that they have served two purposes: first, as the catalysing factor uniting a group of States opposed to the alleged misbehaviour of another State (by taking sanctions and prompting other countries to adopt the same course of action, the State taking the initiative—the US in the case of Afghanistan, the UK in the case of the Falklands/Malvinas—intended to rally other States behind its censorious attitude); second, as a symbol of public exposure and condemnation of the States allegedly misbehaving (they were not so much intended to damage the delinquent State in the economic field—the history of international relations speaks volumes for the actual ineffectiveness of economic sanctions—but primarily to dramatize and articulate the condemnation of a certain form of behaviour and, by the same token, 'delegitimize' it, or, to put it differently, to prove to world public opinion that the 'delinquent' State was wrong inasmuch as it had acted contrary to internationally accepted standards).

From this point of view the sanctions may be said to have been relatively effective. On other scores they have not achieved any major results.

[38] For the Soviet view that Western 'sanctions' for the invasion of Afghanistan were unlawful, see the interview with President Brezhnev of 13 January 1980 (translated in *The Current Digest of the Soviet Press* 32, no. 2 (13 February 1980), p. 1) as well as the statement published by the news agency Tass on 30 December 1981 in *Foreign Broadcasting Information Service, Daily Report, Soviet Union* 3, 12 March 1982. A 6.

[39] For the declarations in the Security Council, see: S/PV.2362, 22 May 1982, p. 38 (Poland); ibid., 2363, 23 May 1982, 8/10 (USSR); ibid., 2363, 23 May 1982, p. 76 (Panama).

Recapitulation and Conclusion

145. At this juncture, it may prove useful to contrast the two basic patterns for enforcing law discussed in some detail in the previous paragraphs. The 'old' law rested on a few fundamental tenets: (1) the unfettered freedom of States to use force; (2) the consequent lack of a clear-cut distinction between enforcement proper (that is, resort to coercive action to compel observance of law) and use of force for realizing one's own interests; (3) the licence to use force without previously having an international authority establish whether a subjective right of the State resorting to force had in fact been violated; (4) the absence of any 'solidarity link' between the injured party and any third State, authorizing the latter to intervene to protect the rights of the former; international wrongs remained a 'private' occurrence between the delinquent State and the aggrieved party, except for those instances where there were already links based on treaties of alliance, in which case an ally might be affected by the wrongdoing and feel authorized to intervene; (5) the lack of any international agency capable of at least co-ordinating resort to force by individual States. In short, traditional law favoured major Powers: minor States derived no protection from general rules and consequently their own safeguard lay in the conclusion of treaties of alliance with one or more Great Powers.

After the unfortuate parenthesis of the inter-war period and the League of Nations experiment, the temporary convergence between the previously hostile Powers (Western countries and the USSR) brought about a consensus to the effect that peace should henceforth constitute the overriding purpose of all members of the world community. Consequently, States agreed that the maintenance of peace should become a public affair, that is to say, a matter of general concern, and that no country should be allowed to break or even jeopardize peaceful relations. The ensuing legal position is as follows: (1) The previously untrammelled right to use force has been suppressed; any use of force except in self-defence is totally banned. It should be noted, however, that the new international law has not abrogated the norms concerning the modalities of the use of force—that is to say, if a State illegally engages in military action, it is bound to respect certain general principles and rules placing restraints on such action (§ 150); the purpose being, of course, to ensure that any breaches of the general prohibitions referred to above do not degenerate into barbarism. (2) There is an international organization, the UN, which, in theory, is endowed with collective responsibility both for enforcing the law in extreme cases (that is, when breaches of international rules jeopardize peaceful relations) and, more generally, for safeguarding peace, irrespective of any action taken by the aggrieved party, hence also in the event of its remaining passive in the face of aggression. Serious international breaches have become 'public' events, which concern the whole international community. (3) Theoretically, the U N has a monopoly of force, in that it should intervene militarily in all the extreme cases just referred to. (4) Whenever international rules are disregarded without the breach falling within the category of 'armed attack', States are not authorized to react by force. Self-help, although still allowed, must be confined to *peaceful* reaction to international wrongs. (5) Even peaceful sanctions must be preceded by resort to other, peaceful, means of conflict-resolution (judicial adjudication, however, is not made compulsory: it may suffice that some peaceful settlement mechanism be used; thus, even contemporary international law has not yet reached the stage typical of domestic legal systems, where ascertainment of legal situations must precede law enforcement). (6) A marked distinction between coercive or non-coercive measures of enforcement—which are lawful—and other instances of use or threat of (military or economic) force—that are unlawful—has emerged. Thus, gradually, international law has come to uphold a distinction which is of fundamental importance and has for centuries been acted upon in municipal legal systems. As in the latter systems, in international law only the supreme collective body, the Security Council, is authorized to depart in exceptional circumstances from this distinction in the interest of the whole community. It can both enforce the law and exercise 'police powers' (see § 129). What unfortunately strongly differentiates the world community from domestic legal systems is both the rudimentary character of the international enforcement machinery and also the fact that this distinction becomes somewhat blurred, in practice, owing to disagreement among States over the exact boundaries of the classes of lawful and unlawful use of force.

Can we say that this legal regime is a great innovation with respect to the previous one? In many respects it is indeed, but in the most important area, that of the condition of major powers, it has left the existing position almost unaffected. While in the past the lack of substantial restraints on the use of force simply confirmed that these Powers were the overlords in the world community, now the law goes so far as to consecrate their might, providing, as it does, that while they must not use force contrary to the Charter, transgression will not invite sanction under Chapter VII of the Charter owing to the veto power conferred on each of them. In spite of this huge shortcoming in the law, the Charter system was designed to afford legal and institutional protection to lesser or middle-sized countries, whenever they were not involved in a fight against one of the major Powers. To this extent the Charter made much headway towards the introduction of some kind of safeguard of peace.

Let us now turn to the actual *operation* of the new system. In practice, the U N has proved ineffective in the field of collective security, primarily because of the East–West rift. As a reaction to this failure, *two major trends* have emerged. First, the collective security system has gradually turned from an enforcement mechanism (as laid down in the Charter) to a hortatory or condemnatory system. Recommendations, non-recognition of unlawful situations, public exposure, and censure have gradually taken the place of collective coercion (§§ 131–4). Second, individual States have gradually endeavoured to 'reappropriate' the rights and powers they had lost, legally speaking, as a result of the creation of the UN. I have already shown how this attempt at reappropriation and the consequent partial return to the old pattern of the world community (the 'Westphalian model') came about. It may now prove useful to the reader to give a brief summary of the *main trends of the practice of major Powers*.

In actual fact, the most powerful Western States and the USSR have acted in such a way as to widen the meshes in the legal fabric of the Charter, either by using force in cases which had not been provided for in effect, or otherwise where the circumstances did not justify the resort to force. It is interesting to note that Western States and the USSR have pursued different policies. The West has followed four paths: first, by maintaining that self-defence, as embodied in Article 51, can be used as a preventive measure (see § 137); second, by asserting the right to collective or individual self-defence in repulsing 'indirect armed aggression' (see § 138); third, by proclaiming that the right to self-defence includes the right to protect one's nationals abroad (see § 140); fourth, by invoking the rules of regional Organizations (cf. § 141).

The USSR, on the other hand, has insisted either on the importance of obtaining the territorial State's consent when what had occurred was not so much an 'armed attack' by third States as a 'counter-revolutionary insurrection' receiving support from abroad (see § 141); or has invoked the right to collective self-defence to help a State suffering from an 'armed aggression' from outside, which had not taken the shape of military intervention from a third State but, at the most, some form of military aid (see § 141).

It seems quite clear that, whereas Western nations have circumvented existing prohibitions by propounding a legal interpretation enabling them to dodge those prohibitions, the USSR has tended to adopt a different course: that of rearranging the *facts*. In other words, the USSR has not formally advanced legal interpretations of the Charter which might conflict with sounder, more commonly accepted ones; rather it has presented the facts in such a way as to lend an apparent acceptability to circumstances which had not been allowed for in the rules. (I have, however, stressed above, at § 138, that in some respects the USSR has also started adopting the Western strategy, at least by *implicitly* suggesting an interpretation of Article 51 which appears to be at variance with the sounder one, previously upheld by the USSR itself.)

However different the strategy pursued by the two blocs, their aim is identical: each single State hopes to 'recover' powers 'expropriated' by the UN Charter.

I should add that another tendency has emerged 'involving' the two *Superpowers* only. If we consider certain more-or-less recent events (such as, for example, the American interventions in Cuba in 1962, in the Dominican Republic in 1965, and in Grenada in 1983; or Soviet intervention in countries in Eastern Europe as well as in Afghanistan), then it should be clear that the two Superpowers are slowly beginning to practise some form of Brezhnev doctrine, for each feels that it is merely exercising one of its rights in using force to protect its vital interests within its own sphere of influence. Naturally this is no more than a tendency, but it cannot be dismissed merely as a violation of existing law, even though it contrasts with the law as it stands—given the nature and stature of the two States in question.

In any case, these observations should have made it clear that, from 1945 to the present day, the differentiation between strong and weak States which the UN sought to bridge by protecting the weaker members has emerged, and is even increasing. Powerful States count on their own force and, should this prove expedient, on political and military groupings; lesser countries must of necessity, rely on military alliances, hence necessarily on one of the two Superpowers.

This imbalance applies to those serious wrongs imperilling peace and security. In the case of lesser breaches, States are again duty-bound to refrain from engaging in military action but do not have any international machinery available for vindicating their rights. The ensuing situation is clear: States, whatever the grouping to which they belong, increasingly take advantage of the loopholes of the Charter system and gradually fall back upon self-help (as pointed out above, the three major areas where legal uncertainty is greater, and where States consequently enjoy greater leeway, are: anticipatory self-defence, self-defence against indirect armed aggression, and intervention at the request or with the consent of the territorial State). Once again we are confronted with a strong tension between the *old* and the *new* pattern of legal order, and once again we must conclude that all too often the old pattern *de facto* ends up gaining the upper hand.

However, one should not play down the role of the UN. For one thing, it renders disputes or frictions which otherwise would remain a 'private' fact between the two States involved, a matter of public concern. Furthermore, the UN provides a political forum where certain disputes reach a peaceful settlement. In addition, even when one of the major Powers is directly involved in a breach of the peace, the UN can, and does, deliver its judgment by passing resolutions designed to expose the misconduct of that Power. In a number of instances the General Assembly has taken one of the permanent members of the Security Council to task for violating the Charter thereby 'enforcing' in some way Article 2.4, even with respect to major Powers.

What is even more important, the U N constitutes the indispensable forum where States can gradually achieve legal change thereby realizing 'positive' peace. By enabling States to agree upon new regulations capable of updating the legal system and rendering it more consonant with the demands of important segments of the world community, the U N sets the stage for the prevention of political and legal disputes. This is, indeed, the major, if indirect, contribution which the U N currently makes to the main-tenance of peace.

Precisely the existence of all these mechanisms for forestalling or settling minor disputes, as well as the *relative* rarity of major frictions and dissen-sions likely to lead to international armed conflicts, enable the world system to operate in a not-too-unsatisfactory fashion, in spite of all its tremendous flaws.

Finally, one should not pass over in silence a major factor which helps to forestall breaches of international law by States: the role of public opi-nion, especially in democratic countries. In this regard, it is fitting to quote the apposite and authoritative remarks of J. L. Brierly, on the enormous importance which international public opinion can and does have for the observance of the 'law of nations'. He noted in 1931 that international public opinion contains an apparent paradox:

It is intrinsically a weaker force than opinion in the domestic sphere, yet it is in a sense more effective as a sanction of the law. For whereas an individual law-breaker may often hope to escape detection, a State knows that a breach of international law rarely fails to be notorious; and whereas again there are individuals so consti-tuted that they are indifferent to the mere disapproval, unattended by pains and penalties, of others, every State is extraordinarily sensitive to the mere suspicion of illegal action.[40]

---

[40] J. L. Brierly, 'Sanctions' (1931), in *The Basis of Obligation in International Law* (Oxford, 1958), p. 203.

Section III

Crucial Issues of Today

10

International Legal Regulation of Armed Conflict

INTRODUCTION

146. THE inhabitants of the island of Utopia, who loathed fighting, considered that war is 'a quite subhuman form of activity, although human beings are more addicted to it than any of the lower animals'.[1] As they were, however, constrained to go to war either to repel invaders or to liberate the victims of dictatorship, the Utopians had contrived a very ingenious way of avoiding fighting. The moment war was declared, they arranged through secret agents for quantities of posters to go up simultaneously at all points on enemy territory. These posters offered a huge reward for killing the enemy king and smaller sums for the elimination of the king's closest associates; the reward for bringing such people alive before the Utopians was double. As people do anything for money—so the Utopians believed and I surmise they were right—the system worked and the inhabitants of Utopia could pride themselves upon disposing of major wars in a most humane way, for they saved thousands of innocent lives at the cost of a few guilty politicians.

Alas, in real life things were already different in Sir Thomas More's time, and they have become even worse today: wars are fought with increasing cruelty and cause suffering to an ever-increasing number of innocent people. Why people who, on the whole, are relatively civilized are so bent on barbarity is a question that keeps puzzling both men of science and all those more generally concerned with maintaining the basic values of human dignity in the face of growing degradation. A short and penetrating answer to this question can be found in an exchange of letters which took place in 1932—when the Second World War already loomed large—between two great figures, Einstein and Freud.[2] At the suggestion of the League of Nations and its International Institute of Intellectual Co-operation, the former invited the latter to try to give an answer to the crucial question of whether there was any way of delivering mankind from the menace of war. The physicist observed that no doubt there were a number of factors which

[1] T. More, *Utopia*, trans. with an introduction by P. Turner (Harmondsworth, 1971), pp. 109 ff.
[2] A. Einstein and S. Freud, *Why War?*, International Institute of Intellectual Co-operation, League of Nations (1933), pp. 11 ff.

helped to explain why nations go to war, including the craving for power of the 'governing class' of every State fearful of losing its national sovereignty; the pressure of those groups which draw enormous benefits from the manufacture and sale of arms; the manipulation by the 'ruling class' of the press, the school, and through them of the emotions of the masses. Still, as Einstein believed, these factors were not sufficient to explain what impelled men to kill and die, why so many men were aroused 'to such wild enthusiasm', why they were ready to sacrifice their lives. To understand the root causes of war one must delve deeper: only 'the expert in the lore of human instincts' stood a chance of solving the riddle.

In his reply, this 'expert' pointed to the 'aggressive or destructive instinct', which in his view was a basic component of human personality, an inherent feature of human behaviour no less than 'Eros' or the 'sexual' instinct; there was little likelihood—he added—of our being able to suppress 'humanity's aggressive tendencies'. Palliatives could be found which might stem the destructiveness of human beings. One such palliative lay in strengthening and enhancing the feeling of community and empathy. Bolstering pacifism was also important; aversion to war was motivated not only by the fact that war 'forces the individual into situations that shame his manhood, obliging him to murder fellow men' and that 'it ravages material amenities, the fruits of human toil, and much besides'. There was a deeper reason why pacifists loathe war: war runs contrary to the two main trends of civilization, namely, 'the strengthening of the intellect, which tends to master our instinctive life' and 'an introversion of the aggressive impulse, with all its consequent benefits and perils'. Freud concluded that some hope could perhaps be set on a growing number of men turning pacifist both on account of man's 'cultural disposition' and of 'the well-founded dread of the form that future wars will take'.

What has happened since 1932—with wars still being fought in so many parts of the world at the time of my writing—amply bears out how sound the views set forth by the two great men were. These views can be taken to constitute the general backdrop against which armed conflict must be assessed. If man is, indeed, strongly drawn to war, what role can be assigned to international legal rules? Does this body of law play into the hands of belligerents or does it instead side with pacifism and put a curb on armed violence?

It has become fashionable to quote the famous observation made in 1952 by Sir Hersch Lauterpacht,[3] to the effect that 'if international law is, in some ways, at the vanishing point of law, the law of war is, perhaps even more conspicuously, at the vanishing point of international law'.

There is a lot of truth in this. As I have already remarked (§ 10), more than any other corpus of legal rules, international law directly and trans-

---

[3] H. Lauterpacht, 'The Problem of the Revision of the Law of War', *B Y I L* 29 (1952), 382.

parently reflects power relations. It only partially restrains States' behaviour. War marks the passage from relatively harmonious relations to armed contention. War is the area in which power politics reach their peak, and in which law relinquishes its control over international dealings. In the daily wrangle between force and law, the latter, of necessity, loses ground, partly because international legal rules hold Armageddon only partially at bay. Moreover international law controls chaos in an utterly unsatisfactory way, for, first, it refrains from imposing trammels on the most dangerous forms of armed violence. Second, all too often existing legal restraints are checkmated by sheer power. This state of affairs is only natural, given the mental disposition of most men and, what is even more important, the division of the world community into self-sufficient and self-seeking nation-States, each of them claiming—as Suarez[4] observed—to be a *communitas perfecta* (a perfect community). One should therefore not expect law to put sweeping restrictions on armed violence, let alone ban it; realistically, one can simply require international law to mitigate at least some of the most frightful manifestations of the clash of arms. This is precisely what the rules on warfare endeavour to do.

CLASSES OF WAR

147. Since time immemorial wars have been armed conflicts involving in their cruelty and devastation the whole population of the contending parties, with civilians suffering no less than combatants. However, for a number of historical reasons, during part of the seventeenth and in the eighteenth centuries (1648-1789), wars tended to take the shape of contests between professionals, conducted as a sort of game and without any direct involvement of the civilian population. This was due to many factors: reaction to the sanguinary and drawn-out wars of the early seventeenth century; the development of costly armies consisting of highly trained professionals, whose death in war would be a great loss for States; the lack of national allegiance in military men entailing a marked reluctance to fight unto the bitter end in defence of the State; the fact that the military profession was almost everywhere an apanage of the nobility, with the consequent feeling of belonging to the same social class common to the officers of all countries; the influence of aristocratic principles of chivalry.

However, the new ideals of the French Revolution and their implementation in this particular field (soldiers were no longer professionals; every citizen became a patriot and a member of a mass army) begot total wars; the devastating armed conflicts in which Napoleon engaged (1792-1815) soon provided an even more forceful negation of Rousseau's maxim that war was not a relationship between man and man but between State and

[4] Suarez's concept of the State as a *communitas perfecta* was emphasized by J. Brierly, *The Basis of Obligation in International Law and Other Papers* (Oxford, 1958), pp. 361 ff., 367 ff.

State, where private persons were enemies only accidentally. The Prussian general von Clausewitz, who had fought against Napoleon, eventually asserted in his treatise *On War* (1832) the need for wars to be life or death struggles involving the whole of the population of the contending States. He was the first to perceive and lucidly expound the difference between the wars of the eighteenth century and the new total war:

> Whilst, according to the usual way of seeing things, all hopes were placed on a very limited military force in 1793, such a force as no one had any conception of made its appearance. War had again suddenly become an affair of the people, and that of a people numbering thirty millions, every one of whom regarded himself as a citizen of the State ... By this participation of the people in the War instead of a Cabinet and an Army, a whole Nation with its natural weight came into the scale.[5]

One should not believe that von Clausewitz's insistence on total war ('absolute war', in his terminology) and its ruthlessness reflected a vicious longing for barbarity. In his view war in its new form had at least two merits. First, the decision to engage in armed conflict was no longer taken by a handful of leaders with no regard whatsoever for the population. Second, the savagery of modern war induced (or at least should have induced) those in command to think twice before engaging in hostilities.

The former proposition is in many respects questionable. Even in modern parliamentary democracies the leaders easily drum up support for any decision they may have made to initiate war for the pursuit of what they consider to be national interests. The waging of wars remains to a large extent in the hands of élites. The latter proposition is also open to criticism. Extreme cruelty in war has not stood in the way of the spread of armed conflict. Let us recall what Hegel wrote in 1837 about the introduction of gunpowder in Europe and the consequent invention of firearms—they democratized fighting, for the use of weapons was no longer monopolized by a limited segment of society with a special social background and a costly training:

> [Gunpowder] was one of the chief instruments in freeing the world from the dominion of physical force, and placing the various orders of society on a level. With the distinction between the weapons they used, vanished also that between lords and serfs.[6]

This is, of course, true. Democratization, however, only resulted in more killing by more persons. In short, there was no substantial progress. Similarly, total war—which in the view of von Clausewitz should have brought about a diminution of armed clashes—in fact merely multiplied

---

[5] Carl von Clausewitz, *On War*, ed. with an introduction by A. Rapaport (Harmondsworth, 1971), p. 384.
[6] G. F. W. Hegel, *The Philosophy of History*, trans. J. Sibree (New York, 1956), p. 402.

human suffering and magnified it to the extent that it has now reached appalling proportions.

Be that as it may, the armed conflicts which spread after the Napoleonic period and are still raging today, belong to the class described by von Clausewitz as total wars.

TRADITIONAL LAW IN A NUTSHELL

148. The bulk of traditional law was either restated and codified, or developed at the Brussels Conference of 1874 and at the Hague Peace Conferences of 1899 and 1907. Interestingly, this law ultimately upheld the 'Rousseauesque', not the 'Clausewiztian' conception. Being based on the assumption that wars are clashes between States' armies, it distinguished between combatants and civilians and sought to shield the latter as much as possible from armed violence. Although, of course, the realities of modern warfare eventually brought about wide cracks in the legal edifice, the fact remains that the basic approach of traditional law was largely 'Rousseauesque', as was pointed out in 1901 by one of the principal framers of that law, the Russian jurist and diplomat Fëdor Fëdorovich de Martens,[7] in an important scholarly study.

The law under consideration essentially resulted from the tension and conflict of interest between: (1) Great Powers and lesser States; (2) Naval Powers such as the U K and France, and other States. (The U K and France were very suspicious of any development in the law of naval warfare which might jeopardize their superiority. They therefore insisted on leaving belligerents as much freedom of action as possible at sea, whereas other States had of course contrary interests and were particularly eager to keep maritime commerce between belligerents and neutral States as unimpeded as possible.); (3) Countries interested in remaining aloof in case of war on the one side, and States pursuing an expansionist policy, and hence bent on war, on the other.

I referred above (§ 25) to certain areas where the major rift—that between strong and weak States—was apparent; let me add now that a handful of powerful States succeeded from the outset in leaving the thorniest issues concerning means and methods of warfare (where they were obviously superior) legally uncontrolled, or at least in watering down the few rules they had to agree upon. In addition, they were keenly interested in restricting the classes of lawful combatants as much as possible and also in extending the rights of occupying powers (see § 25). The less powerful countries (consisting of a few European plus Latin-American nations) constantly strove to enact rules calculated to restrain the military superiority of the Great Powers and to protect their own nationals and territory in case of

[7] F. F. de Martens, *La Paix et la guerre* (Paris, 1901), pp. 368-9.

enemy invasion. The whole corpus of law established in this period basically arose out of the tensions between those two groups. As we shall see, however, it was the stronger countries that left their basic imprint on law.

The rules worked out in 1874 and enacted by the 1899 and 1907 Conferences as well as the customary law which had previously evolved, can be summed up as follows.

Only *interstate* armed conflicts were regulated. No rule was adopted concerning the conduct of hostilities within the framework of civil wars. Actual fighting by insurgents remained, therefore, under the sway of domestic criminal law (unless the State concerned granted the rebels the recognition of belligerency: see §§ 146, 163).

Detailed rules on *neutrality* were laid down: the law of neutrality governs the relations between belligerents on the one side and third States on the other. The interests of the former are clearly at variance with those of the latter: no belligerent wants third States to help its adversary by lending military or economic support; each belligerent is, therefore, interested in barring any dealings between third States and its enemy. By contrast, neutral States are keen to maintain unrestricted commercial dealings with the contending parties without, however, becoming embroiled in the armed conflict. The attitude of neutrality adopted by the US towards the countries engaged in the Napoleonic wars (1804-15) and, subsequently, the stand of England and other European countries in relation to the American Civil War (1861-65) greatly contributed to the development of a set of rules striking a fairly felicitous compromise between conflicting interests.

These were the main principles governing neutrality: (1) neutral States must refrain from giving any direct or indirect assistance to either belligerent; in particular they must prevent their territories from being used in the interest of one of the contesting parties (for example by enlisting troops); (2) belligerents must refrain from using the neutral territory for any warlike action and, in case their troops take refuge in neutral territory, must acquiesce in their internment by the neutral State. However, (3) belligerents have the right to search and visit, and to seize, neutral vessels carrying contraband (that is, such goods as may assist the enemy in the conduct of war) and, in addition, they are entitled to blockade the enemy coast, thus preventing access to it by any vessel, including those of neutral States. It should be noted that neither at The Hague, in 1899 and 1907, nor in other international forums was it possible to reach agreement on what categories of neutral goods constituted 'contraband', liable to seizure by belligerent warships. This in the end left belligerents free to designate as 'contraband' not only articles of undisputed military character, but also any other goods which, in their view, might serve the interests of the enemy. Thus a serious blow was struck against the interests of neutral States which considered their commercial dealings as vital.

Both war on *land* and *naval* war were regulated in great detail (air warfare in 1899 was still in its infancy—balloons appeared of little military value;

see below). The law covered the whole gamut of war, from the opening of hostilities to the conclusion of peace treaties, including the conduct of hostilities in the field and at sea, the treatment of war victims and civilians.

The concept of *lawful combatants* was legally defined. The compromise solution reached by Great Powers with lesser States (see § 25), lay in granting the status of lawful combatant to regular armies, plus militia and volunteer corps, provided the latter category fulfilled the following four conditions: that they were commanded by a person responsible for his subordinates; that they wear a fixed distinctive sign recognizable at a distance; that they carry arms openly; and that they conduct their operations in accordance with the laws and customs of war. For another class of combatants (namely 'the inhabitants of a territory not under occupation who, on the approach of the enemy, spontaneously take up arms to resist the invading troops without having the time to organize themselves') two conditions only were required: that is, to carry arms openly and to respect the laws and customs of war (see further § 152–3).

The expansion of the class of combatants was manifestly the major concession made by Great Powers to small countries. In actual practice, however, in the period between 1907 and 1939 wars were mainly fought by regular armies and on a few occasions only did other lawful combatants take part in hostilities on a large scale. In short, for a number of historical reasons, small countries did not in practice take advantage of the gains they had obtained on the normative level.

International regulation of *means of warfare* is the acid test for the interests behind the body of law governing warfare and international dealings in general. It is apparent from a survey of the various provisions restricting or banning the use of weapons that only those agencies of destruction which were either relatively ineffective or might imperil the life of their very users were proscribed. Thus explosive projectiles weighing under 400 grams and dumdum bullets were prohibited as belonging to the former category, whereas the other banned category covered such weapons as poison or poisonous weapons, asphyxiating or deleterious gases, and automatic submarine contact mines.

Really important and effective weapons were not banned, however inhuman they might be. This applies particularly to aircraft. In 1899 the Hague Conference adopted a Declaration prohibiting the discharge of explosives from balloons for a term of five years. However, in 1907 there were already indications of the importance that balloons and similar aerial devices might have for warlike purposes, and it was therefore agreed to 'prohibit, for a period extending to the close of the Third Peace Conference [presumably five years, but the Conference was never convened] the discharge of projectiles and explosives from balloons or by other new methods of a similar nature'. The impact of the Declaration was weakened, first by this proviso, and, second, by the fact that it was signed by a few countries only. It did not bear the signatures of such major Powers as France, Germany, Italy, Russia, and Japan, with the consequence that, as the British Manual on Land Warfare of 1912 put it, the Declaration was 'practically without force'.[8]

Apart from a few specific bans, the law of warfare included the general principle, first stated in 1899 and reiterated in 1907, that 'it is expressly forbidden to employ arms, projectiles, and material calculated to cause unnecessary suffering'. The principle, however, was very loose and lent itself to the most divergent interpretations. In practice, it was taken to proscribe such minor arms as lances with a barbed head, irregularly-shaped bullets, projectiles filled with broken glass, and the like. Another general principle which evolved in this period was that prohibiting indiscriminate weapons (that is weapons which do not distinguish between combatants and civilians) or the indiscriminate use of weapons. But this was too vague to function as a workable standard of behaviour (except in extreme cases).

Like the provisions on means of warfare, most of those on *methods of warfare* tended to favour strong States. In this area one should distinguish between two sets of rules: those meeting the needs of all belligerents, regardless of the power they wielded; and those which instead, were calculated to favour, directly or indirectly, the stronger States. The former includes such rules as those prohibiting treachery (Article 23 *b* of the Hague Regulations); the killing or wounding of enemies who have 'laid down their arms or, no longer having any means of defence, have surrendered at discretion' (Article 23 *c*); the declaration that no quarter will be given, in other words that even the defeated enemies willing to surrender will be killed (Article 23 *d*); the improper use of flags of truce, of national flags, or of the military insignia and uniform of the enemy, the distinctive signs of the Geneva Conventions; and, lastly, pillage. Similarly, to this class belongs the rule allowing 'ruses of war' and 'the employment of measures necessary for obtaining information about the enemy'. All these norms are clearly intended to introduce a minimum of fair play into the conduct of hostilities and actually serve the interests of all parties.

By contrast, when it comes to the rules prescribing how belligerents must behave in areas where civilians are located—areas which normally constitute the greatest part of the battlefield—it becomes apparent that the international regulation grants scant protection either to civilians or to the weaker belligerent. In short, belligerents must not attack, either from land or from sea, 'undefended towns, villages, dwellings, or buildings' (Article 25 of the Hague Regulations). However, the concept of 'undefended town'

---

[8] *Land Warfare—An Exposition of the Laws and Usages of War on Land for the Guidance of Officers of His Majesty's Army*, by J. E. Edmonds and L. Oppenheim (London, 1912), p. 24 nt. b.

was not defined, nor was a procedure envisaged for the reaching of an agreement between the contending parties about the 'undefended' status of a certain locality. As a consequence, an invading Power could refuse to consider a locality as 'undefended' even if it had been declared such by the adversary.

No less loose and defective were the rules governing the attack on 'defended' localities: Article 26 of the Hague Regulations merely provided that 'the officer in command of an attacking force must do all in his power to warn the authorities before commencing a bombardment, except in cases of assault', and Article 27 provided that 'all necessary steps must be taken to spare, as far as possible' churches, works of art, hospitals, and historic monuments.

More satisfactory were the rules protecting *war victims*, namely prisoners of war, the wounded, the sick and the shipwrecked, whether they belonged to the enemy or to one's own side. In this area the Hague codification made great headway, for it was clearly in the interest of all States, irrespective of their status and military strength, to lay down rules protecting those who no longer took part in armed hostilities.

The weakest point of traditional international law concerned the *means for ensuring compliance with the laws of warfare*. No third-party institution existed, nor was a third State or any independent commission ever entrusted with the task of scrutinizing the behaviour of belligerents. In the final analysis, each of them took upon itself the task of unilaterally determining whether the adversary abided by the law, and of enforcing it in case of disregard.

Three devices were available and were in fact used to a great extent: (1) Belligerent reprisals (for example the maltreatment of prisoners of war, the unlawful bombardment of 'undefended' localities or of buildings immune from attack, etc.). They were a barbaric institution, ultimately leading to the killing of innocent combatants or civilians, punished for the misdeeds of their fellow countrymen. In addition, they lent themselves to abuses owing to the absence of any impartial verification of violations by the enemy. (2) Criminal punishment of enemy combatants or civilians guilty of 'war crimes', that is, serious violations of the laws of warfare. This institution too, was questionable on a number of counts: first, because it was open to abuse, and second, because normally trials of war crimes were initiated after the war by the victor against nationals of the defeated country (whereas if proceedings were instituted during the hostilities, the adversary could easily retaliate by similarly prosecuting and punishing the enemies in his hands). (3) The payment of compensation for any violation perpetrated. Plainly, compensation was requested by the victor once the war was over, while the defeated had no means of doing likewise.

A distinguishing trait of traditional law is that the applicability of international conventions on warfare to individual armed conflicts was always uncertain and precarious. Indeed, all these conventions included the so-called *si omnes* clause, whereby they applied to an armed conflict on condition that *all* the belligerents were contracting parties. Consequently, it was sufficient for one belligerent not to be bound by a certain convention for it also to become inapplicable to the relationships between the other belligerents *inter se*. It follows that only customary law—hence the most general but also the loosest body of legal rules—was undisputedly applicable in any war.

To conclude, traditional international law tended to favour strong and middle-sized powers at least in three major areas: those of means of combat, methods of combat, and devices for inducing compliance with law.

NEW DEVELOPMENTS IN MODERN ARMED CONFLICT

149. In the period following the Hague codification, a series of events occurred which rendered it defective or inadequate in many respects.

In the first place, new classes of combatants emerged. During the Second World War partisans and resistance movements played a remarkable role in certain European countries occupied by Germany (Yugoslavia, France, Italy, The Netherlands, Poland and the Soviet Union). They were not formally legitimized by existing law, partly because they operated in territories under military occupation (and under the Hague rules, militias and volunteer corps were only lawful outside such territories), and partly because they often lacked one or more of the four requirements mentioned above (§ 148). In particular, they normally did not carry arms openly, nor did they wear a distinctive sign recognizable at a distance. After the war a general feeling emerged among the allies that resistance movements had acted for politically sound reasons, and that some provision should therefore be made in future for granting them legitimacy. When, subsequently, guerrilla warfare spread throughout the colonial countries, the majority of States felt that guerrillas, who normally do not fulfil all of the four conditions referred to above, should be upgraded to the status of lawful combatants.

Second, war developed in two opposite directions: the 'wars of the rich', that is armed conflicts engaged in by highly developed countries using sophisticated weapons of mass destruction, and the 'wars of the poor', struggles for national liberation waged by liberation movements in colonial or occupied territories and usually conducted by guerrillas. It should be noted that both classes of war (which often co-existed, as in the case of the Vietnam conflict between 1964 and 1974), have resulted in a staggering increase of civilian losses. In modern wars non-combatants are those who suffer most from armed violence: civilian casualties have increased out of all proportion to military casualties.

Third, new agencies of destruction took pride of place: aircraft, first used in the war between Italy and Turkey (1911-12), then in the First World War, proved of tremendous importance and effectiveness in the Spanish Civil War (1936-9) when German planes participated massively in the fighting. It subsequently became a major instrument of combat. Technological developments led to the creation and use of the atomic bomb (on 6 and 9 August 1945), and subsequently to the manufacture and stockpiling of nuclear bombs. The arsenals of great and small Powers (the latter furnished by the former) have become bigger and bigger, with the addition of bacteriological and chemical weapons and, more recently, of the neutron bomb.

Fourth, the emergence of two Superpowers after the Second World War, and the balance of terror brought about by the existence of nuclear weapons, has made civil wars more and more widespread: Great Powers fight each other by proxy, providing military assistance to the various factions struggling within the territory of sovereign States, mostly in Third-World countries, where historical and social conditions—chiefly tribal and political dissensions—generate clashes between opposing groups, and facilitate the eruption of civil tumult.

Fifth, the laws of neutrality were ignored more and more frequently, and the whole institution of neutrality gradually fell into decline. This process began during the two World Wars, when the rules on neutrality turned out to afford very little protection to those States wishing to hold aloof and actually put them in a condition no less hazardous than that of belligerents. (In the Second World War both the USSR and the US were still neutral States when they were first attacked by Germany and Japan respectively.) Further factors were the establishment of the UN (which rested on the concept that, if the need arose, any member State could take armed action against an aggressor) and the proliferation of security pacts when it became apparent that the UN collective system was ineffective. A decisive blow to neutrality was struck by the creation of political groupings and alliances, each of them, sooner or later, siding with one of the belligerents during armed conflicts, which rendered the duties of impartiality, in particular the duty not to assist either side militarily, obsolete. Furthermore, States increasingly considered that the impediments to commercial relations between neutrals and belligerents were economically disadvantageous and not warranted by the new circumstances.

Finally—and here the hackneyed expression 'last but not least' is, alas, appropriate—the danger of all-out nuclear warfare has become increasingly paramount. This danger raises the question of the extent to which the laws of warfare are applicable. Or, is this new kind of war utterly beyond the pale of law, or even the very negation of law and humanity?

THE NEW LAW

General

150. All these developments prompted States to revise and update the traditional rules on warfare (by contrast, they did not feel the need to make the laws of neutrality more consonant with modern times). The legislative process started in 1949, when four Conventions on war victims (on the wounded and sick in the field; on the wounded, sick, and shipwrecked at sea; on prisoners of war; on civilians) were adopted by a Diplomatic Conference. In 1977 another Diplomatic Conference adopted two Protocols, one on international armed conflicts, the other on internal armed conflicts. They extensively revised and updated both the Hague Regulations of 1907 and the Geneva Conventions of 1949. At present, the laws of warfare consist mainly of these two sets of international legislation, plus a number of customary rules, some of which were consecrated in the 1977 Protocols.

Three general remarks should be made at the outset. First, the new law which emerged after the Second World War in the form of both customary rules and treaty provisions, has not destroyed or supplanted the old law; rather, it has generally elaborated and supplemented it, or lent it greater clarity and precision. One ought never to lose sight of this point when examining and appraising the new norms governing armed conflict.

Second, the new law does not substantially depart from the 'Rousseau-esque' conception of armed conflicts, on which the traditional law rested (see § 148). It does, of course, endeavour to take account of the fact that modern wars increasingly tend to become life or death—'total' conflicts. Consequently, the new rules take into consideration the growing involvement of both civilians and civilian installations (factories, etc.) in the war effort. What matters, however, is that even the new body of rules has not abandoned the basic tenet that a distinction must always be made between combatants and persons who do not take part (or no longer take part) in hostilities, and also between military and civilian objectives.

Third, the '*si omnes* clause' (see § 148) has been gradually abandoned in modern treaties on warfare. Since the majority of the Hague Conventions has turned into customary law, and recent agreements such as the four 1949 Geneva Conventions on war victims, as well as the 1977 Protocols explicitly apply in case of armed conflict to the States parties irrespective of whether or not one of the belligerents is a contracting party, it has become less easy today for belligerents to claim that they are free to disregard the existing law.

151. Before setting out the fundamentals of the present legal regulation, it may be fitting to point to the main political and ideological positions underlying the drafting of the treaties mentioned above.

A characteristic feature of the 1949 deliberations is that, except as regards the issue of civil war, there was basic agreement among the majority of States. A desire to avert a recurrence of the horrors of the Second World War naturally led all countries, regardless of their ideological or political leanings, to favour a more effective humanitarian protection of war victims. States were also basically in agreement on a further point—the advisability of avoiding any regulation on actual combat. Both the means of warfare and the conduct of hostilities on the battlefield were left aside. The political tensions resulting from the Cold War, the existence of a new tremendous agency of destruction, the atomic bomb, which at that time only the two Superpowers possessed, the feeling that any discussion on weapons and methods of warfare might wreck the whole negotiation, all prompted the participants in the Conference to concentrate on the humanitarian side of armed conflict.

To be sure, a number of divergences and conflicts of interest emerged but as a rule they did not concern major issues. The main bone of contention was the regulation of civil wars. By civil strife socialist countries, led by the USSR, primarily meant colonial wars. Consequently, they strongly favoured the extension of the whole body of humanitarian law of armed conflict to those wars. In particular, they were keen to extend the rules on lawful combatants to internal wars, which entailed the granting of the status of legitimate belligerents to insurgents, who became thereby entitled to prisoner-of-war treatment on capture. This, of course, meant giving increased status to peoples fighting against colonial powers and, indeed, legitimizing their struggles. Western countries strenuously and successfully opposed the attempt. The upshot of the ensuing diplomatic tug-of-war was the adoption of a famous provision (Article 3 common to the four Geneva Conventions; see § 164), which was only humanitarian in scope and denied insurgents both international status and special rights and privileges. (The Soviet delegate called Article 3 'a Convention in miniature' and this telling expression has since turned into a trite characterization of the provision.)

The political and ideological setting was, of course completely different between 1974 and 1977, the years spanning the Geneva Diplomat Conference. Socialist States were much stronger than in 1949 and, what is even more significant, developing countries now formed a fairly united front willing to push their own aspirations and proposals through the Conference. The Vietnam conflict had just ended, but colonial wars were still raging, particularly in the Portuguese colonies. Yet despite the political and ideological split of the world community, in some areas there was something uniting States over and above their various political leanings—the fact of whether they belong either to the class of militarily strong Powers or to that of weak countries. Thus, on some basic issues there was an alignment which cut across political and ideological groupings and lumped together States of different 'philosophical' tendency.

The major ideological divisions, emerging during the Conference, concerned three issues: the upgrading of wars of national liberation to the class of international armed conflicts proper (see § 161); the treatment to be meted out to guerrilla fighters on the one hand, and mercenaries on the other (see §§ 153-4); the legal regulations of civil strife (see §§ 163-5). On these three issues the various groupings split very soon (however, on the first one and on the third one, Eastern European and Third World countries adopted positions which were not wide apart). By contrast, on other topics, (such as the protection of civilians from armed hostilities; methods of combat; reprisals; possible restrictions on the use of weapons, etc.) a rift emerged—more or less marked, depending on the specific issue—between Great and middle Powers on the one hand, and lesser States on the other.

FUNDAMENTALS OF THE CURRENT REGULATION OF ARMED CONFLICT

INTERSTATE CONFLICTS

Lawful Combatants

152. As stated above (§ 148) traditional law regarded as lawful combatants the members of regular armies, as well as militias or volunteer corps fulfilling four specific conditions. In addition it made allowance for the whole civilian population taking up arms on the approach of the enemy, provided two specific conditions were met. In 1949 the Third Geneva Convention added in Article 4.A.2 the category of 'organized resistance movements, belonging to a party to the conflict and operating in or outside their own territory, even if this territory is occupied', provided they fulfilled the same four conditions established in 1899 for other irregular combatants (a fifth condition was spelled out in 1949: stipulating that the combatants must be linked to a Party to the conflict).

After 1949 the question of guerrilla fighters (that is, irregular combatants resorting to guerrilla warfare within the framework of interstate wars or wars of national liberation) became increasingly important. At the same time, the question of mercenaries came up. Both problems were dealt with during the 1974-7 Conference.

Guerrillas

153. Since the 1960s socialist and Third World States have insisted in the General Assembly that guerrilla fighters should be treated as lawful combatants entitled to prisoner-of-war status on capture, even though they do not meet all the five requirements laid down in customary international law, as reflected in Article 4 of the Third Geneva Convention of 1949. In their view freedom fighters by definition cannot wear uniforms, nor can they have a distinctive sign recognizable at a distance; rather they must conceal themselves among civilians and take the adversary by surprise. A number of resolutions to this effect has been passed by the General Assembly, in spite of the opposition of Western countries. In the 1974-7 Geneva conference the debates were complex and protracted, but eventually led to the adoption of a compromise formula laid down in a particularly convoluted provision, namely Article 44. This stipulation leaves unaffected three of the requirements provided for in 1899 and 1949 for other categories of combatants (namely, being linked to a Party to the conflict; being under a responsible command; and complying with the laws of war), while it reduces the two other criteria (carrying a distinctive sign recognizable at a distance, and carrying arms openly) to one: that combatants 'are obliged to *distinguish themselves from the civilian population* while they are engaged in an attack or in a military operation preparatory to an attack' (Article 44.3, first sentence). Thus the two traditional requirements are relaxed to the general condition of 'distinction from civilians' (presumably by a sign or any appropriate outward token, or by openly carrying weapons) and, in addition, combatants are only required to comply with this condition during an armed attack or immediately prior to it. Furthermore, if captured by the adversary, irregular combatants not fulfilling the condition do not forfeit their status of lawful combatants; consequently, they continue to be entitled to prisoner of war treatment, although they are liable to punishment for violating Article 44.3.

The requirements just mentioned were further relaxed with regard to such situations as wars of national liberation and military occupation. With respect to these situations the second sentence of Article 44.3 only requests that a combatant should *carry his arms openly* '(a) during each military engagement, and (b) during such time as he is visible to the adversary while he is engaged in a military deployment preceding the launching of an attack in which he is to participate'.

Thus guerrillas fighting in wars of national liberation or in occupied territory are favoured in two respects: first, the requirements exacted from them are *less stringent* than those necessary for irregular combatants fighting in 'normal' situations; second, they must fulfil these requirements under circumstances ('military engagement', etc.) which are *narrower* in scope than those for which guerrillas in 'normal' fighting must fulfil their conditions. However, in another important respect Article 44 is more exacting, or stricter with guerrillas fighting in 'special' situations: if irregular combatants not satisfying the requirements of the second sentence of Article 44.3, are captured in the course of a war of national liberation or in occupied territory, they forfeit their status of lawful combatants and cannot therefore enjoy prisoner of war treatment. Let us take the illustration given by Aldrich[9] a distinguished jurist who greatly contributed to the elaboration of Article 44. He mentioned the case of a guerrilla fighting in an occupied territory, who disguises himself as a civilian; if he is stopped and searched by occupying troops and suddenly draws his weapon and opens fire on the soldiers, on capture he will be deprived of prisoner of war status provided it can be proved that he was engaged in a 'military deployment preceding the launching of an attack'. Only if he was not so engaged must he be treated as a prisoner of war.

Mercenaries

154. In recent years the number of mercenaries has become conspicuously large in Africa, where (usually white), they are used both by the ruling élites (for internal security, intelligence, the training of special commandos, etc.) and by foreign powers as tools for organizing or strengthening movements to destabilize African regimes. Many an African State has taken a strong stand against the latter practice. Accordingly, both in the UN and at the Geneva Conference of 1974–7, African States claimed, with the support of other developing countries and of the socialist group, that mercenaries should be treated as unlawful combatants (hence not entitled to the treatment of prisoners of war on capture). Western countries retorted that mercenaries fulfilling the various requirements of international law should be regarded as legitimate combatants, lest an ideological element be introduced into the laws of warfare, which would be contrary to their basic humanitarian principle of equality of treatment.

The growing insistence on this issue by countries in the UN and the Organization of African Unity (OAU) found official recognition in the adoption of Article 47 at the Geneva Conference. The provision states in para. 1 that 'a mercenary shall not have the right to be a combatant or a prisoner of war' and then gives, in para. 2, the following definition of a mercenary:

'any person who (*a*) is specially recruited locally or abroad in order to fight in an armed conflict; (*b*) does, in fact, take a direct part in the hostilities; (*c*) is motivated to take part in the hostility essentially by the desire for private gain and, in fact, is promised, by or on behalf of a Party to the conflict, material compensation substantially in excess of that promised or paid to combatants of similar ranks and functions in the armed forces of that Party; (*d*) is neither a national of a Party to the conflict nor a resident of territory controlled by a Party to the conflict; (*e*) is not a member of the armed forces of a Party to the conflict; and (*f*) has not been sent by a State which is not a Party to the conflict on official duty as a member of its armed forces'.

[9] G. Aldrich, 'New Life for the Laws of War', *AJIL* 75 (1981), 773–4.

Conduct of Hostilities

Means of Warfare

155. So far international law has adopted a dual approach to the question of banning or restricting the use of weapons: it has laid down general principles prohibiting the use of certain categories of weapons designated by their general characteristics, and special bans on selected weapons. The general principles to which reference has already been made (§ 148), have not played a significant role in recent international practice for they are so loose as to be almost unworkable, save in extreme situations.

Specific bans on specific weapons have proved more useful. They list the arms on which there is a general prohibition and describe the objective properties of the weapons to be prohibited. Certain of the weapons banned in such a manner have already been mentioned (§ 148): namely, poison or poisonous weapons, dumdum bullets, explosive projectiles weighing less than 400 grams, asphyxiating gases. In 1925 the Geneva Protocol had prohibited the use of chemical and bacteriological weapons. In 1972 the ban on bacteriological means of warfare was restated and strengthened by a specific Convention designed to prohibit the manufacture and stockpiling of these agents of destruction.

More recently, the use of three categories of weapons has been proscribed by a Convention adopted in 1980, to which three Protocols were annexed, prohibiting non-detectable fragments; mines, booby traps, and other devices; and incendiary weapons, respectively. Strikingly, the First Protocol banning the use of 'any weapon the primary effect of which is to injure by fragments which in the human body escape detection by X-rays', concerns weapons which in fact do not exist. When the first move to ban such weapons was made, it was erroneously believed that US military forces had used them in Vietnam. Although it was later made clear that the weapons had actually not been used or even manufactured and that no State planned to include them in its arsenal, the ban was enacted, probably because major military Powers wished to show their readiness to make concessions and, in any case the issue was harmless (but the ban can serve the purpose of discouraging States from engaging in the manufacture of the weapon in question). As for the other arms covered by the Convention, the clear opposition of Western countries to any major encroachment upon their freedom of action and the extremely prudent attitude of socialist countries which eventually came to join the major Western Powers, greatly inhibited the Mexican and Swedish efforts to enact effective prohibitions. It seems, indeed, improbable that the Convention will command sufficient support to be ratified by a significant number of States.

The prohibition of specific weapons by specific bans or restrictions has two undoubted advantages. First, since the relevant international proscriptions refer to weapons by describing their objective features, a high degree of certainty is provided about the kind of weapons outlawed. By the same token, the prohibitions and restrictions are capable of providing safe normative guidance which is effective, even in the absence of an enforcement authority: as can be seen from the fact that, generally speaking, the various prohibitions of specific weapons have been respected even though there has been the occasional violation.

The specific-ban approach presents, however, two major drawbacks. First, as we saw before (§ 148), so far, international bans have concerned only those weapons which proved to be of minor military effectiveness or which, although militarily effective, might also present a risk to the belligerent using them. Accordingly, not only did bombing from aircraft fail to be prohibited, but—what is of course more important—no specific ban on atomic and nuclear weapons has ever been enacted.

On this class of weapons the opinion of major military Powers is to some extent divided: Western nuclear States (the US, the UK, France) claim that nuclear weapons are not prohibited *per se*. To quote the 1956 US Military Manual:

The use of explosive 'atomic weapons', whether by air, sea or land forces, cannot as such be regarded as violative of international law in the absence of any customary rule of international law or international convention restricting their employment.[10]

By contrast, the USSR has repeatedly stated—at least until the mid-1970s—that the 'first', and indeed even the 'second' use of atomic and nuclear weapons are contrary to international law, and (in 1961 and 1972) voted for the UN General Assembly resolutions to this effect. A slightly different position is taken in the 1974 Military Manual of the GDR which states that

The employment of nuclear weapons is contrary to international law, to the extent that it is not made as an unavoidable response to an imperialistic aggression through nuclear weapons.[11]

In 1982 the USSR formally committed itself in the UN General Assembly not to be the first to use nuclear weapons.[11a] One can infer from this pledge that the Soviet Union now takes the view that resort to those weapons is not illegal *per se*: indeed, were the use of nuclear weapons in any case prohibited, it would not be necessary to assume a unilateral obligation on the matter. As for the People's Republic of China, it seems that so far it

[10] *The Law of Land Warfare*, Department of the Army (Washington, DC, July 1956), p. 18.

[11] 'Regeln der Kriegführung A4', in DDR, *Handbuch militarisches Grundwissen* (1968), 5th edn. (Berlin, 1972), p. 47.

[11a] See the statement made by Gromyko in 1982, in UN doc. A/S-12, PV.12, pp. 22–23/25 ('The Soviet State solemnly declares: the USSR assumes an obligation not to be the first to use nuclear weapons. This obligation shall become effective immediately, at the moment it is made public from the rostrum of the UN General Assembly').

has not yet clearly stated its position concerning the legality or illegality of nuclear weapons (there are, however, strong indications that it regards the use of nuclear weapons as lawful under general international law; indeed, China too has recently made a special pledge not to be the first to use those weapons).[11b]

On the other hand, scant support can be drawn from State practice. The only elements of some weight are the protest lodged with the US Government on 10 August 1945, through Switzerland, by the Japanese Imperial Government,[12] which agreed that the atomic bomb dropped on Hiroshima was contrary to international law since it 'produced suffering not inferior to that caused by other weapons specifically prohibited by international law', and the famous decision handed down in 1962 by the Tokyo District Court in the *Shimoda* case,[13] in which, however, the Court confined itself to passing judgement upon the lawfulness of the specific case of the bombings of Hiroshima and Nagasaki and did not claim to make a general pronouncement concerning atomic or nuclear weapons. The Court concluded that that bombing was unlawful for it was contrary both to the principle prohibiting indiscriminate attacks on undefended towns, and to the principle forbidding the use of weapons causing unnecessary suffering.

This being so, the contention—which I share—that the use of nuclear weapons is prohibited by the international principle on indiscriminate weapons, and that on unnecessary suffering (except of course as a response to an armed attack by another country using nuclear weapons), is bound to remain a scholarly view of little or no consequence. Ultimately, the hard fact is that the major Powers consider themselves legitimized to use nuclear weapons under extreme military circumstances; consequently, a realistic solution can only be found in disarmament treaties.

A second shortcoming of the specific-ban approach is that even the bans on minor weapons can be easily by-passed by elaborating new and more sophisticated weapons which, while they are no less cruel, do not fall under the prohibition owing to new features. Furthermore, the States which are most likely or capable of dodging the bans are, for obvious reasons, the more industrialized ones. As a result, the gap between technologically developed States and less advanced countries is marked in this field as well, and likely to widen even further.

Methods of Combat

156. International regulation on the subject of methods of combat is very defective indeed. Following the spread of air warfare, which rendered the

---

[11b] See the statement made on 11 June 1982 by the Chinese delegate to the Special General Assembly of the UN (text reproduced in *China and the World*, Bejing, 1983, p. 16).

[12] See *JYIL* 8 (1964), 251-2.

[13] Ibid., 212 ff.

concept of 'undefended localities' still more uncertain, and in any event utterly obsolete, State practice has gradually brought about the emergence of three fundamental principles: (1) it is prohibited to attack civilian objects alone or to hit military and civilian objects indiscriminately; (2) when launching an attack, precautions must be taken to spare civilian objects; (3) in case an attack on military objectives cannot but cause incidental loss of civilian life or destruction of civilian objects, such losses or destruction must not be out of all proportion to the military advantage. However, all three principles were so loose as to lend themselves to the most divergent inter-pretations. For one thing, for a long time the very concept of military objective was not clearly defined, and could therefore be extended at dis-cretion. This circumstance, of necessity, weakened the principle about in-discriminate attacks. Second, 'precautions' cannot be defined in precise terms either. In this respect too, States retain great latitude. Consequently the second principle also turns out to be rather weak. Third, 'proportion-ality' is by definition very questionable, except in extreme cases (for exam-ple, if in order to destroy a tiny garrison controlling a bridge, the adversary annihilates a whole village surrounding the place where the garrison is located). As was rightly pointed out by an outstanding American scholar, R. Baxter, 'proportionality'

calls for comparing two things for which there is no standard of comparison. Is one, for example, compelled to think in terms of a certain number of casualties as justified in the gaining of a specified number of yards? Such precise relationships are so far removed from reality as to be unthinkable ... One rebels at the thought that hundreds of thousands of civilians should be killed in order to destroy one enemy soldier who may be in their midst. But under more reasonable circumstances, how can a proper ratio be established between loss of civilian life and the destruction of railway carriages?[14]

Although the three principles referred to above are too vague and contain too many loopholes, they still provide a standard for at least the most glaring cases. One should not lose sight of the fact that were they lacking, no restraints on military power would exist and any war would soon turn into even worse carnage than the wars we have known so far.

The principles under consideration were clarified and given legal preci-sion—to the extent, of course, that this was feasible in view of the open or covert opposition of major military Powers—in Protocol I of 1977.

A few illustrations of the trends emerging in the Conference may suffice. Article 52.2, for example, lays down a general definition of military objectives ('Those objects which by their nature, location, purpose or use make an effective contribu-tion to military action and whose total or partial destruction, capture or neutrali-

[14] R. Baxter, 'Criteria of the Prohibition of Weapons in International Law', *Festschrift für U. Scheuner* (Berlin, 1973), p. 46.

zation, in the circumstances ruling at the time, offers a definite military advantage'). This definition is so sweeping that it can cover practically anything. More useful are the definitions of 'indiscriminate attacks' (Article 51.4 and 5), and 'precautionary measures' to be taken when launching an attack (Articles 57 and 58), or the various provisions on civilian objects (Articles 52-6), non-defended localities (Article 59) and 'demilitarized zones' (Article 60).

Many of the relevant rules met, however, with the opposition of a number of strong military States (for instance, the UK, France, the US). Some of them have voiced great concern or taken exception to the workability of the rules, and seem unlikely to ratify the Protocol (at least, without far-reaching reservations). It seems, therefore, realistic to conclude that the most significant of those rules merely constitute contractual undertakings which will become binding on the ratifying States only. In other words, although they build upon, expand, and give precision to customary law, they themselves have not yet become generally binding principles.

One important advance made in 1977 should not, however, be passed over in silence. A rule was adopted prohibiting what was described as '... the use of methods or means of warfare which are intended or may be expected to cause such damage [i.e. widespread, long-term and severe damage] to the natural environment and thereby to prejudice the health and survival of the population' (Article 55). This provision was supported by practically all States. Its enactment had been preceded by various pronouncements by States during the Vietnam war to the effect that weapons damaging the environment were unlawful or should be banned. In addition, this rule is the outgrowth of greater concern in the world community for the environment, regardless of whether the threat occurs in times of peace or of war. We could therefore, claim that that provision already reflects a general consensus of States and thus is binding on all members of the world community.

Protection of War Victims

157. The protection of all those persons who do not take part in hostilities (civilians) or, having engaged in combat, are no longer in a position to do so (prisoners of war, the wounded, sick, or shipwrecked), is the subject of extensive and detailed international legislation, to be found both in the four Geneva Conventions of 1949, and in Protocol I of 1977. Under the Conventions civilians are satisfactorily protected to the extent that they are in the hands of the adversary either from the outset of the hostilities, or after the occupation of enemy territory. By contrast, those who happen to be on the theatre of military operations, are only safeguarded by Protocol I (to which the major military Powers are not yet party).

What are the reasons for the difference between the section of the laws of warfare protecting the victims of war (with the exception just mentioned) and the other sections, such as that concerning means and methods of combat? Humanitarian considerations have counted more in this area than in others, where they have been outweighed by military demands. Plainly, it lies in the interest of major military Powers to afford strong protection to war victims, while they are less concerned with prohibitions or restraints on the conduct of hostilities. On the other hand, small countries as well are interested in expanding the protection of war victims, if only for humanitarian reasons.

Means of Ensuring Compliance with Law

(1) Reprisals

158. As noted above, reprisals constitute the most rudimentary and widespread means of inducing the adversary to abide by the law. While traditional international law did not place any restraints (except for those in time of peace: § 143), the 1949 Geneva Conventions banned reprisals against 'protected persons' (prisoners of war, the wounded, sick, or shipwrecked, and civilians (who found themselves in the hands of the enemy; consequently, reprisals against civilians were allowed in the theatre of military operations). These bans have by now turned into customary law.

The 1974–7 Conference extended the ban to a series of civilian persons or civilian objects finding themselves on the battlefield (Articles 51.6; 53 c; 54.4; 55.2; 56.4 of Protocol I). However, the strong opposition of States such as France and Australia, and the misgivings entertained by a number of other States lead one to believe that those provisions remained treaty law, and will consequently bind only the States which ratify or accede to the Protocol (without entering reservations).

This, of course, is a deplorable state of affairs, for reprisals are a primitive instrument through which violence escalates into barbarity. They are open to the worst abuses and, in addition, play ultimately into the hands of major military Powers. States favourable to reprisals contend that, despite their shortcomings, they constitute the only effective sanction available to belligerents. This argument only proves that the humanization of war has still a long way to go, and that no effort should be spared to strengthen and expand the existing weak restraints on military force.

(2) Penal Repression of Breaches

159. In the past the prosecution and punishment of those guilty of war crimes has normally been carried out by the adversary, on the basis of the principle of 'passive nationality' (the victims of breaches were nationals of the State conducting the trial). Since the First World War the prosecution has also been effected by allies, on the basis either of the principle of territoriality (the crime was committed on their territory) or of the principle of passive nationality mentioned above (it is sufficient for the victim to have the nationality of an allied country). Although various national legislations also made provision for punishment on the basis of the principle of '*active* nationality' (the law-breaker had the nationality of the prosecuting State), in actual practice scant use was made of this principle, for obvious reasons.

The 1949 Geneva Conventions marked a great advance both as regards the extension of substantive law (new categories of war crimes were added) and of procedural law. They set up a very advanced system for repressing violations by States. This system was based on, first, the duty of any contracting State (whatever its status in a given armed conflict, hence even in the event of its being a neutral country) to search for, arrest and bring to trial any person accused of 'grave breaches'; second, the alternative duty to hand those persons over for trial to another contracting State, provided the latter made out a *prima facie* case. Thus, the principle *aut judicare aut dedere* was upheld. The relevant provisions represented a momentous departure from customary law, for the Conventions laid down the principle of *universality* of jurisdiction (a contracting State could bring a person to trial regardless of his nationality, of the nationality of the victim, and of the place where the alleged offence had been committed). It seems probable that it was precisely the very bold character of the regulation which rendered it ineffective in actual practice. The provisions remained a dead letter.

The functioning of the penal repression of violations of the laws of war can be assessed better in its merits and shortcomings if considered in the light of the fundamental distinction drawn by Röling between 'individual' and 'system' criminality.[15] The former encompasses crimes committed by combatants on their own initiative and for 'selfish' reasons (rape, looting, murder, and so on). The latter refers to crimes perpetrated on a large scale, chiefly to advance war effort, at the request of, or at least with the encouragement or toleration of, the government authorities (the killing of civilians to spread terror, the refusing of quarter, the use of prohibited weapons, the torture of captured enemies to obtain information, and so on). Normally 'individual criminality' is repressed by the national authorities of the culprit (army commanders do not like this sort of misbehaviour, for it is bad for the morale of the troops and makes for a hostile enemy population). By contrast, 'system criminality' is normally repressed only by international tribunals (of the Nuremberg and Tokyo type) or by the national jurisdiction of the adversary.

There are, of course, exceptions. As pointed out by Röling, the case of the US lieutenant Calley 'a typical example of system criminality', was an exception urged upon the US authorities by American and foreign public opinion.

By and large, repression of 'individual criminality' is a more frequent

---

[15] B. V. A. Röling, 'The Significance of the Laws of War', in *Current Problems of International Law*, ed. A. Cassese (Milan, 1975), pp. 137-9.

occurrence than that of 'system criminality', for the simple reason that the latter involves an appraisal and condemnation of a whole system of government, of misbehaviour involving the highest authorities of a country.

(3) *Protecting Powers*

160. The 1949 Geneva Conventions codified and improved on international practice concerning the designation of 'Protecting Powers' by belligerents for the purpose of safeguarding their interests as well as impelling the adversary to abide by international law.

In a nutshell, the Conventions provided that each of the belligerents could appoint a third State as 'Protecting Power'. But for the State to accomplish its tasks the consent of both belligerents was necessary. Thus the 1949 system hinged on a 'double-decker three-sided' relationship: the two belligerents and two third parties. Once a triangular agreement was reached, a third party could act as a 'Protecting Power' on behalf of each belligerent and scrutinize the implementation of the Conventions. (Nothing, of course, ruled out the possibility of one third State acting as Protecting Power for both belligerents.) As the consent of all the States involved was necessary for the appointment and functioning of Protecting Powers it follows that if consent by one of them was withdrawn the Protecting Power ceased to act. A significant advance of the 1949 Conventions lay in the provision of 'Substitutes for the Protecting Powers'. Of the three possibilities envisaged by the Conventions, the third stood out on account of its mandatory character: under Article 10/10/10/11 para. 3 the Detaining Power (that is, the State detaining the enemy civilians, the wounded, the shipwrecked, or the prisoners of war) was duty-bound to accept 'the offer of the services of a humanitarian organization, such as the International Committee of the Red Cross to assume the humanitarian functions performed by Protecting Powers under the present Convention'. As was rightly pointed out by Abi-Saab, this obligation

... introduces a greater degree of automaticity in the system by making it possible in principle to have an entity exercise a certain measure of supervision over the implementation of the Conventions in all circumstances, regardless of the agreement of the parties or the goodwill of the detaining power.[16]

In actual practice the Protecting Powers system proved a (relative) failure. It was resorted to only in three cases: in 1956, in the Suez conflict (only, however, between Egypt on the one hand and France and the UK on the other); in the short Goa affair in 1961; and in the Indo-Pakistani war in 1971, although India soon withheld its consent. The various causes for its failure include belligerents' fear that they would recognize each other as a

[16] G. Abi-Saab, 'The Implementation of Humanitarian Law', in *The New Humanitarian Law of Armed Conflict*, ed. A. Cassese, i (Naples, 1979), p. 322.

result of the appointment of Protecting Powers, the desire not to sever diplomatic relations, and the reluctance of the International Committee of the Red Cross to step in and offer to take on the role of substitute (or quasi-substitute).

The system instituted in Article 5 of the First Protocol of 1977 substantially takes up the 1949 system. It spells out that the consent of all the parties concerned is all important. Consent is made the linchpin of the system, and any automatic obligation, even that laid down in Article 10/10/10/11 para. 3 of the 1949 Conventions is done away with. Also (in para. 3) it sets up a procedure for facilitating the appointment of Protecting Powers: it eliminates some of the practical or political obstacles to the appointment of Powers, by specifying in paras. 5 and 6 that the designation and acceptance of Powers does not affect the legal status of the parties to the conflict or of any territory, and that diplomatic relations can be maintained by the belligerents despite the functioning of Powers.

WARS OF NATIONAL LIBERATION

The Assimilation of Wars of National Liberation to International Conflicts

161. For many years Third World countries, strongly supported by socialist States, have urged in the UN that wars of national liberation be upgraded to international armed conflicts, with the consequent application to them of all the rules of warfare. Western countries, by contrast, insisted that those wars were merely internal conflicts; therefore their upgrading would mean that one particular class of domestic strife would be treated differently from the others. Such differentiation, they added, would be based on merely ideological considerations (the struggle for self-determination against colonial, racist, or alien regimes), and would introduce into international law the concept of *bellum justum*, or just war, luckily discarded after its being predominant in the Middle Ages. The Third World and socialist countries, mustering a comfortable majority, had their views approved by the Geneva Conference in 1974. In the final session, in 1977, Western States attenuated or even forwent their oposition, both because they preferred to take account of the wish of the majority, and because, meanwhile, two territories belonging to the last great colonial empire, namely Angola and Mozambique, had gained political independence, with the consequence that the rule adopted in 1974 seemed destined to lose at least part of its political impact.

Therefore, when the relevant provision (Article 1.4) was put to a vote 87 States voted in favour, one against (Israel) and 11 abstained (all of which were Western countries, except for Guatemala). The result of the vote should not make us jump to conclusions, however. It is apparent from the declarations made by various countries that in actual fact only one State, namely Israel, totally rejected the provision. The States which abstained voiced misgivings about the possibility of applying the provision without difficulties and differences of opinion. Though they challenged the political and practical wisdom of the rule; they did not dismiss it out of hand as inapplicable in the future. In other words the few States which voiced misgivings about the rule were not motivated by a strong opposition to it, but rather considered that the rule was *bad law*. Arguably the result of the vote, and the tenor of the 'reservations' entered by some States make it clear that even these had come to accept that the rule represented a *new law of the international community*—although, as I have just emphasized, in their view it was not 'good' law.

Another important factor supporting the general character of the rule is that at least three delegations (Egypt, Greece, and Australia) emphasized that the provision actually embodied a general norm which was binding on all States in that it codified a previous practice. These declarations are important both *per se* and also because no other delegation felt it necessary to challenge them. The conclusion is therefore warranted, that in 1977 agreement was reached in the Conference to the effect that wars of national liberation falling within the three classes mentioned in Article 1.4 were to be regarded as international armed conflicts. The general consent consolidated and gave shape to an emergent customary rule—evolved in the UN—which, however, did not crystallize as a fully fledged international norm until the Western countries (one of the three major segments of the international community) adhered to it. The adoption of Article 1 testified to the formation of a rule binding on all the States participating in the Conference (irrespective of whether or not they ratified the Protocol), save for Israel, which consistently rejected Article 1.4.

To the foregoing considerations one might object that Western States refrained from opposing the provision in 1977 not because they intended to abide by it but only because they planned either to refrain from ratifying the Protocol or, in case of ratification, to enter a reservation on the provision. It is easy to rebut this possible objection on the grounds that if this were so, one fails to understand why certain Western States which had voted against the rule in 1974 abstained or even voted for it in 1977. If they had been opposed to it in 1974 one would have expected them to vote against it once more in 1977. In fact the change in attitude of the Western countries had been brought about by two factors: first, the gradual disappearance of colonial empires, and the consequent removal of a major bone of contention; second, their becoming convinced that, after all, the rule in question was not dangerous for humanitarian law since it safeguarded all the basic principles of this law. (This motivation transpired most clearly in the statements of the British and Japanese delegations.)

Jus in bello

162. The fact that Article 1.4 embodies a rule of customary law is not devoid of practical consequences on the legal plane. It follows from this rule that States covered by Article 1.4 are enjoined to apply to the categories of wars of national liberation at least the fundamental principles of customary law with respect to the conduct of hostilities and protection of war victims governing interstate conflicts.

One might object that this conclusion has only theoretical value, for the two major countries against which Article 1.4 was actually aimed, to wit Israel and the Republic of South Africa, did not become bound by it, the former on account of its explicit decision to opt out, the latter primarily because it did not participate in the final session of the Geneva Conference (it took part in the 1974 session only and, needless to say, cast a negative vote when the rule was adopted). Consequently even the substantive rules of customary law on warfare do not apply to the struggles between the PLO and Israel, between SWAPO and the South African authorities in Namibia, and between the various South African liberation movements and South Africa. However, as I have already pointed out, international rules often have a significance transcending their legal force; they possess an 'agitational' or 'rhetorical' value, which explains why States are so eager to enact them despite the fact that the rules may have scant effectiveness as legal standards of behaviour. *Qua* 'rhetorical' value they can serve the useful purpose of making it possible to expose the conduct of States which do not live up to them. Article 1.4, however, has a legal scope too. It is not confined to the occurrences in which the two aforementioned States are involved; it can apply to other, fresh situations as well, witness the Soviet occupation of Afghanistan, which no doubt comes within the purview of the rule although the USSR has not ratified the Protocol and will probably refrain from doing so in the near future, as well as the Indonesian occupation of East Timor. To all these situations both Article 1.4 and the general principles on warfare which this article renders operative, can be deemed applicable.

If this Article has not been applied, this cannot be taken to mean that States do not feel bound by it. For, in the aforementioned instances, the States concerned first, claimed that they were not faced with a war of national liberation, and subsequently found various legal justifications for the use of military force. In the case of Afghanistan, the invading State has claimed that it had been requested by the lawful authorities to enter the country in order to put down insurgency or foreign interference; in the case of East Timor, Indonesia claimed that the island was, in fact, under its sovereignty and that, therefore, the fighting there was merely a case of civil strife. Thus, the general rule on wars of national liberation has not been deemed applicable for the simple reason that in the opinion of the States concerned the requisite circumstances were not present. This only proves that although the rule has undisputedly evolved, the lack of any central agency capable of pronouncing on its concrete application greatly weakens its purport.

It should be added that those provisions of Protocol I which do not crystallize or reflect general rules but have merely contractual force, only apply to wars of national liberation if two conditions are met: first, the (colonial, racist, or occupying) Power against which the war is conducted is a party to the Protocol; and second, the national liberation movement fighting for self-determination makes the declaration provided for in Article 96.3, by which it undertakes to apply the four Geneva Conventions of 1949 and the Protocol. Plainly, the first requirement is unlikely ever to be met. It follows that only general rules on warfare will apply.

INTERNAL ARMED CONFLICT

General Features of the Legal Regulation of Civil Strife

163. At present, civil strife is viewed by international law from three different viewpoints: (1) the rights and obligations of third States with regard to the State where an internal armed conflict has broken out; (2) the conditions on which insurgents can claim international standing and the extent to which they consequently possess rights and obligations; (3) the extent to which international law regulates the fighting going on between the incumbent Government and the rebels.

I have already dwelt on the first two issues (see § 46). It is now appropriate to turn to the third one. We should, however, remind ourselves (see § 46) that the whole approach of international law to civil strife rests on an inherent clash of interests between the 'lawful' Government on the one side (which is of course interested in regarding insurgents as mere bandits devoid of any international status) and rebels, on the other side (naturally eager to be internationally legitimized). Third States may, and actually do, side with either party, according to their own political or ideological leanings, and this, of course, further complicates the question.

All rules governing the struggle between the lawful Government and insurgents have one main feature in common: they do not grant rebels the status of lawful belligerents; in the eyes of both the Government against which they fight and of third States, rebels remain criminals infringing upon domestic penal law. Consequently, if captured, they do not enjoy the status of prisoner of war but can be tried and executed for the mere fact of having taken up arms against the central authorities. Insurgents can be upgraded to the status of lawful combatants only if the incumbent Government decides to grant them the so-called 'recognition of belligerency'. Obviously, this recognition has only been accorded in extreme situations. (For example, the declaration made on 17 June 1979 by four members of the Andean group (Colombia, Venezuela, Bolivia, and Peru), to the effect that they recognized both sides in the Nicaraguan civil war as 'belligerents' was not in fact intended to produce the legal consequences of this type of recognition, nor did it achieve them.)

The obsolescence of the recognition of belligerency (mainly owing to the desire of the Governments involved in civil commotion to wipe out rebellion as soon as possible, as well as to the interest of the third States in either holding aloof or meddling *de facto* in the conflict without, however, going to the length of granting insurgents international legitimation) underlines the fact that rebels are in a greatly inferior position in relation to the central authorities against which they fight. One should not jump to the conclusion that if rebels come to possess international rights and duties, under certain circumstances (§ 46) this achievement automatically entails the acquisition of the status of lawful combatants. As we have seen (§ 46) on becoming international legal subjects they are enabled to enter into international agreements and to send or receive diplomatic missions, on the one hand, and are duty-bound to respect foreigners living in the areas under their control, on the other. The acquisition of international status also means the right to demand respect for certain international humanitarian rules on armed conflict and the obligation to abide by them. This does not mean, however, that these fighters legally cease to be criminals for the Government concerned—however abused this state of affairs may be.

Another important feature of the corpus of rules concerning internal armed conflict is that most of them aim at protecting non-combatants only, that is civilians who do not take part in hostilities and may directly or indirectly suffer from armed violence, the wounded and sick as well as those who, having taken part in the hostilities, are no longer willing, or in a position, to fight. Methods of combat are not regulated, except to the extent that they must aim at sparing civilians. In practice, there are almost no restraints on the armed engagements of Government authorities and rebels *inter se*. States have decided to leave fighting substantially unrestricted on the clear assumption that, being militarily stronger than insurgents, they may quell rebellion more easily by remaining untrammelled by law. This concept is proving increasingly fallacious, for, at present, rebels are assisted in various ways, especially militarily, by third States, and armed violence is therefore carried out with great intensity and cruelty on both sides.

Customary Law

164. Owing to its ruinous effect and the magnitude of its armed hostilities, the Spanish Civil War (1936-9) acquired features comparable in several respects to an international war proper. This prompted the contending parties and several European States to affirm that certain general rules protecting civilians in interstate wars were applicable to this conflict as well, and to all similar examples of civil strife. Thus, a very interesting phenomenon took shape, which has become a major trend of the present century: the increasing extension to civil wars of the principles applicable to international armed conflicts. The rules on which general consent emerged were: the ban on deliberate bombing of civilians; the prohibition on attacking non-military objectives; the rule concerning the precautions which must be taken when attacking military objects; the rule authorizing reprisals against enemy civilians and consequently submitting them to the general conditions exacted for reprisals.[16a]

The four rules in point apply to any internal armed conflict, provided it has the characteristics of the Spanish Civil War. That is to say, the insurgents must exhibit the following features: an organized administration effectively controlling a portion of the territory of the State; and organized armed forces capable of abiding by international law. Internal armed conflicts having a lesser degree of intensity, for example, instances of minor rebellions, or uprisings which do not take on the proportions of a civil war proper, are not covered by the rules.

The formation of general norms on civilians was substantially borne out by the unanimous adoption by the General Assembly in 1968 of resolution no. 2444 (XXIII), and, again, in 1970, when resolution no. 2675 (XXV) was passed. Interestingly, on a par with these UN resolutions, recent practice has reaffirmed the applicability to civil wars of at least some general rules on civilians. Such applicability was urged by the International Committee of the Red Cross on several occasions (for instance, in 1964 during the conflict in the Congo and during the 1966–9 Nigerian civil war), on none of which did it arouse any significant opposition.

Unfortunately these fairly satisfactory conditions of law are not matched by its observance in practice. It is dispiriting to notice that the Government and rebels of the same State—even though they pay lip-service to current legal standards, and in spite of the fact that, after all, the civilians suffering from the conflict are fellow-nationals—rarely protect non-combatants as requested by law. This has been the case in recent occurrences such as the Nigerian conflict and the civil wars in Nicaragua and El Salvador. A possible explanation is that, first, civilians often take sides in domestic strife and actually contribute, at various levels, to the struggle, and, second, that in many States (chiefly in Africa) the population is split into conflicting ethnic and cultural groups which consequently do not share the feeling of belonging to one and the same country.

Another body of customary rules has evolved out of a provision common

---

[16a] See A. Cassese, 'The Spanish Civil War and the Development of Customary Law Concerning Internal Armed Conflict' in *Current Problems of International Law* cit., pp. 287 ff.

to the four 1949 Geneva Conventions, namely Article 3. However, this Article, has a much broader field of application than the general rules on civilians, for it applies to any internal armed conflict, even to those which do not reach a high level of intensity. Article 3, which makes a point of leaving the legal status of insurgents unaffected, is meant to protect only the victims of hostilities, namely 'persons taking no active part' in them, to whom it grants a set of basic humanitarian safeguards.

First, non-combatants must not be attacked; in other words, they must not be identified as a military target and can never be the object of deliberate attacks. Furthermore, the contending parties must not resort to measures intended to intimidate or terrorize the civilian population. These prohibitions clearly follow from the provision banning the infliction of violence on the life and persons of non-combatants. In this connection, it is interesting to recall that in a document of 30 January 1970, the Legal Bureau of the Canadian Government stated *inter alia* that Article 3 outlaws 'acts of the type occurring at My Lai'.[17] This statement referred to the ban on physical violence against civilians, stemming from Article 3.

Second, pursuant to Article 3, the taking of hostages is prohibited. This practice, it must be emphasized, has frequently been resorted to during civil wars, including the Spanish conflict; the relevant provision is, therefore, of great value.

Third, all reprisals involving violence to the life and persons of non-combatants, or outrages upon their personal dignity, are forbidden.

Fourth, if members of the armed forces of the adversary, or civilians belonging to the opposing party and suspected of supporting it, are arrested and detained, or are put into internment camps, they must be treated humanely. In particular, no discriminatory treatment can be meted out to them, nor can they be submitted to torture, or to cruel, humiliating or degrading measures. In the event of their being brought to trial, all judicial safeguards provided for in para. 1 *d* of Article 3 must be observed.

Finally, the wounded and sick, including those belonging to the adversary, must be collected and cared for.

State practice developed after 1949 (including the adoption of a similar provision in 1954: Article 19 of the Hague Convention on the Protection of Cultural Property) shows that Article 3 was invoked, reaffirmed, and relied upon on a number of occasions. Even when it was disregarded in actual practice, no State admitted violating it. This is no matter for surprise, for Article 3 essentially enshrines a handful of humanitarian principles proclaimed by States in other contexts, such as the various treaties on human rights.

---

[17] The Canadian statement is in *C YIL* 9 (1971), 301.

The fact remains, however, that the instances of violation or disregard for the provisions of Article 3 greatly outnumber the instances of compliance. The list is long and includes such cases as the fighting in Malaya (1949-57); Kenya (1952-60); and Algeria (1954-62). 'La Question' (1957), the famous booklet published by the French journalist Alleg,[18] on the torture practised by the French Army in Algeria made known to the whole world how France infringed upon the basic human rights proclaimed in Article 3. Other cases are Cyprus (1954-9); the Congo (1960-1); the Yemen (1962-9); Nigeria (1967-70); Nicaragua (1978-9); El Salvador (1979-83). True, all these instances of non-observance have not been such as to erode the rule, for the latter has been consistently upheld by States (similarly, domestic criminal laws are not obliterated by their daily violation). The jurist concerned with humanitarian demands is, however, justified in concluding that a lot of pressure is still needed to impel States and rebels to live up to international standards protecting human life and dignity.

Treaty Law

165.　The sad history of how the Geneva Protocol II of 1977 was mutilated and stripped of some very significant provisions at the eleventh hour is well known. What matters here is to emphasize that although nearly all its provisions were adopted by consensus, and although the Protocol itself was the subject of consensus approval, strong and unequivocal objections were raised by a number of Third World countries. This group included States such as Nigeria, Sri Lanka, India, Indonesia, Mexico, Ghana, Sudan, Zaïre, Guatemala, the Phillippines, Uganda—as well as Chile, which made a 're-servation' actually calculated to hamstring the Protocol, as far as its possible application to Chile was concerned. Some of these States went so far as to declare that the Protocol was 'superfluous' (Mexico), 'pointless' (India), 'quite unnecessary' (Uganda), and even that it 'did not involve any international agreement but simply a concession on the part of States which agreed to apply it to their own nationals' (Sudan). The number and content of the objections was such as to lead the Turkish delegation to state that the consensus was only apparent.[19]

The Protocol exhibits a general feature differentiating it from the rules generated by Article 3 and putting it on the same footing as the various rules on civilians which emerged as a result of the Spanish Civil War: it only covers large-scale armed conflicts, that is to say, civil strife presenting all the characteristics of intensity, duration, and magnitude of the Spanish and Nigerian civil wars. It does not apply to 'situations of internal disturbances and tensions, such as riots, isolated and sporadic acts of violence and other acts of a similar nature'. Thus, the progress made in 1977 turns out to be limited on a threefold score: first, on account of the paucity of the rules evolved; second, because these rules do not cover all classes of internal

[18] H. Alleg, *La Question* (Paris, 1957).
[19] For the various statements on Protocol II, see *Diplomatic Conference on Humanitarian Law of Armed Conflict, Official Records*, vii. 199, 203, 251, 201, 250.

armed conflicts, but only those above a certain 'threshold'; third, because the Protocol is unlikely to enlist wide support and will, therefore, become binding on a few States only. (Indeed on 1 April 1986, nine years after its adoption, it has been ratified by only fifty (out of about 170) States. Moreover one of them, El Salvador, is not heeding it in the least in the civil strife which has been raging there since 1980, and no attempt is being made by other contracting States to press for its application.) All the same, the Protocol represents the maximum which States participating in the Geneva Conference, and particularly Third World countries, were prepared to concede. To attain a more satisfactory general regulation of civil wars it will be necessary to wait for the appearance of a more favourable attitude on the part of States.

CONCLUDING REMARKS

166.   There is no denying that over the years mankind has witnessed steady progress in the sophistication, the devastating effects, and cruelty of weapons and methods of combat. Illusions about a 'permanent peace' can no longer be entertained, and one watches with astonishment the succession of barbarous armed conflicts and the lack of any real advantage for mankind; indeed, Hegel's famous proposition that Thucydides' 'immortal work' on the Peloponnesian wars was 'the absolute gain that mankind drew from that struggle'[20] could not be repeated for recent wars, for they have not even had the advantage of being narrated by a great historian. (It has, however, been argued that recent armed conflicts have had the 'merit' of stimulating industrial and technological progress. But this can hardly be considered an 'advantage', compared with the suffering brought about.)

International legal control of warfare has kept pace with the developments in organized armed violence only to a limited extent. Major military Powers have not accepted sweeping restraints, with the consequence that this body of law is beset with deficiencies, loopholes, and ambiguity. These observations, I believe, answer the question raised before (§ 146) about whether, in the final analysis, international law plays into the hands of Great Powers, or whether it is, instead, calculated to protect lesser States. Here, as in other areas, international law cannot but mirror the constellation of power of the world community. Accordingly, to a large measure it benefits militarily strong countries, simply by omitting extensive, clear-cut and workable restrictions on means and methods of warfare, and on the effective monitoring of military misbehaviour. By the same token it also includes a number of rules which protect victims of armed conflict, as well as a few norms specifically meeting the entreaties of lesser States. Thus the

[20] Hegel, op. cit., 266.

laws of warfare, although ultimately more beneficial to militarily powerful States, do not neglect the smaller ones altogether.

A realistic assessment of the present condition should not beget despair. After all, as early as 1764, Voltaire, to whom we owe one of the most incisive analyses of war, wrote: 'famine, plague, and war are the three most remarkable ingredients of this vile world',[21] adding that unlike the first two, which came from Providence, war emanated from the 'imagination' of men. How could law dispose of so important an 'ingredient'? Besides, one should not forget the wise teaching of Scholem that 'Reason is a dialectical tool that serves both construction and destruction, *but has had more notable successes in destruction*'.[22] Nevertheless, legal rules, however weak and defective, do restrict the behaviour of States and introduce a modicum of humanity into utterly inhuman conduct. The absence of normative standards would be even more regrettable: it would leave strong military Powers—or for that matter, any State, even the poor ones provided they were supported by one of the Great Powers—free of any trammel. Furthermore, it is precisely the nature of the laws of warfare referred to above (§ 146) which makes it clear that here, more than in any other area, legal standards possess a significant meta-juridical value: they serve as a moral and political yardstick by which public opinion can appraise if, and to what extent, States misbehave. This role of legal rules can be of great help, especially if soundly and impartially used by non-governmental groups and associations.

[21] Voltaire, *Dictionnaire philosophique* (1764) (Paris, 1909), p. 203 (under: *Guerre*).
[22] G. Scholem, *On Jews and Judaism in Crisis: Selected Essays* (New York, 1956), p. 31.

International Protection of Human Dignity

INTRODUCTION: THE BIRTH, AFTER THE SECOND WORLD WAR, OF INTERNATIONAL CONCERN FOR HUMAN RIGHTS

167.   To paraphrase a famous political document, one could say that since 1945 the world has been haunted by a spectre: that of the doctrine of human rights, which has been troubling and upsetting some, inflaming and thrilling others, whether members of cabinet or diplomats. In fact, after the Second World War this doctrine became, for some States, one of the significant postulates of their foreign policy, of great use when blaming or denouncing other countries, or guiding their actions within international organizations. To other nations, of course, this doctrine has become an incubus instead: it serves as a yardstick by which their behaviour is gauged and censured in international forums.

The arrival of 'human rights' on the international scene is, indeed, a remarkable event because, as a number of political scientists have pointed out, including Bull and Hoffmann,[1] it is a subversive theory destined to foster tension and conflict among States. Essentially it is meant to tear aside the veil that had in the past covered and protected sovereignty, giving each State the appearance of a fully armoured titanic structure, perceived by other States only 'as a whole', and whose inner mechanisms could not be tampered with. Today the human rights doctrine forces States to give an account of how they administer justice, run prisons, treat their nationals, and on so. Potentially, therefore, it can subvert their domestic order and, consequently, the traditional configuration of the international community as well.

On a closer examination, however, this doctrine was not the first to sow seeds of protest against the 'Westphalian model'. As far back as the First World War a politico-legal postulate had been advanced challenging certain facets of the main fabric of the 'family of nations', namely the principle of self-determination of peoples. I have already shown (§ 80) how this principle, particularly in its anticolonialist version, sapped the foundations of the

---

[1] H. Bull, *The Anarchical Society: A Study of Order in World Politics* (New York, 1977), pp. 135–53; S. Hoffmann, 'Reaching for the Most Difficult: Human Rights as a Foreign Policy Goal', *Daedalus*, 112 (1983), 33–4.

community of sovereign States for the very reason that it legitimized certain revolutionary forces, in particular peoples oppressed by colonial or alien Powers. After the Second World War the doctrine of self-determination was joined by that of human rights. In conjunction with each other, they have gradually eroded the international order and legitimized the entry of new 'actors' onto the international scene, whether they be peoples (see § 51-6), or individuals (see § 57). Later on their common challenging force justified their gradual amalgamation—to the extent that self-determination was included in the 1966 U N Covenants on human rights as the prologue and basis for the rights in question.

On the whole, one can say that within the international community the two doctrines under consideration have acquired the value and significance which within the context of domestic systems, had formerly belonged to Locke's theory of a social contract, Montesquieu's concept of the separation of powers, and Rousseau's theory of the sovereignty of the people. Just as these political ideas corroded and undermined absolute and despotic monarchy, democratizing the foundations on which kingdoms rested, so the two doctrines we are discussing have lent, and still lend, tremendous impetus to the democratization of the world community.

Why then did sovereign States support and even advocate these two 'theories' at an international level, knowing full well that they diverged radically from the political philosophy of State sovereignty and the basic principle on which the 'Westphalian model' rested? What political and ideological motives can have induced certain members of the international community to propound ideas which could, sooner or later, undermine and disrupt their own authority?

I have already attempted to describe (§§ 30, 80) the historical factors underlying the emergence of the principle of self-determination. Now let us find out which factors helped to launch the concept of human rights on the international scene. To do so we must first retrace our steps and re-examine, if very briefly, the degree of consideration granted to individuals by traditional international law.

168. The basis of traditional international law was reciprocity, as is indeed still the case with the bulk of modern international law (§ 11). Individuals were only taken into consideration *qua* citizens of a given State; if they suffered damage abroad, their interests were concretely safeguarded only to the extent to which their national State decided to exercise diplomatic protection. Individuals were mere 'appendices' of the State to which they belonged, simple pawns in its hands, to be used, protected or sacrificed according to what was dictated by State interests.

There were, however, a few exceptions, which were mentioned in the previous pages: the treaties prohibiting the slave trade in the nineteenth century, and those banning both the slave trade and slavery as such in the present century (§ 33); the I L O conventions (§§ 12, 33, 57) and the various treaties protecting religious, ethnic, and linguistic minorities, agreed upon after the First World War (§ 33). These treaties, although founded to a great extent on humanitarian considerations, were also motivated by the self-interest of the contracting States. We have seen that the pressure to put a stop to the trade in black slaves came in part from those European countries which no longer had colonial interests in the Americas and were consequently keen to end the flow of cheap manpower to other countries. In the case of I L O conventions, guaranteeing uniformity of treatment to workers in all major areas of the world prevented certain countries from taking unfair advantage in the international market of low labour costs at home. The treaties on minorities (with Czechoslovakia, Greece, Poland, Rumania, and Yugoslavia) as well as the peace treaties including clauses on minorities (those with Austria, Bulgaria, Turkey, and Hungary) were to some extent politically motivated: those European countries which had ethnic, linguistic or religious affinities with groups living in other countries were eager for these groups to be respected and to be immune from undue hindrance and interference. What is even more important—as President Wilson pointed out at the Peace Conference on 31 May 1919, in an attempt to rebuff the opposition of States where minorities existed—the international protection of minorities aimed at safeguarding peace, besides attenuating the often harsh consequences of the territorial partitions effected in Europe by the Great Powers.[2] Even so, it remains true that one of the motivations behind these three classes of treaty was the concept that certain groups or categories of individuals ought to be protected by international law for their own sake.

After the Second World War international protection of human beings as such increased at a staggering pace. Individuals were no longer to be taken care of on the international level *qua* members of a group (minority or particular category); they began to be protected *qua* single human beings. Furthermore, the international standards on the matter were no longer motivated, even in part, by economic interests, although they were often dictated by political considerations.

Why did things change so drastically? The main reason was the shared conviction, of all the victorious powers, that the Nazi aggression and the atrocities perpetrated during the War had been the fruit of a vicious philosophy based on utter disregard for the dignity of man. One means of preventing a return to these horrors was the proclamation at all levels of certain basic standards of respect for human rights. This view was propounded with greatest force by the Western powers (in particular the US), for the simple reason that their whole political philosophy and indeed the

[2] W. Wilson, in League of Nations *Official Journal*, Special Supplement, 73 (1929), 46–8.

fundamental legal texts of some of their national systems were based on a 'bill of rights'. Therefore, it came naturally to them to project their domestic concepts and creeds onto the international community.

The basic approach to the question of human rights was twofold: the victors pursued, on the one hand, the development of international criminal law to meet the immediate need of bringing to justice and punishing German and Japanese war criminals who had committed inhuman acts not covered by the traditional laws of warfare; on the other hand, they pursued the elaboration of a set of general principles on human rights designed to serve as guidelines for the UN and its member States, with a view to being gradually implemented and elaborated upon through traditional normative means, that is to say, treaties.

These two approaches, although distinct, were in fact complementary, both stemming from the desire to punish those guilty of inhuman acts and, by the same token, prevent the recurrence of similar acts in future by establishing a set of standards to be observed even in peacetime.

In the following paragraphs I shall examine the two trends separately. It should, however, be said from the outset that the first part of the strategy (namely the elaboration of international criminal law prohibiting inhuman acts and providing for the punishment of offenders), did not yield much fruit in the long run, for a number of reasons which we shall look at. By contrast, the other trend has gradually brought about the creation of an impressive body of law, to some extent matched by an improvement in actual practice.

INTERNATIONAL PROHIBITION OF CRIMES AGAINST HUMANITY

169.   During the Second World War the Allies became aware that some of the most heinous acts of barbarity perpetrated by the Germans were not prohibited by traditional international law.

The laws of warfare only proscribed violations involving the adversary or the enemy populations, whereas the Germans had also performed inhuman acts for political or racial reasons against their own citizens (trade-union members, social-democrats, communists, Jews, gypsies, members of the church); against citizens of the allies (for example Italian Jews in the period before Italy's surrender in 1943 and French Jews under the Vichy regime (1940-4)); against nationals of States not formally under German occupation and, therefore, not protected by the international rules safeguarding the civilian population of occupied territories: this applied to Austria, annexed by Germany in 1938, and Czechoslovakia (following the Munich Treaty in 1938, the Sudeten territory was annexed by Germany, and the rest of the country became the so-called Protectorate of Bohemia and Moravia, in 1939). The Germans also harassed and murdered stateless Jews and gypsies. In addition, in 1945 such acts as mere persecution for political or racial purposes were not prohibited, even against civilians of occupied territories.

In 1945, at the strong insistence of the US, the Allies decided that a better course of action than simply to execute all the major war criminals, would be to bring them to trial. The London Agreement embodying the Charter of the International Military Tribunal included a provision under which the Tribunal was to try and punish persons guilty, among other things, of 'crimes against humanity'. These were defined as:

... murder, extermination, enslavement, deportation, and other inhumane acts committed against any civilian population, before or during the war, or persecutions on political, racial, or religious grounds in execution of or connexion with any crimes within the jurisdiction of the Tribunal [i.e. either 'crimes against peace' or 'war crimes'], whether or not in violation of the domestic law of the country where perpetrated.

It is apparent that one major shortcoming of this definition is that it closely links crimes against humanity to the other two categories of off-ences. As was rightly remarked by Schwelb,[3] this association meant that only those criminal activities were punished which 'directly affected the interests of other States' (either because these activities were connected with a war of aggression or a conspiracy to wage such a war, or because they were bound up with war crimes, that is crimes against enemy combatants or enemy civilians). Plainly, in 1945 the Allies did not feel that they should legislate in such a way as to prohibit inhuman acts on the grounds of their inhumanity regardless of their consequences or implications for third States.

Despite this limitation, the creation of the new category of 'crimes against humanity' was a great step forward. First, it indicated that the international community was widening the category of acts considered of 'meta-national' concern, which came to include all acts running contrary to those basic values of respect for human dignity which are, or should be, considered inherent in any human being (in the notion of 'crimes against humanity', humanity did not mean 'mankind' or 'human race' but 'the quality' or 'concept' of man). Second, inasmuch as crimes against humanity were made punishable even if perpetrated in accordance with domestic laws, the 1945 Charter showed that in some special circumstances there were limits to the 'omnipotence of the State' (to quote the British Chief Prosecutor Sir Hartley Shawcross) and that 'the individual human being, the ultimate unit of all law, is not disentitled to the protection of mankind when the State

---

[3] E. Schwelb, 'Crimes Against Humanity', *BYIL* 23 (1946), 195.

tramples upon his rights in a manner which outrages the conscience of mankind'.[4]

The International Military Tribunal gave application to the Charter provision dealing with 'crimes against humanity'. In so doing, it indubitably applied *ex post facto* law; in other words, it applied international law retroactively, as was stressed by the defence counsel.[5] The Tribunal gave two justifications for its application of the Charter. First, it stated that it was 'the expression of international law existing at the time of its creation; and to that extent [was] itself a contribution to international law'. This, however, was not the case so far as crimes against humanity were concerned, and, indeed, it is striking that the Tribunal did not consider it fitting to argue its general view with regard to this class of offences. The second proposition of the Tribunal—chiefly articulated with regard to 'crimes against peace' (see §§ 34, 35) but also applicable to the offence under consideration—was that 'the maxim *nullum crimen sine lege* is not a limitation of sovereignty, but is in general a principle of justice'.[5a] This proposition is no doubt valid for grave atrocities and inhuman acts. In the case of newly established crimes, however, the courts were wise to refrain from meting out the harshest penalty, namely the death sentence, to defendants found guilty of these new crimes only (this view was forcefully defended by Röling, the Dutch member of the Tokyo International Tribunal, in his dissenting opinion).[6]

Only two defendants were found guilty of crimes against humanity exclusively: Streicher and von Schirach. The former, who had been for some time *Gauleiter* (district leader) of Franconia and had published an anti-Semitic weekly, was found guilty of incitement to persecute Jews; although he had started his anti-Jewish activities as early as 1933, the Tribunal found that he had engaged in the persecution of Jews in connection with war crimes, for he had urged the extermination of Jews in the Eastern European countries occupied by Germany. He was sentenced to the death penalty and hanged. The other defendant, von Schirach, had been *Gauleiter* of Vienna in which capacity he had participated in the deportation of Jews to Eastern European ghettos—a policy which, as the Tribunal stressed, he had not himself initiated, however. His crimes were considered as coming under the jurisdiction of the Tribunal because he had committed them in connection with and execution of the annexation of Austria by Germany. This, in the view of the Tribunal, had been the result of a conspiracy to commit aggression, and hence a crime against peace. He was sentenced to twenty years imprisonment.

[4] Sir Hartley Shawcross, in *Speeches of the Chief Prosecutors at the Close of the Case Against the Individual Defendants* (London, 1946), p. 63.

[5] See *Trial of the Major War Criminals before the International Military Tribunal, Nuremberg 14 November 1945–1 October 1946, Official Documents*, Vol. 1 (Nuremberg 1947), pp. 168–70.

[5a] See *Trial* etc. cit., p. 219.

[6] B. V. A. Röling, in *The Tokyo Judgment*, ed. B. V. A. Röling and C. F. Ruter, ii (Amsterdam, 1977), pp. 1048 ff.

In the wake of the major war trials momentous changes in international law took place. A conspicuous number of international instruments were drawn up embodying the prohibition of crimes against humanity, at least certain of which improved and extended the London Agreement.

The Peace Treaties with Italy, Romania, Hungary, Bulgaria, and Finland included terms providing for the punishment of these crimes. On 11 December 1946 the General Assembly unanimously adopted a resolution 'affirming' the principles of the Charter of the Nuremberg International Tribunal and its judgment. On 10 December 1949 the General Assembly adopted the Convention on Genocide, the first international treaty prohibiting genocide in peace as well as war. And on 12 August 1949 a Diplomatic Conference adopted the four Geneva Conventions on War Victims, which greatly expanded the categories of war crimes so as to cover many instances of crimes against humanity as well, and which, in addition, made it incumbent upon all contracting States either to prosecute and try, or to extradite, persons accused of serious breaches of the Conventions (see § 159).

It is a matter of regret that this tremendous normative development was not matched by the implementation of the relevant rules. Both in time of peace and in the course of the wars which have been waged since 1945 atrocious acts against humanity have been committed, in particular acts of genocide. The world community has, however, remained silent, or, rather, time and again public opinion has uttered its indignation and dismay, but Governments have preferred to hold aloof and not take advantage of their right to demand the discontinuance of the crime and the punishment of the wrongdoers. Only in very few instances (for example the *Eichmann* and the *Barbie* cases) have men been tried for crimes against humanity. But there were special historical and moral motivations behind Israel's and France's action and in any case Eichmann's and Barbie's crimes had been perpetrated before and during the Second World War. In all other instances, self-interest and power politics gained the upper hand.

In conclusion, so long as there is no collective sense of solidarity and no joint interest in respect for fundamental standards of behaviour on human dignity, the prospects for a satisfactory implementation of the whole body of law concerning crimes against humanity remain poor indeed.

THE INTERNATIONAL PROTECTION OF HUMAN RIGHTS BY THE UN

The U N Charter

170. Let us now turn to the efforts made by the international community to promote respect for human dignity on a more general and 'day-to-day' basis. (For lack of space, I shall not go into regional organizations such as the Council of Europe and the Organization of American States. In so far as the UN is concerned, I shall only dwell on the principal doctrines on human rights propounded by the various groupings within the Organization and the basic lines of action adopted by the main UN bodies. Both specific cases of UN 'intervention' on the matter, and the practical details of UN action must, of necessity, be left outside the picture.)

As pointed out above, the lead was taken in 1945 by Western countries and chiefly by the US. President Roosevelt in his message to Congress of 6 January 1941 had already listed the 'four freedoms' which he saw as important goals of future US foreign policy:

In the future days, which we seek to make secure, we look forward for a world founded upon four essential human freedoms. The first is freedom of speech and expression—everywhere in the world. The second is freedom of every person to worship God in his own way—everywhere in the world. The third is freedom from want—which, translated into world terms, means economic understandings which will secure to every nation a healthy, peaceful life for its inhabitants—everywhere in the world. The fourth is freedom from fear—which translated into world terms, means a world-wide reduction of armaments to such a point and in such a thorough fashion that no nation will be in a position to commit an act of aggression against any neighbour—anywhere in the world.[7]

The lofty concepts enunciated by Roosevelt were taken up in the Atlantic Charter of 14 August 1941 and then amplified by the US delegation to the Dumbarton Oaks Conference in 1944. In the 'US Tentative Proposals for a General International Organization' of 18 July 1944, it was suggested that the General Assembly of the UN should be responsible for

initiating studies and making recommendations for ... the promotion of the observance of basic human rights in accordance with the principles or undertakings agreed upon by the States members of the International Organization.

It is apparent from this proposal that, from the outset, even the very State which championed the inclusion of human rights among the matters under the jurisdicion of the UN proceeded with utmost caution and took pains to spell out that the Organization should have limited powers only, and that in particular the standards on human rights by which member States should be guided were to be first accepted by them through the traditional process of treaty-making. (The American restraint was clearly motivated by domestic reasons: the constitutional problems, which the acceptance of international obligations on human rights might raise, but also, and more importantly, the fact that in the US in 1945 various racist laws were in force—and continued to be until the 1960s—which might easily expose the US Government to international censure and scrutiny, if internationally

[7] See US *Hearings Documents*, 77th Session of Congress, 1st Session.

binding obligations on human rights were enacted through the UN Charter).

At the Dumbarton Oaks Conference (August–October 1944), the initial opposition of the UK and the USSR led the US to water down its proposals even further. In fact the provision on human rights produced by the Four Powers (US; USSR; UK; and China), was rather weak. However, when the San Francisco Conference (April–June 1945) began, the four Sponsoring Powers were confronted with a spate of bold amendments, mostly emanating from Latin-American countries. This, as well as the conversion of the USSR to the cause of human rights (this State put forward specific proposals on the matter, particularly on non-discrimination and self-determination of peoples) led the Four Powers to consider it advisable to strengthen their proposals.

In the course of the San Francisco Conference three alignments emerged. On the one hand, there was a group of vocal Latin-American countries (chiefly Brazil, Colombia, Chile, Cuba, the Dominican Republic, Ecuador, Mexico, Panama,and Uruguay) plus a few Western States (Australia, New Zealand, and Norway) and Third World nations, such as India. These countries put forward amendments substantially calculated to lay down an obligation to respect human rights. The second group of States included major Western Powers, which though favourable to the promotion of human rights, opposed the attempts to expand the sphere of action of the UN and to lay down any definite obligation to respect human rights. The US took a lead on this score, by strongly objecting to the broadening of Article 56 and also by insisting on the need to lay down a safeguard clause protecting State sovereignty (namely, the proviso which later became Article 2.7 on domestic jurisdiction). One can finally discern a third group, consisting of socialist countries (Byelorussia, Czechoslovakia, and Ukraine) led by the USSR which, although substantially upholding the restrictive attitude of the second group just mentioned, distinguished itself by the fact that it stressed the importance of the right of peoples to self-determination (a right which major Western countries, plus such colonial powers as Belgium, strongly opposed).

In addition, the USSR put forward proposals clearly showing that there were contrasts between East and West even in areas where there seemingly was agreement. Thus, for instance, when the four Great Powers met in San Francisco and discussed the proposal that the UN should promote 'respect for human rights', the USSR suggested that this should be followed by the words: 'in particular, the right to work, and the right to education'. The US and the UK opposed this proposal, on the grounds that if it was specified which rights were to be protected, then others should be added — in particular the right to freedom of information and freedom of religion. Similarly, when at San Francisco the report of Committee II/3 came to be discussed, the Soviet delegate drew attention to the part played by the USSR in improving on the Dumbarton Oaks proposals and specifically mentioned the principle of respect for human rights. He only spoke of economic, social, and cultural rights, however.

The upshot of the lengthy discussions at San Francisco was that the first group of States did not obtain any substantial gains, while the other two groups reached a compromise which, to some extent, accommodated their mutual demands.[8] The compromise consisted of the following provisions: (1) no specific obligation to take separate action for the promotion, let alone the protection, of human rights was upheld (Article 56); (2) the right of self-determination of peoples was proclaimed (Articles 1 and 55), but only as a guiding principle for the Organization and in the emasculated version of self-government; (3) the powers of the General Assembly in the field of human rights, already very weak (they amounted to making recommendations and studies) were further limited by the proviso of Article 2.7 (on domestic jurisdiction); (4) the relevant Charter provisions were inspired by the conviction that respect for human rights should be furthered as a *means of safeguarding peace*. The major concern of the countries which had come through the Second World War was that all possible steps ought to be taken, directly or indirectly, to prevent international armed conflicts and to keep the peace. Human rights were seen and understood in this light.

Evolution of the UN Action

General

171. Faced with this normative framework, member States of the UN were called upon to decide how to make use of the loose formulas of the Charter. Broadly speaking, two possible courses of action were open to them. They could either confine themselves to using the General Assembly as a 'regular diplomatic conference' and accordingly draft conventions or stimulate States to pursue certain objectives by addressing general recommendations to them, in keeping with a liberal construction of Article 2.7. Arguably, this would by no means have been a poor performance, for the mere fact of detailing and spelling out in international instruments the human rights and fundamental freedoms for the promotion of which States should strive, constituted a major accomplishment.

Alternatively, a less moderate course of action was open to States. By placing a strict interpretation on Article 2.7 they could go beyond the mere preparation of international standards and call States to account at least in

---

[8] The various statements and proposals made in the UN and quoted above are in UNCIO, vol. 3, p. 603; vol. 6, pp. 296 ff.; vol. 8, pp. 56, 80-1, 85, 90-1. Some of them are also cited by R. B. Russell, *A History of the United Nations Charter* (Washington, DC, 1958), pp. 304 ff.

case of massive infringements of human rights. To this effect, they could emphasize that the General Assembly could act as the 'conscience of the world': in addition to its 'quasi-legislative' functions it would be given the task of watch-dog for the purpose of forestalling or castigating egregious deviations from basic standards on human rights.

In the following pages we shall see that the UN gradually took the second path.

The changes in the majority in the UN in the course of time enable us to speak of three different phases in the evolution of this organization. I shall endeavour to pinpoint the philosophy and strategy of human rights championed in each of these stages by the majority prevailing at any one time in the General Assembly.

The first stage, which dated from the adoption of the Charter to the late 1950s, was characterized by Western dominance. The second, which started with the strengthening of the socialist group in 1955 and with its taking the lead of Third World countries, had as its main feature the need for the West to come to terms with the other two groups, with the consequent striking of a number of compromises. The third stage, started around 1974, was marked by the prevalence of developing countries. It launched a new doctrine of human rights, which eventually gained the upper hand and aimed at supplanting the views previously upheld by the General Assembly.

THE FIRST STAGE OF INTERNATIONAL PROTECTION OF HUMAN RIGHTS (1945 TO THE LATE 1950S)

The Influence of the Western 'Doctrine' of Human Rights

172. In the first years after the adoption of the Charter, the Western political philosophy easily prevailed. It can be summarized as follows:

(1) Although it is not really possible to rank human rights in order of preference, civil and political rights appear to be of primary importance, especially certain rights such as freedom of thought and religion, which distinguish democracies from authoritarian States.

(2) Self-determination constitutes only a general principle, not a full right of peoples.

(3) International treaties laying down obligations in the field of human rights should be as clear and precise as possible; woolly and generic terminology should be avoided, as should treaties which place too many restrictions on the freedom of individual States (lest the treaties fail to be ratified by a significant number of States).

(4) It is not sufficient to approve international treaties to protect human rights; of equal importance is the establishment of an international moni-

toring mechanism to check that these measures are being respected by the ratifying States, for without some kind of international supervision, treaties are not only of little practical use but are mere propaganda.

(5) The promotion of human rights is an end to be pursued in its own right and is not at any cost to be subordinated to that of friendly relations between States.

The political and ideological motives of the Western powers are clear. The Western historical and political tradition, based as it is on respect for civil and political rights induces Western countries to underscore the importance of this class of rights in the international arena as well.

At the same time, to single out this particular class for attention is to concentrate on an area in which socialist countries are at a disadvantage; human rights can therefore be used as an ideological weapon against Eastern European States. The insistence on international monitoring mechanisms also has an ideological basis, at least up to a point: it springs first of all from the belief that a rule can be called legal in so far as it lays down clear standards of behaviour accompanied by strict and effective sanctions (see §62). But to stress the importance of international scrutiny once again underlines the crucial importance of civil and political rights—these being the only ones to which such scrutiny can be applied. (International monitoring of the application of economic and social rights—clearly a slow and gradual process—is both less feasible and perhaps of comparatively lesser importance.) Finally, there are also ideological and political considerations behind the Western preference for international treaties on specific sets of human rights rather than resolutions. Treaties require ratification and leave Western countries free to withhold their assent. Furthermore, treaties are, or should be, more strictly and precisely worded than resolutions and lend themselves less to generic formulations of an essentially political nature. Finally, treaties give States all the time they need for consideration and for overcoming any possible internal difficulties of a constitutional or political kind before ratification. (Singularly, the U S is one of the Western countries which has ratified fewest conventions on human rights: even today it has only ratified the least significant ones.)

Moving Towards International Legislation

173. The first phase was characterized by efforts on the part of the General Assembly to draw up an international document on human rights which would be acceptable to all U N members: to States as dissimilar ideologically and politically as the U S and the U S S R; to nations with such different economic and political structures as the Western countries on the one hand and Ethiopia, Saudi Arabia, and Afghanistan on the other; to countries upholding differing religious philosophies, ranging from Christian (the nations of the West and Latin-America), to Muslim (like Saudi Arabia, Afghanistan, Turkey, Pakistan, etc.), Hindu (like India) and Buddhist (like China).

It was therefore necessary to find the lowest common denominator, as regards the conception of both the relationship between State and individual and of basic human rights. The attempt to forge a single, collective stand, a general 'philosophy' of human dignity, was successful, although agreement was only reached after lengthy discussions. The ensuing political document, the Universal Declaration of Human Rights of 10 December 1948, has two basic characteristics, one to do with its formal structure and the other with its content.

In formal terms, it is not legally binding, but possesses only moral and political force. In other words, it is simply a recommendation to States. About the content of the Declaration a bit more needs to be said. On the whole, the view of human rights expressed in it is *Western*. More space and importance are allotted to civil and political rights than to economic, social, and cultural rights, and of the rights of peoples no mention at all is made (the right of self-determination is completely absent). The position taken with regard to colonized peoples, who have been partially or completely denied their right to freedom, is purely formal. Nor does the Declaration say anything about economic inequalities between States, or consider the fact that some of them, being underdeveloped, will find it hard to grant full freedom to their citizens, and in any case will not be in a position to guarantee certain basic rights, such as the right to work, to education, to suitable housing, etc.

How did the West succeed in imposing its 'philosophy'? The socialist countries, though putting up a strong resistance to the fact that so little importance was being attributed to economic, social and cultural rights, were in a minority. All they could do was abstain. Moreover, they had not yet fully worked out a clear strategy of their own on the subject. As for the Third World, it was at this stage to a large extent made up of Latin-American countries with a Western outlook; the remaining countries simply did not have the strength or authority to stand up to the Western powers, which incidentally numbered among their delegates influential figures such as Eleanor Roosevelt and René Cassin.

In spite of its limitations, the Declaration was, however, of great importance in stimulating and directing the international promotion of human rights. It formulated a unitary and universally valid concept of what values should be cherished by all States within their own domestic orders. It was not enthusiastically supported by one particular category of States, namely the socialist countries; yet neither the latter nor developing nations regarded the Declaration as something from which they felt estranged—rather, they looked upon it as a document containing a basic valid nucleus in need of completion. Consequently their subsequent efforts were directed not at eroding, let alone jettisoning, the Declaration, but rather at filling its gaps.

The Tendency to Overrule the Objection of Domestic Jurisdiction

174. During this period the UN tended to reject the objection of State sovereignty put forward by a number of States, and discussed various questions concerning human rights. In general, however, the questions at issue were large-scale, flagrant violations of human rights, rather than isolated cases, and the UN justified its 'intervention' on the grounds that these violations constituted a threat to peace and to friendly relations between States. The line taken was one of 'intervention' (justified in the same terms as those used while drafting the UN Charter: respect for human rights purely as a means of securing peace) thereby dispelling misgivings that the organization would suffer from a paralysing fear of trespassing on State sovereignty.

The Cold War

175. The Cold War had started even before the adoption of the universal Declaration and the Convention on Genocide in 1948. As friction between the two blocs became increasingly serious, the question of human rights was drawn into the ideological struggle between East and West. Some Western countries found that they could use human rights as a stick to beat the socialist countries with, to show up the merits of Western democracy and the demerits of the socialist system. Thus the campaign for human rights came to be given a different justification from that which had inspired the drawing up of the Charter. In the dark years of the cold war concern for human rights was justified—at least by some Western countries—by the ideological and political confrontation with the socialist block.

THE SECOND STAGE (1960 TO THE MID-1970S)

The Socialist 'Doctrine'

176. Two important political events heralded the beginning of the second phase: the strengthening of the socialist group in 1955 owing to the admission of four Eastern European countries to the UN and the fact that the cold war began gradually to draw to an end. The socialist States became more and more vocal and assertive and began to make their presence more strongly felt, often with the support of a growing number of developing nations which joined the Organization in the late 1950s and early 1960s.

Above all, the socialist group perfected its doctrine and strategy and the West began to find itself on the defensive. The entire second stage can be said to be marked by the confrontation and the occasional convergence in the UN of two schools of thought: that of the West and that of socialist countries, supported by the Third World.

Briefly, the main points of the socialist 'doctrine' were as follows. The UN Charter and later UN documents have led to the emergence of a universal principle by virtue of which all States must respect human rights without distinction of race, sex, language or religion. To comply with this principle and with the international conventions which spell it out, States must take the necessary legislative steps at a national level. Once this has been done, respect for human rights is an internal question: it is for the laws of each State to recognize human rights; responsibility for safeguarding these rights rests with the authorities of the State. Nationals of a State must rest content with bringing any alleged breach of human rights before State authorities, without being allowed to petition international agencies. It is not for other countries or for the UN to interfere in this process; rather they must observe the *following principles.* (1) No intervention must be made in the internal affairs of States. (2) Care should be taken to prevent the international protection of human rights from endangering peace or friendly international relations. (3) The role of the UN should be limited to the elaboration of international instruments for ratification (or in the case of recommendations, for consideration) by States, leaving individual countries to deal with the practical application at a national level. It should be stressed that socialist nations have a definite preference for treaties, perhaps because the latter are only binding on those countries which give their consent to them (by ratification or adhesion) and because they usually have no political or moral force prior to consent. (4) The UN should concern itself with individual countries only in exceptional circumstances, that is, only when a State commits serious, repeated and systematic violations of human rights, going against the universal principle mentioned before and endangering peace and friendly relations between States. (5) In the interest of furthering human rights, it is of prime importance that improvements should be made in the international situation. (International tension, the arms race, etc., are factors which have a detrimental effect on human rights; consequently, one way of promoting respect for these rights is by fostering friendly and peaceful relations between States.)

It should be added that the preference of socialist countries is clearly for economic, social, and cultural rights; the right of self-determination; and the right of equality (with the consequent prohibition of discrimination, especially racial discrimination). Of special interest is the socialist doctrine of self-determination of peoples, as it was elaborated, in the wake of Lenin's teaching (see §31), by certain prominent jurists from the GDR (Arzinger,

Steiniger and Graefrath).[9] Although they pay lip-service to the notion that the right to self-determination belongs to all peoples, in practice they contend that *external* self-determination means the right to get rid of colonial or foreign domination, while *internal* self-determination means the free choice of socialism. As was stressed by Graefrath, 'the extensive interrelated norms of internal and external self-determination ... demand especially in our time that the peoples should have the liberty (1) to establish a socialist order of society, (2) to overcome the imperialist limitations of the right to self-determination in a socialist revolution, and (3) to free themselves from the fetters of the capitalist world market'. It is plain that in the view of the jurists and diplomats of Eastern European countries the right to self-determination cannot apply to the peoples of these countries, for they have already 'opted for socialism'. For these countries, then, self-determination ultimately amounts to the right to be free from any undue interference by other States.

It is evident that the socialist doctrine is ideologically and politically motivated. Its ideological roots are to be found in Marxism. As for its political motivations, clearly 'self-determination of peoples' implies the destruction of the Western colonial empires and the gradual undermining of 'capitalist' countries; equally, the struggle against racial discrimination implies a criticism of those Western political systems where racism is *de facto* tolerated or those countries (like South Africa) supported by the West where racism has become official government policy. It is equally apparent that the rejection of any intervention by other States or international organizations in the internal affairs of socialist countries constitutes a defence against outside pressure to demand respect for civil and political rights. Furthermore, the refusal to allow individuals access to international supervisory bodies serves to protect these countries from any international scrutiny, which might prove embarrassing.

International Legislation

177. The three main groups of States basically agreed on the need to translate the general principles of the Universal Declaration into legally binding instruments. Thus Covenants on Civil and Political Rights (with an Optional Protocol) and on Economic, Social, and Cultural Rights were adopted in 1966. (In 1965 a Convention on Racial Discrimination had been passed by the General Assembly at the instigation of developing countries.)

---

[9] B. Graefrath, 'A Necessary Dispute on the Contents of the People's Right to Self-Determination', *Bulletin of the GDR Committee on Human Rights* (1981), pp. 11, 14. (See here for quotations from the works of R. Arzinger and P. A. Steiniger.) See also DDR-*Völkerrecht* 1982, i. 121–4, 150–5.

A brief glance at the choice of rights favoured and the formulation of the respective measures is enough to see that socialist and developing countries had by this time won the upper hand—even if they had, of course, to reach a compromise with the West on more than one point.

There was also considerable agreement—though some Western countries dragged their feet—that the principle of self-determination should be given international recognition on a 'legislative' level. For the West this simply meant proclaiming a general principle to serve as a guideline for individual States to follow gradually. The other countries, on the other hand, wanted a clear legal obligation to be laid down which would be binding and immediately applicable. Compromise was finally reached and the principle was proclaimed, in identical terms, in both Covenants (Article 1).

Furthermore, the right of property does not figure in either Covenant. That is, it was no longer considered a value worthy of international protection on a universal level. This omission went along with the trend to erode and revise the international customary law which in the past had protected the private property of foreigners, requiring 'prompt, adequate, and effective' compensation in the case of expropriation or nationalization (see § 202).

In addition, for the first time in an international legal document we find the concept that formal or legal equality makes little sense if deep practical inequalities exist. This being the case, it appears right to give legal sanction to certain types of distinction when they come into being as a consequence of practical inequalities. Thus, Article 2.3 of the Covenant on Economic, Social, and Cultural Rights lays down that developing countries can establish to what extent they mean to allow foreigners the economic rights specified by the Covenant. In other words, they are authorized to discriminate between nationals and foreigners (so long as this is justified by the country's economic circumstances and is not discrimination against citizens of a particular State, and so long as this refusal to award the same status to foreigners and nationals does not lead to serious violations of other human rights).

Finally, socialist States as well as a number of Third World countries succeeded in weakening the system of international scrutiny of the application of the two Covenants proposed by the West, and also in making at least the most incisive part of it 'voluntary' or 'optional' (supervision of observance of the Covenant on Civil and Political Rights, exercisable on individual request, is foreseen in an Optional Protocol and not in the Covenant itself).

It should be added that the socialist and developing countries also played a decisive part in deciding which rights were to be given special protection through a specific international convention. It is certainly no accident that a draft treaty on religious freedom—a subject dear above all to certain

Western democracies—has been brought before the UN time and again without success, whereas the three Conventions on racial discrimination, on apartheid and on the non-applicability of statutory limitations to war crimes and crimes against humanity, respectively—subjects towards which the Western attitude was distinctly lukewarm, if not downright hostile— were passed by the General Assembly in no time at all.

Supervision

178. International mechanisms for ensuring compliance with the rules protecting human rights were created during this period. Something should be said about why they appeared to be necessary.

Clearly, in general the best means of ensuring respect for a right is to back it up with legal guarantees to be administered by a court of law. I have, however, already mentioned that in the international community the judicial settlement of disputes is often rendered all but impossible by the lukewarm attitude of some major Western States, and the opposition of socialist countries and a large part of the Third World (see §§ 112-13). In the case of human rights, opposition to international adjudication is even stronger for reasons I set forth above (§§ 115, 167-8). The need to strike a compromise between State sovereignty and the requirement that international standards on human rights be complied with by States, led to the establishment of a number of monitoring mechanisms—which, as pointed out above (§§ 115-16), are much weaker than international adjudication.

The principal mechanisms created in this period were of two kinds: those established by international treaties and those set up by UN resolutions. As regards the former, it is sufficient to mention the procedures created by the 1965 Convention on Racial Discrimination and by the Covenant on Civil and Political Rights of 1966, with its Optional Protocol. The latter mechanisms were set up in 1967 by Resolution 1235 (XLII) of the Economic and Social Council (ECOSOC), and in 1970 by Resolution 1503 (XLVIII) of the same body.

The Conventions mentioned above established three supervisory procedures: (1) A procedure based on the examination of reports periodically submitted by States. (It is of course, the weakest and it is no coincidence that it is precisely the form of scrutiny applicable to all contracting States.) (2) The procedure which can be set in motion by a contracting State against another party. (It can work only with regard to those States which, in addition to ratifying the Convention, have also accepted a special clause providing for the procedure. So far it has not yielded any results, for obviously States refrain from engaging in 'inter-State' complaints.) (3) The procedure operating at the request of individuals or groups of individuals. (Like the previous one, it is provided for in an 'optional clause', but it has proved effective, within the limitations inherent in any supervisory mechanism: see §§ 115-16.)

The two procedures set up by ECOSOC are both complex and somewhat cumbersome. They operate at the request of individuals or groups of individuals and deal with 'a consistent pattern of gross violations' only, (that is, not with individual or sporadic infringements). The one established in 1967 is public, for the discussion of the gross violations of human rights referred to in the 'communications' of individuals, is made in public sittings of the UN Commission on Human Rights. The other procedure by contrast, is confidential, for only its final outcome is made public. Both procedures depend upon several UN bodies such as the Subcommission for the prevention of discrimination and protection of minorities, the Commission on Human Rights, and ECOSOC (plus possibly a Commission of Investigation).

It may prove interesting to ask ourselves how it was that the socialist and Third World majority, both of which are in principle reluctant to accept international supervision, particularly in the area of human rights, eventually bowed to the establishment of the two ECOSOC procedures which, unlike the similar ones provided for in the Conventions referred to above, are *not* optional.

The idea of setting up the first monitoring mechanism in 1967 came from the Third World countries, with the support of the socialist countries. The USSR and Tanzania proposed the establishment of some kind of international procedure capable of exercising constant pressure on two racist countries, South Africa and Rhodesia, arguing that the General Assembly having proved itself inadequate, more specific controls were required. Moreover, the two groups of States in question intended to link the action of the UN on human rights to the struggle against colonialism. To this end they sought to create a mechanism to ensure respect for the right of self-determination. This goal met with the opposition of numerous Western countries, which insisted that the question of decolonization should be kept distinct from that of human rights. These countries also felt that it would not be right to centre criticism on two States only, as this would be a serious discrimination between these States and all the other ones equally guilty of serious violations of human rights. The outcome of the lengthy ensuing debates and negotiations was a compromise: a supervisory mechanism was established, but its sphere of action was extended to *all* States, in spite of the opposition of the socialist countries.

Why was a new and more complex procedure established in 1970? There were basically two reasons. First, immediately after the creation of the first procedure in 1967, the Subcommission on Minorities had singled out two countries, Greece and Haiti, as guilty of serious violations of human rights. This caused considerable concern both among the Western nations allied to Greece and among the socialist countries which, in spite of the short-term benefits they might derive from the accusations of the Subcommission against a NATO member, saw the dangers of a precedent which could in the future be used against them. As a result, the Commission on Human Rights concluded in 1968 that the Subcommission's allegations were not based on sufficient evidence, and shelved the question. It therefore became necessary to think up a new mechanism for examining allegations against States, which would provide more adequate protection for State sovereignty.

The second reason for the creation of the 1503 procedure was that the previous one had had certain failings and inconsistencies; it was therefore proposed to clarify it.

Under the new system, the entire proceedings were to be confidential (on the proposal of Tanzania), thus protecting the States involved from the public eye for as long as possible. On the other hand, the procedure was made more rigorous and complex, although, incidentally, also more long-winded and involved.

What have these two international control mechanisms achieved in practice? It should first of all be stressed that when evaluating international bodies of this kind, with so fragile a basis as a resolution of a U N organ (a simple majority in ECOSOC could abolish either procedure from one day to the next) and with such wide-ranging functions, one should not overstress the short-term results. The achievements, if any, can only be seen in the long run.

Bearing this in mind, we can see that the procedure set up in 1970 has not yet achieved a great deal. On the contrary, as a consequence of the confidential nature of its hearings, it has tended to be used as a shield behind which countries accused by the Subcommission have hidden (in more than one case States accused in public hearings under the terms of procedure 1235, have insisted on the question being considered confidentially). The 1235 procedure has had better results. Several States have been requested to put an end to the grave violations of human rights of which they have been accused, namely, Israel, South Africa, and Rhodesia (singled out by other U N bodies too), and in 1974 an enquiry was started with reference to Chile. (For more recent developments see § 182.)

The UN's Widening Sphere of Action and Increasing Disregard of Domestic Jurisdiction

179. As a result of the growing network of international legislation and the establishment of the above-mentioned control procedures during this period, the conviction gradually took hold among U N members that 'intervention' in the affairs of single States is fully justified, so long as serious and large-scale violations have been committed. With this reservation— important though it may be—the U N is authorized to concern itself with the state of human rights in individual countries, regardless of whether the alleged violations are a threat to peace or to friendly relations between States. This development was an important turning-point for the U N. Respect for human rights became an end to be pursued in its own right, and not merely as a means of keeping the peace.

THE THIRD STAGE (THE MID-1970S TO THE PRESENT DAY)

The Third World 'Doctrine' of Human Rights

180. As pointed out above, the third stage is dominated by the Third World. In the early 1970s developing countries managed to elaborate their own philosophy and strategy of human rights. Thanks to their numerical superiority and their vociferousness, they managed to propound their own aspirations without necessarily needing the support of socialist countries. However, in practice, this support was usually forthcoming, with the result that the West increasingly stood on the defensive.

As we shall see, Third World dominance makes itself felt in every area of the UN's concern with human rights, but fears expressed by some authors that this new situation has gradually entailed a complete suppression of Western ideals are, as we shall see, groundless. In important respects the majority in the UN has not gone so far as to disregard basic Western demands, particularly as regards implementation and emphasis on certain categories of grave violation, such as torture, forced 'disappearances', etc.

The attitude of many developing countries towards civil and political rights is one of indifference, sometimes even hostility, for three main reasons. First, fully to recognize the importance of this category of rights could undermine or weaken the authority of the government in such countries. Developing nations are often torn by conflict between different groups and factions and in some cases even by tribal wars. Their principal aim, at least in this post-colonial period, must be to strengthen the authority of the State and not to favour centrifugal tendencies which could benefit from full recognition of the rights and freedoms of the individual.

The second reason is economic. Developing countries need a strong central government if their economies are ever to get off the ground. With economic growth and the well-being of their populations as their aim, their tendency is rather to concentrate power in the hands of the government than to limit it by fostering the rights of the individual. The restriction of certain rights and liberties seems to these countries to be justified by the need to give precedence to economic and social rights. To give a few examples: restrictions on freedom of movement and expatriation are justified by the need to stop the 'brain drain'; limitations on personal freedom and the right to start a family can be justified by the need to slow down the birth rate; limitations on the rights and freedoms of trade unions (the right to strike, for example), can be justified by the urgent need for economic development and industrialization, etc. In other words, not being in a position to protect all human rights, and often having to choose between civil and political rights on the one hand and economic and social rights on the other, these countries prefer to favour the latter at the expense of the former. (The preference for economic and social rights also follows from the inherent character of these rights: as was rightly stressed by Hoffmann,[10] they contribute to the 'build-up of State structures', whereas civil and political rights involve placing restraints on those structures.)

In the third place, the social structure typical of many African and Asian countries is that of a community with a leader exercising undisputed power. The freedom-authority dialectic which we find in the Western European tradition ('In all governments, there is a perpetual intestine struggle, open or secret, between Authority and Liberty; and neither of them can ever absolutely prevail in the contest,' Hume wrote in 1742)[11] is therefore alien to the culture of most of these countries. From a cultural point of view, the idea of a ruler with unlimited powers arouses neither criticism nor repulsion ('The African concept of government is personal, not institutional. When the word "Government" is said the African thinks of the leader not, as the British, of a big building in which debates are held', Nyerere wrote in 1961).[12] The leader expresses the needs of his people and stands up for their interests and they in turn submit to his will. In short, a curtailment of individual rights and freedoms to the benefit of the centralized authorities, which for a westerner brings to mind a whole tradition of rebellion against absolute authority, often appears neither irrational nor to be condemned.

These three arguments are put forward, more or less explicitly, by many developing countries to justify their lukewarm attitude towards civil and political rights. However, it cannot be denied that some of them have a motive of a different kind: their opposition to these rights springs from the need to bolster autocratic regimes, which are fairly common in the Third World. The arguments mentioned above are used as an ideological justification for despotic and authoritarian forms of government, to protect those in power from unwelcome interference from the UN.

The developing countries' doctrine of human rights is based on the following points. (1) In the present state of affairs at least, the realization of economic, cultural, and social rights is to be considered, if not an absolute priority, at any rate a major priority. (2) To this end, the present international economic system must be altered, as it is to a large extent responsible for the undeveloped condition of the poorer nations and hence for the lack of recognition of fundamental rights in these countries. The establishment of a less unjust international order will be reflected inside these States. (3) When one of them is accused of violating civil and political rights, it makes no sense to criticize or condemn it; instead, the economic and social

[10] S. Hoffmann, *Duties Beyond Borders* (Syracuse, 1981), p. 103.
[11] D. Hume, 'Essays, Literary, Moral, and Political', in *Essays and Treatises on Several Subjects*, i (Edinburgh, 1804), pp. 27 ff.
[12] J. Nyerere, 'The African and Democracy', in *Africa Speaks*, ed. J. Duffy and R. A. Manners (Princeton, NJ, 1961), p. 33.

causes must be found and the domestic–international context for these violations understood. Only by changing this context and eliminating the causes can the violations be brought to an end. It therefore appears counterproductive—according to these States—for the UN to denounce or condemn certain States for alleged grave violations of human rights. It should try instead to bring about a change in international economic relations, thereby contributing to removing the objective conditions which lead to violations. (4) There do exist exceptional cases of countries in which, for example, the government pursues a declared policy of racial discrimination (South Africa; Rhodesia from 1965–80) or denies the right of self-determination (Israel); the organized international community should concentrate on these exceptional cases, which involve grave violations of all kinds of rights. (5) In fostering respect for human rights, resolutions of the UN General Assembly should be preferred to treaties. This choice is dictated in part by the consideration that it is easier to make other States accept Third World views when they do not take the form of legally binding instruments. But developing countries also have a definite preference for resolutions because they are more flexible and adaptable than treaties, more suitable for general pronouncements laying down loose principles for action than precise legislative instructions (see § 70).

Virtues and Defects of the Developing Countries' Strategy

181. The opinions of the developing States have in a very short time come to prevail in the UN thanks in part to the support of the socialist countries. The turning point was 1974, when a series of important documents concerning the New International Economic Order was approved. These documents make the reform of the international economic and social order a precondition for greater respect for human rights in developing countries, although they avoid making more than passing reference to human rights. The new view was, however, expressed with specific reference to human rights in a resolution approved by the General Assembly in 1977. This resolution had been proposed by Argentina, Cuba, Yugoslavia, the Philippines, and Iran (Resolution 32/130). In short, it sought to make it clear, once and for all, that when considering important and delicate matters such as human rights, one cannot take an abstract and meta-historical view but must look into the general factual and economic context of human rights.

While these points can be regarded as significant contributions to a meritorious approach to human rights, they should not, however, blind us to the undeniable limitations and ambiguities of the Resolution, and of the whole underlying philosophy. First, one should at once be put on one's guard by the fact that the countries which took an important part in framing the Resolution included Third World States which had (and in some cases, still have) authoritarian governments. It cannot be ruled out that they were motivated in part by the desire to quash the Western proposal to create the post of UN High Commissioner with the job of making sure that human rights were respected. The 'neutralization' of the High Commissioner and the simultaneous evolution of the strategy expressed in Resolution 32/130, which chiefly stresses social and economic rights, could have been thought up by these authoritarian governments as a means of distracting international attention from the grave violations of human rights committed in their own countries.

In the second place, it is admittedly important to stress the difference between developed and developing countries both because this can serve to highlight the sins of some of the former (colonialism, attempts to deny the right to control natural resources to developing peoples, etc.) and because it is true that many breaches of human rights in the latter are largely determined by their backward condition. Nevertheless, there is the risk that, as a result, too little attention is paid to certain classes of grave violations of human rights on the part of some Third World countries, in particular, violations which are not among those listed by the Resolution. For example torture, genocide, denial of the most elementary civil and political liberties, etc. They appear to be the fruit of unjustified and arbitrary forms of authoritarian rule; they are not dictated by conditions of economic underdevelopment, but are the consequence of abuses perpetrated by individuals or groups.

Third, the Resolution does not throw enough light on a phenomenon which is by no means uncommon in developing countries and which is often the cause of grave infringements of human rights. Specifically, it sometimes happens that the ruling minority has the backing of large-scale foreign interests and pursues ends which are not for the good of the whole population. This minority often uses the support of foreign nations or powerful foreign economic interests to oppress the population. The authoritarian methods of these Governments are to some extent the result of underdevelopment, but cannot be eliminated by economic aid alone, which, in any case, will often be used by the ruling élite to strengthen the repressive structures; also required is international condemnation of the authoritarian nature of the government.

International Legislation and Control

182. What have been the consequences of this new strategy of human rights? Briefly, it can be said that its chief result has been to stimulate the formulation of new rights, namely the right to development (which, according to some, is a right of the individual, according to others, of peoples; see § 214); the right to peace; the right to a just and fair international order (already foreshadowed in the 1948 Universal Declaration); the right to a healthy environment, free from pollution.

A great deal has been achieved in the way of drawing up international conventions. In 1979 the Convention on the Elimination of Discrimination against Women was adopted and in 1984 an important Convention on Torture was passed, after many years of protracted discussions.

By contrast, it has appeared difficult to draw up international conventions in three fields characterized by widespread practices contrary to the protection of human dignity: the rights of detainees (especially political prisoners); politically motivated 'kidnappings' and 'disappearances'; and the declaration of a 'state of emergency', as a means of seriously limiting human rights for long periods of time. On these three subjects the UN has, however, carried out studies and investigations and also approved resolutions.

On the other hand, the new strategy has not had a negative effect on the international control mechanisms already in existence. The supervisory procedures foreseen by international conventions have begun, or continued, to function, sometimes with important results.

Of the two procedures instituted by resolution, the 'confidential' one (created in 1970) has not achieved a great deal, while the other one (set up in 1967) has led to the formulation of recommendations to several States. For example, the Commission on Human Rights has made recommendations concerning Kampuchea (since 1980), Morocco (for violation of the right of self-determination of the Saharoui people, 1980-1), Guatemala (since 1980), Bolivia (1980-1), Equatorial Guinea (since 1979), El Salvador (since 1980), Iran (since 1982), Poland (1982-3) and Afghanistan (since 1983). It should be added that sometimes after debates in the Commission, the General Assembly has 'intervened' directly, for example in the cases of Chile, El Salvador, Bolivia, Morocco and Guatemala. Since 1980 the General Assembly has also passed resolutions on the violation of the right of people to self-determination in Afghanistan.

UN ACTION: TENTATIVE STOCK-TAKING

Comparison and Contrast Between the Different 'Philosophies' of Human Rights

183. What conclusions can be drawn about the work of the UN just examined? We should distinguish between two different levels, that of the 'doctrines' put forward by the various groups of States between 1945 and the present day; and that of the actual legislative and institutional action taken. To be sure, the two levels are closely connected and influence each other. Nevertheless, it is useful to draw a distinction, if only for the sake of clarity.

As regards 'doctrine', in the preceding pages we have seen how the Western view, which used to be dominant in the UN, has given way to the conception held by socialist countries and the Third World. We should not lose sight of the fact that, although the three principal 'doctrines' have influenced each other to some extent, they have not only remained distinct but are also, in a way, opposed to each other. There remains a fundamental rift between two different schools of thought, that of Western States and that of developing and socialist countries. The former has had the great merit of advocating projecting domestic bills of rights onto the international level, thereby pushing for the world-wide recognition of certain basic values hitherto only upheld within the national setting of a few countries. The latter doctrine, which has occasionally entailed the neglect of civil and political rights, must be given credit for having prompted the UN to promote a deep sense of social justice and of indignation against 'structural violence', in particular those historical situations (such as colonial or neo-colonial exploitation and apartheid) which deprive whole groups of people of basic rights and freedoms. As was rightly pointed out by Röling, the UN

... has been instrumental in bringing about a new concept of world justice based on the universal recognition of human rights. The implementation of this new concept of justice has contributed to conflict and violence in many parts of the world in that it calls for a fundamental change in international relations, the abolition of traditional privileges of the rich part of the world and the granting of rights whose exercise clashes with substantial interests of States that formerly ruled the world.[13]

In other words, the UN has succeeded in moving from a static concept of human rights (conceived as a means of realizing international peace) to a dynamic concept which goes as far as to promote violence and the disruption of the status quo for the sake of introducing social justice and respect for the dignity of man (this, as Röling has correctly emphasized, is what happened in the case of apartheid and Rhodesia, where the UN willingly promoted rebellion against structural violence in the form of white rule).

Let me now go back to the conflict between the two main approaches to human rights. This conflict has not led to a deadlock. In fact, in spite of the many differences within the General Assembly, an essential body of opinion has emerged which is now shared by all three groups of States. Let us now consider this phenomenon somewhat more closely.

It can, I think, be said that all groups of States agree on the following essential points:

First, the dignity of human beings is a basic value which every State should try to protect, regardless of considerations of nationality, sex, etc.

---

[13] B. V. A. Röling, 'Peace Research and Peace-Keeping', in *UN Peace-Keeping: Legal Essays*, ed. A. Cassese (Alphen aan den Rijn, 1978), p. 251.

Second, it is also necessary to aim at the achievement of fundamental rights of groups and peoples.

Third, there is full agreement on condemning racial discrimination, and, in particular, apartheid, which is universally considered (and rightly so) to be one of the most repulsive and inhuman features of the present age. It is significant that the Convention on Racial Discrimination (1965) has been ratified by more countries than any other international instrument on human rights: 124 countries had ratified it on 1 January 1986. In particular, as regards apartheid, even Western countries—which rely heavily on South African exports of four key minerals (chromium, manganese, vanadium, and platinum) essential to their industry and defence—are beginning to realize how loathsome the policy of discrimination pursued by the authorities in that country is, and are increasingly calling for radical changes. Indicative of the mood emerging in the West, and also of the motivations behind it, is the statement made in 1982 by the influential American, Robert McNamara.[14]

Fourth, even though some States may find it hard (either for economic and social reasons, or for organizational and political reasons) to grant full respect for human rights, no State must perpetrate grave, repeated and large-scale violations of whole categories of human rights. When this does occur, the international community is justified in 'intervening', by addressing recommendations and solicitations to the country concerned, or by helping it to put an end to the practices criticized.

It is thanks to the opportunities afforded by the UN for States to come together to exchange views and to try to reduce the area of conflict, that it has been possible to develop a common approach, at least on the basic points just listed.

Legislative and Institutional Achievements

184. As regards practical achievements, the results of the co-operation and compromise between the different groups of States over the last thirty-five years should not be underestimated.

First, numerous conventions have been made. In other words, an international legislative framework has been created which is binding on a large number of States and regulates the most important aspects of human rights and fundamental freedoms.

Generally speaking, these conventions have had the widespread support of the three main groups of States. Very few have been drawn up without the support of all three groups. One such exception was the 1968 Convention on the Non-Applicability of Statutory Limitations to War Crimes and Crimes against Humanity;

[14] R. S. McNamara, 'South Africa Threatens to be the Middle East of the 1990s', *International Herald Tribune*, 25 October 1982, p. 5.

another the 1973 Convention on the Crime of Apartheid. In both cases the initiative of the Afro-Asian and socialist countries did not meet with the approval of the West. As a result, although the Conventions at issue were adopted by the General Assembly, they have only been ratified by a relatively low number of States (respectively 28 and 83 on 1 January 1986); neither convention has been ratified by a Western country.

A second positive feature of this legislative activity is that it has also led to the gradual emergence of certain important customary norms: for example, the principle forbidding grave, repeated, and systematic violations of human rights (see §86); the rules banning genocide and racial discrimination; the norm prohibiting denial of the right of peoples to self-determination, as well as the rule prohibiting torture. It should be noted that these rules are not only binding on all States belonging to the international community, whether they have ratified conventions on the subject or not, but they also impose obligations *erga omnes*, as has been stressed by the International Court of Justice.[14a] Moreover, some of them have also acquired the status of *jus cogens* (see §96).

As for the international scrutiny of observance of human rights, the balance sheet is undoubtedly less optimistic. Although a few important monitoring procedures have been instituted, so far they have not yielded any conspicuous results. However, in assessing these procedures one ought to bear in mind that the existing international mechanisms for inducing States to discontinue violations are only measures of 'supervision' (that is they are neither legally binding nor coercive: §§115, 116); consequently they can only be effective by exerting moral, psychological and political pressure and by making use of public opinion (in the country concerned and in the whole international community). It follows that their effects can only be appraised in the long run.

A general appraisal of the UN's action in this field should not, however, pass over in silence two trends, to which Condorelli[15] has rightly drawn attention, which show the limitations from which the UN action still suffers: first, the regionalization of the protection of human rights (very often the extreme difficulty of reaching satisfactory results at the universal level because of the numerous divisions and conflicts existing between the various groupings, has made it advisable to fall back on the regional level, where greater ideological or political homogeneity makes it possible to make more headway), and the 'optionalization' of supervisory mechanisms (that is, the fact, emphasized above in §177, that often the reluctance of socialist and Third World countries to submit to international scrutiny has made it necessary to make 'optional' the clauses on supervision included in inter-

---

[14a] See ICJ, *Case Concerning the Barcelona Traction, Light and Power Company, Limited* (Second Phase), *Reports 1970*, p. 32, paras 33–4.

[15] L. Condorelli, *Droit international public*, i (Geneva, 1984–5), p. 102.

national conventions for the protection of human rights: acceptance of monitoring mechanisms does not follow from the ratification of the convention, but only from the further step constituted by the specific acceptance of these clauses). These two trends clearly show that we are still a long way from the universal acceptance of standards of behaviour on human rights and the attendant devices for inducing compliance with them.

FINAL REMARKS

185. I have already stressed—although emphasis was probably not required—that if one appraises the achievements of international institutions in the light of the current massive violations of human rights the former may easily appear to be a drop in the ocean. As in other instances, the words of writers come to mind: in a play by Shaw,[16] a man announces to Caesar that the library of Alexandria, the first of the seven wonders of the world, is in flame and, to stir up the seemingly unsolicitous emperor, adds: 'What is burning there is the memory of mankind'; to which Caesar replies: 'A shameful memory. Let it burn.' Arguably, the words of Caesar hold true for the long chain of misdeeds in the field of human rights perpetrated for so many years by States (but also by private groups such as terrorist organizations): they make up a shameful memory indeed and mankind would perhaps better pass them over in silence lest future generations, inspired by past models, engage in even worse misconduct. Yet, it may easily be observed that the knowledge of horrors may be salutary if it produces the determination to prevent their recurrence. To revert to our specific subject, awareness of the daily trampling of human rights and of the relative impotence of international organizations should not beget passivity, but rather, more commitment. In addition, it would be mistaken to discount the achievements of international institutions. In the face of the engrained bent of Governments and private groups to infringe upon human dignity, how could international bodies—dominated as they are by States—be expected to have a greater bearing on States' conduct?

In particular, a balanced assessment of UN action should not disregard the following fundamental fact. This world organization has gradually knocked down the old principle that the relationships between State agencies and individuals come exclusively within the purview of State sovereignty, and that accordingly, no outside authority may meddle therein. As the Chilean delegate to the General Assembly said as early as 1948, 'human rights [are] ... not the private concern of each State, but the common heritage of mankind, a heritage which should be defended'.[17] Nowadays

[16] G. B. Shaw, 'Caesar and Cleopatra' (1898), in *Nine Plays* (New York, 1936), pp. 406-7.
[17] The declaration of the Chilean delegate (Mr Cruz Ocampo) is in GAOR, III, Part I, Committee VI, p. 723 (meeting of 2 December 1948).

gross breaches of human rights are of concern to the international community at large wherever they occur, be it in a large or in a small country, in the 'First', the 'Second', or the 'Third' World.

Given the present structure and composition of the international community, what has been achieved by the UN constitutes the most that could be expected. Steps forward will certainly be taken, but only slowly and only if a collective effort is made at all levels—not only by Governments, but also, and above all, unofficially, by individuals, groups, associations, and 'non-governmental bodies'.

12

The Law Governing International Economic Relations

GENERAL

186. INTERNATIONAL economic relations are usually the hunting ground of a few specialists, who often jealously hold for themselves the key to this abstruse admixture of law and economics. The road we must now take, when not beset with pitfalls, is interspersed with inaccessible fortresses. It is, however, indispensable at least to undertake a foray into this ever more important area; as the French Foreign Minister Cheysson observed on 27 July 1983, talking of the problems confronting developing countries, 'in the next years the freedom of our nations will be much more threatened by economic limitations than by dangers of military nature'.[1] Even if one does not altogether share this appraisal, the fact remains that economic problems are destined to be at least as important as military questions.

The complex and multifaceted character of this subject-matter makes a twofold caveat necessary. First, on a few points my exposition will, of necessity, be somewhat technical and dry: the reader is invited to be patient and not to be discouraged too quickly. Second, in this area more than in any other it proves necessary to simplify and schematize reality in order to delineate the main trends of the various relevant institutions. In particular, I shall have to over-simplify in dealing with the attitude of the various groupings and alignments: in actual fact, political realities are more complex and multifarious than they will be made to appear. The remarks I am about to set forth are therefore to be taken *cum grano salis*.

PREDOMINANCE OF THE *LAISSEZ-FAIRE* PRINCIPLE UNTIL THE FIRST WORLD WAR

187. In the years following the birth of the international community, economic relations between States as well as those between nationals of the various States were hardly the subjects of international regulation. This is easily understood if one recalls that until the beginning of this century States did not concern themselves with all the various facets of economic life, but preferred to leave private entrepreneurs free to engage in commer-

---

[1] Text in *Le Monde*, 29 July 1983, p. 6.

cial and financial transactions with foreigners. The principle of freedom prevailed. One of its consequences was that as far as its domestic economic set-up and its international economic policies were concerned each State could do as it pleased.

During this period (between the seventeenth and the nineteenth centuries) two conflicting tendencies in the economic policy of States took shape: *protectionism* and *free trade*. The former trend was intended to safeguard the development of countries in need of protecting their fledgling industry from foreign competition. Some States (chiefly Germany and the U S) chose to erect national barriers to international trade by imposing customs dues and taxes on the importation of foreign goods. Free trade was, by contrast, supported by those States (chiefly the U K and France) which had already developed their industry and were therefore eager to export their goods to foreign markets. They advocated the need to do away with any impediment to the free flow of commodities; accordingly, they eliminated barriers to trade at home and demanded that they be dismantled by foreign countries.

It is against this general background that the legal developments of this period should be considered.

The conflict between protectionism and free trade stimulated the conclusion of treaties of commerce and navigation which deal with the treatment to be granted in each contracting State to nationals of the other States involved. Very often it was established that citizens of one party enjoyed on the territory of another the same commercial and civil rights as the nationals of the latter. In the case of trade a special clause, the 'most-favoured-nation clause' was devised, under which a State automatically granted to the other contracting party all the rights and benefits it accorded to the third State it treated best. It followed from this clause that each contracting party was to treat in the same manner all foreigners having the nationality of States with which it had treaty relations. As was rightly emphasized by the Austrian author Sommer,[2] the *reciprocal, unconditional, and absolute* clause, which, as we shall see, was adopted by States such as the U K, was the embodiment of the philosophy of free trade, which, in turn, derived from the ideology of equality propounded in the Age of Enlightenment (all traders must be placed on the same footing, whatever their nationality: any legal or institutional hindrance constituted a discrimination contrary to the principal of equality and to its corollary of free competition). Clearly, a general adoption of such a clause would have introduced untrammelled freedom of trade; for, indeed, the primary purpose of the most-favoured-nation treatment was to compel as many States as possible to remove trade barriers so as to allow the citizens of all coun-

[2] L. Sommer, 'Die Staatsideologischen Voraussetzungen des Kampfes gegen die Meist-begünstigungskausel', *Zeitschrift für öffentliches Recht* 16 (1936), 265 ff.

tries to compete freely. However, this practice ran counter to the interests of those States which had opted for protectionism. It is therefore only natural that not all States were ready to uphold such a clause and its far-reaching consequences.

Certain countries (the US, Japan, and a few Latin-American countries such as Argentina) therefore decided to qualify it by making the most-favoured treatment *conditional*: any favour, privilege or immunity granted by one of the contracting parties to third States would be extended to the nationals of the other contracting party if the latter State met all the requirements under which those favours, privileges or immunities had been accorded by the former State to the nationals of the third countries. Thus, for example, in a treaty of commerce between Japan and the US, the US extended to Japanese nationals in the field of importation, exportation, and transit of goods the same treatment it accorded to the most-favoured nation (say, the UK) on condition that Japan granted US nationals the same commercial favours (e.g. low import duties) which the UK accorded to the goods of US nationals.

The success of the two different types of clause varied in time. The US held on to the conditional clause to favour the expansion of its economy until 1923, when it finally opted for the unconditional clause. In Europe the fortune of the latter clause had its ups and downs according to the predominance of protectionism or free trade, but it became firmly embedded after 1860, when the UK altogether dropped the protectionist policy it had followed during the preceding years, and Napoleon II decided to adopt free trade.

Another development, on which industrialized countries presented a united front (whereas there were clashes between them and economically backward countries) concerned the treatment of foreign investment. Customary rules soon evolved to the effect that the principle of 'sanctity of private property' so steadfastly upheld at home should also hold true in international relations. In consequence, economically advanced countries, to which the persons investing in foreign countries belonged, gradually developed the rule that foreign property must be respected and protected and was not to be expropriated except for purposes of public necessity, without discrimination and subject to the payment of appropriate compensation. Whenever capital-importing States refused to comply with this rule, the Governments of the nationals whose property had been expropriated resorted to diplomatic or judicial protection or else to the use of force (thus, for instance, as mentioned above, § 26, the UK, Germany, and Italy mounted a military expedition against Venezuela in 1902 to force it to pay its dues to nationals of the three countries concerned). We have also seen (§ 26) that the attempts by the Argentinians Calvo and Drago, as well as the compromise proposals put forward by the American Porter, to contrive legal mechanisms for loosening the impact of international law on the capital-importing countries, ended in failure.

In conclusion, it can be contended that in this period international law refrained from extensively regulating the economic and commercial inter-action between States. Only one customary rule evolved, that on foreign private property. In the field of trade and commerce, on the other hand, the major issues were regulated by treaty. The relative lack of international regulation plainly favoured the economic development of the more powerful States. It is no coincidence that the only area in which general rules evolved was one where the interests of powerful countries normally coincided: the protection of foreign investment.

THE INTER-WAR PERIOD

188.   After the First World War the existing legal regime began to break up. The previously established rules were not repealed or radically revised; rather, they were challenged by a number of States and thus what used to be taken for granted became a matter for discussion.

The principal point of friction concerned the protection of foreign prop-erty. The emergence of the USSR in 1917 had an immediate and conspi-cuous impact upon this area, for the new Government nationalized all foreign property, confiscating banks, the merchant fleet, and insurance busi-ness, etc. On 13 February 1918, the US lodged a protest with the Soviet Government on behalf of fourteen allied and associated Powers and six neutral States, stating that they all

considered that the decrees on the repudiation of Russian State debts, the confis-cation of property and other similar measures were without effect as regards their nationals.[3]

Subsequently, at the Brussels Conference on Russia of October 1921, the delegates passed a resolution to the effect that

The forcible expropriations and nationalizations without compensation or remuner-ation of property in which foreigners are interested is totally at variance with the practice of civilised States. Where such expropriation has taken place, a claim arises for compensation against the Government of the country.[4]

Between 1918 and 1925 the USSR entered into a series of treaties with various European States providing for some form of indemnity or compensation for the nationalized assets. Thus the USSR was eventually forced to bow to the economic and political pressures of other States and grudgingly comply with the prevailing international standards.

[3] See *Correspondence Between His Majesty's Government and the French Government Re-specting the Anglo-Russian Trade Agreement*, 1921 Cmd 1456, p. 8.
[4] Text in McNair, *International Law Opinions*, i (London, 1946), p. 9.

Similar considerations apply to Mexico. However, the case of Mexican nationalizations is rather more interesting because the arguments advanced by this country to justify its behaviour were quite new at the time (and indeed they are substantially the same as those put forward at present by developing countries). The US, one of the foreign countries affected by the nationalizations, furious at the Mexican move, was able to elaborate and expand the traditional Western doctrine by specifying the criteria which, in its view, a State must meet for expropriation to be lawful under international law. It is clear that two fully-fledged doctrines are at work in this area, both of which deserve to be examined, if only briefly.

By a decree of 18 March 1938, the Mexican Government seized the property of oil companies which belonged chiefly to American, British, and Dutch nationals. The three Powers involved reacted indignantly. The US took the opportunity to insist on its claims for the settlement of the dispute arising from the Mexican Agrarian reform of 1927, under which assets belonging to US citizens had been nationalized together with Mexican agrarian property. A diplomatic correspondence ensued between Mexico and each of the three States. After a delay of a few years, Mexico agreed to pay the indemnities requested by the nationalized countries, plus, of course, the interests.

Let us now briefly consider the Mexican justification, as it was expressed in a note from the Mexican Foreign Minister to the US, dated 3 August 1938:

... There does not exist, in international law, any principle universally accepted by countries, nor by the writers of treatises on this subject, that would render obligatory the giving of adequate compensation for expropriations of a general and impersonal character. Nevertheless, Mexico admits, in obedience to her own laws, that she is indeed under obligation to indemnify in an adequate manner; but the doctrine which she maintains on the subject, which is based on the most authoritative opinions of writers of treatises on international law, is that the time and manner of such payment must be determined by her own laws.[5]

In sum, Mexico propounded the following view: first, there is no international obligation to pay compensation when expropriation of foreign property is not discriminatory; second, it expressed a readiness to pay 'adequate compensation' so as not to contravene its own legislation; third, the modalities of payment were to be determined by domestic legislation solely. As we shall see, this is, to a very large extent, the view set forth in the UN resolutions on the New International Economic Order of 1974 (see §§ 202 and 213). At that time, however, the Mexican doctrine was received with utter vexation by the US, which replied with a note of 22 August 1938, signed by Secretary of State Hull, which included the following statement:

[5] Text in G. H. Hackworth, *Digest of International Law*, iii (Washington, 1943), p. 658.

I do not hesitate to maintain that this is the first occasion in the history of the western hemisphere that such a theory has been seriously advanced. In the opinion of my Government, the doctrine so proposed runs counter to the basic precepts of international law and of the law of every American republic, as well as to every principle of right and justice upon which the institutions of the American republics are founded. It seems to the Government of the US a contention alien to the history, the spirit and the ideals of democracy as practiced throughout the independent life of all nations of this continent.

If such a policy were to be generally followed, what citizen of one republic making his living in any of the other twenty republics of the western hemisphere could have any assurance from one day to the next that he and his family would not be evicted from their home and bereft of all means of livelihood? Under such conditions, what guarantees or security could be offered which would induce the nationals of one country to invest savings in another country, or even to do ordinary business with the nationals of another country?[6]

The skilled blend of indignation against the repudiation of one of the basic 'ideals of democracy' and of threats about the discontinuance of investments in Mexico, tellingly underlines the position of Great Powers current at the time.

The US Government took this opportunity to formulate its doctrine of compensation. In the same note, Mr Hull stated that 'no Government is entitled to expropriate private property, for whatever purpose, without provision for prompt, adequate, and effective payment therefor'. This famous formula was subsequently considered by Western countries to encapsulate the basic requirements for lawful expropriations.

These first notes of dissonance in State practice—to which others should be added, such as the agrarian reform in Romania in 1921 which in the view of Hungary resulted in the expropriation of foreign assets without adequate compensation—were, to some extent, echoed in legal literature. The overwhelming majority of jurists supported the official view propounded by Great Powers. However, a few distinguished commentators disagreed: the British Sir John Fischer Williams and Brierly, the Italian Cavaglieri, the Belgian Rolin and the Frenchman Duguit.[7] They contended that, unless obligated by a treaty, under general international law States were free to expropriate property without compensation (or without adequate compensation) provided they did not discriminate against foreigners or their property. By and large, the refutation of any international duty on the matter rested on the doctrine of State sovereignty. Suffice it to quote the words of Fischer Williams, one of the most perceptive and arti-

---

[6] Text in *AJIL* 32 (1938), Suppl., p. 192.

[7] J. Fischer Williams, 'International Law and the Property of Aliens', *BYIL* 9 (1928), 1 ff.; J. L. Brierly, *The Law of Nations*, ed. Sir Humphrey Waldock 6th edn. (Oxford, 1963), p. 284; A. Cavaglieri, in *Revue générale de droit international public* 38 (1931), 296; A. Rolin, in *Revue de droit international et de législation comparée* 8 (1927), 438 ff., 466 ff.; L. Duguit, ibid., 469 ff.

culate of the jurists concerning themselves with this issue. In his view the asserted duty would have entailed an inadmissible 'truncation' of the 'legitimate authority' of the State. He put it as follows:

If States have not the same freedom to deal by law with the property of aliens as with the property of their own nationals, by what act or omission of their own have they been deprived of it? Whiteacre belongs to a British subject: the British Parliament is sovereign to expropriate him how and when it pleases. The British subject sells Whiteacre to an alien: Parliament has lost a portion of its former power. But Parliament has done nothing and has omitted nothing. On what principle must it suffer an abridgement of its authority by the act of third parties—a British vendor and an alien purchaser—both of whom are in this respect persons subject to its power?[8]

This attack on the 'principle of the intangibility of foreign property' should not be passed over in silence, for it harbingers the strictures on that principle voiced after the Second World War by a number of developing countries. However, it will be clear to the reader that the motivations behind the criticisms of the prevailing view voiced by Fischer Williams and the other jurists referred to above were different from those underlying the Third World assault on the duty of compensation. The Western jurists of the 1920s and 1930s, perhaps unwittingly, made a plea for the authority of the State to intervene in economic life and protect the interests of the whole population, even at the expense of single individuals—be they nationals or foreigners. In other words, they wished to take account of a new phenomenon: the growing presence of the State in a domain until recently reserved to individuals alone, and the need for it to redress social and economic imbalances or at any rate cater more intensely and positively for the common good. By contrast, developing countries are impelled to expropriate foreign property because their natural resources are to a very large extent in foreign hands and one of the ways of achieving rapid economic advance lies in appropriating foreign assets without this constituting an excessive financial burden for the expropriating State. In this case the contrast is no longer that between common good and State authority versus private property (be it national or foreign), but rather between economic development and sovereignty over national resources versus foreign exploitation of these resources. It is therefore not surprising that under the terms suggested by Fischer Williams and the other jurists, the nationalizations carried out by developing countries after the Second World War would have been contrary to international law: indeed, according to those jurists, if 'in fact the whole or nearly the whole of the particular class of property affected [was] held by foreigners' one could not claim that the expropriation was justified, for in fact it was discriminatory.

[8] Fischer Williams, op. cit., 15-16.

189. The disruption of economic relations was much greater in the field of trade. After the war, the US tried to re-introduce the principles of free trade. They were advocated by President Wilson in his Fourteen Points (1915) and indeed in 1923 the US, as I emphasized above, dropped the 'conditional' most-favoured-nation clause it had consistently upheld for so long. However, the economic crisis which broke out in the aftermath of the war and escalated into the great slump of 1929 led most countries to adopt drastic measures at home and to engage in fierce protectionism as far as international trade was concerned. At home the intervention of State authorities proved necessary to avert a worsening of the economy. As a result (in the words of three French specialists, Carreau, Juillard, and Flory) 'individuals lost command of international economic relations to the profit of nation-States. From a private-law world one passed on to a public-law world. The private order in the field of international economic relations, obtaining before, yielded to a system where the State was omnipresent'.[9] Correspondingly, in the international field protectionism manifested itself both in trade and in monetary exchanges.

States established customs dues to protect their national commodities, or restrictions on imports, and to boost the national economy they granted financial aid to exports or resorted to 'dumping' (the sale abroad of goods at lower prices than on the national market). Protectionism was also extended to the monetary field in the form of currency control: States unilaterally devalued their currency to make their goods more competitive on the international market, or introduced exchange controls designed to protect their own foreign exchange resources. Thus they introduced the requirement that foreign funds held in the State be surrendered against payment in local currency at the official rate of exchange, although the local currency was less valuable on the free market than the foreign funds surrendered. They also established multiple currency practices for different commercial transactions (a certain rate of exchange for commercial transactions, another for tourism, yet another for financial handlings, etc.), or floating exchanges. These measures were calculated to influence the exchange value of the national currency with regard to foreign currencies in such a way as to favour national products (for example, by increasing the value of the national currency when it came to buy foreign goods).

Finally, it should be added that during this period States also found it convenient to enter into international agreements on economic matters. Most of them were, however, bilateral in character for there was little chance of bringing together a group of States willing to agree upon common policy lines. Many bilateral treaties were designed to lay down quotas in trade or customs duties applicable to the contracting parties. This, while it gave

[9] D. Carreau, P. Juillard, and T. Flory, *Droit international économique*, 2nd edn. (Paris, 1980), p. 72.

some stability to the economic interaction of the States concluding such agreements, could not but enhance the lack of equality among members of the world community, for the plain reason that what applied as between a pair of States was not applicable between other States.

THE MAJOR TURNING-POINT AFTER THE SECOND WORLD WAR: THE DOMINANCE OF THE US AND ITS NEO-LIBERAL OUTLOOK

190. The Second World War left Europe in a shambles: the economies of both Western European countries and the USSR had been either disrupted by the fighting or converted to the war effort. Japan, too, was on its knees. The only big Power whose territory had been spared by invasion or bombardment and whose economy had been boosted by the war was the US. After the war, it had become by far the most powerful State militarily and it was in its interest to increase its economic power by allowing its capitals to be invested abroad and by expanding its economy on a world scale. To some extent, the UK—the only European big Power whose territory had not been invaded by the Germans—shared the American concern, although it saw as its primary and immediate goal the rebuilding of its economy and the gradual achievement of full employment, rather than the conquest of foreign markets. The US was therefore forced to seek some degree of compromise with the British demands. However, owing to its economic and military superiority, it easily gained the upper hand. The US economic expansion on European territory and in the Far East was of course salutary, at least in the short run, to the countries disrupted by war. They could not but benefit from the flow of US capital into their markets and hence keenly welcomed the restructuring of international economic relations propounded by the US. To implement the new scheme it was, however, necessary to dismantle all the barriers which over the years had been erected in the world community by States increasingly bent on protectionism. Thus the US launched a free trade and free market philosophy, which forced other States (except for the USSR) to accept. What is more significant still, it succeeded in having three important international institutions established for the purpose of creating the necessary mechanisms for realizing that philosophy on a multilateral, stable and continuing basis. One institution, the International Monetary Fund (IMF), was given the task of ensuring international monetary stability: it was to ensure that single States did not alter international trade conditions by monetary contrivances (such as unilateral devaluations of their currencies) designed to protect the national economy at the unfair expense of foreign countries. In addition, it was designed to help finance temporary balance-of-payment deficits of Member States, provoked by fluctuations in the prices of products on the international market or by domestic problems (such financing was clearly to serve as a device for preventing States from finding themselves constrained to resort to protectionism). A second organization was given the task of mobilizing and collecting money from private sources on the international capital market, with a view to lending it to those States most in need of foreign investment. This was the International Bank for Reconstruction and Development (the Bank). The third institution was intended to abolish traditional tariff restrictions on free trade which greatly hampered free competition on the world market: it was the General Agreement on Tariffs and Trade (GATT).

In the following paragraphs I shall try to show how these three institutions were set up and how they operate in practice. It must be stressed right at the outset that since the mid-1950s they have gradually been facing a new problem, largely unknown in 1944-5: that of the development of newly independent countries. As a result of the gradual accession of colonial countries to political independence after the mid-1950s the question arose of how to promote their industrialization and, more generally, their economic progress. This is generally referred to as the *North–South question*. The IMF, the Bank, and GATT, not specifically geared to the promotion of development in backward nations, were forced to face the new situation, for which they were scantily equipped. As we shall see, this was a gradual process, and one which was, to a considerable extent, influenced by their terms of reference and by their guiding postulates (which to a large extent were on a collision course with the doctrines advocated by underdeveloped countries: free market and free competition principles are hardly reconcilable with 'welfare State principles', whereby 'preferential treatment' and 'positive discrimination' are to be accorded to disadvantaged nations). All three institutions slowly attuned their policy, at least in part, to the new problem, albeit in a manner which developing countries have considered inadequate.

PROMOTION OF CURRENCY STABILITY: THE INTERNATIONAL MONETARY FUND

191. In the period between the second half of the nineteenth century and the First World War international monetary relations had been fairly smooth thanks to the 'gold standard', through which all international transactions were made either in gold or in national currencies whose value was assessed in gold. Moreover, there were no obstacles to the exchange of one national currency for another or to the transfer of national currencies abroad. This was indeed the golden age of free trade philosophy: the economy of the richer countries was boosted by the lack of any monetary impediments to the financial transactions of private enterprises. Things changed radically after the First World War when the economic crisis brought about by the conflict, and subsequently exacerbated by the Great Depression of 1929–30, led most States to adopt protectionist measures in the monetary field as well. The 'gold standard' gradually declined; in 1931 it was dropped by the UK and Governments increasingly adopted measures to protect employment. The general slump caused a decrease in international trade, causing States to resort to various protectionist measures (see § 189). In short, what was called the 'beggar my neighbour policy' obtained in the monetary field.

After the Second World War, as a reaction to these tendencies and so as to ensure its own economic expansion on world markets, the US proposed a scheme called the 'White plan', after Treasury Under-Secretary White. The plan was revised in the light of Keynes's proposals—submitted at an earlier date by the British economist on behalf of the UK—and became the 'Articles of Agreement', or the treaty establishing the IMF. The treaty was concluded in 1944 and entered into force on 27 December 1945.

Duties of the Member States

192. The previously unrestricted sovereignty of States in monetary matters was seriously limited in the Articles of Agreement by a set of obligations. (1) By agreement with the IMF the currency of each member was assigned a *par value* expressed in terms of gold or in terms of the US dollar of the value in effect on 1 July 1944. (Some countries defined their currencies in terms of the dollar under their national legislation, and, in addition, the dollar was already the most widely used currency.) Each country undertook to maintain this par value for its currency. Gold was the common denominator of the system in that exchange rates were pegged to a par value in gold. It should be stressed that this practice was made possible by the fact that the US, under its legislation, had undertaken to convert US dollars into gold at a fixed rate of 35 dollars per ounce. In this way a fixed parity between US dollar, gold and the various currencies was established. Plainly, this arrangement was designed to ensure a relative stability in foreign exchange. (2) Changes in par value could be made only to correct a 'fundamental disequilibrium' in the balance of payments after consultation with the IMF and with its concurrence (cumulative changes up to ten per cent of the initial par value did not require concurrence). (3) Each member State had to ensure that foreign exchange dealings between the currencies of other Members and its currency which took place on its territory be based on parity. The maximum and minimum rates for exchange transactions were not to differ from parity by more than one per cent in the case of spot transactions or, in the case of other exchange transactions, by that margin exceeding one per cent which was considered reasonable by the Fund. (4)

Member States were to refrain from introducing restrictions on payments or transfers for current international transactions as defined by the Articles, multiple currency practices, or discriminatory arrangements, unless authorized by the Articles or approved by the Fund. (5) Member States were to subscribe the quotas assigned by IMF, to be paid to IMF partly in gold (25%), partly in the State's currency (75%).

The quotas of the initial members were fixed by a Schedule to the Articles of Agreement on the basis of a number of criteria (national gross product; monetary reserves; average exportations; difference between the lowest and highest importations in a five-year period 1934–38; etc.). By way of example, the following quotas were listed in the Schedule (figures are given in millions of US dollars): US 2,750; UK 1,300; France 450; India 400; Canada 300; The Netherlands 275; Brazil 150; Chile 50; Iran 25; Peru 25; Iraq 8; Nicaragua 2, etc.). The quotas of those who acquired membership at a later stage were determined by the Fund. The whole of the quotas makes up the Fund's capital (but the Fund can borrow and it has reserves).

The Right to Draw Foreign Currency from the Fund

193. As a sort of countervailing measure to the limitations on their sovereignty referred to above, member States had the right to draw the currency of another member from the fund whenever they needed it to correct temporary disequilibria in their balance of payments. In exchange for such currency the requesting State must give the Fund the equivalent in its national currency or in gold, plus a modest commission (in the former case, the State drawing on the Fund's resources was expected to repurchase its own currency within three to five years).

The purpose of this right was to allow member States to overcome their balance of payments difficulties without being compelled to resort to all those protectionist measures the IMF was set up to prevent. Its exercise was, however, made subject to a few conditions, on which it is for the Fund to pass judgment (Article 5, Sect. 3).

The Organizational and Power Structure of the Fund

194. The Fund, although it is a UN Specialized Agency, differs radically from the UN as regards both its composition and its decision-making process. It is largely dominated by the Western industrialized countries. (The USSR and the other Eastern European countries are not members, except for Romania and Hungary which joined the Fund in 1972 and 1982, respectively; Cuba left the Fund in 1964. Poland applied for membership in 1981, but in 1985 its application was still being considered by the Fund.[9a]

[9a] See IMF, *Annual Report of the Executive Board for the Financial Year Ended April 30, 1985* (Washington D.C., 1985), p. 66.

(Yugoslavia has been a member of the Fund for years.) The reason for the socialist countries holding aloof will soon become apparent.)

The central organ is the Board of Governors, consisting of a Governor and an alternate appointed by each member State (membership runs at present to 148 States). Most of the Fund's powers are vested in the Board of Governors, which can delegate them to the Executive Board, which at present is made up of 22 Directors, six of whom are appointed by the five countries having the largest quotas (the US, the UK, the FRG, France and Japan) plus Saudi Arabia and sixteen, who are elected at two-year intervals by the other members through the formation of 'constituencies'.

If the 'usual' or 'traditional' voting system was adopted, the majority in control of the Fund would not differ from that in the UN. However, the 'weighted voting' has been adopted, and consequently the voice of the wealthiest countries is stronger than that of the others. Each member is allotted the same basic number of votes namely, 250; additional votes are allocated in proportion to a country's quota (one vote for any part of the quota exceeding 100,000 US dollars) or, since 1972, to a country's 'special drawing rights' (see below).

Thus at present the following countries have the following votes in the Executive Board: US: 19.29; UK: 6.69; FRG: 5.84; France: 4.85; Japan: 4.57; Saudi Arabia: 3.47; Spain (elected by seven Latin-American countries plus Spain): 4.77; The Netherlands (elected by Cyprus, Israel, The Netherlands, Romania and Yugoslavia): 4.35; India (elected by four Asian countries): 3.03; Tanzania (elected by 18 African countries): 2.96; China: 2.60; Argentina (elected by six Latin-American countries): 2.51; Niger (elected by 23 African countries): 1.95.

As a consequence, most important decisions can actually only be made with the consent of the big industrialized countries.

However, recent modifications have somewhat decreased the role of major Powers. For a number of decisions a special majority of either 70 or 85 per cent of the total voting power is now required. In addition, there is also a tendency towards the practice of consensus (see § 108), all of which tends to give greater importance to lesser States.

The Evolution of the IMF

195. Since its establishment the Fund has undergone various modifications owing to changes in world economic conditions. I shall stress only a few general tendencies.

Three main trends can be discerned. First, the tendency to loosen the initial rigidity of the system for ensuring the lack of any alteration of exchange stability: the access of members to the Fund's resources has been rendered less difficult and the obligations concerning the maintenance of the fixed parity of currencies were first relaxed, then abrogated. Second, the Fund has gradually turned from a monetary institution into a lending institution (although to some extent lending was always basic to the Fund: as J. M. Keynes is reported to have said 'You have to understand that the Bank is a Fund, and the Fund is a Bank'—i.e. the Fund gives overdrafts as loans). Third, the Fund, which at the beginning was largely dominated by Western industrialized States, has increasingly opened up to Third World countries, at least in a number of respects (see below).

Although these three trends are closely intertwined and should therefore be considered as a whole, for the sake of clarity I shall examine the most important ones separately. It will be apparent, however, that some of the developments listed under one of the three headings should equally be considered under one of the others.

A first change occurred when the scheme of Stand-by Arrangements was devised: members in need of foreign currency for the adjustment of their balance of payments could obtain assistance after making a declaration stating their economic policy and objects. The fund granted its help within certain limits and for a certain period of time. Plainly, this practice was intended to facilitate the access of members to the Fund's resources.

The same purpose was achieved in 1969, when the Fund was given authority to issue Special Drawing Rights (SDRs) through the adoption of an Amendment to the Articles of Agreement. The SDRs form a reserve asset that the IMF can allocate to members. States entitled to benefit from the special drawing rights can be allocated foreign currency to meet balance of payment outflows. At the request of the member in need of reserves because of balance of payment problems, the IMF designates another member having a strong balance of payments position; the latter receives a transfer of SDRs from the requesting State and, in return, provides a freely usable currency to it. One of the differences between this scheme and that provided for in the Articles of Agreement is that under the former the transfer of SDRs and the consequent allocation of convertible currency is not made conditional on an assessment by the Fund of the economic policy of the States needing foreign currency.

A radical revision was carried out in 1978 when a second Amendment of the Articles of Agreement was adopted. In short, gold was dethroned as the common denominator of the 'par value' regime in international monetary transactions; the official price of gold was abolished and States were allowed to refer to its market rate in their mutual relations; members were no longer obliged to make payments to the Fund in gold, not even in regard to their quotas, or vice versa; it was at the Fund's discretion to sell the gold in its possession or return it to the member States; also the role previously allotted to gold was now given to the special drawing rights. Since 1 January 1981, they have been valued on the basis of a 'weighted basket' of the five principal currencies: dollar, Deutschmark, yen, French franc, and pound sterling (this means that a SDR is the sum of 0.54 dollar (42%); 0.46 Deutschmark (19%); 34 yen (13%); 0.74 French franc (13%) and 0.071 pound sterling (13%); the per cent 'weight' of each currency varies). This complex calculation on the basis of the currencies of the most undustrialized countries allows the SDR to be used as a unit of account in private and public transactions, thereby ensuring a relative stability in exchange rates. The new role which the SDR acquired for those countries which have pegged their currencies to the SDRs was, in practice, achieved by allowing members to ensure the stability of foreign exchange in one of the following manners: by keeping the value of the national currency in terms of the SDR (or any other denominator except gold) chosen by the State; through agreements with other States by which they agree upon the value of their currency in their mutual relations; and through other exchange arrangements. As a result of this new regime, which granted States much freedom, some of them have chosen the free floating of their currency (for example this applies to the US dollar, the pound sterling, and the yen); others have opted for a joint floating (this applies to the currencies included in the European Monetary System), or for a multitude of other arrangements. Moreover, a member is free to determine the external value of its currency under the exchange arrangements of the member's choice.

While these last measures mark the new drive of the IMF towards greater liberty of member States in their choices in monetary matters, other changes, including developments in the IMF's regulatory authority, show how the Fund was gradually turned more and more into a lending institution. Cases in point are: the *Compensatory Financing Facility*, established in 1963 and expanded in subsequent years, which is designed to provide additional resources to States exporting primary products and which encounter problems due to temporary shortfalls in their exports' receipts; the *Extended Facility*, established in 1974, which in turn grants assistance for longer periods of time and in larger amounts than normal to States which suffer serious deficits in their balance of payments owing to structural maladjustments in production, trade or prices.

The gradual opening of the Fund to developing countries took place in three different respects: first, through an increase in the lending of financial resources to Third World countries; second, through the growing participation of these countries in the decision-making process in the Fund; and third, through the growing influence of developing countries on the drafting of provisions regulating the Fund and the use of Fund's resources.

The Contribution of the I M F to Free Trade

196. It will by now be apparent that the Fund has been greatly instrumental in allowing international trade to flow unimpeded by monetary distortions and by similar protectionist practices. To this extent the Fund has made for the expansion of the trade of industrialized countries, where it has also protected employment. If in recent years the Fund has experienced a deep crisis, this is mainly due to the world economic situation, which has taken a turn for the worse for a number of reasons, among which rising inflation in industrialized countries is paramount.

It is also apparent that the Fund has gradually moved from a position of substantial neglect of developing countries to one of increasing receptivity to their problems, taking steps both to help them and to give them a greater share in the decision-making process in the Fund machinery. This development accounts for the mass participation of Third World countries in the Fund (on the other hand, it could be argued that it is precisely such participation which has greatly increased the Fund authorities' awareness of the problems besetting the South). Many developing countries remain, however, rather sceptical about their chances of deriving greater gain from the I M F; as we shall see in the next chapter, they pin their hopes on other international mechanisms to achieve their aim of promoting rapid development and industrialization at home. They are indeed aware that the Fund, in spite of its numerous changes, has not undergone a root and branch revision and remains, to a large extent, an instrument for the free trade of industrialized States.

A more radical view of the I M F is taken by Eastern European countries which, as was mentioned above, have failed to join the Fund (with the exception of Hungary and Romania). The attitude of the more extreme of these countries is summarized in the following terms in the G D R Manual of International Law of 1982:

The I M F is the most important instrument of State monopoly in the field of international monetary policy, which the imperialistic States have established after the Second World War under the domination of the U S ... The objects and tasks of the I M F mentioned in the Articles of Agreement have proved in practice to pursue the expansion of capital-interests of the major imperialistic countries.[10]

Thus, we are confronted with an international institution which does not rest on the common consent of all three major segments of the world community but commands the unqalified support of only one of them, and is seen by many members of one of the others as an unsatisfactory mechanism which may perhaps serve their cause, but only in the long run, while it is strongly opposed by a number of countries belonging to the third group.

[10] D D R-*Völkerrecht* 1982, ii. 84.

MOBILIZATION OF INTERNATIONAL CAPITAL: THE BANK FOR INTERNATIONAL RECONSTRUCTION AND DEVELOPMENT

197. As stated before, after the Second World War one of the principal problems was to find capital for the reconstruction of Europe and the economic development of all the other countries affected by the war. At the same time, it was in the interest of the U S, whose economy had achieved a buoyant recovery during the war period, to invest abroad the private capital accumulated over the years.

The *traditional* means of providing foreign capital to needy countries had proved unreliable in the inter-war period: capital raised by States or by private business corporations through sales of securities in foreign capital markets had turned out to be scarcely rewarding to the lenders, for often the borrowers were overburdened with prior debts and consequently widespread defaults ensued. Investments by foreign private undertakings often did not provide a profitable outlet for the capital resources of the investors: frequently there was no certainty about the profitability of the investment owing to a lack of information on the economic structure, etc. of the country where the investment had been made. Furthermore, no actual scrutiny was possible of the way capital was used, and, in addition, there was the risk that the receiving State would decide to nationalize foreign assets. Finally, as regards State-to-State lending, it frequently led to interference on the part of the lender in the domestic affairs of the borrower, and at any rate was either politically motivated or encumbered with political overtones.

In 1944, at the Bretton Woods Conference, the leading States of the world thought it necessary to devise a system devoid of all these faults and capable of ensuring a constant flow of capital, under safe conditions, to the areas of the world where money was badly needed. As a result, the Bank was created.

The Bank is an inter-governmental organization (it later became a Specialized Agency of the U N), corporate in form, all its capital stock being owned by its member States which subscribe to shares of 100,000 U S dollars each. Only one-tenth of the Bank's authorized capital is paid in; of this part, two per cent is paid in gold or U S dollars, and the remainder in the member's own currency. Nine-tenths of the Bank's capital stock are not paid in, but may be called for by the Bank if they are required to meet its obligations arising from borrowing or guaranteeing loans. The Bank draws its lending resources either from its own paid-in capital or from money it borrows from private sources through the sale of Bank obligations to investors on capital markets. This second way of acquiring capital for investment has become increasingly important, and one can therefore conclude that one of the unique features of the Bank is that, while being an inter-governmental organization, it mainly relies upon private investors for its financial resources.

The Bank lends the money thus collected to member States, to 'political subdivisions thereof', or to business enterprises in the territory of members. If, however, the borrower is not a Government, the loan must be guaranteed by the Government in whose territory the project financed by the loan is located. The Bank's loans must, generally speaking, be for high-priority productive purposes; they must be used to meet the foreign exchange requirements of specific projects. While initially the long-term loans were for a period of ten or twenty years, at present they are granted for a period of twenty-five to thirty-five years (this is much better, particularly for poor countries, where the outstanding debt is very heavy and it is therefore difficult to reimburse loans over a relatively short period); there is a ten-year initial grace period (that is a period during which no reimbursement is due), and the rate of interest is usually 6.25 (somewhat lower than, but related to, market rates); in addition, the Bank charges a service charge of 0.75 per cent per annum.

An important feature of the lending policy of the Bank is that before making a loan, it carefully investigates the economic situation of the borrower to determine if it is 'creditworthy' and in a position to meet its obligations under the loan. Once the loan is made, the Bank makes arrangements to ensure both that its proceeds are only used for the purposes for which the loan was granted, and that due attention is paid to economy and efficiency.

The organizational and power structure of the Bank is similar to that of the IMF. It is therefore unnecessary to dwell on it at great length, except to say that it consists of a Board of Governors and a Board of Executive Directors, plus a President (who in practice, under a sort of unwritten rule, is always a US citizen). The weighted voting system is adopted (under Article V.3 *a*, 'each member shall have two hundred and fifty votes plus one additional vote for each share of stock held').

It should be stressed that, since the US organized in 1948 the so-called Marshall plan for the purpose of providing European countries with capital earmarked for the reconstruction, the Bank has increasingly departed from the aim of lending money for reconstruction and concentrated instead on the supply of capital to stimulate or step up economic growth in the borrowing countries.

CRITICISM BY SOCIALIST AND THIRD WORLD COUNTRIES

198. Socialist countries have criticized the Bank on the same grounds as those on which they have found fault with the IMF: in their view the Bank is a typical capitalist institution which pursues, on an international level, purposes typical of a free-market and free-competition society, and which is, in addition, strongly dominated by the most powerful Western industrialized State, namely, the US. In other words, it is mainly for ideological reasons that socialist States oppose the Bank. There are, however, also political grounds: in their view, should they participate in the Bank's functioning and take advantage of its loans, they would sooner or later become subservient to private capital and its underlying economic interests. But there is yet another reason for socialist opposition. As we have seen above, before granting any loans the Bank carefully investigates the conditions of the borrower and demands stringent requirements of profitability for the loans to be made; even after the money has been lent, a close watch is kept on how the whole project is carried out. In the case of socialist countries, this would mean that an international institution with a capitalist outlook and philosophy could interfere in their State-run economic systems. Finally, if socialist States were to participate in the Bank, they would find themselves in a minority position in relation to Western States, for the Eastern European bloc includes only two highly industrialized countries (the USSR and the GDR), while the West numbers at least ten (see § 194). It is therefore not surprising that the USSR, even though it took part in the Bretton Woods Conference, and even subscribed its capital share, has never participated in the Bank, while Poland, Czechoslovakia, and Cuba, also among the founding members, withdrew in 1950, 1955, and 1960, respectively. At present only Hungary and Romania are members of the Bank (in addition, of course, to Yugoslavia).

The attacks of Third World countries have been less ideological and more strongly geared to the inadequacy of the Bank to meet their demands for economic development. They have taken the Bank to task on several grounds. First, especially in the past the type of loan granted and the requirements to be met by the borrowing party often failed to take account of the singular conditions of developing countries. To build up an adequate infrastructure, these countries need to devote their resources to projects which are not profitable under the Bank's criteria: housing, health services, education, transport, communication. In these and other areas poor countries need to invest a lot of money without drawing immediate financial benefit. For many years (until McNamara's Presidentship) projects in these areas were not, or only rarely, eligible for the Bank's loans, since the profitability criterion could not be adequately assessed. Only recently has the Bank started to finance projects for agriculture and rural development, nutrition, housing, education, and family planning: in short, now emphasis is beginning to be laid on investments which can have an impact on the well-being of the destitute in backward countries. Yet numerous problems remain. Thus before granting a loan, the Bank investigates the economic situation of the borrower as well as, in the case of States, the degree of its outstanding foreign debt and the present and prospective conditions of its balance of payments. Now, the general economic backwardness of developing countries leads them to rely on high borrowing from foreign capital with a view to establishing the minimum conditions necessary for industrialization and for better exploitation of natural resources. In addition, the decline in the price of the primary commodities they produce adversely affects their balance of payments. As a consequence, the basic conditions required by the Bank are seldom met.

A further reason for criticism by the Third World is that the Bank's interest rate is too high and that the loan is usually made in hard currency (not in the currency of the requesting State) in order to cover that part of the development project which calls for the disbursement of foreign currency. It follows that the borrower is of necessity led to use the money borrowed to buy industrial or other equipment manufactured by industrialized countries; thus (developing countries claim) lending to developing countries may ultimately become as beneficial to industrialized States as to the borrowing nations.

A second cluster of strictures refers to interference in domestic affairs of the borrowing country, which the Bank can indulge in owing to the policy lines it has decided to follow. This sort of interference is, of course, not a political attitude deliberately chosen by the Bank's most influential members or by Bank officials, but is the necessary concomitant of the Bank's philosophy, geared to free market and free enterprise principles. In its lending policy the Bank tends to favour private enterprises, while it markedly dislikes public or semi-public corporations, and before a loan is granted, it has been known to go so far as to request the transformation of a public enterprise into a private one, more profitable and competitive under market standards. Furthermore, the Bank influences the economic area to which the financed project relates, in order to ensure that the context in which it works be as profitable as the project itself. Thus, for example, the Bank sometimes requires a more or less detailed regulation of tariff in case of power production projects; or, in cases such as projects concerning roads, railways or port construction, it requires changes in the administrative structure of the relevant apparatus of the borrowing State. As the Bank itself has conceded, as a rule the political situation of the requesting State is also considered before granting a loan—at any rate, the Bank will consider the political situation to the extent that it could impinge upon the profitability of the loan. Consequently, political instability or, more generally, conditions of uncertainty (something very common in Third World countries) may have an adverse impact on the decision to grant a loan.

Finally, a third line of attack relates to the developing countries' lack of opportunities for influencing the Bank's decision-making process. The weighted voting-system does not, of course, do justice to their numerical majority and leaves the major decisions in the hands of the Western industrialized countries, whose interests do not necessarily coincide with, and indeed very often collide with, theirs.

THE PRACTICAL RESULTS OF THIRD WORLD CRITICISM: THE ESTABLISHMENT OF THE IFC AND THE IDA

199. The Bank has not turned a deaf ear to Third World demands and has tried to adopt measures calculated to accommodate their urgent requests, albeit to a limited extent.

First, it has changed certain of its lending techniques. Thus, it has made the loan terms longer, and started differentiating between the interest rates requested from industrialized countries and those from developing countries (the rate for loans granted to the former is higher by 0.50). In addition, it has begun to grant at least part of the loan in local currency. But more significant steps were taken with the creation of two agencies specially designed to take account of the needs of developing nations: the IFC and the IDA.

The International Finance Corporation

The IFC was established in 1956. From 1950 on, developing States had repeatedly requested in the UN that a Special UN Fund for Economic Development (SUNFED) be set up. As this institution was considered by the West to conflict with its own interests (see §207), the solution they fell back on was the IFC.

The IFC is an affiliate of the Bank and its structure is that of the Bank (except for the Director General of the IFC, the Bank's representatives also work for the IFC under the same voting-system). Its principal aim is to promote private foreign investment, particularly in developing countries, by participating in private loans and other investments and, when private capital is not available, by supplementing private investment from its own resources. The resources available to the IFC are made up of the subscribed capital of member States plus the money borrowed from the Bank (it can borrow from the Bank up to a limit of four times its own unimpaired subscribed capital and surplus). It uses these resources to make investments in private industrial enterprises, particularly in developing countries, in the form of capital shares, convention loans or loans with equity features. In other words, the IFC is distinguished from the Bank by the fact that (1) its funds only come from public sources; (2) in its financial operations it does not require any Government guarantee; (3) it not only provides but also mobilizes risk capital for investment in developing countries, thereby taking account of the urgings of the Third World (as we shall see, at §207, one of their demands was that the money to be lent to them be only public capital). However, certain IFC features have aroused the opposition of the Third World. For instance, the lack of any Government guarantee for the promotion of private investments has been perceived as a device which could lead to unacceptable forms of investment (although Article III.3 of the Articles of Agreement provides that a State can object to a loan made by the IFC on its territory, Governments fear that any objection might discourage future investments). However, what is even more unacceptable to developing nations is the fact that the IFC is essentially an inter-governmental organization acting as a bank for the purpose of stimulating and providing private investment. In other words, as was noted by Touscoz, a distinguished French commentator, the IFC is 'an organization having speculation as its main purpose; it is an organization capitalistic in character serving the interests of big private enterprises'.[11] Rather than provide a big volume of capital, it aims at introducing in economically backward nations certain investment techniques and even a certain 'philosophy of enterprise'. It is therefore only natural that a number of developing countries should feel somewhat dissatisfied with its operations.

The International Development Association

The IDA was established in 1960 on the initiative of the US. The first proposal to set up an international institution granting development loans on terms more liberal than those then available was thrown out by the US Senator Monroney of Oklahoma in the US Senate in February 1958. According to Touscoz, the principal concern of Senator Monroney was to find a solution to an American domestic problem: that of using foreign non-convertible currencies accumulated by the US in the developing countries which had received US food assistance and 'paid' for it in local currency. Since the US feared that any use of such money in bilateral assistance might arouse the charge of interference in domestic affairs, Senator Monroney thought of a 'multilateral' utilization through an international institution.

Like the IFC, the IDA is an affiliate of the Bank, and avails itself of its structure. Its financial resources consist of capital subscribed by the member States and by supplementary contributions from several members. (On one occasion the Bank transferred money to the IDA and two non-member States—Switzerland and New Zealand—made a number of interest-free loans.)

[11] J. Touscoz, 'Le groupe de la Banque Mondiale face aux exigences du développement', *Revue belge de droit international* 6 (1970), 39, 33-4.

The IDA operates by making loans for a term of 50 years, with a ten year initial grace period, no interest charge, and a service charge of 3/4 of one per cent per annum. The areas on which the IDA has concentrated are first electric power supply, communications, and transportation, and, second, agriculture and education.

Besides the length of the term of loans and the lack of any interest rate, one other feature of the IDA's operations was designed to uphold some Third World requests: that of greater participation of Third World countries in the decision-making process. This was achieved by dividing member States into two categories, one consisting of countries subscribing their quota in convertible currency, the other made up of countries allocating only ten per cent of their subscription in convertible currency and the remainder in national currency. The latter, manifestly composed of countries destined to be recipients of the IDA's loans, has additional voting-rights. As a result, the former category disposes of 64 per cent of the voting-rights (the US having 26 per cent and the UK 10.75), the latter disposes of 36 per cent.

However, the fact remains that the majority is firmly kept in the hands of the industrialized countries, and, in addition, the IDA to a large extent operates under the criteria proper to the Bank. This circumstance accounts for the lukewarm attitude of developing countries.

LIBERALIZATION OF INTERNATIONAL TRADE: THE GENERAL AGREEMENT ON TARIFFS AND TRADE

200. The combination of international currency stability and the institutionalized mobilization of private capital to promote the free flow of investment to countries short of money, did not suffice for the realization of the grand design launched by the US and other leading Western Powers in the post-war period (see § 190), which constituted a bold projection onto the world community of a pattern of economic order typical of capitalist countries. The free enterprise, free market, and free competition postulates would have become empty words if protectionism in trade had survived. Hence, after the establishment of the IMF and the Bank, the need soon arose to complete the foundations of the new economic order by abolishing trade barriers. Once this undertaking was accomplished, complete equality between private (and public) business seemed a possibility.

In 1947 a new scheme was set up in the shape of GATT. This Agreement, unlike the Articles instituting the IMF and the Bank, did not create an international organization, although over the years an organizational structure did evolve. This structure operates in between the 'sessions' of the Contracting Parties, held twice a year at Geneva and, unlike the IMF and the Bank, is based on the equal voting power of each Party (in other words, not on the weighted voting-system). This structure has gradually grown, so much so that at present GATT can be considered to be an international organization indistinguishable from other similar agencies.

The core of GATT is the set of obligations which the Agreement imposes on the contracting States—a very complex network of stipulations, so complicated and technical that Gardner, a noted American jurist, has wittily remarked that 'only ten people in the world understand it [i.e. GATT], and they are not telling anybody'. Similarly, Senator Millikin said at a Senate hearing that 'Anyone who reads GATT is likely to have his sanity impaired.'[12]

The first obligation is that of granting all other parties the most-favoured-nation treatment in the field of imports and exports (that is, to treat other GATT members in the same manner as the country which is given the most favourable conditions). Under Article I, this clause applies to the following matters:

customs duties and charges of any kind imposed on or in connection with importation or exportation or imposed on the international transfer of payments for imports or exports; the method of levying such duties and charges; all rules and formalities in connection with importation and exportation; internal taxes or other international charges of any kind in excess of those applied, directly, or indirectly, to like domestic products.

What differentiates the clause contained in the Agreement from the 'most-favoured nation' clause provided for in previous years, is that the later clause is multilateral, covers a broad range of subjects, and is made subject to a system of scrutiny designed to oversee whether it is complied with by members of GATT.

Why was this clause deemed necessary for the purpose of achieving free trade? Clearly, if the clause is loyally applied by a great number of States, it follows that discriminations between them tend gradually to fall down and a regime of equality in their trade relationships is established.

If, say, France must grant all other members the most-favoured treatment, this means that in relations between France and all GATT members the same dues will apply as those in force between France and the country it treats best. Thus there will be complete equality between all countries concerned. Similarly, if Japan is to grant the same treatment to all GATT members as to the most-favoured nation, this implies that between Japan and all the other members there will be complete equality. It may, however, happen that France gives a better treatment to a third country than the one accorded by Japan to the nation it favours most. In this case, difference of treatment between France and Japan, *inter se* will ensue, for the former will extend to the latter (and to all other countries) a better treatment than the treatment granted by Japan to France. It follows that the operation of the clause

[12] R. Gardner, *In Pursuit of World Order* (New York, 1966), pp. 148–9; E. D. Millikin, in *US Senate Hearings* (1951), *Senate Finance Committee*, 92.

does not necessarily beget *complete* equality among all members of GATT. In practice, however, this imbalance is somewhat tempered by the fact that, on the whole, the granting of commercial treatment is based on reciprocity. Therefore, at least when members of GATT accord each other special advantages, these advantages extend to all other members. If, say, Sweden and Algeria enter into an agreement providing, on a mutual basis, for special facilities as regards imports and exports of certain commodities, each of them must extend the same treatment to all other members of GATT. (This, however, does not imply that between two other GATT members, say Mexico and Italy, the imports or exports of the same commodities are subject to the same regime. In other words, even in this case equality is not absolute.)

The clause is supplemented by another obligation, prescribing that foreign goods be treated no worse than domestic goods under internal taxation or regulation measures. Thus, while the most-favoured-nation clause is designed to provide a non-discriminatory treatment for the imports from different foreign countries, this obligation (laid down in Article III) puts foreign goods on the same footing as those produced domestically. The obligation, it is plain, strikes at the very heart of the protectionist tendency of most States.

These two obligations are closely related to, and supported by, the general obligation gradually to reduce customs duties by way of bilateral or multilateral negotiations (Article XXVIII, *bis*). In practice, the first four negotiations were conducted bilaterally, whereas later on a multilateral approach came to be preferred (Kennedy round: 1963-7; Tokyo round, 1973-9).

While these are the principal obligations laid down in the Agreement, they are attended by further obligations calculated to strengthen the principles of non-discrimination and equality of treatment in other specific areas where States tend to depart from free trade postulates. Thus, Article XI.1 prohibits quantitative restrictions on both imports and exports (such restrictions are often introduced to protect national products from foreign competition); Article VI.1 forbids dumping (that is, the practices 'by which products of one country are introduced into the commerce of another country at less than the normal value of the products'), if 'it causes or threatens material injury to an established industry in the territory of a contracting party or materially retards the establishment of a domestic industry'. Article XVI.4 restricts the freedom of States to grant subsidies, particularly export subsidies.

When imposing all these obligations, the framers of the Agreement were, of course, aware that special situations existed of which they ought to take account. This is why they provided for a set of exceptions, some of which were laid down in the original Agreement, whereas others were added in subsequent years when the practical operation of GATT rendered them necessary. The exceptions can be grouped under three different headings.

Some are general in character and are aimed at *general situations*. Thus Article XXV stipulates that the contracting parties, acting jointly, may by a specific vote waive an obligation laid down in the Agreement. Article XIX provides for the use of temporary restraints on imports if the latter are causing serious injuries to domestic industry. Furthermore, Articles XII to XIV permit the use of quotas on imports in case of balance of payments' crises. Finally, Articles XX and XXI provide for exceptions for the purpose of implementing national health and safety regulations as well as those pertaining to national security.

A second group of exceptions aims at allowing the maintenance of *preferences* between members of special regional groupings. These exceptions in particular concern such groupings as customs unions (for instance, the EEC) and free-trade areas (for example, EFTA).

They are stipulated in Article XXIV, which allows these two categories to derogate from the principles of most-favoured-nation treatment and non-discrimination. The former kind of association is allowed to establish duties and other restrictions towards third countries not higher or more restrictive than the general incidence of duties and restrictions of the separate constituent countries prior to the establishment of the customs unions. As for the latter category of association, its members are allowed to keep duties and restrictions not higher or more restrictive than they were before the establishment of the free-trade area.

A third group of exceptions relates to *developing countries*. Of course, the elimination of trade barriers may prove detrimental to their economy, because the backwardness of their industrial development and the consequent higher costs of production (see §205) cannot but render their products less competitive than those from highly industrialized countries. In order not to collapse, Third World countries therefore need some protection for their economy, in the form of trade barriers on their imports and preferential treatment for their exports. This requirement was provided for both in 1947 and, with greater sensitivity to the problems of the 'have-nots', in 1965, when a Protocol amending the General Agreement was adopted. As a result of the combination of the Agreement and the Protocol, developing countries are now allowed: (1) with a view to promoting the establishment of particular industries to modify or withdraw tariff concessions previously made for manufactured products of industrialized countries; (2) to impose quantitative restrictions on the importation of foreign goods in order to safeguard their financial position and ensure an adequate level of monetary reserves. Industrialized counries, in their turn, have undertaken first, to accord high priority to the reduction and elimination of barriers to products of particular export-interest to developing countries; second, to refrain from introducing, or increasing the incidence of, customs duties or non-tariff import barriers on those products; third, to refrain from imposing new fiscal measures which could hamper significantly the growth of consumption of primary products which are wholly or mainly produced in the territory of developing countries.

However, none of these devices was flawless: in particular, they did not rest on a general and permanent legal basis designed to guarantee developing countries that the devices would not be disregarded by industrialized nations. This legal basis was set up in 1979, at the end of the Tokyo round, by a decision passed outside the relevant rules governing the amendment procedure to the GATT. The decision laid down an important derogation from the Agreement in that it authorized contracting States to disregard the 'most-favoured-nation' clause in their relations with developing countries. More exactly, this so-called 'enabling clause' authorized contracting States 'to accord differential and more favourable treatment to developing countries, without according such treatment to other contracting parties'. The clause applies to: (1) the Generalized System of Preferences (adopted during the second UNCTAD held in New Delhi in 1968; it had various gaps, which were eliminated in 1979); (2) non-tariff barriers; (3) preferences among developing countries (regional or inter-regional arrangements set up by developing countries *inter se*); (4) special treatment for the 'least developed developing countries' (there are about thirty of them, including Afghanistan, Bangladesh, Burundi, Chad, Lesotho, Somalia, Uganda, and Upper Volta). As Yusuf has rightly emphasized,[13] the 'enabling clause' has the drawback that it does not legally oblige industrialized countries to grant the treatment it provides for to developing nations. However, the clause

removes one of the main obstacles which developed countries claimed would prevent them from granting differential treatment to underdeveloped States, namely their obligations under the most-favoured-nation clause of GATT ... Consequently, differential treatment for and among developing States is no longer a temporary, and undesirable, exception to the equality of treatment under the GATT, but an accepted norm of behaviour in international trade relations. As such, it meets a fundamental concern of developing countries by legitimizing at the international level one of their long-standing aspirations.

The Position of Socialist and Developing Countries

201. I pointed out that GATT, like the other two international institutions mentioned previously, responded to a free market and free enterprise orientation; in other words, it was primarily established to further the economic interests of Western industrialized countries. This raises the question of the reaction of the other two segments of the world community.

[13] A. A. Yusuf, 'Differential and More Favourable Treatment: The GATT Enabling Clause', *Journal of World Trade Law* 14 (1980), 488 ff.

As for *socialist countries*, their participation in GATT is in principle impeded by their very economic structure: they operate State enterprises (private enterprises make up a very peripheral part of their economic set-up); furthermore, they utilize State trading corporations for practically the whole of their international trade and these corporations monopolize all such trade. In short, both the bulk of agricultural and industrial activity and all commercial intercourse with foreign countries are operated by the State. This being so, GATT principles can hardly be considered compatible with socialist systems. For one thing, often the conduct of business is not carried out according to principles of competitiveness but in accordance with political principles and in the light of economic planning. The same consideration applies to State monopoly of importation and exportation. The basic philosophy of GATT is that once trade barriers have been dismantled, all private enterprises of any member State should be put on a footing of equality in their trading activity and thereby achieve that competitiveness which represents the guiding principle of any economic undertaking in the West. This, however, cannot occur in socialist countries as they do not have a plurality of competing enterprises to boost. On the other hand the abolition of trade barriers to foreign business could seriously jeopardize some non-competitive local corporations, thereby running counter to the economic interests of the country.

All these considerations stand behind the socialist States' refusal to join GATT and behind their decision to form 'regional' organizations such as COMECON (Council of Mutual Economic Aid), established in 1949 for the co-ordination of the economic development of the Soviet Union and the other Eastern European countries. (Outer Mongolia, Cuba, and Vietnam joined the Organization, while Albania *de facto* dropped out in 1962 and Romania in 1975.) Nevertheless, GATT authorities, with great flexibility and a pragmatic spirit, allowed certain socialist countries gradually to join on a case-by-case basis and under arrangements specific to each State: Czechoslovakia, a founding member, was allowed to remain in GATT on certain conditions; Yugoslavia joined it progressively, over a period stretching from 1959 to 1966, when its participation became definitive; Poland adhered in 1967, Romania in 1971, and Hungary in 1973. These various arrangements have proved mutually satisfactory: the acceding States have benefited from all the liberalization measures established within GATT (and this proved beneficial in that it opened up profitable outlets to their products), while they themselves have been requested to increase their trade with the other contracting parties, to liberalize their monopoly of foreign trade and to stop discriminatory trading practices.

In spite of these overtures, GATT remains to a large extent alien to the socialist economic philosophy, as it proved by the fact that the biggest Eastern European country, the USSR, has kept clear of it.

The position of *developing nations* towards GATT is somewhat similar to that of socialist countries, although the former are motivated by different considerations and participate in the Conference on a larger scale than the socialist States. In spite of the changes introduced in 1954–5 and in 1965 to accommodate their views, GATT is still looked upon by developing countries as an institution which meets their demands in a rather unsatisfactory way. There are, no doubt, various specific points which arouse the criticisms and misgivings of the Third World. Thus they feel that one of their primary objectives—the elimination by industrial countries of tariffs on manufactures and semi-manufactures from their own countries which would boost the fledgling industry of backward nations; the elimination, again by industrial States, of quotas and discriminatory internal taxes on exports of developing countries—has not been fully achieved by GATT. However, as Abi-Saab has rightly emphasized,[14] the basic grounds on which developing countries feel estranged from and critical of GATT is that this organization and the legal regime of international trade it is intended to promote are based on two principles, both of which they challenge. The first is the full-employment orientation (liberalization of trade was seen by the framers of the Agreement as a means of reaching and maintaining full employment in industrialized countries). The second doctrine is that of non-discrimination ('the idea that optimum allocation of international resources can only be achieved through multilateral and non-discriminatory international trade'). Both postulates are, however, incompatible with the goals of backward countries: these, first, do not aim at full employment but rather at economic growth (in their conditions of low-level productivity, full employment cannot be the primary target, for it presupposes at the very least widespread industrialization or a rational exploitation of agriculture, which is precisely what these countries are striving to achieve); second, in view of their backwardness, developing countries would like international economic relations to be restructured on the principle whereby sweeping obligatory differential treatment should be effected in their favour.

THE EVOLUTION OF THE INTERNATIONAL REGULATION PROTECTING FOREIGN INVESTMENT

202. In the period after the Second World War three major developments occurred in the field of international protection of foreign property: the number of nationalizations soared; differences on the legal regulation of the consequences of nationalization deepened; several devices were contrived for accommodating, if only in a tentative and provisional way, the conflicting interests of capital-exporting and capital-importing countries. Let us consider each of these developments in turn.

[14] G. Abi-Saab, *UNCTAD: the Issues and their Significance* (Uppsala, 1968), p. 3.

The seizing of foreign assets, a relatively rare phenomenon in the inter-war period, increased steeply after the Second World War.

In the years 1946-8, the new socialist countries (Poland, Czechoslovakia, Yugoslavia, Hungary, Bulgaria, and Romania) seized foreign properties and undertakings. Then, developing countries took the lead, in an impressive crescendo: Iran in 1951 (with the famous nationalization of the Anglo-Iranian Oil Company, mainly in the hands of British capital; the downfall of Prime Minister Moussadegh in 1954 and the concurrent agreement for compensation laid the British claims at rest); Egypt in 1956 (with the no less famous nationalization of the Suez Company, the ramifications of which are all too well known); Cuba in 1959; Sri Lanka in 1963; Indonesia in 1965; Tanzania in 1966; Bolivia in 1969; Algeria in 1971; Somalia between 1970 and 1972; Chile in 1972; Libya in 1978.

The second development was the widening of the chasm on existing law. While Western States held on to the customary rules as evolved after the First World War and, in particular, stressed the need for compensation to be 'adequate, prompt, and effective', from the late 1960s onwards, the Third World, supported by socialist countries, contended that only 'adequate', or 'appropriate' compensation was due, and that the modalities of its determination were to be left to the nationalizing State. Their doctrine, still not fully developed in 1962, when the famous General Assembly resolution on permanent sovereignty over natural resources was passed (Resolution 1803-XVII), was set forth in 1974 with the adoption of the Charter of Economic Rights and Duties of States by the General Assembly (Resolution 3281-XXIX). Article 2.2 *c* of the Charter stipulates:

Each State has the right ... to nationalize, expropriate or transfer ownership of foreign property, in which case appropriate compensation should be paid by the State adopting such measures, taking into account its relevant laws and regulations and all circumstances that the State considers pertinent. In any case where the question of compensation gives rise to a controversy, it shall be settled under the domestic law of the nationalizing State and by its tribunals, unless it is freely and mutually agreed by all States concerned that other peaceful means be sought on the basis of the sovereign equality of States and in accordance with the principle of free choice of means.

Most Western States either voted against this provision or abstained, and made it clear that in their view it did run counter to existing law. By contrast, in the view of Third World and socialist countries it consecrated the new law. The Charter provisions on nationalization, while not binding on Western countries, had a significant impact on traditional international law. They showed that the customary rules on the seizure of foreign property are no longer considered binding by two major segments of the world community. This being so, can one still speak of customary international law? The answer is yes, on condition that it be specified that such law tends to become 'particular' law, that is, law applicable to one segment only of the world community (see § 14); the other two groups consider themselves bound by the new provisions. More precisely within the U N they solemnly claim that they intend to reject outright the traditional legal regulation. In their actual dealings, however, they sometimes behave in consonance with those assertions, but on other occasions they are more cautious, or even uphold standards not very different from those laid down in the old law. As, however, any legal regulation of nationalization of foreign property is basically designed to govern relations between capital-exporting countries on the one side and capital-importing countries on the other (that is between developed, or relatively developed, and developing countries), the present legal position turns out to be extremely unsatisfactory. It simply shows the lack of rules which are binding on the two main groups of States likely to be concerned.

Be that as it may, in actual practice, States have sought to avoid harsh conflicts by resorting to *devices and compromises* which to some extent accommodate the demands of both categories of States, although, of course, on more than one occasion one of the parties concerned has accepted the *de facto* or legal settlement only grudgingly, whereas in other extreme situations (as in the case of Moussadegh's Iran or Allende's Chile), the capital-exporting country has allegedly resorted to devious means in order to bring about the toppling of the nationalizing Government. After all, it is in the interest of both parties not to stretch things too much but to try to reach a compromise: in case of total disagreement, if the country of the investors does not want to use extra-legal pressure, its nationals end up seeing their own interests sacrificed, with great loss as regards their property. Similarly, nationalizing or expropriating countries do not gain much from a refusal to negotiate, or from a break in negotiations, for the other country concerned can retaliate by discontinuing its assistance, if any, or by discouraging private investment in other ways (indeed, the famous Hickenlooper Amendment of 1963 to the Foreign Assistance Act of 1961, enacted in the U S at the request of the U S Senator, and named after him, was precisely designed to suspend assistance to any Government dispossessing U S nationals of their property without due compensation, until such time as this Government had taken 'the appropriate steps').

The contrivances most frequently used have been the so-called *lump sum agreements* (normally resorted to by socialist countries: they are international treaties by which the nationalizing State allocates a single sum of money determined on the basis of various criteria and normally meeting the conflicting requests of the two States concerned half-way). In other cases (as in that of the nationalization of the Suez Canal Company, when a settlement was reached in 1958), an agreement is concluded whereby a sum not entirely meeting the claims of the dispossessed foreigners is paid in instalments over a period of several years. In other instances the dispossessing State grants compensation in kind. (This happened in the Bolivian nationalization of 1969, when Bolivia compensated foreign countries through the sale of gas to them.)

Another means of avoiding the consequences of expropriation or nationalization was devised by the Bank in 1965. It is the 'Convention on the settlement of investment disputes between States and nationals of other States', which was elaborated by the Bank, and entered in force in 1966. The parties to an investment dispute are given the option to resort to conciliation or arbitration and I C S I D, the International Centre for Settlement of Investment Disputes, has been set up to provide machinery for settling disagreements. The Convention, on the other hand, does not give a detailed definition of the rules by which the dispute shall be settled— under Article 42.1 the Arbitral Tribunal provided for in the Convention simply applies 'such rules of law as may be agreed by the parties'. In the absence of such agreement, it applies 'the law of the Contracting State party to the dispute' (including its rules on the conflict of laws) and such 'rules of international law as may be applicable'.

Finally, another way of forestalling disputes between the deprived individuals and foreign countries is very widespread today: capital-exporting States set up a national agency responsible for providing insurance protection for private investment abroad. Suffice it to mention the US agency OPIC (Overseas Private Investment Corporation), established in 1969 as a self-supporting corporation and totally owned by the US Government. It provides insurance to American enterprises investing abroad against three classes of non-commercial risk: inconvertibility of foreign currency into dollars; expropriation of investment by the host Government; war, revolution, or insurrection. By covering the risks of private business, this and similar State agencies protect private investment abroad; in case of nationalization without due compensation States are in a position to decide freely whether to intervene directly with the nationalizing Government or to refrain from doing so on political grounds.

Interestingly, recent State practice, as it has taken shape in bilateral treaties, tends to uphold traditional standards; in the case of nationalization provision is made for compensation under criteria very close to the old 'prompt, adequate, and effective' standard. This has been amply demonstrated by two Dutch scholars, Verwey and Schrijver,[15] who have scrutinized 181 treaties concluded between 1946 and 1982 by industrialized States with developing countries, as well as 14 treaties made, between 1950 and 1982, by developing States *inter se* (for example by India and Afghanistan, by Kuwait and Sudan, by Egypt and Sudan, by Romania and Gabon, by Korea and Sri Lanka). It is, of course, difficult to say whether this practice constitutes an

[15] W. D. Verwey and N. J. Schrijver, 'The Taking of Foreign Property Under International Law: A New Legal Perspective?', *NYIL* 15 (1984), 3 ff.

exception to the principles adopted by the majority of States in the UN (that is to say, whether it was provided for contractually and motivated by special considerations), or whether, on the contrary, it confirms that traditional law has not in fact been eroded by UN resolutions. Both views have been put forward, the former by an Indian jurist, Chowdhury,[16] the latter by three Dutch scholars: Peters, Schrijver, and de Wart.[17]

CONCLUDING OBSERVATIONS

203. After the Second World War the Western industrialized States led by the US devised and put into practice a coherent global plan for the promotion of economic development along the lines of a free enterprise and free trade philosophy. This system worked fairly well, at least until the crisis of 1973, when the Middle East war, the oil crisis, and the accentuation of the inflationary tendencies of Western economies proved that the general pattern of the world economic order contrived in 1944-5 was no longer adapted to current needs. Until that turning-point the scheme had been satisfactory, primarily for Western countries, but with 'spill-over' effects for other countries as well. As has been stressed by Carreau, Juillard, and Flory,[18] the neo-liberal system allowed a yearly rate of growth of world trade at an average rate of eight to ten per cent. The value of world exports multiplied by 50 from 1939 to 1978, passing from 25 billion US dollars to nearly 1,300. This growing volume of exchanges was financed without any major crisis by the international monetary system until 1970.

A few major achievements, however, should not lead us to pass over in silence two important deficiencies. First, the rebuilding of the world community on a neo-liberal basis was achieved at the price of a deep rift between the West and the socialist bloc. Indeed, as we saw above, the paramountcy of Western economic philosophy in international institutions impelled socialist countries to keep to themselves and form their own groupings. Thus no universal arrangement has been set up in a field where West and East might have undertaken a constructive dialogue.

The other shortcoming is even more serious. Since the 1950s, when former colonial territories began to gain political independence, it has become increasingly clear that the great problem of current international economic relations is the removal of the ever widening gap between wealthy and poor countries: in short, the promotion of economic and social development in the Third World. Existing international institutions, although they

[16] S. R. Chowdhury, 'Permanent Sovereignty over Natural Resources', Paper submitted to a seminar convened by the ILA and the Centre for Research on the New International Economic Order (Oxford, 1982), p. 95.
[17] P. Peters, N. J. Schrijver and P. J. I. M. de Wart, 'Permanent Sovereignty, Foreign Investment, and State Practice', Report for the ILA Committee on Legal Aspects of a New International Economic Order (1982), p. 27.
[18] D. Carreau, P. Juillard, and T. Flory, op. cit., 83.

have endeavoured to come to grips with at least some of the thorniest problems of development, have not, however, been able to give a satisfactory answer and, what is more important, have done very little towards achieving a solution. As a consequence, developing countries supported by the other group of dissatisfied, socialist States, have become politically estranged from these institutions. On the other hand, bilateral efforts by both Western and socialist countries with a view to promoting development by means of bilateral arrangements have turned out to be 'disadvantageous' to the countries at the receiving end (more often than not political strings are attached and in the end the grantee is tied to the political alignment to which the grantor belongs—a result increasingly considered unacceptable by Third World countries).

Thus, in the field of economic relations more than in any other, disagreement among the three groups of States (often within each grouping as well, for, as pointed out above, the various alignments referred to so far are more complex, multifaceted and varied than appears at first sight) is marked to such an extent that the differences seem almost unbridgeable. The 'have-nots' have, however, taken the lead in recent times, if only on the plane of rhetoric and of political action, and are striving to restructure the economic foundations of the world community. It is to this subject-matter that I shall devote the next chapter.

13

International Promotion of Development

THE TRADITIONAL SETTING

204. THE reader is by now familiar with one of the main traits of the 'old' international community, namely its lack of any 'community duty'. Traditional law was geared to States' freedom and formal equality and no attention whatsoever was paid to factual inequalities. Minor States, if they wished to survive, were forced to ally themselves to major ones, or, more often than not, to become tributaries to them. Consequently, any ties of solidarity involved small groups of States only and were, in addition, motivated by political or ideological reasons.

Against this general background, the colonial relationships stood out. The patterns along which powerful European countries benefited economically from the natural resources of colonial territories are well known. Nevertheless, it may prove useful to the general reader to get a broad (though necessarily over-simplified) view of how the colonial pattern developed economically. The following remarks to some extent apply also to Latin America, long under the *de facto* domination of industrialized countries.

It is well known that colonial expansion was decisively stimulated by the advent in the eighteenth century of industrial development in Europe, chiefly in the UK (which witnessed rapid industrial growth in the period 1780–1840). As the UK had few natural resources of its own (among these coal and iron) but was capable of manufacturing goods at a relatively high pace and convenience, it found it useful to import primary commodities (sugar, coffee, tea, rubber, cocoa, wool, nitrates, copper and so on). Thus it proved of immense value to the Western economy to invest in colonial territories or in such backward countries as the Latin-American nations, which had been independent since the early nineteenth century, for the purpose of extracting the raw materials which were available there. The impact of advanced economic activity on the archaic structure of underdeveloped territories resulted in the creation of what the economist Furtado[1] termed in 1964 a 'dual' or 'hybrid' economy. Two different patterns of economic activity came to exist side by side, namely, a dynamic and modern sector, export-oriented and based on the capitalistic model, and the general sector of the economy, essentially based on pre-capitalistic structures and geared to subsistence agriculture. The former sector was con-

[1] C. Furtado, *Development and Underdevelopment* (Berkeley, 1964), pp. 127–40.

trolled by foreign enterprises but availed itself of local labour. Colonial penetration, based on the recruitment of local manpower, had a favourable impact on the standard of living of the population in the region where foreign enterprises were set up. It stimulated a certain amount of economic activity, and had other useful side-effects in such areas as health, sanitation, or infrastructures (lines of communication, transport, harbours, telegraphs, etc.). In spite of these beneficial effects, no structural modification in the overall economic system of the 'receiving' countries was brought about. In the main, Western economic dominance produced the highly adverse effect of not promoting a global and self-sustaining development process involving all economic sectors. The economic structure of backward nations remained 'dual'. Indeed, with the passage of time this character became even more conspicuous. Later on, according to the same economist, in certain underdeveloped countries such as Brazil (politically independent since 1822), more complex structures evolved. Their economy gradually came to consist of three sectors: the traditional area where subsistence (agricultural) activities predominated; the sector geared to foreign trade (production and export of raw materials); and a sector of light industry producing articles of general consumption such as textiles and processed foodstuffs, earmarked for the domestic market.

The condition of underdeveloped countries worsened after the First World War. The US became the leading economic force in the world and, owing both to its consistent protectionist policy and its vast natural resources, its requirement of imported primary commodities consistently diminished. This attitude resulted in the steady decline of exports from underdeveloped nations which, in its turn, further accentuated the economic imbalance between North and South.

Before considering how after the Second World War international legal institutions were made better geared to the needs of development by newly independent States, it may prove useful to set forth—in addition to the general remarks already formulated—a few observations concerning the main features of the economic structure of the Third World. This will help the reader better to assess how the international community has reacted to the enormous problems of backward countries.

THE MAIN FEATURES OF DEVELOPING COUNTRIES' ECONOMIC STRUCTURE

205. It is, of course, an arduous task to set forth the principal economic characteristics of emergent countries in a concise manner, if only because those nations differ widely. They include China (one billion inhabitants), India (600 million) and Brazil (120 million), as well as Grenada (100,000), Swaziland (600,000), and Nauru (10,000). They range from States such as

Bangladesh and the Central African Republic, with a very backward and rudimentary economic structure, to countries such as Nigeria, Venezuela, India, Indonesia, and Singapore, where considerable progress towards industrialization has been made and at least one sector of the economy has advanced along lines similar to those prevailing in Western nations. By the same token, developing countries comprise both nations whose economies are based on free market and free competition principles and nations with a centrally planned economy (Cuba, Vietnam, Mongolia, Romania, etc.).

This huge variety notwithstanding, a few generalizations are possible, with the usual caveat that they tend to over-simplify reality.

First of all, let me point out that the existence and degree of underdevelopment may be assessed on the basis of a number of factors. According to economists all these factors suffer from various flaws, the least questionable of them probably being the criterion of per capita income. It would appear that developed countries have an average per capita income of about 3,600 US dollars per annum, while the average per capita income of poor countries is around 265 US dollars per annum. (Different figures are quoted in a recent book;[1a] from 8,000 to 15,000 US dollars per capita for the rich countries and from 70 to 1500 US dollars per capita for the poor.) Underdeveloped countries make up about seventy per cent of the world population.

Let us turn now to the principal characteristics of an undeveloped economy. They may be summed up as follows: (1) The dominant economic activity is agriculture (while in developed countries industrial production prevails). (2) Often two sectors coexist: one export-orientated, which is more advanced, and another, based on subsistence activities (the 'dual' or 'hybrid' character referred to above, §204). (3) Both agriculture and manufacturing are often conducted on a family basis, that is, primarily in family-sized, cottage-type units, rather than in industrial productive units. (4) The industrial and agricultural equipment is primitive, or at any rate not very sophisticated. As a consequence, the labour productivity is low and the output relatively poor. (5) So-called 'concealed unemployment' prevails. That is to say, 'the situation prevails in which the number of workers employed would be reduced without causing a fall in production, even without a change in the stock of capital and technique of production used' (Napoleoni).[2] (6) There is a low level of capital stock; the accumulation of capital necessary for the acquisition of better industrial equipment and more generally for productive investment, does not take place, for two principal reasons. First, the low productivity of labour does not bring about that excess of production over consumption which allows private saving (in

---

[1a] M. Bertrand, *Refaire l'Onu: un programme pour la paix* (Geneva, 1986), p. 79.

[2] C. Napoleoni, *Economic Thought of the Twentieth Century*, trans. and ed. A. Cigno (London, 1972), pp. 145 ff.

other words, industrial and agricultural output primarily serves to ensure the subsistence of workers.) Second, that part of the national product not earmarked for the subsistence of the labour force often goes to a small wealthy élite, normally made up of landowners, a few industrial entrepreneurs, and political leaders.

These features create what economists have called 'the vicious circle of poverty'. In the words of a distinguished scholar:

To increase income per capita it would be necessary to increase productivity, which in turn would require a fast rate of accumulation of capital and therefore a substantial excess of production over subsistence consumption; but this surplus is very small because income per capita is so low in the first place. The existence of this vicious circle condemns underdeveloped countries to a practically stationary situation, which is all the more hopeless because the excess of output over subsistence consumption is not only small but, in many cases, also destined for the 'affluent consumption' of the wealthy classes.[3]

In addition, the initial economic imbalance becomes greater and greater. This is because of the existence of what economists call 'conglomerative factors'. One such cluster revolves round the fact that the industrialization of an area presupposes a number of infrastructures (communications, electric power, public administration, training of local manpower, supplies of piped water, etc.), which, in turn, make further investment profitable. The lack of industrialization and of all the ancillary facilities in developing countries makes it more advantageous for capital-exporting States to invest in industrialized areas: indeed, even the availability of cheap manpower in developing countries does not outweigh the profitability of investment in areas where a whole range of infrastructures already exists. Second, conglomerative factors also operate with regard to the demand of workers operating in industry: if a factory is set up in a backward area, the workers' earnings cannot be spent only on purchasing the factory's output; there consequently arises the problem of creating a market, which itself can then further stimulate economic activity. The optimum solution lies in setting up, instead of one big factory, a number of small industrial units capable of producing a wide range of products to be sold to the workers. However, below a minimum size modern factories are not profitable. It follows that the installation of a new factory in a developing country may be attended by the lack of an adequate domestic market, so that all the beneficial effects of industrialization fail to materialize.

The upshot of these circumstances has been incisively described by Napoleoni:

[A] development process starting under modern technological conditions requires a very large initial investment in order to create, all at once, all those conditions that

[3] Ibid., 147.

make an investment profitable. It is precisely for this reason that underdeveloped countries find it so difficult to get the development process off the ground and remain trapped in the vicious circle of poverty.[4]

A further complicating factor is the steady increase in population in developing countries. In a report to the UN, Prebisch (then Secretary-General of UNCTAD) stressed in 1964 that economic growth was likely to be largely absorbed by the growth of the population. He pointed out that:

Nearly half of the capital invested in the developing countries is needed to provide for the increase in population, thereby limiting the resources available for substantially and steadily raising the overall level of living. Unless the present tempo of population growth slows down, it would take eighty years at an annual rate of growth of 5 per cent for the developing countries to reach the current average per capita income level of Western Europe, and approximately forty years more for them to reach that of the US. For the least advanced countries, accounting for one half of the population of developing areas, the period required to reach the present western European level would be of the order of two hundred years.[5]

When this distinguished Chilian economist wrote these lines, the annual growth rate of the population of developing countries was about 2.4 per cent. Twenty years later, thanks among other things to the birth control measures applied by a number of countries (chiefly China), the rate has decreased to between 2.0 and 2.1. In spite of this significant achievement, the condition of developing countries remains dramatic, if only because the annual rate of economic growth has declined to two per cent.

THE EMERGENCE AFTER THE SECOND WORLD WAR OF A DRIVE TOWARDS ASSISTING LESS DEVELOPED COUNTRIES

206. A host of factors contributed to awakening feelings of solidarity in the international community and, in particular, an awareness of the compelling need to help backward countries move towards economic and social progress. First, there was of course the gradual dismantling of colonial empires, which unveiled the real conditions of colonial territories and made it clear that the latter, while politically independent, were in urgent need of comprehensive assistance. Second, the increasing impact of socialist ideologies on international relations convinced statesmen that one should not turn a blind eye to cruel realities, the more so because, to a large extent, they had been brought about by European countries. Third, developing countries themselves evolved an increasing awareness that they ought vociferously to claim their moral right to achieve better living conditions and more say in international affairs. Fourth, there was the concept, shared

[4] Ibid., 148.
[5] R. Prebisch, *Towards a New Trade Policy for Development*, Report by the Secretary-General of UNCTAD (E/Conf.46/3, 1964), p. 5.

after the Second World War by all major actors on the international scene, that the root causes of armed confrontation lay also in economic and social conflict, and that consequently one of the means of forestalling war was to take due regard of those conflicts (this was spelled out in Article 1.3 of the UN Charter). Finally, the UN, whose role has been of incalculable importance in bringing all the major segments of the world community together so as to allow those more sensitive to social justice to influence the others, as well as in providing the institutional framework for channelling the first attempt at international solidarity.

Since 1945 international efforts for the promotion of development have made great strides forward and undergone various changes. It seems therefore appropriate to put them in historical perspective, by dividing the whole range of international action into a few periods, corresponding to certain major turning-points (with the usual caveat, however, about periodization being an arbitrary process).

Stage 1 (1946 to the early 1960s): Technical and Financial Assistance

207. It was Lebanon which in 1946 started the whole business of technical and financial assistance by proposing in the General Assembly the creation of 'advisory boards' charged with providing 'expert advice' to developing countries. Socialist countries reacted rather coolly, observing that machinery was already available in the UN and that the setting up of new bodies would increase the Organization's expenses. However, the support of Western States, though somewhat lukewarm, enabled the General Assembly to pass a resolution (Resolution 52-I) providing for the furnishing of technical advice to UN members who requested it. A major turning-point occurred in 1949 when, on the initiative of the US, the General Assembly adopted a resolution (304-IV) establishing the Expanded Programme of Technical Assistance (EPTA) which (1) involved other organizations of the 'UN family' such as FAO, ILO, etc; (2) was financed by a special fund, contributed voluntarily by member States; (3) was administered by two special organs, the 'Technical Assistance Committee' (TAC) and the 'Technical Assistance Board' (TAB); (4) provided technical assistance at the request of Member States and on the basis of agreements concluded with the requesting State. Assistance mainly consisted in furnishing expert advice (by experts sent to the recipient State), the individual training of local personnel, the provision and dissemination of technical information, and the supply of equipment for demonstration purposes.

Interestingly, after some initial opposition, the attitude of socialist countries gradually became co-operative. In 1953 the USSR decided to participate in the programme, and other Eastern European States soon followed suit. However, the socialist financial contributions were made in inconvertible roubles, which, of course, could only be used in Eastern European countries for the buying of supplies and equipment there, for the use of socialist experts, or for fellowships to be used by people from developing countries in Eastern Europe. As a commentator pointed out, 'in a way, these contributions were converting the multilateral character of the Expanded Programme into a kind of bilateralism and permitting the contributors to use their meagre assistance more for their own aims and profits'.[6]

The very limited scope of this kind of assistance, compared with the enormous range of needs in developing countries, is all too evident.

Meanwhile, another project was being lobbied by developing countries, increasingly aware of the inadequacy of existing international institutions such as the IMF (§§ 191-6) and the Bank (§ 197) in settling their problems. As early as April 1949 Rao, the Indian president of the UN Subcommittee on economic development, had produced a report on 'Methods of Financing Economic Development in Underdeveloped Countries',[7] in which he proposed the setting up of a UN Special Fund that he called SUNFED (Special UN Fund for Economic Development). This institution was to avail itself of public capital (as opposed to the Bank, which, as we have seen above, mainly relied on private sources) and use it either by making donations to developing countries or by granting long-term loans with a very low interest rate (unlike the loans of the Bank). The purpose of the institution was therefore to collect public money to be used not with profitability criteria but with a view to facilitating the economic growth of backward nations. Finally, the projected agency would have worked on the principle of equal voting (that is, not under the weighted voting-system). Thus developing countries would have had a say equal to that of industrialized ones (while in the IMF and the Bank they were outvoted).

The socialist countries reacted favourably, although they stressed that in their view the more urgent task was to remove the restrictions on the commercial exchanges of developing countries. As for Western industrialized nations, certain of them, such as the US, the UK and Canada, declared that they were ready to support the project on condition that substantial progress in world disarmament be made—clearly a condition destined to torpedo the Fund, for the obvious reason that existing conditions did not allow negotiations on disarmament to make much headway. Other Western countries such as France, Denmark, Norway, the Netherlands, Luxembourg, Italy, and Japan, were more forthcoming, although they did not contribute much on the practical side to the implementation of the project. The opposition of the Bank, consulted at the request of some industrialized

---

[6] U. Kirdar, *The Structure of the UN Economic Aid to Underdeveloped Countries* (The Hague, 1966), p. 42.
[7] See UN document 1949, II/A, 3.

States, as well as the scant interest of the West, gradually wrecked this all-important scheme.

Substitutes for SUNFED were, as far as the Bank was concerned, the IFC (§ 199) and, for the UN, the Special Fund set up in 1958 under Resolution 1240-XIII. This Fund was entrusted with financing projects calculated to explore the need for, and to plan the use of, capital investment in developing countries. It was an independent subsidiary body of the UN under the authority of ECOSOC and the General Assembly, and was financed by voluntary contributions of member States. It was not to lend money to developing countries, but only to provide relatively small grants (allocated free of charge) destined to finance pre-investment projects. The fund provided assistance with the exploration of the natural resources of developing countries and helped to create the conditions necessary for making investment feasible or more effective. The various means for achieving this end were: survey and feasibility studies; the establishment of local research institutes as well as of local institutions for developing vocational and technical skill in the recipient countries.

It will be clear that the Special Fund was markedly different from SUNFED. While the latter was to be created in order to provide money for investment, the former merely sought to furnish a new kind of technical assistance. All it had to do was pave the way for investment, which was to be made through the existing channels (bilateral aid, or borrowing from the Bank). Thus, the creation of the Fund did not mark a real turning-point in the quest for effective devices to help developing countries in their economic take-off. In addition, the financial participation of States was relatively small (the major participant was the US which, however, made its contribution subject to the condition that it should not exceed 40 per cent of the total contribution).

Although the Special Fund was a meagre 'ersatz' for SUNFED, it possessed three characteristics which corresponded to the demands of the Third World: (1) developing countries were not in a minority position: the Governing Body consisted of nine representatives of the States providing assistance and of an equal number of delegates from developing countries; (2) the Fund drew upon public funding, not private sources (for it was fed by the voluntary contributions of member States of the UN); (3) its primary object was to allocate non-reimbursable grants.

Stage 2 (from the early 1960s to 1973): Trade Not Aid

208. Various factors contributed to changing the UN approach to development in the early 1960s. First, it had become apparent that the existing scheme was totally inadequate for coping with the far-reaching problems of developing countries. Second, these problems were becoming more and more acute. The prices of the primary commodities they produced (cocoa, tea, coffee, pepper, olive oil, sugar, wheat, tobacco, bananas, rubber, tin, bauxite, copper, iron ore, mercury, petroleum, tungsten, nickel, manganese ore, etc.) were steadily declining on the world market, while at the same time there was a steady increase in the price of manufactured or semi-manufactured goods (that is goods which poor countries had to import both to meet their growth requirements and also to create the infrastructure necessary for promoting foreign investment). As a consequence, a decline in the exports of developing countries and an increase in their imports took place, with the result that their balance of payments deficit worsened at staggering speed. Thus it became imperative for less advanced countries to reconsider the whole international economic system and to propose measures which, instead of being mere palliatives, could come to grips with the substance of international relations. Third, the accession to political independence of a great number of formerly dependent African and Asian States rendered the Third World more vocal and pugnacious, and, what is even more important, made for the emergence of a wholesale 'doctrine' of development, a doctrine which poor nations soon endeavoured to translate into international standards and institutions.

Developing countries followed a four-pronged strategy: (1) they created a new institution calculated to promote negotiation on matters such as trade (UNCTAD, established in 1964); (2) they prompted existing economic and financial institutions to adjust their policies, so as to make them more responsive to the needs of developing countries (the Bank, the IMF, and GATT were impelled to adopt new measures favouring the 'have-nots'); (3) they reshuffled the UN institutions: in 1965 the United Nations Development Programme was established; (4) in 1966 they set up UNIDO, a special institution designed to promote their industrial development.

Let us briefly consider each of these four developments in turn.

UNCTAD

209. The first UN Conference on Trade and Development was held in 1964 under the auspices of the UN, and was attended by practically all members of the world community (120 States). After three months of hard and protracted labours, it adopted a set of resolutions which laid down the basic principles on which the institution was to work in future. The General Assembly then decided to establish the Conference as one of its institutions, to be convened at intervals of no more than three years, and also set up a permanent executive body, the 'Trade and Development Board' (consisting of fifty-five members elected by the Conference, to meet twice yearly), as well as a Secretariat, headed by a Secretary-General (appointed by the UN Secretary-General and confirmed by the General Assembly).

Among the general principles laid down by the Conference the following stand out:

(1) 'Economic development and social progress should be the common concern of the whole international community'. Accordingly, all countries pledged themselves:

to pursue internal and external economic policies designed to accelerate economic growth throughout the world, and in particular to help promote in developing countries a rate of growth consistent with the need to bring about substantial and steady increase in average income in order to narrow the gap between the standards of living in developing countries and that in developed countries [Principle I V].

Thus, a general political philosophy was propounded whereby the development of less advanced countries was of concern to everybody, in particular to industrialized nations. While until that time backward countries had merely requested to be assisted as a concession on the part of advanced States, now they proclaimed that they were entitled to international help.

(2) A new idea was launched, that of an international division of labour (Principle V).

(3) Existing trade barriers hampering the access of primary products of developing countries were to be eliminated by developed countries (Principle V I I).

(4) A further important measure was to be the stabilization of the price of primary commodities so as to avoid their fluctuation and decline to the detriment of producers (Principle V I I).

(5) Finally, developed countries were requested to grant commercial concessions to developing countries, in particular the most-favoured-nation treatment, without, however, requiring any concession in return from developing countries. In other terms, the most-favoured-nation clause ought not to be reciprocal when applied to less advanced nations. Furthermore, technologically advanced States were invited to make preferential concessions, both tariff and non-tariff, to developing countries, and the latter were to be allowed not to extend to the former preferential treatment in operation amongst them (Principle V I I I).

In short, the liberal, free-market approach was to be dropped as far as developing countries were concerned, and they had to enjoy a 'discriminatory treatment', that is a treatment different and more advantageous than that existing between developed countries. This was, indeed, a conspicuous departure from the basic principles which had governed international relations until that time.

It is apparent from the foregoing that U N C T A D does not constitute a 'traditional' international organization, nor has it brought about a set of standards legally binding on all the participating States. U N C T A D is, rather, a felicitous combination of a body of general guidelines destined to serve as a blueprint for action, and a political forum where developed and developing countries meet on an equal footing, exchange views, and gradually try to implement these guidelines. The establishment of UNCTAD marks the real divide in international action for development, for it was in 1964 that developing countries became aware that aid was no longer sufficient and that it was necessary to come to grips with the basic causes of international disequilibrium. Subsequently, it was within UNCTAD that backward States gradually evolved their new philosophy of development and, as we shall see, came to formulate a global strategy, which was expounded in 1974, thus changing from a specific sector (that of international trade) to an overall approach to economic relations between North and South.

More specifically, UNCTAD is important in the following three respects. First, as emphasized by Abi Saab,[8] its real significance

... is reflected ... in the forces which brought it into being but which were given more shape and self-awareness through it. Thus for the first time a vast grouping of all the underdeveloped countries was formed and is learning to co-operate and to act as one bloc in defence of their common interests. The importance of this factor is not reduced by the occasional awkwardness and deviation which are part and parcel of any process of learning.

A second merit of UNCTAD lies in 'educating world public opinion, especially in developed countries' as to the conditions and causes of underdevelopment in the Third World, so as to persuade industrialized States to take action at least to reduce the most glaring international economic injustices.

The third, and perhaps most important, merit of UNCTAD is its piecemeal construction of a set of international standards designed to expand and apply the general guidelines set forth in 1964.

One of the areas where the effects of pressure by UNCTAD are most visible is that of commodity agreements, that is, those multilateral treaties calculated to impinge upon the free play of international market forces controlling the sale of primary commodities or raw materials (see § 208) by developing countries.

Precisely because developing nations are mostly geared to monocultures, that is, to the exploitation of one basic natural resource, for many years a crucial issue has been the stabilization of the international price of such commodities. Since the early 1960s the terms of trade of raw materials have deteriorated, for a number of reasons: (1) the influence of natural causes (weather, vegetal diseases, etc.) on the production of such resources; (2) the inherent instability of the international market, which moves in unpredictable cycles; (3) the tendency of industrialized countries to replace

---

[8] G. Abi-Saab, *UNCTAD: the Issues and their Significance* (Uppsala, 1968), p. 24.

natural products such as rubber and fibres with synthetic products; (4) the tendency of developed countries to draw on goods they themselves produce. UNCTAD has strongly pressed for the conclusion of agreements designed to eliminate or attenuate short-term market instability by preventing or moderating pronounced fluctuations in the price of those commodities. Urged on by UNCTAD, States felt impelled to undertake commodity agreements (no novelty in 1964 since an agreement on wheat had been concluded as early as 1949) because this was the best way to guarantee sovereignty over natural resources and stable earnings from them.

The Impact of the New Strategy on Existing International Institutions

210. The new economic philosophy advanced by developing countries in 1964 ran contrary to all the 'classical' principles on which international economic affairs had been based until then. It therefore proved necessary to adjust GATT, the Bank, and the IMF to this new philosophy.

I have shown that after 1964 changes were introduced to the IMF (§ 195), to the Bank (§ 199), and to GATT (§ 200). As the reader will remember, these changes were not considered sufficient by developing countries.

The UN Development Programme

211. In 1966 the deficiencies which emerged in the administration of the UN activities for the promotion of development made it necessary to set up a centre unifying and effectively co-ordinating all those activities. To this end the United Nations Development Programme (UNDP) was established by General Assembly Resolution 2029-XX.

The Expanded Programme and the Special Fund were merged under the authority of a Governing Council composed of forty-eight members, twenty-seven of which were developed, and twenty-one developing, countries. Furthermore, the assistance previously granted by the various specialized agencies with relative autonomy was reduced. The Programme was made responsible for their co-ordination, and projects were to be carried out under the supervision and direction of the bodies responsible for the Programme. In addition to reorganizing and streamlining the bodies entrusted with promoting development, the UNDP shifted its action from a planning based on specific projects to a planning geared to given countries. The UNDP now indicates for each country the amount of assistance available and the recipient Government selects the projects it considers most useful.

The UN Industrial Development Organization

212. UNIDO was set up by a Resolution of the General Assembly (2152-XXI) passed on 7 November 1966. It was created as a subsidiary body of the General Assembly, but its increasing importance led the UN to turn it into an autonomous organization having the status of a specialized agency. This development occurred in 1979, when a draft treaty was adopted by a Diplomatic Conference at Vienna (by now the treaty has been ratified by over one hundred States; in August 1985 UNIDO started working as a specialized agency).

The 'primary objective' of the Organization is 'the promotion and acceleration of industrial development in the developing countries with a view to assisting in the establishment of a new international economic order' (Article 1). UNIDO does not provide, nor does it lend, money to developing countries for their industrialization. It merely carries out studies and surveys; provides technical assistance; co-ordinates the UN activities in this field; provides a forum where industrialized and developing countries can meet and conduct negotiations; and serves as a clearing-house for industrial information and, in particular, promotes the exchange of experience and technological know-how of industrially developed and developing countries with different socio-economic systems.

In spite of the relative modesty of UNIDO's activities, a major bone of contention was its financing. Western and socialist States favoured a system whereby ordinary expenditures for the administration, etc. should be met from assessed contributions, whereas technical assistance should be covered by the voluntary contributions of States. Developing countries pleaded instead for expanding the former category so as to cover operational activities of the Organization as well. The ensuing tug of war ended in a compromise solution, whereby the 'regular budget' (covering expenditures to be met from assessed contributions) provides for administration, research, and other regular expenses of the Organization, as well as for *some* operational activities (provided their cost does not exceed six percent of the whole 'regular budget'), whereas the '*operational* budget' (consisting of voluntary contributions) provides for the bulk of expenditures for technical assistance and other related activities. Interestingly, some socialist countries (the USSR, Poland, Czechoslovakia, Hungary, and the GDR) made a joint declaration of principle (not to be considered as a reservation, as they themselves pointed out) to the effect that the provisions allowing some operational activities to be covered by the 'regular budget' were contrary to the principle whereby such activities should be financed through voluntary contributions.[9]

It is significant that in spite of the opposition of industrialized countries, for the first time in the UN system at least part of operational activities for promoting development are to be paid out of the 'regular budget' of the Organization. This is an important step towards the concrete recognition by developed countries that their financial contribution to development does not depend on their generous disposition but follows from a general duty.

[9] See UN document A/Conf.90/CRP.3, 7, April 1979.

Stage 3 (1974 to the Present): The New International Economic Order

213. In 1973 a few major developments precipitated a radical change in the 'normative' make-up of international law of development.

Following the 1973 Arab–Israeli conflict, the Arab oil-producing countries decided upon a boycott of industrialized countries. This measure seriously worried the West, which became aware of its weakness in this particular field, and also aroused in the oil-exporting Arab countries a realization of their strength: they understood that they could now hold their own in a confrontation with the two traditional politico-military centres of power (Western and Eastern European States). This state of affairs emboldened the Arab countries, and developing nations in general, to put forward more audacious and far-reaching demands concerning the reshaping of international economic relations.

Two more general phenomena also favoured the growing assertiveness of developing countries. First, the Cold War, whose adverse consequences had plagued the world community since the early 1950s, had lost some of its chill, turning into a minor 'war of attrition'. This, of course, allowed the third great segment of the community to come to the fore without hindrance and, what is even more important, circumstances propitious to Third World demands began to receive more attention from the two blocs. The other major development was the substantial demise of traditional colonialism. (By 1973 practically all colonial empires had been disrupted and the scattered remnants were about to be swept away by the great tide of independence—save, unfortunately, for Namibia.) This allowed developing countries to concentrate more and more on so-called neo-colonialism, whose essence is, in the words of Nkrumah, Ghana's former leader, 'that the State which is subject to it is, in theory, independent and has all the outward trappings of international sovereignty. In reality its economic system and thus its political policy is directed from outside.'[10]

The first move towards the international proclamation of a set of radically innovatory standards was made by President Luis Echeverria of Mexico at the third UNCTAD in Santiago in 1972. The Conference endorsed his proposal and entrusted a Working Group, chaired by the Mexican jurist and diplomat J. Castañeda, with the preparation of a draft Charter laying down the economic rights and duties of States. While the Charter was being drafted, the Algiers Conference of Non-Aligned Countries of September 1973 gave greater impetus to the demands of emergent nations. The final Economic Declaration adopted by the Conference emphasized, among other things, the importance of the Arab oil boycott and the role of the association of oil exporting countries (OPEC) as a model on which to

[10] K. Nkrumah, *Neo-Colonialism: The Last Stage of Imperialism* (London, 1965), ix and xiii.

proceed ('The results obtained in the hydrocarbons sector, which was previously exploited for the sole benefit of the transnational oil companies, demonstrate the power and effectiveness of organized and concerted action by producing and exporting countries.' All developing countries producing raw materials were consequently called upon to grip the levers of price control by realizing a cartel covering all the basic raw materials which they produced.) It was argued that such an association ought to be one of the major instruments for securing 'the establishment of a new international economic order which would meet the requirements of genuine democracy'.

At the demand of Algeria, which took up a French request with alacrity and gave it a radical bent, a special session of the General Assembly was devoted in 1974 to the elaboration of the basic principles of a new international economic order. The General Assembly adopted by consensus, but amidst the sweeping 'reservations' of Western countries led by the US, two resolutions, one (Resolution 3201-S.VI, of 9 May 1974) containing a Declaration on the Establishment of NIEO, the other (Resolution 3202-S.VI, of 16 May 1974) containing a Programme of Action on the Establishment of NIEO. While these two texts contain loose formulations and were drafted in the form of general guidelines and objectives and did not claim to impose a set of binding standards of action, the Charter of Economic Rights and Duties of States, adopted by the General Assembly on 12 December 1974 (Resolution 3281-XXIX), was couched in a language more akin to international legislation. This, as well as the fact that its provisions were more specific than those of the two previous instruments, led to a split in the General Assembly. When a vote was taken, a few Western industrialized countries voted against (Belgium, Denmark, the FRG, Luxemburg, the UK, and the US) while others abstained (Austria, Canada, France, Ireland, Israel, Italy, Japan, the Netherlands, Norway, and Spain). What happened was very significant, politically and ideologically: the Charter, born from a combination of Afro-Asian and Latin-American countries, was strongly supported by all the socialist States, while it aroused intense opposition in the Western bloc. Consequently, the new text reflected the aspirations and demands of two segments only of the world community, which greatly weakened its 'normative' force.

What are the *main tenets* of the NIEO, as they are laid down in the 1974 Charter? They can be summarized as follows:

(1) One of the principal reasons why developing countries endure increasingly worse conditions is because they do not actually control their own natural resources which are in fact in the hands of foreign corporations, usually in the form of multinational concerns (§ 58). The latter use Western technology to exploit those resources and reap the bulk of the benefits, leaving developing countries a relatively small proportion of the profits. Consequently, developing countries must 'exercise full permanent sovereignty, including possession, use, and disposal, over all its wealth, natural

resources, and economic activities' (Article 2.1). Two consequences naturally flow from this principle: first, the countries under discussion must be entitled to regulate and control the activities of multinational corporations operating within their territory (Article 1.2 *b*); and second, they must be free to nationalize or expropriate foreign property on conditions favourable to them; accordingly they must only pay 'appropriate compensation' (see §§ 187, 188, 202).

(2) Developing countries should set up associations of primary commodity producers similar to OPEC and all other States must recognize this right and refrain from applying economic, military, or political measures calculated to restrict it (Article 5).

(3) More equitable conditions of trade should be established for the purpose of favouring developing countries. To this effect 'stable, remunerative, and equitable prices' for raw materials should be provided for, especially by means of arrangements and by the conclusion of long-term multilateral commodity agreements. Measures should be taken to achieve a substantial increase in the foreign exchange earnings of those countries, a diversification of their exports and the acceleration of the rate of growth of their trade; the system of generalized non-reciprocal and non-discriminatory tariff preferences to developing countries should be enlarged. Furthermore, the net amount of financial flows to developing countries should be increased (Articles 6 and 14).

(4) Of course, the economic take-off of backward countries cannot take place without an injection of modern technology. It was therefore to be expected that transfer of technology to developing countries should be requested as a primary necessity (Article 13.2).

(5) In the view of the Third World, all the above measures, while strictly necessary, do not mean that 'traditional' economic and technical assistance from the industrialized countries should be discontinued: far from it, it should be increased and, what is even more important, it should not have any strings attached. As Article 17 puts it, States should extend 'active assistance' to underdeveloped countries 'consistent with their development needs and objectives, with strict respect for the sovereign equality of States and free of any condition derogating from their sovereignty'.

For the time being the NIEO largely amounts to a set of standards of achievement possessed of political and rhetorical value only. These standards concern goals which industrialized States ought to endeavour to pursue, although they are under no legally binding duty so to do. The whole body of standards which has come to be called NIEO leads a sort of twilight existence. It is no longer a set of political demands put forward by individual States, for it has already obtained the official consecration of the highest organ of the world community, the UN General Assembly, and there it has aroused a very broad measure of consent in two major groups of States. However, it has not yet ripened into a body of binding rules. Time alone will show whether this evolution will take place, and in what form.

We should now briefly mention the first steps taken to implement the principles on the NIEO. Soon after the adoption of the basic texts on the

NIEO, the Philippines proposed in the UN that an effort at progressive development of international law should be made so as to turn the postulates of the NIEO into legally binding rules by dint of the adoption of a multilateral treaty. This proposal, however, did not arouse unreserved favour. Particularly among Western countries, a fundamental disagreement emerged over the basic issue of whether the principles of the NIEO were already in existence as international legal phenomena, or whether it was suitable to undertake any progressive development thereof. Discussions on this issue have been dragging on for many years in the UN General Assembly, and it is plain that there is still a large measure of dissent.

To show how the views of States differ, it may prove interesting to mention the attitude adopted by various States in the General Assembly in 1980.[11] Among developing countries, States such as the Philippines, Mali, Chile and India strongly pressed for a rapid effort towards progressively developing the main principles of the NIEO. By contrast, China suggested caution ('in principle, [the Chinese] delegation favoured the step-by-step approach: at the outset it would be possible to study and investigate the fundamental principles and substance of the question, while consolidation and the consideration of specific legal norms could be tackled at a later stage').

Also among Western countries differing views emerged. For example States such as the Netherlands and Canada suggested that it was sensible and appropriate 'at the current stage to focus attention first on those basic principles which appeared to have been commonly accepted as cornerstones of the legal framework of a new international economic order'. Other countries such as the US, the UK, France, the FRG, and Italy contended that the question of codification was premature in view of various ongoing international negotiations on development issues, and expressed scepticism about the feasibility of any effort at translating the NIEO into legal rules.

By contrast, Eastern European countries exhibited a united front—without, however, showing any enthusiasm for the proposed exercise. Speaking on behalf of all the COMECON countries, the GDR stated that it supported the draft resolution proposed by the Philippines, 'on the understanding that the Declaration and Programme of Action on the Establishment of a NIEO, the Charter of Economic Rights and Duties of States, and other documents referred to [in the draft resolution] had the nature of recommendations'. The GDR spokesman went on to point out that those

---

[11] For the various statements, see: A/C6/35/SR.68, paras 18, 22, 24 (Philippines); SR.69, para. 2 (Mali); SR.70, para. 2 (Chile); SR.71, paras 23-7 (India); SR.70, para. 16 (China); SR.70, paras 27 and 34 (The Netherlands); SR.71, paras 14-17 and SR.75, paras 79-82 (Canada); SR.71, paras 18, 22, and SR.75, paras 77-8 (the US); SR.75, paras 84-8 (the UK); SR.75, para. 71 (France); SR.71, paras 30-3 (the FRG); SR.75, paras 74-5 (Italy); SR.75, paras 72-3 (the GDR). See also SR.70, paras 44-5 (USSR).

'documents undoubtedly had, and could continue to have, a bearing on international economic relations. The question whether those progressive recommendations would constitute the basis for legal norms of a binding nature should be decided after a careful and comprehensive analysis of the practical implementation of the recommendations. Such an analysis should take due account of the diversity of economic relations among States and the position of the socialist States explained in connexion with the adoption of the documents in question'.

Nevertheless, some progress was subsequently made, albeit very slowly. So, by 1983 the United Nations Institute for Training and Research (UNITAR), had 'identified' seven principles pertaining to the NIEO, and the General Assembly subsequently endorsed this 'identification'. In 1984, at the request of UNITAR, an important 'Analytical Study' was prepared on the matter by Abi-Saab.[12] All we can do is hope that the General Assembly will gradually elaborate general standards endowed with binding force, along the lines suggested in Abi-Saab's study.

THE ATTEMPT TO SUPPLEMENT THE NIEO BY INTRODUCING THE RIGHT TO DEVELOPMENT

214. Even before the principles proclaimed in 1974 were laid down and subsequently reiterated and expanded in various General Assembly resolutions and in the resolutions of other international bodies, the whole corpus of ideas and standards constituting the NIEO was brought to bear on two special areas: the law of the sea and human rights. As for the former, I shall show in Chapter 14 how the concept of the common heritage of mankind evolved after 1967, eventually to be upheld in the 1982 Convention. At this point I shall therefore confine myself to the field of human rights. In this area the influence of the new outlook made itself felt in that it was forcefully asserted that individuals, peoples, and (developing) States have a right to development.

The idea of such a right was first propounded in 1966 in the General Assembly by the Foreign Minister of Senegal.[13] In 1972 it was eloquently taken up and elaborated upon by Kéba M'Baye, the then Chief Justice of Senegal, in a famous lecture and subsequently in various statements made as head of the Senegalese delegation to the UN Commission on Human Rights.[14] The concept in question was widely upheld by developing and

---

[12] G. Abi-Saab, *Analytical Study on Progressive Development of the Principles and Norms of International Law Relating to the New International Economic Order*, UN document A/39/504, Add.1, 23 October 1984.

[13] See GAOR, 21st Session, 1414th Mtg., 23 September 1966, para. 228.

[14] K. M'Baye, in *Revue des droits de l'homme* 2 (1972), 502 ff.

socialist countries as well as by a few Western States, and has now become one of the principal catchwords of the UN and has also been embodied in a number of resolutions.

It is apparent that the affirmation of the 'right to development' had various motivations. First, it was a means of reformulating the whole problem of the international law of development in terms of a 'fundamental right'; this served to bring the demand of developing countries for a restructuring of the world economic order into focus and indeed to dramatize such a demand: clearly, if you speak of a 'right' it follows that there must exist a 'duty' falling upon somebody. Second, the new concept served to bring the whole momentum of the human rights doctrine—a doctrine much in the limelight and to which the West is highly sensitive and receptive—to bear on all the problems of international economic relations, thereby forcing Western countries, notoriously devious in this field, to come out into the open. Thus, the whole panoply of ideas, standards, patterns, concepts, and machinery normally used for the human rights area came to be applied to a territory on which the industrialized countries did not wish to tread. Third, at least for some of the developing and socialist countries warmly supporting the right to development (assuredly not for Senegal), ventilating this right constituted a useful tool in the political and ideological struggle between blocs. It helped the introduction of elements calculated to divert the attention of States and UN bodies from gross violations of human rights (in their view, it does not make sense to put too much emphasis on violations of such rights in developing countries, for, as long as their right to development, which should have the highest priority, is not implemented, they must of necessity rely on fragile structures which cannot fully respect either civil and political rights or economic, social, and cultural rights). Furthermore, emphasis on the right to development afforded a good opportunity to attack the Western industrialized countries, for it is mainly with them that responsibility for transforming such a right into reality lies.

The concept of 'right to development' undisputedly reflects a serious and totally justified preoccupation, namely that of promoting the development of backward countries. However, what may seem wrong is to transpose into the area of human rights the need to impose upon industrialized countries the duty to promote the economic advancement of poor nations. For, on analysis, the concept of 'right to development' proves not susceptible of being translated into legal terms as a human right, either *de lege lata* or *de lege ferenda*. It cannot be regarded as a right of individuals, for, as Abi-Saab correctly pointed out, then the right would amount to 'the aggregate of the rights recognized in the [two UN] Covenants, especially the social and economic and cultural rights'[15] and consequently the concept of a

[15] G. Abi-Saab, 'The Legal Formulation of a Right to Development', in *The Right to Development at the International Level*, ed. R.-J. Dupuy (Alphen aan den Rijn, 1980), p. 63.

'right to development' would not make much sense: to bully the West into promoting its realization it would suffice to impel States to ratify and comply with the two UN Covenants. On the other hand, it is not correct either, to consider the right as a 'collective right' belonging to peoples of developing States, in conformity with the approach taken, among other things, by the 1981 'African Charter of the Rights of Men and Peoples' (Article 22). Indeed peoples, as distinct from States, cannot be legal subjects of international rights (except for the case of those peoples possessed of a representative organization which find themselves in the condition of being oppressed by a colonial country, a racist regime or a foreign occupant, and are consequently endowed by a specific international rule with the right to self-determination: see §§ 54–6). In the case of peoples of sovereign States (say, those of Ghana, or Algeria, or Chile), how can one contend that these peoples, as distinct from the Governments which actually participate in international dealings on their behalf, are the legal subjects of the right to development? The right to self-determination can be invoked by peoples with respect to States because there is a representative apparatus (a liberation movement) distinct from that of the oppressive State or Government, and this apparatus in some way looks after and voices the interests and aspirations of the people oppressed, and can therefore claim international legal status. Things are different in the case of peoples of developing sovereign States. Hence, on close analysis the 'right to development' cannot but benefit States. Only *developing States* could invoke such a right and claim respect for it. If that is the case, it no longer makes sense to speak of a 'human right'.

Consequently the launching of the whole concept and phraseology of the 'right to development' has proved misguided. Admittedly, the fact that in the case of development concepts based on human rights have been utilized, has helped to spread two important ideas: first, development does not merely amount to economic growth, but also involves a 'human dimension'; second, development concerns not mere Governments, but the whole population, and consequently should not be to the sole advantage of ruling élites. Nevertheless, not only for the sake of clarity but also to avoid misleading abuses, it would have been politically sound and well-advised to concentrate on the gradual translation of the NIEO into legally binding rules, thus turning the principle on co-operation (see § 87), in its significance as 'postulate of international solidarity', into operational standards of behaviour. Only after this had been achieved would developing countries benefit from an effective 'right to development'.

I should add that it is, however, unrealistic to think that at this juncture the whole diplomatic action initiated by developing and socialist States might be given a different turn. Such diplomatic moves are like avalanches: they cannot be stopped; and an attempt to divert their course might prove counter-productive. Yet, in the case at issue it would be salutary to avoid all efforts at contriving formulas to apply the 'right' to individuals or peoples, and to focus instead on the need gradually to implement the 'right' by bringing into effect all the postulates of the NIEO.

In point of fact, it seems that some States are beginning to realize that it would be more realistic to take the approach to which I have just alluded. Thus, in 1980, it was pointed out in the General Assembly by the Chinese delegate that 'the new international economic order would also entail new concepts in international economic law, which would thus be called upon to uphold *the developing countries' right to development*, to do away with the old structure of formal equality and to establish international economic relations on the basis of the equal and sovereign rights of States and such principles as equality and mutual benefit'. On the same occasion the representative of the FRG spoke of 'the obligation to promote the economic development of developing countries', observing that it 'was not expressly mentioned in the [UN] Charter, [but] had become an important principle of the existing international order'. He immediately added, however, that 'unfortunately, that *moral and political responsibility*, which was incumbent upon all States, was not assumed by all'.[16]

A TENTATIVE STOCK-TAKING

215. If one looks back to what has been accomplished since the Second World War in the international community to remove developing nations from their ghetto, the achievements are undoubtedly epoch-making. For one thing, the realization that the 'haves' should assist the 'have-nots' has solidly taken root, with the attendant feeling of social solidarity which had never before manifested itself on the international scene. For another thing, a whole corpus of standards, and a host of institutions have been set up with a view to putting solidarity into practice. Furthermore—and this is perhaps even more important—in many backward countries actual development has taken place over the years. As was stressed in 1977 by the President of the Bank, McNamara, in his address to the Bank's Board of Governors, the past record of development is impressive:

Indeed, historically, it [development] is without precedent. Never has so large a group of human beings—two billion people—achieved so much economic growth in so short a time.

In the quarter century from 1950 to 1975 the average per capita income of the developing world grew at over 3% a year. The present industrialized countries, at a comparable stage in their own development, required a much longer time to advance as far, and attained an annual per capita growth of only 2%.

[16] The statement of the Chinese delegate is in UN document A/C.6/35/SR.70, para. 13. For the statement of the delegate of the FRG see ibid., SR.71, para. 30 (my italics).

Nor was the achievement exclusively economic. Important social progress was made as well. Average life expectancy, for example, was expanded from about 40 years to 50 years. Though 50 is still 30% lower than the longevity currently enjoyed in the industrialized nations, it took Western Europe a century to achieve what the developing nations did in 25 years.[17]

However, three major deficiencies can still be discerned. First, the body of standards has to a great extent remained on a political plane. In other words, it has not taken the shape of legally binding, hence *operative*, rules. This is, of course, but the 'normative' reflection of a political problem. Those standards have not commanded the support of the three major segments of the world community. As I pointed out above (§ 213), the Western industrialized States have not come to share the political philosophy of development launched in 1973–4 by the Third World, and this, of course, has had adverse consequences for the 'peripheral States'. As for socialist countries, although they have indeed supported the demands of poor nations, their contribution to development has been relatively insignificant, first, because only a few of them have reached a degree of industrialization comparable to that of major Western States, and second, because even the more industrialized socialist nations prefer to grant assistance to backward countries on a bilateral basis, hence often with political strings attached.

The second main deficiency lies at the heart of the action for promoting development. Between the late 1960s and the beginning of 1970 a group of enlightened Western intellectuals stressed that the assistance provided by industrialized countries either directly or through international institutions did not actually improve the lot of the vast majority of people in poor countries. Admittedly, this assistance to some extent promoted the economic growth of backward States, but this ultimately benefited the rich strata of the recipient countries, while the underprivileged remained in dire conditions.

The idea of the 'basic needs', was therefore launched by arguing that economic assistance to Third World countries should be geared to the basic needs of the whole population, in the form of commodities such as food, housing, education, etc. Interestingly, a similar stand was taken by McNamara after he became President of the Bank in 1960. He repeatedly stressed that there was both 'uneven growth among countries, and misdirected growth within countries'; in particular he emphasized that growth did not benefit the poor and that a most disturbing trend in development was the decline in the rate of growth of *per capita* income in the poorest countries. In 1977 he forcefully put it as follows:

The truth is that in every developing country the poor are trapped in a set of

---

[17] R. S. McNamara, *Address to the Board of Governors*, 26 September 1977 (Washington, DC, 1977), pp. 5, 10, 11.

circumstances that makes it virtually impossible for them either to contribute to the economic development of their nation, or to share equitably in its benefits.

They are condemned by their situation to remain largely outside the development process. It simply passes them by.

Nor are we talking here about an insignificant minority. We are talking about hundreds of millions of people. They are what I have termed the absolute poor: those trapped in conditions so limited by illiteracy, malnutrition, disease, high infant mortality, and low life expectancy as to be denied the very potential of the genes with which they were born. Their basic human needs are simply not met.[18]

In many important speeches McNamara accordingly underscored the need for 'policies specifically designed to reduce the deprivation among the poorest 40 per cent in developing countries'. To him this prescription was motivated by the need to avert 'the political risks' of rebellion. As he put it: 'Social justice is not merely a moral imperative. It is a political imperative as well.'

The reasons why economic growth does not benefit the poor were tellingly expounded by a number of leading figures from the Third World, such as the Pakistani Mahbub ul Hak, a senior official of the World Bank, formerly in charge of economic planning in Pakistan at the time of General Ayoub Khan; the Egyptian Samir Amin, of the UN Institute in Dakar for Development Planning, or Albert Tevoedjre, a national of Benin, working as the director of the ILO's International Institute for Labour Studies. All these Third World figures (to whom Abi-Saab, the leading Egyptian jurist can be added), have rightly argued that economic growth in poor countries is not enough as long as it is not attended by a radical redistribution of power and wealth there, so that economic progress also entails social progress for all. They have therefore attacked the policy followed in many developing countries, where authoritarian power structures use economic advancement, including foreign economic aid, to prop themselves up.

Suffice it to report here what Mahbub ul Hak related about his own experience in Pakistan. In 1968 after convincing President Khan as to the iniquities of current economic growth, he was asked to draft a new emergency plan to redress the most glaring inequalities, but the President was soon toppled. Ul Hak comments as follows:

One of the bitter lessons he must have learned was that the alliances of privileged groups that he had forged to promote accelerated growth were totally unwilling to let him trim their privileges and that he had few political alliances at his disposal to engineer a meaningful change.[19]

A third stricture has been voiced by certain radical critics which concerns

[18] R. S. McNamara, *Statement to the Board of Governors of the Bank* (Washington, DC, 1972), pp. 3–4.
[19] M. ul Hak, *The Poverty Curtain: Choices for the Third World* (New York, 1976), p. 7.

the very model of development upheld in backward countries. Many Third World nations tend, sometimes unwittingly, to adopt patterns of development and behaviour typical of Western countries where consumerism is the dominant feature. Those critics postulate instead a style of life and also a configuration of needs more consonant with local traditions, or at any rate less oriented towards consumption patterns. This sort of misgiving has been voiced by, among others, Ivan Illich. After forcefully contending that 'the plows of the rich can do as much harm as their swords', he points out:

Rich nations now benevolently impose a straitjacket of traffic jams, hospital confinements and classrooms on the poor nations, and by international agreement call this 'development'. The rich and schooled and old of the world try to share their dubious blessings by foisting their pre-packaged solutions on to the Third World. Traffic jams develop in Sao Paulo, while almost a million northeastern Brazilians flee the drought by walking 500 miles. Latin American doctors get training at the New York Hospital for Special Surgery, which they apply to only a few, while amoebic dysentery remains endemic in slums where 90 per cent of the population live. A tiny minority gets advanced education in basic science in North America—not infrequently paid for by their own governments. If they return at all to Bolivia, they become second-rate teachers of pretentious subjects at La Paz or Cochibamba. The rich export outdated versions of their standard models.[20]

Needless to say, this criticism hits not only industrialized countries but also the poor countries themselves, for, as Illich rightly emphasizes, 'underdevelopment is a state of mind'. The alternative he propounds is based on jettisoning the industrialized countries' pattern, and opting for another model. By way of illustration: developing countries need buses, not a multitude of private cars; paramedics, not medical doctors; safe drinking water, not high-priced surgery; community food storages, not expensive kitchen equipment, and so on. More generally, the belief is now growing that an altogether different model of development is needed, which has been called 'self-reliant' or 'independent' development. It is based on options and methods devised by the needy countries themselves and, even more important, on actions primarily undertaken by those countries, in an effort to promote development 'from inside' (e.g. through an agrarian reform or the more rational exploitation of agriculture).[21]

I said above that if one compares the situation prevalent in poor countries before the Second World War with what has been accomplished since then the achievements are certainly astounding. I should add, however, that if one compares these undisputed successes with the appalling conditions in which the greatest part of the population of those countries still live, one is

---

[20] I. Illich, 'Outwitting the "Developed Countries"', in *Underdevelopment and Development*, ed. H. Bernstein (London, 1978), pp. 357, 359, 361.

[21] See J.-P. Cot, *A l'épreuve du pouvoir—Le Tiers-mondisme pour quoi faire?* (Paris, 1984), 49-75.

overwhelmed by a profound feeling of dejection. The problems still to be faced are so immense, and of such a decidedly political and economic dimension, that the jurist is left feeling like one of those intellectuals of whom a well-known writer said that they amused themselves painting still lives on the walls of a sinking ship.[22] Yet despite the enormity of the tasks and the gaping chasm between what has been done and what remains to be achieved, I believe the sediment of hundreds of years of inequality and oppression can be washed away.

[22] B. Brecht, 'Fünf Schwierigkeiten beim Schreiben der Wahrheit', in *Mutter Courage and ihre Kinder* (Berlin, 1956), p. 89.

14

From Sovereignty to Co-operation: The Common Heritage of Mankind

GENERAL

216. IN our search for an Ariadne's thread to lead us through the intricacies of international relations we stumble upon a new concept creeping in and out of the interstices of international reality: the 'common heritage of mankind'. It designates a new way of distributing wealth in the world community and, as the reader may have guessed already, has been propounded by developing countries. To grasp all its implications it is necessary first to take a look at the traditional principles regulating the appropriation of things and territory.

We shall see that these principles were based on the postulates of sovereignty, whereas the new trends emerging in the world community are intended to meet—admittedly amidst evident conflicts and contradictions—the demands of co-operation and, indeed, constitute an original scheme for co-operation. The concept of the common heritage of mankind is therefore strongly indicative of the tensions and clashes between the 'old' and the 'new' law and consequently repays close scrutiny.

TRADITIONAL PRINCIPLES CONCERNING THE APPROPRIATION OF TERRITORIES

217. In 'classical' international law the 'physical dimension' of State activity was regulated in fairly simple terms: the earth, sea, and air were divided up into areas subject to the sovereign authority of States on the principles that: (1) whoever possessed a territory and exercised actual control over it acquired a legal title; (2) as far as *terrae nullius*, that is, areas subject to no one, were concerned, mere discovery on the principle 'first come first served', was not enough, for actual display of sovereignty coupled with the intent to wield authority, were needed. On the strength of these principles the whole planet became gradually subject to the rule of one or other sovereign State. The air above each territory was considered subject to the sovereignty of the territorial State *usque ad sidera*, namely, up to the stars, but, of course, this stipulation was only theoretical in nature, for

States did not possess any means of exercising *de facto* control over outer space.

The only exception to this partition among competing claims was that pertaining to the high seas, which were subject to the principle of freedom as a *res communis omnium*, that is, a thing belonging to everybody.

It is apparent that the distribution of space among the various members of the world community was inspired by aggressive individualism and a *laissez-faire* attitude: whoever had the physical means of acquiring a portion of territory on land was legitimized by law to claim sovereign rights over it. As a consequence, the more powerful—militarily and economically—a State, the greater its chance of acquiring a bigger territory. Of course, possession of a huge territory often made for the military and economic strength of the State, and was instrumental in its becoming even bigger. Consequently, the fact that the high seas were considered a 'common good' should not lead us to believe that this legal regime had been the outcome of feelings of solidarity. Had a State, or group of States, proved strong enough to claim the exclusive right to use the high seas, it would have had no hesitation in depriving the other members of the world community of access to it. Furthermore, *res communis omnium* means that every State is authorized to use a certain good for its own purposes and in its own interest. The *res communis* concept is not community-orientated, but geared to the self-interest of each and every member of the community. In addition, whereas the high seas were in theory open to all States, in practice poor countries did not greatly benefit from the economic, commercial, and military advantages accruing from their use, or at any rate they benefited from them to far less an extent than powerful countries. Similarly, the fact that sovereign rights over territorial waters and the air space above State territory were bestowed by international law on any country (except of course for the landlocked States in the case of territorial waters) regardless of its economic conditions, did not mean that States were in effect equal. However, the automatic attribution of those sovereign rights was a 'democratic' way of, at least legally, levelling out inequities between States.

THE MODERN EXTENSION OF STATE SOVEREIGNTY: THE CONTINENTAL SHELF, THE CONTIGUOUS ZONE, THE EXCLUSIVE ECONOMIC ZONE

218. It should not be assumed that this direction of the world community is the hallmark of the past solely. State sovereignty, nationalism, and *laissez-faire* attitude extend as far today and indeed constitute a significant feature of the present international community. Individualistic and sovereignty-orientated acquisition of territory, or of control over territory, has manifested itself in various forms: (1) in the subjection of the continental shelf to the sovereignty of the coastal State (see Article 1 of the 1958 Convention on the matter and Articles 76-7 of the 1982 Convention on the Law of the Sea; under Article 76.1 'the continental shelf of a coastal State comprises the sea-bed and the subsoil of the submarine areas that extend beyond its territorial sea [i.e. beyond 12 nautical miles] throughout the natural prolongation of its land territory to the outer edge of the continental margin, or to a distance of 200 nautical miles' from the coast); (2) in the establishment of the contiguous zone (see Article 24 of the 1958 Convention on the Territorial Sea and Article 33 of the 1982 Convention on the Law of the Sea; the contiguous zone, which 'may not extend beyond 24 nautical miles' from the coast, is an area where the coastal State may exercise the control necessary 'to prevent infringement of its customs, fiscal, immigration or sanitary laws and regulations within its territory or territorial sea', as well as 'punish infringement of the above laws and regulations committed within its territory or territorial sea'); (3) in the customary recognition of exclusive fishing zones off the coast of some States, beyond their territorial sea; (4) in the establishment in the 1970s of the exclusive economic zone, which stretches up to 200 nautical miles and denotes an area where the coastal State has the exclusive right to explore and exploit 'the natural resources, whether living or non-living, of the waters superjacent to the sea-bed and of the sea-bed and its subsoil' (see Articles 55-7 of the 1982 Convention on the Law of the Sea).

That the 'territorial' principle of national appropriation has to a great extent shattered the principle of freedom of the high seas is hardly surprising. As R.-J. Dupuy has stated, 'two great winds have never ceased to blow over the seas: the wind from the open sea, that of freedom, and the wind from the land, that of sovereignty'.[1] It is an indisputable fact that in recent times developing countries have found it more convenient and better suited to their interests to insist on the concept of sovereignty. They hold the view that, at a time when technology increasingly brings to light mineral and fishing resources lying off their coasts, the principle of freedom would only benefit powerful States, endowed with huge fleets and consequently able to fish thousands of miles away from their own coasts. True, developing countries might have suggested that the resources in the exclusive economic zone should be used and administered by the UN, or by another international agency, so as to ensure that the proceeds be equitably shared by under-developed countries, and in particular by those of them most in need of economic and financial resources. Out of sheer self-interest, however, they have preferred to discard any idea of solidarity or joint utilization of resources and to opt for a nationalist approach.

[1] R.-J. Dupuy, *The Law of the Sea: Current Problems* (Dobbs Ferry, 1974), p. 14.

THE CONCEPT OF 'COMMON HERITAGE OF MANKIND' AS A NEW GUIDING PRINCIPLE FOR THE JOINT EXPLOITATION OF NATURAL RESOURCES

The Emergence of the Concept

219. It was in 1967 that this concept was first propounded in an international forum as a standard by which to establish a new regulation for the exploration and exploitation of the resources of the high seas. It was forcefully championed by the Maltese ambassador Arvid Pardo. (Pardo noted in his statement of 1 November 1967 to the First Committee of the General Assembly, that the notion had been used previously, in July 1967, by the 'World Peace Through Law Conference', an international gathering of private persons.)

Ambassador Pardo specified that fresh developments in the field of oceanography as well as technological progress were making it possible to benefit from the immense wealth existing on the sea-bed and the ocean floor beyond national jurisdiction. In short, the abyss of the ocean was full of concretions, commonly called nodules, irregularly spherical in shape like potatoes, ranging from 0.5 to 25 centimeters in diameter, and containing manganese, iron, cobalt, copper, nickel or lead. Equally vast were the resources lying beneath the ocean floor: petroleum, gas, and sulphur deposits (later on, however, it was discovered that petroleum resources were not exploitable for technical reasons, mainly owing to the great depths at which they were located). Since the 1958 Convention on the Continental Shelf provided in Article 1 for the exploitability criterion, by which each coastal State was entitled to extend its sovereign rights over the sea-bed as far as it could exploit it (see § 218), the Maltese diplomat felt there was the danger that at least the more powerful States would gradually expand their national jurisdiction. These countries might find it profitable to do so both for obvious economic reasons and also for security and defence considerations (tracking devices to detect enemy nuclear submarines could be installed in suitable areas of the deep seas and the ocean floor; the installation of fixed military equipment on the ocean floor might prove useful, for example in the deployment of anti-ballistic missile systems; furthermore mobile near-bottom nuclear missile systems could be developed which, while immune from detection, could provide immense offensive capability). This process, Ambassador Pardo stated:

... will lead to a competitive scramble for sovereign rights over the land underlying the world's seas and oceans, surpassing in magnitude and in its implications last century's colonial scramble for territory in Asia and Africa. The consequences will be very grave: at the very least a dramatic escalation of the arms race and sharply increasing world tensions, also caused by the intolerable injustice that would reserve the plurality of the world's resources for the exclusive benefit of less than a handful of nations. The strong would get stronger, the rich richer, and among the rich themselves there would arise an increasing and insuperable differentiation between two or three and the remainder. Between the very few dominant powers, suspicions and tensions would reach unprecedented levels. Traditional activities on the high seas would be curtailed and, at the same time, the world would face the growing danger of permanent damage to the marine environment through radioactive and other pollution: this is a virtually inevitable consequence of the present situation.[2]

In Pardo's view, the only sensible alternative to these disastrous consequences was the establishment of an international legal regime to ensure that the sea-bed and the ocean floor were exploited solely for peaceful purposes, and for the benefit of mankind as a whole. Clearly, at the outset, Pardo's primary concern was for the peaceful exploitation of these areas and for the economic advantages deriving therefrom. However, the diplomat soon added (particularly in his statements to the General Assembly of 29 October 1968, and of 20 March 1969 and in the statement to the Consultative Assembly of the Council of Europe of 3 December 1970) that the international regime to be established along the lines proposed by Malta should also aim at stimulating scientific research in marine areas and at preventing pollution. Consequently, the resulting picture eventually revolved around five points. (1) The sea-bed and the ocean floor were to be excluded from the possible appropriation or use of individual States. In other words, unlike the high seas, they were not to be made a *res communis omnium*, an area which anybody could exploit and use, but were to belong to mankind as a whole (as was later stated in the UN by the delegate of Peru, 'humanity [is] the only owner of the area and its resources').[3] (2) Control and administration of the exploitation of the area was to be entrusted to an international agency, which would use the resources of the area in the interest of mankind. In the view of Malta (a view subsequently shared by other developing countries such as Tanzania and a group of thirteen Latin-American States)[4] this meant that the revenue from such exploitation should primarily go to developing countries, admittedly after defraying the cost of exploration and exploitation and after setting aside a certain sum for the protection of the marine environment. (3) The sea-bed and the ocean floor were not to be used for military purposes. (4) Measures were to be taken to protect the environment and prevent pollution. (5) Marine research was to be promoted.

[2] A. Pardo, *The Common Heritage: Selected Papers on Oceans and World Order, 1967–74* (Valletta, 1975), pp. 31, 64, 85.
[3] See UN document A/AC.138/SC.I/SR.36, p. 47.
[4] The draft put forward by thirteen Latin-American countries is in UN document A/AC.138/49.

Clearly, the Maltese proposals were very bold and innovative. As Pardo put it, somewhat too enthusiastically, in his statement of 29 October 1968 to the First Committee of the General Assembly: the common heritage concept was 'the key that will unlock the door of the future'. The concept radically departed from the traditional sovereignty-oriented *laissez-faire* approach, geared to national self-interest and totally oblivious of the common good, and in particular of the condition of the 'have-nots'. As Pardo noted at the initial stage of the UN Sea-bed Committee, the 'common heritage' was a 'socialist concept'. However, as we shall presently see, this declaration was challenged by socialist countries. It was also stated that the concept was an attempt to replace the idea of freedom by that of justice. It seems more likely that the concept was, in fact, inspired by a 'welfare State' philosophy, according to which existing economic and social inequalities were to be eliminated by the joint efforts of the 'haves', both through a feeling of solidarity and also because of an awareness that in the long run the result would be beneficial to all members of the community.

To the extent that it was geared to a new mode of distributing wealth, the 'common heritage' concept was motivated by the interest of poor countries in keeping the hands of rich States off a newly discovered source of wealth and endeavouring to profit as much as possible from it themselves by taking advantage of the technology of industrially advanced States. To this extent, the design of developing countries was part of a political struggle of one group of the world community against another. However, the concept had also other important facets: it propounded the peaceful use of the ocean floor, the protection of the environment, and the promotion of marine research. In this respect, the proposals of developing countries coincided with the interests of the whole of mankind, for it clearly lay in the interest of developed countries as well, to meet the three points just mentioned.

The gist of the Maltese proposal was, however, immediately perceived by developed countries as being the new mode of distribution of ocean riches. It is hardly surprising that the latter's reaction was lukewarm. The USSR and the other socialist countries expressed misgivings and tried to gain time. A delegate from a socialist country observed that 'Obtaining profit without working is against socialism. It is just like an absentee-landlord theory.'[5]

Pardo went out of his way to explain to them that it was in their interest to accept his proposals. In his speech of 20 March 1969 to the Legal Subcommittee of the Committee on the Peaceful Uses of the Seabed and the Ocean Floor—a body set up by the General Assembly at the instigation of Malta—he pointed out:

[5] The statement of a socialist delegate is mentioned by S. Oda, 'New Law of the Sea and Common Heritage of Mankind: Some Comments', in *Legal Aspects of the New International Economic Order*, ed. K. Hossain (Oxford, 1980), p. 171.

... The socialist world does not have easy access to the world's oceans. It is bounded by the icy Arctic in the north and by closed or marginal seas the significant, but limited, resources of which it must share with others. The socialist world cannot realistically count on being able to participate significantly and securely in the exploitation of the immense non-living resources of the bed of the world's oceans except under international aegis. Hence to put the matter bluntly and undiplomatically: in preventing the establishment of a viable and effective international regime, should this in fact be the policy determined upon, the socialist world would lose what is possibly a unique opportunity to secure equal access to resources which will certainly become increasingly valuable in the peaceful competition between different social systems.[6]

Gradually the Soviet Union changed its attitude. Thus, interestingly, in 1971 it submitted to the UN a draft treaty on the use of the sea-bed for peaceful purposes which proposed (in Article 8) that:

The industrial exploration of the sea-bed and the subsoil thereof and the exploitation of their resources shall be carried out for the benefit of mankind as a whole, irrespective of the geographical location of States, whether coastal or land-locked, and taking into particular consideration the interests and needs of the developing countries.[7]

However, no details were given as regards the tricky questions of the issuing of licences for the exploitation of the resources and the distribution of benefits.

As for Western developed countries, their attitude was no less reserved. True, as early as 1967 President Johnson of the US had indicated in his message to Congress his determination to work with all nations to develop the seas for the benefit of mankind'.[8] However, this did not mean that the US or, for that matter, any other industrialized countries—the only States possessing the technology necessary for the exploitation of the areas in question—were willing to share the revenues of such exploitation equally with developing countries. Much less were developed States disposed to accept the proposal that a large share of the profits deriving from that exploitation should go to developing countries.

Much debate ensued within the General Assembly between 1967 and 1970. Most States came to accept the notion of 'common heritage of mankind' although only gradually, and amidst strong resistance (for instance, in 1969 countries such as Bulgaria, Czechoslovakia, France, Italy, and even Ethiopia, expressed the view that the concept at issue was vague, lacked legal content, and was subject to varying interpretations. And Poland con-

[6] Pardo, op. cit., 85.
[7] The Soviet draft of 1971 is in UN document A/AC.138/43 and A.84.21, Annex.
[8] President Johnson's statement is quoted by L. Henkin, *Law for the Sea's Mineral Resources* (New York, 1968), p. 52.

sidered discussion of the concept outdated and impractical).[9] Faced with the opposition, or at least the lukewarm attitude of industrialized countries, Third World nations soon realized that a major danger in strategy lay in permitting industrialized countries to start to exploit the areas unilaterally pending the hammering out of an international treaty. Consequently they had the General Assembly adopt a resolution (2574-D-XXIV, of 15 December 1969), which declared:

... pending the establishment of the aforementioned international regime:

(a) States and persons, physical or juridical, are bound to refrain from all activities of exploitation of the resources of the area of the sea-bed and ocean floor, and the subsoil thereof, beyond the limits of national jurisdiction;

(b) no claim to any part of that area or its resources shall be recognized.

The passing of this resolution was, however, a Pyrrhic victory, for it was adopted by a vote of sixty-four in favour (developing countries plus Sweden), twenty-eight against (Western and socialist countries, plus Ghana and Malta, which probably considered that the text was not strong enough), and twenty-eight absentions (African, Asian, and Latin-American countries plus Greece, Israel, Romania, Spain, and Turkey). Developed States made it clear before or after the vote that they did not regard themselves as in any way bound by the resolution.

Despite this setback for the Third World, the discussions that took place in the UN and, above all, the debate that led in 1970 to the adoption (by 108 votes to none, with fourteen abstentions) by the General Assembly of the landmark resolution 2749 (XXV) containing the 'Declaration of Principles' on the matter, made it clear that a general consensus of opinion on at least a few major points had been achieved. First, there was general acceptance of the principle that the sea-bed and the ocean floor beyond national jurisdiction must not be subject to appropriation by States, and that no State must claim or exercise sovereign rights over any part thereof. Second, a broad consensus of interpretation evolved of the concept of 'common heritage of mankind', which clearly indicated, in the view of developing countries, that the area under consideration was not a *res communis omnium*, in other words, that States were not entitled to make competitive use of its resources. This, it should be emphasized, was not considered by developed States as contrary to their own interests, for their conception of 'common heritage of mankind' simply implied that States willing to exploit the resources of the area unilaterally, had to do so not only in their own interest but also on behalf of the world community as a whole (for example, by earmarking some of the profits for less developed States). Third, in the period under consideration substantial agreement was

---

[9] The statements made by Bulgaria and other countries are mentioned in *Yearbook of the United Nations 1969*, p. 61.

reached on the idea that the exploitation of the resources was to be carried out in accordance with the international regime to be established. Furthermore, agreement was reached on the need to use the area exclusively for peaceful purposes, to pay due regard to marine research and to prevent 'damage to the flora and fauna'. However, the subject on which dissent persisted concerned the specific way of utilizing the resources; the structure and powers of the international agency to be established; the role of private enterprise; and the criteria for the sharing of profits. As for the main bone of contention, the resolution merely stated that the legal regime to be established in the new treaty of a universal validity should

... ensure the equitable sharing by States in the benefits derived therefrom [i.e. from the orderly and safe development and rational management of the area and its resources], taking into particular consideration the interests and needs of the developing countries, whether land-locked or coastal.

The Common Heritage of Mankind Concept in the 1982 Convention on the Law of the Sea

220.   Let us now take a quick look at how the concept of common heritage of mankind has been enshrined in two treaties, the Convention on the Moon and Other Celestial Bodies of 1979 and the Convention on the Law of the Sea of 1982. For the sake of clarity I shall start with the latter, which is also the more important.

Article 136 of the Convention on the Law of the Sea provides that 'The Area [i.e. the sea-bed and ocean floor and subsoil thereof, beyond the limits of national jurisdiction] and its resources are the common heritage of mankind'. Article 137 then goes on to specify that no portion of the area and its resources can be appropriated or made subject to State sovereignty, that 'all rights in the resources of the Area are vested in mankind as a whole, on whose behalf the Authority [i.e. The International Sea-Bed Authority, an organization instituted under Articles 156–91 of the Convention] shall act' (para. 2). The provision then stipulates:

These resources are not subject to alienation. The minerals recovered from the Area, however, may only be alienated in accordance with this Part [of the Convention] and the rules, the regulations and procedures of the Authority.

No less strictly, para. 3 provides:

No State or natural or juridical person shall claim, acquire or exercise rights with respect to the minerals recovered from the Area except in accordance with this Part [of the Convention]. Otherwise, no such claim, acquisition or exercise of such rights shall be recognized.

Thus, the legal regime of the Area and its resources is only and exclusively regulated by the Convention, which rules out any regulation or control by individual States.

In addition to excluding national appropriation and providing for an equitable sharing of resources, the Convention includes other features characteristic of the 'common heritage' concept, namely the peaceful use of the Area (Article 141), the promotion of marine scientific research (Article 143), and the protection of the marine environment (Article 145).

The regime of exploitation of the Area established by the Convention can be summarized as follows. All activities of exploration and exploitation of the Area must be organized, carried out and controlled by the Sea-bed Authority (whose Assembly is made up of all the contracting States, while the Council consists of thirty-six States selected in accordance with special criteria laid down in Article 161). The activities shall be carried out either by the Enterprise (an organ of the Authority charged not only with the exploration and exploitation but also with transporting, processing, and marketing the minerals recovered from the Area), or by State parties, or by State enterprises, or by natural or juridical persons having the nationality of, or being controlled by, a State party. In case the various activities are carried out by entities other than the Enterprise, the former may do so only after receiving an authorization for production from the Authority. Each area for which an entity applies shall be divided into two parts: one to be exploited by the applicant, the other by the Enterprise (either by itself, or in joint venture with the interested State or entity). The financial terms of the contracts to be concluded by the aforementioned entities with the Authority are regulated in detail by Article 13 of Annex III to the Convention. In short, a contractor must pay a fee 'for the administrative cost of processing an application for approval of a plan of work in the form of a contract', a fixed annual fee from the date of the contract's entry into force, and also, as from the date of commencement of commercial production, either a production charge or the fixed annual fee, whichever is greater. In addition, the contractor is duty-bound to transfer technology and scientific knowledge to the Enterprise (Article 144).

The Convention, however, does not specify how the sharing of benefits shall occur. It merely provides in Article 160 that the Assembly, 'the supreme organ of the Authority', shall consider and approve

... the rules, regulations and procedures on the equitable sharing or financial and other economic benefits derived from activities in the Area and the payments and contributions made pursuant to Art. 82 [providing for the payment of contribution in kind by coastal States in respect of the exploitation of the non-living resources of the continental shelf beyond 200 nautical miles], taking into particular consideration the interests and needs of developing States and peoples who have not attained full independence or other self-governing status.

Thus, once more the precise determination of such sharing or the criteria for undertaking it have been postponed until the Authority's activities begin, thereby opening the door to exploitation.

Despite this gap—which was no doubt necessary in order to achieve a very broad measure of agreement on the establishment of the legal regime of the Area—this regime is of enormous importance because for the first time a complex and detailed set of regulations for the exploitation of immense wealth has been laid down at an international level. Nevertheless, it contains two shortcomings which should not be overlooked.

First, Chile's proposal that the Convention itself should proclaim that the provision on the common heritage of mankind belongs to *jus cogens*, was rejected because of the strong opposition of industrialized countries.[10] This refusal implies that a conspicuous and important segment of the world community believes that it is not illegal to enter into international agreements derogating from the legal regime established by the 1982 Convention. As this regime obviously presupposes the universal consent of all member States of the international community to become operative, the rebuffal of that proposal casts a dark shadow over the future of the regime.

However, the other flaw is even more serious. To a large extent it is closely bound up with the former, and is indicative of the same trend of industrialized countries to 'opt out' of (or rather, not to submit to) the international regulation established in the Convention. A number of prominent developed countries have recently passed laws allowing national companies to initiate unilateral exploration and exploitation of the ocean floor and its resources until such time as the Convention enters in force for each of them (the US in 1980, with implementing regulations of 1981 and 1982; the FRG in 1980 and 1982; the UK and France in 1981; Japan and the USSR in 1982).

Admittedly, all of these laws provide in terms that their regime is only provisional and that it will be repealed as soon as an international convention becomes binding on each State concerned. Furthermore, they set the same time-limit (1 January 1988) before which no exploitation can begin and only exploration can be undertaken. Finally, most national legislation (excepting the French) stipulates that part of the proceeds of the exploitation shall be set aside for use by an international authority or by developing countries.

The fact, however, remains that the controversy surrounding this legislation shows that a number of prominent States, while being prepared to grant a small amount of the proceeds of their unilateral deep sea-bed mining to developing countries, do not accept the quintessence of the 'common heritage' concept, namely: (1) the fact that it is for an international autho-

---

[10] See Conference document MC/14, 29 August 1979 as well as G/P/9, 5 August 1980.

rity to decide how the ocean floor should be explored and exploited, and to what extent the benefits deriving from such activity should go to developing countries; (2) the duty of industrialized countries to transfer their technology and know-how to the international authority, and through it to poor countries.

It could be argued that all those national legislative acts are contrary to the present drive of the international community towards solidarity. One might even go so far as to maintain that those acts are at odds with existing international principles, in particular with the 'principle' concerning the common heritage of mankind. Alternatively, one could point out that those laws are contrary to the principle whereby until a treaty is ratified States must refrain from acts which would defeat the object and purpose of the treaty (reliance upon this principle might be warranted by the fact that the resources of the sea-bed are exhaustible). However, in the light of the hard truth that those countries rank among the holders of real power in the world community and are unlikely to back down from their present position, the objections voiced above are likely to strike the reader as merely the idle musings of a jurist.

The Moon and Other Celestial Bodies as Common Heritage of Mankind

221.   Until the launch in 1957 of the first rockets and satellites into outer space (that is, the space around the earth beyond an altitude of about 100 miles), States all agreed that each had jurisdiction over the air above its own territory. However, as soon as the USSR and the US began to launch rockets and to orbit satellites, a consensus of opinion instantly emerged to the effect that they were not to ask for the authorization of the States above whose territory the satellites were orbiting. All States bowed to the technological superiority of the two Superpowers and gave up their (theoretical) right of jurisdiction over the outer space above their respective territory. As a consequence, outer space was immediately considered as a *res communis omnium*, that is, open to everybody for exploration and use. The dangers following from the possible orbiting by the Superpowers of weapons of mass destruction, as well as the fact that in practice, for many years, only the two Superpowers would make use of outer space, prompted UN members to rally round certain major points of agreement. After a few years of discussion, the UN General Assembly unanimously adopted a very important Resolution (1721-XVI, of 20 December 1961) followed by Resolution 1962-XVIII of 13 December 1963, and on 27 January 1967, by a Treaty on Outer Space. The Resolution and the Treaty embodied the following fundamental principles: (1) outer space and celestial bodies were not subject to national appropriation by claim of sovereignty, by means of use or occupation, or by any other means; (2) the 'exploration and use of outer space', including the moon and other celestial bodies, was to be carried out 'for the benefit and in the interests of all countries, irrespective of their degree of economic or scientific development, and shall be the province of all mankind'; (3) outer space must not be used to put into orbit round the earth, or station in any other manner, objects carrying nuclear weapons or other weapons of mass destruction; (4) the moon and other celestial bodies were to be used exclusively for peaceful purposes.

In other words, as far as outer space was concerned, States did not go beyond the concept of *res communis omnium*. Except for the ban on orbiting weapons of mass destruction and damaging the environment (Article 9 of the Treaty), outer space was subjected to a legal regime akin to that of the high seas. The notion that the exploration and use of outer space is 'the province of all mankind' (Article 1 of the Treaty) is an emphatic proposition which should not lead one to believe that outer space is subject to the legal regime of the 'common heritage of mankind'. In fact, the Treaty did not impose on States exploring and using the area in question specific duties to the effect that such activity should be carried out in the interest of all mankind. And it is common knowledge that each of the Superpowers is using outer space primarily, if not exclusively, in its own interest (except, of course, for certain duties of co-operation undertaken by treaty with a few other countries).

Some headway was made a few years later with regard to the moon and other celestial bodies. The successful landing on the moon in 1969 of a US spacecraft and the fact that moon rocks were brought back to Earth alerted States and world opinion to the question of the exploitation of resources existing on celestial bodies. Long discussions and negotiations ensued in the UN Legal Subcommittee on the Peaceful Uses of Outer Space and led on 5 December 1979 to the passing by the General Assembly of the Agreement Governing the Activities of States on the Moon and Other Celestial Bodies.

The idea of considering these resources as the 'common heritage of mankind' was propounded in 1970 by Argentina, which put forward a draft agreement ably illustrated by its delegate A. A. Cocca.[11] In short it was proposed that 'all substances originating in the Moon or other celestial bodies' should be regarded as 'natural resources' belonging to the common heritage of mankind. (Subsequently, in 1973, following the broader proposals of Egypt and India, Argentina extended the concept so as to cover the moon itself and the other celestial bodies proper.) In the Argentinian draft the common heritage concept implied that the benefits from those resources should be 'made available to all peoples, without discrimination of any kind', with particular attention being paid to the needs of developing coun-

[11] See UN document A/AC.105/C.2/L.71 and *corr.* 1.

tries, while at the same time paying due regard to 'the rights of those [countries] undertaking these activities' (i.e., the exploration and use of resources on celestial bodies). However, no precise guidelines as regards the specific modes of sharing the profits were forthcoming.

Strikingly, in a proposed draft treaty of 1971 the USSR failed to refer to the concept of common heritage.[12] It only emphasized that no right of ownership could be claimed over the moon, its surface and subsoil by States and other entities exploring it. Thus the focus of the Soviet draft was on the idea that the space environment was a *res communis omnium*: everybody could use it but nobody could appropriate it. In 1973 the USSR submitted a document expressing misgivings about the concept of common heritage. In its view, the term 'heritage', or the equivalent term 'inheritance' used in Soviet civil law, were inseparably bound up with the concept of ownership: without the concept of property and property rights those of 'inheritance' and succession were meaningless. Now, according to the 1967 Treaty on Outer Space, celestial bodies could not become any person's thing or any person's property. The Soviet document went on to say that 'consequently, portions of the surface or subsurface of the moon cannot be the object of civil law transactions ... Nor can they, quite naturally, be the object of succession. A thing that belongs to nobody cannot pass into any person's possession by succession'. The Soviet document concluded that celestial bodies, being 'the province of all mankind' under the 1967 Treaty, were 'available for the undivided and common use of all States on earth, but [were] not jointly owned by them'. These words appear to indicate that the USSR preferred the concept of *res communis omnium* to that of common heritage. It should, however, be added that the USSR also declared itself willing to reach a 'satisfactory compromise' on the matter. (It is interesting to note that in a subsequent working paper Argentina rebutted what it called the 'philosophical or philological analysis' of the Soviet document, pointing out, among other things, that one should speak of a 'common property' of the moon and other celestial bodies in the sense of 'beneficial ownership' (*dominio util*) that is, ownership comprising joint enjoyment, receipt of the fruits, and profit).

Initially, the US was not enthusiastic either about the concept. Admittedly, in 1958 President Eisenhower had called upon States 'to promote the peaceful use of space and to utilize the new knowledge obtainable from space science and technology for the benefit of mankind'. This statement had been echoed by C. Lodge, the US delegate to the UN on 2 September 1958, when he said that it was the intention of the US for 'outer space to be used for the benefit of all mankind'.[13] These statements were, however,

[12] See UN document A/8391 4 June 1971. The Soviet document of 1973 is in A/AC.105/196, Annex I.

[13] The declaration by C. Lodge is in *Introduction to Outer Space: An Explanatory Statement by the President's Science Advisory Committee* (Washington, DC, 1958), p. 1.

advisedly couched in loose terms, and in practice did not commit the US to any position, save for the view that the outer space could not be appropriated by anybody. The US changed its stand after Argentina tabled its proposal, and in 1972 it submitted a working paper upholding the concept of common heritage.[14]

International pressure and a series of proposals by countries such as Egypt, India, Iran, Brazil, Chile, Indonesia, Mexico, Nigeria, Romania, Sierra Leone, and Venezuela, eventually led to the adoption, in 1979, of a few provisions of the Treaty upholding the common heritage concept both for the moon and other celestial bodies and for their natural resources (Articles 4.1; 6; 11 and 18). These provisions embody the five elements characteristic of the common heritage concept, namely, (1) the exclusion of a right of appropriation; (2) the duty to exploit the resources in the interest of mankind in such a way as to benefit all, including developing countries; (3) the duty to explore and exploit for peaceful purposes only; (4) the duty to pay due regard to scientific research; (5) the duty duly to protect the environment.

The significance of the adoption of the Treaty, great though it is, should not be overestimated as far as the common heritage concept is concerned. In fact the Treaty commanded unanimous support because the crucial point, that of how to share the benefits deriving from the exploitation of resources in outer space, was left open. The Treaty merely postponed the question, by providing in Article 11 paras. 5 and 7, that an 'international regime' was to be established as soon as the exploitation of the natural resources of the moon was about to become feasible, and that one of its main purposes was:

... an equitable sharing by all States Parties in the benefits derived from the resources, whereby the interests and the needs of the developing countries, as well as the efforts of those countries which have contributed either directly or indirectly to the exploration of the moon, shall be given special consideration.

Mention should also be made of the interpretation of the expression 'equitable sharing' insisted upon by the US whereby the choice of 'equitable' instead of 'equal' means that all States need not be put on an equal footing, but better treatment should be reserved to the States actively engaged in exploring or otherwise exploiting outer space. This interpretation, it is plain, may further weaken the concept of common heritage as advocated by developing countries, by watering down one of its basic implications, namely, that the profits of the exploitation of natural resources should primarily accrue to the Third World. By the same token, no provision was made for a moratorium on the exploitation of the resources pending the drafting of

[14] The US document is in A/AC.105/C.2 (XI), Working Paper 12. See also A/AC.105/196, Annex 1.

the treaty establishing an international regime. The developing countries had consistently demanded that such a moratorium be set up, but the US had no less consistently and successfully opposed it.

CONCLUDING REMARKS

222. The introduction of the concept of common heritage of mankind no doubt represents a great advance in the world community. In particular, as I emphasized above (§216), it marks the passage from the traditional postulate of sovereignty to that of co-operation. In other words, the expression 'common heritage of mankind' succinctly expresses—with all its merits and limitations—the 'new model' of world community which has gradually emerged since 1945.

Although it has not yet displayed all its potential, the concept has already changed legal habits and institutions and introduced momentous new notions as regards the right to appropriate certain resources, their peaceful use and joint exploitation, and the need to promote scientific research and protect the environment. These are lasting and by now undisputed achievements which accrue to the benefit of all mankind, both of the rich and of the poor. By contrast, the real linchpin of the concept, the idea of equitable sharing of profits, both in the extreme formulation of Malta and other States (§219)—a formulation subsequently echoed by such countries as Sri Lanka (for which the system should imply that 'each country would contribute according to its capacity and each would receive according to its needs')[15]—and in the more moderate versions propounded by others, was advanced in the exclusive (or primary) interest of developing countries. It is therefore hardly surprising that it has been strongly opposed by industrialized States. That idea has not yet acquired a world-wide legal status: as we have seen, it was embodied, in very loose terms, in the 1979 Treaty on the Moon (but its actual implementation has been postponed until the future drafting of another treaty) and subsequently, with a somewhat less general and vague wording, in the 1982 Convention on the Law of the Sea. However, a few developed countries have already passed legislation on deep-sea mining which is, to a large extent, inconsistent with the relevant provisions of the Convention of 1982. In other words we are here in the presence of a concept which arouses political antagonism and which, for lack of a consensus of opinion in the world community, proves difficult to put into a concise and legally binding form. It seems probable that it stands no chance of being accepted by industrialized countries until it has been duly emasculated so as to take account of their interests.

---

[15] The statement by Sri Lanka was made in 1980, in the UN General Assembly, on the occasion of the discussion on the NIEO: see A/C.6/35/SR.70, para. 20.

However important the common heritage concept may be for the future co-operation among nations, let us not forget that the approach championed by developing countries is based on a contradiction. It is indeed striking that at the very time developing countries appropriated the exclusive economic zone, they also declared that the ocean beyond that zone was part of the common heritage of mankind. It has been objected that the former area might also have been declared part of the same heritage. But national self-interest prevailed, no doubt because in the exclusive economic zone coastal States, even the poor ones, were able to exploit their own resources directly. In the area beyond the zone, the 'have-nots', being totally unable to engage in highly technical forms of exploration and exploitation, urged that the States able to do so should act in the interests of everyone.

That this contradiction exists cannot be denied. One cannot expect States to behave in a logical, rational and consistent manner. States are primarily motivated by self-interest, although in some instances, as in the one under consideration, the self-interest they pursue may, in the end, prove to be short-term only. This criticism should not, however, overshadow the important fact that in other respects the concept of common heritage has served the interests of humanity at large and that consequently, by putting it forward, developing countries have acted as the mouthpiece of the whole of mankind.

15

Epilogue

223. WE have now come to the end of our journey. It has been long and tiresome at times—at least for the writer who, unlike the reader, has been unable to benefit from those moments of relaxation which, according to tradition, in the Middle Ages allowed amanuenses to write relieving glosses on the margin of laboriously transcribed manuscripts ('thank God, it is growing dark and soon I'll get some warm soup', and similar frivolities). I surmise that the reader is impatiently counting the remaining pages. Let me therefore quickly try to set forth a few concluding observations. I shall restrict myself to reviewing the four general themes of this book, which have coloured the warp and weft of my analysis. As stated in the Preface, they are: first, the unhomogeneous character of present international law, a law created by three competing groups of States, each inspired by a different ideology and by specific interests; second, the coexistence in the world community of two distinct patterns of legal order, one—that of traditional or classical law—characteristic of the origins of the community, the other—that of the new law—born after the First World War to a large extent under the aegis of the 'newcomers': socialist and developing countries; third, the role which, given the present rifts and dissensions, law can play in a community still dominated by sovereign States, and the extent to which it serves as a significant factor in transactions between those omnipotent juggernauts; fourth, and last, the place assigned to individuals, to private groups and to non-governmental organizations—the pariahs of the international community—in the present world order, and the extent to which they may claim a hearing from rulers, whether in their own country or abroad.

INTERNATIONAL LAW IN A DEEPLY DIVIDED WORLD: DIFFERENCES AND CONSEQUENCES AMONG THE MAIN GROUPS OF STATES

224. At the beginning of this book I pointed out that one of the principal features of the international law which evolved after the First World War is the fact that it is essentially the body of rules of a deeply split community. Not only do the three main segments of this community have a different concept of international law and attribute a different role to it, but they also endeavour to give it a shape according to their own interests. Alternatively, when confronted with rules they are unable to remould, they try at least to interpret them in the manner most useful to their own interests. I have shown that there are not many areas in which the views of the three groups chime in unison. Areas of dissent are: the classes of international legal subjects (§§43 and 59), the law-making processes (§§94-107), the devices for settling disputes peacefully (§§110, 112, 119) the mechanisms for enforcing law (§145), the forms of protection of human rights (§§170-85), some features of international control of armed conflict (§§151-66), the regulation of international economic relations (§§190-201), the ways of helping developing countries free themselves from their present backwardness (§§215-16), and the means of exploiting natural resources located in areas not subject to the sovereignty of anyone (§§219-22).

As I duly stressed (§96), international law itself eventually registered and consecrated on a normative level the fact that the world community is split into different segments: the provision on *jus cogens* contained in the 1969 Vienna Convention on the Law of Treaties stipulates that to become a peremptory norm of general international law, a rule must be 'accepted and recognized by the international community of States as a whole'. In other words, only if the three main segments of the world community are in agreement with each other can a general norm be regarded as belonging to *jus cogens*.

As was pointed out above (§145), it should be added that in at least two areas—that of use of force and that of armed conflicts—there has been a 'reshuffling of the cards', as it were, in the sense that an almost imperceptible convergence between the major Western Powers and the USSR has gradually materialized. It follows that, at least with regard to some features belonging to these two areas, divisions and conflicts cut across the three fundamental groupings. We are confronted with a rift between powerful States (be they from the West or the East) on the one side, and lesser countries (whatever the ideological or political grouping to which they belong), on the other. This antithesis constitutes a highly significant 'deviation' from the 'normal pattern' of ideological and political split, a deviation which can easily be accounted for if one thinks of the strategic and military interests underlying the legal regulation of the two areas referred to above.

One ought not, however, to overemphasize the present divisions of whatever 'class', lest one fail to understand why in spite of all the rifts the legal gearing of the world community works fairly smoothly and allows a minimum of coexistence and co-operation. It is undoubtedly true, as Judge de Lacharrière has lately, with great shrewdness, noted, that not only each group of States but even each individual State pursues the 'legal policy' which best suits its own goals on a world-wide level, and that to this effect it chooses from the panoply of devices made available by international law those which best further its own interests.[1] Yet the fact remains that these

---

[1] G. de Lacharrière, *La Politique juridique extérieure* (Paris, 1983), pp. 13 ff.

policies do not result in utter chaos or in a permanent state of conflict, but are relatively harmonized in international relations. To be more specific, there are three factors which make for a modicum of social and legal coexistence and co-operation.

First, although each sovereign State is unquestionably a monad, it has, nevertheless 'doors and windows': it communicates day by day with other States, for the very simple reason that it needs to do so. Even the most powerful States such as the US and the USSR cannot estrange themselves from international interaction but need to maintain a certain degree of association, if only to protect their nationals living abroad, sell their goods to other States, buy the commodities they need, enter into agreements providing for the stationing of their troops in foreign countries, try to influence the policies of other nations in international institutions such as the numerous world organizations, and so on. Even more compelling are the reasons urging middle-sized and lesser States to entertain international relations and consort with other countries: more pressing economic and commercial needs, the necessity to get together for the purpose of creating agencies capable of providing defensive 'umbrellas' in case of aggression by other States, etc. All these multifarious relations need of course a medium through which they can be effected. International law plays precisely this role. In spite of all its weaknesses and inadequacies, this body of law discharges the important task of providing a channel through which international relations are effected with relative smoothness.

In turn, this body of law contributes to making States 'system-conscious' (in Hoffmann's terminology),[2] that is, 'aware of the existence and structure of the whole' and by and large co-operative within the framework of pre-established patterns of behaviour.

The second factor is the existence of a core of general principles on which all States, whatever their ideological leanings and political bent, have come to agree. They are the eight principles considered in Chapter 6, which by now have become the 'tables of the law' for the international community. It is precisely on account of their being accepted by all international subjects that I have chosen to label them 'universal' so as to underline their essential characteristic. Admittedly, as I have shown (§§91-2), in their practical application even these principles are subject to divergent interpretations, especially as regards their co-ordination, that is the rank to be assigned to each of them in their mutual relations. This unquestionably weakens their role. The fact is that conflicts and discussions cannot be simply swept under the carpet. They resurface again, no matter how skilfully they are glossed over. What matters in the case of the eight principles is that at least their

[2] S. Hoffmann, *The State of War: Essays in the Theory and Practice of International Politics* (New York, 1965), p. 91.

gist is not called into question, and this is really important given the present world structure.

In addition to these principles, all States substantially agree upon at least *one* of the modalities for producing internationally binding rules, namely treaty-making (but on custom there is no unbridgeable rift either). All of them have eventually come to accept—in one way or another (§ 103)—the bulk of the 1969 Vienna Convention (see § 105) and this allows them peacefully and smoothly to set the standards by which their relations have to be legally controlled.

The third factor is the existence of a number of international organizations, chiefly the UN, where States from any grouping or alignment can get together and discuss, negotiate, and possibly harmonize their views. True, these institutions sometimes lend themselves to mere exercises in rhetoric. Furthermore, even the most important of them, the UN General Assembly, now increasingly indulges in the highly questionable practice of begetting ever greater numbers of resolutions, as if to conjure up problems and provide for their solution on paper served to settle them in real life. In spite of this tendency to hypertrophy, of an otherwise useful instrument, the mere fact that debates take place and that the debaters are accredited representatives from all over the world, is of incalculable importance. Within international forums differences both at a political and at a legal level are narrowed. Thus, for instance, as shown above, over the years there has been a gradual convergence of views on various important issues such as the principal modes of peaceful settlement of disputes (§§ 115-19), the humanitarian law of armed conflict (§ 151), human rights (§§ 183-4), and so on. As long as there are channels through which States can exchange their views and give vent to their remonstrances and expostulations, the present risk of conflicts of interest degenerating into armed clashes will at least not increase.

THE OLD AND THE NEW PATTERNS OF WORLD LEGAL ORDER

225. Throughout this book emphasis has been laid on the coexistence in the world community of two different patterns of legal order. The first to evolve took shape at the dawn of present international law. It reflects the markedly primitive and highly individualistic features characteristic of the community for about two and a half centuries, features which remind us of the earlier stages of human collectivities (tribes and similar groupings which existed long before central authorities established themselves on a firm basis and rulers developed institutions for the daily and painstaking control of the conduct of their subjects). I hope that it will be helpful to the reader if I now recapitulate and summarize the principal distinguishing traits of the 'model of Westphalia'—to use a phrase to which I have repeatedly referred (see, in particular, the Introduction). They can be described as follows. (1) The world community consisted largely of sovereign States, which monopolized control over the entire earth as well as over that part of the sea which could be appropriated. Each regarded itself as a 'perfect community' (see § 146), and was consequently unwilling to bow to the authority of any other Power: they were all *communitates superiorem non recognoscentes* (communities not recognizing any superior authority). (2) Force was the primary source of legitimation: the principle of effectiveness held sway. (3) The three 'legal functions' (law-making, settlement of disputes, and law-enforcement) were decentralized to such an extent that each individual member of the community took upon itself the task of discharging them—plainly, in a manner commensurate to its real power. (4) No legal trammels were imposed on the use of force, with the consequence that the bulk of legal rules, for example, those protecting territorial sovereignty, political independence, the right to protect their own nationals and so on, were only respected by powerful States to the extent that this did not run counter to their own interests. It follows that international legal standards afforded a protection which was provisional and precarious (which is why lesser States resorted so often to treaties of alliance and promoted a balance of power between the stronger States). (5). Responsibility for international wrongful acts was a 'private affair' involving the delinquent State and the victim only. To the remainder of international subjects breaches of international standards of behaviour were something extraneous, in which they were not authorized to meddle. Clearly, no joint interest in compliance with law existed. Only those directly and immediately injured by a wrong were entitled to take the remedial steps provided for by law. (6) The contents of legal rules were 'neutral' in the sense that they placed all States on a footing of legal equality and did not take account of factual disparities or imbalances. (On this score, those rules represented an unequalled embodiment of the eighteenth century doctrine of equality, which did not look upon human beings or collective entities in their socio-economic setting but considered them as abstract phenomena existing outside history and society.) (7) What is also typical of this period is that international law amounted to a body of rules designed essentially to cushion States' coexistence, that is, to ensure that they could live together, side by side, with a minimum of attrition and the occasional joint effort to achieve something which was useful to a group consisting of more than two States. But enduring relationships involving groups of States were few and far between: when they occurred, they were primarily motivated by military reasons, such as defence.

By contrast, the international legal system, which gradually evolved after the First World War (and especially after the Second World War) has the hallmark of novelty and, in particular, tends to mould international rules

on domestic legal systems. In the course of this book I have tried to pinpoint the various features pertaining to the most recent stages of evolution
of the world community: the so-called 'UN Charter model'. It may be
useful briefly to sum them up and even if it turns out to be a rather dry
enumeration, I hope it will nevertheless be of some help to the reader.
These features are: (1) the mushrooming of international organizations
which, without dethroning sovereign States, have, however, come to play a
significant role not only as meeting-points for international subjects, but
also as mechanisms for exercising leverage on individual States; (2) the
granting of a limited role to single human beings or to groups of people in
the international arena—a development unthinkable at the beginning of
this century—and the consequent removal (admittedly, a partial and perhaps ephemeral removal) of individuals from the ghetto of 'objects' of
States' conduct to the status of entities having at least a walk-on part in
international affairs; (3) the assignment of a fairly extensive role to organized
peoples subject to such oppressive Powers as colonial States, racist regimes
or foreign occupants—a notable departure from the old pattern, indicating
that from a club of rulers we are increasingly turning into a community
where certain limited groups of governed peoples are also allowed to have
a say; (4) the imposition of sweeping restrictions on resort to military and
even economic force by States; (5) the gradual emergence of values designed
to limit at least the broad import of force as the exclusive legitimizing
criterion in international relations; with the consequent evolution, as a
countervailing factor to the principle of effectiveness, of the postulate
whereby newly developed situations which are contrary to given basic international standards, ought not to be formally recognized by States in
spite of their effectiveness; (6) the establishment of a set of devices calculated
to facilitate the fulfilment of the three 'legal functions' of the international
community, by promoting the creation of new standards of behaviour, the
settlement of differences, and enticements or compulsions on States for
greater compliance with international norms; (7) the fact that while previously there were no proper legal principles of a universal character directing the conduct of all the members of the international community (§ 76),
since the 1960s some such principles have gradually emerged, which represent the backbone of the whole corpus of international rules; (8) the emergence of something which would have been inconceivable before the First
World War, namely, a concern for the rights of individuals, and the gradual
formation of a corpus of international rules enjoining States to grant
human rights and fundamental freedoms to any human being under their
jurisdiction.

A further distinguishing trait of the present pattern is that (9) certain
values have emerged which States have decided to invest with pre-eminent
legal force: peace, and the protection of human dignity from outrageous

manifestations of human cruelty such as genocide, racial discrimination (in particular apartheid), slavery and practices verging on slavery, torture, and other large-scale and glaring violations of human rights. To these values States have attached a number of legal consequences: first, they are embodied in customary rules which lay down obligations *erga omnes* (see § 12); second, the norms relating to them belong to the corpus of *jus cogens* (see § 96); third, disregard for these values does not constitute a private business of the delinquent State and the victim, but amounts to a 'public affair' involving the whole international community: any member State can step in and claim respect for law, even though it has not suffered any direct injury from the wrongful act; fourth, at least in respect of certain of them (peace, the prohibition of genocide) international rules now provide for the personal responsibility of the State officials who engage in such prohibited acts, in addition, of course, to the traditional responsibility of the State to which those individuals belong and on whose behalf they act; fifth—but here we are still witnessing the emergence of common consent among States and can therefore not yet speak of hard and fast binding rules—in respect of certain of the above values one can speak of a particularly serious responsibility falling upon the shoulders of the States which depart from them; thus, in the case of aggression, genocide, large-scale disregard of human rights, forcible denial of the right of self-determination, States are gradually taking the view that they constitute international crimes of States (as opposed to delicts or ordinary wrongs); consequently, to react to those violations, steps of a more serious nature than ordinary sanctions are allowed, such as joint retaliatory measures.

Finally (10), as we saw above (§§ 28, 206-15), contemporary international law has torn to shreds the myth of the legal equality of States and set itself the task of concerning itself with economic and social inequalities. Thus it has developed a whole set of rules aimed at introducing greater justice into international relations, for instance by helping backward countries to do away with the misery in which their populations have lived for so long. This new law has also had an impact both on the rules governing the appropriation of territories and property and on those concerning exploitation of natural resources. The consequence has been the emergence of the crucial concept of 'common heritage of mankind', which is calculated not only to restructure international attitudes towards appropriation, but also to set the stage for the realization of 'world welfare conditions'—parallel to some extent to what the welfare State wished to achieve on the domestic level in the 1930s and 1940s.

226. To sum up and contrast concisely the old and the new 'model' it may prove helpful to use certain concepts expounded as early as 1862 by a well-known German thinker and politician: Ferdinand Lassalle. According to him, in dealing with legal institutions one ought always to distinguish between the 'actual relationships among social forces' and the 'theoretical and paper law':[3] it is the former which really matter. Whenever there is a discrepancy between the two, the former is destined to prevail and the latter is of no consequence, regardless of the efforts of jurists and politicians. Just as an apple tree does not turn into a fig tree simply because the owner puts a tag on it to this effect and orders everybody to regard it as a fig tree (the next year the fruit it bears will be apples, not figs), in the same way legal rules remain a dead letter if they contradict the 'real state of affairs', the 'actual relations among social forces'. Let us now apply these concepts to the world community. It is clear that in the period of the 'Westphalian model' there was full coincidence between the 'real relationships among social forces' and the 'paper law'. As I emphasized above (§ 10), international legal rules fully reflected the constellation of power, and mirrored the interests of major States. Traditional international law made up a 'realistic' body of legal rules, for it actually sanctioned the existing power relationships. Consequently there was no major tension between the legal precepts and the body politic (or, to put it more precisely, between the dominating figures in it). With the change-over to the 'Charter model' a gap between the real position of States in the world community and the aspirations and demands of the (weak) majority—as embodied in the new law—has increasingly materialized. To a large extent law is no longer a faithful reflection of the existing constellation of power, but incorporates a large body of 'oughts', that is to say, of imperatives which are a far cry from political and economic realities. Law has become less 'realistic' and more 'idealistic'. We should ask ourselves whether the sagacious observations of Lassalle about the impossibility of turning an apple tree into a fig tree by a nominalistic alteration of reality also hold true for the present world community (see *infra*, § 232).

227. An illustration of the tension between 'realistic' and 'idealistic' law may prove useful to the reader.

Traditional international law did not provide any safeguard of the *environment* as such: it only prohibited damage to the environment of other States, in keeping with the fundamental principle that the sovereign rights of other States were to be respected. Huber, the distinguished arbitrator, in his award on the *Island of Palmas* case, stated that 'Territorial sovereignty ... involves the exclusive right to display the activities of a State. This right has as a corollary a duty: the obligation to protect within the territory the rights of other States, in particular, their right to integrity and inviolability

---

[3] F. Lassalle, *Was Nun? Zweiter Vortrag über Verfassungswesen,* 3rd edn. (Leipzig, 1873), pp. 12–13.

...'.[4] More specifically, in another famous case, the *Trail Smelter* case (decision of 11 March 1941), a US–Canada court of arbitration stated that 'under the principles of international law ... no State has the right to use or permit the use of its territory in such a manner as to cause injury by fumes in or to the territory of another or the properties or persons therein, when the case is of serious consequence and the injury is established by clear and convincing evidence'.[5] It is apparent that the protection of environment was not pursued *per se*: consequently, any State was free to damage *its own* environment (provided its action did not entail harmful consequences for other States), as well as any areas under no State jurisdiction, such as the high seas. Recently, however, the protection of the environment *per se* has become the subject of treaties and resolutions by international organizations so numerous that it can be argued that a general rule has evolved (or is at least in the process of evolving). Under this rule (1) every State must refrain from damaging the environment, whether its own, that of other States, or areas not subject to State jurisdiction; (2) every State has the right to claim respect for the environment, regardless of whether or not it has derived any damage from the wrongful action of another State resulting in injury to the environment. Plainly, international law has thus moved from a rule geared to sovereignty and reciprocity to a rule upholding 'community values' and establishing 'solidarity links'. The latter does not obliterate the former, but expands it, makes it more responsive to current needs and—what is even more important—does away with the sovereignty-orientated approach. However, in practice, States comply only with the old rule, which is firmly rooted in the traditional structure of the international community. By contrast, the new rule, permeated with 'idealistic' demands, is hardly able to take off, and actually is not observed in point of fact (so much so that a number of jurists voice doubts about its having acquired the hallmarks of a legally binding rule).

228. After reviewing the main features of the new international law, we should now see how the unique coexistence of the old and new pattern in the international legal order can be explained. As I have emphasized, the old and the new models coexist, for the latter has not succeeded in supplanting the former, which resurfaces again and again for the simple reason that the fundamental structure of the world community has remained unchanged since the first stages of development of the community. The new pattern has merely superimposed itself on the old one. A significant illustration of the continuous emergence—especially in times of profound tensions and conflict—of the 'Westphalian model' relates to the use of force.

---

[4] The passage of the arbitral award on the *Palmas* case is in *Reports of International Arbitral Awards*, 2, p. 839.
[5] For the passage from the judgment on the *Trail Smelter* case, see ibid., 3, p. 1907.

As I stressed above, there is now a sweeping ban on the use of force, with two well-known exceptions: collective measures of enforcement provided for in Chapter VII of the UN Charter, and self-defence. Following the failure of the Charter system, and in marked deviation from it, the so-called 'peace-keeping forces' have been established by the UN. However, they do not act as 'international policemen' capable of intervening by means of the threat or use of coercion: they can only act *with the consent* of the State on whose territory they intend to undertake their action. State sovereignty—which the Charter had endeavoured to do away with, at least in this area—thus resurfaces again. Similarly, self-defence, which within the context of the Charter ought to constitute the exception, has become the norm: States have increasingly been dragged back to the old system of self-help. In these and similar instances the tension between the two poles of State sovereignty and community demands, is eventually resolved in favour of the former.

There are many historical reasons for this, but one of the principal ones is that the new forces which have advocated and pushed 'modern' international law through are not powerful enough to supplant the traditional protagonists and replace the old structures. As we have seen, the bulk of the new institutions has been set up on the initiative or at the request of socialist and developing countries—although occasionally, as in the case of the 1945 ban on force, they have resulted from the exceptional concordance of all States motivated by a series of unique events, such as the Second World War. In other instances, such as that of international protection of human rights, the initiative has been taken by the West. Leaving aside this last area (where, of course, it is precisely Western countries which press for novelties), and the prohibition of war (on which there is still a large measure of agreement), the fact remains that most devices making up the 'new' international law have been accepted rather reluctantly by the more powerful developed States. Socialist and Third World nations are unable to impose new forms and techniques of international relations on Western industrialized countries, the more so because some socialist States, chiefly the USSR, are keen to maintain economic links with the West, and, in addition, need Western co-operation to try to reach agreement on disarmament.

Furthermore, in some areas (the use of force, and the international regulation of armed conflict) their interests to a large extent converge with those of major Western Powers (see § 145). In addition, developing countries are often weak; they are also divided—some of them being under the political influence of the East, others being too dependent on Western economic assistance to be able to impose new patterns of behaviour.

The 'conservative' drive of many Western countries is also motivated by their insistence on the need to couple normative changes with parallel developments in the field of implementation. Socialist and, to some extent, developing nations object that it is not always necessary to create new *remedies* along with new *rights* (see §71). Western States retort that the opposition to international means of scrutiny in the fear that they might be used for encroaching upon domestic jurisdiction, rests on a desperate attachment to sovereignty. Indeed, this excessive adhesion to sovereignty constitutes, so they argue, a major stumbling-block to a sensible and rational evolution of the international legal order. It is indeed true that the position of socialist and developing countries is somewhat contradictory, since on the one hand they push through bold innovations—which inevitably entail significant restraints on States' freedom of action—and, on the other, cling to, and even inflate, their sovereignty. (However, as I shall shortly point out (§232), there are certain well-identifiable political and historical motivations behind their tendency to extol sovereignty.) Be that as it may, all these differences have led to a radical rift which cannot but stand in the way of further progress.

229. There is a second and perhaps deeper reason why the new law has not displaced the previous pattern. I have already stressed that the old structure was acutely individualistic. To be able to obliterate the traditional setting fresh legal institutions ought to be founded on true international solidarity. However, in reality this is not the case, not even within each particular group. In order fully to appreciate this point it may be useful to avail ourselves of the concept of solidarity developed as early as 1893 by the French sociologist Durkheim.[6] With regard to social groups, mainly within a domestic setting, he rightly distinguished between 'mechanical solidarity', based on affinities, and 'organic solidarity' resting on division of labour. The former unites people showing strong similarities and sharing ideals, creeds, inclinations, and likings. The latter is based on the differences among members of a group and unites them on the strength of their ability to accomplish diverse but all equally necessary tasks, and as such is the manifestation of marked interdependence. Within modern States we discern both classes of solidarity and, indeed, it is precisely their combination which accounts for the progress of States in so many areas. In the international community both catégories of solidarity do exist, but only to a very limited degree. Mechanical solidarity is to be found within each of the three main groups, particularly among developing countries. Two points should, however, be emphasized. First, no real solidarity exists between any two groups, for, as I have repeatedly pointed out, they actually fight, or at least glower at, one another. Can anyone say that Western and socialist countries have congenial relations or that Western and developing countries share common goals? Even socialist and Third World countries, which frequently support each other and join efforts to change the international community along lines more suitable to their interests, occasionally do not see eye to eye

[6] E. Durkheim, *De la division du travail social* (1893) (Paris, 1978), pp. 35 ff.

on major issues (see, e.g. §§ 219 and 221). Second, even within the group showing the greatest degree of homogeneity and solidarity, on close scrutiny these common traits appear to be the manifestation of a fairly transitory stage. Although the basic interests of members of the group tend to be in unison, they are likely to diverge drastically as soon as the momentary convergence of interests comes to an end. Let me give two typical examples.

The first is taken from the negotiations for a new law of the sea. At a certain stage, when the legal regime of the exclusive economic zone (§ 218) was still under discussion, Lesotho, a very poor land-locked State, suggested that one united African economic zone be established, to the advantage of the members of the whole continent and not of each coastal State (whose zone of necessity would have varied according to the characteristics of its coast).[7] It was no doubt a bold proposal which, if successful, could have enhanced the ties of solidarity between African countries and strengthened their co-operation. It was, however, rejected by the other States (including the other African countries) and the nationalistic and sovereignty-oriented allocation of the exclusive economic zone was effected among the various coastal States.

A second illustration is taken from the work of the IMF in favour of developing countries. In 1975 the IMF decided to sell up to 25 million ounces of fine gold for the benefit of developing countries which were members of the Fund. The proceeds of the sale beyond the former official price of gold were to be used for financing balance of payments loans on concessional terms to developing countries through a Trust Fund. However, in the negotiations on the setting up of the Trust Fund, developing countries—to use the words of a distinguished commentator, Sir Joseph Gold— 'successfully proposed that not all the proceeds of the sale of gold that was to be undertaken, in excess of the former official price, should be transferred to the Trust Fund. The portion notionally attributable to developing members on the basis of quotas [that is, that part of the profits corresponding to the proportion of a developing member's quota on 31 August 1975, to the total of all quotas on that date] should be distributed to these members and not transferred to the Trust Fund. The proposal was made notwithstanding acceptance of the principle that loans through the Trust Fund were to be for the benefit of the poorer developing members. The proposal of developing members was advanced with the protestation that they should not have to contribute to the welfare of their own kind.'[8] Thus, acting on the principle that only industrialized countries should bear the brunt of economic efforts for helping poor nations, a few Third World States avoided

---

[7] The statement made by Lesotho is in: IIIrd Conference on the Law of the Sea, *Official Records*, ii, IInd Committee, 20th Mtg., 30 July 1974, para. 53.

[8] Sir Joseph Gold, in *Indian Journal of International Law*, 21 (1981), 511-12.

shouldering the burden of sharing some of their economic advantages with poorer States.

So much for 'mechanical solidarity'. The other category of solidarity, the 'organic' one, is also terribly ineffective on the world scene. States have not achieved much as regards international division of labour, either in the economic or in any other field. Rather, they are eager to avoid allocating certain tasks to a particular State or group of States (except for the 'duty' of giving economic assistance to backward countries in their development, which Third World countries would like to foist upon industrialized nations, while the latter are, of course, stolidly recalcitrant). States fear that such allocation might render one or more countries excessively powerful and consequently dangerous. As a result, we witness the proliferation of international institutions vested with specific tasks; within the institutions' main bodies, however, control over the fulfilment of those tasks is not allotted to one member or to a group of members but to all of them jointly.

Upon close analysis it is apparent that the lack of international solidarity originates in the same basic phenomenon which ultimately unites the old and the new patterns, the cornerstone of the whole edifice of international law as it has developed since the Peace of Westphalia: in other words, the all-pervasive role of State sovereignty. In spite of all the bold innovations I have taken pains to outline in the previous pages, the fact remains that since its inception the world community has always been made up of sovereign States confronting one another in the international arena. States are still the overlords and preserve all the characteristics they possessed ever since they came into being. To a large extent they still are the 'puppeteer' in whose hands international legal institutions are all too often mere puppets.

In addition, the paradox to which Parry drew attention: 'of the simultaneous power and impotence of the individual State'[9] (in other words, its omnipotence—within its borders—over all human beings living there and its relative helplessness outside its own frontiers, with respect to other fellow States) is as valid today as it was in the seventeenth century.

230 To find out the deeper reasons for the disturbing state of affairs described above, one must of course turn to history, political science, and social psychology. History helps to explain why, towards the thirteenth century, mankind, at that time dominated by feudal lords, gradually became encapsulated in nation States, and authority was increasingly parcelled out between sovereign rulers, each governing a distinct community over a certain territory, and each excluding any outside authority from the territory

---

[9] C. Parry, 'The Function of Law in the International Community', in *Manual of Public International Law*, ed. T. Sørensen (London, 1968), pp. 5-6.

under its domination. History and political science together help us to understand why nationalism and its corollary, State idolatry, instead of diminishing, are at present on the increase, and why socialist States and developing countries emphasize the 'dogma' of sovereignty more than other nations. But philosophy and anthropology too provide us with tools indispensable to the understanding of current international realities.

Thus, for example, the distinction drawn by Bergson in 1932 between 'closed' and 'open' societies[10] can prove of great help for the purpose of grasping the present working of the world community. To this French philosopher a 'closed society' is essentially the natural society, based on the community and convergence of instincts, emotions and natural tendencies: the tribe, the city, and later the State. The chief feature of this society is as much 'that of embracing a certain number of individuals as that of excluding the others'. A 'closed society' is always opposed to other similar societies and is dominated by the 'war instinct': 'its members live together, indifferent to all the others, always ready to attack the others or to defend themselves, constrained in sum to a fighting posture ... The two opposing maxims *homo homini deus* [any man is a god to another man] and *homo homini lupus* [any man is a wolf to another man] are easily reconciled. When the former is set forth, one thinks of some fellow countryman. The latter relates to foreigners.' By contrast, the 'open society' embraces, 'in principle' all mankind. However, according to Bergson, a gradual transition between the two is not on the cards: 'from the closed to the open society, from the city to mankind one shall never move by dint of an enlargement. They do not partake of the same essence.' Nevertheless, there is no gainsaying that men show a strong tendency to search for an 'opening society', in other words, a tendency to try to realize certain basic postulates of humanity.

The tension between the 'closed' and 'open' societies and the basic motivations underlying the functioning of the former have been investigated in depth by students of social psychology. Notably, the analysis of the unconscious has demonstrated that the congregation of people united by common links of language, traditions, historical and cultural background, economic conditions, etc. *necessarily* goes hand in hand with the emergence of feelings of strong aversion and hostility towards outside groups and nations. This happens at all levels of human society, from the family to the nation-State. No one can deny this fact, even if one does not share the interpretation which has been advanced (according to which, the tendency to dislike aliens both expresses a form of narcissism—that is, something of an auto-exaltation which loathes anything different from itself, which is perceived as a sort of implied criticism—and also constitutes a form of

[10] H. Bergson, *Les Deux Sources de la morale et de la religion* (1932) (Paris, 1982), pp. 283–307.

aggressiveness, an essential and inherent part of any human being's mind).[11]

231. To conclude, several reasons, in particular the fact that the world community is still made up of sovereign States, explain why so many traits of traditional international law still survive in the world community—relics of a past era which can at any time resurface and display all their potential force. Nevertheless, the signs of an emerging pattern must not be played down. The various innovations I have already listed are clues to a possible evolution of the present world community. Some of them are admittedly peripheral, others are overpowered by the harsh realities of the 'old' international community as soon as States consider that self-interest ought to prevail. Nevertheless they constitute scattered proof of a new path which States will probably take one day, albeit step by step and by a process which will require many years to reach completion. To the impassioned observer they bear the same significance as the few tiny and seemingly disparate novelties which, according to an Italian writer, one day presented themselves to Christopher Columbus towards the end of his long voyage in his anguished and often hopeless quest for a new world (the 'quality of the earth the sounding-rod brought up with it; the shape and the colour of the clouds; the air, become gentler and warmer; the wind, no longer impetuous and steadfast; a floating stick; a little branch with its berries on still red and fresh':[12] a multitude of small tokens, which, taken together, seemed even to the most diffident man—as Columbus replied to his inquiring companion Gutierrez—to engender 'great and good expectations').

THE ROLE OF LAW IN THE WORLD COMMUNITY

232. I noted above, albeit in passing, that law plays a significant role in the world community. Admittedly, one might discount the importance of the few international courts and emphasize that often unlawful behaviour goes unpunished because 'private' self-interest still overrides 'public' concern for compliance with law; nevertheless the enormous wealth of treaties which all States enter into, and the number of international organizations through which they co-operate, should constitute sufficient evidence of the fact that sovereign States take account of legal standards in their international dealings and endeavour to comply with them as much as

[11] The psychological interpretations referred to above are those put forward by Freud in his essays *Massenpsychologie und Ich-Analyse* (1921), repr. in S. Freud, *Das Unbewusste, Schriften zur Psychoanalyse*, ed. A. Mitscherlich (Frankfurt am Main, 1960), pp. 246–7 (Chapter 6), and *Das Unbehagen in der Kultur* (1929), ibid., 386–7 (Chapter 5), where the important concept of 'Narzissmus der kleinen Differenzen' is elaborated.
[12] G. Leopardi, 'Dialogo di C. Colombo e di P. Gutierrez (1827), *Operette morali*, in *Opere*, ii (Bari, 1928), p. 149.

possible. I have also emphasized (§ 145) that on careful analysis the enforcement procedures turn out to be less defective than is normally claimed. On the whole, it can be said that even in those areas where it is more difficult to induce States to abide by law (I refer, of course, to politico-military relations, particularly when States' vital interests are at stake), even there States proceed with great caution, for a number of reasons: the pressure that can be exercised on the delinquent party within the UN, the weight of world public opinion, the need not to wreck good relations in the economic, commercial, and political fields, the necessity not to alienate the sympathy of countries with which the wrongdoer may have political and ideological affiliations, and the like.

If then law is regarded as one of the factors which States take into consideration when planning and carrying out their foreign policy, we may ask ourselves whether there is some truth in the current view that international law is more useful to small or weak States which are consequently more eager to invoke it, than to Great Powers.

On the face of it, this proposition is too sweeping. Thus, for instance, the present international regulation of economic relations does not favour developing countries. Similarly, the rules on the use of force do not protect lesser countries, but play into the hands of powerful States, in particular the five permanent members of the Security Council, for the latter can resort to force with impunity, in breach of the UN Charter (save for the political, psychological or moral safeguards referred to above, which, however important, do not form part of the body of law to which I am referring now).

Another area of law where smaller countries are at a disadvantage is that of settlement of disputes. If differences arise between one such country and a Great Power or even a middle-sized State and no pre-established and compulsory machinery of conciliation or arbitration exists, the former country can only rely on UN mechanisms. These, as we saw above (§ 114), are primarily concerned with disputes the continuation of which may endanger peace. Indeed, as has been repeatedly stressed, the UN's paramount concern is not so much for the rule of law or respect for justice, as for the maintenance of peace. Consequently, if the Security Council or the General Assembly consider that the dispute is not likely to jeopardize international peaceful relations, the State in question is at a loss on how to achieve a satisfactory solution. Even if the UN bodies step in and apply pressure to the bigger State for the purpose of impelling it to come to terms with the other party, the former State may turn a deaf ear to UN exhortations and, in actual fact, leave things as they stand.

It is apparent from these and similar illustrations that international law does not necessarily favour smaller countries. This is only natural if one is reminded that the corpus of international legal rules has been primarily shaped by Great Powers and that if smaller countries have wrenched a number of concessions and advantages, this has been achieved after a laborious tug of war.

Yet the proposition made above has some truth in it. It is true that a few areas of international law do protect smaller countries. To be more precise, this function is fulfilled by: (1) some substantive rules, and (2) by the bulk of the international mechanisms existing in the international community.

As for the rules, let me insist on those concerning territorial integrity and political independence, normally lumped together under the label of rules on State sovereignty. Needless to say, these norms address themselves to all States and are consequently meant to protect the interests of all, be they big or small. However, in practice they turn out to be of greater use to smaller States. Big States have plenty of guns and armed men at their disposal to discourage any other country from infringing upon their territorial and 'political' rights; to them the rule on sovereignty is but the formal reflection of their capacity to wield exclusive authority within their borders and to keep out potential intruders. For the smaller or weaker nations, on the other hand, the rule in question constitutes a much more important form of protection in itself, for it does not necessarily mirror the effective power to drive out potential intruders. In a case of infringement a weak country cannot rely on its own military strength, but it can raise hell in the international community, particularly in international political institutions such as the UN or regional organizations: there, the violation of its rights can be exposed, and this eventuality, in itself, should discourage bigger States from engaging in unlawful actions.

The other segment of international law which may prove exceedingly helpful to smaller States is the whole body of international institutions operating in various fields and at various levels (inter-governmental organizations, other interstate agencies, etc.). I have already emphasized (§ 25) that it was precisely the practice of international diplomatic conferences in the nineteenth century which led smaller States to play a greater role by contributing to the framing of international rules. Now those conferences have been to a large extent rendered permanent and, what is more, institutionalized. Stable machinery has been set up providing forums where States can get together and discuss international issues, and put pressure on other States. Of incalculable importance also is the part played by the secretariats of those organizations, which, as a rule, accomplish in a fairly impartial way important tasks of study, research, investigation, scrutiny, etc. For lesser States all this represents a sort of safety net which is, on the whole, capable of averting major risks to their security and independence, and, in addition, places at their disposal the necessary tools for fulfilling a role to which their military and economic strength would not be commensurate. In a word, these institutions allow them to have a say even in areas where naked force and military superiority alone would otherwise constitute the legitimizing factors. These international institutions democratize the world community (it is no coincidence that the repeated criticisms recently levelled at the UN and similar agencies often emanate from people and bodies close to one or another of the Great Powers; they frequently reflect the political interest of those who utter them). To be sure, they are unable 'to turn apple trees into fig trees' (to take up Lassalle's image referred to above), or, in other words, they do not possess the authority of actually changing by legal fiat, the existing powers' relationships to the benefit of backward and developing countries. However, they can, and in fact do, gradually graft new shoots on the old 'apple tree' or, to put it differently, they are instrumental in eroding, step by step, the traditional configuration of the world community, so as to narrow down the gap between the 'Westphalian model', reflecting the 'real power relationships', and the new 'ideals' of the 'Charter model' which are, to a large extent, if anything, still at the stage of 'theoretical or paper law'.

233. It should be added that there are two factors destined to heighten the role of international legal institutions. First, the tremendous tensions created in the world community by the existence of weaponry capable of destroying the whole earth several times over and the correlative mutual distrust of the two Superpowers, cause men and States to live in a permanent condition of anxiety, but also increase the value of existing international machinery for facilitating negotiation and agreement. International permanent forums of a political nature, particularly those specializing in matters of disarmament such as the Geneva Conference on Disarmament, or the bilateral negotiations between the US and the USSR at Geneva, Vienna, or in other venues, become crucial council chambers where the lot of mankind is determined.

The second general trend is the emergence of far-reaching centrifugal forces within nation-States. Minorities are more and more vocal; ethnic groups in any part of the world (not only in Africa or Latin America, but also in Europe) vociferously claim respect for their identity as well as a measure of autonomy, and often even international status; groups based on the most varied affiliations tend to form within States, to branch out into the international community, and even set up their own international network. These and other collectivities tend to disrupt the fabric of nation-States. For good or for bad, they tend to introduce into the world community a sort of anarchy which in the long run may jeopardize the present framework of international relations. Existing international institutions could serve a very important purpose by channelling and directing all these centrifugal forces; they could make room for peaceful integration by accommodating competing demands within an orderly framework—

without, however, completely doing away with the interstate structure of the world community.

234. In contrast to the two aforementioned trends, a tendency exists in the international community which might, in the very long run, erode the role and importance of international inter-governmental institutions: the tendency towards *regionalization*. It is common knowledge that regional (economic or political) institutions have been created in various areas of the world, chiefly in Western and Eastern Europe (the European Economic Community and COMECON, respectively), in Latin America (the Organization of American States, as well as the various smaller groupings such as the Latin-American Free Trade Association, the Andean Pact, the Caribbean Free Trade Association) and in Africa (where, in addition to the Organization of African Unity a few smaller organizations exist of a primarily economic nature such as the East African Community, the Economic and Customs Union of Central Africa, and the Economic Community of West African States). The reasons behind the drive towards the setting up of these institutions are obvious: within areas where States tend to share common political values, economic outlook, and cultural background, it is much easier to achieve integration (both at the political, economic, and at the normative and institutional level) than in the world community at large. Among these organizations the European Economic Community stands out as an exemplary model of integration.

The EEC is based on close economic and political cooperation. So far, it has achieved a common market (albeit incompletely: a custom union, and a common commercial policy). In addition, it has set up an important scheme for the association of developing countries (and a remarkable group of such countries has indeed associated itself to the EEC through the Lome Conventions). At present the Community is striving to attain greater monetary and economic integration. 'Supranationalism' is the distinguishing feature of the Community. This concept indicates the following principal features: (i) some of the Community bodies are not composed of Government representatives (the Commission, the Parliament, and the Court); (ii) under certain conditions Community organs can bind member States by a majority or weighted majority vote; (iii) the Community may take decisions immediately binding on natural or legal persons within the national legal systems of member States.

These radically innovative characteristics of the EEC should not, however, lead one to believe that the Community has gradually turned into a sort of federal State. Far from it, the more the Community has endeavoured to expand its supranational role, the more member States have endeavoured to retain and even enhance their control over Community institutions. This striking phenomenon has not escaped the attention of observers.

Thus, for instance, in 1979 Dahrendorf pointed out that 'European union has been a remarkable *political success*, but an equally remarkable *institutional failure*. So far as the substance of European co-operation is concerned, we have gone a long way forward; so far as the framework for taking common decisions is concerned, we have locked ourselves into procedures and institutions which at times do more damage than good.'[13] The same contradictory phenomenon has been explained by Weiler, in 1982, in the following terms:[14] while there has been an advance in '*normative supranationalism*' (which is 'concerned with the relationships and hierarchy which exists between Community policies and legal measures on the one hand and competing policies and legal measures of the member States on the other') there also has been a diminution of '*decisional supranationalism*' (which 'relates to the institutional framework and decision-making processes by which Community policies and measures are, in the first place, initiated, debated, and formulated, then promulgated and finally executed'). Weiler rightly emphasizes that the two developments are closely correlated, in the sense that the price the Community has had to pay for its expansion in scope and in the impact of its decisions on the legal systems of member States has been the greater control member States have over the decision-making process. To quote Weiler's own illustration: take the tricky and sensitive issue of 'supremacy of Community law' over national law: member States yielded to the gradual affirmation of the supremacy of Community law, but on condition that they are able to control the making of such law, hence also to block it.

It should be added that in spite of these difficulties and tensions the European Economic Community stands out as a model institution not only for the economic and political integration of member States but also since it constitutes an exemplary model for relations with developing countries. The Lome Convention (in its three successive formulations) with the associated ACP (African, Caribbean, and Pacific) countries, is a novel attempt at devising a forward-looking pattern of relations between industrialized and underdeveloped countries. (See, for example, the important scheme of compensatory financing of shortfalls in commodity exports proceeds of developing countries, a scheme which has three variations: STABEX, SYS-MIN, and the Protocol on ACP Sugar.)

As I stressed above, regional integration might in the long run erode international law in the sense that it might gradually make inter-governmental institutions proper, superfluous. The process will, however, be a very slow one, owing to the resilience of State sovereignty, as proved by the contradictory developments in the European Economic Community, to which I have just made reference.

[13] R. Dahrendorf, *A Third Europe?*, 3rd Jean Monnet Lecture (Florence, 1979), p. 8.
[14] J. Weiler, 'The Community System: The Dual Character of Supranationalism', *Yearbook of European Law* 1 (1981), 271, 273, 291-2.

THE POSSIBLE CONTRIBUTION OF INDIVIDUALS AND PRIVATE GROUPS

235. Students of anthropology and related sciences have rightly stressed that 'the substitution of the power of the community for that of the single individual has marked the decisive step towards civilization'.[15] Indeed, while in primitive societies there are no limitations on the satisfaction of individuals' demands, except for the restraints imposed by nature and the naked force of other individuals, at later stages in the development of the community, the collectivity somewhat monopolizes the fulfilment of individuals' needs, in particular it monopolizes the use of force. Centralization has no doubt represented an important advance in history; it has proved no less important than its counterpart in religious thinking, namely, monotheism—the ideological reflection of the gradual suppression of minor rivalling authorities. The formation of the collectivity *par excellence*', the modern nation-State, has compounded this long process towards civilization. However, as is plain to everybody, States also monopolize the whole life of individuals; the latter often have no say whatsoever, particularly in international relations. These are in fact administered by the power structures existing at the top of any nation-State, namely, Governments, which all too often have scant regard for the needs of individuals. Indeed, Nietzsche was not all that far off the mark when he described States as the most stony-hearted of stone monsters.[16] This raises the question of whether single human beings or non-governmental groups can nevertheless play a part in interstate transactions.

I am, of course, thinking not so much of the role of individuals *qua* representatives of States, who are bound by the instructions of their Governments, and whose leeway is therefore limited.

However, any observer of international diplomatic conferences knows that even there, certain personalities stand out, and often prominent diplomats are able to bring singular force and eloquence to their task and therefore influence the delegates of other countries. Suffice it here to mention Pardo, the Maltese ambassador, whose contribution to the concept of 'common heritage of mankind' has already been mentioned (§ 219). Another illustration, taken from the past, is the role played at the Hague Peace Conference of 1899 by the German delegate, Zorn (when he was appointed, Jellinek, the leading German jurist at the time wrote that it was indeed remarkable to see that Germany took the Peace Conference so seriously as to designate two delegates, one of whom had just published a book on the advantages

[15] S. Freud, *Das Unbehagen in der Kultur*, cit., 370 (Chapter 3).
[16] *Thus Spoke Zarathustra*, in *The Portable Nietzsche*, ed. W. Kaufmann (Harmondsworth, 1982), p. 160. (Actually Nietzsche used the terms 'the coldest of all cold monsters': 'Staat heisst das kälteste aller kalten Ungeheuer'; *Also Sprach Zarathustra*, in *Sämtliche Werke*, vol. VI (Stuttgart, 1964), p. 51.)

of war, whereas the other (Zorn) was famous for rejecting international law).[17] However, in spite of his theoretical inclinations, Zorn soon emerged at the Conference as an eloquent champion of compulsory settlement of legal disputes and, in particular, of the establishment of a Permanent Court of Arbitration. When his Government instructed him to oppose the setting up of the Court, he went so far as to refuse to comply and subsequently managed to convince the German Foreign Minister, von Bülow, to change his mind and support the creation of the Court. By his action Zorn thus succeeded in rallying the support of one of the Great Powers, without which the Court would never have seen the light[18] (see § 112).

Not very different is the role of those individuals who, acting at the instruction of their Government, have been instrumental in prompting States to be more responsive to the rule of law. An example which springs to mind is that of F. Lieber, a German academic who emigrated to the US in the nineteenth century. (At the request of the American President he worked out a code for the conduct of the American army in the field, in which he welded together a deep sense of humanity, legal draftsmanship, and balanced judgment, thus setting a landmark for the future development of rules governing the conduct of military operations.)

Apart from these instances, the urgent question today is whether human beings can have a say when they do not act as Government representatives or at the request of Governments. Undisputedly a number of individuals have fulfilled such a role in the past, when international relations were less complex and when—more important still—relations within States were less complicated, for the ruling classes were more homogeneous.

To give but one illustration of the influence individuals can exert on the conduct of Governments, suffice it to recall the role played by the Swiss citizen H. Dunant, who happened to witness the horrors caused by the battle fought at Solferino (a small town in the north of Italy) between the Austrian and Franco-Sardinian armies, in 1859, and was so upset by the ensuing suffering that he initiated a movement for the protection of war victims. His humanitarian action actually led to the formation of the International Red Cross and the elaboration of Conventions on the protection of the wounded and the sick.

Today, however, it is much more difficult for a single individual to exert that much influence on the conduct of his or her Government, much less on foreign Governments. A more important role can therefore be played by groups who exhort States to live up to international rules.

236. In point of fact, several non-governmental organizations have discharged and are discharging important tasks both by pressing States to

---

[17] G. Jellinek, 'Zur Eröffnung der Friedenskonferenz' (1899), in *Schriften*, 542–3.

[18] On Zorn's participation in the Hague Conference see the work by Zorn himself: *Deutschland und die beiden Haager Friedenskonferenzen* (Berlin, 1920), pp. 23 ff., also A. K. White, *Autobiography*, ii (London, 1905), pp. 308 ff.

adhere to international standards and by carrying out investigations and research which it would be more difficult for States or intergovernmental bodies to undertake. Organizations such as *Amnesty International*, the *International Commission of Jurists* and the *Anti-Slavery Society* stand out for their remarkable record of action and achievement. They do not aim at replacing States in the fulfilment of the latter's functions; they only *spur* States on to do something which they are frequently recalcitrant to do. As has been rightly said, they act as the conscience of mankind: their means of action are investigation, exposure, and exhortation. Other organizations such as the *International Committee of the Red Cross* operate on a different level: they not only encourage Governments to do something, but also act directly on a transnational level for the benefit of the wounded, the sick, the shipwrecked, and all those in need of help as a result of natural disasters or of armed conflicts—those man-made and no less disastrous cataclysms.

Other private bodies have as their goal the dissemination of ideals for the liberation of individuals and groups from their condition of misery and oppression: they set out to speak directly to individuals and peoples so as to increase their awareness of their rights. As the Argentinian poet Cortazar said of one of these organizations, the 'Permanent Tribunal of the Peoples', they strive to translate the theoretical and normative notions of basic human rights into intuitions, into 'palpable, immediate, and daily certainties in the life of many millions of women and men still astray in a mental desert and in an enormous prison of mountains and plains'.[19]

In other cases, however, the deep dissatisfaction which enlightened individuals feel with the conduct of certain Governments, has led them to try to '*replace*' States, albeit in a rudimentary and primarily symbolic way, in the discharge of their 'sovereign' functions. Groups of persons have indeed felt that it was their moral duty to speak out when States kept silent—not only the Government directly concerned but also other States, which preferred to stay silent out of considerations of *Realpolitik*. It is not surprising that the Governments most directly concerned have reacted angrily: they have seen the claims of individuals to act as their (partial and temporary) replacements as an usurpation of their sovereign prerogatives. Let me give just two examples.

The first relates to the Vietnam war in which the U S was engaged from 1964 to 1974. It was increasingly claimed that U S military action frequently involved methods contrary to the basic principles of humanity. However, when it became clear that no Government was willing to speak out against the U S (except for the Eastern European countries, whose ideological position made these outbursts suspect), a group of leading intellectuals, spearheaded by the philosopher Bertrand Russell, decided to set up a 'tribunal'

[19] J. Cortazar, 'Avant-propos', in *Un tribunal pour les peuples*, ed. E. Jouve (Paris, 1983), p. 12.

to pass judgment on the violations allegedly perpetrated by the US. While the US Government completely ignored the 'Russell Tribunal', the position of the French Government is interesting, because this Government was not directly involved in the war, and indeed had adopted a political stand critical of American conduct. After the French refused to grant a visa to one of the members of the 'Tribunal' (the Yugoslav historian Dedijer) to enter France, where the 'Tribunal' was to hold its proceedings, another member, Jean-Paul Sartre, addressed a letter to the French President, Charles De Gaulle. In his reply of 25 April 1967,[20] De Gaulle stated that although the Government shared some of the concerns of the 'Russell Tribunal' and although, of course, there was full freedom of thought and assembly in France, he would not allow the 'trial' to take place on French territory, for he was duty-bound to prevent an ally from being the 'object of a procedure at odds with international law and usages'. In his view, 'the administration of justice, in principle as well as in its execution, belongs only to the State'. As to Lord Russell and his friends, they 'were not vested with any international authority nor had they received any international agency'; therefore, he would not allow them to conduct the 'trial'. We are manifestly confronted here with two conflicting conceptions of justice: according to one, justice can only be carried out by State authorities; according to the other, private individuals without any formal legitimation may exercise moral authority and pass a verdict which, although devoid of legal value, may carry ethical and psychological weight. The fact that the 'Russell Tribunal' did hold its session (in Sweden) and that it continued its action in the subsequent years, when it called to account other States allegedly culpable of international crimes, testifies to the need for individuals to voice their views whenever Governments remain silent. It stands to reason that, since the force of such 'kangaroo courts' lies in their moral authority alone, the greater their authority and independence, the more effective is their impact on world public opinion and, consequently, on Governments.

A second example of the attempt of individuals to take over when Governments do not respond to the compelling demands of humanity is the 'Charter 77 Movement', which arose spontaneously in Czechoslovakia in 1977. A group of persons, claiming that the Czechoslovak authorities did not abide by the two UN Covenants on Human Rights ratified by that country, got together to draw up a document where they listed all the deviations from the standards laid down in the Covenants. In this instance, the task of exercising scrutiny over the conduct of State authorities in order to determine whether they comply with international norms—a task normally devolving upon either international supervisory bodies or domestic courts—was shouldered by a group of citizens. Here again the Government

[20] De Gaulle's letter is reprinted in J.-P. Sartre, *Situations*, viii (Paris, 1972), pp. 43-5.

concerned refused to acknowledge the movement any authority, and took steps to disband the group.

To sum up, despite the tendency of sovereign States to dispense with the contribution of individuals or even to gag them, individual input can be significant (provided, of course, they do not lend themselves to becoming tools in the hands of opposing international alignments). Indisputably sovereign States still are, and will for a long time be,[21] the authorized mouthpieces of the human collectivities over which they hold sway: the twilight of the gods is far off! However, in times of emergency, when power politics try to stifle the voice of moral conscience and only lend their ear to guns, mankind can express its fears and demands through groups of persons invested with no official power. Though no doubt we live in gloomy times, yet as individuals, we can have a say, if we are not too submissive. After all, we should not forget what a great French writer said in 1942, namely that 'on all essential problems—I mean thereby those that run the risk of leading to death or those that intensify the passion of living—there are probably but two methods of thought: the method of La Palisse and the method of Don Quixote'.[22]

[21] See the splendid paper by H. Bull, 'The State's Positive Role in World Affairs', *Daedalus* 108 (1979), 111 ff.
[22] A. Camus, *Le Mythe de Sisyphe* (Paris, 1960), p. 16.

Select Bibliography

IN this bibliography I shall indicate only those works in English or French which appear to me most significant (a number of works in other languages have already been quoted in the references relating to various chapters). In addition, I shall primarily mention legal writings, without, however, neglecting historical works or essays and books taking a political science approach.

GENERAL WORKS

Legal

Three classical works should first of all be mentioned: D. Anzilotti, *Cours de droit international*, i, trans. G. Gidel (Paris, 1929); J. L. Brierly, *The Law of Nations*, ed. Sir Humphrey Waldock, 6th edn. (Oxford, 1963); G. Scelle, *Manuel de droit international public* (Paris, 1948).

Other standard works are: I. Brownlie, *Principles of Public International Law*, 3rd edn. (Oxford, 1979); N. Quoc Dinh, P. Daillier, and A. Pellet, *Droit international public*, 2nd edn. (Paris, 1980); H. Thierry, J. Combacau, S. Sur, and C. Vallée, *Droit international public*, 4th edn. (Paris, 1984).

Of great importance are some general courses given at the Hague Academy of International Law: M. Sørensen, Hague *Recueil* 101 (1960-III); H. Waldock, Hague *Recueil* 106 (1962-III); R. Jennings, Hague *Recueil* 121 (1967-II); E. Jimenez de Arechaga, Hague *Recueil* 159 (1978-I); R.-J. Dupuy, Hague *Recueil* 165 (1979-IV); M. Virally, Hague *Recueil* 183 (1983-V).

Political Science

S. Hoffmann (ed.), *Contemporary Theory in International Relations* (Englewood Cliffs, 1960); id., *The State of War: Essays in Theory and Practice of International Politics* (New York, 1965); R. Falk, *Legal Order in a Violent World* (Princeton, NJ, 1968); id., *The Status of Law in International Society* (Princeton, NJ, 1970); I. L. Claude, jun., *Swords into Plowshares*, 4th edn. (New York, 1971); H. Bull, *The Anarchical Society: A Study of Order in World Politics* (New York, 1977); P. Reuter and J. Combacau, *Institutions et relations internationales* (Paris, 1980); S. Hoffmann, *Duties Beyond Borders: On the Limits and Possibilities of Ethical International Politics* (Syracuse, 1981); M. Merle, *Sociologie des relations internationales*, 3rd edn. (Paris, 1982); C. Zorgbibe, *Les Relations internationales*, 3rd edn. (Paris, 1983). See also A. Truyol y Serra, 'Genèse et structure de la société internationale', Hague *Recueil* 96 (1959-I), 557 ff.

HISTORICAL EVOLUTION OF THE INTERNATIONAL COMMUNITY

B. V. A. Röling, *International Law in an Expanded World* (Amsterdam, 1960), A. Nussbaum, *A Concise History of the Law of Nations*, 2nd edn. (New York, 1962),

C. H. Alexandrowicz, *An Introduction to the History of the Law of Nations in the East Indies* (Oxford, 1967); F. S. Northedge and M. J. Grieve, *A Hundred Years of International Relations* (New York, 1971); J. Droz, *Histoire diplomatique de 1648 à 1919*, 3rd edn. (Paris, 1972); J.-B. Duroselle, *Histoire diplomatique de 1919 à nos jours*, 8th edn. (Paris, 1981); R. Ago, 'The First International Communities in the Mediterranean World', *BYIL*, 53 (1982), 213 ff.

INTERNATIONAL SUBJECTS

C. N. Okeke, *Controversial Subjects of Contemporary International Law* (Rotterdam, 1974), J. A. Barberis, 'Nouvelles questions concernant la personnalité juridique internationale', Hague *Receuil* 179 (1983-I), 157 ff.

THE ATTITUDE OF STATES TOWARDS INTERNATIONAL LAW

General Works Expounding the Different Perceptions of International Law

O. J. Lissiztyn, *International Law Today and Tomorrow* (Dobbs Ferry, 1965); L. Henkin, *How Nations Behave*, 2nd edn. (New York, 1979).

Western Countries

O. J. Lissitzyn, *International Law Today and Tomorrow* (Dobbs Ferry, 1965); R. Higgins, *Conflict of Interests* (London, 1965); G. de Lacharrière, *La Politique juridique extérieure* (Paris, 1983).

Socialist Countries

F. I. Kozhevnikov (ed.), *International Law* (Moscow, 1962), G. Tunkin, *Theory of International Law* (London, 1974).

Developing Countries

J. Castañeda, 'The Underdeveloped Nations and the Development of International Law', *International Organization* 15 (1961), 38 ff.; G. Abi-Saab, 'The Newly Independent States and the Rules of International Law: An Outline', *Howard Law Journal* 8 (1962), 95 ff.; R. P. Anand, 'Role of the "New" Asia–African Countries in the Present International Legal Order', *AJIL* 56 (1962), 383 ff.; M. Sahovic, 'Influence des états nouveaux sur la conception du droit international', *AFDI* 12 (1966), 30 ff.; G. Abi-Saab, 'The Third World and the Future of the International Legal Order', *Revue égyptienne de droit international* 29 (1973), 27 ff.; A. S. Osman, 'The Attitude of Newly Independent States Towards International Law: The Need for Progressive Development', *Acta Scandinavica Juris Gentium* 48 (1979), 15 ff.; T. O. Elias, *New Horizons in International Law* (Alphen aan den Rijn, 1979), 21–34, 159 ff.; Wang Tieya, 'The Third World and International Law', *Ch Y L* (1983), 6 ff.

GENERAL PRINCIPLES

R. Bierzanek, 'Legal Principles of Peaceful Coexistence and their Codification', *Polish Yearbook of International Law* (1966-7), 17 ff.; G. Arangio-Ruiz, 'The Normative Role of the General Assembly of the United Nations and the Declaration of Principles on Friendly Relations', Hague *Recueil* 137 (1972-III), 528 ff.; G. Abi-Saab, 'The Third World and the Future of the International Legal Order', *Revue égyptienne de droit international* 29 (1973), 39 ff.

THE LAW-CREATION PROCESSES

T. Sørensen, *Les Sources du droit international: étude de la jurisprudence de la Cour Permanente de Justice Internationale* (Copenhagen, 1946); M. Virally, 'La valeur juridique des recommandations des organisations internationales', *AFDI* 2 (1956), 66 ff.; R. Ago, 'La codification du droit international et les problèmes de sa réalisation', *Mélanges Guggenheim* (Geneva, 1968), 93 ff.; T. Minagawa, '*Jus Cogens* in Public International Law', *Hitotsubashi Journal of Law and Politics* 6 (1968), 16 ff.; R. Baxter, 'Treaties and Custom', Hague *Recueil* 129 (1970-I), 25 ff.; J. Castañeda, 'La valeur juridique des résolutions des Nations Unies', Hague *Recueil* 129 (1970-I), 129 ff.; T. O. Elias, 'Modern Sources of International Law', *Essays in Honour of P. Jessup* (New York, 1972), 34 ff.; S. Rosenne, 'Bilateralism and Community Interest in the Codified Law of Treaties', *Essays in Honour of P. Jessup* (New York, 1972), 202 ff.; R.-J. Dupuy, 'Coutume sage et coutume sauvage', *Mélanges Rousseau* (Paris, 1974), 75 ff.; T. O. Elias, 'Modern Sources of International Law', *Essays in Honour of P. Jessup* (New York, 1972), 34 ff.; R.-J. Dupuy, 'Droit déclaratoire et droit programmatoire: De la coutume sauvage à la "soft law"', Société Française de droit international, *L'Élaboration du droit international* (Paris, 1975), 132 ff.; G. Gaja, '*Jus Cogens* beyond the Vienna Convention', Hague *Recueil* 172 (1981-III), 285 ff.; R. Jennings, 'What is International Law and How Do We Tell It When We See It?', *Annuaire suisse de droit international* 37 (1981), 59 ff.; P. Weil, 'Towards Relative Normativity in International Law?', *AJIL* 77 (1983), 413 ff.; T. Minagawa, 'Essentiality and Reality of International *Jus Cogens*', *Hitotsubashi Journal of Law and Politics* 12 (1983), 1 ff.; P. Reuter, *Introduction au droit des traités* (Paris-Genève, 1985); S. Bastid, *Les traités dans la vie internationale—Conclusion et effets* (Paris, 1985).

SETTLEMENT OF DISPUTES

J.-P. Cot, *La Conciliation internationale* (Paris, 1968); H. Waldock (ed.), *International Disputes: The Legal Aspects* (London, 1972); J. Stone, *Fact-Finding in the Maintenance of International Peace* (New York, 1970).

ENFORCEMENT

H. Waldock, 'The Regulation of the Use of Force by Individual States in International Law', Hague *Recueil* 81 (1952-II), 415 ff.; A. Ross, *The United Nations: Peace and Progress* (Totowa, New Jersey, 1966), 228 ff.; S. Hoffmann, 'International Law and the Control of Force', in K. Deutsch and S. Hoffmann (ed.), *The Relevance of International Law* (New York, 1971), 34 ff.; M. Virally, *L'Organisation mondiale* (Paris, 1972), 413 ff.; C. Leben, 'Les contre-mesures inter-étatiques et les réactions à l'illicite dans la société internationale, *AFDI* 28 (1982), 9 ff.

ARMED CONFLICT

The Old Law

L. Oppenheim and H. Lauterpacht, *International Law*, ii, 7th edn. (London, 1955).

The New Law

G. I. A. D. Draper, 'The Geneva Conventions of 1949', Hague *Recueil* 114 (1965-I), 63 ff.; C. Zorgbibe, *La Guerre civile* (Paris, 1975); E. Roucounas, 'Les infractions graves au droit humanitaire: L'article 85 du Protocole additionnel aux conventions de Genève', *Revue hellénique de droit international* (1978), 57 ff.; A. Cassese (ed.), *The New Humanitarian Law of Armed Conflict*, (2 vols., Naples, 1979 and 1980); D. Schindler, 'The Different Types of Armed Conflict According to the Geneva Conventions and Protocols', Hague *Recueil* 163 (1979-II), 17 ff.; S. Nahlik, 'L'extension du statut de combatant à la lumière du Protocole I de Genève de 1977, Hague *Recueil* 164 (1979-III), 171 ff.; G. Abi-Saab, 'Wars of National Liberation in the Geneva Conventions and Protocols', Hague *Recueil* 164 (1979-IV), 353 ff.; G. I. A. D. Draper, 'The Implementation and Enforcement of the Geneva Conventions and the Two Additional Protocols of 1977, Hague *Recueil* 164 (1979-III), 5 ff.; M. Bothe, K. Partsch, and W. Solf, *New Rules for Victims of Armed Conflicts* (The Hague, 1982).

General

H. Bull, 'War and International Order', *Essays in Honour of C. A. W. Manning* (Oxford, 1973), 116 ff.; G. Best, *Honour Among Men and Nations* (Toronto, 1982); M. Howard, *The Causes of Wars and Other Essays* (London, 1984).

INTERNATIONAL PROTECTION OF HUMAN DIGNITY

R. St. J. Macdonald, 'The United Nations and the Protection of Human Rights' in R. St. J. Macdonald, D. M. Johnston and G. L. Morris, *The International Law and Policy of Human Welfare* (Alphen aan den Rijn, 1978), 203 ff.; L. Henkin (ed.), *The International Bill of Rights* (New York, 1981); L. B. Sohn, 'The New International Law: Protection of the Rights of Individuals Rather Than States', *The American University Law Review* 32 (1982), 1 ff.; P. Alston, 'A Third Generation of Solidarity Rights: Progressive Development or Obfuscation of International Human Rights Law?' *Netherlands International Law Review* 29 (1982), 307 ff.; S. Hoffmann, 'Reaching for the Most Difficult: Human Rights as a Foreign Policy Goal', *Daedalus: Journal of the American Academy of Arts and Sciences* 112 (1983), 19 ff.

LEGAL CONTROL OF INTERNATIONAL ECONOMIC RELATIONS

H. Gros Espiell, 'The Most-Favoured-Nation Clause: Its Present Significance in GATT', *Journal of World Trade Law* 5 (1971), 115 ff.; H. Gros Espiell, 'GATT: Accommodating Generalized Preferences', *Journal of World Trade Law* 8 (1974), 342 ff.; A. A. Yusuf, 'Differential and More Favourable Treatment: The GATT Enabling Clause', *Journal of World Trade Law* 14 (1980), 488 ff.; D. Carreau, P.

Juillard, and T. Flory, *Droit international économique*, 2nd edn. (Paris, 1980); Sir Joseph Gold, 'Developments in the International Monetary System, the IMF, and International Monetary Law since 1971', Hague *Recueil* 174 (1982-I), 107 ff.

INTERNATIONAL LAW OF DEVELOPMENT

M. Virally, 'Vers un droit international du développement', *AFDI* 11 (1965), 3 ff.; G. Abi-Saab, *UNCTAD: The Issues and Their Significance* (Uppsala, 1968); G. de Lacharrière, 'L'influence de l'inégalité du développement des états sur le droit international', Hague *Recueil* 139 (1973-II), 227 ff.; K. Hossain (ed.), *Legal Aspects of the New International Economic Order* (London, 1980); A. A. Yusuf, *Legal Aspects of Trade Preferences for Developing States: A Study in the Influence of Development Needs on the Evolution of International Law* (The Hague, 1982); B. V. A. Röling, 'The History and the Sociological Approach of the NIEO and the Third World', *Thesaurus Acroasium* 12 (1982), 181 ff.; M. Benchik, *Droit international du sous-développement* (Paris, 1983); M. Bennouna, *Droit international du développement* (Paris, 1983); G. Abi-Saab, *Analytical Study on the Progressive Development of the Principles and Norms of International Law Relating to the New International Economic Order*, UN document A/39/504/Add.1, 23 October 1984, 28 ff.; C. Tomuschat, 'International Commodity Agreements', *International Encyclopedia of Comparative Law*, xviii (Tübingen, n.d.).

THE COMMON HERITAGE OF MANKIND

R.-J. Dupuy, *L'Océan partagé* (Paris, 1979), 135 ff.; C. Q. Christol, 'The Common Heritage of Mankind Provision in the 1979 Agreement Governing the Activities of States on the Moon and Other Celestial Bodies', *International Lawyer* 14 (1980), 429 ff.; A. A. Cocca, 'The Advances in International Law Through the Law of Outer Space', *Journal of Space Law* 9 (1981), 13 ff.; T. Treves. 'Continuité et innovation dans les modalités de gestion des ressources minérales des fonds marins internationaux' in R.-J. Dupuy (ed.), *La Gestion des ressources pour l'humanité: Le Droit de la mer* (The Hague, 1982), 63 ff.; A. C. Kiss, 'La notion de patrimoine commun de l'humanité', Hague *Recueil* 175 (1982-II), 109 ff.; R. Wolrum, 'The Principle of the Common Heritage of Mankind', *Z.aöRuV* 43 (1983), 312 ff; J. Combacau, *La droit international de la mer* (Paris, 1985); R.-J. Dupuy and D. Vignes (eds.), *Traité du Nouveau Droit de la Mer* (Paris, 1985).

Of special importance is an essay in German, on which I have drawn heavily: W. A. Kewenig, 'Common Heritage of Mankind: Politischer Slogan oder völkerrechtlicher Schlüsselbegriff?', *Festschrift für H.-J. Schlochauer* (Berlin, 1981), 385 ff.

Index of Subjects

(References are to *paragraphs*, not to pages)

international organizations
early 37, 48
international legal personality 43, 48
powers 48
rights and duties 48
International Red Cross 228
international rules
distinction between universal, general and
particular 14
international subjects 1
international trade 187, 189, 190, 200
interpretation of treaties
in traditional law 104
under the Vienna Convention 105
intervention
as a means of enforcement 122
for the protection of nationals abroad 124,
140
see also non-interference
investment abroad
new legal trends 188
old law 187
see also protection of foreign investment

jus cogens 8, 66, 96
and general principles 90
and human rights 84
and the law of the sea 220
jus dispositivum 8

Kantian tradition 13, 74

laissez-faire principle
until the First World War 25, 187
lawful combatants *see* armed conflict
League of Nations 32
legal fictions in international law 45, 83, 133
lump sum agreements 202

mediation 111
see also disputes
mercenaries 154
minorities
treaties for the protection of 33, 168
monism 7
Monroe doctrine 23
moon
and common heritage of mankind 221
legal regime 217, 221
most-favoured-nation clause 187, 189
see also General Agreement on Tariffs and
Trade, UNCTAD
multinational corporations
question of their international legal personality, 58
and new international economic order, 213

municipal law
domestic implementation of international
law 5, 6
need for international law to rely on 4
relations with international law 4, 5
theories on the relation with international
law 7
nationalizations *see* protection of foreign investment
national liberation movements
features distinguishing them from insurgents 51, 56
recognition 54
rights and duties 55
national treatment 187
negotiation 111
see also disputes
neocolonialism 213
neo-liberal trends 190
neutrality
old law 148
new law 149
new international economic order 213
non-coercive measures
by individual States 142-4
collective 131-5
non-discrimination
principle 201
non-European States
in the 'old' international community 20, 21
non-governmental organizations (NGOs) 228
non-integration of international subjects 2,
226
non-interference in domestic affairs
and human rights 85
principle of 85
non-intervention *see* non-interference in
domestic affairs
non-recognition
and the UN 133
non-recognition of acquisition of territory
by force 83
Stimson doctrine 133
within the system of Holy Alliance 22
normative role of GA resolutions 95, 107
Nuremberg Tribunal 34

obligations *erga omnes* 12
OPIC 202
outer space 217, 221

Pact of Paris *see* Briand-Kellogg Pact
particular law 14, 202
patterns of world legal system 13
see also 'Charter model', international
community, 'Westphalian model'